NAEYC Standards and Outcomes	Chapter and Topic	Relevant Student Activities and Discussion Topics
STANDARD 3: Observing, Documenting and Assessing to Support Young Children and Families	Chapter 4-*How to Observe Children* Chapter 1-*Why Guidance Matters*	**Practical Application:** The Mysterious Case of the Spinning Peg (with Discussion Questions), Ch. 4, page 87
3a. Understanding the goals, benefits, and uses of assessment.		How Does My Observation Become a Plan? Ch. 4, page 86
3b. Knowing about assessment partnerships with families and with professional colleagues.		How Observation Supports Positive Guidance, Ch. 4, page 84
		TeachSource Video: Infants and Toddlers: Daily Health Checks, Ch. 4, page 82
3c. Knowing about and using observation, documentation, and other appropriate assessment tools and approaches.		Identifying Personal Biases, Ch. 4, page 81
		Appropriate Observational Instruments and Checklists, Ch. 4, page 85
3d. Understanding and practicing responsible assessment to promote positive outcomes for each child.		Creating a Workable Strategy to Gather Usable Information, Ch. 4, page 87
		Responding More Objectively to Individual Children, Ch. 4, page 84
		Practical Application Case: The Spoiled Child—Myth or Reality? (with Case Discussion Questions), Ch. 1, page 10
STANDARD 4: Using Developmentally Effective Approaches to Connect with Children and Families	Chapter 1-*Why Guidance Matters* Chapter 8-*Building Relationships through Positive Communication* Chapter 9-*Fundamental Causes of Positive and Negative Behavior* Chapter 11-*Mistaken Goals, Motivation, and Mindfulness*	**Student Activities:** Be safe, be respectful, be responsible practical application exercises, Ch. 1, page 21
		TeachSource Video: Curriculum Planning: Implementing DAP, Ch. 1, page 6
4a. Understanding positive relationships and supportive interactions as the foundation of their work with children.		Cultural Transition Tips for Teachers, Ch. 5, page 123
		How Does Culture Affect Adults' Styles of Interaction? Ch. 5, page 125
4b. Knowing and understanding effective strategies and tools for early education.		**Practical Application Case:** "I'll Leave You Here Forever" (with Discussion Questions), Ch. 8, page 205
4c. Using a broad repertoire of developmentally appropriate teaching/ learning approaches.		**Student Activities:** Practical application of positive communication, Ch. 8, page 225
4d. Reflecting on their own practice to promote positive outcomes for each child.		**TeachSource Video:** Language Development: Infants and Toddlers: Communication Development, Ch. 8, page 200
		Compare Negative Commands to Positive Requests, Ch. 8, page 212
		Crucial Conversations and Conflict Resolution, Ch. 8, page 219
		Take Time to Think before You Respond to Biting, Ch. 10, page 257
		Remove the Child from a Problem Situation, Ch. 10, page 262
		Adapt Objects, Events, and Attitudes to Remove Causes of Problem Behavior, Ch. 10, page 266
		Dealing with Genitalia-Related Issues, Ch. 10, page 254
		Prevention and Quick Response Techniques, Ch. 10, page 271

Continues on next page

NAEYC Standards and Outcomes	Chapter and Topic	Relevant Student Activities and Discussion Topics
STANDARD 5: Using Content Knowledge to Build Meaningful Curriculum 5a. Understanding content knowledge and resources in academic disciplines. 5b. Knowing and using the central concepts, inquiry tools, and structures of content areas or academic disciplines. 5c. Using their own knowledge, appropriate early learning standards, and other resources to design, implement and evaluate meaningful, challenging curricula for each child.	Chapter 2-*Historical Perspectives and Guidance Theories* Chapter 7-*Designing Developmentally Appropriate Environments Inside and Out* Chapter 10-*Effective Guidance Interventions*	How Does the Environment Nurture Appropriate Behavior? Ch. 7, page 165 The Vital Role of Play in Childhood, Ch. 7, page 166 How Will I Design a DAP Environment? Ch. 7, page 167 What Effect Does the Classroom Environment Have on Guidance? Ch. 7, page 167 Developmentally Appropriate Activities, Materials, and Routines, Ch. 7, page 170 Planning for Positive Behavior Checklist, Ch. 7, page 168 What Is Special about a DAP Environment? Ch. 7, page 171 How Do Schedules Support Positive Behavior? Ch. 7, page 173 How Can I Improve Transition Times? Ch. 7, page 175 Supporting Physical Development, Ch. 7, page 177 Supporting Social/Emotional Development, Ch. 7, page 178 Supporting Cognitive Development, Ch. 7, page 178 The Nurturing Social Environment, Ch. 7, page 184 What about Physical Punishment? Ch. 7, page 187
STANDARD 6: Becoming a Professional 6a. Identifying and involving oneself with the early childhood field. 6b. Knowing about and upholding ethical standards and other professional guidelines. 6c. Engaging in continuous, collaborative learning to inform practice. 6d. Integrating knowledgeable, reflective, and critical perspectives on early education. 6e. Engaging in informal advocacy for children and the profession.	Chapter 2-*Historical Perspectives and Guidance Theories*	**Practical Application Case:** Boba Rebear and Salty Green Paper (with Discussion Questions), Ch. 5, page 110 **Student Activities:** Practical application via children's books, curriculum materials, and case study, Ch. 5, page 130 **TeachSource Video:** Multicultural Lessons: Embracing Similarities and Differences, Ch. 5, page 101 Understanding Children and Families in the Context of Their Communities, Ch. 5, page 98 Unconditional Acceptance, Ch. 5, page 99 Striving against Bias and Discrimination, Ch. 5, page 100 NAEYC Code of Ethical Conduct, Ch. 5, page 107 What Is Our Ethical Responsibility? Ch. 5, page 105 How Can We Teach Young Children to Resist Bias? Ch. 5, page 102 How Does Culture Affect Early Social and Emotional Development? Ch. 5, page 97 Examples of "DAP" and "Not DAP" Settings, Ch. 5, page 113 How Can I Spot Bias, Stereotypes, and Myths? Ch. 5, page 104 How Multicultural Is My School? Ch. 5, page 104

Source: *NAEYC Professional Preparation Standards*, copyright © 2011 by the National Association for the Education of Young Children. The complete position statement can be accessed at [URL]www.naeyc.org/files/ncate/file/NAEYC Initial and Advanced Standards 3_2011.pdf

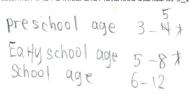
preschool age 3-4* (5)
Early school age 5-8*
School age 6-12

Positive
Child
Guidance

8TH EDITION

Darla Ferris Miller

Open-ended-activity

BOX

葉, 小石, 小枝

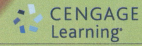

CENGAGE
Learning·

Australia • Brazil • Japan • Korea • Mexico • Singapore • Spain • United Kingdom • United States

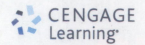

Positive Child Guidance, 8th Edition

Darla Ferris Miller

Product Director: Marta E. Lee Perriard

Product Manager: Mark Kerr

Content Developer: Kate Scheinman

Product Assistant: Julia Catalano

Media Developer: Erik Fortier

Marketing Manager: Jennifer Levanduski

Art and Cover Direction, Production Management, and Composition: MPS Limited

Manufacturing Planner: Doug Bertke

Photo Researcher: PreMedia Global

Text Researcher: PreMedia Global

Copy Editor: Patricia Daly

Text Designer: Diane Beasley

Cover Designer: Diane Beasley

Cover Image: Gettyimages/AID/a.collectionRF

Library of Congress Control Number: 2014940082

Student Edition:

ISBN-13: 978-1-305-08899-3

ISBN-10: 1-305-08899-9

Cengage Learning
20 Channel Center Street
Boston, MA 02210
USA

Cengage Learning is a leading provider of customized learning solutions with office locations around the globe, including Singapore, the United Kingdom, Australia, Mexico, Brazil, and Japan. Locate your local office at: **www.cengage.com/global**

Cengage Learning products are represented in Canada by Nelson Education, Ltd.

To learn more about Cengage Learning Solutions, visit **www.cengage.com**

Purchase any of our products at your local college store or at our preferred online store **www.cengagebrain.com**

Printed at CLDPC, USA, 08-18

Brief Contents

Preface   xviii

PART ONE	Preparing for Positive Guidance	2

1 Why Guidance Matters   2

2 Historical Perspectives and Guidance Theories   22

3 Understanding Children's Behavior   40

PART TWO	Valuing the Uniqueness of Each Child	80

4 How to Observe Children   80

5 Serving Culturally Diverse Children and Families   94

6 Understanding Children with Ability Differences   132

PART THREE	Preventing Behavior Problems	164

7 Designing Developmentally Appropriate Environments Inside and Out   164

8 Building Relationships through Positive Communication   198

9 Fundamental Causes of Positive and Negative Behavior   226

PART FOUR	Positive Interventions	252

10 Effective Guidance Interventions   252

11 Mistaken Goals, Motivation, and Mindfulness   274

Appendix   309

Glossary   315

References   323

Index   349

Contents

Preface   xviii

PART ONE   Preparing for Positive Guidance   2

1   Why Guidance Matters 2

1-1   Child Rearing in Today's World   3

1-2   What Is Developmentally Appropriate Practice?   5

TEACHSOURCE VIDEO: Curriculum Planning: Implementing Developmentally Appropriate Practice in an Early Childhood Setting   6

POSITIVE FOCUS 1.1: The Core of DAP   6

1-3   Why Is Positive Child Guidance Training Important for Parents, Caregivers, and Teachers?   7

1-3a   Who Should Be Responsible for the Well-Being and Guidance of Children?   7

POSITIVE FOCUS 1.2: Professional Early Childhood Jobs Are Increasing   7

POSITIVE FOCUS 1.3: Sadly, Quality Child Care Is Not Available to All Families   8

1-3b   Committing to Becoming the Child's Resource Team   8

TEACHSOURCE VIDEO: A Parent's Viewpoint: Parent-Teacher Communication   9

TEACHSOURCE DIGITAL DOWNLOAD: POSITIVE FOCUS 1.4: Handy Tips for Effective Home/School Partnerships   9

PRACTICAL APPLICATION CASE: The Spoiled Child—Myth or Reality?   10

1-4   What Is the Purpose of Child Guidance?   10

1-4a   Does This Book Have a Special Point of View on Guidance?   11

1-5   Short-Term Objectives for Child Guidance   12

1-5a   Do Children Have Rights?   14

1-5b   How Do We Tell the Difference between Enforcing Reasonable Safety Rules and Being Overprotective?   16

1-6   Long-Term Goals for Child Guidance   16

1-6a   The Nurturing Environment and Long-Term Development   17

BRAIN FACTS: What Can We Learn from Neuroscience? Warm and nurturing social relationships improve learning and behavior   17

TEACHSOURCE DIGITAL DOWNLOAD: POSITIVE FOCUS 1.5: Guide for Adult Role Models   18

TEACHSOURCE VIDEO: Benefits of Preschool   18

1-6b   Why Should Children Be Involved in Maintaining and Protecting Their Environment?   19

1-6c   Children—Our Investment in the Future   20

Summary 20

Key Terms 20

Student Activities 21

Related Resources 21

2 Historical Perspectives and Guidance Theories 22

2-1 Historical Perspectives 23

    2-1a How the Modern World Has Influenced Thinking about Child Guidance 24

    TEACHSOURCE VIDEO: **Piaget's Stages and Educational Implications** 26

    BRAIN FACTS: What Can We Learn from Neuroscience? Children develop empathy and learn skills by watching role models 27

    TEACHSOURCE VIDEO: **Montessori Education** 28

2-2 The Child in Society 29

    2-2a How Life Is Different for Children in Today's Changing World 30

    2-2b Preparation for Participation in a Democracy 30

    TEACHSOURCE DIGITAL DOWNLOAD: POSITIVE FOCUS 2.1: **Critical Skills for Good Citizenship** 31

    2-2c How Early Influences Affect Children and Their Learning of Appropriate Behavior 31

    2-2d The Strain of Changing Disciplinary Traditions 32

2-3 Philosophies of Guidance 32

    PRACTICAL APPLICATION CASE: Bringing Home a Baby Bumblebee 33

    2-3a Is a Child's Personality Mostly the Result of Nature or Nurture? 34

    2-3b What Do Researchers Say about the Origin of Intelligence and Personality? 34

    2-3c How Do I Know Which Philosophy Is Right? 37

Summary 38

Key Terms 39

Student Activities 39

Related Resources 39

3 Understanding Children's Behavior 40

3-1 Typical Ages and Stages 41

    TEACHSOURCE DIGITAL DOWNLOAD: POSITIVE FOCUS 3.1: **How Does Guidance Change to Match Development?** 42

    POSITIVE FOCUS 3.2: **Erik Erikson's Psychosocial Stages of Human Development** 43

3-2 Infants (Birth to 12 Months) 45

    3-2a Do Infants Intentionally Respond by Crying? 45

    3-2b Can Babies Misbehave on Purpose? 46

    3-2c Infant Brain Development 46

    3-2d Reflex Responses and Unconscious Conditioning 46

    BRAIN FACTS: What Can We Learn from Neuroscience? Research is shedding new light on infant brain development 46

    3-2e Conditioning 47

    3-2f Operant Conditioning 47

    3-2g Metacognition 48

    3-2h How Do Babies Develop Control of Their Actions? 48

3-2i Why Do Babies Cry? 48

3-2j When Do Babies Begin Learning Language? 49

3-2k Can Babies Understand Body Language? 49

3-2l How Do Trauma and Chronic Stress Affect an Infant's Brain Development? 50

3-2m How Do Babies Develop Trust? 50

BRAIN FACTS: What Can We Learn from Neuroscience? Reliable, responsive care and affection supports a baby's developing brain 50

3-2n What Is Learned Helplessness? 51

BRAIN FACTS: What Can We Learn from Neuroscience? Play supports children's brain development 52

3-2o How Do I Answer Parents' Sleep Questions? 52

3-2p Which Is Best: Flexible Spontaneity or Predictable Routines? 53

3-2q What Are Interaction Styles? 53

TEACHSOURCE DIGITAL DOWNLOAD: POSITIVE FOCUS 3.3: Interaction Styles 53

3-2r What Do We Mean by Secure Attachment to Caregivers? 54

3-2s Why Do Babies Cling? 55

3-2t Separation and Stranger Anxieties 56

3-2u How Do Babies Perceive Themselves and Their Surroundings? 57

3-3 Toddlers (12 Months to 3 Years) 57

3-3a Can Toddlers Control Their Feelings and Actions? 57

3-3b How Does Awareness of Cause and Effect Develop? 58

3-3c Toddlers Need to Explore Their Surroundings 58

3-3d Safety Is a Major Issue in Toddler Care 58

3-3e How Does Verbal Communication Begin? 60

3-3f What Kind of Language Experiences Are Good for Toddlers? 60

3-3g Stranger and Separation Anxiety 61

3-3h How Can I Make Friends with a Shy Toddler? 61

3-3i Why Are Toddlers So Possessive? 61

3-3j Why Do Some Toddlers Become So Attached to Security Blankets, Pacifiers, and Other Cuddlies? 61

TEACHSOURCE VIDEO: Pre-K Funding Cuts 61

3-3k Why Are Toddlers Stubborn One Minute, Then Clingy the Next? 62

3-3l Are Toddlers Aware of Themselves? 63

3-3m Why Do Toddlers Get So Excited and Happy when They Imitate Each Other? 63

3-4 Preschoolers (3 to 5 Years) 64

3-4a Can Preschoolers Make Plans and Decisions? 64

3-4b Talking to Preschoolers about Sensitive Issues 64

3-4c Communicating Successfully with Preschoolers 65

3-4d Teaching Preschoolers to Use Words to Express Their Feelings 65

3-4e Friendships Are Important to Preschoolers 66

3-4f How Do Preschoolers Learn to Accept Responsibility? 66

PRACTICAL APPLICATION CASE: "I'm Never Gonna 'Vite You to My Birth'ay!" 67

TEACHSOURCE DIGITAL DOWNLOAD: POSITIVE FOCUS 3.4: Avoiding Stress and Burnout 68

3-4g How Can I Support Independence in Preschoolers? 68

3-4h How Can I Help Preschoolers Follow Rules? 69

BRAIN FACTS: What Can We Learn from Neuroscience? Play develops children's brain function enabling self-discipline 69

3-4i How Do Preschoolers Develop a Positive Sense of Self? 70

3-4j Should Children Be Encouraged to Compete? 71

3-5 Early School-Agers (5 to 8 Years) 71

3-5a Why Do Early School-Agers Ask So Many Questions? 71

TEACHSOURCE VIDEO: 5–11 Years: Lev Vygotsky, the Zone of Proximal Development, and Scaffolding 72

3-5b Why Do They Get So Angry if They Don't Win? 72

3-5c Why Do They Call Each Other Names and Say Hurtful Things? 72

PRACTICAL APPLICATION CASE: The Big Boys and the Very Muddy Day 73

TEACHSOURCE VIDEO: Making a Great Teacher 74

3-5d How Can I Earn the Respect of School-Agers? 74

3-5e Why Do Early School-Agers Resist Going to Child Care? 74

3-5f Why Do Early School-Agers Get So Upset about Fairness? 75

3-5g Why Do They Insist on Picking Their Own Clothes? 75

3-5h How Can We Help Early School-Agers Develop Initiative? 75

3-5i How Can We Support the Early School-Age Child's Self-Esteem? 76

3-6 Older School-Agers (9 to 12 Years) 76

3-6a Why Do Older School-Age Children Argue So Much? 76

3-6b How Can I Get Older School-Agers to Trust and Respect Me? 76

3-6c Why Do Older School-Agers Try So Hard to Be Popular? 77

3-6d The Role of Media in the Lives of Older School-Age Children 77

3-6e Puberty 77

3-6f How Can We Support Older School-Agers' Self-Esteem? 78

Summary 78

Key Terms 78

Student Activities 79

Related Resources 79

PART TWO Valuing the Uniqueness of Each Child 80

4 How to Observe Children 80

4-1 Identifying Personal Biases 81

TEACHSOURCE VIDEO: Ensuring High Quality through Program Evaluation 82

4-1a Responding More Objectively to Individual Children 82

TEACHSOURCE DIGITAL DOWNLOAD: POSITIVE FOCUS 4.1: Objective Observations and Subjective Interpretations 83

4-2 The Observation Sequence 83

BRAIN FACTS: What Can We Learn from Neuroscience? Assessment helps us create effective learning environments 84

4-2a How Observation Supports Positive Guidance 84

4-2b What Do I Need to Get Started? 85

4-2c How Will I Use My Observations? 85

4-2d How Does My Observation Become a Plan? 86

4-2e What if My Plan Does Not Work? 86

4-2f How Can I Be Sure My Plan Is Working? 87

PRACTICAL APPLICATION CASE: The Mysterious Case of the Spinning Peg 87

4-3 Observation Strategies 87

    4-3a What Is an Anecdotal Record? 88

    TEACHSOURCE DIGITAL DOWNLOAD: POSITIVE FOCUS 4.2: **Evaluation Using Anecdotal Records** 88

    TEACHSOURCE DIGITAL DOWNLOAD: POSITIVE FOCUS 4.3: **Evaluating Using Home Observations** 89

    4-3b What Is a Running Account? 89

    4-3c What Is Time Sampling? 89

    TEACHSOURCE DIGITAL DOWNLOAD: POSITIVE FOCUS 4.4: **Evaluation by Time Sampling** 90

    4-3d What Is Event Sampling? 90

    TEACHSOURCE DIGITAL DOWNLOAD: POSITIVE FOCUS 4.5: **Evaluation by Event Sampling** 90

    4-3e Which Method of Recording Observations Works Best? 91

    TEACHSOURCE VIDEO: **Preschooler Social and Emotional Development** 91

Summary 91

Key Terms 91

Student Activities 92

Related Resources 92

5 Serving Culturally Diverse Children and Families 94

5-1 Culture Gives Meaning to Our Lives 95

    5-1a What Is Ordinary Culture? 96

    5-1b Does Everyone Have Culture? 96

    5-1c How Does Culture Affect Early Social and Emotional Development? 97

5-2 Understanding Children and Families in the Context of Their Communities 98

    5-2a Bronfenbrenner Suggests We Visualize the Child's Inner Self 98

    5-2b Unconditional Acceptance 99

5-3 Prejudice, Racism, and Discrimination 100

    5-3a Where Did Prejudice Come From? 100

    5-3b When Does Discrimination Begin? 101

    5-3c What Are Early Signs of Prejudice? 101

    TEACHSOURCE VIDEO: **Multicultural Lessons: Embracing Similarities and Differences in Preschool Education** 101

    5-3d How Can We Teach Young Children to Resist Bias? 102

    5-3e The Antibias Curriculum 102

    TEACHSOURCE DIGITAL DOWNLOAD: POSITIVE FOCUS 5.1: **What We Can Do to Help Children Resist Bias** 103

    5-3f How Can I Spot Bias, Stereotypes, and Myths? 104

    TEACHSOURCE DIGITAL DOWNLOAD: POSITIVE FOCUS 5.2: **How Multicultural Is My School?** 104

    5-3g What Is Our Ethical Responsibility? 105

    POSITIVE FOCUS 5.3: **Guidelines for Learning to Spot Bias in Books and Other Media** 105

TEACHSOURCE DIGITAL DOWNLOAD: POSITIVE FOCUS 5.4: **How Can We Empower Children from Diverse Cultural Backgrounds?** 107

POSITIVE FOCUS 5.5: **NAEYC Statement of Commitment to Professional Ethics** 107

5-4 How Culture Shapes Guidance 108

PRACTICAL APPLICATION CASE: Boba Rebear and Salty Green Paper 110

BRAIN FACTS: What Can We Learn from Neuroscience? Healthy brain development requires nurturing social interaction and environmental experiences 112

TEACHSOURCE DIGITAL DOWNLOAD: POSITIVE FOCUS 5.6: **How Do Young Children Learn About Their Role in the World?** 113

5-5 Respecting Cultural Differences 116

Barbara's Special Gifts 116

BRAIN FACTS: What Can We Learn from Neuroscience? Poverty too often damages young children's developing brains 117

TEACHSOURCE DIGITAL DOWNLOAD: POSITIVE FOCUS 5.7: **Take Time to Think before You Judge Others** 118

5-5a What Things Should I Know So I Can Be More Considerate to People from Other Cultures? 119

5-5b How Can I Help Parents from Other Cultures Feel More Comfortable? 119

5-5c Will These Tips Keep Me from Culturally Offending Anyone? 121

5-5d Honoring Families' Religious Beliefs and Customs 122

5-5e How Can I Help Children through Difficult Cultural Transitions? 123

POSITIVE FOCUS 5.8: **Cultural Transition Tips for Teachers** 123

POSITIVE FOCUS 5.9: **Welcome Children with English as a Second or Other Language (ESOL)** 124

5-5f How Does Culture Affect Adults' Styles of Interaction? 125

5-5g How Does Culture Affect a Person's Learning Approach? 125

5-5h How Does Culture Affect Social Role Expectations? 126

5-5i How Does Culture Shape Our Use of Language? 127

5-5j How Does Culture Shape Our Intellectual Approach? 128

Summary 129

Key Terms 129

Student Activities 130

Related Resources 130

6 Understanding Children with Ability Differences 132

6-1 How Can I Guide Children with Ability Differences? 133

TEACHSOURCE DIGITAL DOWNLOAD: POSITIVE FOCUS 6.1: **Nurturing Children with Learning Differences** 134

6-1a What Do Children with Ability Differences Need? 134

6-1b Why Should We Include Children with Ability Differences? 134

6-1c Do Children with Ability Differences Need DAP? 135

TEACHSOURCE VIDEO: **5–11 Years: Developmental Disabilities in Middle Childhood** 135

TEACHSOURCE DIGITAL DOWNLOAD: POSITIVE FOCUS 6.2: **DAP Concepts We Follow to Support Children with Ability Differences** 135

POSITIVE FOCUS 6.3: **Why Is Inclusiveness Important?** 136

BRAIN FACTS: What Can We Learn from Neuroscience? Nurturing brain development in children with special needs   **136**

6-1d Helping Children Treat People with Ability Differences with Respect   137

POSITIVE FOCUS 6.4: **Choosing Books that Support Children with Diverse Abilities**   **137**

6-1e Does a Different Appearance Affect a Child's Life?   138

6-1f How Should I Handle Teasing and Bullying?   140

POSITIVE FOCUS 6.5: **Bullying Hurts Children**   **140**

6-1g How Can I Support the Child with an Ability Difference?   141

TEACHSOURCE DIGITAL DOWNLOAD: POSITIVE FOCUS 6.6: **Support Children with Ability Differences**   **141**

TEACHSOURCE VIDEO: **Shaken Baby Syndrome**   **142**

POSITIVE FOCUS 6.7: **Understand Parents of Children with Ability Differences**   **142**

6-1h How Can I Support Parents of Children with Ability Differences?   142

6-2 Laws and Programs for Children with Ability Differences   **143**

PRACTICAL APPLICATION CASE: "Thank Heaven for Sarah"   **144**

6-2a What Are the IEP and IFSP Processes?   145

6-2b What If My Program Isn't Required to Provide an IEP?   145

6-2c What If My Program Doesn't Accept Children with Ability Differences?   146

6-3 How Do Various Health Conditions Affect Behavior?   **146**

6-3a What Type of Ability Differences Am I Most Likely to Encounter?   146

POSITIVE FOCUS 6.8: **Troublesome Problems that Interfere with Learning**   **146**

6-3b Hearing Impairment and Deafness   147

6-3c Sensory Processing Disorder   147

TEACHSOURCE DIGITAL DOWNLOAD: POSITIVE FOCUS 6.9: **Guide Children Who Are Deaf or Hard of Hearing**   **147**

TEACHSOURCE DIGITAL DOWNLOAD: POSITIVE FOCUS 6.10: **Guiding Children with SPD**   **147**

6-3d Down Syndrome   148

6-3e Fetal Alcohol Spectrum Disorders   149

TEACHSOURCE DIGITAL DOWNLOAD: POSITIVE FOCUS 6.11: **Guiding Children with Down Syndrome**   **149**

TEACHSOURCE VIDEO: **Fetal Alcohol Syndrome**   **149**

TEACHSOURCE DIGITAL DOWNLOAD: POSITIVE FOCUS 6.12: **Children with ADHD Have Special Challenges**   **150**

6-3f Attention Deficit/Hyperactivity Disorder (ADHD)   150

TEACHSOURCE DIGITAL DOWNLOAD: POSITIVE FOCUS 6.13: **Guiding Children with ADHD**   **151**

TEACHSOURCE VIDEO: **Autism and a Bike**   **152**

6-3g Intellectual Disability (ID)   152

TEACHSOURCE DIGITAL DOWNLOAD: POSITIVE FOCUS 6.14: **Guiding Children with Intellectual Disability**   **152**

6-3h Pervasive Developmental Disorders   153

TEACHSOURCE DIGITAL DOWNLOAD: POSITIVE FOCUS 6.15: **Guiding Children with Autism**   **153**

6-3i Tourette's Syndrome   155

TEACHSOURCE DIGITAL DOWNLOAD: POSITIVE FOCUS 6.16: **Guiding Children with Autism 155**

TEACHSOURCE DIGITAL DOWNLOAD: POSITIVE FOCUS 6.17: **Children with Tourette's Syndrome 156**

TEACHSOURCE DIGITAL DOWNLOAD: POSITIVE FOCUS 6.18: **Guiding Children with Tourette's 156**

6-3j Bipolar Disorder 156

TEACHSOURCE DIGITAL DOWNLOAD: POSITIVE FOCUS 6.19: **Children with Bipolar Disorder 157**

TEACHSOURCE DIGITAL DOWNLOAD: POSITIVE FOCUS 6.20: **Guiding Children with Bipolar Disorder 157**

6-3k Oppositional Defiant Disorder and Intermittent Explosive Disorder 158

TEACHSOURCE DIGITAL DOWNLOAD: POSITIVE FOCUS 6.21: **Children with ODD 158**

TEACHSOURCE DIGITAL DOWNLOAD: POSITIVE FOCUS 6.22: **Children with ODD and IED 158**

TEACHSOURCE DIGITAL DOWNLOAD: POSITIVE FOCUS 6.23: **Guiding Children with ODD and IED 159**

6-3l Conduct Disorder 159

TEACHSOURCE DIGITAL DOWNLOAD: POSITIVE FOCUS 6.24: **Children with Conduct Disorder 159**

TEACHSOURCE DIGITAL DOWNLOAD: POSITIVE FOCUS 6.25: **Children with Conduct Disorder Typically Demonstrate 160**

Summary 160
Key Terms 161
Student Activities 161
Related Resources 162

PART THREE Preventing Behavior Problems   164

7 Designing Developmentally Appropriate Environments Inside and Out 164

7-1 How Does the Environment Nurture Appropriate Behavior? 165

7-1a Three Key Elements of Prosocial Behavior 165

TEACHSOURCE DIGITAL DOWNLOAD: POSITIVE FOCUS 7.1: **Prosocial Behavior Consists of Positive Social Relations 166**

7-1b The Vital Role of Play in Childhood 166

7-2 How Will I Design a DAP Indoor Environment? 167

7-2a What Effect Does the Classroom Environment Have on Guidance? 167

7-2b What Effect Does DAP Have on Child Guidance? 168

TEACHSOURCE DIGITAL DOWNLOAD: POSITIVE FOCUS 7.2: **Planning for Positive Behavior Checklist 168**

7-3 Creating a Calm, Peaceful Classroom Atmosphere 169

POSITIVE FOCUS 7.3: **Skills for Citizenship in a Democracy 169**

7-3a Developmentally Appropriate Activities, Materials, and Routines 170

7-3b Why Is Consistency Important? 170

7-3c What Is Special about a DAP Environment? 171

TEACHSOURCE DIGITAL DOWNLOAD: POSITIVE FOCUS 7.4: Analyze Classroom Traffic Patterns 171

TEACHSOURCE DIGITAL DOWNLOAD: POSITIVE FOCUS 7.5: Use Picture Symbols to Demonstrate Behavior 171

7-3d How Do Schedules Support Positive Behavior? 173

POSITIVE FOCUS 7.6: How Can I Promote Prosocial Behavior? 173

TEACHSOURCE VIDEO: 2–5 Years: Play in Early Childhood 173

Preschool Full-Day Child Care Schedule 174

TEACHSOURCE DIGITAL DOWNLOAD: POSITIVE FOCUS 7.7: How Can I Improve Transition Times? 175

PRACTICAL APPLICATION CASE: William and the Nature Walk 176

7-4 How Will I Design the Outdoor Environment? 177

7-4a Supporting Physical Development 177

7-4b Supporting Social/Emotional Development 178

7-4c Supporting Cognitive Development 178

TEACHSOURCE DIGITAL DOWNLOAD: POSITIVE FOCUS 7.8: Expand Outdoor Learning 179

POSITIVE FOCUS 7.9: Design a DAP Playground 180

7-4d Environmental Elements of a DAP Playground 180

TEACHSOURCE VIDEO: Obese Children 182

7-4e What Is a Green Playscape? 182

TEACHSOURCE DIGITAL DOWNLOAD: POSITIVE FOCUS 7.10: Design a Green Playscape 183

7-5 The Nurturing Social Environment 184

7-5a The Importance of Playful Learning 184

7-5b Creating a Cooperative Setting 185

TEACHSOURCE DIGITAL DOWNLOAD: POSITIVE FOCUS 7.11: What Is Involved in Toilet Learning? 186

7-6 The Nurturing Adult 186

POSITIVE FOCUS 7.12: Tips for Being a Nurturing Adult 186

7-6a What about Physical Punishment? 187

POSITIVE FOCUS 7.13: Never, Ever Spank! 188

POSITIVE FOCUS 7.14: Guiding School-Aged Children 188

BRAIN FACTS: What Can We Learn from Neuroscience? Corporal punishment and brain development 189

BRAIN FACTS: What Can We Learn from Neuroscience? Verbal abuse and brain development 190

POSITIVE FOCUS 7.15: Why Do Parents Spank? 191

7-6b How Does a Nurturing Adult Respond to Aggression? 191

7-6c Can Children Learn Appropriate Behavior through Imitation? 191

TEACHSOURCE DIGITAL DOWNLOAD: POSITIVE FOCUS 7.16: Ask These Questions about Annoying Behaviors 192

TEACHSOURCE DIGITAL DOWNLOAD: POSITIVE FOCUS 7.17: Positive Role Model Checklist 192

TEACHSOURCE DIGITAL DOWNLOAD: POSITIVE FOCUS 7.18: Five Tips for Teachers and Caregivers 193

7-6d Can I Be Both Assertive and Caring? 194

7-6e Am I Willing to Protect Individual Rights? 195

Summary 196

Key Terms 196

Student Activities 196

Related Resources 197

8 Building Relationships through Positive Communication...198

8-1 Building a Foundation for Positive Communication 199

8-1a How Can I Support Early Communication Skills? 199

TEACHSOURCE VIDEO: Infants and Toddlers: Communication Development 200

8-1b How Do Young Children Communicate? 200

BRAIN FACTS: What Can We Learn from Neuroscience? How Do Babies and Young Children Learn Language? 201

8-1c How Does American Sign Language Support Child Guidance? 202

8-1d Why Is Communication Important for Child Guidance? 202

TEACHSOURCE DIGITAL DOWNLOAD: POSITIVE FOCUS 8.1: Communication Supports Positive Guidance 203

8-1e How Does Attentive Listening Nurture a Sense of Belonging? 203

TEACHSOURCE DIGITAL DOWNLOAD: POSITIVE FOCUS 8.2: Listening Attentively 204

8-1f Three Basic Human Needs Underlying Requests for Help 204

TEACHSOURCE DIGITAL DOWNLOAD: POSITIVE FOCUS 8.3: How Do Children and Adults Communicate Their Needs? 204

PRACTICAL APPLICATION CASE: "I'll Leave You Here Forever" 205

8-1g Appropriate Responses to Requests for Action or Information 205

8-1h Appropriate Responses to Requests for Understanding and Attention 207

8-1i How Should I Respond to Requests for Inappropriate Interaction? 208

8-1j Do Listening and Helping Strategies Work with Babies and Toddlers? 210

8-2 Addressing Underlying Feelings 211

8-2a When and How Should Adults Express Their Feelings to Children? 211

TEACHSOURCE DIGITAL DOWNLOAD: POSITIVE FOCUS 8.4: Giving "I Messages" 211

8-3 Positive Instructions versus Negative Commands 212

TEACHSOURCE DIGITAL DOWNLOAD: POSITIVE FOCUS 8.5: Positive Requests versus Negative Commands 213

8-4 Characteristics of Assertive Communication 213

8-4a Key Factors in Assertive Communication 214

TEACHSOURCE DIGITAL DOWNLOAD: POSITIVE FOCUS 8.6: How Can I Be Authoritative Rather Than Authoritarian? 217

8-5 Characteristics of Nonproductive Communication 217

8-5a How Do These Stereotypes Show Up as Problems? 217

8-6 Resolving Confrontations Peacefully with Conflict Resolution 219

TEACHSOURCE DIGITAL DOWNLOAD: POSITIVE FOCUS 8.7: Crucial Conversations 220

TEACHSOURCE DIGITAL DOWNLOAD: POSITIVE FOCUS 8.8: **Adult Expectations for Help** 222

8-6a When Is a Critical Conversation Needed? 223

TEACHSOURCE DIGITAL DOWNLOAD: POSITIVE FOCUS 8.9: **Ways Children Can Make Amends** 224

8-6b Should We Force Children to Apologize? 224

Summary 224
Key Terms 225
Student Activities 225
Related Resources 225

9 Fundamental Causes of Positive and Negative Behavior 226

9-1 Moral Development Builds a Core for Positive Behavior 227

9-1a Building Moral Intelligence 228

POSITIVE FOCUS 9.1: **Moral Intelligence** 228

POSITIVE FOCUS 9.2: **Develop Moral Development** 229

9-1b How Do Young Children Learn Right from Wrong? 230

POSITIVE FOCUS 9.3: **Kohlberg's Theory of Moral Development** 230

BRAIN FACTS: What Can We Learn from Neuroscience? Brain Development and Moral Behavior 231

TEACHSOURCE VIDEO: **Early Childhood: Positive Guidance** 232

9-2 Methods to Support Children's Moral Development 232

9-2a Set Limits 232

9-2b Model Appropriate Behavior 232

TEACHSOURCE DIGITAL DOWNLOAD: POSITIVE FOCUS 9.4: **Authoritative Demandingness** 233

9-2c Rely on Democratic Processes 233

9-3 Defining Negative Behavior 233

9-3a What Do We Mean by Functional and Dysfunctional Behaviors? 234

9-3b The Adult-Centered Definition of Misbehavior 235

9-3c The Child-Centered Definition of Misbehavior 235

9-4 Temperament 235

9-4a How Do Infants Show Differences in Temperament? 236

POSITIVE FOCUS 9.5: **Rothbart's Inventory of Babies' Temperament Differences** 236

9-4b How Can We Support the Spirited Child? 237

TEACHSOURCE DIGITAL DOWNLOAD: POSITIVE FOCUS 9.6: **The Spirited Child Has Intensity** 237

TEACHSOURCE DIGITAL DOWNLOAD: POSITIVE FOCUS 9.7: **The Spirited Child Has Persistence** 238

TEACHSOURCE DIGITAL DOWNLOAD: POSITIVE FOCUS 9.8: **The Spirited Child Has Sensitivity** 239

TEACHSOURCE DIGITAL DOWNLOAD: POSITIVE FOCUS 9.9: **The Spirited Child Has Perceptiveness** 239

TEACHSOURCE DIGITAL DOWNLOAD: POSITIVE FOCUS 9.10: **The Spirited Child Has Adaptability** 240

PRACTICAL APPLICATION CASE: Is a "Really Good Spanking" Really Good? 241

9-5 Underlying Causes of Problem Behavior 241

    9-5a Inappropriate Expectations 241

    9-5b Misunderstanding Expectations 242

    9-5c Immature Self-Control 242

    9-5d Silly Playfulness, Group Contagion 243

    9-5e Boredom 244

    9-5f Fatigue and Discomfort 245

    9-5g Desire for Recognition 246

    9-5h Discouragement 246

    9-5i Frustration 247

    9-5j Rebellion 248

    TEACHSOURCE DIGITAL DOWNLOAD: POSITIVE FOCUS 9.11: **Conditions That Set the Stage for Rebellion** 249

Summary 250

Key Terms 250

Student Activities 250

Related Resources 251

PART FOUR Positive Interventions   **252**

10   Effective Guidance Interventions 252

10-1 Ignore Mildly Annoying Behavior That Is Not Against the Ground Rules 253

    10-1a Focus Attention Elsewhere 254

    10-1b Discreetly Redirect Slightly Annoying Behavior to More Positive Substitute Behavior 254

    10-1c Assist the Child in Recognizing the General Effects of Positive Behaviors 254

    10-1d Dealing with Genitalia-Related Issues 254

    TEACHSOURCE DIGITAL DOWNLOAD: POSITIVE FOCUS 10.1: **Take Time to Think Before Reacting to Genital Touching** 255

10-2 Immediately Interrupt Behavior That Is Harmful or Unfair 256

    10-2a What Do I Do about Biting? 257

    TEACHSOURCE DIGITAL DOWNLOAD: POSITIVE FOCUS 10.2: **Responding to Toddler Biting** 257

    TEACHSOURCE DIGITAL DOWNLOAD: POSITIVE FOCUS 10.3: **Take Time to Think before You Respond to Biting** 258

    10-2b Intervene as Firmly as Necessary but as Gently as Possible 259

    10-2c Maintain Objectivity 260

    BRAIN FACTS: **What Can We Learn from Neuroscience? Children's Brains and the Development of Self-Control** 260

    10-2d Remove the Child from a Problem Situation 261

    PRACTICAL APPLICATION CASE: **Will and the Cream Cheese Wonton** 262

10-3 Assertively Shape Positive Behavior 263

    10-3a Teach Ground Rules 263

    10-3b Clarify Expectations 264

    TEACHSOURCE DIGITAL DOWNLOAD: POSITIVE FOCUS 10.4: **Positive and Specific Statements of Our Expectations** 265

    10-3c Maintain Consistency 265

10-4 Adapt Objects, Events, and Attitudes to Remove Possible Causes of Problem Behavior 266

10-4a Offer Assistance and Encouragement 266

10-4b Give Undivided Attention 267

TEACHSOURCE VIDEO: Guidance for Young Children: Teacher Techniques for Encouraging Positive Social Behaviors 267

10-4c Redirect Inappropriate Behavior Firmly and Respectfully 268

TEACHSOURCE DIGITAL DOWNLOAD: POSITIVE FOCUS 10.5: Prevention Techniques 268

10-4d Clearly Express Appropriate Feelings 270

10-4e Explain the Natural Consequences of Unacceptable Behavior 270

TEACHSOURCE DIGITAL DOWNLOAD: POSITIVE FOCUS 10.6: Appropriate Verbal Expressions of Adult Feelings 271

10-4f Provide Persistent Follow-Up 271

10-4g Emphasize Unconditional Caring and Affection 271

10-4h Maintain and Express Confidence That a Problem Will Be Resolved 272

10-4i Protect Children's Dignity and Privacy 272

10-4j Be Willing to Start Over to Forgive and Forget 272

Summary 272

Key Terms 272

Student Activities 273

Related Resources 273

11 Mistaken Goals, Motivation, and Mindfulness 274

11-1 Can Misbehavior Be Caused by Mistaken Goals? 275

11-1a Mistaken Goal Number One: Attention-Seeking Behavior 276

TEACHSOURCE DIGITAL DOWNLOAD: POSITIVE FOCUS 11.1: Addressing Emotional Causes of Misbehavior 276

11-1b Mistaken Goal Number Two: Controlling Behavior 277

TEACHSOURCE DIGITAL DOWNLOAD: POSITIVE FOCUS 11.2: Be Alert—Stop Bullying! 279

11-1c Mistaken Goal Number Three: Disruptive Behavior 279

TEACHSOURCE DIGITAL DOWNLOAD: POSITIVE FOCUS 11.3: To Support Emotional Growth 279

BRAIN FACTS: What Can We Learn from Neuroscience? Intrinsic Motivation versus Extrinsic Motivation 280

11-1d Mistaken Goal Number Four: Withdrawn, Passive Behavior 283

11-2 Can Behavioral Problems Indicate Child Abuse or Neglect? 284

11-2a How Can Child Abuse Fatalities Be Prevented? 284

POSITIVE FOCUS 11.4: Child Abuse Fatalities 284

11-3 Meeting Adult Needs 285

TEACHSOURCE DIGITAL DOWNLOAD: POSITIVE FOCUS 11.5: Coping Techniques for Child Educators/Teachers/Caregivers 286

11-4 What Is the Difference between Punishment and Guidance? 286

TEACHSOURCE DIGITAL DOWNLOAD: POSITIVE FOCUS 11.6: What Is Punishment? 286

PRACTICAL APPLICATION CASE: "Please Wear This Dress!"   288

11-4a   Think Twice before You Give Time-Out   289

11-4b   Consider "Time-Away" for Tantrums and Other Troubles   289

TEACHSOURCE DIGITAL DOWNLOAD: POSITIVE FOCUS 11.7: Should I Ever Use Time-Out?   289

TEACHSOURCE DIGITAL DOWNLOAD: POSITIVE FOCUS 11.8: What Is the Difference between Punishment and Guidance?   289

11-5   Accepting the Consequences of One's Behavior   290

11-5a   Natural Consequences   291

11-5b   Logical Consequences   291

TEACHSOURCE DIGITAL DOWNLOAD: POSITIVE FOCUS 11.9: Examples of Logical Consequences   291

11-5c   Avoid Rescuing Children from the Consequences of Their Own Actions   292

11-5d   Sometimes Intervening Is Not Rescuing Children   292

11-5e   Should We Ask Children to Apologize?   293

TEACHSOURCE DIGITAL DOWNLOAD: POSITIVE FOCUS 11.10: Ways Children Can Make Amends   293

11-6   Motivation for Behavior—Maslow's Hierarchy   294

TEACHSOURCE DIGITAL DOWNLOAD: POSITIVE FOCUS 11.11: Maslow's Hierarchy of Emotional Needs That Motivate Behavior   294

11-6a   How Can I Support the Child's Development of Self-Esteem?   295

11-7   External Reinforcement   295

11-7a   What Is Behavior Modification and How Should It Be Used?   297

11-7b   Behavior Modification Does Not Work All the Time   298

11-8   How Can We Expand Children's Social–Emotional Intelligence?   299

TEACHSOURCE VIDEO: Preschool: Emotional Development   299

POSITIVE FOCUS 11.12: Ten Habits of Emotionality Intelligent People   299

11-8a   How Do We Teach Children Social–Emotional Intelligence?   300

11-9   Moving toward Mindfulness   300

POSITIVE FOCUS 11.13: Components of Social–Emotional Intelligence   301

11-9a   What Does Mindfulness Mean?   301

11-9b   How Can Mindfulness Help Me?   302

TEACHSOURCE DIGITAL DOWNLOAD: POSITIVE FOCUS 11.14: Mindfulness of the Environment   302

POSITIVE FOCUS 11.15: Mindfulness of the Body   303

POSITIVE FOCUS 11.16: Mindfulness of the Environment: Awareness of Movement   303

POSITIVE FOCUS 11.17: Mindfulness through Focus on Breathing   304

POSITIVE FOCUS 11.18: Mindful Contemplation   304

POSITIVE FOCUS 11.19: Practicing Mindfulness   305

Summary 306

Key Terms 306

Student Activities 306

Related Resources 307

Appendix   309

Glossary   315

References   323

Index   349

Preface

Not too long ago, one of my granddaughters screamed at her little sister for interfering in her elaborately arranged doll play. Relying on positive guidance techniques, of course, I said, "April, Rosie is crying. She wants to talk about how she felt when you said angry words to her."

April looked up blankly, like someone coming out of a deep concentration, and said, "I didn't hear myself say angry words." I have been thinking a lot about my sweet April lately. We, too, have times when we don't hear ourselves. Guiding children effectively demands focus and self-discipline from adults. Becoming successful in child guidance is not just about memorizing new information—it is about processing information, becoming self-aware, and sometimes changing lifelong habits. None of these things are easy. Like April, first we have to hear ourselves saying angry words.

I've been a classroom teacher (from infants and toddlers to middle school), a child care director, an early childhood professor, and a supervisor of student teachers. A lot has changed in my years of watching teachers and children. But some things have not changed. Today, there are still teaching staff who intimidate young children to keep them quiet and make them mind, mistakenly thinking it will help children learn.

Our Shared Quest through This Text

Most adults who interact with children have good intentions and want only the best for children. Our shared quest, as early childhood educators, is to find authentic best practices that will really work for us on a day-to-day basis. Our genuine hope is to support children's development and enhance their lives. We all want to be successful. It is my sincere hope that this book will bring new levels of success in child guidance.

The guidance methods presented here are not my invention or discovery. I have spent four decades observing, studying, working with, and learning about children and families. I've learned by studying people such as Piaget and Adler and Montessori—but I've also learned from coworkers like you who so generously share your ideas by presenting at conferences and writing journal articles. In this book I offer you my best effort at bringing together all of the practical child guidance expertise, research, and wisdom I can distill in these pages in a simplified, organized, easy-to-read format.

Critical Assumptions

Positive Child Guidance offers a comprehensive plan for guidance. Every part of the text clearly fits within the ideals of developmentally appropriate practice (DAP).

The methods here are based on the following critical assumptions. Guidance must

- Be respectful and build self-esteem
- Accommodate individual differences
- Support self-reliance and self-discipline
- Match the child's developmental level
- Be referenced to the child's cultural community

Three Philosophical Perspectives

- **Maturationists**—Arnold Gessell advanced the maturationist belief that development is a biological process occurring automatically in predictable stages over time. This perspective provides useful guidance tools with the warning that taken too far it may be used as an excuse for *permissive,* "hands-off," or neglectful guidance.
- **Behaviorists**—Theorists such as John Watson, B. F. Skinner, and Albert Bandura contributed greatly to the environmentalist perspective of development, which proposes that the child's environment shapes learning and behavior. This perspective provides useful guidance tools for responding to very specific kinds of behavior problems. Its strategies are not developmentally appropriate, however, for responding to all guidance situations. In fact, use of behaviorist methods without children's active cooperation risks placing the adult in the manipulative and controlling *authoritarian* role.
- **Constructivists**—Jean Piaget, Maria Montessori, and Lev Vygotsky helped develop the constructivists' view, in which young children are seen as active participants in the learning process. Because active interaction with the environment and people is necessary for learning and development, constructivists believe that children are partners in their own learning. The constructivist philosophy is a natural match for the *authoritative* adult guidance role in the developmentally appropriate classroom.

Obviously, *Positive Child Guidance* leans toward the constructivist perspective.

Audience for This Text

This text is written primarily for community college students, although many universities have adopted it over the years for beginning early childhood education courses. Community college students are remarkably diverse. One class may include students struggling with English, honors program students, students getting help to bring their basic skills up to college level, and returning adults whose maturity and work habits cause them to excel academically.

I intentionally developed *Positive Child Guidance* to appeal to many levels of adult learners. This book offers the theoretical and philosophical foundations of guidance in a relatively jargon-free writing style. There are readable, practical anecdotes and interesting photographs to make chapters more enjoyable for students who struggle. There is also, however, enough "meaty" information provided and enough stimulation of critical thinking to create intellectual challenge for more experienced students.

Organization of the Text

The text has been organized into four parts:

(1) Preparing for Positive Guidance
(2) Valuing the Uniqueness of Each Child
(3) Preventing Behavior Problems
(4) Positive Interventions

This organization follows the guidance approach of the text:

- Chapters 1–3 start off the text by looking at goals for children and reviewing theories of learning and child development.
- Chapters 4–6 provide information on how to value children by observing, recognizing, and understanding their unique qualities.
- Chapters 7–9 discuss how to prevent problems by planning DAP settings, building strong relationships, and supporting moral and social intelligence development.
- Chapters 10 and 11 give practical details on learning how to ignore, redirect, or intervene in inappropriate behavior and address the mistaken goals underlying persistent unproductive behavior.

New And Updated For The Eighth Edition

Positive Child Guidance, eighth edition, focuses on supporting children's development and enhancing their lives through developmentally appropriate guidance methods. *Positive Child Guidance* offers a comprehensive plan for guidance. Every part of the text embraces the ideals of developmentally appropriate practice (DAP). This new edition includes critical advances in research and addresses the cultural changes that are changing the way babies and children are cared for today.

Features

NEW Colorful Design and Larger Trim Size
This edition is a full-color text with an appealing interior design and larger trim size to help enhance student learning.

UPDATED Learning Objectives
Learning Objectives correlated to the main sections in each chapter show students what they need to know to process and understand the information in the chapter. After completing the chapter, students should be able to demonstrate how they can use and apply their new knowledge and skills.

NEW Standards Included with Each Chapter
New and improved coverage of NAEYC standards includes a chapter-opening list to help students identify where key standards are addressed in the chapter. NAEYC and DAP icons are integrated throughout the text, and the NAEYC standards correlation charts help students make connections between what they are learning in the textbook and the standards.

NEW Brain Facts Boxes
These new boxes provide students with current neurological findings that affect our understanding of how children learn and how we can most effectively guide them.

NEW Colorful Icons
Integrated throughout the book, marginal icons draw student attention to content that relates to NAEYC, DAP, BRAIN, DIVERSITY, CHALLENGING BEHAVIOR, and CRITICAL THINKING content.

NEW TeachSourceDigital Downloads
Downloadable and often customizable, these practical and professional resources allow students to immediately implement and apply this textbook's content in the field. The student downloads these tools and keeps them forever, enabling preservice teachers to being to build their library of practical, professional resources. Look for the TeachSource Digital Downloads label that identifies these items.

NEW TeachSource Video Cases
The TeachSource videos feature footage from the classroom to help students relate key chapter content to real-life scenarios. Critical-thinking questions provide opportunities for in-class or online discussion and reflection.

MindTap for Education is a first-of-its kind digital solution that prepares teachers by providing them with the knowledge, skills, and competencies they must demonstrate to earn an education degree and state licensure, and to begin a successful career. Through activities based on real-life teaching situations, MindTap elevates students' thinking by giving them experiences in applying concepts, practicing skills, and evaluating decisions, guiding them to become reflective educators.

Practical Application Emphasis
Every chapter has at least one Practical Application Case Study that demonstrates important concepts addressed in the chapter. Additionally, numerous Examples designated

throughout the text help students grasp how their new competences can be applied in real-world situations.

Clarification of the Role of Behavior Modification in Positive Guidance

Extrinsic motivation, using tokens, prizes, and praise as reinforcement, can be very effective in specific kinds of situations, but, used incorrectly, can seriously undermine intrinsic motivation. Guidelines are provided for supporting intrinsic motivation and using extrinsic motivators wisely.

UPDATED Coverage on Moral Development

Early childhood programs can play an important role in the development of moral values that are essential for successful citizenship in a democracy. Positive guidance is based on caring for children respectfully and assertively—developing their internal motivation to live healthfully, to respect others, and to be responsible for their actions.

UPDATED Marginal Key Terms and Definitions

To support student learning, key terms and their definitions appear in the text margins adjacent to boldface key terms where they first appear in the text. At the end of each chapter, a list of the key terms appears, and at the end of the book, there is a comprehensive glossary of key terms.

UPDATED Quotations

Throughout the text relevant quotes from well-known philosophers, educators, and writers illuminate the content of the chapters and inspire students.

UPDATED Web-Based Resources

Students today use the Internet as a handy tool to follow their own curiosity and learn more about specific topics that interest them. In every chapter students will find recommended websites relevant to the topics being discussed.

Chapter-by-Chapter Highlights

Chapter 1—Why Guidance Matters

- Material revised connecting text to DAP fundamentals
- Timely information on children and families today
- Statistical update on child care for families
- Ground rules expressed as "Be healthy, be respectful, and be responsible"

Chapter 2—Historical Perspectives and Guidance Theories

- New information on how current research on mirror neurons affects today's perspective on guidance.

Chapter 3—Understanding Children's Behavior

- Updated information on key theories of child development
- Updated section on infant development
- New data on the impact of chronic stress on the development of brain architecture
- Updated information on caregiving styles
- New information on the important role of play in child development

Chapter 4—How to Observe Children

- New video on insuring high quality through program evaluation
- Updated strategies for integrating observations with DAP
- Discussion of using neuroscience to better understand children's development

Chapter 5—Serving Culturally Diverse Children and Families

- New guidelines for learning to spot bias in books and other media
- New listing of underrepresented cultural groupings that rarely appear in children's learning materials, books, and media

- New research findings on the devastating impact of poverty on child development
- New research findings on the beneficial effect of DAP learning environments on babies and young children
- Updated statement of NAEYC code of ethics and listing of DAP cultural objectives

Chapter 6—Understanding Children with Ability Differences

- New research findings on the special vulnerability to chronic stress faced by differently abled children
- The term *ability difference* is used instead of the term *disability*
- The term *inclusion* is added in opposition to the idea of exclusion
- Bullying and teasing are addressed by developmental levels as well as gender

Chapter 7—Designing Developmentally Appropriate Environments Inside and Out

- DAP connections integrated throughout this chapter
- In-depth information on designing indoor and outdoor environments
- Innovative section on green playscapes and what research says about them
- New video on childhood obesity and the value of outdoor play
- Updated research on the negative impact of physical punishment
- Update on abusive head trauma and related issues

Chapter 8—Building Relationships through Positive Communication

- New research findings on the development of language in infants and toddlers
- Strategies for using sign language with toddlers to reduce communication frustration and to enhance brain development
- Methods for creating a sense of belonging among children
- Methods for addressing crucial conversations and resolving conflicts peacefully

Chapter 9—Fundamental Causes of Positive and Negative Behavior

- An overview of the seven essential values of moral intelligence
- New research showing how developing brain structures affect moral development

Chapter 10—Effective Guidance Interventions

- Practical DAP strategies for solving day-to-day guidance issues

Chapter 11—Guiding Children from Mindless Mistaken Goals to Mindful Responsibility

- New research findings on conditions that affect intrinsic and extrinsic motivation
- Strategies for dealing with children's use of rude or inappropriate language
- Material on helping children accept the consequences of their behavior
- Update on effective uses of behavior modification
- Research update on emotional intelligence
- Ten habits of emotionally healthy people
- Mindfulness exercises for young children

In addition, to help students build skills and relate theory to practice, *Positive Child Guidance,* eighth edition, offers the following:

- Color photos that make the content of chapters come to life
- Emphasis on developmentally appropriate practice (DAP)
- Boxes that present real-life stories, charts, examples, tips, and strategies
- Unique planning for positive behavior checklist
- Relevant studies, emerging social issues, and challenges
- Sample dialogues among teaching staff, parents, and children
- Developmentally appropriate activities to promote positive behavior
- Research findings related to the brain and the emotions
- Ways teachers can support prosocial development

Ancillary Materials

MindTap™: The Personal Learning Experience

MindTap for Miller, *Positive Child Guidance*, eighth edition, represents a new approach to teaching and learning. A highly personalized, fully customizable learning platform, MindTap helps students to elevate thinking by guiding them to

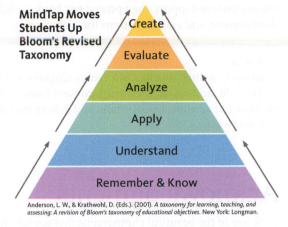

MindTap Moves Students Up Bloom's Revised Taxonomy

Create

Evaluate

Analyze

Apply

Understand

Remember & Know

Anderson, L. W., & Krathwohl, D. (Eds.). (2001). *A taxonomy for learning, teaching, and assessing: A revision of Bloom's taxonomy of educational objectives.* New York: Longman.

- Know, remember, and understand concepts critical to becoming a great teacher
- Apply concepts, create tools, and demonstrate performance and competency in key areas in the course
- Prepare artifacts for the portfolio and eventual state licensure, which are necessary to launch a successful teaching career
- Develop the habits to become a reflective practitioner

As students move through each chapter's Learning Path, they engage in a scaffolded learning experience that is designed to move them up Bloom's Revised Taxonomy, from lower- to higher-order thinking skills. The learning path enables preservice students to develop these skills and gain confidence by

- Engaging them with chapter topics and activating their prior knowledge by watching and answering questions about TeachSource videos of teachers teaching and children learning in real classrooms
- Checking their comprehension and understanding through *Did You Get It?* assessments, with varied question types that are autograded for instant feedback
- Applying concepts through mini-case scenarios—students analyze typical teaching and learning situations and create a reasoned response to the issue(s) presented in the scenario
- Reflecting about and justifying the choices they made within the teaching scenario problem

MindTap helps instructors facilitate better outcomes by evaluating how future teachers plan and teach lessons in ways that make content clear and help diverse students learn, assessing the effectiveness of their teaching practice, and adjusting teaching as needed. The Student Progress App makes grades visible in real time so students and instructors always have access to current standings in the class.

MindTap for Miller, *Positive Child Guidance*, eighth edition, helps instructors easily set their course since it integrates into the existing learning management system and saves instructors time by allowing them to fully customize any aspect of the learning path. Instructors can change the order of the student learning activities, hide activities they don't want for the course, and—most importantly—add any content they do want (e.g., YouTube videos, Google docs, links to state education standards). Learn more at www.cengage.com/mindtap.

PowerPoint® Lecture Slides

These vibrant Microsoft® PowerPoint lecture slides for each chapter assist you with your lecture by providing concept coverage using images, figures, and tables directly from the textbook.

Online Instructor's Manual with Test Bank

An online Instructor's Manual accompanies this book. It contains information to assist the instructor in designing the course, including sample syllabi, discussion questions, teaching and learning activities, field experiences, learning objectives, and additional online resources.

For assessment support, the updated test bank includes true/false, multiple-choice, matching, short-answer, and essay questions for each chapter.

Cognero

Cengage Learning Testing Powered by Cognero is a flexible online system that allows you to author, edit, and manage test bank content from multiple Cengage Learning solutions; create multiple test versions in an instant; and deliver tests from your LMS, your classroom, or wherever you want.

Acknowledgments

Many of the beautiful photographs that appear on these pages were graciously provided by the families and staff of Montessori Country Day School of Houston and The Preschool at Claremont United Methodist Church. Margaret Ellison, Marisol Sharp, Jeri Bolman, and a number of teachers spent many hours collecting photographs and communicating with parents to make it possible for the photographs to appear here in this text. These professionals have my full appreciation for their efforts.

I also appreciate the inspiration, creative input, and feedback I received for this edition from my dear friend Ginger Rothe, former *Newsday* editor. I received help and support from two daughters, Michelle and Cynde, both of whom are professors. Michelle holds a doctorate in cognitive psychology from the University of California at Los Angeles and is professor of psychology at Northern Arizona University. Cynde holds a master's degree in fine arts from the University of California at Irvine and is an associate professor at Chaffe Community College.

Mark Kerr, executive editor, and Kate Scheinman, senior content developer, brought a new vision to this edition. I feel fortunate to have worked with them and the other professional and skillful staff at Cengage Learning.

Most of all I sincerely thank the early childhood faculty who contributed to the readability, accuracy, and usefulness of this book by critiquing it and adding their own ideas and suggestions. These expert reviewers provided a remarkably perceptive level of insight, good judgment, and experience, pushing *Positive Child Guidance* to become a better and more useful text. They include

Susan, Barber, Stephen F. Austin State University

Johnny Castro, Brookhaven College

Stephanie Daniel, J. Sargeant Reynolds Community College

Angel Fason, Mississippi State University

Benita Flores, Del Mar College

Teresa Frazier, Thomas Nelson Community College

Marissa Happ, Waubonsee Community College

Jill Harrison, Delta College

Jo Jackson, Lenoir College

Jennifer Jacobs, University of Cincinnati

Mary Larue, J. Sargeant Reynolds Community College

Mary Olvera, Surry Community College

Diane Plunkett, Fort Hays State University

Brigitte Vittrupe, Texas Woman's University

Elizabeth Watters, Cuyahoga Community College

Dedication

This book was inspired by and is dedicated to my parents, Evolee and Roy Ferris. "Papa Roy" did not live to see the book completed, but he had great interest in and enthusiasm for its writing. Because he grew up the youngest child of a troubled single parent during the Great Depression, he spent much of his adult life struggling to learn how to be a good parent and to let his children know that he loved them. When he read the beginning draft of the first edition of this book, his eyes got a bit misty, and he said, "You've said some important things in here. I'm really proud of you." Of course, no child ever outgrows the need to know she has made her parents proud.

As my late husband, Tommy Miller, and I reared our daughters, we, too, struggled to learn how to be good parents and let our children know they are loved. We have four wonderful grandchildren, Fiona, April, Rosa, and Quinn. Today I feel awe as I watch our next generation learning and growing. Their parents are also learning and growing as they go step-by-step through the joyous, exhausting, scary, magical adventure of child rearing.

About the Author

Darla Ferris Miller holds a doctorate in early childhood education, Texas and Mississippi teaching credentials, and the American Montessori Society Early Childhood, Infant and Toddler Certification. She was a vice president, a division chair, and a professor at North Harris College. Dr. Miller has also served in a wide range of roles within the field of child care and development. She has been caregiver, early childhood teacher, center director, teacher trainer, and consultant, and she has worked with children from infancy to middle school. Dr. Miller's publications include the following:

Miller, D. F. (2014, Summer). Spiritually responsive education and care: Nurturing infants and toddlers in a changing society. *Montessori Life*, *26*(2), 48–52.

Miller, D. F. (2011, Fall). Montessori infant and toddler programs: How our approach meshes with other models. *Montessori Life*, *23*(3), 34–39.

Miller, D. F. (2004, Spring). Science for babies. *Montessori Life*, *16*(2), 26–29.

Miller, D. F. (2004, Winter). Early crusade planted seeds for NHC infant-and-toddler teacher education initiative. *Montessori Life*, *16*(1), 18–22.

Miller, D. F. (1993). *L'éducation des enfants une démarche positive*. (French translation of *Positive Child Guidance*). Ontario, Canada: Institut des Technologies Télématiques.

Miller, D. F. (1990). Room to grow: How to create quality early childhood environments. In L. Ard & M. Pitts (Eds.), *Room to grow: How to create quality early childhood environments*. Austin: Texas Association for the Education of Young Children.

Miller, D. F. (1989). *First steps toward cultural difference: Socialization in infant/toddler day care*. Washington, DC: Child Welfare League of America, Inc. (Continuously in print from 1989 to 2005 and was termed a Child Welfare League "classic" book.)

CHAPTER

1

Why Guidance Matters

naeyc Standards

The following NAEYC Standards are addressed in this chapter

Standard 1 **Promoting child development and learning**

1b Knowing and understanding the multiple influences on early development and learning

1c Using developmental knowledge to create healthy, respectful, supportive, and challenging learning environments for young children

Standard 2 **Building family and community relationships**

2a Knowing about and understanding diverse family and community characteristics

2b Supporting and engaging families and communities through respectful, reciprocal relationships

Standard 4 **Using developmentally effective approaches to connect with children and families**

4a Understanding positive relationships and supportive interactions as the foundation of their work with young children

Objectives

After reading this chapter, you should be able to do the following:

1-1 Identify contemporary issues in child guidance.

1-2 Discuss the relevance of developmentally appropriate practice (DAP).

1-3 Explain why parent and professional training is key to child guidance.

1-4 Analyze the purpose of child guidance.

1-5 List short-term objectives for child guidance.

1-6 List long-term objectives for child guidance.

1-1 Child Rearing in Today's World

At dawn every weekday morning all across the country, from bustling cities to tiny rural communities, mothers and fathers struggle to begin another workday. In millions of homes and apartments, parents hurry to feed and dress babies and young children. Without a minute to spare, they grab diaper bags and satchels, buckle little ones into car seats, climb onto buses, or push strollers into elevators. They head for a variety of child care arrangements ranging from homes of relatives to registered family day homes to proprietary, religious, and government-funded child care centers; early childhood programs; and schools. Stress begins early for today's parents and children.

The world is changing dramatically, but children still need protection, nurturance, love, and guidance. Whether a parent is a full-time homemaker or a business executive with an urgent 8 a.m. appointment makes little difference to a toddler who plops in the middle of the floor and cries because he doesn't want oatmeal for breakfast. **Child guidance** is a challenging task for any parent, but if parents work outside the home, managing their children's behavior may be more complicated, and they may rely a great deal on early childhood professionals to support their children's social and emotional development (Brazelton, 1985; Lederman et al., 2010; Lester & Sparrow, 2010).

Practical day-to-day responsibility for guiding the next generation is shifting from parents alone to parents, communities, and early childhood personnel working

naeyc

child guidance
Contrived methods for external control as well as interaction with and extension of the development of naturally unfolding internal mechanisms and motivations for self-control and self-discipline.

dual-earner couples
Couples in which both partners are gainfully employed.

DIVERSITY

parents single parents
Mothers, fathers, grandparents, or guardians rearing children alone.

family structures
Various arrangements of people living together with children and possibly other generations of relatives.

together. Today, there are fewer full-time homemakers caring for children and rapidly increasing numbers of exhausted **dual-earner couples**, **single parents**, grandparents, stepparents, and other arrangements of employed households juggling work while rearing young children (Williams & Boushey, 2010).

At the same time that **family structures** are changing, more and more research has surfaced highlighting the critical importance of early experiences for the long-term development of a child's personality, character, values, brain development, and social competence (Bernal, 2008; Gopnik, 2010; Liu, Mroz, & van der Klaauw, 2010). Never before has there been such acute awareness of the influence early caregivers have on young lives, and never before has there been such need for people outside the family to assume major involvement in the process of child rearing (Mishel, Bernstein, & Shierholz, 2012; Nelson et al., 2007).

Mothers below the poverty level have always relied on grandmothers, other relatives, and friends to lend a hand in child rearing so they could make a living and keep food on the family table. But for most families a half-century ago, "babysitting" was just a break from the usual business of child rearing carried on by a mother who probably did not work outside the home. Having someone other than a family member look after the children usually lasted only briefly. People assumed that any untrained but reasonably responsible teenager or neighbor could give adequate care to a baby or young child.

Today, however, most babies and young children have parents who work part- or full-time outside the home, whether they live with one or both working parents. Child care is not a brief interruption in child rearing but a central part of it. Many babies spend most of their waking hours in some form of child care as early as the first weeks of life (Forum on Child and Family Statistics, 2009; Friedman, Melhuish, & Hill, 2009; Mishel, Bernstein, & Shierholz, 2012).

These changes place new pressures on parents and on early childhood professionals. Working parents must face the stress of juggling home and work obligations. Fathers find that modern lifestyles present a new level of involvement for them in caring for and managing their children. Early childhood professionals find that more and more is expected of them from parents and from society.

Additionally, more households than ever are being shared by three or even four generations. Adult children often stay at home or return home, and the elderly live

This teacher gives a warm morning greeting. The teacher's affection and attention welcome the parent and child and ease their feelings of stress as they separate from each other.

© Cengage Learning 2013

so much longer that many families care for parents as well as children (Galinsky, Aumann, & Bond, 2009). Working parents' time and finances are often strained to the breaking point. In the United States, welfare reform pressures low-income single mothers to be employed, although their earnings may be meager and their child care costly (National Association of Child Care Resource and Referral Agencies, 2009).

Even parents who are full-time homemakers find that contemporary lifestyles bring new stresses to child rearing. Many feel that their toddlers and preschoolers benefit from participating in professionally run early childhood programs.

Parents and early childhood professionals worry about discipline: "How do I get kids to clean up after themselves?" "How can I keep toddlers from biting and pulling hair?" "What should I do when preschoolers call each other hurtful names?" "Am I being too strict?" "Am I being too lenient?" "How can I manage my own feelings of anger and frustration when children throw tantrums?"

Self-discipline and self-control do not automatically appear out of thin air. Competent, well-behaved children do not just happen. Dedication and skill on the part of parents and early educators help children reach their full potential. Effective guidance prevents behavior problems, supports children's health, safely channels negative feelings, and builds a solid foundation for children's future participation in society.

Child guidance is the very challenging process of establishing and maintaining responsible, productive, and cooperative behavior in children. Parents and early educators must devote a great deal of time, effort, and persistence to help children become considerate and self-disciplined members of society. *Knowledge of the natural stages of child development is the most powerful tool to guide youngsters through this process of maturing.*

1-2 What Is Developmentally Appropriate Practice?

This book provides answers focused on **developmentally appropriate practice**, referred to as DAP. Detailed information about DAP can be obtained through the **National Association for the Education of Young Children** website.

> If our American way of life fails the child, it fails us all.
>
> —*Pearl S. Buck*

DAP developmentally appropriate practice
Early education and care that is carefully planned to match the diverse interests, abilities, and cultural needs of children at various ages and that is carried out with respect for and in cooperation with their families.

naeyc National Association for the Education of Young Children (NAEYC)
A professional organization for early childhood educators dedicated to improving the well-being of all young children, with particular focus on the quality of educational and developmental services for all children from birth through age 8. (See Developmentally Appropriate Practice, Figure 1.1.)

FIGURE 1.1

Developmentally Appropriate Practice

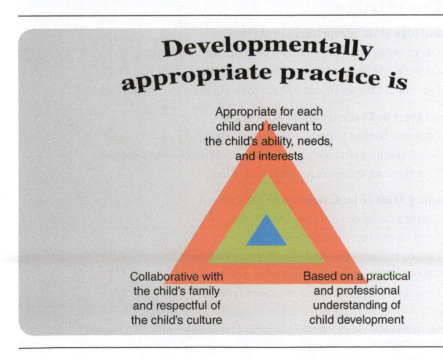

Developmentally appropriate practice is

Appropriate for each child and relevant to the child's ability, needs, and interests

Collaborative with the child's family and respectful of the child's culture

Based on a practical and professional understanding of child development

© Cengage Learning®

TeachSource Video

Curriculum Planning: Implementing Developmentally Appropriate Practice in an Early Childhood Setting

Watch this Video Case and the bonus video offered; then study the five Viewing Questions provided and answer the following four questions.

1. What are three activity centers you saw in the case?
2. Why should the teaching staff know about the child?
3. How many desks did you see?
4. What is the difference between a teacher-initiated and a child-initiated activity?

A caring community of learners is created as children work and play together. Children learn to help each other and to respect each other's needs.

DAP As children mature through natural stages of development, their social, physical, emotional, and intellectual needs and interests change dramatically. Activities, materials, and events are individualized and adapted to be "just right" for their needs. In DAP, a teacher's methods change not only according to ages and stages, but also according to individual differences in children's personalities and interests. One child may have a tremendous interest and curiosity about dinosaurs—another child may think dinosaurs are "nasty." She may be fascinated in exploring seeds and plants and in figuring out how food grows.

Every part of this book is written to support DAP by supporting positive, respectful, and empowering relationships among adults and children. See Positive Focus 1.1.

Positive Focus 1.1 — The Core of DAP

1. Knowledge Must Inform Decision Making
   a. Demonstrate knowledge of child development and learning
   b. Observe and discover each child as an individual
   c. Learn about the social and cultural contexts in which children live

2. Goals Must Be Challenging and Achievable
   a. Empower families to participate in goal setting
   b. Select teaching strategies to promote individual children's progress
   c. Communicate children's progress to families

3. Teaching Must Be Intentional to Be Effective
   a. Create a caring community of learners
   b. Teach to enhance development and learning
   c. Plan curriculum to achieve important goals
   d. Assess children's development and learning
   e. Establish reciprocal relationships with families

Adapted from National Association for the Education of Young Children (NAEYC), Washington, DC, www.naeyc.org/dap/core.

1-3 Why Is Positive Child Guidance Training Important for Parents, Caregivers, and Teachers?

In today's world, most children do not spend the first years of their lives only at home. They are up with the alarm clock, their days are structured and scheduled, they come in contact with many adults other than their parents, and they must learn to get along with other children in groups. Modern parents need help in developing skills for effectively guiding young children and preventing behavior problems. Adults may not have time to deal with a toddler throwing a tantrum and refusing to get dressed or a pouting preschooler who insists that everyone in the whole world hates her. Parents need support so that behavior problems do not place additional strain on family life that may already be stretched thin from the stresses of contemporary living (American Psychotherapy Association, 2008; Galinsky, Aumann, & Bond, 2008;Heckman, 2006; McClowry, Snow, Tamis-LeMonda, & Rodriquez, 2010; Snow, 2009). See Positive Focus 1.2.

Early childhood professionals need study and practice to develop effective child guidance skills. They will provide important support to family life. Teachers and caregivers can never replace caring parents. Parents have an irreplaceable influence on their children's lives because of the emotional bonds that are a part of being a family. Although caregivers must never compete with or infringe on this special parent–child relationship, they can be a tremendous support to both children and their families. Parents are the first and most important teachers children will ever have. But early childhood professionals have a growing importance in today's world.

Parents are becoming more aware of the critical importance of their child's development in early childhood. When they look for child care, they are likely to look for teacher training and program accreditation.

1-3a Who Should Be Responsible for the Well-Being and Guidance of Children?

It is in the world's best interest if all adults accept responsibility for the well-being and guidance of children. In past centuries, children were thought to be their parents' property. In Western Europe just over a century and a half ago, babies were not considered to be real persons. It was not even thought necessary to report their deaths (Aries, 1962). In a modern democracy, however, children are understood to be human beings with inalienable human rights. Governmental agencies are set up with responsibility to protect the welfare of young children because children are future citizens. Failure to address children's early needs costs government millions of tax dollars later in remedial education, indigent support, and the prosecution and incarceration of convicted criminals (Belfield & Levin, 2007; Lakhanpal & Ram, 2008; Muennig, 2006; Muennig et al., 2009; Schweinhart, 2004).

Professional Early Childhood Jobs Are Increasing

Positive Focus 1.2

Employment in preschool teaching and formal early childhood program teaching is expected to grow by 25 percent over the 2010–2020 period, much faster than the average for all occupations. Growth is expected due to a growing public awareness of the importance of early childhood education and the growing population of children ages 3 to 5. In other words, over the coming decade, jobs will be available for well-trained early childhood professionals.

Adapted from Bureau of Labor Statistics (2012–2013). Bureau of Labor Statistics, U.S. Department of Labor, 2012–2013 Occupational Outlook Handbook, Accessed 9/28/2013, http://www.bls.gov/ooh/

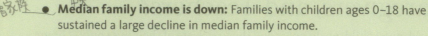

Positive Focus 1.3   Sadly, Quality Child Care Is Not Available to All Families

- **Poverty is up.** Over the past decade, the percentage of children living in families below the poverty line has increased.
- **Median family income is down:** Families with children ages 0–18 have sustained a large decline in median family income.
- **Secure employment is down:** Parents today are less likely to be securely employed than they were in 2001.
- **Publicly funded enrollment progress has <u>stalled</u>.** Despite solid improvement in the 1990s, we have failed to sustain a pattern of enrollment growth. Public funding for preschool programs across the United States fell by an unprecedented $500 million in the 2011–2012 school year.

Land, K. C. (2012). Foundation for Child Development. 2012 Child Well-Being Index (CWI); New York, NY. Accessed online 9/28/2013, http://fcd-us.org/our-work/child-well-being-index-cwi

> If a man empties his purse into his head, no one can take it away from him. An investment in knowledge always pays the best interest.
>
> —*Benjamin Franklin*

parent–teacher resource team
Teachers and parents working together as a cooperative, respectful, and cohesive partnership.

naeyc

DAP requires that teachers value the unique qualities of each child as well as the special role of children's parents.

Business and industry have an interest in the welfare of young children because today's children will become tomorrow's workforce, and competitiveness in world markets depends on the availability of capable, responsible workers. Civic groups, churches, schools, and you and I are also responsible for children's welfare. Good citizenship obligates us to look toward the future well-being of humanity rather than focusing only on our own personal interests. We can help our community build a brighter future by joining with others to inform and encourage better child care and education.

Throughout the United States, there is growing recognition that investing efforts and resources to better the lives of children is not only humane, but is also very cost effective. Children are open to ideas and experiences. It is possible to bring about meaningful changes in their lives and to have real influence on their long-term development of values and character traits. As adults, we tend to be more rigidly set in our habits and potentials. If we are to continue to enjoy the benefits of living in a democracy, then we should help all children learn personal responsibility and respect for others so they will know how to function properly as adults. See Positive Focus 1.3.

1-3b Committing to Becoming the Child's Resource Team

Parents are children's first teachers—and they are children's teachers throughout childhood and, to some extent, even into adulthood. Parents have an important opportunity to make a huge difference in their children's lives. If we are to reach our goals, we must partner with the people ultimately responsible for the children in our care—the parents. To be effective in guiding children, teachers and parents must work as a cooperative and cohesive team. Mothers, fathers, grandparents, guardians, and teachers should communicate frequently and respectfully about the child's needs.

For effective **parent–teacher resource teams**, we give families opportunities for communication and a strong sense of empowerment. Parents are accustomed to being in charge of their children.

© Cengage Learning 2013

They want to know their children's activities and progress. Some parents fear that they will be perceived as too intrusive if they ask how their children are doing. Other parents, especially those lacking in education, may feel intimidated by teachers. And some parents whose children are particularly challenging may avoid interacting with teachers for fear of being blamed for their children's inappropriate behavior.

Teachers can open the channels of communication with all of these parents by treating them with respect. Teachers can show respect for each parent by conveying in everything they do that each child has strengths and is valued. They can empower parents by allowing them to have a meaningful voice in the child's education.

Teachers work in partnership with families, establishing and maintaining frequent two-way communication. See Positive Focus 1.4.

The parent–teacher resource team can brainstorm together what changes in the child's environment are needed from time to time. Will parents need to unplug the television at home to ensure more quality time? Will the teacher need to increase individual attention for a challenging child? How will the team communicate day-to-day changes in children's health and emotional well-being? How can the team nurture budding learning in a certain area? Or work on a negative habit pattern that has begun to develop?

Copyright © 2016 Cengage Learning

▶❚❚ TeachSource Video

A Parent's Viewpoint: Parent-Teacher Communication

Watch this Video Case on parent communication, and then answer the following questions:

1. Why do you think parents are so eager for information about their child's day?

2. Name three examples of information the teacher in this video described sharing with parents.

3. Did the teacher seem to resent parents' eagerness for information? Why or why not?

Handy Tips for Effective Home/School Partnerships

Positive Focus 1.4

For Parents

- Communicate with teachers
- Read to children every day
- Read in front of children daily (set an example)
- Talk often about how learning helps people
- Take time to really listen to children
- Play with children; allow children to lead in play activity
- Monitor and support play with friends
- Give children responsibilities and make sure they succeed
- Allow children to make choices within reasonable boundaries
- Make boundaries and expectations very clear in advance

For Teachers

- Convince parents that involvement is valuable
- Develop a simple parent involvement plan
- Know that extensive plans overwhelm
- Start a simple classroom newsletter for parents
- Take time to really listen to parents
- Use labeled folders to send work and notes home
- Invite parents and grandparents to be school volunteers
- Teach parents how to make easy learning games
- Display children's work and invite parents to see it

TeachSource Digital Download

The Spoiled Child—Myth or Reality?

It is a glorious day at the park. Bright sunshine is radiating just enough warmth to balance a flag-snapping breeze. This sudden evidence of spring has drawn families and children outdoors like a magnet. Sitting on the grass alongside a large sandbox is a cluster of grown-ups who are laughing and talking as they watch their youngsters squealing and running or digging eagerly in the sand.

Al and Tamara's 4-year-old son Joel makes gleeful whooping sounds as he chases his 2-year-old brother Eddy with a wriggling bug he has found in the sand. Eddy screeches and dives onto his dad for protection as his mother beseeches Joel to "stop being so wild."

As he skids to a stop, Joel inadvertently smashes into a double stroller holding the Rodriguez twins. While Al escorts his boys back to their buckets and shovels, Tamara bends down with Elena Rodriguez to make sure the 1-year-old twin girls are okay.

Several other parents have stopped talking and are watching attentively as Elena adjusts the little girls in their stroller and smoothes their crisp red dresses with identical embroidered collars.

Other mothers are amazed that the twins have not cried. Tamara takes one little girl by the hand and says, "Shall we get them out and let them play for a while?"

"Oh, no," says Elena, "They would get filthy. They know that they have to stay in the stroller." Al comments that his boys were never that "good." They would have pitched a fit to get out and get right in the middle of the dirt.

Several other parents chime in with awestruck comments about how good the twins are. Elena responds, "I knew with twins and me working that they had better not get spoiled. In the child care center I use, they are very strict about not spoiling the kids. They only pick up the babies to change and feed them. The babies cried for a few days right at first, but now they're just no trouble at all."

The conversation about Elena's twins trails off as other parents scatter to chase after straying toddlers and respond to their children's cries of "Watch me," "Push me in the swing again," and "Look at my sand castle!" As Tamara rushes to Eddy to remind him not to eat sand, she feels a surge of envy for Elena and her "good" babies who are never any trouble.

Case Discussion Questions

1. What do people really mean when they label babies either "spoiled" or "good"?

2. What appear to be Elena's priorities and values in caring for her children? What are her daughters learning about their role in the world? Why is that a problem?

3. Why do you think the staff in Elena's child care center were opposed to holding, rocking, and playing with babies? Does frequent holding and cuddling create a setting in which adults are warm, nurturing, and emotionally available to the children? Why is this important to children's development?

4. How do you feel about Al and Tamara's relationship with their children?

5. List, in order of importance, the 10 characteristics you personally value and admire most in a person (for example, kindness, sense of humor, energy, intelligence, enthusiasm, and so on). Are these the same characteristics you expect caregivers to model in their interactions with babies and young children? Describe a real situation in which you demonstrated the characteristic that you most value.

6. List the 10 characteristics you like least in a person. Are these characteristics that you have seen caregivers demonstrate in their interactions with youngsters? Describe a real situation in which you demonstrated a characteristic that you would not want children to imitate.

7. Al and Tamara have a different cultural background from Elena. Do you think their cultural background may have had an effect on their child-rearing style? If so, how?

1-4 What Is the Purpose of Child Guidance?

The early childhood setting, whether in the home or in a child care center, is a miniature community in which children develop and practice the basic skills they will need to cope as they go through school and then finally enter the big, wide world. Child guidance builds a foundation on which everything else in the child's life is built, including social interaction with others, learning, and emotional development. By their very nature, babies come into this world helpless and self-centered. Guidance transforms them into full-fledged, functioning members of society.

1-4a Does This Book Have a Special Point of View on Guidance?

This book has been written specifically for those **adults** who make an invaluable contribution to society by caring for and teaching the youngest and most vulnerable—our children. The book is intended as a foundation for effective problem solving and as a guide for adults as they strive to meet the developmental needs of children from infancy through early childhood. *Every child has unique needs. Consequently, no single guidance strategy will be appropriate for all children at all ages.*

This book addresses typical characteristics and needs of children as they proceed through developmental stages. It provides a broad range of practical, effective, and flexible guidance methods that are based on principles of honest communication and assertiveness. The focus is on respect for the dignity and human rights of the infant and young child. Guiding children effectively always takes effort. But the methods presented here promise to make the process less frustrating and more satisfying for both adult and child.

Many child guidance authors have focused mostly on behaviorist learning theory, a view that learning can best be explained as the result of externally reinforced (or rewarded) behavior. External control in the form of ignoring negative behavior and rewarding appropriate behavior is referred to as behavior modification. If used well in certain types of situations, it can be extremely useful.

For many people, however, discipline means simply giving rewards and punishments to control children's behavior externally. Many schools rely completely on competitiveness, grades, stickers, and time-outs to motivate and control children. A problem with reliance on external control is that children may respond only when they know that rewards or punishments are close at hand. They may not learn to behave appropriately simply because it is the "right" thing to do.

Additionally, rewarding children for behaving a certain way raises several sticky issues. Because human beings of all ages are infinitely complex, the praise or prize that reinforces one child may embarrass, bore, or alienate another. Doling out privileges and prizes may place an adult in the role of a stingy gift giver, rather than that of a democratic guide and role model, and may stimulate competition rather than cooperation among children. Doling out attention and praise as reinforcement risks implying to children that compliance is a condition for affection and that only "good" children are valued.

Planning for positive child guidance should not rely only on strategies for external control but instead should support the child's naturally unfolding motivation for self-control. Children should be helped to become self-directed and less dependent on others to manage their behavior. As they grow toward adolescence and adulthood, they must begin to make critical choices about what to do and how to behave.

Because imitation of adult modeling is an important way young children learn, how adults cope with stress and frustration is critical. Children tend to do what we *do* rather than what we *say to do*. Remember, the purpose of child guidance is to support the growth of effective life skills—not just to control annoying behaviors.

Positive, persistent assertiveness takes more deliberate patience than intimidating children into obedience by scolding, screaming, or spanking. And it definitely requires

adult

One who seeks not to gain control over children but rather to guide them effectively, while setting for them first-hand examples of appropriate coping and assertive negotiation.

© Cengage Learning 2013

When using positive child guidance, teachers enjoy and appreciate the individual qualities of each child.

naeyc

a great deal more thoughtful effort than allowing children to "run wild." But taking the time to guide children properly will give them the skills they need to be successful not only in school, but also throughout their future lives. In today's world, all children deserve attentive, self-esteem–building guidance.

Early childhood programs are training grounds where very young people practice the skills they will need for effective living. The personal characteristics and capabilities needed for survival in an autocracy or anarchy are very different from those needed for life in a democracy. Early child guidance begins with the development of self-respect, awareness of and consideration for the rights of others, and recognition that persons of all ages, colors, and creeds should be treated with respect.

The ultimate goal of child guidance is the child's development of inner responsibility, self-confidence, and self-control. Inner discipline, based on a desire to be a cooperative community member, is very useful to adult life in a democracy. A democracy doesn't function very well if its citizens act only to gain rewards and avoid punishments. Of course, democracy is not helped by laissez-faire anarchy in which people recklessly trample the rights of others in their search for self-indulgence.

This book outlines practical, workable steps for creating a cooperative, respectful community of children and adults. Behavior modification is addressed not as the foundation of child guidance, but rather as a single, carefully placed stone in a solid structure of positive guidance. Maturation is addressed not as an excuse to relinquish responsibility for child behavior, but as a powerful tool for understanding and responding appropriately to various stages of child behavior. The method presented is one of assertive and respectful enforcement of cooperatively developed rules and persistent protection of individual rights.

Aggression, passivity, and manipulation are identified as hindrances to positive child guidance. They trigger negativity, even rebellion, in children, and they set an example for behaviors that are hindrances to successful participation in democratic community life. *The role of the adult, in this book, is that of one who seeks not to gain control over children but rather to guide them effectively, while setting for them a first-hand example of appropriate coping and communication.*

In this model, the adult guards the well-being and individual rights of children and stimulates their development of inner control by creating a functioning democratic community of children and adults. Positive child guidance involves guiding children as firmly as necessary, as gently as possible, and always with respect.

1-5 Short-Term Objectives for Child Guidance

objective
Immediate aim or purpose.

The short-term **objective** for child guidance is deceptively simple. Children will be helped to follow the same basic values for decent and responsible behavior that are applicable to all persons living in a democracy. To accomplish this, we can use the following guidelines to determine the appropriateness of children's day-to-day behaviors and help them learn the difference between right and wrong:

- Behavior must not present a clear risk of harm to oneself or others.
- Behavior must not infringe on the rights of others.
- Behavior must not unreasonably damage the environment, animals, objects, or materials in the environment.

To communicate these values effectively and to translate them to the comprehension level of young children, they must be greatly oversimplified. By oversimplifying them, young children can be guided to make sense of what otherwise may seem to them to be an endless number of unrelated little rules. By lumping rules into three basic categories, young children can be helped to remember and understand basic principles for appropriate behavior: be healthy, be respectful, and be responsible. These principles should be stated as reminders before more specific class rules are stated. These principles—be healthy, be respectful, be responsible—lay the groundwork for children to think about the consequences of their behavior. Children then develop specific class rules to guide their day-to-day behavior. Class rules are based on the same principles behind laws and social expectations in the adult world.

By teaching basic principles of appropriate behavior, we are helping children learn to think for themselves: "Is my choice healthy? Is my choice respectful? Is my choice responsible?" We could never create enough class rules to cover every possible inappropriate situation children could get into. Even if we could create lists of rules for every possibility, we wouldn't be able to remember them all. Instead, we teach children to think about potential consequences before they act. Children become responsible and cooperative members of their community of children.

Children will need many daily reminders:

- Be *healthy*! Wash your hands before snack.
- Be *respectful*! Wait for your turn.
- Be *responsible*! Put your trash in the trashcan, not on the ground.
- Be *healthy*! The fence is not safe for climbing. The fort is safe for climbing.
- Be *respectful*! Please wait for your turn on the slide.
- Be *responsible*! Please take a paper towel and wipe up your spill.

"Remember—be healthy—sand is for digging, not for throwing. Sand hurts if it gets in your eyes."

Positive daily reminders recognize appropriate behavior. For example,

- "Thank you for being healthy. You have chosen a nutritious snack."
- "Thank you for being *respectful*. I heard you say 'Excuse me.'"
- "Thank you for being *responsible*. You put your blocks away."

By the time the children are 5 or 6 years old, we can review behavior principles and then invite children to collaboratively develop class rules. At that age, they can help write and post the basic guidelines and then develop class rules that are related to these three main categories. For example, children can think of three class rules that would help classmates remember to respect the rights of others:

- "Don't look in someone else's locker (cubbie) without asking."
- "Don't tell someone she can't play kickball because she is a girl."
- "Don't shove when you are waiting for the bus."

In addition, we help teach children how to rephrase their rules into positive *do* statements instead of negative *don't* statements. For example,

- "Ask before you look in someone else's locker (cubbie)."
- "Help friends feel included."
- "Say 'excuse me' if someone is in your way."

Remember that the reason for these guidelines—be healthy, be respectful, be responsible—is to teach basic values for membership in a community. You can reword these statements, translate them, express them in sign language, or

"Thank you for hanging up your backpack so nicely."

DIVERSITY

use your own special way to communicate these values to children. Our words should match children's individual levels of development.

We teach children to protect themselves and others from harm, respect the rights of others, and avoid unnecessary damage to surroundings. We guide them to make choices that are healthy, respectful, and responsible. Whether a child is in the United States, Canada, Mexico, Korea, Kenya, France, or anywhere else on the globe, these three guidelines are important to being a cooperative member of a community.

Stating principles for appropriate behavior is easy. Evaluating behaviors in real children in specific cultural settings can be a great deal more difficult. Evaluation requires us to think.

A well-coordinated 5-year-old is leaning back on two legs of his chair. Let's analyze the situation:

Be healthy

- Is a fall likely?

Be respectful

- Is the walkway between tables blocked for other children?

Be responsible

- How sturdy are the chairs?
- Are breakable things nearby?

If we haven't created a class rule about children leaning back in their chairs, should we make a rule? How will children be involved in thinking about behavior consequences and creating class rules?

Personal judgment, practical experience, and knowledge of individual children and their capabilities will determine how we answer these questions and how we go about setting rules and enforcing discipline. I hope you will answer these questions with enough compassion to see every situation through children's eyes and enough courage to be true to your sense of fair play and good judgment.

1-5a Do Children Have Rights?

Children have rights just like any other human being in a democracy. There are times when children need the opportunity to figure out how to defend themselves appropriately against an assault on their rights. At other times, they need direct teaching to show them how to defend their rights appropriately. Sometimes, they simply need someone bigger to defend them from hurtful behavior. But in all cases, children's rights deserve our attention.

Children Have a Right to Be Safe

Adults should be very strong-minded about protecting every child's right not to be hit, kicked, bitten, or shoved. It is never okay to allow a child to be kicked because he did it first and "deserved to get a taste of his own medicine." It is never okay to bite a toddler back "so that he will learn what biting feels like." A cliché that happens to be true is, "Two wrongs do not make a right." The only thing that revenge really does is bring about more hurtful behavior. Adults should monitor children carefully and consistently so that aggression can be prevented or interrupted immediately when it does occur.

Children Have a Right to Avoid Unnecessary Discomfort

Children have a right to eat lunch peacefully without an unnerving noise level caused by children around them screaming and yelling. They have a right to listen to a story without being squashed by others who are struggling to see the pictures. And they have a right to build sand castles without getting sand in their eyes because gleeful playmates are shoveling sand into the air just for the fun of it.

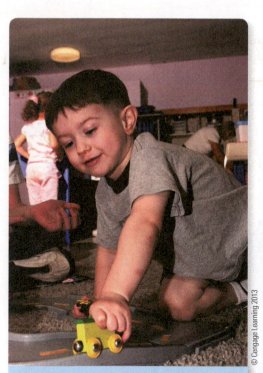

This little boy has a right to focus on his imaginative play without needless interruption. Other children should ask, "May I play with you?"

© Cengage Learning 2013

Although newborns begin with a kind of thinking that limits them to a self-centered (or egocentric) view of the world, children gradually learn that others have feelings. A 1-year-old may try to give his pacifier to an older child who is crying, or a preschooler may run to tell a teacher that her friend got pushed off the swing. Adults who are consistently sensitive to the comfort needs of children set an emotional tone in which children are much more inclined to be sensitive to each other. Additionally, we talk often to children about how others might be feeling:

- "How did Monique feel when you took her crayon? How would you feel if she took your crayon?"
- "I wonder how Ravi felt when you shoved him?"
- "What does Junior feel when you chase him? Is he having fun or is he feeling scared?"

Children Have a Right to Their Possessions

Adults sometimes impose on children very strange views of sharing. In the adult world, government provides precise laws related to possession and ownership. Law forbids others from tampering with one's possessions without permission. Social customs follow the same rule. If I take a cart in a grocery store and begin doing my shopping, it would be extremely rude and surprising for another shopper to snatch that cart away and dump my groceries because she wanted "a turn" with the cart. I would greatly appreciate a store manager (authority figure) who intervened politely but assertively and redirected the offending shopper to other available carts. Oddly enough, a child in preschool who complains because another child grabbed the tricycle or snatched the container of crayons he was using is often not helped but instead chided for "tattling" and for "not sharing."

A child's personal possessions are his own, and others should not tamper with them without asking the child or at least letting the child know that, for example, "I'm going to move your blocks over there." Objects that are available for shared use belong to the person using them at any given time (until, of course, that use infringes on the rights of others). In a home setting, if one child is watching television, another should not be allowed to march in and change channels without asking. In a group setting, a puzzle belongs to the child who chose to work with it, and no one else should be allowed to touch that puzzle without permission from the child who chose it first. Sharing is really sharing only if it is voluntary.

Children Have a Right to Fairness

Fairness is a concept that emerges slowly in children during the preschool and early elementary years. Even before that concept is well developed, however, children deserve fair treatment, and they need to observe role models of integrity and fairness. If one child is allowed to have a picture book during naptime, then it is unfair to deny that privilege to another child without some logical reason or explanation.

By the time children are around kindergarten age, they can sometimes be heard proclaiming loudly, "Hey, that's not fair." Although their logic is still rather limited and their actual concept of fairness may be hazy, they are likely to complain if the action of an adult or another child appears to them to be blatantly unequal or out of compliance with a rule. Sometimes, if an adult carries out a disciplinary action that appears arbitrary and capricious to a child, the child will immediately begin enforcing that action on other children, partly as revenge and partly in imitation of the adult. For example, a teacher angrily snaps at a child and yanks

Each day of our lives we make deposits in the memory banks of our children.
—Maya Angelou

© Cengage Learning 2013

Children begin life without any self-control, so we assist them in their journey toward responsible adulthood by nurturing their mastery of self-control.

his lunch box out of his hand because it is not yet time for lunch. A few minutes later, the child mimics the adult's behavior and tone of voice, yanking away a smaller child's toy and snapping, "Gimme that, you baby!"

1-5b How Do We Tell the Difference between Enforcing Reasonable Safety Rules and Being Overprotective?

Just about every interesting activity or environment has some element of risk. Imagine for a moment trying to create an environment that has absolutely no possibility for any kind of accident. Unfortunately, a child can potentially misuse, fall off, throw, choke on, or bump into just about any kind of equipment or material that can be named. The only perfectly safe environment would probably be an empty room with padded walls and floor, and some child would undoubtedly find a way to get hurt there too. Of course, a padded cell would not offer many opportunities for exploration and skill development. So in an interesting, challenging environment, safety is always a matter of compromise. The difficulty for many teachers and parents seems to be in deciding what level of risk is acceptable and reasonable and what level is not.

Children feel a sense of pride and dignity when they succeed in mastering a difficult challenge that has a bit of risk involved. No baby ever learned to walk without risking a fall, and no child ever learned to jump off a step, climb a tree, roller skate, or ride a bicycle without risking a bump or bruise. Some pediatricians assume that children who make it through childhood without so much as a broken finger have been overprotected. The acceptability of risk must be weighed against the severity of possible outcomes. If the worst thing that could reasonably result is a 2-foot fall onto a thick gymnastic mat, then the risk seems very acceptable. If the child could possibly fall 10 feet onto brick pavement, then there is a clear risk of harm; that kind of accident could result in serious or permanent injury to the child.

Adults must be diligent about creating healthy environments for young children. Environments should be checked and double-checked routinely for hazardous equipment, toxic plants or substances, and dangerous but tempting situations. Then, but only then, can adults step back and allow children the freedom to negotiate challenges independently, under a watchful eye but without hovering control.

1-6 Long-Term Goals for Child Guidance

goal
Overarching purpose or aspiration.

If children are to become responsible, they must learn to control their actions and impulses. Unfortunately, self-control is not an easy thing to teach. Children begin life without any self-control whatsoever, so our most critical long-term **goal** is to assist them in their journey to responsible adulthood by nurturing their mastery of self-control.

Children are not simply lumps of clay to be shaped by caregivers. They are born with individual potentials and personality traits. They are also, however, profoundly influenced by the people, experiences, and events they encounter, especially during the first years of their lives (Bouchard & McGue, 2003; Champagne & Mashoodh, 2009; Crosnoe et al., 2010). The effect of the environment on children, interestingly, is reciprocal. Children have a tremendous impact on the behavior of the adults in their lives. Instead of being passively shaped by adults, children are actively involved in the experiences that influence their own development. Adults behave differently with different children. The actions and appearances of individual children trigger different emotions and reactions in individual adults.

temperament
Clusters of personality traits with individual and distinctive behavioral patterns.

Children are born with individual and distinctive behavioral patterns. These clusters of personality traits are referred to as **temperament**. The temperament of an infant or child has an influence on how adults will care for her. Also, the quality and style of the care that adults provide have a strong influence on that continually developing temperament. A child affects her caregivers and they affect her; both change and are changed by their interactions (Bradley & Corwyn, 2008; Miner &

Clarke-Stewart, 2008; Park & Rubin, 2008; Rubin, Burgess, & Hastings, 2002). All these influences, both internal and external, ensure that no two people will ever be exactly the same. We must help children appreciate their differences.

Even when two children's behavior is similar, their gender, size, or appearance may trigger different adult reactions. A thin, frail infant girl may evoke more protective, nurturing behavior in adults than would a loud, robust infant boy, who may evoke more roughhousing and active playfulness in caregivers. A child who appears defiant may be treated sternly, whereas a child who appears contrite may be treated indulgently after an identical incident. A cycle emerges in which the child begins to anticipate a certain kind of interaction with others so he behaves accordingly, actually triggering the expected interaction. What began as incidental action and reaction settles eventually into habit, attitude, and personality. The bottom line is, of course, that early experiences make a difference in children's lives.

We play a critical role in shaping children's future lives. Our long-term goal for guidance is our most important contribution: equipping children with the skills and attitudes they need for happy, responsible, and productive adult life.

Courtesy of the Miller Smith Family

Affection and attention foster the long-term development of children's potential to become competent, confident, cooperative people.

1-6a The Nurturing Environment and Long-Term Development

High-quality early childhood settings look so simple that it is easy to underestimate the importance of the interactions that take place there. An appropriate environment for young children is relaxed and playful. Children follow their own curiosity as they freely but respectfully explore objects, toys, and materials in the environment. They move about, chatter peacefully, laugh, and occasionally argue as they explore human social interactions and learn reasonable limits. Homes where children are expected to be seen and not heard or formal school settings with pupils sitting rigidly and silently following teacher instructions and listening to teachers talking are not examples of DAP environments.

BrainFacts

What Can We Learn from Neuroscience?

Warm and nurturing social relationships improve learning and behavior

- Oxytocin is a hormone that increases empathy, trust, and ability to "read" others' feelings (Kosfeld, Heinrichs, Zak, Fischbacher, & Fehr, 2005).
- Oxytocin is released in our bodies at high concentrations during positive social interactions (Fischer-Shofty, Levkovitz, & Shamay-Tsoory, 2012).
- Oxytocin reinforces memory and aids learning (Ferrier, 1980; Hurlemann et al., 2010).
- Our natural "fight or flight" response to conflict excites us to strike back or run away. Oxytocin calms us and triggers a "tend and befriend" response that causes us to reach out to others for support and help (Fischer-Shofty, Levkovitz, & Shamay-Tsoory, 2012; University of Haifa, 2013).
- Reaching out to others strengthens social bonds and gives us a healthy way to cope with conflict.

Positive Focus 1.5

An appropriate role model teaches children positive behavior by serving as an example

Children learn social skills by imitating others

Guide for Adult Role Models

- Treat everyone with dignity and respect at all times.

- Rely on communication, persistence, and patience rather than on force.

- Respond assertively to misbehavior with both firmness and gentleness.

- Use problem-solving strategies to identify the causes of misbehavior.

- Plan and prepare appropriate activities, materials, and routines.

- Give unconditional affection and affirmation.

- Communicate in an honest, polite, and straightforward manner.

- Protect every child's individual rights.

- Celebrate differences.

- Really listen.

TeachSource Digital Download

Video supplied by BBC Worldwide Learning

▶❚❚ **TeachSource** Video

Benefits of Preschool

Watch this Video Case on preschool attendance, and then answer the following questions:

1. What effect did preschool attendance have on the children described in this video?

2. In this video, did you see teachers presenting flash cards and worksheets to children between the ages of 2 and 5? What activities did you see?

3. Did the video state that preschool-attending children from low-income families benefit more than or less than preschool-attending children from wealthier families?

The rote memorization in lessons with workbooks, flashcards, and worksheets is definitely something many young children can master. But it will take coercion, pressure, prizes, or extravagant praise to keep them on task. Even then, the abstract concepts they will have memorized are just gobbledygook. Their young brains are not developed well enough to know what the facts mean. Even toddlers can memorize and repeat chants and rhymes with long words, but they are unlikely to have a clue about their meaning. If too much time is spent in such questionable ventures as rote memorization, the loss of time for more wholesome hands-on, sensory learning experiences can interfere with the essential business of early childhood. Children will have plenty of time for more meaningful memorization in later childhood, adolescence, and college. See Positive Focus 1.5.

DAP learning environments help children reach their full potential. The healthy development of the whole child requires social, emotional, and physical development through whole-body exploration and play. The foundation of early learning is self-directed exploring, practicing, constructing, pretending, and problem solving (Coplan, Rubin, & Findlay, 2006; Elkind, 2007; Pellegrini, 2009). Experience truly is the best teacher for young children (Brown & Vaughan, 2009; Dewey, 1959; Fleer, 2009).

In family settings where parents have strong bonds of love for and attachment to their child, they will quite naturally respond to the cries and smiles given when a child needs attention. A healthy, well-developing baby or child gives many signals or cues to indicate needs. A sensitive, caring parent uses trial and error to discover what will work to stop the child's crying and to keep the child happy and comfortable. This same give-and-take can be the heart of group care. Teaching staff express warmth through behaviors such as physical affection, eye contact, tone of voice, and smiles.

If we see child care as a tedious chore made easier by ignoring children's cries and by avoiding emotional attachment, then nature's way of ensuring healthy development is undone. Caregivers and teachers who do not find joy in working with children should consider a different career.

1-6b Why Should Children Be Involved in Maintaining and Protecting Their Environment?

Even the youngest children need to begin learning how to take proper care of their clothing, toys, dishes, and any other objects they handle. This is their little world and they need to care for it as independently as possible. Very young children can learn to say *environment* and know generally what it means. I remember a preschool teacher who was from Alabama and had her own special pronunciation for *environment*. A cute little 3-year-old boy's mother came to class one day totally mystified and asked the teacher if she could see the "varmint." She told the puzzled teacher that her son talked often of cleaning the "varmint" and she just wanted to see what kind of varmint that they had.

Very young children can learn to put their toys back on the shelf, put their shoes and clothing in the correct spots, and pass out cups and napkins. They can accept responsibility. Children must have the freedom to make small mistakes. They discover connections between their behaviors and unwanted outcomes. Children learn to clean up after knocking over a cup of milk or spilling paint. Without the sting of blame or punishment, children can be helped to focus their attention on the results of their actions and learn how to do better. Stained clothes will soon be forgotten, but a child's independent accomplishment will be treasured, and the benefit of the experience of independence may stay with a child for life.

Although it is essential to keep a reasonable perspective about orderliness, remember that responsibility, manners, and good citizenship require all of us to have respect for our surroundings. We all share the resources of this planet and have an obligation, therefore, to use them wisely and well. Early child guidance prepares children for good citizenship. When a child remembers to use one paper towel at a time and then throw it away, he is preparing for membership in adult society where everyone benefits if forests logged to make paper towels are replanted, water used in factories is cleaned before being dumped, and fish and game are taken according to lawful limits and seasons.

In the first years of life, children can gradually learn to take only what they need, use it with care, and then restore it (put it away) when they have finished using it. Toys, games, and learning materials should be arranged in an orderly manner on low shelves that are accessible to children. Even a very young child can learn to replace a puzzle if it has its own place on a shelf or in a puzzle rack. A stack of heavy puzzles crammed on a shelf makes it difficult or impossible for a child to take any but the top puzzle. Additionally, the number of learning materials available at any one time should match the capacity of the children. More is not always better.

Watch children carefully. Can they get materials from the shelf easily? Can they easily return the item to the correct spot? If they cannot, if the shelves are crowded or confusing, there may be too much available. Simplify the shelves and rotate in new materials as children tire of the old ones. Adults serve as role models for care of the environment so children learn that things are easier to find if they are always returned to the same spot.

Children should be stopped firmly but kindly when their behavior is damaging to the environment. While playing outdoors, children may innocently break limbs off shrubs, smash birds' eggs, or peel bark off trees. Teaching them about nature and the value of plants and animals assists them in building respect for living things and in accepting **responsibility** for their own actions. Indoors, children playfully smash riding toys into table legs and stuff tissues down the sink drain just to see what happens. These actions should immediately be interrupted in an understanding but matter-of-fact way. Children shown how tables are sanded smooth and painted or how pipes bring water into and out of our homes will be more likely to understand and care for their environment appropriately.

responsibility
Individual accountability and answerability.

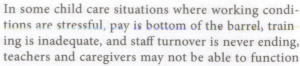

In some child care situations where working conditions are stressful, pay is bottom of the barrel, training is inadequate, and staff turnover is never ending, teachers and caregivers may not be able to function consistently at a level that parents would want their children to emulate (Ackerman, 2006). Parents, early educators, and public policy makers are becoming acutely aware of the significance of early experience on long-term development. Too often, in past years, it has been assumed that child care need be little more than a kindly but custodial parking lot for youngsters. Growing evidence from the study of human development indicates that the first years of life may be the most, rather than the least, critical years in a child's emotional, physical, and intellectual growth (Bongers et al., 2008; Branje et al., 2010; Pagani et al., 2010; Schweinhart, 2004).

Child care centers, preschools, mother's-day-out programs, and other early childhood settings have the potential to help parents create a better future for children and for society in general. To have resources, support, and high expectations from communities, the child care profession must come to be viewed as an integral part of our educational system. Assuring that every child, regardless of income, has a chance at quality early care and education is not a luxury but is rather a necessary step toward building America's future workforce (Clampet-Lundquist et al., 2003; Evans & Schamberg, 2009; Findlay, 2010; Lipina & Colombo, 2009; Meyers & Jordan, 2006; O'Donnell, 2006; Vandell et al., 2010).

Because early experiences are so important to healthy development, child care outside the family takes on special significance. The first question parents should ask as they examine child care alternatives is, "Are the adults in this setting warm, nurturing, and emotionally available to the children?" And because imitation and firsthand experience, rather than direct teaching, are the major avenues for learning in young children, the next crucial questions parents might ask are, "Do I want my child to absorb the personality traits, communication styles, and problem-solving behaviors of the adults here?" and "Do these adult role models set an example for behavior that I value and want my child to imitate?"

© Cengage Learning 2013

Assuring that every child, regardless of income, has a chance at quality early care and education is not a luxury, but rather a necessary step toward building America's future.

Summary

- Contemporary family life brings special stresses and strains to children and families.
- To be effective in guiding children, teachers and parents must work as a cooperative, respectful, and cohesive team.
- Teachers should see themselves as a support system for families.
- This book provides child guidance strategies consistent with developmentally appropriate practice, referred to as DAP.

- Caregivers trained in DAP provide nurturing attention and interaction that helps infants, toddlers, and young children develop to their full capacity.
- The long-term goal of positive guidance is to support the development of responsible, self-disciplined human beings.
- Short-term objectives safeguard children's well-being, respect individual rights, and protect surroundings.

Key Terms

adult

child guidance

developmentally appropriate practice

dual-earner couples

family structures
goal
National Association for the Education of Young Children
objective

parent–teacher resource team
responsibility
single parents
temperament

Student Activities

1. Interact with one or more preschoolers, reminding them, "Be healthy; wait for your turn to go down the slide," "Be respectful; use only words to tell John you are angry," or "Be responsible; put your wrapper in the trash can."
   a. Practice until the phrases begin to come to you naturally.
   b. How do preschoolers react to rules?
   c. What have you learned?

2. Sit down with a group of children who are 5 years old or older. Using the ideas discussed in this chapter, help the children develop their own list of classroom rules.
   a. Did they develop rules for respecting others?
   b. Did they develop rules for healthy behavior?
   c. Did they develop rules for protecting the environment?
   d. How do kindergartners and school-agers react to rules?
   e. What did you learn?

3. Explore using "Be Healthy, Be Respectful, Be Responsible" with one or more toddlers.
   a. Write down notes about your experience.
   b. Compare your notes with those of other students.
   c. How do toddlers react to rules?
   d. What have you learned?

Related Resources

Readings

Hallowell, R. (2007). *Crazy busy: Overstretched, overbooked, and about to snap! Strategies for handling your fast-paced life.* New York: Ballantine Books.

National Association of Child Care Resource and Referral Agencies. (2012). *Parents and the high price of child care: 2012 update.* Arlington, VA: NACCRRA. Retrieved September 30, 2013, http://www.naccrra.org

Seccombe, K. (2011). *Families and their social worlds* (2nd ed.). Upper Saddle River, NJ: Pearson.

Websites

National Association for the Education of Young Children NAEYC is a large nonprofit association serving early childhood education teachers, staff, administrators, trainers, college educators, families of young children, policy makers, and advocates.

Child Care Aware This organization helps families learn more about the elements of quality child care and how to locate programs in their communities. Child Care Aware also provides child care providers with access to resources for their child care programs.

The Children's Defense Fund This child advocacy and research group was founded in 1973 by Marian Wright Edelman to advocate on behalf of children.

The National Child Care Information Center This organization is a national resource that links information and people to ensure that all children and families have access to high-quality comprehensive child care services.

2

Historical Perspectives and Guidance Theories

naeyc Standards

The following NAEYC Standards are addressed in this chapter

Standard 1   Promoting child development and learning

1b Knowing and understanding the multiple influences on early development and learning

Standard 5   Using content knowledge to build meaningful curriculum

5a Understanding content knowledge and resources in academic disciplines

Standard 6   Becoming a professional

6d Integrating knowledgeable, reflective, and critical perspectives on early education

After reading this chapter, you should be able to do the following:

2-1 List historical perceptions about children.

2-2 Describe the child's role in contemporary society.

2-3 Contrast major guidance philosophies and approaches.

2-1 Historical Perspectives

Child care and guidance practices have changed drastically through the years. Many child care traditions from the past would seem strange, even cruel, to modern parents. For example, swaddling, the snug wrapping of infants in strips of cloth or blankets, is an ancient custom that has persisted for centuries in many parts of the world. Snugly wrapping newborns in blankets is considered to be a very appropriate tradition in most modern cultures, but the old practice of swaddling was intended to control the baby's movement and routinely continued until the child was old enough to walk.

John Locke in 1699 described the customary child care of his day and how a baby was

rolled and swathed, ten or a dozen times round; then blanket upon blanket, mantle upon that; its little neck pinned down to one posture; its head more than it frequently needs, triple crowned like a young page, with covering upon covering; its legs and arms as if to prevent that kindly stretching which we rather ought to promote . . . the former bundled up, the latter pinned down; and how the poor thing lies on the nurse's lap, a miserable little pinioned captive. (cited in Cunnington & Buck, 1965, p. 103)

In western Europe during the first half of the eighteenth century, infants were seen as not only somehow less human than older people, but also somewhat expendable. A wealthy mother usually sent her newborn infant to the care of a hired wet nurse, who was expected to breastfeed and care for the child, often at the expense of the life of the wet nurse's own infant. Infant mortality rates reportedly reached as high as 80 percent in some areas as wet-nurse mothers, to ensure their livelihood, gave birth to stimulate the production of breast milk, then sent their own infants to poorly maintained foundling homes (Weiser, 1982).

The writings of Rousseau toward the end of the eighteenth century both influenced and reflected a change in the cultural perception of childhood. He insisted that "everything is good as it comes from the hands of the Author of Nature" (Rousseau, 1893, p. 1). He argued that, rather than being an evil creature who must have sin beaten out of him, the young child is born good and innocent. He believed that the harsh discipline techniques of that day, which were intended to provide the child salvation from original sin, tainted the child rather than provided healthy, normal growth. Rousseau's prescription for child care included breastfeeding by the natural mother, fresh air, loose clothing, and a minimum of interference from adults.

DIVERSITY

Certain tribes of Native Americans in the 1900s particularly valued physical toughness in their children. To build up the child's resistance, newborns were plunged into cold water several times at birth, regardless of the weather. The Native Americans' version of swaddling was to fasten the baby securely onto a cradleboard that could be conveniently worn, hung inside the lodge, from a tree branch, from a saddlebow, or wherever family members were clustered. Babies were not released from the confines of cradleboards until they were able to walk (Weiser, 1982).

American mothers of European descent sent their infants and young children to the neighborhood widow or spinster for care and teaching. In these "dame schools," a baby might nap on a quilt in a corner of the kitchen while older children practiced reading from the New Testament (Weiser, 1982). Farm and slave children were valued as a source of free labor. Toddlers barely able to walk were assigned chores and held accountable for them. By the early 1900s, momentum had begun to build for promoting the scientific study of the development of children and the dissemination of pertinent information to parents. Some of the writings of that day foretold trends in thinking about young children. For example, a book produced by the Institute of Child Welfare at the University of Minnesota in 1930 included the following warning to parents:

The parent who has the ideal of complete and unquestioning obedience, and who is forceful and consistent enough to obtain it, is likely to have a child who, when he goes to school, distresses a good teacher and delights a poor one by always doing what he is told and furthermore by always waiting to be told what to do. His whole attitude is that of finding out what authority requires and then complying, an attitude which, if maintained, is apt to result in incompetence, inefficiency, and unhappiness in adulthood. (Faegre & Anderson, 1930, p. 45)

Photo courtesy of the Ferris Family

The early 1900s brought changes in people's beliefs about childhood and their expectations for children.

2-1a How the Modern World Has Influenced Thinking about Child Guidance

During the twentieth century, ideas about children were influenced by two world wars, alternating periods of economic depression and prosperity, and by growing scientific interest in child development research. At the end of World War II, Maria Montessori wrote such books as *Peace and Education* (1971) and *Reconstruction in Education* (1968) to express her view that the hope for world peace lay in a new education for young children. Montessori (1971) wrote:

Certainly we cannot achieve [peace] by attempting to unite all these people who are so different, but it can be achieved if we begin with the child. When the child is born he has no special language, he has no special religion, he has not any national or racial prejudice. It is men [sic] who have acquired all these things. (p. 6)

In the late 1940s and into the 1950s, researchers began to unlock some of the mysteries of the common belief that experiences of the first years of life were inconsequential to later development; this idea was pushed aside by more complex theories explaining the development of intelligence and personality. These new theories placed greater emphasis on early social interaction and exploration of the physical environment (Erikson, 1963; Harlow & Zimmerman, 1959; Piaget, 1952, 1962, 1963, 1968, 1970; Skinner, 1953). In the 1960s, research into the learning processes of children from birth to school age flourished, and an estimated 23 million books on child rearing were sold during the mid-1970s (Clarke-Stewart, 1978). Since the 1970s, there has been a mushrooming of parental as well as scientific interest in the processes of child growth and development (Champagne & Mashoodh, 2009; George et al., 2010; Pagani et al., 2010; Peters et al., 2010; Rao et all, 2010; Vandell et al., 2010).

John Dewey

John Dewey's (1859–1952) approach to education relied on learning by doing rather than learning through rigid lecture-based lessons, tedious memorization, and recitation of memorized material, which were all standard practices of that period.

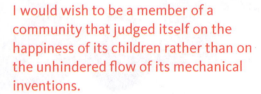

I would wish to be a member of a community that judged itself on the happiness of its children rather than on the unhindered flow of its mechanical inventions.

—*Thomas Moore*

Dewey's significance for educators lies in several key areas. His innovative exploration of thinking and reflection inspired continuing development and research by others such as Carl Rogers. Dewey's belief that education must engage with and expand experience to be meaningful has had a powerful effect on today's views of education.

Additionally, he raised awareness and concern for the development of learning environments in which students were able to actively interact with learning materials and find a concrete framework for continued practice of learning concepts. And most importantly, his passionate belief in democracy propelled him to advocate for schools that developed good citizens so that democracy could thrive (Caspary, 2000).

Alfred Adler

Alfred Adler (1870–1937) developed a social constructivist view of human behavior based on value-oriented psychology. He believed human beings were capable of working cooperatively, living together peacefully, striving for self-improvement and self-fulfillment, and contributing to the common welfare of the community. He believed that people were not passive victims of heredity or environment but actively constructed their beings through their social interactions, experiences, and developing perceptions of the world. He saw human beings as constantly striving to compensate for their feelings of inferiority.

Adler's ideas are similar to those of Abraham Maslow, who envisioned individuals as striving toward self-actualization, toward the full realization of their potential (Maslow, 1970). Adler, like Sigmund Freud, believed that a person's personality was largely developed in the first five years of life. Adler's concepts for the guidance of young children include the following:

- Mutual respect is based on a belief that equality is the inalienable right of all human beings.
- Reward and punishment are outdated and less effective than logical consequences.
- Acting instead of talking in heated conflict situations avoids arguments and resolves problems more quickly.
- It is appropriate to withdraw from provocation but not appropriate to withdraw emotionally from the child.
- Teaching and training take time and patience.
- Adults should never do for a child what she can do for herself.
- It is critical to recognize and understand a misbehaving child's goal.

Carl Rogers

Carl Rogers's (1902–1987) theory of personality evolved out of his work as a clinical psychologist and his deep respect for the dignity of all human beings. The clinical methods he developed focused specifically on the humane and ethical treatment of persons. He believed that human beings have an underlying "actualizing tendency" that motivates them to achieve their potential.

Over the years, educators, philosophers, and scientists have influenced our views on child guidance.

The idea of self is central to his theory. He believed that the self is constructed through interactions with others. A child's self-concept is strongly influenced by the perceptions of those around her. Thus valuing a child and treating her with dignity and respect would help her construct a strong, positive self-concept. Disrespectful, humiliating, and dehumanizing treatment would damage the child's development of self-esteem. Rogers argued that, to reach their full potential, human beings must have positive regard from others that eventually leads to the development of positive self-regard.

Robert R. Carkhuff

Robert Carkhuff took the abstract theories of Carl Rogers and developed a systematic set of guidelines for effective interpersonal skills. The impact of his work has been dramatic. Numerous existing programs teaching appropriate interpersonal skills have been derived from this original source.

George Michael Gazda

George Gazda (1931–) took the work of Carkhuff and modified it further to create an effective system for solving classroom management problems and motivating children to change their inappropriate behaviors. His work focuses on effective strategies for perceiving and responding, ineffective communication styles, nonverbal behaviors, confrontation, and anger. Gazda defined strategies for teachers that correct behavior problems while strengthening children's self-concept and self-esteem.

Jean Piaget

Jean Piaget (1896–1980) studied the development of intelligence in children and proposed a theory based on four predetermined stages of mental growth. His studies have had a major impact on the fields of psychology and education. Piaget spent much of his professional life listening to children, watching children, and studying research reports from other cognitive psychologists. He concluded that children's learning was progressively constructed by the children themselves through their interaction with their environment. He believed that children's logic for thinking and problem solving was initially very different from the logic they would use later as they grew stage by stage toward adulthood. Children simply don't think like adults.

Piaget believed that children are little scientists who constantly create and test their own theories of the world. Children are not empty vessels to be filled with knowledge (as had been believed) but instead are active builders of their own knowledge. Like John Dewey and Maria Montessori, Piaget took child learning very seriously. Montessori and Dewey set out to reform education, but Piaget tried only to understand and explain how children think and learn. Piaget, nonetheless, has had a profound effect on education throughout the world.

Lev Vygotsky

Lev Vygotsky (1896–1934) is remembered primarily for identifying what he called the "zone of proximal educational development" (sometimes referred to as the ZPD, ZoPED, or simply "the Zone"). He believed that children develop by exposure to skills, words, concepts, and tasks that are a little beyond their ability but within a "zone" of possible achievement. He believed that adults play an important coaching role in helping the child grasp this new knowledge or ability during these teachable moments.

▶❙❙ **TeachSource** Video

Piaget's Stages and Educational Implications

Watch this Video Case on Piaget's stages, and then answer the following questions:

1. Is the child's thinking the same as an adult's? Why or why not?

2. What sort of experiences help young children learn best?

3. In the video, young children gave incorrect answers. Should teachers keep explaining the materials until each child memorizes the correct answer? Why or why not?

What Can We Learn from Neuroscience?

Children develop empathy and learn skills by watching role models

- Researchers have found that certain brain cells activate both when we perform an action and when we watch another perform the same action (University of California–Los Angeles, 2010).
- These "mirror neurons" help us feel what someone else must be feeling, as if we were in their shoes. 相手のことを考える
- Mirror neurons stimulate the development of empathy.
- Mirror neurons also pass skills down from generation to generation by prompting children to observe what others are doing and to imitate it.
- Young children with conduct problems may have reduced responses in their mirror cells that cause early vulnerability (Cell Press, 2013; Lockwood et al., 2013).
- Exemplary environments help vulnerable children learn empathy and develop effective learning strategies (Lockwood et al., 2013; Rushton, 2011).

Vygotsky believed that children developed primarily from their interactions with adults and also from those with other children. Vygotsky believed that child learning was inseparable from human history and culture. He believed that psychological development was the process of children learning how to use the ideas and tools developed by people throughout history such as language, number concepts, music, art, and so forth. He emphasized that language was the most important of the cognitive tools passed down through the centuries. Without language, children cannot fully develop self-awareness. Without self-awareness, children cannot think about, evaluate, anticipate, and control their behavior. Words become the framework through which we think, perceive, experience, and act (Berk & Winsler, 1995).

Vygotsky believed the overarching goal of education was to generate and lead development. He believed that development occurred through the processes of social learning, social interactions, and the internalization of culture. Vygotsky emphasized the critical importance of prior knowledge for making sense of new experiences and situations. Everything has to be taught in context of what the child already knows. The child's culture, family background, and current skill level determine her curriculum (Luria & Vygotsky, 1992; Smagorinsky, 2007; Vygotsky, 1978).

© Cengage Learning 2013

A century ago Maria Montessori began advocating that children needed respectful guidance and hands-on learning in carefully planned environments.

Maria Montessori

During a terrible time of world war, Maria Montessori (1870–1952) proposed the idea

▶❚❚ TeachSource Video

Video supplied by BBC Worldwide Learning

Montessori Education

Watch this Video Case on the Montessori method, and then answer the following questions:

1. Montessori teaches what kind of discipline?

2. Is the environment structured or unstructured?

3. Do teachers assign the children's Montessori activities or are children encouraged to choose their own Montessori activities?

that "mankind can hope for a solution to its problems . . . only by turning its attention and energies to the discovery of the child" (*The Discovery of the Child*, 1986, pp. ix–x).

Montessori observed children's capacity for repetition of activities that matched their development and interests. She saw that children needed hands-on learning in a carefully planned environment. She designed small, child-sized furniture and simple, attractive, sensorial learning materials children could use independently to develop cognitive, physical, practical life, and social skills. Her focus was on independence and respect for the child (Kramer, 1976; Standing, 1957).

Montessori's ideas about the importance of the young child's absorbent mind, internal motivation, respectful teacher role, and sensitive periods for learning have been profoundly influential to mainstream early childhood education (Lee, 2005).

Friedrich Froebel

Friedrich Froebel (1782–1852) transformed our thinking about early childhood education. Froebel realized that play was the engine that naturally drove learning in young children. He set about finding ways to guide children's natural desire to play and to help them find additional meaning in their play. He created learning materials for children that he called "gifts"—small balls, rods and rings, wooden building blocks, rectangular tiles, and such. He invented games for children to play using these objects that would help them discover new concepts (Froebel, 1887, 1907).

Stimulating children's learning through interaction with these play objects was the focal point of Froebel's innovative demonstration kindergarten. His intention was for the materials to engage the child's intellect, creativity, and natural spirit of playfulness. Soon educators around the world took note of Froebel's gifts, or *Gaben,* as he called them. His idea was a huge success (Corbett, 1988).

Today we would expect developmentally appropriate early childhood programs to have wooden building blocks as essential classroom learning materials. Certainly there are other early childhood learning materials we use today that have evolved directly or indirectly from Froebel's original gifts.

Urie Bronfenbrenner

Urie Bronfenbrenner (1917–2005) worried that the unpredictability and instability of modern family life was undermining the well-being of our children. Bronfenbrenner developed a bioecological model to explain expanding worries about school failure and behavioral, social, and emotional problems in children.

According to Bronfenbrenner's bioecological theory, when relationships in the immediate family break down, children fail to develop the tools they need to thrive as they grow up and move out into other parts of the community—school, religious groups, social organizations, and eventually work. Bronfenbrenner

© Cengage Learning 2013

Montessori designed small, child-sized furniture and simple, attractive, sensorial learning materials that children could use independently to develop cognitive, physical, practical life, and social skills.

argued that technology has changed our society, but we have not responded to compensate for the negative effect of the work world on our families (Henderson, 1995).

Bronfenbrenner pointed out that, to develop well, young children need constant, stable, reciprocal interaction with attentive and caring adults. Children who don't get this kind of high-quality care eventually look for attention in inappropriate places. Children's deficiencies show up in adolescence as antisocial behavior, lack of self-discipline, rebelliousness, and lack of initiative.

To help solve some of the problems he identified, Bronfenbrenner cofounded Head Start. At the beginning, Bronfenbrenner convinced the other cofounders that Head Start would be most effective if it involved not just the child, but also the family and community. Parent and community involvement were unheard of at the time, but that became a cornerstone of Head Start and proved to be critical to its success. We know now that developmentally appropriate practice must include parent involvement (Addison, 1992; Bronfenbrenner, 1990).

Bronfenbrenner convinced his fellow cofounders that Head Start would be most effective if it involved not just the child, but also the family and community. Today parent involvement is a basic principle in developmentally appropriate practice.

DIVERSITY

2-2 The Child in Society

Children occupy a very special niche in contemporary society (Gutek, 1997; Hoffman & Manis, 1979; Wyness, 2006). They are dressed in fancy clothing, photographed, given countless objects (toys) made especially for children, fed special foods from tiny glass jars, and equipped with elaborate contraptions designed for sitting, swinging, strolling, eating, and crawling. Compared with previous cultures, children today are pampered and indulged. A bright-eyed baby decked out in a designer outfit, wearing scented leak-proof disposable diapers, and riding in the latest stroller will bring oohs and ahhs from shoppers in a supermarket and comments such as, "Oh, isn't it adorable! Look at its little shoes and its tiny earrings!"

The practice of referring to infants (and sometimes toddlers) with impersonal pronouns such as *it* tells us a lot about our perception of babies. The use of such descriptors as *it* and *thing* in reference to children gives a subtle indication that babies are not perceived as real persons. Several centuries ago, impersonal references to children were even more pervasive than they are today. Children were commonly referred to as "it" well into early childhood: "In this age [birth to seven years] it cannot talk well or form its words perfectly, for its teeth are not yet well arranged or firmly implanted" (*Le Grand Proprietaire,* cited in Aries, 1962, p. 21). At present, despite remnants of belief that infants are somewhat less than fully human, we place a great deal more emphasis on the value and importance of individual children's lives than we did in the past.

Parents may refer to a fetus as an "it" before the child's birth, but parents almost never refer to their baby as "it" afterward, especially after they have come to know and love the child. Strangers are always more likely to refer impersonally to a baby or child. For example, a newspaper account of an alleged brutal child abuse murder quoted a district attorney explaining to shocked citizens why the murder victim, a two-year-old boy, had been given back to his natural mother after having been removed since early infancy for neglect: "Most reasonable people . . . might say the decision to put it [the child] back was probably a bad call. . . ." (Krupinski & Weikel, 1986). When asked about the use of impersonal references for babies, people often explain that "it" is used because the baby's sex may not be known. Interestingly, in discussing older children and adults, even if that person's gender is not known, it would be considered highly inappropriate to refer to that person (a salesperson, a mail carrier, or an acquaintance's teenager) as an "it." Only after a person dies is that person's body referred to as an "it."

2-2a How Life Is Different for Children in Today's Changing World

Children today are not only valued, but are also usually thought to have a fairly carefree existence, in contrast to earlier generations' use of child labor. In past years, young children have generally been allowed to spend a good portion of their days playing, fooling around, romping in the sunshine, and generally finding their own occupations (sometimes in front of a television set). Child care has brought new levels of structure to many children's lives. In many early childhood programs, this structure has enriched children's lives and assisted in their development of healthy and productive habits. In other child care settings, children spend a considerable amount of time sitting, waiting, being scolded, standing in line, and taking part in activities that are initiated and controlled by adults and are carried out by groups of children in lockstep (Findlay, 2010; National Association of Child Care Resource and Referral Agencies, 2009, 2010; U.S. Census Bureau, 2010).

You don't really understand human nature unless you know why a child on a merry-go-round will wave at his parents every time around—and why his parents will always wave back.

—William D. Tammeus

Because many affluent parents are having fewer children and waiting until their professional careers are well established before having them, there is new pressure on some children to live up to the "fast lane" expectations of their parents. In the push for "superbabies" and superior children, many youngsters may be given gymnastics, music lessons, dance lessons, tutoring, and yoga before they even start kindergarten. Their lives may become so full of enrichment activities that they run out of time to lie in the clover and experience wonder as they watch clouds go by. In an era when parents feel pressured to create a superchild, they may inadvertently destroy some of the wonder and magic of early childhood.

Occasionally, the young child's role in contemporary society approaches that of a pet or a possession rather than a person deserving respect and dignity. From time to time, that role may mean that the child is indulged, pampered, forgotten, rushed, and pushed. She may be expected to be perfect, or be coerced to play the violin or show off other skills on cue to impress family or friends.

autocracy
Control by a single person having unlimited power.

Our growing knowledge of and emphasis on early childhood has put youngsters on a pedestal. But, of course, being on a pedestal has distinct disadvantages. Being on a pedestal means that every move one makes is watched, judged, and managed. Early childhood experts have growing concerns that children are not being allowed the freedom to "just be children" (Bodrova & Leong, 2010; Elkind, 2003; Ladd, 1996).

By playing and learning in a culturally diverse, developmentally appropriate learning environment, children develop citizenship skills, self-reliance, responsible work habits, and ability to cooperate in teamwork.

2-2b Preparation for Participation in a Democracy

Settings where young children live, work, and play (whether in a home or a child care facility) function as their small version of society. As has been discussed previously, interaction in family, school, and caregiving communities helps children learn how to participate later in adult community life. Child guidance is the process by which adults help children learn appropriate ways to function as part of a group. In an **autocracy**, people would need to learn only blind obedience to function appropriately.

Critical Skills for Good Citizenship ❯

1. **Concept of citizenship**—being cooperative, having a sense of fair play, and respecting the rights of others

2. **Initiative and self-reliance**—being a self-starter, a lifelong learner, and a creative problem solver

3. **Appropriate work habits**—having established patterns of accomplishing tasks, taking pride in the accomplishments, and accepting responsibility for the results

4. **Ability to cooperate in teamwork**—willingness to put aside one's immediate interests for the good of the team

TeachSource Digital Download

A dictator who demands submission dominates people. In an **anarchy**, everyone follows his or her own desires and interests. Chaos prevails because no one governs. In a **democracy**, however, educated, responsible citizens are needed to provide effective self-governance through active participation.

The guidance practices carried out by adults can help children learn how to participate in a democracy by developing the necessary skills. See Positive Focus box 2.1.

2-2c How Early Influences Affect Children and Their Learning of Appropriate Behavior

During the 1970s and 1980s, researchers began studying how various approaches in early childhood programs affect children's development of characteristics, attitudes, and values. However, some educators have been focusing on personal development and citizenship as a part of early learning and guidance for more than 100 years. John Dewey wrote dozens of books describing his theories of learning as a part of daily living. His world-famous school, which included preschool and kindergarten and opened in 1894, was specifically designed to foster the characteristics that are essential for living in a democracy (Dewey, 1966).

It is essential for those parents, caregivers, and teachers who supervise young children to recognize that guidance is not just a process for getting children to behave appropriately today, but rather a process for helping children learn to live happy, productive lives. Guidance strategies cannot be judged only on the merits of how expedient they are at the moment; judgment must also consider how effective they are in instilling functional living skills that relate to the real world.

Disciplinary tactics are aimed at controlling children's behaviors, often by the use of punishment. Guidance procedures are focused on the development of children's self-control and self-discipline. They rely on authentic experiences, logical consequences, and intrinsic rewards. Positive guidance is not a bag of tricks for coaxing or coercing children to do what we want them to do.

In a democracy, people have rights. If I break a law by driving faster than the speed limit, I still have rights. A police officer is authorized to use only as much force as is appropriate and necessary to stop me. She is forbidden to hurt me, harass me, or humiliate me as a punishment or to get back at me for what I did. In fact, many police officers patiently persist with recalcitrant lawbreakers by politely but firmly insisting, "I know you don't like being pulled over, sir, but you were exceeding the speed limit. May I see your license?"

If officers of the law behaved the way some adults do in handling misbehaving children, we would be shocked. Imagine an officer yanking a driver out of the car, angrily shaking the driver while yelling at her, and snapping, "If you ever do this again, I'll use a paddle on you and you won't be able to sit down for a week!" We would probably feel very angry and misused. Children feel that same way too. It takes time and practice for children to grasp rules, but they can learn to be good citizens by the same technique that our judicial system is supposed to use: persistent and consistent guidance that is as firm as necessary but as respectful as possible.

anarchy
Absence of any form of control; chaos and disorder.

democracy
The principles of social equality and respect for the individual within a cohesive community.

Children desperately need to know—and to hear in ways they understand and remember—that they're loved and valued by mom and dad.

—Paul Smally

One hundred years ago, a strong back and a willing attitude were generally considered all one needed to make a living. Today, success requires a complicated set of skills and attitudes.

Photo courtesy of the Ferris Family

2-2d The Strain of Changing Disciplinary Traditions

Changing the way we deal with misbehaving children is not easy. During our own childhoods, we absorbed a great deal of unconscious information about how adults are expected to interact with children. It is as if we have mental videotapes of disciplinary interactions stored in our brains ready for instant replay at any time. Without thinking, we suddenly hear the voices of adults from our own childhoods as we scold the young children in our care.

Guidance methods that were acceptable generations ago are not useful for preparing today's children for life in the future. In past generations, conformity and obedience to authority were important to economic success. In our children's future, collaboration, creativity, innovation, and open-mindedness will be critical, not conformity and obedience. *Today, our guidance methods must teach children to think, not just to obey* (Collins & Halverson, 2009; Trilling & Fadel, 2009).

The world is changing at an astonishing rate. As it changes, children need different kinds of experiences to prepare them for the future. A hundred years ago, children were not expected to prepare for a technological world where adaptability and flexibility were more valued than adherence to set routines. Minorities and women were not expected to prepare for the likelihood that they would be competing ambitiously in the business world. And women were not expected to prepare for the distinct possibility that they would, at some time or other, function as head of household and sole breadwinner.

Once we recognize the necessity for updating strategies for guiding and teaching children, it can be difficult to change our old habits. Unfortunately, we adults experience confusion and stress when the methods for dealing with children that intellectually begin to seem logical and right do not match the methods we experienced and lived in our own childhoods. Beliefs cannot be turned on and off like a light switch. Instead, they must be studied and practiced for years.

Human beings, adults and children alike, are influenced by life experiences. But as human beings, we also have the ability to make choices, to take control of our lives, and even to make unexpected changes in our life journey. We are not merely leaves floating in the stream of life. Instead, we are fish, strongly influenced by currents and tides but free to swim upstream if we have the strength and motivation. We can choose to break old habits and establish new ones, but it is not easy. It requires stamina, determination, and a great deal of persistent practice over time.

2-3 Philosophies of Guidance

Culture plays an important role in shaping parents', teachers', and caregivers' philosophies about children and child rearing. A person's philosophy affects her perception of children, how they learn, what their intentions are, and why they behave as they do. Ideas about child guidance that immediately seem logical and appropriate or sound ridiculous have been filtered by the set of beliefs and assumptions that make up one's philosophy.

Although parents, teachers, or caregivers may think that they have no particular philosophy, it is likely that they simply have never really analyzed how their beliefs compare with those held by others. Some people may mistakenly assume that

Bringing Home a Baby Bumblebee

In a medium-size neighborhood child care center, a group of preschool-age children cluster around their teacher and sing with her. They snatch invisible bumblebees out of the air and pretend to trap them in their clasped hands as they sing:

"I'm bringing home a baby bumblebee. Won't my mommy be so proud of me? I'm bringing home a baby bumblebee—bzzz bzzz bzzz bzzz. Ouch! [slap] He stung me!"

In another part of town, in a child care center located in a tiny building that is part of a low-income housing project, a group of children sit on chairs around long tables as they enthusiastically sing:

"I'm bringing home a baby bumblebee. Won't my mama be surprised of me? I'm bringing home a baby bumblebee—bzzz bzzz bzzz bzzz. Ouch! [slap] He stung me! I'm squashing up the baby bumblebee. Now there's bumblebee blood all over me. I'm wiping off the blood of the bumblebee. Now there's no more blood all over me."

In still another part of town, in a tastefully decorated private preschool, a third group of children sit cross-legged on the floor in a circle singing happily with their teacher:

"I'm bringing home a baby bumblebee. Won't my daddy be so proud of me? I'm opening up the window carefully, so my bee can fly away free—bzzz bzzz bzzz bzzz. Bye bye, baby bumblebee."

(See Miller, 1989, for more information on differences in linguistic code in toddlers.)

Case Discussion Questions

1. Do you think that songs and games parents and child care workers use to entertain children pass cultural perceptions from one generation to the next?
2. What are your own cultural perceptions of children? Do you see children as innocent and pure, to be protected from anything violent, scary, or disgusting? Do you see children as regular people who enjoy raucous humor to get their aggressions out? Do you see children as "born sinners" who sometimes can have evil or cruel impulses?

3. Compare versions of songs and stories you have heard. Do the different versions of the songs reflect cultural experiences of children you know?
4. Why do you think the third teacher in the example replaced the word *mommy* or *mama* with the word *daddy*?
5. Do you think that children growing up in inner-city slums might like different songs and games than other, more sheltered children who have not experienced the discomfort and fear associated with poverty?
6. If the interactions described above really are what Vygotsky called dialogues, what cultural values might the children figure out from the wording of the different songs?
7. Are songs and stories ever purposely used by adults to instill in children an awareness of cultural values? What songs can you think of?
8. Identify a song or story you would feel uncomfortable using with children. What would you do to change it? Why?

Each child is part of some kind of family, community, and culture or blend of cultures. His family, community, and culture form a basis for how he perceives the world.

everyone in the world naturally shares their underlying beliefs about how things should be and why they are as they are. The process of acquiring appropriate behavior is a learning process just as surely as the process of learning to read and write is. It is, therefore, essential for us to explore various philosophies related to how and why learning takes place.

2-3a Is a Child's Personality Mostly the Result of Nature or Nurture?

One of the oldest debates related to children is the old nature versus nurture controversy. People who believe that *nature* has the stronger effect believe that children become whatever they become owing to heredity, inborn traits, and inner motivation. People who believe that *nurture* has more effect believe that children become whatever they become owing to parental guidance, teaching effectiveness, television, and other external influences (Asbury & Plomin, 2005; Cohen, 1999; Kagan, 2004; Sameroff, 2010).

Whenever adults compare children, they can hardly resist venturing opinions about how children grow to be so different. Some will say, "Jennifer was born to be a little terror! She's just like her dad, never still for a minute," or "Rahul will undoubtedly be a talented musician. He has inherited musical ability from both sides of his family." These people emphasize the importance of children's internal nature in their development. They believe that children are predestined at birth to certain talents and personality traits because of genetic inheritance or inborn characteristics.

Others disagree. They say things such as, "Of course Ming Li has become potty trained so early. Her child care teachers have trained hundreds of toddlers. They know how to do it." Or they say, "If that was my child, he wouldn't be whining and sucking his thumb. His parents must be overindulgent or he wouldn't behave that way." These people emphasize the importance of external nurturing in the development of children. They believe that children are all born pretty much the same, and their differences evolve because of differences in their treatment and teaching.

In the past, cultural perceptions dictated that personality and potential were inborn. Some people even worried that an adopted child could carry a "bad seed." Human nature is such that we adults are often tempted to take credit for a child's accomplishments and exemplary behavior but blame failures and unacceptable behaviors on inborn traits of the child.

DIVERSITY

As research into human learning has mushroomed over recent years, a dawning awareness has spread about the importance of everyone and everything the child encounters in the child's development. The pendulum has swung to the extreme—whereas once people blamed fate for however a child turned out, now people try to create "better" babies by leaping ahead in the educational process and mistakenly trying to get babies, toddlers, and preschoolers to memorize abstract curriculum that is intended for older children.

DAP

Cognitive stimulation is to mental development much like food is to physical development. If enough food is not available, development will be stunted. However, forcing too much food (or the wrong foods) on a child is not good. We should make appropriate quantities of developmentally appropriate learning experiences available and respect the child's readiness for learning. In DAP, learning experiences are like the Three Bears' porridge: always *just right*. Never too much, never too little, never too advanced, never too simple, always just right for the child's developmental level, cultural background, and personal interests.

behaviorists
Those holding the view that the environment is the primary determinant of human behavior and that objectively observable behavior constitutes the essential psychological makeup of a human being.

maturationists
Those holding the view that internal predisposition, physiological characteristics, or inherited traits account for the essential psychological makeup of a human being.

constructivists
Those holding the view developed by Piaget and Vygotsky that our personality and intelligence comes from both inborn cognitive structures and external experiences.

2-3b What Do Researchers Say about the Origin of Intelligence and Personality?

If human thinking could be neatly separated into simple categories, we would find three primary positions:

1. The **behaviorists** (also called empiricists) believe that behavior and learning result from external forces such as reinforcement; they focus on external strategies for guidance.

2. The **maturationists** believe that behavior and learning hinge on internal processes such as maturation and motivation; they focus on nonintrusive ways to support children's naturally developing self-control.

3. The **constructivists** believe that behavior and learning result from the interactions between internal development and external environment; they study child development, observe the child, and prepare a developmentally appropriate environment. They positively and proactively guide the child's inner development of self-control and respect for others.

The Behaviorist Approach

The behaviorists incorporate the seventeenth-century tradition of John Locke, who viewed the newborn's mind as a tabula rasa, or empty slate. These theorists—the behaviorists, positivists, and empiricists—believe that human learning comes from outside the learner. They believe that environment accounts for nearly all that a person becomes.

Watson (1930), Skinner (1953, 1974), and others have theorized that human beings are really products of their environments. People become scholars or cat burglars not because of their genetic makeup or by choice, but because their environment has conditioned them to behave as they do. Subscription to this view has powerful implications for parents and educators. It implies that human beings can be molded or shaped by controlling environmental experiences. This view also shifts emphasis away from focus on human will and predisposition.

Behaviorists view the development of appropriate behavior as the responsibility of the adult. The adult is responsible for identifying and selecting specific behavior goals for the child. Then the adult observes the child and monitors spontaneous behaviors that are slightly closer to the desired goal behavior, reinforcing each subsequent step closer to the desired goal by giving praise, treats, or **tokens**. The adult maneuvers the child's surroundings to **modify** (or change) specific behaviors in the child.

Behaviorists leave nothing to chance. They choose goal behaviors, select reinforcers, and even plan a reinforcement schedule of when, how often, and under exactly what circumstances reinforcers will be given. Behaviorist views are all focused on the idea that learning is an external process and that learning takes place in a child as a result of influences from the child's environment. Child guidance is seen as an adult-directed process.

These little girls confidently study an insect. According to the constructivist point of view, nature lays the groundwork for a child's potential, but nurturing makes it possible for the child to achieve that potential.

tokens
Objects (for example, stars, points, stickers) given to children for performing specified behaviors; these objects are then exchanged at prearranged times for children's choice of activities or items from a menu of rewards (for example, toys, special food treats, field trips).

modify
The process of bringing about a change. In behavior modification, modifying is the process of changing a specific behavior through external reinforcement of some kind.

The Maturationist Approach

From a point of view opposite to that of the behaviorists, the maturationists borrow from the tradition of Plato. These maturationists, innatists, and nativists believe that learning emerges from within. These educators and philosophers have theorized that human beings are born to be whatever they become; the human infant in this conception is like the rosebud, naturally unfolding into a preordained blossom as long as it is kept healthy. Well into the 1920s and 1930s, Arnold Gesell, a researcher at Yale, maintained that children's external environment did not control developmental outcomes. He claimed that children's own genetic and biological characteristics determined their intelligence and personality (Gesell et al., 1940).

The maturationists view the development of appropriate behavior as a natural

Behavior modification leaves nothing to chance. Behaviorist teachers choose goal behaviors, select reinforcers, and plan a reinforcement schedule of when, how often, and under exactly what circumstances external reinforcers will be given.

process. They believe that as long as basic needs are met, the child will automatically develop the social skills, intelligence, and physical control necessary to behave properly. They see the role of the adult as that of a facilitator. The adult studies children, carefully observing and monitoring their behaviors and abilities. When there is a problem, the adult steps in to help the child understand what has happened in a specific situation and help the child resolve the problem as independently as possible.

Maturationists perceive that learning comes from inside the child. They believe that the processes of learning cannot be rushed. Adults view themselves as role models, guides, and consultants. They believe children are ultimately responsible for their behavior. Personality and growth traits inherited genetically and the child's own willpower play an important role in the maturationists' views on how children learn to behave appropriately. Maturationists see the development of proper behavior as a child-directed process.

Obviously, this type of perception has broad implications for parents and educators concerned with guiding children. If early experiences are relatively inconsequential to later development, then adults need be concerned only with providing the basic necessities for safety and health—custodial care—in the earliest years. This view implies that growth and learning proceed according to internal rules of physiological growth and as a result of personal decision making, not specific environmental circumstances.

The Constructivist Approach

Debate over the previous two contrasting views of human learning (the nature versus nurture controversy) has been complicated by a growing body of research compiled toward the end of the twentieth century by the constructivists, who believe that human learning results from the interaction between the learner and his environment.

Much research has made it clear that environmental factors influence human development (Bloom, 1964; Chomsky, 1965; Hunt, 1976; Kagan, 1971; Kagan & Moss, 1962; Kagan et al., 1978; Kohlberg & DeVries, 1987; Piaget, 1952, 1962, 1963, 1970, 1983; Swann, 2009; Vardin, 2003; Warash et al., 2008). But the research also supports the importance of individual readiness, personal learning styles, and mutual interaction as a part of the process. These factors have gained scientific credibility and are now recognized as part of neither a maturational nor a behaviorist view of learning.

Piaget (1952), for example, termed himself a constructivist. He asserted that infants are born with predispositions to certain kinds of thought and behavior but that they must create their own knowledge through stages of interaction with the environment. *Play* is the concept we use to refer to this early exploratory interaction with the environment.

According to the constructivist point of view, children create their own learning. We are only their guides.

© Cengage Learning 2013

Vygotsky's sociocultural theory of development states that children learn through social interactions in their culture. This approach is much different from Piaget's theory that children act on their environment to learn. Vygotsky said that children interact through "dialogues," and through these social and cultural interactions children learn the values of their society (Luria & Vygotsky, 1992; Vygotsky, 1962; Woolfolk, 2004).

Children come into the world with potential, but potential is not a guarantee of any level of achievement. The child is born to learn, but without appropriate support from the environment, no learning can take place (Bodrova & Leong, 2010). This way of thinking about young children reminds parents and child care providers to produce high-quality early experiences so that optimal experiences can be made available. Researchers have further emphasized the importance of early environments by showing that a baby's brain uses information from sensory experiences to design its own architecture. A kind of mapping takes place inside the brain with astounding rapidity as the number of synapses (or connections) among brain cells multiplies by the trillions in a very few months (Fifer et al., 2010; Friedman, Melhuish, & Hill, 2009; Hayne, 2007; Sai, 2005).

Ethologists are researchers who study behaviors in terms of natural processes and in natural settings. They have refined the idea of sensitive periods for learning in which environmental stimuli can have a maximum impact on learning. Hunt (1976) described what he called the "match." He said that a match must be created between a child's level of readiness and the exact level of difficulty or discrepancy in a specific learning situation before optimal learning can take place (Hess, 1972; Lamb, 1978, 1981; Lorenz, 1966; von Frisch; 1974).

If interactions in the environment are too difficult, children become frustrated and discouraged. If they are too easy, children become bored. Children actively seek out materials and activities that match their ability level. They enjoy and learn well from an environment that offers a fairly wide range of difficulty and in which they are allowed the freedom to choose toys, games, and interactions matched to their ability level, as well as the freedom to reject materials or activities that seem too easy or too difficult.

In terms of child guidance, the constructivists believe that children can learn to behave appropriately only when they have inner maturity as well as suitable external influences. Adults must study children and plan carefully, but they must also focus on the child's own interests and abilities. A few areas of child guidance seem more responsive to external behaviorist control or internal maturationist development. Mindless habits a child really wants to change can probably be treated quickly and effectively through behaviorist strategies. Long-standing problems that seem to have deeply rooted emotional causes are sometimes best treated with maturationist support of the natural processes of development.

The constructivist approach integrates the processes for inner and outer development. Constructivists see child guidance not as an adult-directed or a child-directed process, but rather as an interaction in which either can lead or follow. It is like a waltz with give and take, leading and following. The adult respects the child's interests and abilities but is also not afraid to take control when necessary. The child feels free to express herself and also knows and respects clearly defined limits. The constructivist approach provides the most broadly useful teaching and learning approach for use in developmentally appropriate programs.

ethologists
Scientists who study the behavior of living creatures under normal conditions. Ethology is the scientific study of animal behavior. (*Note:* Ethnology is the study of the characteristics of cultures.)

2-3c How Do I Know Which Philosophy Is Right?

Within any group of people who care for and teach young children, there will be many successful and effective adults who tend to lean a bit toward either a more maturationist or a more behaviorist view of early growth and development. Developmentally appropriate practice, however, a predominant view in the field of early childhood education, revolves around the basic assumption that early development results from the interaction between children's inner capacity and motivation and their external environment.

Two basic assumptions fundamental to the procedures throughout this book are the following:

1. Children develop skills and concepts best by interacting in a nurturing, developmentally appropriate environment.
2. The way children interact in their environment is triggered by their particular stage of development as well as their own interests and motives.

DIVERSITY

DAP

failure to thrive syndrome
Causes a wasting away of the child's body. This condition can result from prolonged absence of emotional nurturance as well as from malnutrition, and affected infants typically show delays in motor and intellectual development.

Babies thrive in warm, nurturing environments.

Photo courtesy of the Jones family

In other words, one might say that typically developing children come into the world ready to learn. They will be motivated to explore the environment around them using their senses, they will seek human social contact, and they will quickly absorb any language they hear. If these components of the environment are easily available, the interactions will foster development in a healthy and natural way (Friedman, Melhuish, & Hill, 2009; Haith & Benson, 2008).

Children who come into the world without all five senses intact, with developmental delays, or with impaired motor or sensory capabilities need special equipment, extra stimulation, and skilled teaching to reach their full potential for development. Children with ability differences do not usually learn as naturally as their peers, but they too can learn.

Tragically, even a healthy infant with enormous potential may suffer terrible effects from a neglectful or non-nurturing environment:

- **Failure to thrive syndrome**
- Developmental delay
- Intellectual disability
- Death

Any of these effects can afflict potentially normal, healthy children if children are deprived of the essential elements of an appropriate environment, which provides nurturing human contact, a sense of being wanted and accepted, the opportunity to share thoughts and feelings with others, and exposure to interesting things they can explore by seeing, touching, tasting, feeling, smelling, and moving around.

The development of an intelligent, responsible human being is not an automatic internal process that takes place whatever the environmental factors, and it is not an external process of molding a pliable child into a predetermined shape chosen by parents and teachers. It is a lively process of give-and-take in which children explore their boundaries and limits. Sometimes they accommodate adult expectations, and sometimes, quite naturally, they resist.

Children come equipped with individual personalities, likes, dislikes, interests, and motives. The role of the adult is to guide, assertively and respectfully, never forgetting that even the youngest child is truly a person with all the rights belonging to any other human being (even the right to be negative and recalcitrant on occasion). In the constructivist perspective, child guidance is intended to give children feedback about the realities of their world, to allow them choices within reasonable limits, and to help them confront the logical consequences of their own actions.

Summary

- Child care and guidance practices have changed drastically through the years.
- Parents who depend on help from others in rearing their children want to be sure their children will receive proper guidance.
- The world is changing, and guidance methods must prepare children to be successful in the world of the future.
- Over the years, educators, philosophers, and scientists have influenced our views on child guidance.

- Adults may have difficulty changing old patterns in dealing with children, but change is possible with motivation and practice.
- Behaviorists believe that behavior and learning come from external forces.
- Maturationists believe that behavior and learning come from internal processes.
- Constructivists believe that behavior and learning come from the interactions between internal and external processes.

Key Terms

anarchy

autocracy

behaviorists

constructivists

democracy

ethologists

failure to thrive syndrome

maturationists

modify

tokens

Student Activities

1. Because behaviorists believe that behavior and learning result from external forces such as reinforcement, they focus on external strategies for managing children's behavior.
   a. Give an example of an external strategy for managing a child's behavior.
   b. When are external strategies for guidance appropriate?
   c. When are external strategies for guidance inappropriate?
   d. Give three examples of learning situations in which behaviorist tokens, stickers, or other rewards are ideal for increasing learning outcomes.

2. Because maturationists believe that behavior and learning hinge on internal processes such as maturation and motivation, they focus on nonintrusive ways to support children's naturally developing self-control.
   a. Give examples of nonintrusive ways to support guidance.
   b. When is nonintrusive support appropriate for guidance?
   c. When is nonintrusive support inappropriate for guidance?
   d. Give three examples of learning situations in which stepping aside and doing nothing is ideal for supporting learning outcomes.

3. Because constructivists believe that behavior and learning result from the interactions between internal development and external environment, they study child development, observe the child, and prepare a developmentally appropriate environment. They positively and proactively guide the child's inner development of self-control and respect for others.
   a. Give an example of developmentally appropriate ways to support guidance.
   b. How are developmentally appropriate practice, the constructionist approach, and the authoritative guidance style similar?
   c. How is the application of logical consequences consistent with the philosophy of the constructionist approach?

Related Resources

Readings

Adler, A. (1998). *Understanding human nature.* Center City, MN: Hazelden Information Education.

Stacy, S. (2011). *The unscripted classroom: Emergent curriculum in action.* St. Paul, MN: Redleaf Press.
This book is written for toddler and preschool teaching staff and encourages them to try innovative teaching strategies.

Seldin, T. (2006). *How to raise an amazing child the Montessori way.* New York: DK Publishing.
This book offers lovely photographs and an easy-to-read presentation written for parents. It offers ideas for parents to encourage and teach helpfulness and shows parents how to set up young children's home environments to encourage learning and positive behavior.

Warash, B., R. Curtis, D. Hursh, & V. Tucci. (2008). Skinner meets Piaget on the Reggio playground: Practical synthesis of applied behavior analysis and developmentally appropriate practice orientations. *Journal of Research in Childhood Education, 22*(4), 441–453.

Websites

Teacher QuickSource®   This is a useful DAP resource for teaching staff who work with infants, toddlers, and children up to age 8. It features a range of creative and appropriate learning activities for each age. You can click on specific activities to find related accreditation standards. Early childhood teachers can find step-by-step activities, materials lists, and outcomes all in one convenient place.

Piaget's Stages of Cognitive Development   This website offers an overview on Piaget in a format that is interactive and fun.

3

Understanding Children's Behavior

naeyc Standards

The following NAEYC Standards are addressed in this chapter

Standard1   Promoting child development and learning

1b Knowing and understanding the multiple influences on early
development and learning

1c Using developmental knowledge to create healthy, respectful,
supportive, and challenging learning environments for young children

Courtesy of Geneviève De Casero

Objectives

After reading this chapter you should be able to do the following:

3-1 Review typical ages and stages of early childhood from birth through age 12.

3-2 Summarize key characteristics of infant development.

3-3 Explain unique concerns of toddler development.

3-4 Analyze critical aspects of preschoolers' development.

3-5 Examine significant features of early school-agers' development.

3-6 Differentiate strategic features of older school-agers' development.

3-1 Typical Ages and Stages

The most important thing to remember when considering the typical ages and stages of childhood is that no child is completely typical. Every child is unique. Although typical or average patterns can be identified, children have individual patterns and rates of development that may be normal but not at all average. An appropriate reason for comparing a child's rate of development with standard rates is to be alert to any consistent differences, or red flags, that may indicate a need for professional screening and possibly some kind of intervention.

Sometimes, by comparing a child's individual behaviors with typical behaviors, we can better understand the child, recognize that the child is only going through a normal phase, and anticipate phases that the child will soon be entering. Adults are often comforted to know that many children at a certain age behave the same way as the child with whom they are dealing. Babies shy away from strangers, toddlers become stubbornly assertive, preschoolers worry about who is or is not their best friend at any given moment, and school-agers reject everything that is not considered cool by their friends. You may or may not be relieved to learn that children frequently outgrow worrisome behavior phases before parents and teachers figure out how to resolve them.

Typical behaviors are clustered together in a sequential order, so a given child's nontypical behaviors might be those found in children at a different chronological age. A 7-year-old who is developmentally delayed may show a wide range of typical preschooler behaviors. However, a gifted 4-year-old who can already read may act a bit like a school-ager in some behaviors but very much like a preschooler in other behaviors. The value of assessing each child individually is to match guidance strategies to the individual child's developmental capabilities and needs but never to label or stereotype the child.

If, for example, a toddler is discovered trying to poke an object into an electrical outlet, the adult may look very concerned and say, "Ouch, that could hurt you. Come play with your toys." But the primary discipline strategy would be to change the environment to protect the toddler more effectively. A specially designed safety guard should be installed to prevent access to the outlet, or the child could be removed to a safer, better supervised, area.

A 5-year-old who is discovered trying to insert an object into an outlet should be handled quite differently from a toddler. The adult must determine whether the child is curious, misinformed, or feeling rebellious. When the adult has a sense of why the behavior has occurred, he might firmly discuss the cause-and-effect dangers of playing with electrical outlets. He should then redirect the child's curiosity by helping the child explore the characteristics of electricity using a safe six-volt battery, wires, and a tiny flashlight bulb. The child's curiosity could be channeled into a whole new area of interest and knowledge by reading books about electricity. She can be taken outside to look at power lines, to talk about how workers protect themselves when they repair dangerous electrical wires, and to make pretend wires out of strings to attach to the child's playhouse.

Our guidance response will be effective if we understand what the child is capable of developmentally and then think about why the inappropriate behavior occurred. The temperament of the individual child, the feelings of the child, and the setting all affect the child's behavior. The important thing to remember is that every child is a unique human being. See Positive Focus 3.1 and 3.2.

As soon as the baby is born, his motor control begins to integrate with his senses.

Photo courtesy of the Bertram family

Positive Focus 3.1   How Does Guidance Change to Match Development?

Stages	Appropriate Guidance
Sensorimotor—Birth to Age 2	
• Development is largely nonverbal.	• Provide responsive, affectionate caregiving.
• Motor control integrates with the senses.	• Provide consistent, predictable routines.
• Children develop the concept of object permanence and the ability to form mental representations.	• Nurture the development of trust by responding promptly to the child's needs.

(Continued)

Preoperational—Ages 2 to 7

- Children's thought is egocentric—they cannot easily take the viewpoint of another.

- Children develop an increasingly refined understanding of cause and effect.

- Children develop the ability to think symbolically and to use language skillfully.

- Children learn the concept of two-way conversation.

- Children cannot reason abstractly or test hypotheses systematically, but they can think logically and see through obviously flawed thinking.

- Children begin to reason abstractly.
- Thinking becomes issue-focused and less egocentric.
- Children can consider hypothetical possibilities.
- Children begin to develop deductive reasoning, depending on educational opportunities and the child's willingness.

- In a caring and consistent way, teach self-help skills such as self-feeding, toilet learning, and dressing.

- Give children opportunities to make choices within reasonable limitations.

- Provide a developmentally appropriate environment for the child to explore and challenge emerging skills.

- As children grow, increase their responsibilities to match their abilities.

- Provide creative activities.

- Give encouragement and deserved recognition to support the development of competence and self-esteem.

- Use class meetings to solve problems.

- Teach conflict-resolution skills.

- Nurture each child to help her discover and develop her own special talents and abilities.

- Provide children support in developing a positive self-identity as their bodies begin to change and mature at different rates.

- Provide support for the development of strong peer relationships and friendships.

- Give children responsibility for tasks that genuinely contribute to the family, classroom, or community.

- Stop any bullying and ensure routine use of conflict resolution.

Atherton, 2005; Donohue-Colletta, 1995; Schaefer & Digeronimo, 2000.

TeachSource Digital Download

Erik Erikson's Psychosocial Stages of Human Development

Positive Focus 3.2

Stage 1: Infants—Birth to 1 Year
Crisis: Trust versus mistrust.
Description: Early in life, infants depend on others for food, care, and affection and must blindly trust caregivers to meet their needs.
Positive outcome: A *sense of hope*—if their needs are met consistently and responsively, infants will not only develop a secure attachment, but will also learn to trust their environment.

(Continued)

Negative outcome: If infants' needs are not met, they will not trust people and things in their environment.

Stage 2: Toddlers—1 to 2 Years

Crisis: Independence versus doubt and shame.

Description: Toddlers begin to develop self-help skills, self-feeding, potty learning, dressing, and so on, at this age. Their self-confidence in this stage hinges on their negotiation of this difficult new territory with caregivers.

Positive outcome: A *strong will*—if caregivers encourage the child's initiative and encourage her when she fails, she will develop confidence.

Negative outcome: If caregivers are overprotective, negative, or disapproving of her newfound independence, she may doubt her abilities or feel shame.

Stage 3: Preschoolers—2 to 6 Years

Crisis: Initiative versus guilt.

Description: Children find a new sense of power and freedom as they develop the motor skills and the language skills they need to become fully engaged in the environment and the social interactions around them. They discover that with this power and freedom comes new adult pressure to control immature impulses and to follow rules.

Positive outcome: A *sense of purpose*—if parents are encouraging, positive, and consistent in guidance, children learn to accept rules without guilt.

Negative outcome: If not, children may develop a sense of guilt and may become clingy and dependent or rebellious and resistant.

Stage 4: School-agers—6 to 12 Years

Crisis: Industry versus inferiority.

Description: School is the critical factor of this stage. Children make a transition from the world of home into the world of community, school, and peers. Home is still important, but succeeding outside the home takes on new importance.

Positive outcome: A *feeling of competence*—if children learn that they can succeed, that others value their work, they develop a sense of competence.

Negative outcome: If not, they will develop a sense of inferiority and may start looking for negative ways to win status with peers.

Courtesy of Geneviere De Casero

School-agers look for ways to win status within their age group. They become aware of who is "popular" and who is not.

Erikson, 1963.

3-2 Infants (Birth to 12 Months)

Babies are fascinating. Their big eyes and rounded contours are specially designed to turn grown men and women to mush (Alley, 1981). Babies are soft and warm and cuddly, but few parents are prepared for the powerful emotions that well up inside them when they, for the first time, have their own child. Some parents feel a jumble of emotions such as tremendous pride, a protectiveness as passionate as a tiger for her cubs, jealousy of any imagined competition for affection, crushing fatigue, fear of failure, and even grief over the loss of infancy as the child grows and matures so quickly.

Parenting is one of the most significant and challenging adventures adult human beings undertake (often with little or no preparation). If additional caregivers are involved in infant care, parents may be relieved of some stresses and strains, but other complex feelings or tensions may emerge. Many a parent has left her baby in a carefully chosen child care center for the first time only to sit in the parking lot, collapsed in tears on the steering wheel of her car.

Fathers, grandparents, and even siblings also fret over the adequacy of anyone helping to care for the new baby. Jenny, a kindergartner in a child care center, talked her teacher into letting her go to the nursery where her 2-month-old brother was newly enrolled. There, she held her baby brother's tiny hand through the bars of his crib for a long time as she carefully watched every move made by the adult caregivers. The employees listened smilingly as the little girl pointed out to them, "You mustn't touch his head right up there where it's soft." Although Jenny was only 5 years old, she felt protective and concerned about her baby brother.

3-2a Do Infants Intentionally Respond by Crying?

Usually, the first kind of upsetting behavior adults must cope with in caring for infants are bouts of crying. A typical circumstance involves the adult trying all the usual problem-solving strategies: warming a bottle, changing a diaper, or rocking. Soon, the adult has done everything she knows to do, but the infant cries even more frantically. Some adults take the infant's crying as a personal criticism of their competence and authority: "How dare this baby accuse me of being a bad father (or mother, or caregiver)!" A howling baby can quickly fray the nerves of even the most patient and devoted adult.

A temptation for many of us is the tendency to project intentional motives on the baby for her crying. We say such things as "She's just crying because she knows I'm a pushover," "She always cries when I try to cook, because she thinks she should be the center of attention," or "She's only crying because she's mad at me. She was born with a fiery temper." These rationalizations may make us feel vindicated for angry or resentful feelings that surge through us as we try to deal with the screaming baby, but they are, nevertheless, inaccurate. Infants do not intentionally do much of anything. They simply react spontaneously and unconsciously to their environment.

Sadly, some adults with virtually no understanding of the processes of child development see infant crying as such a clear example of intentional "bad" behavior. They attempt to punish the infant for his crying in the mistaken belief that they are helping their babies learn to be "good." Child protective services workers and other social agents too often deal with parents who begin shaking, hitting, and spanking babies in the first 2 years of life—a terribly dangerous and inappropriate practice.

A long-standing folk belief in some cultures is that responding quickly to babies and holding or playing with them will result in "spoiling" and will make the child excessively demanding and dependent. Sometimes caregivers are tempted to leave babies in cribs or playpens for the sake of convenience or to put them on a rigid schedule for feeding, changing, and sleeping, regardless of the baby's crying.

We know now that lots of holding, touching, talking, and playing with babies is critical for their brain development and emotional well-being. Do not ever hesitate to give comforting and attention to babies. Holding, touching, talking, and playing do not "spoil" infants.

3-2b Can Babies Misbehave on Purpose?

Regardless of many common misconceptions, in the first months of life, infants have no capacity for consciously intentional behavior. They are not able to think about or plan actions to get desired results. Until they have **object permanence** (the mental ability to envison persons, objects, or events that are not in sight), they cannot "think" or "know" that any action will bring about a desired result (Piaget, 1968). They can react or respond only in a very unconscious way to internal feelings such as pain or hunger and to external **stimuli**—sensations the infant sees, feels, hears, tastes, or smells.

3-2c Infant Brain Development

Even in toddlers, some behaviors that may seem intentional are actually **unconscious reactions** based on the child's having absorbed connections or relationships among day-to-day experiences. Unrelated objects, events, and sensations become connected. We might expect any 9-month-old to show curious interest in a brightly colored, shiny can. If the baby immediately fusses and struggles for the can of soft drink she sees in her mother's hand, though, it is pretty clear her unconscious day-to-day experience has led her to expect a sip whenever she sees a soft drink can.

3-2d Reflex Responses and Unconscious Conditioning

In newborns, almost all actions are simple reflexes over which the child has no control. Infants blink, startle, grasp an object placed in the palm of the hand, and root toward a nipple, but not because they choose to do those things. They do them simply because their brains are designed to make certain behaviors happen automatically. From the moment of birth, however, babies carefully study their environment, at first by staring and eventually by using all their senses. Babies gradually progress beyond reflex behavior. They begin to recognize and associate things they see, feel, hear, taste, and smell with other meaningful sensations or events. A hungry breast-fed infant will become very agitated when she is held near her mother's breast. The feel, smell, and sight of the breast are closely associated with the memory of the sweet taste of milk. This is called **unconscious conditioning**.

object permanence
The knowledge that something hidden from view is not gone forever but rather is in another location at that time and likely to reappear.

stimuli
Something taken in through the senses that might incite activity or thought; something seen, smelled, heard, felt, or tasted; an incentive for action.

unconscious reactions 無意識に働く
Actions that are unplanned, devoid of forethought. 反応

unconscious conditioning
A response developed through the use of all the senses; an association of things seen, felt, heard, tasted, and smelled with other meaningful sensations or events.

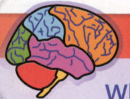

BrainFacts

What Can We Learn from Neuroscience?

Research is shedding new light on infant brain development

- Brain development that takes place before age 1 is more rapid and extensive than previously realized (Meltzoff & Gopnik, 2013; Meltzoff, Williamson, & Marshall, 2013).

- Early brain development is more vulnerable to environmental influence than was previously known (Dilger & Johnson, 2010).

- The influence of early environment on brain development is long lasting (Gallagher, 2005).

- The environment affects not only the number of brain cells and the number of connections among them, but also the way these connections are *wired* (Lewis & Carmody, 2008).

- There is increasing evidence of the negative impact of infant stress, inadequate nutrition, and infection on long-term brain development (Gerhardt, 2004; Shonkoff & Phillips, 2000).

3-2e Conditioning

To a baby, hearing keys rattle means someone is leaving, being placed in a stroller means going for a walk, or hearing the rustle of plastic wrap means getting a cookie. This kind of learning is generally categorized as **classical conditioning**. Looking at a balloon does not by itself make babies cry (seeing a balloon is an unconditioned stimulus). Loud noises, however, certainly do make babies cry (crying in response to a loud bang is a naturally occurring stimulus–response connection). If a baby has been frightened and has cried on several occasions when balloons have popped, then the baby may begin to cry whenever she even sees a balloon. This is associative learning.

Researchers have documented classical conditioning (pairing an unconditioned stimuli with a naturally occurring stimulus–response connection) in newborns. Usually what is documented is a rather rough kind of learning called **pseudoconditioning**. Studying early responses is difficult because so little of the newborn's movement can really be called voluntary (Fifer et al., 2010; Rosenblith & Sims-Knight, 1985). However, research tells us that from birth, classical conditioning is a part of the child's day-to-day learning (Domjan, 2003).

3-2f Operant Conditioning

Operant conditioning is different from classical conditioning. It occurs when the child's own voluntary actions are reinforced by positive stimuli (pleasurable rewards such as food, a feeling of accomplishment, or an interesting sensation). In operant conditioning, the focus is not on positively reinforcing the child; the focus is on positively reinforcing very specific behaviors.

Because this book is called *Positive Child Guidance*, everything you will read here is opposed to using negative stimuli (punishment) with children. Even the early behaviorist experimenters admitted that negative conditioning made their mice nervous. Positive reinforcement worked more effectively (Baron, 1998).

It is important to note that we are not the only ones who reinforce children's behavior. Stimuli in the environment condition young children too. For example, 9-month-old José has learned from crawling around his environment that the dog barks if you pull his ears; chewing on the remote control makes something happen to the TV; and crawling under the coffee table means a bumped head. Behaviors learned through operant conditioning continue so long as they get positive or negative reinforcement. If they are not reinforced, they usually disappear (Bauer, San Souci, & Pathman, 2010; Hayne 2007).

Newborns automatically cry as a response to the discomfort of being hungry. Older babies and toddlers learn to whimper or make a "fake" crying sound to signal that they are hungry. In the classical conditioning example previously described, babies became excited by sensations that unconsciously reminded them of being fed. In operant conditioning, however, hungry babies learn to repeat whatever behaviors have in the past resulted in their being fed. For example, if a breast-fed infant is nursed whenever she pulls at her mother's blouse, then that action (pulling) may become an unconscious but **learned behavior** that she repeats whenever she is hungry.

A baby first turns toward a nipple in response to an unconditioned rooting reflex. Then, over time, the pleasurable reward of warm milk stimulates more active and goal-oriented rooting. Eventually, the sight of the nipple, the feel of being placed in a nursing position, or other sensory **cues** (the smell of milk or the sound of a voice) will trigger rooting and sucking. An adult who is unfamiliar with a specific baby may inadvertently cause her to become frustrated and cry simply by holding her, without feeding her, in a position that she associates with nursing.

classical conditioning
Teaching a new response triggered by a new stimulus by pairing it repeatedly with a stimulus for which there is a physiological reflex (sometimes called Pavlovian conditioning). This term derives from an experiment originally performed by Ivan Pavlov in which a bell was rung just as food was offered to a hungry dog. Soon the dog would salivate at the sound of the bell whether or not food was offered, demonstrating that the association had become learned.

pseudoconditioning
The pairing of an unconditioned stimuli with a naturally occurring stimulus–response connection.

operant conditioning
A kind of learning that occurs when a spontaneous behavior is either reinforced by a reward or discouraged by punishment. For example, mice that go through a maze the wrong way get a shock. If they go the right way, they get some cheese. So they eventually learn to go the right way every time.

learned behavior
An action repeated because it produced a favorable response or was taught via the reinforcing response of another. This develops rapidly in the early stages of cognitive growth.

Operant conditioning occurs when the child's voluntary actions are reinforced by positive stimuli. This little girl chose her own puzzle. Each time she gets pieces together correctly, she is positively reinforced with a feeling of accomplishment.

© 2013 Cengage Learning®

3-2g Metacognition

Infants in the first year of life may need many repetitions of unfamiliar sensations, actions, and events to form associations. But by the end of their first year, they have learned through conditioning to expect specific responses to accompany many different sensations (see above). This kind of learning is an unconscious conditioning process. Although unconscious, conditioned learning continues to take place throughout life. (Advertisers spend millions of dollars every day trying to control our buying behavior through classical and operant conditioning—hoping we'll make our buying decision unconsciously.) Years will pass before an infant will develop the ability to consciously and intentionally control his own behavior, a process we call **metacognition**.

When a child has developed metacognition, he will be able to think about his own thinking processes and develop strategies to help him manage his own behavior. Children between 3 and 6 years old are only beginning to develop metacognition. Janah, age 4, was beginning to use her developing metacognition when she put glue into her mittens before she put them on because she was worried that she might lose them. School-age children have a much better developed ability to plan strategies. Babies and toddlers possess none of these skills; they just spontaneously react to the positive and negative sensations in their world.

metacognition
The ability to reflect on or evaluate one's behavior or actions.

cephalocaudal growth
Development in a pattern from the head downward, toward the feet (head to toe).

proximodistal
Development in a direction from closest to the body's trunk to the farthest, such as controlling the muscles of the trunk, then the muscles down the arms, and finally the hands (close to far).

habituated
The process of becoming accustomed to frequent repetition or pattern of behavior.

3-2h How Do Babies Develop Control of Their Actions?

The first muscles babies can actively control are those around the face and head. A newborn can move her eyes to follow objects, she can suck effectively, and she can turn her head. Muscle development proceeds from head to toe and from the trunk to the extremities: **cephalocaudal** (top to bottom) and **proximodistal** (close to far). At first, infants are only able to control a few mouth, eye, and neck muscles.

Gradually, an infant expands body control downward into the trunk (she learns to turn over), outward through the arms to the hands (she learns to bat at objects and then to grasp them), and finally down the legs to the feet (she learns to crawl and then walk). Tiny muscles of the hands and fingers will not be fully developed for years (then she will finally be able to use her fingers to button her sweater, tie her shoelaces, and write her name).

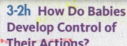

3-2i Why Do Babies Cry?

In the child's first year of life, behaviors result almost exclusively from internal developmental characteristics along with gradually increasing conditioned learning. If a baby cries for a prolonged period, that behavior does not stem from manipulativeness, maliciousness, or any other kind of conscious intention but rather from internal discomfort, stress, or fatigue or from externally conditioned routines. Babies cannot be held responsible or blamed for their behavior. It is more realistic to think in terms of relieving the cause of a crying infant's unhappiness if the problem is internal or of changing adult routines or the environment if the problem is external.

Adults are the ones who establish routines and habits in infants through day-to-day basic care patterns. Infants become **habituated** (accustomed) to those patterns and object loudly when routines are abruptly broken. If an infant is accustomed to being in constant contact with her mother's

Muscle control begins closest to the body and gradually moves from head to toe, cephalocaudal, and from the trunk out to the fingertips and toes, proximodistal.

Courtesy of the Bertram Family

body, she will cry pitifully when she is left alone in a quiet room. If an infant is accustomed to quiet isolation, he may be terrified by sudden placement in a noisy, bustling child care center.

Psychologists define stress as the process of recognizing and responding to perceived threat or danger (Dwiveldi, 2000). While working directly with infants over the years in various child care facilities, I have on several occasions seen babies who seemed especially upset by a separation or by a stark upheaval in their care arrangements. In spite of attentive caregivers, the infants (ranging from 2 to 9 months of age) appeared to slip from a long period of anguished, relentless crying into a period of quiet depression with only languid whimpering.

The infants withdrew from social contact, avoided eye contact, lost appetite, refused to play, slept too much or too little, and, apparently as a result, appeared noticeably less healthy after a time. After various lengths of time (ranging from days to months), each of these babies eventually recovered spontaneously and became responsive, robust, and playful. Today, almost a decade later, even the one of those infants most severely affected gives every appearance of being a bright, healthy, and well-adjusted young girl. Nevertheless, stress should be considered in dealing with children of any age and avoided or eased whenever possible.

Careful planning of basic care and nurturing routines that can be maintained consistently will help protect the child from abrupt and upsetting changes. When changes in routines must occur, careful planning and gradual orientation should take place—especially before drastic upheavals in child care arrangements—to avoid subjecting babies to unnecessary stress (Evans & Schamberg, 2009; Gallagher, 2005; George et al., 2010; Trad, 1991).

stress
The process of recognizing and responding to threat or danger.

Don't forget that compared to a grownup person every baby is a genius. Think of the capacity to learn! The freshness, the temperament, the will of a baby a few months old!

—May Sarton

3-2j When Do Babies Begin Learning Language?

Babies begin hearing the muffled sounds of their mother's words while they are still in the womb. They are born ready to pay attention to language. When loving caregivers talk to their babies, they typically use a special lilting speech pattern called "Motherese." Researchers have observed this rhythmic, high-pitched Motherese across languages and believe it is essential for infants to acquire language (Cutler & Mehler, 1993; Murty, Otake, & Cutler, 2007). Don't ever be afraid to talk baby-talk to babies. Just remember to drop the baby-talk when the baby is no longer a baby!

3-2k Can Babies Understand Body Language?

From birth, children respond to facial expression, tone of voice, and body movement. Long before a child understands language, she reacts to cues such as body language, inflection, tone, and volume that are part of an adult's speech. The following story about Betty Jo and Jeremy illustrates this point.

Betty Jo, the lively young mother of 5-month-old Jeremy, comes to pick up her son from the family day home where he is cared for during the day. She chats with other parents picking up their children as she zips Jeremy into his snowsuit. Jeremy makes a funny sound and his cheeks turn red as it dawns on Betty Jo that she will have to change his diaper.

Everyone downwind of Jeremy is, by this point, quite aware that the diaper is definitely more than just wet. As other parents chuckle, Betty Jo jokingly but energetically scolds Jeremy for being so rude after she has gone to all the trouble of bundling him up to go home.

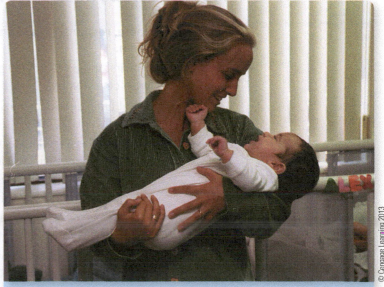

Long before he understands words, he responds to facial expression, tone of voice, and nonverbal body language.

© Cengage Learning 2013

Although the little boy clearly does not understand all her words, he unmistakably interprets her fake scowl and sharp tone to mean that she is angry with him. He turns his face away from her and sobs. Betty Jo is quite startled by his reaction. Because he did not know how to talk, she assumed he would not have any idea what she was saying.

3-2l How Do Trauma and Chronic Stress Affect an Infant's Brain Development?

Constant exposure to stressful environments can dramatically change the way an infant's or young child's brain develops, making the child more prone to emotional disturbances and less able to learn. Children exposed to severe, prolonged stress may develop learning disabilities and emotional and behavioral problems (for example, attention deficit disorder, anxiety, and depression). They also may become more vulnerable to medical problems such as asthma, immune-system dysfunction, and heart disease (George et al., 2010; Gunnar et al., 2001; Lipina & Colombo, 2009; Miner & Clarke-Stewart, 2008; Muennig et al., 2009; Pransky, 1991; Prothrow-Stith & Quaday, 1995; Shore, 1997).

3-2m How Do Babies Develop Trust?

According to Eric Erikson (1963), trust developed in infancy is a primary foundation for healthy emotional attitudes that are needed throughout life. Basic care patterns offer our first opportunity to demonstrate our trustworthiness to an infant. Whenever the infant experiences internal distress, she automatically responds by crying. In time, through operant and classical conditioning, she can come to expect a dependable response from the adult caregivers in her life. This trust in the predictability of her environment and in the responsiveness of her primary caregivers helps the baby develop a sense that she is valued and that she can affect her surroundings, the first step toward the development of positive self-esteem. The child knows she is greatly valued by the way she is treated.

appropriate touch
Suitable for the occasion and the person affected, nonexploitative, and having no concealed intention; physical contact that is casual, affectionate, reciprocal, and welcome, but never sexual or controlling.

Appropriate touch has a powerful calming and bonding effect for babies and young children (Honig, 2005; Mantagu, 1986). Infants need a great deal of physical

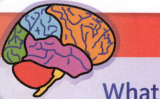

BrainFacts

What Can We Learn from Neuroscience?

Reliable, responsive care and affection supports a baby's developing brain.

- The first three years of life present a particularly sensitive period for human brain development.
- Infant brain development is an active process that requires a supportive environment (Wilson, 2002).
- Giving babies affectionate, reliable care and freedom to explore a safe environment fuels their brain development.
- Trauma and continual stress produce high levels of hormones in babies, which can change the growth of their brains (Marshall, 2011).
- "Children whose environment is hostile or lacking in nurture end up thinking with a very different brain" (Cairns, 2002, p. 46).
- Babies with secure attachments to consistent caregivers handle occasional stress without experiencing a flood of stress hormones (Luijk et al., 2010).
- Active, responsive learning environments entice babies to explore, which strengthens brain networks.

contact. Not only does physical contact help them feel calm and organized, but also it is necessary for their growth and development. A pacifier, rocking, swinging, and cuddly toys calm babies because they mimic the sensations he felt when nursing, being held, rocked, or cuddled by the parent. But these are just substitutes. What the baby needs most is authentic physical contact—holding, carrying, playing, hugging, and rocking.

3-2n What Is Learned Helplessness?

Babies who are caught in a flow of events that are unpredictable and clearly outside their control may develop an unfortunate style of response termed learned helplessness (Comer, 2004; Honig, 2000; Honig & Wittmer, 1997; Seligman, 2004, 2006). Heartbreaking but very instructive studies of the créche, a Romanian orphanage run by French nuns, helped researchers more fully understand the devastating impact of learned helplessness. Babies in this orphanage were adequately fed, clothed, and kept warm and dry, but the babies stayed in cribs with only uninteresting white crib bumpers and white ceilings to look at. There were few playthings and no structured activities. Caregivers were not aware that talking directly to and interacting with babies was necessary.

Because the babies were fed and changed on a schedule, there was no motivation for caregivers to respond to the babies' cries, so the babies soon learned that there was no use in crying. In effect, the children had no influence on their environment. Nothing that happened to them hinged on either spontaneous or learned actions on their part. They had no incentive to function in any way other than as passive objects in the environment, and in fact, their behavior was soon not much livelier than that of a potted plant. These babies did not learn to sit up until a year old or walk until 4 or 5 years old. By age 6, their IQs were about 50, which is half the normal IQ and well into the range of serious mental retardation (Dennis, 1973).

Adults who care for babies should be down on the floor laughing, talking, singing, playing, and interacting with the babies, not sitting in rocking chairs talking to other adults while babies are bored and alone in their cribs. Sometimes adults rationalize this inappropriate behavior by saying, "You shouldn't hold babies and play with them all the time. They'll turn into spoiled brats! It's better for them to learn to entertain themselves."

learned helplessness
A person's inability to take action to make his or her life better, arising out of a sense of not being in control.

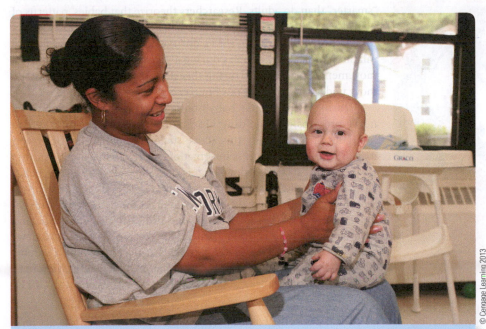

Holding, touching, talking, and playing is critical for her brain development and emotional well-being. It does not "spoil" the baby.

BrainFacts

What Can We Learn from Neuroscience?

Play supports children's brain development:

- Play provides the context for healthy brain development (Fantuzzo & McWayne, 2002; Rushton & Larkin, 2001; Steglin, 2005).
- Babies, toddlers, and children from all socioeconomic backgrounds and cultures naturally play (Trawick-Smith, 2006).
- Play develops the foundation for memory, language, math, analytical, and symbolic thinking (Berk, 2009; Corsaro, 1988; Kim, 1999; Levy, Wolfgang, & Koorland, 1992).
- DAP environments stimulate purposeful and constructive play (Bergen, 2002).

Obviously, the fundamental needs of an infant for the kind of care that will foster development of social, emotional, intellectual, and physical growth must take priority over convenience for adults. Quality child care involves a great deal of effort and hard work. Although overindulgence and overprotection do undermine child guidance, lazy or haphazard care is never in the best interest of children (Bronson, 2001).

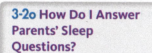
3-2o How Do I Answer Parents' Sleep Questions?

Although it is upsetting to parents, newborn night-waking has developmental benefits. Sleep researchers have discovered that infants sleep "smarter" than do adults. Researchers theorize that babies' patterns of light sleep and frequent waking help infants' brains develop by allowing their brains to remain active during sleep. In fact, blood flow to infants' brains nearly doubles during a phase of sleep called rapid eye movement (REM) sleep. During this stage of sleep, our eyes actually move under our eyelids as our brain exercises (Sears et al., 2005, 2011).

During REM sleep, a baby's body increases its manufacture of nerve proteins, the building blocks of the brain. Learning is also thought to occur during this active stage of sleep. The baby's brain may use this time to process information taken in while awake, storing what is useful and discarding what is not. Some sleep researchers believe that infant REM sleep acts to stimulate the developing brain, promoting mental development. And we thought the baby was just fussy!

Parents often ask early childhood professionals about sharing their beds with their children. Bed sharing, or *cosleeping*, with a newborn supports breastfeeding. But great care must be taken. If parents choose to have a young infant sleep in their bed, they must be sure to do the following (Lindsay, 2002; Okami et al., 2002; Sears et al., 2011):

- The baby sleeps on his back (unless the doctor says otherwise).
- The baby does not come in contact with soft surfaces or loose covers.
- The sides or edges of the bed do not present entrapment possibilities.
- The bed is not also shared with other siblings.
- The adults do not smoke or use substances such as alcohol or drugs.

© Cengage Learning 2013

Babies should eat whenever they are hungry and sleep whenever they are tired. We respect their needs while gradually nudging them toward eating at mealtime and snack time and sleeping at nap time and bedtime.

Parents also ask about having their preschoolers sleep with them or get in bed with them during the night. Studies show no evidence of negative long-term problems from bed-sharing so long as both parents are comfortable with the arrangement (Donohue-Carey, 2002; Hauck et al., 2003; Sears, 2008; Sears et al., 2011).

3-2p Which Is Best: Flexible Spontaneity or Predictable Routines?

Two opposing priorities for infants have been described in this chapter. The reader might well ask at this point, "Should I provide consistent, reliable routines or respond flexibly and spontaneously to cues from the baby?" On one hand, external environment (the infant's physical surroundings, daily routines, and patterns of interacting with others) is important because infants shape future expectations through day-to-day experiences. On the other hand, an infant's internal sensations and needs are important as a basis for adult responses because internal sensations and natural urges stimulate the child to initiate behaviors and to explore making things happen. Balancing these two opposing needs makes sense, but each individual teacher will develop and apply a personal educational philosophy (addressed in Chapter 2).

This book proposes the constructionist perspective, which describes an interweaving between external forces and internal processes. In terms of guiding young children, this process is called positive child guidance, an assertive gentle nudge method. A caregiver can be very responsive to and respectful of cues (indications of interest or need) from a child while gradually nudging the child toward routines that are socially appropriate and convenient for the adult.

A 6-month-old will be encouraged to follow her inner drives to explore the sensory qualities of her environment by feeling, squishing, pounding, and smelling her food as she tastes it. However, she will be gently, gradually, and persistently nudged over time to handle food in a more traditional manner. She will learn to use eating utensils and eventually to have polite table manners.

3-2q What Are Interaction Styles?

In a domineering authoritarian-style setting, a baby would be forced to eat passively and not touch the food at all. In a permissive-style setting, where adults abdicate responsibility, they would shrug and accept the belief that children are hopelessly slovenly in their eating habits and nothing can be done about it. In a respectful authoritative-style setting, adults set reasonable but slightly challenging expectations for the child based on needs, interests, and abilities. Adults help the child learn by modeling a behavior for her, giving her freedom to try on her own, and encouraging her first clumsy attempts to master the skill. See Positive Focus 3.3.

external environment
The physical surroundings or conditions around a child that influence his or her growth, development, and learning. A young child's environment can be described as everything the child sees, hears, touches, or experiences.

internal sensations
The physical feelings that are caused by one or more of the sense organs being stimulated. The feelings sensed by one's own body such as hunger or fear.

positive child guidance
Relying on the "developmental interactionist" perspective to create guidance that is primarily based on an interweaving between external forces and internal processes.

cues
Indications of interest or need.

authoritarian style
Interactive (or control) style relying on one-way communication, rigid rules, and punishment—"the sledgehammer."

permissive style
Interactive (or control) style relying on neglect, abdication of responsibility, or over-indulgence—"the doormat."

authoritative style
Interactive (or control) style relying on two-way communication, collaboratively developed rules, and positive guidance—"the guide."

Positive Focus 3.3

Interaction Styles

The Authoritarian Style

- "Do it because I said so."
- "I don't want to hear any more about it."
- "Do as you're told!"

Authoritarian adults tend to communicate in commands. Their one-way communication does not permit the child to air her concerns or express her opinions. The authoritarian adult relies on punishment. Rules are rigid. There is no negotiation.

In this environment, children may become sullen, withdrawn, aggressive, quarrelsome, self-destructive, and unable to make responsible decisions. Both cognitive and social skills may lag developmentally (Baumrind, 1967; Kawamura, Frost, & Harmat, 2002; Maccoby, 1992).

(Continued)

The Permissive Style

- "Gee, I hope you're not going to fall off that 8-foot fence."
- "I'd rather pick up your clothes myself than listen to whining."
- "Here, darling, have more chocolates—unless you prefer ice cream."

Adults may be permissive in an indulgent, child-centered way, or they may be permissive in a negligent, uninvolved, adult-centered manner. Both forms of permissiveness hurt children. When children are left to their own devices, allowed to follow impulses without limits, and given no expectations, they have great difficulty learning positive social skills (Johnson et al., 2008; Leung, Lau, & Lam, 1998; Maccoby, 1992).

Children in an indulgent environment tend to become self-centered, bossy, and impulsive. They are more likely to have low levels of self-control, self-esteem, and achievement.

Children treated in the negligent–permissive, uninvolved interaction style, however, are often harmed most of all. These children may develop very aggressive or destructive behavior patterns. These behavior patterns tend to persist over time, causing low academic achievement and dysfunctional, antisocial, hostile, or even delinquent behavior (Bullock & Dishion, 2003; Dishion & Bullock, 2002).

The Authoritative Style

- "Samantha, please stop."
- "When you shake the hamster cage, Fluffy feels frightened and his water spills."
- "Would you like to get fresh water for Fluffy so you can help him feel better?"

The authoritative style of interaction is characterized by respect, fairness, warmth, open communication, reasoning, consistency, and involvement. *Adults give reasons for rules, are open to negotiation, but never abdicate their final responsibility for making decisions even when they have to say no.* Children are given authentic and appropriate choices, are asked for opinions, and are genuinely heard.

Many positive character traits have been correlated with the authoritative style. These include independence, creativity, persistence, mature social skills, optimism, academic competence, original thinking, leadership skills, achievement motivation, self-control, and effective decision-making skills (Aunola, Stattin, & Nurmi, 2000; Baumrind, 1967, 1978; Kaufmann et al., 2000; Raikes, 1996; Steinberg et al., 1994).

3-2r What Do We Mean by Secure Attachment to Caregivers?

The attachment of babies to their adult caregivers is a critical part of their overall healthy social and emotional development. Early studies looked only at mother–infant relationships because that was the only interaction that was considered to be of importance. Freud focused on the attachment of infants to the mother and theorized that the baby considered her a "love object" simply because she provided pleasurable sucking and warm milk. He believed that the process of weaning, whether it was too rigid or too lenient, set the emotional tone for all of the child's future relationships with people and institutions.

Erikson (1963) revised and updated Freud's theory. He believed that experiences in the first year of life gave infants a general point of view about the world, either the positive reaction of trust or the negative reaction of mistrust. He theorized that not only interpersonal relations but also competence in learning was affected by the baby's relationship to the mother. Exploration is essential for skill development, but babies have the confidence to explore the environment only when they have an adult who serves as a "secure base."

The authoritative style of interaction is characterized by respect, fairness, warmth, open communication, reasoning, consistency, and involvement.

Konrad Lorenz (1966) discovered a kind of attachment in certain birds (ducks, chickens, and so on) that he called **imprinting**. The ducks he studied became attached to whatever, or whomever, they saw moving near them when they hatched. Baby ducks that attached to "Papa" Lorenz not only followed him around as they grew up but also tried to mate with his leg when they reached maturity. Ethologists (scientists who study behaviors in naturalistic surroundings) do not pretend that human beings behave instinctively as ducks do, but they do theorize that some early experiences or attachments have long-term impact on human behavior.

Bowlby (1958) and Ainsworth (1973) studied the processes of human attachment as researchers experienced a dawning awareness that biologic mothers were not the only people who could develop important emotional relationships with infants. When discussing attachment, writers began to use the word *parent* instead of *mother* to reflect awareness of the effect of father–child relationships. Gradually, the term *caregiver* came into use to indicate awareness that babies could develop multiple loving attachments to grandparents, older siblings, and other consistent child care providers outside the family, as well as to adoptive and foster parents.

3-2s Why Do Babies Cling?

Attachment must be recognized by caregivers as a valuable part of babies' early development rather than an inconvenience to be avoided. Elise, a mother with a highly successful career, picked up her 11-month-old son from his child care center one afternoon. The little boy eagerly crawled to his mother and pulled himself up by holding onto her legs. As he clutched at her skirt, clung to her legs, and whined to be picked up, Elise breathed a dismayed sigh, looked helplessly at the infant-room teacher, and said, "Look at him. He just clings to me. What am I doing wrong?"

Elise was not aware that her son was only showing the normal indications of healthy emotional ties to his mother, which Ainsworth called **secure attachment**. When babies

imprinting
A kind of early bonding in an animal's development that normally results in significant recognition ability and social attraction to members of its own species, especially to its mother.

secure attachment
Healthy emotional ties to caregiver. Typical signs include brightening at the sight of caregiver, visually following caregiver's movements, smiling or vocalizing to get attention, holding out arms to be picked up, or clinging to the caregiver. Babies develop emotional bonds to the significant caregivers in their lives.

Babies develop emotional bonds to the significant caregivers in their lives.

brighten at the sight of a caregiver, visually follow that caregiver's movements, smile or vocalize to get attention, hold out their arms to be picked up, or cling to the caregiver, they are showing the typical signs of healthy attachment.

Babies who turn or crawl away when a caregiver returns after an absence may be expressing the angry, rejected feelings that accompany a disrupted or poorly formed attachment. Babies who alternately cling and reject, or show a push–pull relationship with the caregiver, may not have built a really secure attachment to the caregiver. *Developing secure attachments is an essential step in the growth of normal social and emotional skills.*

The positive child guidance concept of the gentle nudge fits well in the area of attachment. Caregivers can best assist infants' healthy social and emotional development not only by allowing and supporting attachment and closeness but also by gradually, as the child seems ready, nudging the child to move out on her own in exploring the environment. A newborn (or a baby in a new child care setting) may need to be held a great deal of the time at first, but gradually he can be enticed to spend increasing amounts of time occupying himself by looking at or playing with interesting mobiles, toys, and other surroundings. By getting down on the floor to play with the baby, a caregiver can be readily available to serve as a "secure base." Having a secure base will help the baby feel confident to explore the environment freely as he learns to roll over and crawl.

3-2t Separation and Stranger Anxieties

Attachment to caregivers serves as a survival mechanism for the species because a helpless infant's safety depends on staying close to a caregiver. It seems logical that an infant would not want to be separated from the caregiver who gives comfort and security. Sometime between 6 months and a year, separation and stranger anxieties begin to appear in many children because of their newly developed cognitive skills. Coincidentally, many parents first begin to rely on child care at about this same time. We adults are able to think and talk about child care arrangements. We may have studied a substitute caregiver's references or investigated carefully a center's license to provide care, but a baby has no way of comprehending all this.

When a baby looks up and sees that her daddy is not in sight, she feels the same way she would feel if she suddenly realized she was alone in the middle of a big department store. The swarms of strangers hovering around trying to be helpful would, at first, only be more frightening. Amazingly, it is not uncommon for parents or child care workers to be heard chiding a crying baby, "Hush! There is no reason for you to cry." If I were riding in an airplane that made an unexpected landing, or if I were pushed out kicking and screaming and left in a strange land with strangers who did not speak my language, I might cry, too, as I watched the plane carrying my family fly away. When the parent is out of sight, the child is unable to realize that daddy is not gone forever.

The more positive experiences a baby has had with meeting new people, the less uncomfortable she will feel when she separates from parents or encounters strangers. In time, the baby develops a concrete understanding that strangers can be relied on to provide care and that, after a while, parents reappear. Pushing the baby into frightening situations is not helpful, but avoiding encounters with strangers altogether is also counterproductive. Gently nudging the baby into pleasurable and trusting relationships with adults other than parents will assist her in developing confidence and an open, positive attitude toward the world.

3-2u How Do Babies Perceive Themselves and Their Surroundings?

In the first months of life, babies have not yet gained a mental conception of themselves as separate individuals. Their perception of their own existence is limited to what they see, feel, taste, smell, and hear. They unconsciously perceive their surroundings as if they were the center of the universe and the people and objects around them were extensions of their own existence. They make no distinction between their own physical being and the surroundings they perceive through their senses.

Caregivers take on a very important role in this context. Caring for a baby means that they literally become a part of that baby's life. Adults facilitate and guide older children whose interests are focused on each other and on their own activities as much as or more than on adults. In the first year of life, however, infants focus an enormous quantity of their interest and energy on interacting with adult caregivers. They depend on adults for every aspect of physical care and safety, as well as for entertainment and affection. Their interest in peers is purely **egocentric**. A 7-month-old may crawl onto a younger baby and casually grasp a handful of hair to feel and taste, then look quite puzzled by the sudden loud, piercing noises emitted by the little friend.

By seeing adults rushing to rescue the younger baby and **modeling** appropriate behavior—softly stroking the offended baby's head while saying to the offender, "Gentle, gentle. Be gentle"—babies can eventually **internalize** more appropriate ways of behaving. Because the baby identifies so closely with the adult caregiver, the baby will automatically mimic behaviors of that adult. Caregivers who respond harshly or aggressively reinforce inappropriate behaviors in babies by modeling loud or rough interactions.

egocentric
Seeing oneself as the center of the universe, self-centered, selfish. This point of view is a perfectly normal developmental characteristic of babies and very young children.

modeling
Providing an example, being a role model. In positive child guidance, the adult is the primary role model.

internalize
The process of taking in experiences and absorbing learning, then making them part of one's own behavior or belief.

3-3 Toddlers (12 Months to 3 Years)

Young toddlers, the 1-year-olds, are amazing human beings. For the first time in their lives, they have become upright bipeds like the rest of us. Also, for the first time, they do not depend on us to bring rattles or squeak toys to them for entertainment. They can walk through, wriggle under, or climb over any obstacle a grown-up can devise to get to the really interesting things that attract their curiosity. Although a toddler can be an adorable timid rabbit one moment, sucking a thumb while peeking from behind a well-worn but snuggly piece of blanket, in an instant she can raise the rafters in a full-fledged tantrum and then crumple in a heap on the floor.

3-3a Can Toddlers Control Their Feelings and Actions?

Young toddlers are totally transparent in their feelings. They are openly affectionate, easily delighted by attention, and full of wonder about their surroundings. They also become confused, frustrated, and overwhelmed by their newfound freedom. One moment they seem ready to take on the world; the next they regress to helpless clingy babies. Their needs are simple: They want food, comfort, affection, and approval and to explore every bit of the huge, booming, wide world around them. As babies, they still respond to their sensations of need by crying, but as growing children, they also begin responding to their own desires by moving out into the environment to get what they want.

Toddlers use their senses (touch, sight, smell, taste, and hearing) to explore the physical attributes of their environment and both small and large muscles to practice physical skills. They still do not consciously plan their actions. They just act. If the toddler feels hungry and the box of cereal in the grocery cart with her looks delicious, she may just rip it open and have a snack, then look hurt when her parents seem shocked by her behavior. Toddlers have the capacity to learn a great deal, but learning takes much repetition and practice.

In each stage of child development . . . there is a central problem that has to be solved . . . if the child is to proceed with vigor and confidence to the next stage.
—Erik H. Erikson

3-3b How Does Awareness of Cause and Effect Develop?

Toddlers have made a huge cognitive leap since infancy in their ability to remember things and in their first crude ability to manipulate ideas mentally. Cause-and-effect relationships become a focal point for toddler learning. Toddlers are fascinated by light switches and will flip the light on and off many times if they are allowed. They watch the switch and the light fixture and mentally connect the cause-and-effect relationship between the two.

Toddlers also tirelessly explore cause-and-effect relationships in social interactions. The toddler will stick her little pointed index finger out to touch the electrical outlet (covered, of course, with a plastic safety cap) and look up at her daddy expectantly as he patiently repeats for the hundredth time, "Stop. Please. That's not for touching." Finally, the little girl will touch the outlet, shaking her head and repeating soberly, "Tah. Tah (Stop, stop)." She is preoccupied with connecting the cause-and-effect relationship between her action and Daddy's words and has totally missed the point that Daddy would rather she did not touch the outlet.

3-3c Toddlers Need to Explore Their Surroundings

Healthy, well-developing toddlers have a curiosity that is boundless. Their desire to explore at times overshadows all other needs. A toddler who is totally immersed in the miseries of teething will stop crying when his mother carries him to the refrigerator and opens the freezer to get his frozen teething ring. For the moment, his pain is forgotten as he watches the frosty air roll out of the freezer and feels the brisk difference in temperature from this strange part of his environment he has never explored before.

Toddlers learn to walk because their fascination with this form of locomotion outweighs their fear of falling or being hurt. They move out into the environment, away from the security of caregivers, because the exhilaration of discovery causes them to throw caution to the wind. Babies might stay in the comfort of their mother's arms forever if it were not for the powerfully motivating activator we call curiosity, which drives toddlers out into the scary but exciting world. Baby birds are comfortable, secure, safe, and well fed in the nest. At some point, however, nature intends them to leap precariously into the air and to flap their little wings until they figure out how to fly—not only a frightening and exhilarating experience for babies, of course, but also a frightening and exhilarating experience for grown-ups to watch.

3-3d Safety Is a Major Issue in Toddler Care

During toddlerhood, a child's motor development far outstrips her capacity to understand, remember, or abide by rules. Because she has not yet developed metacognition, she cannot look at a situation and then think about and plan for the potential consequences of her own behavior in that situation. Toddlers are still a bit unsteady in their walking, running, and climbing, and they are compelled to taste, feel, smell, and manipulate every interesting object they encounter. All this adds up to toddlers being vulnerable for accidents (Centers for Disease Control and Prevention [CDC], 2008).

Unless toddlers are constantly and diligently supervised, they can inadvertently swallow objects and poisonous substances, fall off or bump into things, and touch things they should not touch. If responding to crying is the first major area of worry for caregivers, then keeping toddlers safe is surely the second big area of stress.

In past years, parents occasionally bragged that they had a toddler so well behaved that the most expensive, fragile, or even dangerous bric-a-brac could be left on the coffee table and the baby would never so much as touch it. They sometimes accomplished that feat by slapping the baby's hand or saying, "No!" sharply whenever the child attempted to touch any forbidden items. These adults believed that by teaching the baby to be still and not touch anything, they were helping him become well disciplined and polite.

Information about the processes of cognitive development, generated by research over the past few decades, has changed this old perception. A delightful poster that is very popular among child care workers pictures a young toddler standing sadly in a playpen. The caption reads "What do you mean, 'Don't touch'? Touching is how I learn." To create a wonderful environment that stimulates development while protecting toddlers from unreasonable risk of harm, adults must childproof all areas before babies ever develop the motor skills to move about.

Toddlers can be independent and safe. This 2-year-old is given a safe set of markers with lids glued with durable marine glue into holes drilled into a solid wooden base. She is able to pull out the markers and then return them to the matched lid without the risk of swallowing lids.

Have you ever heard a parent or child care worker say, "I don't intend to spend my life picking toys up off the floor. I let them have one or two toys and that's it"? Babies and toddlers scrutinize every sensory aspect of each object. How does it taste? How does it feel? How does it sound? And then they tire of it. They need variety in textures, weights, colors, sounds, and other properties in the objects they are allowed to explore. The same two or three plastic squeak toys simply won't meet their brain's complex developmental needs (Birkbeck, 2009; Van Herwegen et al., 2008).

The period of early toddlerhood is a special period in a child's life for social, intellectual, and motor skill development. Direct sensory exploration of the physical environment serves as a key requirement for optimal development. Keeping toddlers in restricted environments that are "hands off," excessively tidy, not childproofed, or downright boring risks losing the child's most valuable opportunity for early learning (Bauer, San Souci, & Pathman, 2010; Friedman, Melhuish, & Hill, 2009; Haith & Benson, 2008; Hayne, 2007).

The ability of very young children to make sense of our feelings from our body language and tone of voice gives us an opportunity to communicate with them without words. Before children have mastered **expressive language**, they have begun to develop **receptive language**. Therefore, if we are honest and sincere in the words we speak, our body language will convey our feelings to the child. If we speak to the child for the benefit of other adults, as if the child were not really present or listening, we may miss an important opportunity to communicate with the child.

From the very beginning, adults should start speaking to babies as if they were (because they definitely are) worthwhile human beings. This has two important benefits for guidance. First, the child will learn early in life to pay attention to adults. Second, adults can begin modeling appropriate communication skills.

Using a kind facial expression and a caring tone of voice, we can speak reassuringly to a young toddler who resists going to sleep: "I know you would rather play with your toys, but it's time for a nap now. Would you like me to rub your back for a minute to help you relax?" Even though the child will not understand all the words, she will sense the adult's caring attitude. She will also have an opportunity to hear language and associate it with objects and events in day-to-day living.

expressive language
Communication with others verbally, in sign language, or in writing.

receptive language
Comprehension of written, signed, or spoken communication expressed by others.

Be a wonderful role model because you will be the window through which many children will see their future.

Thomas Mckinnon

3-3e How Does Verbal Communication Begin?

Toddlers seem to explode into language. At a child's first birthday, she may know only words such as "mama," "dada," and "baba" for bottle. He will understand many words before he is able to say them. Within a few months, the child may know how to say dozens of single words plus a number of holophrases (phrases made of words that are joined and used as if they were inseparable single words). "Gofieys" may mean, "Go to a fast food restaurant and get French fries." "Sousite" may mean, "Let's go outside to play."

The child soon learns to mix and match words or holophrases to create two-word sentences. Soon, the child's speech begins to sound like strange text messages—including only a few key letters in important words and leaving out unimportant words completely: "Doggy bih (big)" "No touch daddy gwas (glasses)." By age 3, the child's speech begins to sound surprisingly like our own (with a few quirks here and there): "My daddy goed to work an he gots a truck."

At birth, the child had little muscular control of her lips and tongue and no comprehension that language existed or had significance. In only three short years, she has learned how to create many different sounds with her lips, tongue, and vocal cords; amassed hundreds of words in her vocabulary; and grasped the basic structure of her native language. Her language comprehension is complex, but not at a conscious level. She has learned naturally and unconsciously simply by listening, practicing, and interacting freely in a supportive environment.

3-3f What Kind of Language Experiences Are Good for Toddlers?

Infants and children of all ages need to hear the rich, lyrical words of adult conversational speech, as well as the musical word patterns in rhymes, songs, and jingles. For maximum comprehension, however, a child must also hear language that is very close to that of her own level of development. This language should be slightly ahead of the child's own level.

If a baby's language development is still limited to the cooing and babbling stage, the adult can effectively communicate through facial expression, tone of voice, body language, imitation of the sounds the baby makes, and introduction of simple words. If the child is using single words, the adult should offer two-word phrases ("All gone," "More milk?").

For maximum comprehension, a child should hear language that is very close to her own level of development. This language should be slightly ahead of the child's own level.

Toddlers may hear and comprehend only a few words in sentences that are above their comprehension. Often, they catch a few accentuated or familiar words from the beginning or from the end of adult's speech. A toddler may innocently respond to the words "You . . . candy . . . mouth" from the adult's complicated sentence, "You need to make very sure you don't put that whole big piece of candy into your mouth." It is better for the adult to say, "Small bite, please." To maximize the toddler's comprehension of important communication, choose key words, speak slowly and clearly, and use facial expression and body gestures to emphasize meaning.

We may be tempted to say to a toddler, "Come here. You need to have your shoelace tied. It could make you trip and fall down." Unfortunately, the toddler may take off running. If a response is needed immediately from the toddler, go to the child, bend down, take the child's hand deliberately, establish eye contact, and then pat the floor expectantly as you articulate firmly and kindly, "Sit, please." Reinforce the child's cooperativeness the instant he looks as if he will comply by smiling warmly and saying, "Thank you!" Then as he sits down and you are tying, explain, "I need to tie your shoe to keep you safe so you won't fall down." Again, smile warmly and say, "Thank you for letting me tie your shoe."

3-3g Stranger and Separation Anxiety

Toddlers show a wide range of reactions to strangers, depending on their own experiences and temperament. Some children go through a distinct phase in which they are terrified of strangers. When confronted by a stranger (or even a less familiar caregiver), many toddlers cling to their parent's or caregiver's clothing, hide their faces, and cry. Other children, especially those who have had broad exposure to many friendly adults since infancy, may show curiosity about new adults, attempt to make friends, and never give any indication of separation or stranger anxiety. Stranger anxiety is often coupled with separation anxiety. Separation anxiety can be seen at any time from infancy through preschool, but it is often pronounced in the second year of life. Children need caregivers' patient emotional support to get them through the ordeal of separation anxiety (Kronenberg, 2010).

3-3h How Can I Make Friends with a Shy Toddler?

To establish a relationship with a shy toddler, respect that child's discomfort. Rather than directly approaching with a big smile and immediately attempting to touch or talk to the child, avoid eye contact at first.

Speak quietly and pleasantly with others around the child while moving a bit closer. If the child is standing or sitting on the floor, sit nearby to be at his eye level. Glance briefly in the child's direction occasionally to see if he is showing curiosity or stress. Smile, but avoid looking directly into the child's eyes until you are confident he feels comfortable with your presence.

After allowing the toddler plenty of time to stare at you, touch the child's hand casually for a moment while glancing briefly in his direction with a smile. Eventually, he will probably indicate his willingness to make friends and allow eye contact. At this point, a diversion in the form of a game or toy may be a perfect way to cement the budding relationship. If no toys are available, sing a song, make up a rhyme, or talk about the child's clothing: "Look at those blue sneakers. You can run fast in those." This distraction will hold the child's interest but not require a great deal of sustained eye contact or active response from him.

empathy
The ability to understand or have concern for someone other than oneself, marked by identification with and understanding of another's situation, feelings, and motives.

3-3i Why Are Toddlers So Possessive?

Young toddlers may step on each other to get what they want, take toys from each other, and scramble to grab food. Sometimes 2-year-olds walk into their child care center in the morning, look suspiciously at their peers, tighten their grip on Dad's hand, and announce defiantly, "My daddy!" Toddlers' behavior does not always seem polite because they do not yet have an ability to mentally put themselves in the place of others. Toddlers do show empathy, but their way of expressing concern is fairly egocentric. For example, a toddler may try to give her pacifier or teddy bear to an adult who is sad.

In time, children develop the ability to recognize that other people have feelings and rights, and they develop the ability to imagine how others would feel if they were treated a certain way. Then it will be possible to teach them manners. Until then, set a good example and tactfully but assertively protect children's rights.

3-3j Why Do Some Toddlers Become So Attached to Security Blankets, Pacifiers, and Other Cuddlies?

Toddlers use various things to help them cope with being little and powerless in a big, fast, scary world. Some adults call toddlers' worn blankets, tattered stuffed animals, pacifiers, or whatever else they snuggle "cuddlies." Child psychologists call them objects for "cyclical self-stimulation."

▶❚❚ TeachSource Video

Pre-K Funding Cuts

Watch this Video Case and answer the questions below.

1. Are most eligible children in the United States enrolled in pre-K programs?

2. According to this video, what do children at this age need?

3. Does pre-K attendance make a long-term difference for children? What is that difference?

© 2013 Cengage Learning®

Toddlers use various "cuddlies" to help them cope with being little in a big world.

Caregivers are sometimes tempted to just call them nuisances. Whatever they are called, when they are lost, they can cause the toddler's emotional world to come crashing down. As strongly as children are attached to these comfort items, they generally begin to lose interest in them by the time they turn 3. Some preschoolers hang onto their cuddlies a while longer, but for many, their attachment at this point is more habit than emotional need.

In most primitive cultures, children stay in physical contact with their mothers' bodies much of the time during their first three years of life. In modern industrialized societies, children are separated from their mothers at birth to be placed in a hospital nursery, put to sleep in a separate crib (sometimes in a separate room), and routinely buckled into high chairs, strollers, and car seats. It is not surprising then that many babies improvise "caregiver replacements" to help them cope. Nipple-shaped objects to suck and soft, warm, fuzzy, or silky objects to touch help infants calm themselves. The child's emotional need for these objects should be respected, although the child can be nudged gently to do without them for gradually increasing periods when these objects have become little more than habit.

Toddlers and children older than 3 should be helped to cope without having a pacifier or thumb "plugged in" for too much of the day. It is difficult for toddlers to practice language with their mouths immobilized. But it is equally important to allow infants plenty of sucking to develop the mouth, lip, and tongue muscles necessary for later speech. Because bottle-feeding requires less muscular effort and coordination to produce milk than breastfeeding, many babies benefit emotionally and physically from the availability of nonnutritive sucking. Pacifiers are healthier for teeth and thumbs and usually easier to wean children from than thumbs.

The American Academy of Pediatrics recommends breastfeeding or bottlefeeding with formula for at least the first year, but adds that it is perfectly normal and healthy for children to have breast or bottle at quiet times up to age 4 or longer (American Academy of Pediatrics Association, 2005). In the absence of breast or bottle, a toddler may find a pacifier or thumb reassuring. We can take good advice from grandmothers, who have been saying for generations, "If you baby a baby when he's a baby, you won't have to baby him all the rest of his life."

social growth
Learning to understand and function appropriately in one's social environment; learning how to effectively interact with others.

emotional growth
Developing self-concept and self-esteem and learning to manage the feelings that affect behavior.

trust
Sense of security; belief that one's needs will be met.

autonomy 自主性
A person's self-reliance, independence, and self-sufficiency. One's capacity to make decisions and act on them.

shame
A negative feeling or emotion of embarrassment, unworthiness, or disgrace.

doubt
A feeling of questioning, uncertainty, and hesitation.

3-3k Why Are Toddlers Stubborn One Minute, Then Clingy the Next?

Erikson (1963) focused on the development of autonomy as the second step in his eight stages of **social growth** and **emotional growth**. After **trust** has been established in infancy, toddlers become immersed in the conflict between **autonomy** and **shame** and **doubt**. Toddlers are able for the first time to do many things that adults consider naughty or destructive. For the first time, adults begin to hold the child responsible for bodily elimination and controlling impulses. The toddler is torn between stubbornly resisting the caregiver and needing to feel loved and protected by the caregiver. He is compelled to explore everything around him with his new capabilities, but is constantly getting into scrapes, making messes, and needing adult help and reassurance.

Adults can help toddlers through this period by being very supportive of the child's need to break away from infancy. To foster autonomy, we should not do anything for the toddler that she could be helped to do for herself. Toddlers can learn to peel their own bananas for a snack, pull up their own socks once the adult gets the sock started, and wash unbreakable dishes (although someone will have to rewash them later for sanitary reasons). Toddlers can be given a small spray bottle with water and a cloth to wash low windows. They can be given small sponges for table wiping, small brooms for sweeping, and other utensils to help maintain the classroom.

Toddlers are interested in processes, not results. They are not interested in achieving specific results and are confused and discouraged by adult concern over results rather than processes. Adults usually do things the most practical way to get the result they want. Toddlers spend long periods in the process of dipping, pouring, and splashing dishes in soapy water, but lose interest before the dishes are actually rinsed and dried.

Sensitive adults will encourage the child's involvement in processes but wait until the child is older to focus on results. Adults should redirect unacceptable behavior rather than make a child feel naughty for following his curiosity and attempting to do things he sees adults doing.

Toddlers are interested in processes, not results. Their focus is on what the dough feels like and what it will do—not what it looks like when they are finished.

3-3l Are Toddlers Aware of Themselves?

When babies look in a mirror, they do not necessarily recognize that the image reflected there is their own. At some point in toddlerhood, they finally discover that the face in the mirror is theirs. If they see an unexpected smudge on the nose in the mirror, they touch their own nose to find out what is there. A younger child will touch only the mirror. According to Amsterdam (1972), self-awareness progresses as follows:

- 6–12 months: Infant in the mirror is perceived as someone else.
- 13–24 months: Babies become wary of image in the mirror.
- 20–24 months onward: Toddlers clearly recognize image as self.

3-3m Why Do Toddlers Get So Excited and Happy when They Imitate Each Other?

Toddlers who have just begun to get a sense of their autonomy tend to be very "full of themselves." If a caregiver gathers 2-year-olds around for a snack, he will often discover that they are entertained by each other. They giggle and poke each other, and inevitably one toddler will begin a gloriously spontaneous action like vigorously shaking her head until her hair stands out all around her head. In an instant, this action spreads into a **group contagion**, leaving the poor adult sitting rather foolishly, tray of snacks in hand, watching a band of toddlers laughing uproariously as they all shake their heads (and perhaps twist their bodies and stamp their feet for good measure). The teacher should breathe slowly, relax, and join in this moment of joy before focusing the children's attention back on snack.

As a toddler begins to recognize her existence as a separate person like the people she sees around her, she begins to develop a **concept** (or picture) of who she is based on feedback, primarily from the adults around her. Sometimes adults make casual comments that are very cutting, such as "You are a little fatty, piggy!" "Why are you always naughty?" "You're hopeless!" "You're an idiot!" Sometimes these hurtful comments come from siblings or other children.

Toddlers are very naive. They tend to internalize what we tell them about themselves through our actions and words. As an older toddler's self-image begins to take shape, we can help her develop a healthy and confident view of herself by being very careful about what we say to her (and what we allow other children to say to her). "How independent you are." "Everybody makes mistakes sometime." "I really like your smile." "I didn't like the hitting, but I will always like you." The toddler's budding self-esteem will serve as a foundation for her growth as a confident, competent, cooperative, and productive human being.

Given consistently nurturing and responsive care, healthy babies develop a high level of "competence" by age 3. Competent preschoolers are much more likely to be successful and well adjusted in school and throughout life (Friedman, Melhuish, & Hill, 2009).

group contagion
Typical toddler group behavior in which one child's gleeful action (for example, foot stamping, head shaking, or squealing) is quickly imitated by the whole group of toddlers.

concept
An idea, understanding, or belief formed by organizing images or mental pictures from specific occurrences and experiences.

3-4 Preschoolers (3 to 5 Years)

3-4a Can Preschoolers Make Plans and Decisions?

Babies think about objects in terms of the way those objects actually feel, look, taste, smell, and sound. Toddlers can conceive of objects both in terms of what they are perceptually and what they stand for symbolically. A baby sees a block only as something to bite, hit, throw, or stack. A toddler can see the block as a toy that is meant for stacking. As children become preschoolers, they are able to see a block as both a physical object and a pretend bar of soap to bathe a doll or a pretend car to zoom around the floor. The block can easily stand as an **abstract symbol** for something else in their imagination.

Preschoolers also become more consciously aware of their own interests and intentions. They look over the options that are available to them and make intentional choices. Although toddlers function primarily by impulse, playing with whatever toy catches their eye for the moment, preschoolers are more inclined to select an activity very carefully and then stay with it longer, sometimes even coming back to play the same game day after day until they finally become bored with it.

Older preschoolers can verbalize what and how they want to play. For example, they may say, "Let's play like this is our house and you are the daddy and he is the baby and that box is the baby bed." They can become very frustrated or angry if things do not turn out the way they expect. Preschoolers often squabble over their conflicting ideas of how their play should go: "I don't want to be the baby. I want to be a truck driver!"

Adults can help preschoolers during this stage by focusing the children's attention on the likely consequences of their actions. Questions should be asked kindly. Adults can gently nudge cause-and-effect thinking by asking, "What might happen if someone ran out into the street without looking?" "Hmmm, I wonder what could happen if you paint without putting a smock on over your clothes?" "How would your friend feel if she never got a turn to be the pretend mommy?" Preschoolers are just beginning to manipulate ideas in their heads. They can learn to weigh consequences and make appropriate decisions before acting.

abstract symbol

An abstract symbol is a person, place, or thing that comes to represent another idea or concept; in general, anything that stands for something else. Dramatic play can help preschoolers express emotional feelings. We cannot take for granted that just because something seems obvious to us it will be obvious to preschoolers. There are a lot of things they don't know yet.

3-4b Talking to Preschoolers about Sensitive Issues

Because preschoolers have an increasing command of language, they benefit from talking about events that have taken place or will take place. Before and after events, they should be invited to talk about that event by parents and teachers. Day-to-day discussions can take place in very simple, concrete terms.

Caregivers sometimes mistakenly try to shield preschoolers from troublesome issues by not talking to children. Children are alert and sensitive to cues around them. They often know a great deal more than adults give them credit for. Children need adult help to understand their world accurately.

A 3-year-old, whose parents often affectionately called her "our sweet baby girl," cried hysterically when an aunt said, "I hear there's going to be a new baby at your house." She had overheard her parents saying that they thought it best for her not to know yet that there was going to be a new baby. She knew, of course, that when they got a new car, the old car vanished, and when she got new shoes, the old ones were dropped unceremoniously into the trash

Dramatic play can help preschoolers express emotional feelings.

can. She could only guess what happened to little girls who she imagined were so naughty that their parents decided to get "a new one."

A 4-year-old boy developed nightmares and bed-wetting after he heard family members crying and talking in somber but hushed tones about how his expectant mother had lost the baby she was carrying. His problem behaviors increased until a psychologist was consulted and discovered that the little boy had been nervously searching in closets and under beds to find the lost baby. He knew that those were places to look when you lost something. He worried that his parents might lose him too!

Adults should give appropriate information at the child's level in a simple, honest, direct manner. Many helpful children's books are available on painful topics such as death, divorce, war, and so forth—topics that too often touch children's lives.

3-4c Communicating Successfully with Preschoolers

By talking to preschoolers in simple, honest terms, we can help them understand and deal with events. We cannot take for granted that just because something is obvious to us it will be obvious to preschoolers. There are many things about this world that preschoolers do not know yet. A caregiver can use simple clear sentences to say, "Marcus, your dad just called on the telephone. He will be late picking you up today. His car won't go so he has to get it fixed. It may be dark when he gets here, but it's okay. I will stay with you. We'll get some cheese and crackers and apple juice and play until he comes." Sometimes adults become so preoccupied with their own issues that they forget to tell children what will happen, causing the child anxiety and/or misbehavior.

Imitating through dramatic play can help children visualize an expected event. Talking through a puppet is a nonthreatening way to get a point across or model appropriate language and behavior. Helping a preschooler laugh at a puppet may dispel anxiety about such things as a parent being late, monsters living under the bed, or lightning that sounds really scary. Taking his aggressions out on the "pretend monster" puppet may help the preschooler feel less helpless and vulnerable. (On another better day we will teach the child the importance of handling classroom toys gently.)

We can frequently prevent problems by anticipating and planning for them, being especially careful not to communicate negative expectations.

> *Aiesha, your friend Tracy will be here soon. Sometimes when she is here it is hard for you to let her touch your toys. That makes Tracy feel sad.*
>
> *Please choose the toys you want to use when you both play together. We'll put the toys you choose in this cardboard box and take them into the backyard. Tracy can play with all the toys in the box. Right?*

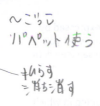

By helping the child positively think through this potential problem before it happens, the child may be able to consciously behave in such a way as to avoid the conflict before it erupts. When a child is angry and upset, it is usually too late to listen to logic.

3-4d Teaching Preschoolers to Use Words to Express Their Feelings

Preschoolers can be guided firmly to use words to get a point across rather than relying on kicking, scratching, and hair pulling. They can be helped to practice appropriate words and allowed to express strong emotions, even anger, through their words. When a preschooler runs to tell parents or teachers about another child's action, instead of being chided for tattling, the child can be encouraged to talk to the other child: "Did you tell Kirin that it was your turn for the swing? Would you like me to go with you to talk to her?"

Adults sometimes try to squelch children's negative feelings. We say things to quiet children such as "Don't cry," "Don't make a fuss," "She didn't really mean to hit you." Maybe the other child really did mean to hit. A child deserves to express her feelings in an honest but respectful way: "I feel angry. I don't like it when you push me off the swing." Preschoolers especially need to be allowed to express their feelings. They can learn that it is okay to feel angry and it is okay to say so, but it is not okay to lash out with words or body in a way that hurts others.

In active listening, the adult reflects what she perceives the child is feeling. "You seem to be feeling a little frustrated with your puzzle. Can you tell me about it?"

Preschoolers can also be helped to verbalize their feelings by having adults **mirror** those feelings. Young children may not realize that they are cranky because they are hot and tired or cold and hungry. Adults can put words to those feelings and assist preschoolers in learning to identify and express what they feel inside by saying, "Brrr, I feel cold! Look at the chill bumps on my arm. Are you cold? Let me feel how cold your hands are."

This mirroring of feelings is called **active listening.** The adult refrains from lecturing, instructing, commanding, or telling (see Chapter 8 for more on active listening). Instead, she listens and sincerely reflects, or restates, what she thinks the child is feeling at the moment. In active listening (a useful communication tool for any age), the adult says things such as "It sounds as if you are really feeling angry with Sofronio," "In other words, what you are saying is that you feel hurt and sad when you don't get to play," "You seem pretty frightened when the other children pretend to be monsters." The point of active listening is not to solve the child's problem for her but only to let her know that she has been heard and to give her a chance to talk about, think about, and confront her own feelings.

mirror

Reflecting the feelings expressed by someone else—repeating what you understood someone to say (see *active listening*).

active listening

A form of attentive listening in which one concentrates on what is being said, then reflects the ideas back to the speaker to show an understanding of what the speaker is feeling and saying.

3-4e Friendships Are Important to Preschoolers

Babies and toddlers are very curious about other children but are most concerned about the adults in their lives. Preschoolers, in contrast, begin to be interested in their relationships with other children. Throughout the rest of childhood, they will rely more and more on their friendships with peers and gradually less and less on their attachment to adults. Between 3 and 5 years of age, children need to learn how to be a friend and how to have friends, a very important kind of learning for the child's long-term social and emotional adjustment in life (Corsaro, 1981; McClellan & Katz, 2001; McElwain et al., 2008).

This can be a very trying stage for adults. Children are elated when they feel liked by peers and emotionally crushed when they imagine that no other child in the whole world wants to play with them. Although some children quickly find a best friend or group of friends with whom they get along very well, other children experience a daily emotional roller coaster as they struggle to establish friendships and deal with peers who barter, as in "I'll be your best friend if you give me your piece of chocolate cake."

Some preschoolers become very cliquish as they decide who is or is not a friend. They say things such as "You can't be our friend because you aren't wearing bows in your hair like us," "You can't play because you're a girl," "You draw scribble-scrabble so you can't color with us." Adults can feel frustrated trying to decide when or how to intervene in these troublesome and hurtful interactions. Children need guidance so they will treat others the way they want to be treated. Meanness should not be tolerated. See Positive Focus 3.4.

3-4f How Do Preschoolers Learn to Accept Responsibility?

Erikson (1963) focused on the need of 4- and 5-year-olds to resolve the emotional conflict of initiative versus guilt. Preschoolers are struggling to become independent of adult caregivers and to find their own limits. Still, they want to please adults, and they feel guilty when they disappoint or anger parents and teachers. An excessive amount of guilt causes discomfort. Some children relieve anxiety by withdrawing from any situations that involve risk of failure, others by pretending to be tough little rebels.

"I'm Never Gonna 'Vite You to My Birth'ay!"

Sarah and Lupita, both 5-year-olds, have claimed a shady spot under a thick magnolia tree on the playground. It is their favorite place to play. They have staunchly defended their little territory against small bands of marauding playmates by insisting, "You can't play. We got here first. This is our house."

Although their teacher does not allow toys from home in the classroom, the students have been allowed to bring their dolls outside with them for their outdoor play period. Sarah has a well-worn Raggedy Ann doll and Lupita has a new, soft plastic baby doll that is wrapped in a pink blanket and looks just like a newborn baby.

They rock their dolls to sleep and carefully place them beside the trunk of the tree, and then they scurry around gathering leaves and sticks to outline a boundary for their playhouse. Sarah finds a large stick and announces that it is the door: "Nobody can come in unless they open this door. Tick tock. Now it's all locked up."

Robby, also 5, has been watching and listening to the girls as he climbs and jumps off a climbing structure "fort" nearby. He cannot resist Sarah's challenge. "I can too get in," he taunts as he dances around the line of leaves and sticks that is the pretend wall of the girls' playhouse. He pokes his foot over the line and darts just out of their reach as he sticks his tongue out, laughing and chanting, "Nanny, nanny, boo, boo!"

Sarah chases and yells at Robby, while Lupita furiously mends the pretend wall. Robby retreats to the top of the climbing structure insisting, "Uh-huh! I could get in there. It's not really your house."

Lupita plants her feet firmly in the grass and stares viciously at Robby, guarding hearth and home, while Sarah runs to tell on Robby.

Robby, of course, loses all interest in Lupita's mean look. He is perched behind a post at the top of the fort watching carefully to see what his teacher, Miss Gresham, will do next.

Miss Gresham bends down on one knee and listens intently as Sarah rants and raves about Robby's alleged offenses. Quietly, Miss Gresham says, "Did you tell Robby how you felt when he messed up your house? Would you like for me to come with you to talk to Robby?" Sarah takes Miss Gresham's hand and quickly leads the way back to the scene of the crime. Robby, meanwhile, is huddled on the fort hoping no one can see him. He forgets that Miss Gresham is tall enough to talk eye-to-eye with him at the highest part of the fort.

With a gentle and reassuring voice, Miss Gresham says, "Robby, let's talk with Lupita and Sarah. I think they're feeling very angry." Robby pauses for just a second, but Miss

Gresham holds her hands out and says, "It's okay, Robby. Sometimes I make mistakes and people get mad at me, too." Robby leans off the fort and Miss Gresham lowers him to the ground. She looks right in his eyes and pats him as she says, "Thanks, Robby." Then she assumes the role of objective referee as the girls tell Robby, in no uncertain terms, "Don't you break our house no more!"

Robby's lip quivers and a big tear begins to slide down his grimy face as he pulls back his shoulders and announces, "You ain't my best friend and I ain't never gonna 'vite you to my birth'ay party!"

Case Discussion Questions

1. Identify characteristics and behaviors of Lupita, Sarah, and Robby that are typical of 5-year-olds.
2. List all the reasons you can think of for Robby's interference with the girls' play. Why were the girls so angry?
3. Do you agree with Miss Gresham's handling of the problem? Explain. What would you have done differently?
4. What might have happened if Miss Gresham had responded to Robby with an angry voice and negative punishment?

© Cengage Learning 2013

Robby pauses for just a second, but Miss Gresham holds her hands out and says, "It's okay, Robby. Sometimes I make mistakes and people get mad at me, too."

Positive Focus 3.4   Avoiding Stress and Burnout

Perfectionism can be a stress trap for educators and parents. Children have bad days. Adults have bad days. In an environment that is basically nurturing and respectful, children learn to deal with occasional shortcomings in their teachers and parents. Adults must learn to cope with their own lapses in meeting the standards they have set for themselves. They must not shrug their shoulders and give up but admit and accept that they blew it and consciously take steps to do better tomorrow. It is helpful to say to the child, "I made a mistake. It's not okay to shout angry things at others. I was wrong. I'm going to try to remember to talk calmly about problems so we can solve them the right way."

The *need to be in control* can be a stress trap. Teaching is an interactive process. In the learning-centered environment, there should be give and take. Sensitive, responsive adults are willing to put aside planned activities when they observe that children are simply not interested. Nurturing adults offer choices within reasonable limits, allowing children their preferences. It is not a sign of failure or weakness for us to admit that we were wrong and the child was right in a given situation. Children who listen, question, and speak up for themselves are better suited to thrive in today's world than blindly obedient children who would never question authority.

People-pleasing is another potential stress trap. Codependent people depend too much on other people's opinion of them. They have an impaired sense of their own worth and spend their lives trying to please others. Remember, we can't please everybody all the time. We should work on defining and trusting our own philosophy and values. We should try hard to use "I" messages (sentences starting with "I feel . . .") to express our feelings to others. We should remember to take good care of ourselves. We can't really nurture children if we allow ourselves to become exhausted trying to please others. We must take proactive steps to avoid physical, mental, and emotional exhaustion. (See Chapter 8 for more about "I" messages.)

Self-doubt clouds judgment and increases stress. We can avoid comparing ourselves with others. Set our own standards and work every day to achieve them. Be a lifelong learner. Open our minds and take advantage of books and other resources to expand our skills and confidence. Learn to trust our judgment. If we make mistakes, learn from them and move on. We can take reasonable risks. When others compliment our accomplishments, we can say thank you rather than being overly shy. It's okay to feel proud. It's most important that we feel good ourselves, not that others notice or approve.

 To develop initiative and avoid guilt, children must be encouraged to achieve independence from adults. Instead of doing things for preschoolers, adults should make it possible for the children to do things for themselves. Adults can simplify tasks and then slowly model simple skills for the child, such as how to turn the faucet on and off for hand washing, how to refill the gerbil's water bottle, how to clip paper to an easel with clothespins, and how to get a jacket zipper started.

3-4g How Can I Support Independence in Preschoolers?

Preschoolers relish the opportunity to be in charge of their own environment. They make many mistakes and often forget to carry out tasks they have agreed to do. Adults can respond best by remembering that the process of learning is much more important than the results of their efforts. Some adults become perfectionists about tasks and say, "It's easier for me to do it myself than to hassle with the kids trying to do it." It may be easier, but it definitely is not better for children. Children need the chance to do for themselves.

With a great deal of practice, encouragement, and patient teaching (one tiny step at a time), preschoolers can learn to carry out many tasks responsibly and well. They will feel so proud of their accomplishments that they will eagerly show initiative in tackling new tasks without having to be prodded every step of the way, as will a child who has fallen prey to feelings of guilt.

3-4h How Can I Help Preschoolers Follow Rules?

Preschoolers can understand simple guidelines: "Be safe! Stop at the gate so a grownup can walk with you across the street." "Be kind! Wait until Carlos is finished with the swing." "Be responsible! Use a sponge to wipe up the tempera paint that has dripped." Preschoolers are **preoperational** (in Piaget's terms), so they perceive rules in a superficial way. They usually follow rules to please adults, not because they fully appreciate the long-term relationship between actions and possible consequences.

Preschoolers still must be supervised closely because they are not always able to follow rules consistently. They continue to need lots of tactful reminders of classroom rules. In their play, they make up rules on a whim and then happily break the rules they have made when it suits them.

If you play a board game with a preschooler such as Candy Land or Chutes and Ladders, you will find that rules clearly don't mean the same thing to a preschooler as they do to a school-aged child or an adult. The child's level of development makes him see the world in a more egocentric way. He shows much more self-restraint than he did as a toddler, but his capacity for self-discipline will continue to grow by leaps and bounds.

Preschoolers begin to make sense intuitively of adult expectations and anticipate what will or will not be allowed in various situations. They tell each other, "Oh! You're gonna' get in trouble." They begin to enforce rules on each other: "You didn't flush. I'm gonna' tell on you." Adults can redirect this overemphasis on enforcement by setting a good example in their own respectful assistance in helping children follow rules.

If adults are punitive and critical and seem eager to *catch* wrongdoers, children will imitate that. If adults request compliance in an assertive and caring tone and then follow through to assure that the child has everything he needs to comply successfully, then other children will imitate that same gentle assertiveness.

Adults can maintain children's interest in rules by sticking with the basic simple ground rules and making sure that children know and follow them. Overwhelming preschoolers with picky rules will alienate and trivialize the whole idea of following rules. Rules mean more to children if they play an active role in deciding on consequences that should follow when the rules are broken.

preoperational
The second stage of cognitive development in Jean Piaget's theory that begins with the achievement of object permanence. This stage is typified by imaginative play, egocentricity, the inability to take another person's point of view, and the belief that the number or amount is changed when objects are rearranged.

Brain Facts

What Can We Learn from Neuroscience?

Play develops children's brain function enabling self-discipline:

- Self-regulation—the ability to control behavior and inhibit impulses—is essential for school success (Bronson, 2000; Ponitz et al., 2008; Rimm-Kaufman & Pianta, 2000).

- Research tells us that positive social relationships not only stimulate learning, they actually affect the physical structure of the brain (Shore, 1997).

- Children develop self-regulation in adult-supported, rather than adult-directed, play activities (Berk, Mann, & Ogan, 2006).

- Children may be hesitant to play if nothing in a classroom resembles their home environment (Heisner, 2005).

Children's awareness of the value of rules increases when they are involved in the guidance process.

- Here are our ground rules: Be safe, be respectful, be responsible.
- Let's make a list of ways we can be safe, respectful, and responsible.
- We'll draw a picture chart of our rules and put it on the wall for everyone to see.

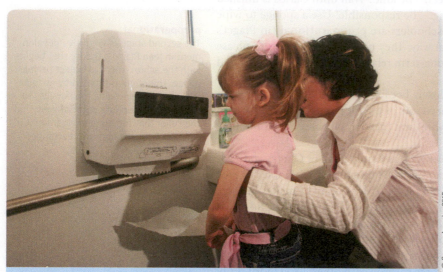

© Cengage Learning 2013

Teachers request compliance in an assertive and caring tone and then follow through to assure the child has everything she needs to comply successfully.

At group time, or in a family meeting at home, children can be invited to help solve simple problems that have occurred, such as pushing and shoving or taking other people's things without asking. Adults can help children by patiently talking about the reasons for rules rather than just saying, "It's a rule because I say so." Understanding why a person should be safe, respectful, and responsible helps children develop moral values (see the section on moral development in Chapter 9).

Stating rules such as "Be safe; the fence is not for climbing" and then proceeding to ignore children who climb on the fence will convince children that grown-ups do not really mean the things they say. Following rules is not only to be safe, respectful, and responsible today, but is also to develop habits that will help the child obey laws as an adolescent and as an adult.

3-4i How Do Preschoolers Develop a Positive Sense of Self?

self-concept
Perception of oneself in terms of personal worth, life and school successes, and perceived social status.

self-esteem
Seeing oneself as a worthwhile individual.

DIVERSITY

DAP

Although the child's self-esteem (or lack of it) has been developing unconsciously since birth, preschool-age children begin to develop a clear, conscious idea of who they are. Self-esteem and self-concept are two closely related concepts. **Self-concept** is one's idea or image of oneself. **Self-esteem** means that one's image of oneself includes a sense of being worthwhile and valuable. Children's ideas about themselves come from others around them, particularly from caregivers. As preschoolers become more adept at language, they also become more susceptible to the opinions of teachers, peers, and others outside the home (Cotton, 1983; Hill & Buss, 2006; Mruk, 2006).

Preschoolers become increasingly aware of their own identity in terms of larger groupings within society. The child may, for the first time, become aware of her ethnicity. Self-esteem can grow from pride in one's ethnic, regional, and religious heritage. Sadly, exposure to prejudice devastates self-esteem and continues the cycle of prejudice and low self-esteem. Low self-esteem causes a child not only to disrespect himself but others also (Derman-Sparks & Ramsey, 2005; Kivel, 2002; Musher-Eizenman et al., 2004; Ramsey & Williams, 2003; Van Ausdale & Feagin, 2001). Every child deserves to learn that he is a respected and valued member of his family and community (see more on teaching tolerance in Chapter 5).

Three-year-olds become aware, for the first time, that their gender is fixed for life; girls will grow to be women and boys will grow to be men. Toddlers may distinguish between girls and boys or mommies and daddies, but they think they can change genders simply by wearing different clothing. Most preschoolers identify strongly with their own gender now and may begin playing only with what they believe to be "boy toys" or "girl toys." No matter how hard politically correct parents have tried to keep their little ones playing with gender-neutral toys, preschoolers have their own minds at this point.

Other parents worry that their physically active daughters may prefer playing rowdy games with the boys or that their sons prefer playing dolls with the girls. Preschool teachers often worry because they want all the children to have well-rounded classroom experiences. Everyone worries, but children generally persist in play that meets their own desires and interests. Their play represents a world they imagine. It isn't ours to force on them. But if preschool-aged boys see daddy having a good time feeding the baby and cooking, they may play house more comfortably than if they have seen only women doing these things. The same may be true for little girls who have watched their mothers play an active role in the community outside the home.

© Cengage Learning 2013

3-4j Should Children Be Encouraged to Compete?

Another factor that affects preschoolers' development of self-concept and self-esteem is competitiveness. Preschoolers have become aware of themselves in comparison to others, so competitiveness first rears its head during the preschool years (Farver, Kim, & Lee, 1995). It can be very tempting for adults to exploit that tendency by saying things such as "Whoever can be the quietest at nap time will get a special treat," "The one who puts away toys the fastest will get to be first in line to go outside," "See if you can get dressed faster than your brother."

These challenges may motivate some children to behave as the adult wishes, but the competition also stimulates friction rather than cooperation among children. Additionally, whenever there are winners there will be losers. Winners may feel stressed and compulsive about continuing to win, and losers may begin to feel inadequate (Watson et al., 2003).

A more appropriate strategy to motivate desired behavior is to encourage children to work together as teams to accomplish tasks. Ideally, a classroom is a **community of learners** who share ideas, talk about and solve problems together, help each other, and cooperate as a team to clean up the classroom so that everyone can have more time for the next activity. In a true community of learners, children see themselves as valued members of an inclusive team.

At the preschool level, competition should only be the child's individual challenges for herself—"I'm going to finish this whole puzzle all by myself"— never to defeat or "beat" peers. Adolescents and adults are better equipped emotionally than young children to understand that in a community of athletes, competitors can compete aggressively, and then winners and losers should shake hands in respect of one another.

These preschoolers are part of a community of learners. They see themselves as valued members of an inclusive group, not as competitors.

There is nothing noble about being superior to some other man. The true nobility is in being superior to your previous self.

—*Hindu Proverb*

3-5 Early School-Agers (5 to 8 Years)

Five- through eight-year-old children are very different from younger children, not only because of their gap-toothed smiles and taller bodies, but also because their thinking and language skills are different.

3-5a Why Do Early School-Agers Ask So Many Questions?

As school-agers become more aware of the world around them, they want to know a simple answer to every puzzling incident. Preschoolers still test things that puzzle them, such as "Do rocks always sink in water?" "What's inside my toy car?" "How high will a swing go?" They ask questions: "What's this?" "What's that?" Early school-agers often ask questions that are really hard to answer, such as "Why can't I have pizza for breakfast?" "What if gravity stopped and everything flew off the earth?" "Why do things look small when they're far away?" "Why did Grandma die?" "What makes the car go?"

community of learners
A group of individuals who share similar educational principles, who work toward common goals, whose activities are linked, and whose collaborative efforts create a synchronized energy in which the power of the group is more profound than that of any one individual. For children, a group that nurtures a sense of belonging among the children and adults in a program in which children learn that all contribute to each other's learning.

▶❚ TeachSource Video

5–11 Years: Lev Vygotsky, the Zone of Proximal Development, and Scaffolding

Watch this Video Case on Lev Vygotsky, and then answer the following questions:

1. What is the zone of proximal development? Give an example.

2. What is scaffolding? Give an example.

be inclined to

collaborative
Cooperative interaction of two or more people who are trying achieve a common goal. Although school-agers may be inclined to compete against each other to be first or best, we can find ways to encourage them to work together as collaborative team members.

Early school-age children are less gullible than preschoolers. They are quick to see discrepancies in adult actions: "You said that nobody could eat or drink unless they sat down at the table. You're somebody and you're drinking coffee." Preschoolers believe just about anything you tell them, but early school-agers question things more analytically. For example, if you say, "You can't eat candy because it is not good for your teeth," a preschooler might protest and beg, but a school-ager will think about that explanation logically and answer with her own rationale, "Okay, then I'll brush my teeth after I eat the candy."

After the early school-ager has asked a persistent series of logical why or why-not questions, parents and teachers often find themselves snapping with exasperation, "Because I said so!" Of course, this is the phrase we hated to hear as children and promised we would never say when we grew up.

3-5b Why Do They Get So Angry if They Don't Win?

Early school-agers make observations and judgments about everything around them. Because of their immaturity, however, their judgment is limited to a simplistic, good-or-bad, win-or-lose view of the world. Naturally, they begin to compare themselves to others. In many settings, competition flares as children struggle to best each other. They constantly fight over who likes whom best. Adults sometimes throw fuel onto this fire by encouraging competition. For example, teachers say, "I will put gold stars on the very best papers and put those papers on the bulletin board for parents' night." This tactic is tempting because early school-agers will practically trample each other to be first or best at anything. However, we should find ways instead to help them learn to cooperate. Learning to be a **collaborative** team member is an important prosocial skill (Watson et al., 2003).

3-5c Why Do They Call Each Other Names and Say Hurtful Things?

Early school-agers have gained skill in expressing themselves with words. They express their anger, frustration, or jealousy loudly. Preschoolers often shove or hit someone who upsets them or bluster, "You're a pooh-pooh head an' I hate you." School-agers are more precise in their words: "Why do you act so bossy? You're not my mother."

In today's environment of casual parent values and the pervasive influence of television and the Internet, young school-agers are using inappropriate language that was unheard of among children a generation ago. A teacher recently told me of shocking language that a beautiful little 5-year-old had used at school. The teacher related this language concern to the parent, who laughed and replied, "Oh, she gets that from me. I say that all the time."

Angry words hurled at early school-agers can wound them deeply, so it is important to help children think about the effects their words have on others. Effectively expressing negative feelings in

Although school-agers may be inclined to compete against each other to be first or best, we can find ways to encourage them to work together as collaborative team members.

The Big Boys and the Very Muddy Day

Mrs. Belk taught first graders in a neighborhood public school for several years. She decided to upgrade her skills by taking a graduate course in psychology at a nearby university. She had only been enrolled in the class for a few weeks, but the professor had already lectured on operant conditioning. What a great idea, she thought: ignore the negative and reinforce the positive.

Mrs. Belk was eager to try some new guidance techniques with several of her more challenging children, especially Chad, a 6-year-old who tended to be her group's ringleader for inappropriate behavior. He seemed to be in a constant state of motion although, he took a medication for hyperactivity.

The past week of school had been particularly stressful for Mrs. Belk. Chad had been even more out of control than usual. It had rained so much that the children had not gotten to play outside. The sun had come out but there were still large mud puddles. When the room was clean, Mrs. Belk asked, "How would you like to go outside?"

To the children's gleeful shouts of, "Yes!" Mrs. Belk answered, "We can go outside on one condition. Everyone has to agree to stay in the dry areas." The children eagerly agreed. As Mrs. Belk walked out into the bright sunlight, she took a deep breath of fresh air and felt a great sense of relief to be outside the stuffy classroom. In seconds, she saw Chad running backward to catch a ball, and splat, he stepped right into the mud. Mrs. Belk stood with her hands on her hips, glaring at Chad and thinking about whether to have him sit on the bench for 10 minutes for breaking the rule she had just made.

She knew that it was a real effort to keep Chad sitting for 10 minutes. Mrs. Belk dreaded a confrontation and decided she did not have the energy to deal with Chad at the moment. She started thinking about what her professor had said about it being helpful to ignore inappropriate behavior—and besides, she thought, maybe his stepping in the mud was really an accident—so she looked the other way and decided to ignore Chad. Within seconds, eager children pulled at her shirtsleeves saying, "Mrs. Belk, Mrs. Belk, look, Chad is in the mud!" Mrs. Belk told them, "Go play and don't pay any attention to Chad."

Within minutes, two of Chad's favorite cohorts, Eddie and Jayden, shrieked as Chad stamped his foot in the mud,

splattering mud on them. They, of course (after they nervously looked back to make sure Mrs. Belk was still ignoring Chad), stamped their feet in the mud, splattering Chad from head to toe. The chase was on with half the class frantically telling Mrs. Belk, "Look, look, look!" and the other half squealing and laughing as the three boys chased and slid in the mud.

Mrs. Belk realized that her "ignoring" strategy was not working. With a look of daggers in her eyes she shouted, "Okay, everybody line up at the door to go inside." All of the children (except Chad, Eddie, and Jayden) hurried to the door and made a straight line. In an angry voice, Mrs. Belk stared straight at the three boys and said, "I'm waiting. Not everyone is ready to go inside." She thought, "There is no way I am going to chase those three around in this mud."

The muddy boys tried hard to look tough, as if they weren't afraid of anything. By this time, however, their shoes and clothes were caked with mud and they were beginning to feel very uncomfortable, anxious, and out of control.

The playground was a mess and the boys were a mess. The situation was no longer salvageable. The principal called their horrified parents to come and get them. There was no easy way for the boys to make amends for their behavior or to save face in front of their friends, parents, and teachers. They had taken part in open rebellion, a serious and scary step for a child and a damaging precedent for future behavior.

Case Discussion Questions

1. What is the difference between ignoring a behavior and ignoring a child?
2. What could Mrs. Belk have done that might have prevented, redirected, or stopped the inappropriate behavior?
3. What do you think the muddy boys were thinking and feeling throughout this episode?
4. What do you think the rest of the children were thinking and feeling?
5. What role do adults play in helping children regulate their behavior? When is children's behavior our responsibility? When is their behavior their responsibility?

---

appropriate words is an important part of learning social skills. Hurtful or demeaning taunts, foul language, and epithets must never be allowed in early childhood programs. In a nonjudgmental way we can teach children that there are some things that may be okay in other settings that are not okay for school. We must never judge the child's parents—even though we may worry about the parents' judgment.

inner self-control
自制心

DAP

無関心

3-5d How Can I Earn the Respect of School-Agers?

Early school-agers can be intimidating to adults. Young children who misbehave can be picked up and carried (kicking and screaming) away from a problem situation. School-agers are too large. They can no longer be controlled by physical restraint. We must be able to rely on the child's inner control.

Parents who used spanking to control young children discover that school-age children may be so emotionally immune to being hit that by this age they respond only with apathy. Or they may be so angered by being treated like a "baby" that an attempt to spank them could trigger outright defiance. Teachers and caregivers will encounter an occasional school-age child who has been subjected to a great deal of rough treatment in her life and has become aggressive, toughened, cynical, and very difficult to manage.

Our best hope for breaking through this tough outer shell is assertive rule enforcement tempered with unconditional affection and open, respectful communication. The surest way out of this emotional trap is for the adult to break the cycle by finding some way to prove to each child that she is liked and respected by the adult. Then, and only then, can the adult begin to gain the children's respect and loyalty. Inner control depends completely on the child wanting to be a cooperative group member. If school-age children see the adult as someone who is absolutely fair, has a sense of humor, is reasonable, and really cares about the needs and feelings of the children, they will be more willing to comply with that adult's wishes.

3-5e Why Do Early School-Agers Resist Going to Child Care?

Child care workers can especially be intimidated by school-age children who have not yet developed inner control. Often, the youngest and least experienced workers are assigned to care for school-age children because they attend the facility only during the early morning and late afternoon hours, summers, and holidays. After school, these children can be exhausted from long hours of sitting on hard desk chairs and feeling pressured to meet adult expectations. During summers and holidays, they may envy friends who are at home or away on vacation.

They may come into the child care setting with resentment for having to be in a "child care for babies." They may especially feel frustration over being expected to play quietly with blocks and puzzles they have outgrown in a room filled with all the trappings of a preschool.

In a typical scenario, school-age children begin to behave wildly. Perhaps they start to throw sand at each other on the playground or stir their graham crackers into their milk, giggling and making a disgusting mush. Inexperienced caregivers may respond in an abrasive and humorless attempt to stop this silly behavior. The children, feeling their oats, become sassy or perhaps stop the behaviors just long enough for the adult to turn her back for a moment. The angrier the adult becomes, the less compliant and cooperative the children will be. This situation can cause the adult to feel frighteningly out of control or helpless, a phenomenon that has an effect on older children that is similar to sharks smelling blood. Effective adults are able to model inner control, even in difficult situations.

Early school-age children will feel more cooperative with teachers who build a relationship with them. Class meetings provide an opportunity for school-age children to think about issues and to give their own opinions. If class meetings are run democratically, with real input from the children, then the children can begin to see rules not as inconveniences capriciously imposed by adults but as necessary protection for the rights and safety of all group members. Of course, it is critical that after-school programs are well planned, with

▶❚❚ TeachSource Video

CBS THE MORNING | EYE ON EDUCATION | "TEACHER OF THE YEAR" ON SECRETS TO HER SUCCESS

© 2013 Cengage Learning®

Making a Great Teacher

Watch this Video Case on great teaching, and then answer the following questions:

1. Name five qualities this teacher believes are important for great teaching.
2. Make a list of other qualities you think might also be important.
3. Why does this teacher create learning activities that match the specific interests of her students?

opportunities for homework, sports, arts, music, dance, and interesting special projects. Bored children are not likely to exhibit self-control and self-discipline, no matter how caring the teachers are.

3-5f Why Do Early School-Agers Get So Upset about Fairness?

Early school-age children are able to see flaws in adult behaviors. "But that's not fair" seems to be the rallying call of early school-age children. Even though they still occasionally break rules themselves, they may become furious when it seems to them that a rule is being enforced inconsistently: "But you didn't make Jerrod go back inside when he threw his book."

At this age, children's concrete operational perspective keeps them from considering extenuating circumstances that are important to adult decision makers. The school-age child may not see it as fair when a child who is new to a school breaks the rules and is simply given an explanation, whereas a child who is expected to know the rules has to deal with a consequence for the same offense. Adults must constantly examine their own biases to determine whether there is any possibility that their treatment of the children is unequal.

Adults should be meticulous about not only their fairness but also their appearance of fairness. If a situation seems unfair to a child, the adult may assist the child's understanding by giving a concrete explanation for the action taken: "When you were younger, you needed many chances to remember rules. Now that you're 7, you know that throwing books is not allowed. Jerrod is only 5 now, but when he is 7 he will have to stop playing, too, if he forgets the rule."

3-5g Why Do They Insist on Picking Their Own Clothes?

The early school years are an important period for children to develop their own identity. They develop a sense of personal identity by observing how others perceive them. They are especially sensitive to criticism or teasing about their appearance or clothing. Early school-agers also begin to worry about their status with other children. They assert their autonomy with parents by insisting on dressing like peers or role models.

Because physical development hinges on the active physical involvement of children in their environment by climbing, jumping, painting, gluing, and so on, parents and teachers can encourage (or require) clothing that is comfortable, washable, and not physically restrictive. It is impossible to be ladylike in a frilly, short dress while climbing a jungle gym, and it is dangerous to climb the jungle gym in heavy, slick-soled cowboy boots. Whatever steps adults take, it is essential to remember how desperately children want to belong, to fit in, and to be viewed as special by their friends.

3-5h How Can We Help Early School-Agers Develop Initiative?

Erikson (1963) identified the emotional crisis for school-age children as one of **industry** versus **inferiority**. One of the enjoyable characteristics of school-age children is their ability to function so much more independently. Young children need direction and help to do new things. School-age children have the capacity to think of their own projects, to gather the needed materials, and then to work independently. They make miscalculations, messes, and mistakes, but they take great delight in having initiated, planned, and built their own crooked airplane, planned their own science project, or created their own art object. Unfortunately, if they receive criticism instead of encouragement for their efforts and accomplishments, they may develop feelings of inferiority ("I'm no good," "Everything I try fails," "My ideas are stupid") and may be discouraged from trying new things.

industry
One's motivation to work constructively, to be diligent and productive.

inferiority
The feeling of being incapable, having a pervasive sense of inadequacy and experiencing a tendency toward self-diminishment.

School-age children have the capacity to think of their own projects, gather needed materials, and work independently.

© Cengage Learning 2013

Adults should not compare children's work according to adult standards. One child's cookies may turn out tough and strangely shaped, but who cares? The purpose of the activity is for children to experience and learn from the process.

3-5i How Can We Support the Early School-Age Child's Self-Esteem?

The big, wide world begins to have tremendous influence on the school-age child. Once she can read, whole new avenues of information are opened. She may see toothpaste ads on television and worry that her teeth are not white enough or see billboards about fire safety and worry that she will burn up in her bed at night. It is not unusual for school-age children to experience nightmares or develop irrational fears: "I'm not going to eat that chicken noodle soup because it has mushrooms, and they might be the poison kind that'll make you die."

We support early school-age children's self-esteem by listening respectfully to their concerns and helping them use their new reading and thinking skills to research topics that concern them. Instead of disputing their misperceptions of the world, we can help them discover on their own the facts of the situation. Instead of making them feel stupid, we empower them to learn about the world on their own. In the process, they discover that they are capable human beings.

> Low self-esteem is like driving through life with your hand-break on.
> —Maxwell Maltz

3-6 Older School-Agers (9 to 12 Years)

concrete operational
In Jean Piaget's theory the third stage of cognitive development, which begins with the ability to analyze thoughts concerning a concrete idea (as opposed to an abstract idea).

3-6a Why Do Older School-Age Children Argue So Much?

As early school-agers become **concrete operational** (at about 7 years of age), they spend more time thinking about the things and events in their world. By 8 or 9 years of age, school-agers are usually able to manipulate thoughts about entire concrete processes. This enables them to mentally evaluate a topic carefully and logically. They detect inconsistencies and gaps in logic. For example, an 11-year-old is likely to say, "Why do I have to wear my bicycle helmet? People have accidents riding in cars, and they don't wear helmets. Besides, if a car ran over my stomach, I'd be squashed anyway and a helmet wouldn't help."

Most children will be adolescents or young adults before they can effectively manipulate abstract ideas and symbols, so they are not yet able to comprehend complex political, moral, or mathematical problems. Although 11- and 12-year-olds may look grown up physically, they still need adult guidance.

Older school-age children love to talk and listen to each other. Young children are more inclined to play together in a physically active way, using language as a supplement to running, jumping, climbing, and playing make-believe games. Older school-age children still enjoy active play but will sit under a tree or get on the telephone and talk for long periods about themselves, school events, and authority figures.

Older school-agers have discovered there really is no Santa Claus and realize grown-ups are not gods but simply human beings who make mistakes. When talking privately with a trusted friend or group of age-mates, school-agers may give an earful of complaints about parents, teachers, and siblings.

3-6b How Can I Get Older School-Agers to Trust and Respect Me?

Older school-age children can be delightful conversationalists. They will listen attentively and respond appropriately in conversations that hold their attention. They can also build new, more mature bonds of affection and loyalty to adults who are willing to listen to them and treat them fairly and respectfully. Older school-age children are especially sensitive to being "talked down to" by adults.

School places new pressures on them. They are expected to assume a higher level of responsibility for their behavior and schoolwork. They will especially appreciate adults who really listen to their thoughts and feelings in an open-minded, nonjudgmental manner.

3-6c Why Do Older School-Agers Try So Hard to Be Popular?

School-age children have a powerful urge to belong to a peer group. They sometimes make up their own clubs or cliques with some semblance of rules and rituals, or even special taboos or requirements in clothing. Younger children may be willing to wear whatever their parents buy for them. School-age children typically want to wear clothes their friends like.

If mom, dad, or teacher prefers a certain style of clothing, shoes, or haircut, the older school-agers may automatically prefer something else. This desire to dress for peers increases but does not reach a peak until adolescence. School-agers' anxiety about whether or not they are popular will only increase as they approach their teenage years.

> No one can make you feel inferior without your permission.
>
> —*Eleanor Roosevelt*

Adults should help children feel secure, valued, and accepted. Self-confidence and self-esteem help children resist peer pressure to experiment with alcohol, sex, or drugs—pressure that many are likely to begin facing at this tender age. Adults can also help children keep material possessions in a proper perspective not only by respecting children's anxiety about peer approval but also by de-emphasizing the value of objects. We can strengthen children's character by focusing attention on valuing people for their character rather than for expensive clothing or playthings.

3-6d The Role of Media in the Lives of Older School-Age Children

Today many school-aged children have their own cell phones, electronic games, and gadgets. They phone, text, and use social networks such as Facebook to talk to their friends. Children this age typically watch an enormous amount of television. But not all media involvement offers children the chance to build the kinds of skills they need to prepare for life. Parents often struggle to find a balance between media and adequate time for family, friends, school, and sleep.

The Center on Media and Child Health, Harvard Medical School of Public Health (2008) strongly recommends keeping computers and televisions out of children's bedrooms. They recommend watching Tivo'd programs, DVDs, and online streaming TV instead of television to avoid commercials that unduly lure children to fatty foods and expensive toys. Parents should strictly limit overall viewing to 1 to 2 hours a day. Hours in front of the TV often result in obesity, inadequate sleep, poor academic progress, and decreased family time.

Caregivers should find out the words of the music children like to make sure it is consistent with desired values. Caregivers should be willing to say "no."

1. **Clarify rules and expectations.** *Know what you do and do not want children to be exposed to. Let children know what your expectations and rules are.*

2. **Use lockboxes or V-chips on computer software.** *To prevent children from seeing certain programs or websites, use the available technology to block unwanted images on the TV or computer.*

3. **Talk to children regularly.** *Of course you already do this, but you may have to ask direct questions to find out exactly what children see, hear, or play on a daily basis (National Association of Child Care Research and Referral Agencies, 2010).*

3-6e Puberty

思春期

As children leave early childhood and move toward adolescence, life sometimes becomes more complicated and stressful. Their bodies seem to take on

As children leave early childhood and move toward adolescence, life sometimes feels more complicated and stressful. A good book and comfy chair bring relaxation for this young girl.

Photo courtesy of the Robertson family

puberty
The period during which the secondary sex characteristics begin to develop and the capability of sexual reproduction is attained. Puberty is followed by a period of rapid physical growth.

a life of their own, growing adult genitalia often far too quickly or far too slowly to suit the confused and disoriented owner of the body.

Puberty may begin earlier than we expect. Breast budding in girls, their first sign of puberty, typically starts around age 10, with some girls starting as early as 8 and others not starting until 13. On average, the first menses occurs just before girls turn 13. A peak growth period for height, weight, and muscle mass occurs about a year after puberty has begun.

Boys enter puberty about a year later than girls. The first sign is enlargement of the testes, which typically happens at 11 but ranges from 9 to 14 years. Boys have a peak growth period about 2 years after the beginning of puberty.

3-6f How Can We Support Older School-Agers' Self-Esteem?

We begin to see little children walking around in very adult-looking bodies, and suddenly we expect them to act like grown-ups. Just as in toddlerhood when 2-year-olds were torn between the security of infancy and the allure of childhood, preadolescents are likely to waver in their feelings about whether to be a little kid or a teenager. One minute the child is sitting on a curb crying over a skinned knee and the next she is choosing her favorite color of lipstick.

Adults must provide a great deal of support, affection, and patience during these years so that school-agers' self-esteem and confidence stay intact. Babies, toddlers, and preschoolers get many hugs because they are little and cute. Adolescents and adults get romantic hugs from the opposite sex. Older school-agers are at an awkward stage and, especially young boys, may be left out of shows of affection altogether. Everybody needs an appropriate (non-exploitative) hug now and then to feel valued and special, and there are many excellent ways other than hugs to express affection. A big smile, sincere recognition, and listening all let the child know we care (Charlesworth, 2011; Gronlund, 1997; Meece, 1997; Steinberg, 1995).

Summary

- Children have individual patterns and rates of development.
- Comparisons should never be used to label or stereotype a child.
- Trust developed in infancy is a primary foundation for the development of healthy emotional attitudes.
- *Spoiling* refers to overindulging and overprotecting children, shielding them from responsibility for their own behavior, and rewarding inappropriate conduct.

- Toddlers strive to achieve autonomy.
- Preschoolers can be helped to express strong emotions in words instead of using their bodies to act out feelings.
- Early school-age children develop an ability to replay events mentally to evaluate experiences logically.
- Older school-agers have a powerful urge to belong to a peer group and be well liked by friends.
- Researchers recommend keeping computers and televisions out of young children's bedrooms.

Key Terms

active listening

appropriate touch

authoritarian style

authoritative style

autonomy

cephalocaudal

classical conditioning

collaborative

community of learners

concept

concrete operational

cues

doubt

egocentric

emotional growth

empathy

expressive language

external environment

group contagion

habituated

imprinting	preoperational
industry	proximodistal
inferiority	pseudoconditioning
internal sensations	receptive language
internalize	secure attachment
learned behavior	self-concept
learned helplessness	self-esteem
metacognition	shame
mirror	social growth
modeling	stimuli
object permanence	stress
operant conditioning	trust
permissive style	unconscious conditioning
positive child guidance	unconscious reactions

Student Activities

1. Interview a first-time parent of an infant or toddler.
   a. What has surprised the parent most in caring for the child?
   b. How can the parent tell when his child is tired? Hungry? Not feeling well?
   c. Ask what has been done to childproof the home so the infant or toddler can explore safely.

2. Interview the parent of a preschooler.
   a. How does the preschooler interact with peers?
   b. Ask about the preschooler's bedtime routine.
   c. Are there any strategies the parent uses to help get the child calmed down and into bed?

3. Interview the parent of a young school-age child.
   a. How does this school-ager handle disagreements with peers?
   b. Does the parent have any concerns about particular behavior issues?

   c. How does the parent respond to behavior issues?

4. Interview the parent of an older school-age child.
   a. What are the child's favorite interests?
   b. How does this child handle disagreements with peers?
   c. How does the child handle frustrations in school?
   d. Is homework a point of contention between the child and parents?

5. Interview the parent of a child of between age 5 and 12.
   a. How many minutes/hours of television does the child usually watch a day?
   b. What kind of television and movies does the child watch most?
   c. What kinds of electronic gadgets and games does the child play?

Related Resources

Readings

Sears, W. (2008). *Nighttime parenting: How to get your baby and child to sleep.* New York: Plume and La Leche League International Books.

Sears, W., M. Sears, R. Sears, J. Sears, & P. Sears (2011). *The portable pediatrician: Everything you need to know about your child's health.* New York: Little, Brown and Co.

Burgess, K., J. Wojslawowicz, K. Rubin, L. Rose-Krasnor, & C. Booth-LaForce. (2006). Social information processing and coping styles of shy/withdrawn and aggressive children: Does friendship matter? *Child Development, 77,* 371–383.

Websites

National Network for Child Care
National Network for Child Care offers practical information and resources that will be useful to you in your everyday work with children.

Zero To Three
Zero To Three informs, trains, and supports professionals and parents to improve the lives of infants and toddlers.

American Academy of Pediatrics
The American Academy of Pediatrics provides information supporting the health and well-being of infants, children, adolescents, and young adults.

CHAPTER

4

How to Observe Children

naeyc Standards

The following NAEYC Standards are addressed in this chapter

Standard 3 **Observing, documenting, and assessing to support young children and families**

3a Understanding the goals, benefits, and uses of assessment

3b Knowing about and using observation, documentation, and other appropriate assessment tools and approaches

3c Understanding and practicing responsible assessment to promote positive outcomes for each child

3d Knowing about assessment partnerships with families and with professional colleagues

© Cengage Learning 2013

Objectives

After reading this chapter, you should be able to do the following:

4-1 Discuss personal biases that affect guidance.

4-2 Follow components of the observation sequence.

4-3 Plan effective observation strategies.

4-1 Identifying Personal Biases

We see children differently because we are different. Everything we perceive with our senses (eyes, ears, and so on) is filtered through layer upon layer of our personal views and biases.

Ava is a bright, gregarious ball of energy. When she was in kindergarten, she popped out of bed every morning before the sun was up because she loved going to school each day. Her teacher, Mr. Costa, seemed to really like her. He often invited her to help with classroom chores such as feeding the goldfish or passing out napkins for snack. Because she learned concepts very quickly, he encouraged her to help other children, a responsibility she took very seriously. Ava liked pretending that she was a teacher, and the younger children thrived on her persistent tutoring. Whenever anyone asked her what she wanted to be when she grew up, she always answered quickly, "A schoolteacher just like Mr. Costa!"

During Ava's first day of first grade, she eagerly tried to get the attention of her new teacher, Mrs. Redwing, and jumped up to help pass out papers. Mrs. Redwing reprimanded Ava for getting up out of her desk without asking and said, "Please stop asking me questions and just sit quietly and listen." Mrs. Redwing thought, "Oh, no, another hyperactive kid. That's all I need."

biases
One's own set of beliefs, values, perceptions, and assumptions that develop from one's upbringing, past experience, and personal philosophy of life; bias can include an unfair preference for or dislike of something or someone.

81

Over time, Ava has become impatient and unhappy. She cries in the morning and tells her father that she does not want to go to school anymore. Mrs. Redwing is upset too. She is becoming more and more frustrated with Ava's behavior, which eventually has become disruptive and, at times, even defiant. Mrs. Redwing has become especially exasperated with Ava's attempts to help other children do their work whenever they have trouble, an action Mrs. Redwing considers a kind of cheating.

One day, Mr. Costa and Mrs. Redwing are sitting in the teacher's lounge drinking coffee. Mr. Costa says, "How is Ava doing this year? I really miss her. What a terrific little girl she is." Mrs. Redwing chokes on her coffee and sputters, "Ava? You've got to be kidding! She drives me absolutely up the wall."

How is it possible for two people to see the same child's behavior so differently? Mr. Costa responds favorably to Ava's energy and spontaneity because she reminds him of himself when he was younger. He values creativity, so he is delighted by Ava's bright mind. In contrast, because of her very strict upbringing, Mrs. Redwing learned early in life to suppress any fidgety impulses she had, so she finds Ava's chattering and bounciness particularly annoying. Her parents would never have tolerated such behavior. These behaviors strike Mrs. Redwing as rude and reckless, even though she can remember resenting her parents' rigidity when she was a child.

4-1a Responding More Objectively to Individual Children

DIVERSITY

TeachSource Video

Ensuring High Quality through Program Evaluation

Watch this Video Case and answer the following questions.

1. Why should a goal be measurable and achievable?

2. Why should teaching staff and administrators be assessed?

3. Describe the actions of the teacher in this video who was recording observations.

4. How can the assessment process be made a positive and supportive experience for those being assessed?

It is inevitable that some children will be more appealing than others to any given adult. Gender, culture, age, experiences, and temperament all affect our biases and shape our perceptions. Our own personality and style cannot be perfectly matched to the needs of every child; however, we can at least be honest about our bias and respectful in our treatment of children, regardless of their differences. Within families, parents sometimes admit that one of their own children seems easier to understand and manage, whereas another child's behavior seems totally confusing. In group settings, an adult may have difficulty admitting that he or she feels more comfortable with children who are small (or large), male (or female), black (or white), or rich (or poor).

To respond more effectively to children's behaviors, we must discover our own areas of bias. What preconceived notions do I have about children? Do I expect certain behaviors from children because of their ethnic, gender, or appearance differences? How can I learn who an individual child really is rather than focus on stereotypes associated with groups or categories of people? Do I tend to have favorite and least favorite children? How do I respond differently to them? How can I become more objective?

One way to increase objectivity is to consciously separate facts from opinions. What do I actually perceive, and what do I interpret intuitively based on my knowledge, experience, and bias? By sorting through our own thinking processes to separate facts from opinions, we can more accurately focus on actual child behaviors and scrutinize our interpretations of the meaning of those actions.

If Mrs. Redwing had separated the facts from her opinions, she might have seen Ava differently. See Positive Focus 4.1.

Objective Observations and Subjective Interpretations

Objective observations (Mr. Costa and Mrs. Redwing both agree that these are accurate facts): Ava talks frequently, begins tasks quickly, completes work before others in class, is active and quick in physical movements, and expresses interest in the progress of classmates.

Mr. Costa's **subjective interpretations**: Ava is very capable in verbal communications; she is a competent, bright student; she is enthusiastic about her schoolwork; she has leadership potential; she cares intensely about others.

Mrs. Redwing's subjective interpretations: Ava ignores the teacher and class rules about talking, she rushes through her work because she does not take it seriously enough, she is overactive, and she worries about the affairs of other children that are none of her business.

When one's opinions are stated separately from observable facts and those opinions are clearly labeled "subjective," it is easier to recognize and deal with personal bias. If we trick ourselves into believing that our opinions are objective facts, then we lose an opportunity to see children as they really are. We can consciously learn to be more objective in our thinking.

TeachSource Digital Download

The following observation is filled with subjective interpretations: "Erik angrily stomped into the kitchen trying to pick a fight with someone. He taunted his sister and hurt her feelings just to see her cry. He hoped she would hit him so he would have an excuse to get her in trouble." These statements are not objective observations. We have no reason to think they are true. We cannot see into Erik's head to look at his intentions or hear his thoughts.

What we can actually see and hear is that Erik "stomped into the kitchen. He looked around with a frown on his face. He pointed to his sister's sandwich and said, 'Yuk, are you going to eat that gooey mess?' His sister began to cry and threatened to hit Erik. Erik said, 'If you hit me, I'll tell mom.'" What we may interpret is that Erik seemed irritable, unhappy, and in a negative mood.

The first opinionated description tempts us to punish Erik for his obnoxious behavior because we assume we know why he behaved the way he did. The second, more objective way of reporting Erik's behavior reminds us that we do not know everything that is going on in Erik's mind and heart. Objective observation encourages us to look further to find out reasons for actions and to better understand troublesome behavior.

objective observations
Describing what happens without making judgments. Objective observations can be seen, heard, smelled, tasted, or touched.

subjective interpretations
Using objective observations to think about and express ideas, explanations, and perceptions of what happened.

Courtesy of Montessori Country Day School

Caregivers invited these toddlers to look at picture books while adults arranged their sleeping cots. What can you see? What can you infer about these children's feelings and needs from their body postures and facial expressions.

4-2 The Observation Sequence

To be effective in working with children, we must become skilled observers so that we can constantly improve the quality of the care and education we provide. Our ongoing observations should result in concrete plans and changes in the curriculum and environment. Child guidance is much more an art than a science.

There is no recipe for treating children that works for all children in all circumstances, but with careful observation, the adult can gather the information needed to make intelligent decisions and to select appropriate methods to prevent or respond to various

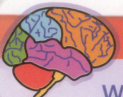

BrainFacts

What Can We Learn from Neuroscience?

Assessment helps us create effective learning environments

- Formative assessment supports brain development by measuring indications of mental growth that help us plan an environment to enhance continued brain development (Imholz & Petrosino, 2012; Popham, 2008).

- Assessment helps us "see" how children's brains are developing over time.

- To flourish in adulthood, children must develop the mental qualities of curiosity, determination, imagination, and self-control (Cooper & Jenson, 2009; Duckworth & Seligman, 2005).

- Assessment can help us document and improve the mental qualities that are needed by citizens in a democracy (Popham, 2008).

- We can change the classroom climate from competition to a supportive learning community whose members collaborate to enhance learning (Barnett et al., 2008; Cooper & Jenson, 2009; Diamond et al., 2007).

- The learning environment should develop children's confidence so they can deal with the real challenges of life (Costa & Kallick, 2014).

- The learning community should help children learn how to live together with civility and respect (Costa & Kallick, 2014).

- Life-long learners find joy in problem solving, curiosity, wonderment, and inquisitiveness (Duckworth & Seligman, 2005).

problems. Later, the adult can observe to evaluate how effective the chosen guidance technique has been in solving the problem.

DAP

4-2a How Observation Supports Positive Guidance

The effectiveness of any effort at resolving a behavior problem depends on the effort being well matched to the child's ability and frame of mind as well as to the circumstances surrounding the behavior. Does the child appear to be feeling angry and destructive or just bored and silly? Is the behavior habitual or a rare event? Is the child capable of benefiting from verbal reminders or is direct physical redirection required? What is the cause of the problem? When, where, and why does it occur? These are all questions that should be answered through careful observation.

Today affordable digital recording technology makes it feasible to record children's behaviors during busy class times to watch and evaluate at a less busy time. A small tripod can be used to stand a video camera discreetly on a shelf at an angle to view an area of the classroom. Some teachers like to keep a smart phone with still photo, video, and voice recording capability in their pockets to pull out for a moment of quick record keeping, just as they would keep notes of an interesting occurrence.

Electronic vignettes can be especially poignant for parents in parent conferences. What parent wouldn't be touched seeing her child involved in meaningful learning activity and joyful interactions with other children? Our technology can give parents vivid images instead of words about our curriculum and methods. When parents are better informed, we are more likely to succeed in our efforts to draw them into classroom and school involvement.

4-2b What Do I Need to Get Started?

There are many excellent developmentally appropriate checklists and observational instruments (assessments) available commercially to assist early childhood professionals in observing children. Go to the NAEYC website for additional information and recommendations on early childhood assessment.

For most parents, caregivers, and teachers, however, the most useful record-keeping tool (and definitely the least expensive) is a simple pocket-size notepad and a pencil. If paper and pencil are available whenever something interesting occurs, it will be a great deal easier to get something written down. No record-keeping instrument of any kind is of value if it stays in a desk drawer or a file cabinet.

With a little pocket notepad, an anecdote can be described before the details are forgotten, tidbits can be added regularly to a running account, or some type of sampling checklist can be maintained. It is easy for us to think, "I don't need to write this down. I'm sure I'll remember it." But then, of course, we forget whatever it was that we were so sure we would remember.

4-2c How Will I Use My Observations?

In DAP, we use our observations for many purposes:

- Communicating with families
- Describing children's development, learning, and progress
- Identifying children's needs and interests
- Improving curriculum, environment, and teaching practices
- Planning program improvement
- Referring children for screening and assessment when indicated

Observations can be just for fun as well as to serve a critical program quality improvement function. Parents love having a chance to know more about their children. They tell grandparents about their toddler's entertaining monkey business and their preschooler's clever comments. Educators enrich families' lives by providing photographs, anecdotes, and child-made keepsakes that share details about children's friendships, accomplishments, skills, and interests.

Families treasure teacher- and/or child-made scrapbooks showing their child's changes over a year's time. Scrapbooks are a terrific way for adults to support the development of children's self-esteem. Photographs and mementos remind the child how much he is valued by parents and educators. Some early educators use folders or help children make construction paper albums to collect anecdotes, pictures, and other items throughout the year for families to share at school events and activities.

We must routinely use observations to determine the right level of activities for children. Is the child eagerly engaged in the puzzle, book, or activity? Or is he looking bored? The activity may not offer a challenge anymore. Does he seem frustrated? The game may be too complicated for his developmental level. Is the group of preschoolers fidgeting and misbehaving during story time? The story may be too long or not lively enough to hold their interest at that age.

We routinely observe children to determine the right level of activities for them. Is each child eagerly engaged in activity? Is she looking bored? Does he seem frustrated?

inferring meaning
Drawing conclusions from evidence perceived by one's senses or through communication.

Observations always come into play when a child is behaving inappropriately. Positive child guidance is a problem-solving method. Adults observe how children are behaving at a given moment, figure out why they are behaving that way, and determine supportive methods to help the child become more responsible and self-disciplined. Positive child guidance cannot succeed without effective and ongoing child observations. It takes concentrated effort and practice to develop keen observation skills.

Interpreting observations is the process of **inferring meaning** from what has been sensed (seen, heard, touched, tasted, or smelled). To interpret what has been observed, knowledge of child development in general as well as recognition of the unique development of an individual child is necessary. An additional help is firsthand experience with other children as well as with the individual child in question. All of this means we should take what we sense at the present and mull it over using all of our past knowledge and experience to create new ideas about why the child may need to behave as he does.

Looking back over observation notes can be surprisingly enlightening. Children grow and change so quickly that we may be startled to look back at our notes about little Bronwyn and see that only three months ago she cried and clung to us when other children were around. Now, she confidently approaches others to initiate play. By seeing a child's progress over time, we can make better sense of the child's immediate behavior and know what help and guidance the child needs to behave more appropriately.

Personal bias must be kept in check while interpreting one's observations. Observation records, particularly objective checklists, may provide convincing evidence that our intuitive assumptions about a particular child have been wrong. Interpreting observations also gives us an opportunity to see things from the child's point of view. We may be annoyed with a child for interrupting our conversations but, after observing him carefully, realize that he deserves to be included more in adult interactions and just needs to be taught how to join a conversation politely.

4-2d How Does My Observation Become a Plan?

In DAP, assessment methods are aligned with appropriate outcome goals. To make an observation plan, we should know what goal we are trying to accomplish. In a doctor's office, a patient is seen and observations are recorded in a chart. The observations of the physician are then carefully interpreted (to make a diagnosis): What is the meaning of the rash? . . . of the fever? . . . of the pain in the left foot? Then, most importantly, a plan is formulated (a prescription) to remedy the problem and accomplish a healthier condition. The doctor prescribes bed rest or an antibiotic.

We observe the child and figure out what we think is wrong. Then we make a plan to make it better. For Rahul—redirection away from the block center. For Wyquelia—an understanding, heart-to-heart talk about hurting people's feelings. For Ja'Miyah—a change in our own behavior toward him, giving him more positive attention and setting up activities that will draw on his interest in helicopters.

4-2e What if My Plan Does Not Work?

After a plan is formulated, the next step is action. Some adults take a fatalistic attitude toward children's misbehavior. They think children will not change and consequently do not bother doing anything other than complain. Young children are avid learners. They learn new habits much more easily than we do. They just need time, effort, encouragement, and a great deal of practice.

Sometimes, even if the plan we attempt does not really work, merely focusing on a child's problem (and caring enough to try to resolve it) may stimulate the child's own awareness of the problem and commitment to correct it. It will be very therapeutic for the child to see evidence from our actions that "I care about you. I am willing to make a real effort to help you learn to use words rather than fists to express your feelings. I won't give up on you."

As long as the action is positive and respectful of the child, it is far more important for us to formulate a plan and do something than it is to worry

All of us are watchers—of television, of time clocks, of traffic on the freeway—but few are observers. Everyone is looking, not many are seeing.

—*Peter M. Leschak*

about being right every time. Perfectionists are often so paralyzed by their fear of making mistakes that they never get around to doing anything. Children can learn valuable lessons from our handling of our own mistakes. They can learn that everyone makes mistakes from time to time and that admitting mistakes is nothing to be ashamed of. We could set a good example by saying, "Joshua, I asked you to hold my hand on our walk to help you remember to stay on the sidewalk where it's safe. I made a mistake. I didn't think about how that might make you feel like a baby. Let's think of a different way to help you be safe."

4-2f How Can I Be Sure My Plan Is Working?

Is what we are doing effective? In the evaluation phase, we make a complete circle and come back to observing. The only way we can be sure we were on target in our first observation, interpretation, plan, and resulting action is to observe again and look for indications that our plan is or is not working. If it is working, we can relax and go on to the next problem. If it is not, we return to square one, collect more information through observation, and develop a new and improved plan of action. This cycle repeats until we find a plan that works.

PRACTICAL APPLICATION CASE

The Mysterious Case of the Spinning Peg

Felicia, an afternoon assistant in an infant and toddler child care center, is sitting on the floor and pulling the string of a "See and Say" toy. Lisa is laughing. Felicia asks, "Where are the fish? Can you see the fish? There they are, seven of them." She laughs and tickles Lisa's tummy. Other toddlers push close to Felicia as they play and interact with her. They watch every move that Felicia makes.

Lisa, who is 18 months old, wanders away from them toward me, the observer, as I sit on the vinyl padded tunnel watching Felicia and Lisa and taking observation notes. Lisa accidentally drops a large plastic peg she is carrying. When it hits the nearby wooden stair, it spins for several seconds. She stares at it with a look of wonder. She carefully picks it up and with great concentration, drops it on the step again, but this time it does not spin. She stares at it, squats beside the stairs, and then proceeds to drop it again and again on the carpet.

It does not spin. She stands up and throws it down on the carpet. It does not spin! She bites it hard and throws it two more times, but still it does not spin. She leaves the peg lying on the floor and walks away. Felicia picks it up and puts it away.

Lisa comes over to me, looks at my writing and at my face. She pats my tablet and then pulls at the pages. She looks very seriously at my eyes. She then walks away. I hear her whine as she walks over to the play sink. She stops abruptly, looks at a plastic fruit, then with great interest she watches it as she drops it to the floor. It does not spin.

She sucks her finger and starts to cry. Felicia picks her up, comforts her, then walks away saying, "You're getting a little fussy. I wonder if you're hungry. Let me see if you get an afternoon bottle."

Case Discussion Questions

1. What are the subjective interpretations you would have made if you had been observing this interaction?
2. When the peg didn't work for her, what else did Lisa try?
3. What did you learn about toddler's persistence?
4. What can you tell about the relationship between Lisa and her caregiver, Felicia?

4-3 Observation Strategies

In DAP, we use assessments to obtain information on all areas of children's development and learning. We need to know about children's cognitive skills, language development, social–emotional development, self-help skills, health, and physical development. Researchers use carefully orchestrated strategies to collect objective data. Those of us who care for young children rarely need such formal methodology.

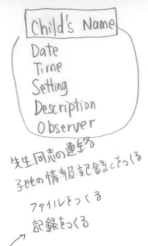

Child's Name
Date
Time
Setting
Description
Observer

先生同志の連絡
子供の情報記録とつくる

ファイルをつくる
記録をつくる

anecdotal record

A short descriptive story about a child's specific behavior event that is of particular interest or concern. This may be first-hand information as observed by child care providers or recorded from second-hand information as provided by parents. It is qualitative, not quantitative data.

We need a workable plan for finding out the what, when, where, and why of children's behavior and learning so that we can respond effectively and appropriately. The following sections describe some useful methods for record keeping. Although many elementary schools have formal assessments they are required to use, some of those tests may only assess academic skills and not cover vitally important social and emotional behaviors. To succeed with young children, we need to observe all areas of the child's development (Bentzen, 2005; Copple & Bredekamp, 2009; McAfee & Leong, 2007; Wortham, 2008).

4-3a What Is an Anecdotal Record?

An **anecdotal record** is a detailed account of a specific episode that is of particular interest or concern. A specific event takes place that catches the attention of the adult. As soon as possible, the adult writes a narrative account; he tells the story of the event. He describes all of the pertinent details that he can recall, such as what he saw, heard, or otherwise perceived with his senses. He includes verbatim quotes whenever possible to further clarify the account. Any personal opinions or interpretations are set apart and clearly identified as observer's comments by such phrases as "It appeared to me that . . ." or "Therefore, it was my impression that . . ." See Positive Focus 4.2.

Positive Focus 4.2 Evaluation Using Anecdotal Records

Following is an anecdotal record of a toddler biting incident:

Observations:

Ricky wandered slowly around the room, whining and shaking his head. After about 5 minutes, he abruptly dropped to the floor and began to cry. Periodically, he stopped crying to sit up, suck his thumb, and twist a tuft of his hair while he looked around, and then he closed his eyes, dropped back on the floor, and began sobbing again.

I picked up a handful of picture books and sat down on the floor beside him. I said, "Ricky, would you like to read a book? Look, it's a book about kitty cats." At first he ignored me, but finally he crawled into my lap and laid his head on my chest as he continued to suck his thumb and make the jerky little sniffing sounds that follow a bout of hard crying. I began to read the story about kittens.

After only a few minutes, Katherine toddled over and plopped into my lap practically on top of Ricky. Before I had even a second to respond, Ricky had grabbed Katherine's face and hair and sunk his teeth into her cheek.

Comments/Interpretations:

Ricky was probably frightened and anxious because he has not been away from his mother very often. He seems to be showing evidence of a great deal of separation anxiety. He may have felt threatened by Katherine's presence because he has no sisters or brothers and may not be accustomed to sharing adult attention with others. I will have to watch Ricky very carefully so that I can help him find ways to cope with his feelings and so that I can anticipate and intervene better in situations where he might hurt another child.

Evaluating Using Home Observations

Home Observations	Comments/Interpretations
Monday, 8:00 a.m.—Celia bit her nails while watching cartoons on television; she had a very tense facial expression. Monday, 3:30 p.m.—Celia and her best friend Joel had an argument; after he told her he wouldn't play with her anymore, she sat by herself on the steps for a long time, biting her nails; again, she appeared very tense. Tuesday, 11:30 a.m.—Celia bit her nails while she waited for lunch; she appeared more bored than tense. Tuesday, 4:30 p.m.—Celia bit her nails the whole time she watched a television cartoon; her whole body appeared to be tense as she sat on the edge of her chair and strained toward the television.	Tension (and possibly boredom) seems to be triggering Celia's nail biting. She was not seen biting her nails when she was coloring, playing with dolls, or putting together puzzles. It may be helpful to redirect Celia to more active play and to discourage her from watching television cartoons.

TeachSource Digital Download

4-3b What Is a Running Account?

In a **running account**, a specific type of behavior is noted each time it occurs. A mother who worries that her child is not eating properly may keep a running account, keeping track of when, where, and what her child eats during and between meals each day. After a few days or weeks, she can begin to see if specific eating patterns emerge. Does the child pick at meals but consume high-calorie junk food during frequent snacks? Does the child eat a well-balanced lunch and afternoon snack but often refuse supper? Does the child eat whatever is offered at home but get into power struggles over food with a caregiver in the child care center? See Positive Focus 4.3.

DAP teaching staff keep necessary materials handy to assure that they routinely record observations necessary to track children's well-being and progress toward goals.

© 2013 Cengage Learning®

4-3c What Is Time Sampling?

The purpose of **time sampling** is to give a periodic snapshot of a certain behavior. In time sampling, a time interval is selected: 5 minutes, 30 minutes, an hour, or other interval. Then, at the designated time intervals, a checklist is marked to show whether the chosen behavior is or is not occurring at that moment. For example, an individual child could be watched at intervals to determine whether he is spending more time actively engaged in play or passively watching others. An entire class could be watched to see how often the reading center is used compared with the block center. This procedure can give factual evidence to support or refute an adult's intuitive impressions about the occurrence of various patterns of behavior. See Positive Focus 4.4.

running account
A detailed commentary describing an event as it unfolds each time it occurs.

time sampling
A recording made at predefined intervals to determine the pattern of occurrence and the general frequency of a certain behavior either in an individual or in the entire group. Setting and sticking with specific time intervals for recording the behavior reduces the influence of observer bias.

Positive Focus 4.4

Evaluation by Time Sampling

Following is a time-sampling checklist used by a preschool teacher to help her study her students' patterns of being **on task** rather than misbehaving, wandering aimlessly, or just watching:

Time	Misbehaving	Wandering	Watching
8:15 a.m.	James, Jill	Suzette, Amy, Tyler	Ben, Ann
8:30 a.m.	James	Amy	Suzette
8:45 a.m.	Amy, Suzette	—	—
9:00 a.m.	Tyler	—	—
9:15 a.m.	—	—	—
9:30 a.m.	—	Suzette	—
9:45 a.m.	Amy, Ben	Jill, Tyler	Suzette
10:00 a.m.	Suzette, Ann	Tyler	Jill, Amy
10:15 a.m.	Suzette	Ann, Tyler, Ben	Amy

Comments/Interpretations

These children have more difficulty staying on task at the beginning and the end of the morning. Their most productive time is between 8:45 and 9:30. Suzette, Amy, and Tyler may need special attention to help them focus on productive activity. James seems able to avoid misbehavior after he settles into productive activity.

on task
Focused on the activities at hand; fully involved in and attentive to productive skill development or learning activity.

event sampling
A recording to determine the precise number of times a specific behavior occurs within a set period, as well as the pattern of occurrence.

4-3d What Is Event Sampling?

The purpose of **event sampling** is to determine the exact number of times a specific behavior occurs. Individual children can be observed for occurrences of a specific behavior, or an entire group can be watched, and a total number of occurrences of a behavior (such as aggression) can be recorded and tallied. In event sampling, a specific action (or actions) is designated for observation. When the behavior occurs, a checklist is marked so that after a given period, the adult can tally the exact number of times the behavior took place. See Positive Focus 4.5.

Positive Focus 4.5

Evaluation by Event Sampling

Following is an event sampling checklist used by a child care worker to determine the individual daily progress of several toddlers in their toilet training (each accident has been recorded as an X):

Toileting Accidents

Names	Monday	Tuesday	Wednesday	Thursday	Friday
Reily	XXX	XXX	XXX	X	
Joseph	XX				
Mariette	XXX	XX	X	X	
Ella	XXXX	XXXXX	XXXX	XXXX	XXXX
Prichart			X	XX	
Bethany	XX		X		

Comments/Interpretations

Ella may not yet be ready for toilet training. It may be helpful to observe Mariette more closely to determine if she is having difficulty at a specific time of day or under specific circumstances.

Reily had difficulty early in the week but managed to stay dry most of the day Thursday and all day Friday. He should probably be watched further to see what happens the following week.

4-3e Which Method of Recording Observations Works Best?

Checklists and narrative accounts can be used as tools for gathering information in many different situations. The particular advantage of narrative accounts is that they create word pictures that may provide insight into a child's behavior far beyond that originally anticipated when the event was recorded.

The adult can look back over several anecdotal records and discover new, previously overlooked relationships or details each time. The biggest drawback to narratives is, of course, that they are very time-consuming and so can be relied on only for recording occasional rather than routine occurrences. Narratives collect **qualitative information**, whereas checklists collect **quantitative information**.

Checklists leave out all of the details surrounding behaviors and focus only on the frequencies and distributions of occurrences. They are especially useful for making comparisons, not only of one child's behaviors to that of other children, but also to the child's own behaviors at other times of day, in other settings, or at an earlier age. The major advantage of checklists is the ease with which they can be used. The major drawback is that a great deal of important information about the extenuating background circumstances of a behavior is not recorded. The checklist examples provided earlier gave a great deal more factual information about many more children than the anecdotal record and the running account; however, you probably feel that you know much more about what Ricky and Celia (described in the narrative accounts) are really like than you do about any of the children listed on the checklists.

▶❚❚ TeachSource Video

01:00:01:40

Preschooler Social and Emotional Development

Watch this video on social and emotional development, and then answer the following questions:

1. What is included in social–emotional development?
2. Describe three examples of social–emotional guidance you saw in the film.
3. List three milestones of early social–emotional growth described in this film.
4. How did the teacher observe, assess, and monitor social–emotional growth?

qualitative information
Unmeasurable descriptive qualities and characteristics of behaviors.

quantitative information
Measurable numerical data and statistical calculations that tell how often or to what degree behaviors occur.

Summary

- Everything that we perceive with our senses (eyes, ears, and so on) is filtered through layers of personal bias.
- One way to increase objectivity is to make a conscious effort to separate facts from opinions.
- Observations help us evaluate how effective a chosen guidance technique has been in solving a problem.

Key Terms

anecdotal record

biases

event sampling

inferring meaning

objective observations

on task

qualitative information

quantitative information

running account

subjective interpretations

time sampling

Student Activities

1. Carry out an observation by creating an *anecdotal record* of the things you see and hear.
   a. Study your observations.
   b. What can you infer from your record?
   c. List three things you might do differently with the child or children on the basis of your observations.

2. Carry out an observation by creating a *running account* of the things you see and hear.
   a. Study your observations.
   b. What can you infer from your record?
   c. List three things you might do differently with the child or children on the basis of your observations.

3. Carry out an observation using *time sampling* to track a specific behavior you have selected.
   a. Study your observations.

   b. What can you infer from your record?
   c. List three things you might do differently with the child or children on the basis of your observations.

4. Carry out an observation using *event sampling* to track a specific behavior you have selected.
   a. Study your observations.
   b. What can you infer from your record?
   c. List three things you might do differently with the child or children on the basis of your observations.

5. Discuss your observations and decide what you might have done more effectively. What worked best? Why?

Related Resources

Readings

Bentzen, W. R. (2005). *Seeing young children: A guide to observing and recording behavior* (5th ed.). Clifton Park, NY: Delmar Learning.

Engel, B., & G. Gronlund. (2001). *Focused portfolios: A complete assessment for the young child.* New York: RedLeaf Press.

Gronlund, G., & M. James. M. (2006). *Focused observations: How to observe children for assessment and curriculum planning.* New York: RedLeaf Press.

Websites

HighScope HighScope is best known for its landmark Perry Preschool Study, a longitudinal study demonstrating the effectiveness of the HighScope Preschool Curriculum and the lasting effects of high-quality preschool education. This site offers research-validated tools for assessment in early childhood education.

Teaching Strategies This company offers assessment resources to programs serving children from birth through kindergarten. Teaching Strategies consistently expands its product offerings to include widely adopted assessment solutions.

Serving Culturally Diverse Children and Families

naeyc Standards

The following NAEYC Standards are addressed in this chapter

Standard 2   Building family and community relationships

2a Knowing about and understanding diverse family and community characteristics

2b Supporting and engaging families and communities through respectful, reciprocal relationships

© 2013 Cengage Learning®

Objectives

After reading this chapter, you should be able to do the following:

5-1 Explain how culture gives meaning to our lives.

5-2 Discuss children and families in the context of their communities.

5-3 Summarize how prejudice, racism, and discrimination damage development.

5-4 Describe how culture shapes child guidance.

5-5 Practice valuing and respecting cultural differences.

5-1 Culture Gives Meaning to Our Lives

The word **culture**, which comes from the Latin root *colere* (to occupy, cultivate, or cherish), refers to the patterns of activity in our lives that give our lives meaning and importance. Culture gives us language, and language gives us the ability to communicate our experiences and express our needs within our community. This capacity to use symbols to express culture is considered a defining feature of human beings.

Culture is something we human beings carry around inside our heads. We can *see* folk dancing, *hear* religious music, *taste* holiday food, *smell* ritual incense, and *touch* handmade clay pots. But those things are only the results of culture; they aren't culture itself.

Culture is something invisible and untouchable in our minds. Culture is made up of the beliefs and traditions passed down from parents to children throughout history by members of groups of people within the larger society who are part of social, religious, ethnic, or any other groups who feel a kinship. Culture is also something we are in the process of creating. We are changing culture day to day as we create new traditions, modify our beliefs, or help our children strive toward different goals in a different environment than we or our parents experienced.

Children are capable of learning to function in more than one cultural context. By creating an environment of unconditional acceptance of different cultures in early

culture

The traditional beliefs and patterns of behavior that are passed down from parents to children by a society; beliefs, customs, practices, and social behavior of any particular cluster of people whose shared beliefs and practices identify the particular nation, religion, ability, gender, race, or group to which they belong.

childhood programs, young children can learn to accept, respect, and behave appropriately in different cultures without giving up their appreciation for and loyalty to their own culture. We call this **cultural competence**.

5-1a What Is Ordinary Culture?

Some people wrongly think culture only means opera, Renaissance paintings, and ballet. Certainly those are a limited part of Western society's culture, but there is a great deal more to culture. Raymond Williams (2001), an early pioneer in the field of cultural studies, argued that culture was "ordinary." He forced an important shift in researchers' thinking about culture. He wrestled the term *culture* away from the "high culture" that was clearly restricted to the rich and powerful members of society, and he broadened the term *culture* to encompass the lived, day-to-day experience of everyday people like you and me.

5-1b Does Everyone Have Culture?

Some traits of human life are transmitted genetically—an infant's desire for food, for example, is triggered by physiological factors within the genetic code. My desire specifically for tortillas and queso fresco with salsa for lunch, however, can't be explained genetically. That is a learned cultural response to hunger. Children learn culture at home, at school, in the community—and even from television—whether we intend for them to learn culture from those particular places or not. That is culture's essential feature—everyone, everywhere is exposed to culture. All socially interacting humans have culture.

Children accept some lessons of culture and keep them throughout life. They reject others and replace them with new ways. Parents and teachers don't always have control over which lessons about culture will be kept and which will eventually be rejected. We do know that the more the child feels valued and respected by parents and teachers during childhood, the more likely he will be to follow parents' and teachers' rules and keep their values as he grows up (Garces, Thomas, & Currie, 2002).

The process through which culture is passed down from one generation to the next is called **enculturation**. It is the process of learning about culture by observing, imitating, practicing, and being taught. Enculturation teaches a child the accepted norms and values as well as the language and skills he needs to become an accepted member of his community.

As part of cultural learning, children pick up **body language** (the gestures, facial expressions, and body postures that people use to communicate along with or instead of speech). Body language, like spoken language, can mean different things in different cultures. For example, winking one eye to indicate a shared secret is an example of body language in North America, but this gesture does not mean the same thing in every country or community. For example, in Japan a wink doesn't mean anything, but in India a wink would be interpreted as a rude, sexual gesture.

Body language is learned and changes over time as part of a culture. Differences in body language can cause confusion, miscommunication, and embarrassment. The best antidote is to be alert to signs that someone is uncomfortable and ask questions. For example, "You looked surprised when I winked. I hope I didn't offend you. In my cultural background, a wink means you and I share a secret. In your cultural background, does a wink mean something different? You have helped me a lot by sharing information with me I didn't know about your culture."

A special concern for young children is their ability to cope with a sudden immersion into an alien culture. Young children tend to adapt much more quickly and easily to an unknown environment than do adults and adolescents, and they definitely learn foreign languages more easily. They can still, however, experience **culture shock** (a feeling of confusion, alienation, and depression that occurs during initial immersion in a new culture). Until the new culture becomes familiar and comfortable, it is customary for children to feel homesick.

If children are learning a new language, they will likely have difficulty communicating and probably make frequent, embarrassing, and humiliating verbal mistakes. This is

cultural competence
Being knowledgeable about different cultures, their daily living practices, cultural values, norms, and traditions; being willing to treat others with appropriate respect regardless of race, ethnicity, religion, ability, country of origin, economic status, etc.

enculturation
The way a culture teaches a child its norms and values so that the child can become an accepted member of that culture. The process of passing culture down to the child not only by direct guidance, but also by her watching and experiencing culture every day from infancy onward.

body language
The gestures, facial expressions, and body postures that people use to communicate along with or instead of speech.

culture shock
A feeling of confusion, alienation, and depression that can result from the psychological stress that typically occurs during a person's initial immersion in a new culture.

usually compounded by feelings of melancholy, fear, and frustration. These feelings can be emotionally stressful. Culture shock usually eases rapidly as the surroundings become more familiar, as long as the new setting is warm and supportive. We need to pay special attention to ensuring that the environment is welcoming and encouraging for the child coming from a different culture.

5-1c How Does Culture Affect Early Social and Emotional Development?

If you observe carefully, you will notice that children from different cultures typically have the usual developmental similarities and also some subtle (or sometimes not so subtle) social and emotional differences. Remembering, of course, that each child is unique—a special, valuable human being.

You might notice, for example, that Chinese and Korean toddlers may tend to show more fearful and anxious reactions than Australian, Canadian, and Italian toddlers in new, stressful situations, such as when they first start child care. Chinese preschoolers will probably have more inner control (or self-regulation) than North American children (Chen et al., 1998, 2003; Gartstein et al., 2006; Rubin et al., 2006; Sabbagh et al., 2006). Cameroonian Nso toddlers from western Africa are likely to show more self-regulation than Costa Rican toddlers when their caregivers ask them to do something or not to do something. And Costa Rican toddlers show more self-control than Greek toddlers (Chen, 2009; Keller et al., 2004).

We think children from different cultural backgrounds develop differently because parents in different cultures treat them differently and expect different things of them. Researchers found that Canadian parents often showed disappointment and disapproval to their toddlers. Chinese parents tended to be warm and accepting to their toddlers. Compared with European-American parents, Chinese and Korean parents were also more likely to closely control their toddlers (Chen, 2009; Keller et al., 2004).

Also, there are differences between native or rural cultures and more technological cultures. Cameroonian Nso mothers were more likely than Costa Rican mothers, who in turn were more likely than middle-class Greek mothers, to keep their babies and toddlers in their arms and on their bodies much of the time. Their physical style of parenting, which involved a great deal of body contact and body stimulation, seemed to speed the child's development of compliance and self-control (Chen et al., 1998, 2009).

Play is naturally the way young children learn, and children from different cultures play differently. An important kind of play that varies across cultures is dramatic play. Western children tend to take part in more dramatic (pretend) behaviors than children in many other cultures. Korean-American preschool children tend to display less social and pretend play than Anglo-American children. Also, when Korean children engage in pretend play, they are likely to act out everyday and family roles rather than the fantasy roles and fairy tale characters of their Western playmates (Farver, Kim, & Lee, 1995). Children from rural areas in Brazil pretend less than those from Brazilian cities (Gosso et al., 2007).

Children growing up in traditional cultures where extended families live together generation after generation tend to be more prosocial (cooperative) in their behavior than children who grow up in big cities, often far from relatives (Edwards, 2000). In big cities, being competitive and being successful may be a higher cultural goal than community harmony. That may cause parents to allow their children to be more coercive and aggressive than children who grow up in rural areas.

In smaller settings where community harmony is most valued, parents socialize their children to be prosocial. Researchers have found that North American children display higher levels of aggression than their age mates in China, Korea, Japan, Thailand, Australia, Sweden, and the Netherlands (Bergeron & Schneider, 2009; Russell et al., 2003; Weisz et al., 1988; Zahn-Waxler et al., 1966).

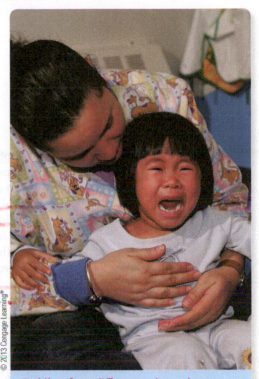

© 2013 Cengage Learning®

Toddlers from different cultures have already absorbed subtle (or sometimes not so subtle) cultural differences. Depending on background, a particular little one may be more likely to be fearful or bold in a new situation.

Culture is involved in virtually all aspects of children's social and emotional development. Cultural values affect how children express their emotions and how they interact with their friends. The most powerful early cultural impact comes from parents and caregivers. But later influences will come from friends as well as the television, school, place of worship, and community.

Even very young children respond to the social and emotional signals from other children. During play, children unconsciously evaluate and respond to the social and emotional characteristics of other children according to their own internalized cultural belief systems. Without even knowing they are doing it, children typically accept children who seem like themselves and reject children who seem different. Young children need nurturing guidance to help them recognize differences, value those differences, and learn to function appropriately in different cultural settings.

5-2 Understanding Children and Families in the Context of Their Communities

Uri Bronfenbrenner, a cofounder of the national Head Start program and a scholar in developmental psychology and child rearing, created a new interdisciplinary field called **human ecology**. Bronfenbrenner (1979, 1988, 1993) and Morris (1998) taught us that a child's development is best understood within the **cultural context** of that child's family and community.

In today's globally competitive industrialized world, it seems that the more we learn about the conditions needed to nurture development, competence, and character, the more we see those exact conditions being eroded. Far too many parents of babies and young children today are battered by time crunches and exhausted by work-induced stress. Families need help and support from early childhood professionals, now more than ever.

5-2a Bronfenbrenner Suggests We Visualize the Child's Inner Self

Bronfenbrenner (1979) and Moen et al. (1995) advised professionals working with children and families to take an ecological perspective. Bronfenbrenner's groundbreaking work combined components of sociology with developmental psychology, creating a new way of approaching and supporting children and families. He realized that the relationships between human beings and their communities were "mutually shaping." He described the individual person's interactive experience as "a set of **nested structures**, each inside the next, like a set of Russian dolls" (Bronfenbrenner, 1979, p. 22). To really understand a child's or parent's inner nature, one has to see within, beyond, across, and through these complicated nesting structures. One has to see how the parents, their workplace, the community, society, schools, and even the economy all interact and all affect children.

Imagine that I use Bronfenbrenner's image of the Russian nesting dolls to help me relate to Ca Nguyen, the mother of a new child in my school. As I talk to her, get to know her, and observe her in different situations, I begin to visualize the tough, assertive businesswoman on the outside, but inside I observe a mother whose confidence can easily be shaken but who wants to do the very best for her child. Inside that, I notice a generous, encouraging neighbor who translates for and helps many members of her community, and very importantly, at the center, I envision the remnants of a young child who lost both parents to the horrors of war several decades ago.

Of course Ca Nguyen is far more complicated than my simple imaginings can construct, and I may be totally incorrect, but by making these observations and taking the time to learn about her and imagine her life from her perspective, I begin to feel

human ecology
The theory that people don't develop in isolation but rather in relation to their family, home, school, community, and society. Each of these constantly changing multilevel environments, as well as the interactions among these environments, is key to a human being's development.

cultural context
The situation or circumstance in which a particular cultural event, action, behavior, or imagery occurs. Actions, events, and behaviors can have different meanings, depending on their cultural context.

nested structures
An individual's interactive experience—how the parents, their workplace, the community, society, schools, and the economy interact and affect children.

empathetic toward Ca Nguyen. Empathy creates warmth, helps broaden trust, and invites further communication. I can now see Ca Nguyen as a complex person, with multifaceted layers in her identity. Importantly, once someone is truly recognized as a complex human being, the person can no longer be pigeonholed as a one-dimensional stereotype.

5-2b Unconditional Acceptance

Cultural knowledge about a child's family and community especially supports child guidance. To effectively guide a child over time, we need to know and understand that child. The strategies for guidance described in this book can, of course, be used in a pinch to assist a child you don't know at all or don't know very well. But to make a real difference in a child's life, you need to have a relationship with that child. The child needs **unconditional acceptance** from you. The child must come to know that you unconditionally accept him as a worthwhile human being. Bronfenbrenner (1994, pp. 118–119) said it best:

> *Somebody's got to be crazy about that kid, and vice versa! But what does "crazy" mean? It means that the adult in question regards this particular child as somehow special— especially wonderful, especially precious—even though objectively the adult may well know that this is not the case.*

It is impossible to unconditionally accept someone if you don't even know her. By learning about the cultural experiences and expectations of a child's family, you can take the first important steps toward open communication with her parents. You don't need a memorized list of typical behaviors for every racial, ethnic, ability, gender, or other potential culturally based grouping known to humankind. You just need the skills of a good listener, an open heart, an open mind, and the willingness to take the time to get to know someone.

Most people love to tell you about themselves. Most people respond well to genuine interest and respect. Learn the parents' names and use them regularly. Try to greet parents in a friendly way before you launch into questions you need to ask. Remember to have a **personal interaction**. Treat each parent as a valuable and worthwhile person who you are happy to see. The home, community, and school are all interconnected, and all have a powerful influence on the developing child. We can't afford to ignore any part of that triangle of influence.

unconditional acceptance
The process of accepting someone as a worthwhile human being; recognition and appreciation without any strings attached.

personal interaction
Reciprocal social activity that should express genuine interest and respect for the other individual.

FIGURE 5.1

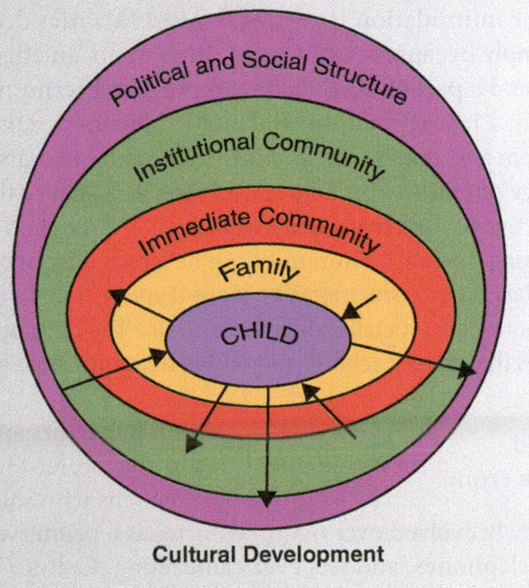

Cultural Development
To see the individual child, we must look across, around, and through the nested structure made up of community, family, and individual within a culture.

Cultural Development

DIVERSITY

DAP

5-3 Prejudice, Racism, and Discrimination

In DAP programs, teaching staff strive against possible bias and discrimination by treating all children with equal respect. Staff create activities and environments that build positive self-identity and proactively teach the valuing of individual differences. Because we live in a democracy, early childhood programs and schools in the United States are required to provide environments free from harassment and/or intimidation directed at any person's race, color, religion, national origin, sex, age, or disability.

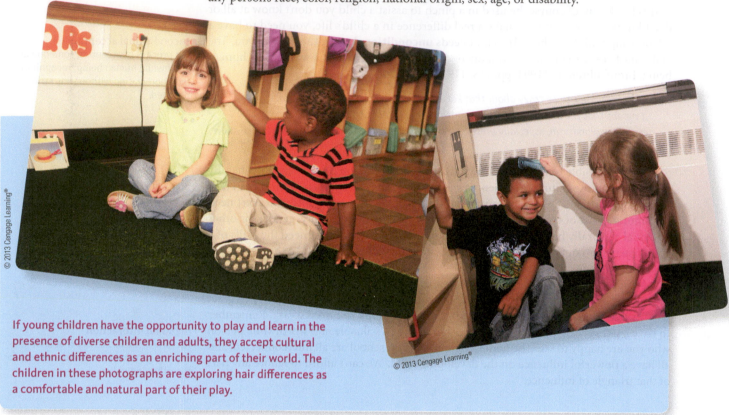

If young children have the opportunity to play and learn in the presence of diverse children and adults, they accept cultural and ethnic differences as an enriching part of their world. The children in these photographs are exploring hair differences as a comfortable and natural part of their play.

© 2013 Cengage Learning®

prejudice
As the name implies, prejudice is the process of prejudging someone. Racial prejudice comprises negative attitudes, beliefs, and rigid stereotypes against an ethnic group that are resistant to change despite contradictory evidence.

racism
A combination of racial prejudice and discrimination. Racism makes the inflexible assumption that individual differences are biologically determined and are therefore unchangeable. Racism does not exist in a vacuum but rather is enacted and reinforced through social, cultural, and institutional practices that endorse the power of one group over another.

sexism
Historically, sexism has been male-driven and accompanied by a belief in male superiority.

Harassment or intimidation is not legal. Most facilities do their best to prevent discrimination simply because it is the right thing to do, an effective and professional business practice, and a part of DAP. Failure to prevent discrimination could result in a devastating lawsuit, a lost reputation, and a failed business. Discrimination damages children's self-esteem and impairs their ability to function in a diverse society.

Our knowledge of culture can help sensitize us and ensure that we make children's experiences supportive of their developing self-image. Even a child in a loving, supportive family within a strong, healthy community can be affected by **prejudice** from the larger society or school. **Racism**, **sexism**, **negative stereotyping**, and **discrimination** harm children physically, emotionally, socially, and intellectually. The developmental progress of the *whole* child requires that family, school, and others treat him as a valued human being.

5-3a Where Did Prejudice Come From?

Destructive cultural behaviors such as prejudice didn't come from thin air. They weren't just thought up one day by a group of evil villains who wanted to create harm in the world. They slowly evolved over many centuries as a primitive **cultural adaptation**, long before cars, telephones, and jets ever came along. Culture is the critical element that has helped human societies survive in diverse locations across the globe—from frozen wastelands to burning deserts, from tropical forests to mountains and plains.

Sometimes, though, adaptations that worked in the early ancestral environment in which they evolved don't necessarily work later as the environment changes. Perhaps some tiny, ancient, primitive tribe, frightened that its very survival depended on making sure everyone stick together and avoid other tribes, was the first to start negative stereotyping and prejudice. Maybe thousands of years ago in a hostile environment it may have seemed logical to shun or fight anyone who looked different or sick. Survival was probably pretty complicated then.

But slowly evolved cultural adaptations such as prejudice can have terribly dysfunctional behavioral effects in today's global cultural environment. *Prejudice hurts children and families and works against our economic interest as a global society. We must end prejudice.*

5-3b When Does Discrimination Begin?

At about the age of 4 years, children begin telling other children they can't play because "you don't have the right kind of sneakers," "you are a girl," or "you aren't wearing a Cinderella ring like we are." Young children don't know better, but it hurts, and it is a rudimentary form of discrimination. That's when we need to use Vivian Paley's (1992) class rule, "You can't say you can't play." This rule fits in our basic rules category "Be respectful." Discrimination may or may not be based on prejudice, although when children interact without adequate adult supervision, discrimination may sometimes escalate into prejudice. Research shows that prejudice leads to hatred.

In fact, research suggests that prejudice and discrimination feed on and enhance each other (Frederickson & Knobel, 1980). Allport (1954) and Milner (1983) wrote about the negative and unreasonable thinking strategies that are characteristic in prejudiced people. Allport refers to these attitudes as "faulty and inflexible," and Milner describes them as "irrational." This inflexibility leads prejudiced individuals to refuse to change their prejudices even when they are faced with contradictory information. Discrimination occurs when hurtful actions are inflicted on others simply because of their association with a particular group. As we work with children using DAP, our learning methods will specifically help children develop flexible thinking strategies. Children will have the capacity as adults to think logically about issues and make rational choices.

5-3c What Are Early Signs of Prejudice?

An early indication of prejudice (or prejudgment) that we need to watch for and squelch is any sign that children are being **stigmatized** (labeled and excluded) on the basis of some different physical characteristic or item of clothing—such as wearing orthopedic shoes, being tall, or wearing a yarmulke (a traditional Jewish head covering). Teachers must take whatever steps are necessary to ensure that finger pointing, teasing, and name-calling don't happen and that all children find their niche.

Direct teaching can help children learn and accept differences. Using multicultural books about others with a wide range of differences is essential for developing empathy in youngsters. You will find a huge selection of delightful children's books in the Appendix of this book that are ideal for helping the children learn to respect differences.

Sometimes children target other children to bully and stigmatize simply because they are looking for a scapegoat. An insecure child trying to justify her own failures or trying to im-

negative stereotyping
To categorize individuals in a group according to an oversimplified, standardized (usually racist or sexist) image or idea that ignores the unique characteristics of the individual.

discrimination
Participation in harmful actions toward others because of their membership in a particular group; the behavioral manifestation of negative prejudice.

cultural adaptation
The process of human societies making cultural changes to better accommodate diverse environments across the globe. Slowly evolving adaptations may have neutral or even maladaptive effects in a rapidly changing cultural environment.

stigmatized
Labeled as socially undesirable on the basis of some specific characteristic; such labeling damages the stigmatized person's self-esteem and excludes him or her socially.

▶❚❚ TeachSource Video

© 2013 Cengage Learning®

Multicultural Lessons: Embracing Similarities and Differences in Preschool Education

Watch this Video Case on multiculturalism. In addition to answering the five viewing questions that follow the video, please respond to the following:

1. In this chapter you read that exposure to culture should not be just an occasional "vacation" for children, but rather a daily experience. Describe three ways the teacher in this video made culture a daily part of the children's learning.

2. Watch the bonus video to listen to the reading of *Cleversticks*. Based on what you have read this chapter, think about this story time in terms of multiculturalism. In your opinion, did this learning experience successfully get the children thinking about a cultural difference? Explain your answer.

scapegoating
Putting blame on another by someone who wants to cause harm or is unwilling to take responsibility for his or her own actions.

group identity
A young child constructs group identity primarily by internalizing whatever that child's family considers important in defining who is "like us." Creating a strong and positive group identity is essential for young children who happen to be part of a cultural grouping that has been devalued or stigmatized by the larger society.

self-identity
The set of characteristics that a person recognizes as belonging uniquely to himself or herself and constituting his or her own individuality.

press her social group may try scapegoating a weaker child to enhance her own social status among her peers. But as Katz's (1981) research shows, children are frequently fickle about the persons they try to stigmatize. That uncertainty often leads children to exaggerate either their negative or positive responses. One exaggerated negative response may be expressed as hatred. It upsets us to see such brutal negative emotions in young children.

To avoid a spiraling negative effect on child guidance for all the children involved, we must stop stigmatizing and scapegoating immediately. Teachers must help the insecure child who was tempted to stigmatize or scapegoat find socially appropriate ways to impress her friends and become more self-confident. Research shows that children with strong self-acceptance are less likely to become prejudiced against others. Prejudiced individuals tend to have low self-acceptance (Fishbein, 2002; Taylor, 2000).

Helping children get along socially in a diverse group is important. The development of prejudice and discrimination in young children harms the development of a **group identity**, as well as **self-identity**. The psychological literature suggests that a group identity emerges between the ages of 3 and 4 years and increases for at least several years after that.

Just sticking diverse children into a classroom next to each other does not necessarily help them learn to get along together, especially if the children always separate into racial or ethnic groups for work, lunch, and playtime. Children often need direct teaching so they can learn to recognize and value positive things about their playmates who look or behave differently. Research does strongly indicate that positive, cooperative, successful social and work interactions among diverse groups of children will reduce prejudice throughout their lives (Fishbein, 2002; Taylor, 2000).

5-3d How Can We Teach Young Children to Resist Bias?

Between the ages of 2 and 5 years, children become aware of their general identity, their gender, and some of the ways in which they are the same as and different from others. Depending on their environment, by the age of 5 years they may already be intensely aware of their cultural identity or only vaguely conscious of it.

This is a time in their lives when children are particularly vulnerable to absorbing both positive and negative attitudes and bias from those around them. It is a critical time to help children form strong, positive self-images and learn to get along with and respect people who are different from themselves. If we want children to feel good about themselves and to respect others, we must learn how to help them resist the biases and prejudices that are still far too prevalent in our society.

Young children innocently ask embarrassing questions, often at exactly the wrong moment: "Why can't I ride in a big chair with wheels like that man?" "Why does that pink boy have little spots on his nose?" "Why is that lady so fat?" "Why doesn't that little girl have any lip?" As part of the enculturation process, we must help children learn about not staring and about remembering that *everyone* has feelings and deserves to be treated with respect even if they look different.

Of course, we should always answer the child's questions about other people's differences honestly. We don't want to do anything that would cause embarrassment to the person who has been pointed out. But we should find a way to assure that the child's questions are answered honestly and at an appropriate age level so there will be no mystery. We know that it is not cute or funny to point out the physical flaws of others, so we will make sure any laughing or egging on by adults or older children is stopped immediately. Our goal is to help children see people who seem different as real people who have feelings inside just like theirs. See Positive Focus 5.1.

5-3e The Antibias Curriculum

DIVERSITY

The antibias curriculum should be approached not as a subject area but as an ever-present thread woven throughout all curriculum areas and throughout each and every day. Louise Derman-Sparks (Derman-Sparks & A.B.C. Task Force, 1989, p. 2), a leader in antibias curriculum, says:

Children learn to value diversity not just through the materials and activities but also from the attitudes that are revealed to them each day in the behavior, words, and body language

What We Can Do to Help Children Resist Bias

- Work on self-awareness of bias.
- Use language that doesn't stereotype anyone (*mail carrier*, *fire fighter* instead of *mailman*, *fireman*).
- Because bias exists, we must counteract it—or else support it through our silence.
- Respond to each child and family in a manner that reflects acceptance and respect.
- Interact daily with each child on a personal level—thus helping to ensure that she feels valued.
- Immediately stop any stigmatizing, rejecting, or bullying.
- Provide materials that illustrate men and women in nontraditional roles.
- Provide materials that illustrate people with ability differences in familiar activities.
- Provide materials that attract children from different cultural backgrounds.
- Provide activities that respect and value many different cultural traditions.
- Help children distinguish between inappropriate feelings of superiority and appropriate feelings of self-esteem and pride in their own heritage.
- Provide opportunities for children to interact with other children who are ethnically, economically, culturally, and in abilities different from themselves.
- Respectfully listen to and answer children's questions about themselves and others. Don't ignore, change the subject, or in any way make the child think she is bad for asking such a question.
- Teach children how to challenge biases about who they are. Give them tools to confront those who act biased against them.
- Use accurate and fair images in contrast to stereotypes, and encourage children to talk about the differences. Help them to think critically about what they see in books, movies, greeting cards, comics, and on TV.
- Let children know that unjust things can be changed. Encourage children to challenge bias, and involve children in taking action on issues relevant to their lives.
- Building a healthy self-identity is a process that continues throughout our lives. Help children get a head start by teaching them to resist bias and to value the differences between people as much as the similarities.

TeachSource Digital Download

of the adults around them. Recognizing this, adults must carefully think about their own behavior, as well as the total classroom environment.

Derman-Sparks talks about classrooms that approach multicultural education as "tourists." On holidays and special occasions they make token efforts to acknowledge that there are various cultural groups in the community or world. Children take canned goods to homeless shelters at Thanksgiving, read about Martin Luther King, Jr. every January, and make tortillas on Cinco de Mayo. But they always go back to business as usual the next day, just like tourists after a vacation at some exotic location. The lesson they learn is that this is our real life and other cultures are something exotic. That is not the lesson we want to teach (Derman-Sparks & Olsen Edwards, 2010; Derman-Sparks & Ramsey, 2006).

The antibias curriculum is something that happens as a part of life—something the children can integrate into their daily physical, social, emotional, and intellectual interactions. As teachers learn about the cultural practices of the families of the various children in the program, some of those cultural practices can be made a part of the day-to-day routines of the program.

If your program serves food, are you just serving regular bread? What about Mexican flour or corn tortillas? Middle Eastern pita bread? Indian naan? Unleavened bread?

Native American fry bread? Of course, finances and convenience will play into your choices, but look at all the options. Grocery stores and supply services are becoming increasingly aware of diverse populations' changing tastes.

How do you greet the children in the morning, and how do you say goodbye? What are the various ways the children say hello and goodbye in their own homes? What if the children learn to say hello and goodbye in different ways at school? Would that be meaningful to your group of children? Or, what about learning different ways to say I'm sorry: for example, in sign language, Spanish, Vietnamese?

An important way in which cultural diversity is represented in the classroom is through the images that are present in the environment. Books, pictures, and other items representing children or family members should feature people of different ethnicities, genders, and ages. Music, art, and literature should be selected to reflect ethnic and cultural diversity and should reflect the lives of children with ability differences and girls in heroic and exciting roles. Children should hear songs from around the world and experience firsthand things like food, clothing, and toys that are typical of other cultures. Culture must be integrated throughout the curriculum in day-to-day activities and materials that stay in the classroom. Culture can't just be dabbled in "tourist style" on holidays (Derman-Sparks & Ramsey, 2006).

DIVERSITY

5-3f How Can I Spot Bias, Stereotypes, and Myths?

No matter how hard we try, in our society today, young children inevitably will be exposed to some racist and sexist attitudes. If these attitudes are pervasive, however, they can distort children's perceptions until stereotypes and myths about underrepresented groups begin to be accepted as reality. See Positive Focus 5.2.

Positive Focus 5.2 How Multicultural Is My School?

Families
- Are we knowledgeable about and sensitive to the cultures of parents?
- Do we connect with children's families, home language, and culture as a foundation for children's learning?
- Do we identify and focus on common goals that we share with parents?
- Do we find supportive, culturally respectful ways to compromise on/resolve issues with parents?

Curriculum
- Do classroom practices demonstrate an understanding of diverse learning styles?
- Do classroom materials accurately represent the life experiences and contributions of different cultural and ability groups and genders?
- Do we encourage all children to participate at their challenge level in all types of learning experiences, regardless of gender, ability, or culture?

Respect
- Do teachers and children value and respect cultural differences?
- Do we treat children fairly? Do we recognize valuable qualities in each child and identify valuable contributions coming from children of different cultural and ability groups and genders?

If a child can be helped to think on a developmentally appropriate level about such things as racism, sexism, and prejudice through picture books, for example, he may then be able to generalize that skill to practical life situations.

We always want to try to surround children with the most unbiased environment possible. But as children begin to develop the skills to think logically, around the age of 4 or 5 years, we need to help them learn how to identify bias. If a child can be helped to think on a developmentally appropriate level about such things as racism, sexism, and prejudice through picture books, for example, he may then be able to generalize that skill to practical life situations.

Raise the children's awareness. Have them help look through the books that are available to the children in your care. Do the books accurately reflect the cultures of the children? The surrounding community? The larger community? Read the guidelines below and use them to analyze your school's books and other **media**. Involve children in making constructive changes. (Could the children be actively involved in a fundraiser?) Everything doesn't have to be changed overnight, but set specific goals. Change only comes with determination.

media
Materials that convey information and cultural expression. Media can bring data by paper (books, magazines), film (videos), computer (cloud storage, Internet, Podcasts, CDs, DVDs, or BluRay), electronic wires or airwaves, (TV, radio), and so on.

ethics
The ideals and the shared conceptions of professional responsibility that reflect the aspirations of a group of practitioners and affirm their commitment to the core values of their field. The basic principles that are intended to guide their conduct and assist them in resolving dilemmas encountered in their field.

5-3g What Is Our Ethical Responsibility?

When we accept responsibility for the care and education of a child, we implicitly promise to follow our profession's **ethics** and look beyond that child's runny nose, messy hair, ability difference, or country of origin to see a precious creation, full of hope and wonder. Only people who are able to approach *all* children with open hearts—people who are ready to give unconditional acceptance to *all* families regardless of creed or color—should enter this important occupation.

It isn't enough just to unconditionally accept the child; we must also unconditionally accept the child's family. Unconditional acceptance does not mean that we think someone is perfect. A parent may have problems and may even be a very difficult person to get to know. The question is, can we get beyond those feelings and unconditionally accept that person as a worthwhile human being? If we cannot find a way to respect that parent, we will not be fully effective in working with and guiding that parent's child. See Positive Focus 5.3.

© 2013 Cengage Learning®

Children can be helped to think about difficult topics through simple picture books. They can learn about treating people fairly no matter how they look or where they come from.

Positive Focus 5.3

Guidelines for Learning to Spot Bias in Books and Other Media

In her antibias education blog, Louise Derman-Sparks offers *An Updated Guide for Selecting Anti-Bias Children's Books* (2013). Following is a summary:

- *Look for stereotypes*—Are underrepresented-group faces depicted as genuine individuals? Do underrepresented-group characters play subservient and passive roles rather than leadership and action roles? Are males the active doers and females the inactive observers?

- *Look for tokenism*—Routinely seeing only one representative of any group in a book teaches young children who is more or less important. Examples of tokenism include books with only one African American child among many white children or having only one book about children with disabilities among many other books.

(Continued)

- *Look for invisibility*—What children do not see in their books also teaches them about who matters and who doesn't in our society. The following people are often invisible in children's books:
  - Families from rural areas
  - Low-income workers
  - Musicians, artists, and writers
  - Children with two dads or two moms
  - People of Arab descent
  - Families who practice religions other than Christianity
  - Families with an incarcerated parent
  - Single mothers or fathers
  - Homeless families
  - Transgender adults and children

- *Check the story line and the relationships between people*—Do white characters in the story possess the power, take the leadership, and make the important decisions? Do people of color, persons with disabilities, and females function in essentially supporting roles?

- *Look at messages about different lifestyles*—Are negative value judgments implied about lifestyles that differ from dominant culture? Do books show diversity within cultural groups—various family structures, living environments, socioeconomic conditions, types of work, and gender roles within the family?

- *Consider the effects on a child's self-image*—Do your book selections imply that some persons are inferior or superior because of their skin color, gender, family income, able-bodiedness, or type of family structure? Will all of the children see themselves and their family's way of life reflected in your book collection?

- *Consider the author's or illustrator's background*—If a story deals with a multicultural theme, what qualifies the author or illustrator to deal with the subject?

- *Check out the author's perspective*—If a book is not about people or events similar to the author or illustrator's background, what qualifies her? Are the author's and illustrator's attitude toward story characters respectful? Do the books in your classroom reflect diverse author and illustrator cultural backgrounds?

- *Watch for loaded words*—A word is "loaded" when it has insulting overtones. Examples of loaded (often racist or sexist) words are *lazy*, *conniving*, *superstitious*, *primitive*, *savage*, and *backward*. Look for use of the male pronoun to refer to both males and females. Although the generic use of *man* was accepted in the past, it is now considered sexist. The following examples show antibias language: *ancestors* instead of *forefathers*; *police officer* instead of *policeman*; *firefighter* instead of *fireman*; *mail carrier* instead of *mailman*.

- *Look at the copyright date*—The realities of our multiracial society and the concerns of underrepresented groups have changed over the years. The copyright dates, therefore, may indicate how likely the book is to be biased, although a recent copyright date is no guarantee of a book's relevance or sensitivity.

Every parent who loves his or her child deserves child care by someone who can respect him or her as a parent. If a parent is unfit, abusive, or neglectful, then authorities should be contacted for intervention. If you are working with parents who are receiving intervention for abuse and neglect, try to find a way to find empathy for the parents' situations. Were they abused and/or neglected as children? Are they overwhelmed economically and/or emotionally? Are they fighting substance addiction? An abusive mate? Sometimes good people have really bad problems. Focus on trying to find something positive in the parents you are dealing with. Let the authorities focus on stopping the abuse and neglect. Our job is to focus on a caring bond of open communication about the education of the child, even if we can't quite muster a sense of respect for the parent.

Some of us have difficulty showing warmth and respect for parents who behave in a way that is foreign to us, live a lifestyle we disapprove of, or are unappealing to us because of hygiene or style of dress. If, however, we can't find a way to respect a parent who is neither abusive nor neglectful, then we must decide whether prejudice is preventing us from accepting that adult as a worthwhile human being. And we must carefully try to see the situation from that parent's perspective. Use Bronfenbrenner's advice and try to see the parent as if she were made up of many complicated layers. Put yourself in her place and try to think through what those layers of culture and experience feel like. Does that parent love her child in her own way? Why can't I accept her? What are my issues? Self-reflection can help us stay on the right track, honoring the crucial role parents play in the education of their children. See Positive Focus 5.4 and 5.5.

DIVERSITY

Positive Focus 5.4

How Can We Empower Children from Diverse Cultural Backgrounds?

- Value the welfare of the children and families and avoid practices that are disrespectful, degrading, dangerous, exploitative, intimidating, or physically harmful to children or their families.
- Respect the rights and dignity of children and adults regardless of their race, gender, religion, ethnicity, national origin, sexual orientation, or ability difference.
- Strive to maintain objectivity, integrity, and sensitivity in carrying out the responsibilities of early childhood education.
- Continually seek knowledge and skills that will update and enhance understanding of issues affecting children and families.
- Take action to report any practice or situation that endangers the mental or physical well-being of children so that the situation can be appropriately resolved.
- Respect the privacy of all children and families.

TeachSource Digital Download

Positive Focus 5.5

NAEYC Statement of Commitment to Professional Ethics

As an individual who works with young children, I commit myself to furthering the values of early childhood education as they are reflected in the ideals and principles of the NAEYC Code of Ethical Conduct. To the best of my ability I will

- Never harm children.
- Ensure that programs for young children are based on current knowledge and research of child development and early childhood education.
- Respect and support families in their task of nurturing children.
- Respect colleagues in early childhood care and education and support them in maintaining the NAEYC Code of Ethical Conduct.
- Serve as an advocate for children, their families, and their teachers in community and society.
- Stay informed of and maintain high standards of professional conduct.

(Continued)

naeyc

- Engage in an ongoing process of self-reflection, realizing that personal characteristics, biases, and beliefs have an impact on children and families.
- Be open to new ideas and be willing to learn from the suggestions of others.
- Continue to learn, grow, and contribute as a professional.
- Honor the ideals and principles of the NAEYC Code of Ethical Conduct.

Name (please print): _____

Signature: _____

Date: _____

This Statement of Commitment is not part of the [NAEYC] Code [of ethics] but is a personal acknowledgment of the individual's willingness to embrace the distinctive values and moral obligations of the field of early childhood care and education. It is recognition of the moral obligations that lead to an individual becoming part of the profession. (For more information, see Feeney, S., & Freeman, N. (1999). *Ethics and the early childhood educator: Using the NAEYC code*. Washington, DC: NAEYC.)

The hard-core avenues for encountering prejudice are usually familiar to all of us in the United States—hate-filled racial prejudice, religious intolerance, gay bashing, needless barriers for persons with ability differences, and gender stereotypes that stop girls and women from reaching their goals. Persons from other countries around the world have also had to cope with varying levels of prejudice—from countries where discrimination is minimal to countries where horrific bloodbaths have taken place in the name of ethnic cleansing.

We may not be as familiar with the term **ethnocentrism** as we are with some of the other terms related to prejudice. Ethnocentrism is very often an unconsciously held assumption that one's own culture is superior to all others. It is the sort of belief that has not been consciously examined or really thought about logically. It is just an unconscious presumption that shows up in the holder's everyday attitudes. Typically, ethnocentric people shun outright prejudice, but their subtle discrimination slips through the cracks as they give evidence of being condescending toward other cultures.

People who are ethnocentric often claim to be open-minded, but they may see cultural traits that are different from their own as meaningless, morally wrong, comical, or just plain peculiar. For example, they may mention to a friend that it's just weird to wear a burka (an all-enveloping cloak worn by some Muslim women) to an American grocery store; they will offer this opinion without even thinking about what that burka means to the woman wearing it.

Ethnocentric people may make jokes about and casually mimic word mispronunciations by an immigrant without really wondering how it feels to struggle in a country where you are trying to learn a second language as an adult. We each need to watch ourselves carefully for ethnocentrism. Some bits of it lurk in each of us, ready to leap out if we don't continually reexamine our cultural assumptions. We each need to regularly think about how it feels to be in someone else's shoes.

ethnocentrism
The deeply felt belief (possibly unconsciously held) that one's own culture is superior to all others. Being unyielding in attachment to one's own way of life and condescending and intolerant toward other cultures. Alien cultural practices are often viewed as being not just different but as silly, weird, evil, or unnatural.

5-4 How Culture Shapes Guidance

The ideas that some North Americans take for granted about the nature of infancy and childhood are different from those held by others in different parts of the world and at different times in history. Other North Americans, some who may be first-generation immigrants, hold dramatically different perspectives. By carefully examining each of our own beliefs and assumptions about children, we can recognize and put into perspective biases and miscommunications that may interfere with our ultimate goal of effective child guidance.

Child care practices have been strikingly different over time for various economic groups. A long period of protected childhood has largely been a luxury of people with middle and upper incomes. Ideas about early childhood have changed according to culture and how much money the family had (Bremner, 1974; Cole, 1950; Glubok, 1969; McGraw, 1941; Neidell, 2004; Osborn, 1980; Reyes, 2007; Rousseau, 1893; Ulich, 1954).

People from different cultural and economic backgrounds frequently hold starkly contrasting views about what proper child care should be. Methods of caring for and educating young children routinely used by families in one community may shock and repel families in another community, and vice versa. A mother in one cultural setting may be astonished that a mother in another setting still allows her 2-year-old to nurse at the breast, whereas the nursing mother may be horrified that the first mother allows her 2-year-old to eat candy and drink soda. In some settings, people expect infants to be taken everywhere the parents go. They think that is good for babies. In other settings, people think it is much better for infants to be left safely at home in their cribs with a babysitter.

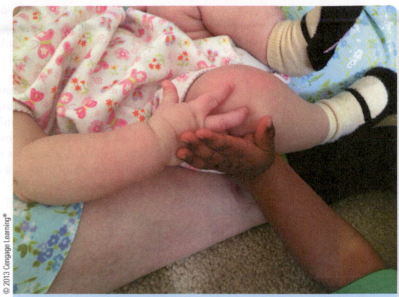

© 2013 Cengage Learning®

Culture plays a key role in defining how parents care for their children.

Guidance strategies believed essential or healthy to growth by some early educators may be considered silly or manipulative by others. Some sincere parents believe misbehaving children should be spanked. Some caregivers believe misbehaving children should be made to sit in a chair for punishment. Many early childhood experts do not like either of those two ideas. Beliefs can vary dramatically among adults who care deeply about young children.

Some people think infants can be made to learn at an accelerated pace by being shown flashcards of letters and numbers. Others think no child of any age should be subjected to flashcards. Social workers, early educators, and child care professionals have often felt the tension among these opposing views. Professionals have sometimes been snagged unknowingly by their own culturally biased inflexibility.

Perception of desirable and appropriate care for children reflects the cultural beliefs of a person at a given time and place in history. The socialization of a new generation reflects the goals, philosophies, and values of the parent generation related to their specific social and economic circumstances. In other words, **culture** plays a key role in defining acceptable methods for dealing with children.

Cultural bias is inescapable. To create a classroom environment that is a small model of a **pluralistic culture**, however, cultural differences must be understood, accepted, valued, and respected. We live in a world where cultures are no longer isolated. People representing countless divergent cultures move around the world every day.

Communication is instant and becoming accessible to almost everyone in the world by cell phone and computer. There is no room for intolerance of cultural diversity. Individuals have a right to keep their own distinctive cultural roots and uniqueness. Each of us has a right to celebrate our own heritage. But we must also make compromises when strong evidence emerges indicating that a culturally based tradition is harmful or ineffective in reaching desired goals (Tomasello et al., 1993).

People used to believe that applying leaches to suck blood out of people cured many diseases. Bloodletting with leaches was discovered to be harmful in most situations, so that tradition needed to go. In many parts of the world, it has been believed that eating such things as the heart of a lion, ground-up elephant trunks, and rhinoceros horns would alleviate impotence and heal disease.

culture
The traditional beliefs and patterns of behavior that are passed down from parents to children by a society; beliefs, customs, practices, and social behavior of any particular cluster of people whose shared beliefs and practices identify the particular nation, religion, ability, gender, race, or group to which they belong.

cultural bias
Unfair preference for or dislike of something or someone based on culture.

pluralistic culture
(See *cultural pluralism*.) Cultural pluralism promotes each group's right to preserve and practice its own cultural traditions without interference or prejudice.

We allow our ignorance to prevail upon us and make us think we can survive alone, alone in patches, alone in groups, alone in races, even alone in genders.
—*Maya Angelou*

Obviously, there isn't much research indicating the effectiveness of ground-up wild animal parts in curing disease or impotence. There is, however, a great deal of research telling us how few endangered animals are left in the world. We must be tolerant of other's choices, but when we want to work together to achieve the same goal, compromise is the magic word.

DIVERSITY

In one country culturally committed to medical products from wild animals but facing world pressures for protecting the remaining endangered wild animals, a creative zookeeper worked out a compromise. He raised funds for the zoo by selling elephant urine, snakeskin, hair shed by lions, dung from tigers and bears, and anything else the predators left behind. The animals weren't harmed and purchasers had their important physical substances from predators at the top of the food chain. Everyone compromised and everyone won.

PRACTICAL APPLICATION CASE

Boba Rebear and Salty Green Paper

The day Ying Ying started preschool he was only 3 and very scared. He didn't know a single word of English. He needed open-heart surgery in an English-speaking hospital, and his doctors urgently needed him to attend preschool to learn some English before the surgery. But poor Ying Ying didn't like the doctors, the hospital, or the preschool, so he cried—oh, how he howled, endlessly it seemed.

The teachers tried patiently to interest him in the soft white bunny in the science center, the wonderful block center, even the food preparation center, but he just sobbed inconsolably. He didn't want to be hugged. He didn't want to be touched. He just cried.

After several days, at circle time, it was Malika's turn to lead the group in a chant. Well, Malika was an amazing child, a beautiful, confident African-American child who loved the spotlight. Of course, she picked her cultural folk favorite, a jazzed-up rhyming version of "The Three Bears." Malika-style, she sashayed right up to the front of the circle and led her chant with uninhibited charm, energy, and talent (not to mention pizzazz):

Once upon a time in a little log cabin
Lived the three bears—CHA, CHA, CHA.
One was the papa, one was the mama
And one was the wee bear—CHA, CHA, CHA.
One day they went a walking in the cool woods a talkin'
And along came a girl, a girl with long hair.
Her name was Goldilocks and upon the door she knocked,
But no one was there; no, no one was there.
So she walked right in and she had herself a chair,
Cause she didn't care, the girl with long hair.
Then home, home, home came the three bears.

Someone's been sitting in my chair, said the papa bear.
Someone's been sitting in my chair said the mama bear.
Hey Boba Rebear, said the little wee bear,
Someone has broken my chair—CRASH!
Then Goldilocks she woke up, she broke up the party,
And she beat it out of there; she beat it out of there,
And that is the story of the three little bears
Boba Re, Boba Re, Boba Ra Ra Ra!

Of course the class responded gleefully, heart and soul, and the classroom fairly rocked with this bebop chant. Ying Ying's sobs were completely drowned out by the ruckus. When the chant ended, it dawned on everyone that Ying Ying wasn't crying anymore. He was standing there looking amazed and actually grinning. Malika yelled out, "Hey, Ying Ying likes it. He stopped crying. Let's do it again."

Apparently, Ying Ying's Chinese cultural background had in no way, shape, or form prepared him for a roomful of children cheerfully boogieing down to a jazzy version of The Three Bears. Malika led the class in the rhyme again. This time Ying Ying shook with laughter. He laughed until he cried. The children enthusiastically "Boba Reed" and "Boba Rood" with every jazzy bone in their bodies over and over. Well, that is when Ying Ying fell in love with Malika.

Malika took Ying Ying under her wing, and he became her constant shadow. Soon he had mastered her cocky walk and learned to speak English, making sure to pronounce his words with an African-American edge just like Malika. He was her "BFF" buddy.

One day when Ying Ying's mother, Mrs. Sung, came to pick him up from school, he was at Malika's side. Mrs. Sung opened her purse and gave Ying Ying a small rectangle of crinkly green tissue. Ying Ying instantly and eagerly popped it into his mouth.

Malika shrieked, "Teacher! Teacher! Ying Ying's mama fed him green paper!" The teacher visited with Mrs. Sung and then said, "Malika, in Ying Ying's country this is a great treat for children. It is made of seaweed and it tastes salty. Would you like to taste?"

Nothing in Malika's cultural background prepared her for eating crinkly green paper. The teacher and Mrs. Sung talked some more with Ying Ying and Malika and decided to wrap some laver (dried, edible seaweed) for Malika to take home to show her parents.

At home that evening, Malika's parents loved the idea of her trying the laver. They even tasted it too. Malika loved the taste of the laver so much that she thought Mrs. Sung should bring more of it one day for all the children at preschool to have a taste of "green paper."

Malika and Ying Ying came from totally different cultural backgrounds, but with the help of supportive teachers and parents, they learned to appreciate, respect, and value each other's cultural background.

Case Discussion Questions

1. What would have happened if the teacher had insisted that the children calm down, sit with their legs "criss-cross applesauce," and sing "nicely" with an "inside" voice?
2. What would have happened if Malika had been sent away from the circle for yelling out at circle time?
3. Which of the following is the more effective way for teachers to respond when an exciting, joyous group activity suddenly turns into an overstimulated and out-of-control activity?
   a. Lecture the children about how and why their behavior is inappropriate.
   b. Begin an even more active activity like dancing to fast music.
   c. End the activity and take the children outdoors.
4. What would have happened if Malika had called Ying Ying a baby and told him to leave her alone and stop following her around all the time?

Cultural predicaments happen frequently in child care centers. For example, a teacher might say, "Mrs. Quiroga, I noticed that you seemed surprised when I mentioned that children, both boys and girls, are encouraged to wear T-shirts, jeans, sneakers, and other such play clothes to school. Did you have a question about that?" Mrs. Quiroga's cultural background may cause her to place an especially high value on dressing her children well. She expected her daughter to wear a neatly ironed, frilly dress to preschool each day. To Mrs. Quiroga, the picture of her daughter, Lupita, wearing a paint-smeared T-shirt and dust-covered jeans, with sand in her hair, evokes an all-too-real image of poverty, not the picture-perfect image of DAP.

Research tells us that play is extremely important to children's social and emotional development, growth, and learning (Bodrova & Leong, 2010; Brown & Vaughan, 2009; Elkind, 2003; Emde et al., 2003; Favez, 2006; McClelland et al., 2000; Raver, 2002; Raver & Zigler, 1997; Warren et al., 2000). Communication is needed to help Mrs. Quiroga understand why her daughter will benefit by being dressed appropriately to paint, play in the sand, crawl around on the floor, use messy substances such as glue, and generally get dirty and have fun. The conference may have several different types of conclusions.

If the teachers agree to respect Mrs. Quiroga's preference that Lupita wear dresses, Lupita will miss out on many important activities or risk ruining her dresses. If Mrs. Quiroga agrees to dress Lupita casually, she may feel disrespected. If, as a parent–teacher resource team, they decide together that Lupita will bring a second set of clothes to school for Lupita to change into for play, the goal will be accomplished and Mrs. Quiroga will feel empowered because her needs have been respected. She will also understand more about *why* it is so important to Lupita's learning and development for her to paint and play with messy materials.

Of course, there is always the chance that Mrs. Quiroga will not understand and will not want to change her cultural viewpoint. She might want Lupita in clean, starched, frilly dresses every day and want to find her spotlessly clean at the end of the day—an impossible task for a DAP learning environment. Our task as early childhood professionals in that case is to continue to communicate as caringly, respectfully, and honestly as we can about what DAP is and what we are trying to accomplish during the day. Patience, persistence, and compromise offer the best chance to work through this obstacle.

Janet Gonzalez-Mena (2008) describes a marvelous compromise reached by parents and child care professionals in one center. African-American parents often express frustration about their children coming home with heads full of sand. Parents whose young children have fine, straight hair have it easy when it comes to brushing and washing out sand. Parents whose children have dense, curly hair (especially if it needs certain kinds of hair conditioning products to be manageable) find it grueling to get the sand out each night.

Many African-American parents complain that sand actually cuts their children's hair. These parents know playing in the sandbox is important, but they also would like to have a clean, presentable child. In one child care center, this long-standing problem was resolved by a particularly clever solution. Parents were invited to send shower caps for the children to wear whenever they played on the playground. The caps were so popular that children of other cultural backgrounds insisted on wearing caps too!

DIVERSITY

Forming effective relationships between families and early childhood professionals means deciding on common goals and working out compromises everyone can accept (Bruns & Corso, 2001; Christian, 2006; Dinnebeil & Rule, 1994; Kalyanpur & Harry, 1999; Kochanek & Buka, 1998; Lynch & Hanson, 1998). Families are more likely to develop effective working relationships with professionals they trust (Dinnebeil & Rule, 1994). Of course, trust is essential to cooperative, effective collaboration between families and educators as they strive to provide positive guidance (Grant & Ray, 2010).

BrainFacts

What Can We Learn from Neuroscience?

Healthy brain development requires nurturing social interaction and environmental experiences.

- Many parents must work one, two, or more jobs to survive financially and are compelled to leave children in the care of persons who may not be able or willing to provide developmentally appropriate care (Evans et al., 2005; Evans & English, 2002; Farah et al., 2006; Feldman & Eidelman, 2009; Luby et al., 2012).

- Healthy brain development in babies requires nurturing attention and extensive social interaction with caregivers (National Scientific Council on the Developing Child, 2004; Rushton & Larkin, 2001; Thompson, 2001).

- Family stress can result in destructive changes in young children's brain development (Bachman, Coley, & Carrano, 2011; Evans & Wachs, 2010; Hsuch & Yoshikawa, 2007; Jyoti, Frongillo, & Jones, 2005; Kochanska, Kim, & Koenig Nordling, 2012; National Scientific Council on the Developing Child, 2005).

- Disadvantaged children often reach school without developing necessary skills (Cook & Wellman, 2004; Hawkins et al., 2008; Lawhon & Cobb, 2002).

- The result can cause devastating delays that harm children's ability to succeed in school, career, and life (Noble, McCandliss, & Farah, 2007; Paulussen-Hoogeboom et al., 2007).

- The achievement gap of disadvantaged children happens long before these children get to school and it is very hard to close thereafter (National Scientific Council on the Developing Child, 2004; Sroufe, 2005; Twardosz, 2012).

- A child's cognitive capacity is not fixed but changeable with appropriate support (Gilkerson, 2001; Kumanyika & Grier, 2006; Pascual-Leone et al., 2005; Ramey & Ramey, 2004; WCCF, 2013).
- Developmentally appropriate care in the first years can prevent achievement gaps, boost school achievement, and create healthier long-term outcomes (Center on the Developing Child at Harvard University, 2011; Decety & Michalska, 2010; Heckman, Pinto, & Savelyev, 2013; Thompson, 2001).

Cultural sensitivity does not include stereotypes about what different groups like and dislike. Differences among people inside a cultural group can be as great as differences between cultural groups (Lynch & Hanson, 1998). Every person should be seen and related to as a unique individual. Some people expect a formal relationship with early education professionals (Schwartz & Ros, 1995). Others expect an informal, friendly relationship (Gonzalez-Alvarez, 1998). See Positive Focus 5.6.

Positive Focus 5.6

How Do Young Children Learn About Their Role in the World?

From birth to school age, children develop basic concepts about how the world works and what their role is in that world. Children get different ideas depending on how we treat them. Following are some typical examples of the way adults treat children in homes and early childhood programs. Of these examples, identify the situations that might reflect cultural practices or traditions in your community. How can we bring DAP and culture closer together? Parent education, compromise, rethinking teaching procedures? What will you do?

Not DAP: If children's environment is rigid and they are herded through the day with no chance for individual choice, they learn that the world is no-nonsense or even harsh and that their individual needs, interests, and ideas don't matter much. This type of learning environment may prepare children to obediently push a broom or stand patiently for endless hours at a conveyor belt in a factory, but it will not necessarily prepare them for self-directed jobs in medicine, scientific inquiry, creative invention, and academic discovery.

Example: Children are all required to sit patiently and quietly at a long table. Everyone waits until all are finished, no matter how long it takes. Children are told and shown exactly how to glue precut pieces of the teacher-planned Christmas tree art activity project onto a paper plate. If a child does this differently than the adult intends, the adult makes the child do it over or the adult does it herself and puts the child's name on it.

DAP: If, in contrast, the environment is flexible and geared to individual needs, choices, and responsibilities, children learn that the world is cooperative and that with persistence and effort, they can affect the world around them.

Example: Craft materials such as paper plates, glue, glitter, cotton balls, and bits of colored construction paper are made available in the art center. Children are not shown an adult model to copy but rather are encouraged to use their own imaginations to create Christmas, Hanukkah, Kwanzaa, Ramadan, or other seasonal decorations. When done, the children responsibly clean up the materials. Unique differences in the finished products are recognized and honored, and all are displayed with pride.

(Continued)

Not DAP: If early authority figures are aloof from the children and control them by issuing frequent imperative commands ("Be quiet," "Sit up straight," "Stand in line," "Don't talk"), children develop a perception of authority figures as omnipotent powers to be obeyed without question, enemies to be rebelled against, ogres to be feared, obstacles to be avoided, or irrelevant annoyances to be ignored.

Example: The adult attempts to maintain total control by having children do everything in unison—they must all sit and wait passively while the adult has children come up to the front of the class one by one to point out letters of the alphabet or say numbers. Children must all line up to wash hands and use the toilet at the same time. Even if their food becomes stone cold, no child is allowed to eat lunch until all are given the signal to begin together. Children may even be required to stand in straight lines on the playground and do calisthenics for exercise (rather than running and playing freely). The adult imagines that no learning is taking place unless she is in charge and the children are quiet, controlled, and attentive.

DAP: If caring adults are warm, responsive, and assertive, children develop a perception of authority figures as dependable and resourceful allies who protect and help.

Example: The adult structures the environment and the schedule to encourage children to function independently and individually and as part of a cohesive group. Children choose learning materials from learning centers and work at their own pace during large, uninterrupted blocks of time. They generally use the restroom according to their own body needs rather than according to group routines. Transitions from one activity to the next are flexible rather than abrupt. If a child finishes lunch earlier than others, she can throw away her trash, sponge off her area of the table, and then curl up and look at picture books until it is time for nap.

Not DAP: If adults treat children as underlings with few rights and are careless, degrading, or threatening in their treatment of children, children learn to treat others with rudeness and aggression and fail to develop self-respect.

Example: Adults often talk to each other as if the children weren't even present, sometimes laughing at or making fun of individual children. Adults order children around without saying *please* or *thank you*. Punishment is meted out according to the adults' moods and whims rather than being based on fair and consistent rules. The adults act as if they are above rules. Adults sit on the tables and shelves, eat and drink while walking around, and shout across the room even though they have told children that those exact behaviors are forbidden.

DAP: If adults treat children as valuable, worthwhile individuals from infancy, children will learn to respect themselves and others.

Example: Adults respond to the needs of children in a timely manner, helping them learn trust. Adults get down at eye level and really listen to children to let them know what they say is worth hearing. Adults use a style of child guidance that is never humiliating, demeaning, or belittling. The child learns self-discipline in a way that is firm, assertive, and self-esteem building. All discipline is based on fair, consistent rules, and adults also show respect for class rules. If children are not allowed to eat, adults don't walk around in front of them drinking coffee and eating a doughnut. If an adult has to stand in a chair to change a light bulb, she explains why it was necessary for her to break a class rule about standing on furniture.

Not DAP: If early caregivers stereotype children by gender, ethnicity, or other characteristics, children internalize the belief that they are limited in what they can achieve.

Example: Adults select only boys to act out the role of the fire marshal in a skit, totally ignoring girls who have their hands raised. Picture books are used that show only one ethnic, cultural, regional, or economic background. Adults take it for granted that all children celebrate Christmas and Easter. A particularly tall 3-year-old is expected to behave more responsibly than a particularly tiny 4-year-old. Children are singled out and treated differently according to how they look, how they dress, or what their parents do for a living.

DAP: If early caregivers see all children as unique individuals who can be helped to reach their own special potential, children develop high expectations for themselves and the self-esteem needed to master challenges they set for themselves.

Example: Children are all seen as unique and valuable individuals. Books, puppets, and dolls are multicultural. Children are helped to appreciate various cultures through food, music, and immersion in diverse cultural practices that expose them to many perspectives. Adults respect and help the children learn about cultural differences in children and their families. Girls and boys are expected to participate fully in all activities, and girls are especially encouraged to be competent and confident.

Not DAP: If the early environment is overly adult-centered and adult-controlled, the child develops a sense of the world as a place where she is helpless.

Example: The adult stands over children, telling them exactly what to do and what will result from each action. Adults see free play at recess as fun but a waste of valuable time. Adults believe that children have little capacity for or interest in learning and so must be taught directly through adult-controlled initiatives.

DAP: If early curriculum is individualized and discovery-oriented, children come to see learning as something actively sought after and knowledge as something one can create. Their learning is spurred by intrinsic curiosity rather than by pressure from parents and teachers.

Example: Early childhood professionals use attractive materials that engage the child's senses, invite her to move her body, and allow her to learn through playful activity. They create an environment that entices the young child to explore, discover, and learn to love learning.

Not DAP: If early role models limit their verbal communication primarily to criticism and commands, then children, who are in the most formative period of their lives for language development, may be discouraged in the development of a level of vocabulary, grammar, and expression that is necessary for later school success.

Example: Adults use worn out clichés, sarcastic overstatements, and meaningless threats. They say things such as "Move, or you're really going to get it!" "Shut up and sit down!" "Hush, I don't want to hear your voice!" "Everybody freeze this instant." "You'd better straighten up and act right." These bossy commands do not require any critical thinking or language expression, only blind obedience.

DAP: If early role models are calm, articulate, accurate, and expressive in their verbal communication with children, and if they are responsive and supportive of children's attempts to express themselves, then children can blossom in their development of communication skills, which form the basis for all later academic learning.

Example: Adults use meaningful statements of cause and effect, descriptions of actual events or consequences, and expressions of honest feelings. The adult's words are relevant to the actual situation. Adults say things such as: "If you stand up at the top of the slide, you may fall down." "If you hurt Genevieve, she may not want to play with you next time." "People have to wash their hands after they use the toilet to keep from spreading germs." "You must walk slowly and quietly here in the library because other people are trying to read." "I feel upset when I see all the pages pulled out of our book." Children are expected to think, understand, predict, and evaluate actions and reactions. Children are exposed to a descriptive and elaborate vocabulary through the adult's expressions.

We each want to be appreciated for all the special qualities inside us and all the possibilities we represent.

If early educators dominate interactions, the family may feel uncomfortable and may not be willing to talk about their needs and concerns (Dennis & Giangreco, 1996; Gudykunst et al., 1996). Domineering teacher styles may be particularly offensive to families from traditional Hispanic, Native American, and Asian backgrounds (Bruns & Corso, 2001; Gonzalez-Alvarez, 1998; Joe & Malach, 1998; Schwarz & Ross, 1995). Resourcefulness in finding community resources and skill in using interpreters are becoming increasingly important for early education professionals. Communicating successfully with diverse families often requires finding community volunteers, family members, computer technology, or professionals fluent in the families' primary language to answer questions and resolve problems (Ohtake, Santos, & Fowler, 2000). Being a sensitive, respectful listener opens the door to understanding the needs and expectations of persons from other cultures.

© 2013 Cengage Learning®

5-5 Respecting Cultural Differences

Accepting cultural differences involves recognition and **respect**. Although few people openly admit to prejudice, most of us consciously or unconsciously lump people together to some extent: Boys are aggressive, the French are romantic, and overweight people are jolly and good-hearted. Some generalizations are patently untrue, and others revolve around some kernel of truth—but every generalization is wrong to some extent. There are boys who are gentle and nonaggressive, French lovers who are clods, and overweight people who are crabby and mean.

Respect means being given the opportunity to be seen as a unique individual rather than as a stereotypical caricature of some larger group. Underneath all the cultural and physical differences, we are all just people. We all want food, comfort, security, fulfillment, and, most of all, the sense of belonging that comes with being valued and respected.

It is possible to urge children to better behavior and more functional habits while clearly letting them know that we accept and respect them as they are. Sometimes adults label children by saying things such as, "Vanessa, you are being so bad. Look how good Jeremy is." This sets an example for stereotyping people whose appearance or behavior is different. We can say instead, "Vanessa, hitting hurts. Use words instead of hitting, please." This way, an unacceptable behavior can be identified without lumping Vanessa into the category of "bad people."

respect
The process of showing regard for the rights and needs of another. To display polite expressions of consideration for another.

Barbara's Special Gifts

A preschool teacher in St. Louis, Missouri, named Barbara Thomson (1989) created a wonderful activity to help children learn not to prejudge. She brought her children to circle time and presented the class with two gifts. One gift was huge and beautifully wrapped with a gorgeous bow on top. The other one was small, ugly, and stained.

The children were asked to choose which they wanted. Of course they all wanted the big, beautiful box. To their surprise, they discovered that the beautiful box held nasty banana peels, old soup cans, and gross apple cores—just garbage, nothing nice at all! The small, ugly box held a delicious special treat made just for the class. As they passed out and munched their wonderful homemade cookies, Barbara asked the children questions about this experience. She talked about how people also have "wrappings" just like the things hidden in the boxes. She asked, "What if someone really nice is 'wrapped' in ugly bad clothes; are they still a really nice person?"

BrainFacts

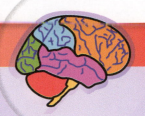

What Can We Learn from Neuroscience?

Poverty too often damages young children's developing brains

- Parents and other caregivers are the essence of the infant's environment, and their protection, nurturing, and stimulation shape early brain development (Marshall, 2011; Paulussen-Hoogeboom, Stams, Hermanns, & Peetsma, 2007).

- Nearly 90 percent of brain growth takes place in a child's first 5 years of life (Marshall, 2011; Twardosz, 2012).

- Interacting with people and objects in the environment wires a baby's brain. Repetition strengthens and refines the wiring (Marshall, 2011).

- Babies come equipped with an irresistible urge to explore and learn (Fischer-Shofty, Levkovitz, & Shamay-Tsoory, 2012).

- The capacity for brain development that enriches the first years of life also makes children vulnerable to harm (Marshall, 2011; Sroufe, 2005).

- What children experience in their social and physical surroundings can either enhance or inhibit the unfolding of their inborn potential (Thompson, 2001).

- Long-term stress, inadequate care, and deprivation create permanent damage to young children's developing neurosensory systems (National Scientific Council on the Developing Child, 2005; Sroufe, 2005).

- Children raised in families coping with the stress of poverty, food insecurity, and community violence typically have more limited vocabulary and undeveloped attentiveness, persistence, impulse control, and cooperativeness compared to children raised in financially secure settings (Hammack et al., 2004; Isaacs et al., 2008).

- Many children lack adequate exposure to environments that promote brain development. This limits brain capacity and can have a life-long negative impact on knowledge and skills (Fischer-Shofty, Levkovitz, & Shamay-Tsoory, 2012; Hawkins et al., 2008).

- Investments in early childhood education can prevent or resolve inequalities that hinder children's development (Poplin & Soto-Hinman, 2006).

- Developmentally appropriate early childhood education helps develop the critical social skills and habits of mind that set the foundation for success in school and life (Thompson, 2001).

- New research on how the growing mind learns confirms the value of NAEYC's constructivist approach, in which environments are designed to gain the learner's attention, foster meaningful connections with prior understanding, and maximize memory through active problem solving (Schiller, 2001; Rushton & Larkin, 2001; Ramey & Ramey, 2004).

Adults should also consider other aspects of cultural exposure. At home, for example, television must be closely monitored because it is a haven for inappropriate material. Young children should not be exposed to television unless all commercials have been removed and the content has been previewed and screened according to the antibias checklist presented previously in this chapter.

Young children should learn terms such as *police officer*, *mail carrier*, and *repairperson* rather than *policeman*, *mailman*, and *repairman*. Teachers, doctors, nurses, and secretaries should be referred to as *he* or *she* rather than in the stereotypical way that implies that all doctors are men and all secretaries are women. Children can learn nursery rhymes and songs in Spanish or Swahili as well as in English. Foods can be offered that sensitize children to regional and national dishes, various ways of preparing foods, and food-related traditions and rituals.

Some of us are obvious in our preference of girls over boys or boys over girls. We unconsciously pit girls against boys. We make comments such as "The boys can go first because all the girls want to do is talk, talk, talk." or "You boys go play. The girls don't like you hanging around causing trouble." Remember, we aren't tourists visiting multiculturalism land on holidays and then going home to business as usual. For effective child guidance, we must transform our classrooms into havens for cultural pluralism. We are creating little democratic communities where all persons are treated with dignity and respect every day!

By age 3, children can recognize and identify different skin colors (Aboud, 2008; Bigler & Liben, 2007; Katz, 1981, 2003; Landreth & Johnson, 1953; Morland, 1972). Babies and young children are very sensitive to subtle body language, tone of voice, and facial expressions, as well as the things we actually say about differences in people. Adults may unconsciously respond more warmly to people who are of similar ethnic and religious backgrounds while snubbing those whose background is different. Sometimes people who are culturally different become invisible to us as we go about our daily business. Maybe we walk right past that office manager sitting in a wheelchair or that African-American woman doctor we stereotypically assumed was a nurse. See Positive Focus 5.7.

DIVERSITY

Positive Focus 5.7

Take Time to Think before You Judge Others

What to Consider

- Do you find yourself having negative thoughts or feelings about a child or parent?

- Does the parent have values, expectations, or communication styles different from your own? Does the child dress, speak, or behave in a way that seems unfamiliar or offensive to you?

- Have you taken steps to evaluate the effectiveness of your program's cultural sensitivity? Have children of different backgrounds had difficulty fitting in?

What to Do

- Respect the uniqueness of each family system. Value every child and parent.

- Remember that a family's cultural differences may relate to their race, ethnicity, religion, nationality, regional heritage, age, wealth, poverty, ability difference, gender, or other cultural difference.

- Don't tell parents what is wrong with their views. Use active listening, involve parents in the program, and always treat them with respect. Acknowledge their values, prior experiences, and cultural knowledge. Identify their strengths and allow them opportunities for recognition and leadership that draw on their individual strengths.

Children need to experience authentic, hands-on DAP learning activities. Young children don't learn well by being told information. Every child needs relevant multicultural experiences, which enable the class to reach true **cultural pluralism** in a diverse school setting.

cultural pluralism
The peaceful coexistence of multiple distinct ethnic, religious, and/or cultural groups within one community or society.

5-5a What Things Should I Know So I Can Be More Considerate to People from Other Cultures?

It would be great to have a simple list of cultural dos and don'ts to memorize that would protect you from offending a parent or coworker of a different background. Unfortunately, life just isn't that simple.

It's great to learn all you can about the cultural ways of other groups. However, individuals are unique, and there is enormous diversity within cultures. Always attributing common characteristics to specific cultural groups tends to create stereotypes—and we certainly don't need any more stereotypes.

DIVERSITY

If you judge people, you have no time to love them.

—Mother Teresa

There are trends or cultural traits common to some—but not all—families of similar cultural backgrounds. African-American and Native American families, for example, tend to place a high cultural value on kinship bonds. They are more likely to rely heavily on extended family members and friends for child care, financial assistance, advice, and emotional support (American Psychological Association, 2003; Dykeman et al., 1996; Lum, 1992; Tower, 1996). It is not unusual for aunts, grandparents, friends, or even older siblings to be the primary care providers for children.

Latino families often express their social enthusiasm through *el abrazo y un beso* (the hug and the kiss). They may mistake other cultures' standoffishness as rejection (Benitez, 2007). Latin American, Asian, and Pacific Island families also rely strongly on the extended family. Asian, Pacific Island, and Native American families may rely on a strict family hierarchy to make decisions. Decisions within Latin American families may be made primarily by the father because of the respect given in his culture to his familial position and the responsibility he bears.

Religion is important to members of many cultures. Southern African-American families especially look to their church communities for spiritual nourishment. Catholicism, the predominant religion for Latin Americans, is a deep source of support and comfort (Benitez, 2007; Rose & Meezan, 1996). Native Americans have strong spiritual feelings about nature and believe they must live in harmony with the earth. The religions of Asians and Pacific Islanders vary greatly, but there is often a common belief that lives are controlled by fate.

Native Americans have great respect for grandparents. Asian grandparents sometimes hold the final authority in child-rearing decisions (Tower, 1996). Sometimes Native American children grow up believing they must restrain their emotions (Lum, 1992; Mcmaster & Trafzer, 2008). Shame has traditionally been used in Asian families as a strategy for disciplining children (Tower, 1996).

Parents and teachers from all cultural backgrounds can learn to talk things over respectfully and, perhaps together, learn more effective methods for reaching child guidance goals together.

5-5b How Can I Help Parents from Other Cultures Feel More Comfortable?

The following cultural tips are often given to teachers to advise them on how to behave politely and courteously and help them avoid embarrassing situations. By all means, try these tips. No one ever complained about too much courtesy. But remember, these bits of information may or may not always apply in real life to every complicated human being you encounter. You still need to get to know the unique individuals you meet to determine what their cultural expectations and needs really are.

DIVERSITY

1. *The Vietnamese gesture for beckoning someone is made by extending the arm with the fingers pointing down and wiggling the fingers.*

Body language differs greatly from culture to culture, and misunderstandings and embarrassment can result when gestures are misinterpreted. For example, the thumb-to-index-finger gesture used in the United States to signal "okay" is considered vulgar in Mexico, but in Japan it is a sign for money. The American gesture used to beckon people (palm up with fingers moving) is considered rude by Vietnamese people because that gesture in their culture is used only to beckon animals. To be safe, it is usually best to avoid using an upward palm to beckon anyone from another culture. Also avoid pointing with your index finger. Those gestures are considered rude in many parts of the world where people opt for other gestures, such as summoning with the palm down and more subtle pointing with the chin or a wave of the palm.

2. *Don't point your finger while discussing negative behaviors of a Hispanic child with his or her parents.*

You probably shouldn't be discussing guidance issues in a child's presence, but if you must, don't wag your index finger at parents (especially Latino parents) during the discussion or you may offend them.

3. *Some African-American cultures expect children to lower their heads and avert their eyes when they are being reprimanded.*

Of course, it's *never* positive guidance to demand that any child look you in the eye while you are correcting him or her. But if a child is African American and is culturally unaccustomed to looking adults in the eye during even positive interactions, gradual, optimistic encouragement in that direction may help her become more comfortable and successful in multicultural settings.

4. *Many African-American parents find it disturbing if not downright insulting to see a teacher touching their preschool or older child.*

A history of institutionalized discrimination may have made African-American communities sensitive and even a bit suspicious. Walking into school and seeing an adult with a hand on their child offends many African-American parents. It draws attention to the child and sends alarm signals that something may be wrong.

DAP involves warm, affectionate interactions between young children and their teachers. With respect, patience, effort, and time, strong bonds of trust develop between teachers and parents. Trust will make it easier for African-American parents to feel comfortable when they see teachers touch their children in appropriate ways.

5. *In many parts of the world—for example, Asia, Eastern Europe, the Middle East, and Thailand—it is considered rude to show the soles of the feet or shoes to others.*

You should avoid crossing your legs in such a way that you expose the soles of your shoes to others in a culturally mixed setting. That's a little thing that may make a big difference. In the housekeeping area, ensure that children put shoes away properly each day. Never allow children to throw shoes at each other.

6. *Use two hands when taking anything from or passing anything to an Asian person, including your business card; using one hand can be interpreted as a sign of disrespect for the receiver. Many Asians will shake hands with both hands as well.*

An Asian parent may give you a business card with pride. Accept it graciously with both hands. If you have a business card, give the parent your business card. In many Asian communities, a business card is regarded as an extension of the individual to be treated with honor and respect. Don't just toss it on your desk.

Perhaps you won't get business cards, but why not take the diaper bag with both hands just to show a little extra politeness and respect? And why not present the child's artwork with two hands instead of one?

7. *When developing a relationship with someone from another culture, take your time. An old Chinese proverb says, "Never talk business before the third cup of tea."*

Americans often launch into business with less regard for relationship-building than for speed and efficiency. This can be confusing and upsetting to people whose culture places more emphasis on politeness than on rushing through business to get the job done quickly. Early childhood professionals can certainly slow down a bit to make their interactions with families more personal.

8. *In many cultures, elders hold a position of great respect and leadership in the family.*

Remember that grandparents and great-grandparents accompanying families may be highly respected by the child's family. Just because that older person is not actively participating in the conversation doesn't mean that she should be treated as invisible. Bring in a translator when possible and if needed. But most importantly, recognize and show respect for elders.

9. *Native American families may take a dim view of Thanksgiving celebrations.*

Some Native American families feel disrespected by Thanksgiving celebrations because Thanksgiving commemorates the coming of European people to North America. Native Americans don't necessarily wish to celebrate something that caused their people to be killed and their culture to be devastated.

Every family's individual religious and cultural perspectives should be respected. Some cultures prohibit foods common in other cultures. Some religions forbid the celebration of birthdays.

Native American cultures typically have religious beliefs that include spiritual reverence in their relationship with nature. For example, some perceive that animals should be mentioned only during seasons when they are present. Speaking of them while they are hibernating or migrating is considered disrespectful.

10. *The left hand is considered unclean in many Middle Eastern cultures.*

Unless members of the Arab culture are handling something considered unclean, they prefer to use the right hand. Moreover, they avoid gesturing with the left hand. In Arab communities, people tend to stand very close to the person they're talking to. The thumbs-up sign, which means "good job" in the United States, is an offensive gesture throughout the Arab world, so be sure to avoid it.

11. *Many Middle Eastern men are forbidden by their religion to shake hands with women.*

To avoid an embarrassing situation, women should avoid offering a handshake to any man they think might be Muslim. A simple nod and "Hi, how are you?" or "Thank you, it was nice to meet you" should be fine instead of a handshake. A Middle Eastern man will offer his hand if he is comfortable with a handshake.

Today's diverse classrooms offer the opportunity for exposure to cultures from around the block and around the world. An open mind and open heart will help teachers grasp nuances of cultures both near and far.

© 2013 Cengage Learning®

5-5c Will These Tips Keep Me from Culturally Offending Anyone?

Unfortunately, no. The world is a very, very big place, and in today's urban settings, there are infinite combinations of cultural backgrounds that can come together. You would need a list the size of an encyclopedia to memorize all the possible ways you might culturally offend or confuse someone from another background.

In addition to languages and ethnic cultures different from your own, you are likely to encounter deaf culture; parents and children with ability differences, religious differences, social and economic differences, and family structure differences; gay, lesbian, bisexual, and transgendered parents and adoptive families; and unfamiliar child-rearing customs unique to different parts of the world (De'Melendez & Beck, 2010; Sparks & Edwards, 2010).

The only really reliable tool is not a memorized bag of tricks, but rather honest, forthright *caring*—being very attentive to make sure parents are comfortable. It is okay to say to a parent (in a genuine, nonthreatening way) something such as, "I am not familiar with your culture, but I want to make sure that the way we care for and teach your child is respectful of your culture." "Please help us do a better job by telling us the things we need to know about your child's special needs." "This is how we usually handle lunch. Are you comfortable with this?" "How can we be more supportive of you and your child?"

We must use thoughtful listening and careful observation of parents' body language to see whether the parents feel uncomfortable, offended, or shocked by something. We must be sensitive to and look for these feelings, and we must encourage conversation. People are often hesitant to express feelings, and they are especially hesitant when those feelings are related to cultural differences. But feelings should be addressed so potential problems can be resolved in a way that is acceptable for all involved.

5-5d Honoring Families' Religious Beliefs and Customs

Unless parents are informed that a program is religious, teachers should focus on supporting multicultural learning in an environment of tolerance and respect that is free of teaching any religious view or doctrine. Teachers, however, should allow children to express their own beliefs and traditions. Children cannot be expected to drop their spirituality at the door when they come to school.

There is a stark difference between children freely expressing their own spiritual feelings and beliefs and teachers instructing children in one set of beliefs without parents' prior knowledge and consent. Allowing a child the freedom to pray, for example, is very appropriate. Instructing children how to pray (without parental knowledge or approval) is not appropriate and is a form of discrimination or disrespect to any families with different beliefs.

Developmentally appropriate programs teach respect for individual beliefs and customs. Every family is unique, and as far as the developmentally appropriate early childhood program is concerned, every family's beliefs and customs are special to that family. By internalizing acceptance and respect for others, children learn an important life skill: They develop the ability to see things from someone else's point of view. This is a crucial social and cognitive developmental milestone.

In recent years, Halloween has become a point of controversy for early childhood professionals. Parents can hold strong opinions about Halloween for a number of reasons. They may love Halloween, object to it for religious reasons, see gruesome costumes as offensive, fear dangers associated with trick-or-treating, or simply dislike commercialism directed at children.

Teachers worry about managing behavior in classrooms filled with children focused on candy and costumes. Teachers also may worry because masks (and sometimes costumes) terrify toddlers and younger preschoolers. Many little ones aren't developmentally able to understand whether people with masks or decorated faces are human beings or monsters.

Developmentally appropriate programs treat all children and families with equal respect and consideration. To do so, it is helpful to provide neutral alternatives for school celebrations and thus ensure relevance for all cultures. For example, a fall costume event or harvest festival geared to cognitive and social skills could replace the traditional Halloween party.

Teachers can support children's creative expression by involving them in creating costumes with grocery sacks, construction paper, tape, glue, and markers. Children who are developmentally ready can make masks and do face painting. In this way, children can be invited to express individual cultural ideas and traditions within boundaries set up by the teacher.

We are each burdened with prejudice; against the poor or the rich, the smart or the slow, the gaunt or the obese. It is natural to develop prejudices. It is noble to rise above them.

—*Author Unknown*

Whenever possible, appropriate materials and activities can be brought into the classroom to help children explore cultural traditions. DAP programs never endorse or teach traditions tied to religious beliefs without prior knowledge and consent of the parents. *Teaching staff trust parents to decide what religious beliefs are right for their child.* Teachers stay focused on ground rules that are based on the core values of democracy: *be safe* (don't unreasonably cause harm to oneself or others), *be respectful* (respect the rights, beliefs, and possessions of others), and *be responsible* (don't unreasonably damage shared property or the natural environment).

DIVERSITY

5-5e How Can I Help Children through Difficult Cultural Transitions?

Cultural differences can cause painful adjustments and misunderstandings regardless of the age of the person making the adjustment. Children can suffer from feelings of stress, fear, embarrassment, and failure. These feelings can be made worse if children are unable to communicate with the people around them. They desperately want to fit into their school environment, but it is difficult to adjust to a new set of values and behaviors in a new culture. See Positive Focus 5.8.

Changes in customs, climate, and foods can also be confusing. If a child is a recent refugee, she may be emotionally struggling to deal with the impact of war, trauma, and death on her family. The child may be very confused about differences in cultural perceptions about punctuality, privacy, and appropriate public behavior. Her parents may be horrified that American child care teachers use their first names with children. The child may be totally confused about what is expected for girls and boys and what kind of relationship she is expected to have with her teacher. Her teacher touches her and hugs her. What does that mean? The child may have no cultural context with which to understand the social cues from her playmates.

Child care providers can help this new child and children like her feel welcomed and at home in the early childhood program by taking some important steps. First and foremost—children's names are integral to their identity in any culture, so it is important to learn to pronounce names correctly. Or, if the child is deaf, learn to sign the child's name correctly.

Ask the parents whether you need to know anything special to use the child's name correctly. For example, in the Vietnamese culture, the surname is first, followed by the middle name, and the given name is last. If a specific name is challenging, help the parents digitally record the name, and then play it for yourself until you can reproduce the name properly. Remember, the sounds our ears didn't hear when we were babies are almost impossible for our brains to detect now, so we have to work very hard at this task. Do what babies do—listen to that sound over and over again.

Cultural Transition Tips for Teachers

Positive Focus 5.8

Bronfenbrenner (1979, 1995) suggests that transitions will be easier for everyone if we ensure the following:

- Cultural sensitivity
- A partnership with parents
- Personal communication
- A shared commitment to successful transition
- Collaborative planning
- Shared decision making between home and school
- Clear goals agreed to by all parties
- Preparation of child for the transition
- The child's transition first made with someone he knows and trusts
- Ongoing open communication between home and school

Teachers should never Anglicize names to make them easier to pronounce. We should not give children nicknames. The children's and their families' names may have been the only authentic cultural possession they had left when they arrived in this country. They will appreciate any efforts to honor their given names. Make it one of your goals to ensure that all children in your class (from toddlers on up) learn everyone's name in the class. There are many games and songs that lend themselves to name awareness in a classroom. Having artwork on the walls at the children's eye level with their printed names, saying the children's names to invite them to choose activities, and telling stories that incorporate the children's names are only a few of hundreds of things teachers can do to raise the children's awareness of names in the classroom. See Positive Focus 5.9.

An awkward situation may occur in which the teacher encounters a child whose name does not transfer well into English—if, for example, the child's name has a pronunciation that is beautiful in his own language but a bit too similar to a profane or obscene word in English. This situation might warrant talking with the parents to see whether they want to think about a nickname. In that case, the *parents* should decide on a culturally appropriate nickname. If the parents treasure the child's name and want to

Positive Focus 5.9

Welcome Children with English as a Second or Other Language (ESOL)

1. Take the new child around and personally introduce him to other children, or have designated children do this.

2. Give the new child special class responsibilities so she feels she is a part of the class.

3. Set a good example of cultural acceptance and respect.

4. Provide contextualized, authentic learning.

5. Let the new child silently observe if he at first feels uncomfortable participating.

6. Partner the new child with a compatible learning cohort.

7. Never pressure a new child to speak; when she does speak, don't overcorrect.

8. Learn some words and phrases in the child's native language; use these with the new child and teach them to the other children.

9. Simplify your English as needed and speak slowly in a clear, normal tone.

10. Repetitive stories, songs, and rhymes allow the new child to practice the rhythms and patterns of language in addition to learning new vocabulary.

11. Role-playing invites the new child to explore lifelike situations so she can have fun practicing the language structures needed for conversation. She can role-play settings in a grocery store or a doctor's office or pretend to make a call to the fire department.

12. Teach the new child the vocabulary and skills he needs to know to participate in group activities and on the playground.

13. Remember, "Students who feel their culture is valued and understood by the school and the larger community tend to do better in school than those who feel it is rejected" (Ashworth, 1992, p. 14).

keep it, that's fine. Then it is the teacher's responsibility to ensure that no child ever teases the child about his name at school. The teacher, of course, will also want to do everything possible to instill pride in the child about his wonderful, proud name. That way he'll know how to handle any future teasing (should it ever occur) outside of school.

5-5f How Does Culture Affect Adults' Styles of Interaction?

Our styles of interaction (sometimes called *styles of control*)—*authoritative, authoritarian,* and *permissive*—are shaped by our cultural backgrounds. We tend to follow the guidance style of our own parents or childhood role models. We can, however, learn more effective guidance styles that we consciously decide to adopt. To make the change, we have to believe—heart, mind, and soul—that the new methods will fit into our own cultural beliefs.

Most of us would not accept new ideas simply because someone tells us to. We have to believe that adopting new ways of doing things will be meaningful in the context of our own lived experiences and in terms of our own cultural view of the world. So, we have to really understand how a different guidance method is going to help children. We want to know if a different method will feel authentic. Will it empower families and strengthen our classrooms? Will it be worth the effort to change deeply engrained habits?

This book explains the process of understanding how and why authoritative, respectful guidance will prepare children to be competent, stress resistant, and prepared to cope with change in the multicultural global economy of today. You are the one who will make the individual decisions about what does and does not fit within your cultural perspective. You will decide what to make part of your teaching style and what to reject. You and I are the ones who must commit to the difficult task of changing habit patterns we no longer want in our lives.

Perhaps my mother and my grandmother believed that pounding on me with a belt would help me behave properly. It is okay for me to reconsider that part of my cultural heritage to see if it makes any sense in today's world. Long-term research shows that harsh discipline usually backfires and causes worse behavior, not better.

Perhaps when I spilled my milk as a young child my father, without even thinking, yelled obscene curse words at me and called me a bad name. Maybe he was out of work, overwhelmed by his life, feeling out of control, and short of temper. I should remember and honor the positive aspects of my upbringing. But I can decide how to let go of patterns I internalized that are not helpful to children's development today. Research tells us that children learn self-esteem when we speak to them as valued human beings.

Some cultural traditions developed from celebrations of the joys in people's lives. Other cultural traditions developed from people trying to cope with the misery in their lives. We human beings are smart enough to determine which traditions to treasure and which to discard. Sometimes we simply need to stop to think, reflect, and consider other points of view.

As you study this book and strive to improve your guidance of children, I hope you will also strive to stay open-minded. Parents you meet will have a diverse r ange of ideas about how children should be disciplined. We shouldn't seem shocked or judgmental if a parent asks us to "spank" little Joe if he acts up. We should matter-of-factly explain our DAP guidelines. We should use nonjudgmental phrases such as, "May I show you some of the things we do at school to help children follow rules?"

5-5g How Does Culture Affect a Person's Learning Approach?

People from different cultures approach learning differently. People from some cultures approach education and educators almost with a feeling of reverence. Learning and knowledge is something that you accept humbly. A professor, a teacher, a parent, or a wise elder from the community should be consulted if you want to *receive knowledge*. The learner could not possibly be presumed to create knowledge. As we know, throughout history a great deal of knowledge has been passed down to younger generations by wise elder generations.

Some cultures approach learning in a radically different way. Just because something has been traditionally thought to be true doesn't convince people in these cultural settings that it is really true. If they want to know something, they may form a focus group or a think tank. They don't ask only wise elders; they do research. They always like to confirm things for themselves. They believe that learning is something anyone can construct. At the rate at which information is changing in our world, I wonder if our great-grandchildren will have to be issued textbooks (electronic, of course) marked with time stamps, like my carton of yogurt—best if used before May 30, 2036.

Children must learn to *construct knowledge* or they will be left in the lurch as they grow up in this diverse, fast-moving technological world. I hope, however, if you are lucky enough to interact with families who treat education and educators with reverence, you will treasure the experience. I will never forget a tiny 2-year-old boy from a Middle Eastern country I taught years ago. I was invited to his home for dinner. To my astonishment, his parents had placed my framed photograph, like a shrine, on his bedside table. My husband, a journalism professor, particularly enjoyed occasional emails he received from one of his international students that always began "Dear Honored Sir." Wouldn't it be lovely if we all revered education *and* supported DAP educational methods?

5-5h How Does Culture Affect Social Role Expectations?

cohesive interaction
Reciprocal teamwork; sticking together to carry out tight-knit group activity.

A particularly interesting cultural difference that is often overlooked is that of individuals' social role expectations See **Fig. 5.2**. Members of some cultures focus on **cohesive interaction**. Their cultural background has prepared them to think in terms of kinship. They tend to gravitate toward group- or team-oriented goals. Children who grow up in cohesive interaction cultural settings often are responsible for caring for other children in the family. They grow up with a strong sense that the community of kinship can be depended on to meet their emotional and physical needs, and they are often extremely attached to their community of origin.

Upper-income Americans are less generous with their money when compared with low-income Americans, who are surprisingly generous with theirs (Piff et al., 2010).

FIGURE 5.2

Cultural Tendencies

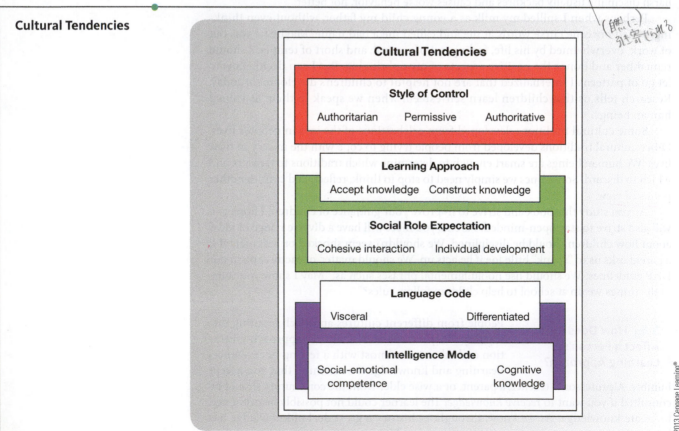

Cultural Tendencies

Style of Control

Authoritarian   Permissive   Authoritative

Learning Approach

Accept knowledge   Construct knowledge

Social Role Expectation

Cohesive interaction   Individual development

Language Code

Visceral   Differentiated

Intelligence Mode

Social-emotional competence   Cognitive knowledge

© 2013 Cengage Learning®

Children growing up in a cultural context where social role expectations tend toward **individual development** and **fulfillment** often are unfamiliar with strong bonds of community kinship. In cultures focused on individual development and fulfillment, a strong nuclear family bond is more pervasive than a wide kinship bond. The family is more likely to rely on itself and less likely to ask for help from others or to give help to others outside nuclear family. Although families may do volunteer work or give to charity, they are much less likely to know what the needs of their neighbors are or to be available to help them. The children are more involved in individual, self-fulfilling work and play and much less likely to have the responsibility of caring for a sibling.

At preschool, the child from a cohesive interaction background would likely look for a group of children with which to actively engage in play. The child from an individual development background might be interested in a puzzle and sit down alone or with another child to try to figure out how to put it together. A cultural challenge for early childhood educators is to help each of these children learn some of the cultural skills of the other child without squashing the unique abilities of either child.

During my research for *First Steps Toward Cultural Difference* (1989), I observed remarkable displays of caretaking by very young children. I saw African-American preschoolers (mostly girls but occasionally even boys) from low-income families look up from their play, notice that a toddler needed something, and instantly drop what they were doing to assist. I did not tend to see that same behavior in privileged, predominantly white children.

Our goal is to help children who are comfortable with cohesive kinship find and build a strong, cohesive kinship at school and then gradually learn that it is okay occasionally to stretch out and experience individual fulfillment. Our goal with the child who is comfortable with individual fulfillment is not only to support that process, but also to help her learn to function well as part of a team. We want her to experience and succeed in situations where she must push aside her own needs for the needs of the group. Being in a multicultural environment will help both of these children have the role models they need to achieve better cultural balance and the ability to function across cultures.

individual development
A particular person, distinct from others in a group, changes, advances, or progresses to a more advanced state.

fulfillment
Completely developing one's abilities and interests; a feeling of pleasure because you are getting what you want from life.

© 2013 Cengage Learning®

Being in a multicultural environment will give each of these children cultural role models so they can learn to function successfully in a broader cultural circle as they grow up.

5-5i How Does Culture Shape Our Use of Language?

Language is a key factor in culture. Obviously, cultures use different languages, but even when different cultural groups use the same language, they are likely to use it differently. In other words, you and a parent may both be speaking English, but culture may cause each of you to use the language in very different ways to express yourself. We know that different regions have their own accents and regional words, but even beyond that, culture shapes the thinking behind the use of words and how those words are constructed into meaningful communication.

To focus on important cultural language differences, I have divided language usage differences into two groups. I call these two groups **visceral** (intuitive) usage and **differentiated** (categorized) usage. You can see these differences if you listen to speech closely (Miller, 1989). For example, if you watch two 3-year-olds digging in the garden, you might overhear the following conversation:

Josie: "Hey, I got bait! You find any bait yet?" えさみつけたよ、Tim、えさみつけた？
Tim: "That's a worm. I feed worms to my box turtle, but he also eats frogs and bugs."
Josie: "This my bait . . . don't you go feeding it to your turtle. I'm going fishing, and I'm gonna catch a whale that will eat your turtle."

visceral 感情を表わにした、直感的の
Proceeding more from instinct than from logical thinking. Characterized by or showing emotion.

differentiated 差別化→区別化
Differences between two or more things that are made apparent and categorized.

→ これはみみずでしょ、このみみずは亀にあげる。亀はかえるも昆虫もたべる

これは、私のえさだから亀にあげないで
今から魚つり行ってくじらみる、くじらはあなたの亀たべるかも

If you think what you have just heard sounds like silly kids' talk, you'd miss some very important insight into Josie and Tim and the way enculturation has structured their use of language. The two children were delighted to find earthworms, but their use of words was different.

When Josie sees the worms, she intuitively lights up and remembers fishing with her grandfather. She intuitively knows the feel of the moist wiggly worms, the smell of the fish her grandfather caught, the sounds of the water splashing against the shore, and the wonder she felt exploring the worms and seeing fish come shooting up out of the water and being yanked to the shore by the long string on her grandfather's fishing pole.

No one in Josie's family has ever spent a lot of time specifically naming or labeling objects for her to learn, so the designation *worm* doesn't leap to her mind today. What does come to her mind is the label she heard in *context* when she was exposed to worms on the fishing trips—"bait." Bait has no dry, memorized mental connection; Josie learned it in the context of richly lived social and emotional experiences.

Tim certainly may have known what bait was, but his thinking style tends toward categorization. He immediately thought of worms as part of the category of foods that his turtle ate—worms, frogs, and bugs. If you asked Tim to name three different kinds of worms, he might be able to think of earthworms, gummy worm candy, and the cartoon worm on *SpongeBob SquarePants*.

Josie might have been quite confused about the connection between the worms in her hands and Tim's grouping that included candy and cartoons. Her brain is not culturally attuned to his perspective. Of course, his brain is not culturally attuned to her perspective either. She energetically and dramatically role-plays an imagined fishing trip in which she catches a giant whale that eats his turtle. He cries and is very bewildered.

Tim's brain has been prepared through his infant and toddler language enculturation to unconsciously, but automatically, differentiate categories. His parents frequently and routinely pointed out objects to him, labeled them, and point out connections, "See . . . the elephant has a long trunk, but the giraffe has a long neck. They both live in the jungle. Where do cows and chickens live?"

Tim's cultural background prepares him to be a particularly capable test taker. (It helps him that tests have been traditionally written and produced by persons of Tim's cultural background.) Josie's cultural background prepares her to be especially capable of expressing herself emotionally in the context of her life experiences. Both will expand their capabilities if they are exposed to cross-cultural experiences in their early years.

5-5j How Does Culture Shape Our Intellectual Approach?

Unfortunately, some teachers and parents may leap to the mistaken assumption that Tim is smarter than Josie. What they may not realize is that there are many kinds of intelligence, and Josie has different capacities and potentials from Tim. By no means should she be considered in any way lesser than Tim. The world needs all sorts of people with all sorts of unique skills and abilities.

Howard Gardner (1983) explained that an essential part of personal intelligence is social–emotional intelligence (see more on this topic in Chapter 11). Pam Schiller (2010) describes social–emotional intelligence as including seven interrelated emotional and social skills. She explains how these skills build a foundation for success and happiness in life.

Lev Vygotsky, a Russian psychologist who emphasized the importance of pretend play as a way for children to learn, was very concerned with social learning. What he described is now often called **authentic learning** (learning taking place in the context of real life). Vygotsky believed that all higher cognitive functions have their origins in social interactions. As we know, schools from our own childhoods all too often objected to social interactions between students ("Stop talking and look at your own work!") and sometimes even interactions with the real world ("Don't look out the window! Your eyes should be on the chalkboard.").

Today's teaching methods have brought new success to schools through improvements such as hands-on sensory learning materials, partnership learning, individualized learning, more flexible scheduling, and peer tutoring. Peer tutoring, for example,

DIVERSITY

social–emotional intelligence (EQ)
The level of one's self-awareness, mood management, self-motivation, empathy, and understanding of one's inner feelings.

authentic learning
A family of research efforts that explain cognition in terms of the relationship between learners and the properties of specific environments. The emphasis of research on authentic learning (or "situated cognition," as it is often called) is to study complex learning, problem solving, and thinking in a realistic environment.

gives children the opportunity to take a leadership role and share their learning in a social interaction (Spielberger, 2004). Using DAP methods in the classroom makes learning more meaningful for children from different cultural backgrounds who have very different learning styles.

As shown earlier in this chapter, increased self-awareness and more well-developed interpersonal skills help individuals decrease prejudice and increase cooperation among diverse cultures. By helping our own diverse group of young children learn to work and play together cooperatively, we can help make the world a better place.

Summary

- Culture is the beliefs and patterns of behavior that are passed on from parents to children.
- A child's development is best understood within the social and cultural context of that child's family and community.
- Unconditional acceptance of a child and her family is the first important step toward open communication.
- It is ethically wrong for early childhood professionals to discriminate based on race, gender, religion, economic status, values, national origin, or ability differences.

- People who are ethnocentric often claim to be open-minded but may see cultural traits that are different from their own as meaningless or peculiar.
- Multicultural education is not a subject area, but an ever-present thread woven throughout all curriculum areas and throughout each and every day.
- Prejudice harms children and damages their development.
- Cultural differences can cause painful adjustments and misunderstandings regardless of the age of the person making the adjustment.

Key Terms

authentic learning

body language

cohesive interaction

cultural adaptation

cultural bias

cultural context

cultural pluralism

culture

culture shock

differentiated

discrimination

enculturation

ethics

ethnocentrism

fulfillment

group identity

human ecology

individual development

media

negative stereotyping

nested structures

personal interaction

pluralistic culture

prejudice

racism

respect

scapegoating

self-identity

sexism

social-emotional intelligence

stigmatized

unconditional acceptance

visceral

Student Activities

1. Gather 12 random children's books. Respond to the following:
   a. Go through the books and count the faces that appear in your books. List all the different ethnicities you identify. Do your books disproportionately represent one ethnic group?
   b. Go through your books and look for any persons with ability differences. Did you find any?
   c. Did the books show any women in nontraditional roles?

2. Identify three safe yet highly sensory objects or activities that you could bring into a preschool classroom to help children understand and appreciate a culture other than their own. For example, making tortillas in class would be a cultural activity that would stimulate the senses of taste, smell, touch, and sight. How would you present these objects or carry out these activities with preschool-aged children?

3. Fred is a new first grader who is transferring into your class today from another school. His is a shy, beautiful child of mixed cultural backgrounds who happens to have a very large birthmark that covers almost half of his face. How will you transition Fred successfully into the classroom learning community and prevent the possibility of his being stigmatized?

Related Resources

Readings

Sparks, L., & J. Edwards. (2010). *Anti-bias education for young children & ourselves.* Washington, DC: National Association for the Education of Young Children.

Vazquez, C. I. (2005). *Parenting with pride Latino style: How to help your child cherish your cultural values and succeed in today's world.* New York: HarperCollins. (Also available in Spanish.)

Wright, M. (2000). *I'm chocolate, you're vanilla: Raising healthy black and biracial children in a race-conscious world.* San Francisco, CA: Jossey-Bass.

Websites

Crossroads Antiracism Organizing & Training
Crossroads was founded to develop new directions in understanding and combating the root causes of institutional racism and to work for racial justice and social equality.

Multicultural Calendar
Multicultural calendars incorporate and explain numerous multifaith, multicultural, and diversity-related holidays and observances.

Understanding Children with Ability Differences

naeyc Standards

The following NAEYC Standards are addressed in this chapter

Standard 1   Promoting child development and learning

1a Knowing and understanding young children's characteristics and needs

1b Knowing and understanding the multiple influences on development and learning

1c Using developmental knowledge to create healthy, respectful, supportive, and challenging learning environments

Standard 2   Building family and community relationships

2a Knowing about and understanding diverse family and community characteristics

2b Supporting and engaging families and communities through respectful, reciprocal relationships

2c Involving families and communities in their children's development and learning

© 2013 Cengage Learning®

Objectives

After reading this chapter, you should be able to do the following:

6-1 Identify strategies for effective guidance of children with ability differences.

6-2 Describe laws and programs critical to providing care and education for children with ability differences.

6-3 List characteristic features of various health conditions and describe how they affect children's behavior.

6-1 How Can I Guide Children with Ability Differences?

This chapter considers children with **ability differences** and **disabilities**. To guide these children and their peers effectively, we need to learn how ability differences affect children and classrooms. Often our own ability to cope with a child's inappropriate behavior improves dramatically when we understand that the child's problems are based on a physical, mental, or emotional problem and are not the child's fault. The child is not being wild, defiant, or stubborn because he or she wants to be. It helps when we understand the child's diagnosis and we have professional information to guide us in meeting the child's needs. We need to know how to nurture children with ability differences (some of whom may have faced physical challenges we can only imagine). We must learn how to talk intelligently with their parents and avoid making offensive or embarrassing mistakes when discussing ability differences. We must help typically developing children become sensitive, considerate, and open to children with ability differences.

We should always give children the benefit of the doubt when we think there *may be* some unknown reason they are behaving the way they are. We will need to learn how to recognize children who may need to be referred for professional screening to assure that their development is on track. We also must learn to recognize children who may have experienced abuse or neglect so the appropriate professionals can check on them.

DIVERSITY

ability differences
Out of the ordinary function in one or more basic activities of life based on medical, physical, cognitive, psychological, or other characteristics. Many believe the term *disabled* focuses on inadequacy and find the term *person with an ability difference* more empowering and appropriate.

disabilities
Word currently used in a diagnostic, clinical, and legal context to describe individuals defined as requiring and eligible for services because medical, physical, cognitive, psychological, or other conditions affect one or more basic activities of life.

Positive Focus 6.1 Nurturing Children with Learning Differences

- Provide unconditional acceptance.
- Focus positively on what the child *can do.*
- Set realistic goals cooperatively with the child, letting her take as much control as possible.
- Support the child in dealing with hygiene, assistive devices, and other concerns as they arise.
- Help the child deal with the emotional ups and downs of his ability difference.
- Recognize that even children with ability differences sometimes behave inappropriately and need to face consequences.
- Learn to deal honestly and caringly with the child's anger and fear, but set reasonable limits on behavior.
- Pay attention to facial expression and body language cues as well as spoken or signed language, and let the child know you care about her feelings.
- Remember that children with ability differences must be treated as much as possible like typically developing children.
- Stay in close contact with parents for suggestions on solving tactical how-to problems and for celebrating triumphs.
- Keep a written record of observations and progress.

TeachSource Digital Download

DIVERSITY

accommodations
Special aids for persons with ability differences that give them access to inclusive activities and environments. Accommodations can include such things as a ramp for a wheelchair, a lowered sink, special door handles, signs written in Braille, a sign language translator, or other changes to help the person with ability differences function equitably with typically developing peers.

learning disability 学習能力
Disorder that affects the brain's ability to receive, process, analyze, or store information.

6-1a What Do Children with Ability Differences Need?

Children with ability differences have as many unique needs as there are children. Some of those specific needs are addressed later in this chapter. See Positive Focus 6.1.

Children with ability differences often need special **accommodations** to help them interact, learn, and play as naturally as possible with their typically developing peers. Accommodations are extremely important. They are the special pieces of equipment or changes in the environment or the schedule that help children with ability differences function better alongside their peers. An accommodation can be as simple as a specially shaped spoon for a developmentally delayed toddler or as complicated as a computer that assists a third grader with a **learning disability** by "sounding out" words for him.

Accommodations give children with disabilities a better chance to fit in and succeed in doing the things their peers do. Professionals may designate what accommodations are required for a specific child with an ability difference. Sometimes teachers and care providers use common sense to create useful accommodations that help children cope better with their surroundings.

6-1b Why Should We Include Children with Ability Differences?

When we encounter a child with significant ability differences, most of us imagine that surely there must be a "special" place "somewhere else" that is especially equipped to deal with this child's different needs. We may feel poorly prepared and frustrated because this child's needs are greater than those of other more typically developing children. Why should we have to deal with striving to meet the needs of children with significant ability differences? There are important reasons why we should provide inclusive care and education. First, we are legally and ethically responsible to provide access to persons with disabilities. Second, we can provide the very best learning environments for all children by helping them learn to work and play cooperatively in diverse settings. Third, including children with ability differences gives them a sense of belonging and acceptance. Through inclusion, they have an opportunity to learn age-appropriate behaviors and skills from their typically developing classmates. They have the chance to practice age-appropriate social skills and to develop friendships with a diverse group of peers.

They get a chance to develop not only self-esteem, but also positive attitudes toward others who have differences.

Help is available. Even privately owned child care centers and schools can help families find access to publicly funded testing, therapists, counselors, social workers, or other resources. Although resources and procedures vary dramatically by areas of the country, local communities are all required to give children with disabilities support to assure them an equal opportunity to get an education. Children with ability differences need parent and teacher advocates to track down potential services.

6-1c Do Children with Ability Differences Need DAP?

Children with diverse abilities need DAP as much as any other children do (Filler & Xu, 2006). See Positive Focus 6.2 and 6.3.

In specific situations, therapists may recommend very structured teaching and guidance strategies for certain children that could seem at odds with DAP. Those strategies are based on the individual child's cognitive, social, or emotional limitations. Any strategies that can be carried out in a respectful way are well within the scope of DAP's intent of individualizing to meet the needs of each child. Any methods that are humiliating, degrading, or dehumanizing to children are not consistent with the ethical foundations of NAEYC or DAP.

Sometimes the recommended strategies involve "pushing" children with certain ability differences to carry out tasks rather than allowing them to proceed at their own pace. This is something we would not find developmentally appropriate with typically developing children. We believe the child is like a rosebud. Give the bud time and a nurturing environment and it will unfold naturally. Unfortunately, disabling conditions make it impossible for some rosebuds to unfold without coaxing. Some children with different needs will not progress without continuous and vigorous nudging.

▶❙❙ **TeachSource Video**

5–11 Years: Developmental Disabilities in Middle Childhood

Watch this Video Case on developmental disabilities, and then answer the following questions:

1. Describe how the typically developing children interacted with Derrick.
2. Was Derrick able to connect with a group of children who were more developmentally advanced?
3. How did Makala and the child she was playing with interact?
4. Was Makala able to connect?
5. Did you sense a respectful, inclusive learning community among the children?

Positive Focus 6.2

DAP Concepts We Follow to Support Children with Ability Differences

- Sincere cultural respect, with every child intrinsically valued for who she is
- A calm, peaceful, and orderly environment with a minimum of distractions
- Regular careful planning to meet *individual* children's needs
- Careful observation and record keeping
- Reasonable but challenging expectations
- Skill development with age-appropriate, authentic, multisensory activities using real objects
- Individualized interactions that let children learn at their own pace
- Clear, simple statements of desired outcomes
- Positive, assertive guidance
- Consistent follow-up on guidance
- Support for a healthy lifestyle—stress reduction, good nutrition, physical exercise, and sufficient sleep

TeachSource Digital Download

Why Is Inclusiveness Important?

Inclusion helps children with ability differences do the following (Halvorsen & Neary, 2009):

- Experience diverse social interactions
- Develop a better understanding of age-mate expectations
- Develop age-appropriate skills by modeling typically developing peers
- Increase social skills and language by practicing with typically developing peers
- Develop self-esteem by feeling included rather than excluded[/BBL]
- Inclusion helps children with typical development do the following:
- Learn to respect differences among people
- Learn how children with ability differences can be models for perseverance and courage in spite of adversity
- Recognize their own strengths and weaknesses
- Learn how children with special needs are similar to all other children
- Value others who may be different in some ways but who also are the same in many ways

Inclusion helps families of children with ability differences do the following:

- Expand their knowledge of typical child development
- Observe age-appropriate skills and social activities
- Get a better perspective to make sense of their children's areas of strength and weakness
- Feel less isolated and more included

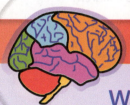

BrainFacts

What Can We Learn from Neuroscience?

Nurturing brain development in children with special needs

- Minor day-to-day stress is normal and even healthy. Severe or prolonged stress is damaging to babies' and young children's brain development (Sprenger, 2002).
- Students with ability differences often experience "toxic" levels of stress because they
  - Feel different
  - Feel socially excluded, stigmatized, or bullied (Tomlinson & Kalbfleisch, 1998)
  - Have impaired coping ability (Davis & Gunnar, 2000)
  - Are expected to do things they can't really do (Given, 2000, 2002)
  - Frequently clash with others because they cannot evaluate and plan appropriate actions (Sprenger, 2002)[BBL_SUB]
- When children with learning differences feel stressed and trapped, their brain functions can downshift into survival mode. In this mode, brains cannot think or learn optimally. Children may say or do things they know are wrong just to avoid dealing with a stressful situation, they may act out, or they may refuse to cooperate (Caine, 2000; Caulfield, Kidd, & Kocher, 2000).

- When any child feels safe, supported, and valued, the brain functions at its best (Jensen, 1998).
- When any child feels unsafe, unsupported, or unwanted, learning is interrupted (Sprenger, 2002).
- Brain differences can affect a child's ability to organize, focus on tasks, attend to details, stay alert, and control emotions (Brown, 2007).

6-1d Helping Children Treat People with Ability Differences with Respect

Children—human beings—fear what they don't understand. Several years ago I observed parents taking their young children through an exhibition of lifelike dinosaurs at Houston's Museum of Natural Science. The exhibit was set up to make you feel as if you had stepped into a foggy primeval lagoon at dawn, just as a bunch of massive dinosaurs had gathered to find food and water. Young children stood about ankle high to these dagger-toothed monsters—the effect was quite dramatic!

As parents brought their young children through the exhibit, I watched the children's reactions. The youngest children who didn't understand that the dinosaurs weren't real interested me most. Many of the toddlers cried and clung to their parents. But some preschoolers immediately became aggressive. The aggressive ones (often little boys, but some girls) marched up to the border around the dinosaurs and planted one foot on the low rail. The child usually menacingly stuck out his fists toward the dinosaurs, making his most daunting growls and snarls. Some spit. A few who had something in hand threw what they had at the dinosaur, much to their parents' dismay. They weren't being bad; they were just reacting to their fear by attacking the source of their anxiety.

These are essentially the same reasons that children pick on a child who is different for some reason. Their immature brain tells them this person is not right, is not the way they expect people to be. Their natural **fight or flight response** causes them to be prepared to run away or to try to hurt the person in some way.

We can help children lose their fear of people who are different by replacing this fear with knowledge and tolerance. We are teachers; we know how to teach. We can take field trips to expose children to people who have differences; we can provide hands-on exploration of ability difference equipment and we can read ability difference-related books. Never underestimate the power of **bibliotherapy**. In this book's Appendix, you will find many thought-provoking, sensitive, and reassuring children's books suggestions; these suggestions are sorted by ability difference, age level, and interest area. See Positive Focus 6.4.

fight or flight response
The body's reaction to a perceived threat or danger. Our bodies react to threats by releasing hormones such as adrenalin and cortisol into our blood stream, which give us a burst of energy and strength to fight or flee. When the perceived threat is gone, our systems are designed to go back to normal levels by means of a relaxation response. But if a child is subjected to constant stress, relaxation is impaired and damage to physical health as well as sleeping, eating, and social and emotional problems may occur.

bibliotherapy
The use of literature by children or adults to aid in processing specific problems (for example, depression, anxiety, stress, frustration). Many libraries have listings of bibliotherapy selections categorized by concerns (divorce, death and dying, new baby, step-parenting, and so on).

Positive Focus 6.4

Choosing Books that Support Children with Diverse Abilities

According to Easter Seals Wisconsin (2008), books should

- Promote respect and empathy for individuals with ability differences
- Use a child's first language
- Promote understanding and acceptance
- Depict individuals with ability differences as complete human beings with the same types of strengths and weaknesses as their peers
- Provide accurate information about ability differences
- Focus on similarities between people with ability differences and typically developing peers
- Show people with ability differences taking on diverse and active roles within the community

(Continued)

- Depict inclusive schools, workplaces, and communities
- Depict people with ability differences from different ethnic and racial backgrounds and from a variety of age groups

In addition, books should not

- Dwell on what people with ability differences can't do, rather than on what they can
- Depict people with ability differences as victims or only as objects of curiosity or seek to evoke pity
- Depict ordinary actions and achievements as heroic when performed by a person with an ability difference
- Depict people with ability differences as helpless or always dependent on others to function in the world
- Use unacceptable ability difference-related language
- Depict people with ability differences as passive observers who take no active role in their schools or communities
- Fail to show people with ability differences participating in activities appropriate for their age group

DIVERSITY

6-1e Does a Different Appearance Affect a Child's Life?

Some ability differences are hidden and can be identified only by a medical expert. Many other ability differences are so obvious that even a baby or toddler immediately recognizes that something is different. Children who live with a different physical appearance face very special challenges.

Some time ago, I visited my 3-year-old granddaughter at her preschool. At the time, my arm was in a surgical cast. As I greeted and hugged my granddaughter, I asked her if she would like to introduce me to her friends. Her bright expression clouded and she said, "Okay, but first I have to go tell them that you are not bad." Surprised, I said, "Honey, why would your friends think I was bad?" She hung her head and said, "You know, 'cause of that." She tapped my cast.

Concern about people who don't look the way the child expects is typical in babies, toddlers, and preschoolers. From infancy, babies' brains are constantly sensing, perceiving, and storing information from the outside world. A newborn begins to show recognition of his mother's face within hours of birth (Sai, 2005; Slater & Quinn, 2001). If a baby, toddler, or preschooler sees a person who doesn't fit the expected image she has established, she may react with curiosity, fear, aversion, or disgust, depending on her age, temperament, and life experiences.

Once a baby, toddler, or preschooler has a fixed idea of what people are supposed to look like, he may scream and cry if he sees unexpected faces such as a person in a Halloween mask, a clown face, or a Santa Claus face. Even someone in a hat or sunglasses may cause a baby distress. Gradually children recognize that different is not necessarily bad. Different can be very good. Although many (if not most) toddlers are terrified of adults walking around in Disney-type costumes, most older preschoolers and young elementary school-agers are delighted by princesses, mice, ducks, and other characters.

Often, as I push my mother in her wheelchair in public places, I make it a point to observe babies, toddlers, and preschoolers stopping to stare at my mom in her chair with wheels. It is especially interesting to see a child in a stroller staring at her, trying to comprehend the connection between her chair with wheels and his chair with wheels. Fortunately, the more often very young children see people in wheelchairs, the more likely they are to include this image in their mental category of normal, acceptable things.

The value of inclusive early childhood programs is not only to challenge children with ability differences by allowing them to live in "real world" environments, but also to allow their peers to grow up knowing that children with ability differences are real people with real feelings who have a lot to offer and who deserve to be treated well. It is our task to help children learn that those with differences can become friends.

The role of physical attractiveness in society has been well documented. Studies have shown that attractive individuals have an advantage in employment settings and are more likely to be acquitted of a crime (Rhode, 2010). This bias for beauty is also apparent toward young children. Research tells us that adults who do not know a different-looking child very well treat the child more harshly and view the child as less competent (Langlois et al., 2000).

Unattractive children are not preferred as playmates by other children and are assumed by their peers and teachers to be less friendly. In addition, teachers expect attractive children to be more intelligent and better behaved than their unattractive peers (Hamermesh & Parker, 2005; Langlois et al., 2000; Vannatta et al., 2009). Studies show that what infants, toddlers, and young children consider attractive is actually a face with very average, symmetrical features and nothing that looks out of the ordinary.

Many of the people who seem most "unattractive" to young children are those who have health problems and ability differences—people we must protect from stigmatizing and discrimination. Every adult who is experienced with young children knows that they can be quite transparent in their insensitivity toward out-of-the-ordinary physical appearances, such as persons with extensive burn scars, facial abnormalities, or severe obesity (Latner & Stunkard, 2003; Lawrence et al., 2006).

In the uninhibited world of childhood, disapproval of unexpected physical features is openly voiced. In interviews with children having visible differences such as facial burn scars, most of the children said they experienced stigmatizing, bullying, and harassment (Lawrence et al., 2011).

If we are kind to them, babies and toddlers will love us innocently and unconditionally, regardless of whether we are odd looking, too fat, too thin; have a large nose or frizzy hair; and even if we sing off key. But every day children are bombarded with messages from television, radio, magazines, movies, friends, and families indicating that there is a right way to look and other appearances are inferior. Every generation adjusts its vision of beauty. Lillian Russell, the famous "bombshell' beauty from the 1800s, weighed 200 pounds, a weight that would now cause her to be shunned by Hollywood (Brown, 1903.)

Early in life children figure out from adult messages that to fit in and be popular you have to be thin and have light skin, symmetrical features, and smooth glossy hair. Girls can't be too tall and boys can't be too short. Between the lines, the messages from media imply that heroes are all tall gorgeous men with bulging muscles, and villains are all dark skinned and ugly, with rough, scarred complexions.

But the fact is that there are some beautiful people who are not at all beautiful inside and there are some obese, scarred, and unsymmetrical people who are intelligent and loving. There are extremely short people who are no different inside than peers who happen to be typical height.

The ax murderers in terror movies often have a face scarred by fire or acne. Stupid or silly people may be obese. The clever heroes are shown as slender, healthy, fair skinned, and flawless. We can help children overcome these damaging stereotypes. To prevent discrimination, children need to learn that handsome people are not always perfect on the inside, and people with different looks might really be worth knowing. The only way to know is to find out what is inside them, not what they look like. Each individual deserves to be discovered as a unique human being.

Courtesy of Geneviere De Casero

Children don't get to choose how they look. But parents, teachers, caregivers, and other children are friendlier and more supportive to children they believe are attractive. Children they believe to be unattractive are not treated as well and may be teased, bullied, stigmatized, or excluded. Tolerance requires us to look beyond superficial appearances so that we can celebrate each child for who he really is inside.

Your assumptions are your windows on the world. Scrub them off every once in a while, or the light won't come in.

—*Isaac Asimov*

6-1f How Should i Handle Teasing and Bullying?

teasing
To annoy, pester, irritate, aggravate, make fun of, or mock playfully.

bullying
To torment physically, verbally, or psychologically by threats, hitting, shoving, name-calling, sarcasm, taking possessions, etc.

Teasing is an inevitable part of childhood. Some teasing is playful and shared among children. Siblings poke and pester each other to many a parent's last straw. Teasing may be very annoying to the recipient, but sometimes it is just part of a game of give-and-take aimed at getting an adult's attention.

But teasing can cross a line and become hurtful, mean, and very damaging **bullying**. Children with severe ability differences are often socially excluded, stigmatized, and bullied. Children who are obese may not be treated the same. We professionals must set an example by treating *all* children respectfully. There are many complicated physiological, sociological, and environmental reasons why a given child might be obese. Blaming the child or the family is cruel and unproductive.

Bullying can look very different between boys and girls. Older school-aged girls tend to be very subtle. A group of popular and attractive girls are likely to strike a wounding blow to an obese classmate simply by walking past her and making rude oinking sounds. Then with exaggerated innocence sweetly batting their eyelashes for the teacher's benefit and saying, "Just kidding." At other times girls can be cruel without saying a word by giving a peer they decide to exclude the silent treatment.

Boys tend to be much more direct. Older school-aged boys grab the "slow" boy's backpack and throw it on top of the lockers where he can't reach it. They run off laughing. They are the same boys who thought it was funny to hide the overweight boy's clothes during summer swim class.

Both boys and girls tend to call other children names that are hurtful. Name-calling is an issue that teachers must address specifically. We will teach children that it is okay to express feelings honestly (e.g., "I'm angry"), but it is not okay to call another person a hurtful name. Often name-calling is targeted at some physical feature over which the child has no control—baldness caused by chemotherapy, hearing aids, leg braces, burn scars, birth marks, unusual height in a girl, unusual shortness in a boy, unusually feminine characteristics in a boy, or unusually masculine characteristics in a girl. See Positive Focus 6.5.

Positive Focus 6.5   Bullying Hurts Children

Bullying must be addressed because it can cause the targeted child to do the following:

- Resist going to school
- Experience learning problems
- Complain of stomach aches or headaches
- Cry frequently
- Become passive or withdrawn
- Have injuries such as unexplained bruises
- Describe himself in negative terms

When you realize that bullying has occurred, do the following:

- Intervene immediately (responsible adults who see bullying and do nothing are bullying partners).
- Supervise carefully because most bullying happens when adults aren't watching.
- Give the child who has been bullied an opportunity to talk privately about her feelings.
- Empower the child who has been bullied by helping him think of ways to solve the problem.
- Model positive behavior by avoiding jokes that stereotype or make fun of people's appearance.
- Teach the child who has been bullied to be assertive and to make eye contact.

- Practice appropriate assertive phrases the child can use such as, "When you throw my shoes in the garbage can, it's unfair and it makes me mad. Stop it!"
- Follow up and stay close by while the child confronts his bullies.
- If the problem persists, consider further guidance and/or screening for children who are chronic bullies.

(Beane, 2000; Beaudoin & Taylor, 2009; Nickerson, Mele, & Princiotta, 2008)

A child with very low self-esteem may feel compelled to pick on, bully, discriminate against, stigmatize, or generally look down on anyone she perceives to be inferior in some way. Dealing with her inappropriate behavior may not succeed until we address the self-esteem shortfall that is triggering it. It is sort of like trying to bail water out of a sinking boat. We need to fix the hole in the boat before we can solve the problem. We need to address the child's self-esteem problem so that she is able to respect herself; then we can help her learn to respect others.

The only disability in life is a bad attitude.
—Scott Hamilton

Children may have mistaken goals that are at the core of their inappropriate behavior. Does the child feel an inordinate need for attention? Has the child felt so hurt he feels a need to hurt back? Is the child feeling a need to rebel against authority? Is the child withdrawing into a world of his own? See Chapter 11 for information on responding to mistaken goals and for more ideas for preventing bullying.

6-1g How Can I Support the Child with an Ability Difference?

Welcome children with ability differences into your heart. Whether you realize it or not, you have a lot to offer a young child with a medical condition or other ability difference. See Positive Focus 6.6.

Support Children with Ability Differences

Positive Focus 6.6

- Learn as much as possible about the child's ability difference.
- Show respect for the child and the family as they struggle to deal with the ability difference in their own way.
- Avoid being overprotective.
- Never do anything for the child that he can reasonably do for himself.
- Refrain from walking on eggshells when guiding the child's behavior.
- Remember that the differently abled child needs calm, assertive positive child guidance as much as does any typically developing child.
- Be optimistic, but have *realistic* expectations in guidance.
- Appreciate the uniqueness of each individual child.
- Never compare children.
- Focus on each child's strengths.
- Identify every child's positive characteristics and assets.
- Show unconditional affection to every child.
- Communicate at eye level, use the child's name, and use appropriate touch to convey respect.
- Teach children to value differences, show compassion, and express caring.
- Prevent bullying and stigmatizing.
- Have a sense of humor.

TeachSource Digital Download

Shaken Baby Syndrome

Watch this Video Case on **abusive head trauma**, or shaken baby syndrome. and then answer the following questions:

1. Why is it dangerous to shake a baby?

2. What might cause an adult to shake a baby?

3. What can parents or caregivers do if they feel out of control?

6-1h How Can I Support Parents of Children with Ability Differences?

Families learning that their baby or young child has a serious medical condition or ability difference go through a great deal of shock and pain. All parents need communication and support, but parents of children with medical conditions and ability differences have special needs and vulnerabilities. Patience, understanding, and encouragement are especially important for these parents. See Positive Focus 6.7.

Parents may hold an idealized image of their child and resist the notion that their child is imperfect and has weaknesses as well as strengths. They may need time to learn that there is no shame in having a special need or an "imperfection." It is healthy to deal with reality and take steps to help the child function with whatever strengths he has.

Many potentially disabling conditions can be prevented or alleviated if they are identified and treated during infancy or earliest childhood, so early screening for developmental problems has special importance. See Figure 6.1.

© 2013 Cengage Learning®

Positive Focus 6.7   Understand Parents of Children with Ability Differences

Parents of children with ability differences often experience a roller-coaster ride of overwhelming emotions:

- **Shock or denial.** The parents may deny that there is any medical condition or ability difference, or they may become preoccupied with thoughts such as "How can this be happening to me?" "Why is this happening to me?" What did I do to deserve this?"

- **Anger.** The parents may feel anger at themselves for "causing" the medical condition or ability difference, or they may direct their rage at others (medical personnel, the spouse, the teacher, the school, or God, and some parents may even feel unconscious anger toward the child).

- **Guilt.** Parents almost always go through a period of feeling that there was something they could and should have done to prevent the medical condition or ability difference.

- **Rejection.** Some parents describe going through a period of hating the idea of the medical condition or ability difference so much that they couldn't stop themselves from withdrawing from the child emotionally for a while; a few even wished the child had never been born.

- **Confusion.** Parents almost always feel confusion after diagnosis of a child's medical condition or ability difference—opinions come from every direction, experts sometimes seem to give contradictory advice, and quack cures may seem unbearably tempting.

- **Fear.** Parents fear the worst for their children; they worry who will take care of a seriously incapacitated child when the parents die or become too old to care for him.

- **Isolation.** Dealing with a child with a profound medical condition or ability difference can cause parents to feel very isolated. Eating out, visiting with friends, having a relaxing vacation, or creating romantic time alone with a spouse becomes so challenging it hardly seems worth it.

- **Envy.** Parents with a severely affected child see other children's accomplishments and can't help feeling envy, resentment, annoyance, and bitterness that is hard to control.
- **Relief.** Parents, especially those who have been struggling for a significant length of time with an undiagnosed medical condition or ability difference, often report they are glad to have a name for their child's disorder. They are relieved to know that their child's problems are not imaginary or caused by bad parenting (Owens & Bassity, 2007, p. 26).

FIGURE 6.1

Planning for Success

We need a plan for success that brings team members together to identify the child's needs, set goals, plan strategies, and track progress.

6-2 Laws and Programs for Children with Ability Differences

Parents and educators should know about the legal rights of children with severe medical conditions and ability differences and the legal responsibilities of educational professionals who work with them. Special education law—the **Individuals with Disabilities Education Act, or IDEA**—requires that students be provided a **free appropriate public education (FAPE)** that prepares them for further education, employment, and independent living. Special education must provide the **least restrictive environment (LRE)**, which is the environment most like that of typically developing children in which the child with a disability can succeed.

Using a program called **Child Find**, state agencies are required to locate, evaluate, and identify children age 3 and older who have disabilities. They must find children regardless of the severity of the ability difference, including children attending private schools and child care centers, highly mobile children such as migrant and homeless children, and children who are suspected of having a disability even though they may be progressing from grade to grade. Disabilities include autism, emotional disorders, hearing impairment and deafness, visual impairment and blindness, intellectual disability, orthopedic impairment, health impairments, specific learning disability, speech or language impairment, traumatic brain injury, developmental delay, attention deficit/hyperactivity disorder (ADHD), and oppositional defiance disorder.

abusive head trauma (AHT)
(also called shaken baby syndrome) A particularly devastating type of child abuse that can be caused by direct blows to the head, dropping or throwing a child, or shaking a child. Head trauma is the leading cause of death in child abuse cases in the United States.

Individuals with Ability Disabilities Act (IDEA)
A law ensuring that eligible infants, toddlers, and children with ability differences receive early intervention and special education and related services. It requires that students be provided a free appropriate public education (FAPE) that prepares them for further education, employment, and independent living. Special education must provide the least restrictive environment (LRE), which is the environment most like that of typically developing children in which the child with an ability difference can succeed.

"Thank Heaven for Sarah"

Sarah taught and cared for a small group of children in her home. She felt strong commitment to her work and believed she made a difference in children's lives. She took great pride in operating her home-based child care program in a professional and responsible manner. She bristled at the term *babysitter* and referred to herself as a teacher, because that is what she believed she was for the babies, toddlers, and preschoolers in her care.

Robert was 3 years old. Sarah had been caring for him for several months and had become very concerned about his behavior. He always seemed to be in conflict with the other children and was biting, hitting, and kicking on a regular basis. Robert almost never used words to express his needs.

Sarah wondered if Robert had some problem that was causing him to misbehave. She watched him carefully and wrote down her observations about when, where, and why he seemed to get into trouble. She noticed his language delay. She began to suspect that Robert might not hear normally. She noticed that all the other children ran to the window when they heard the garbage truck, but Robert did not react. One day, Sarah stood quietly behind Robert and said very softly, "Robert, it's time for lunch." Although other children quickly responded, Robert never looked up from his blocks.

Sarah approached Robert's parents about her concerns on several occasions. She showed them her observation notes. She said, "I'm certainly not an expert about hearing, but I'm wondering if Robert could have a hearing problem. Has his pediatrician ever tested his hearing?" Robert's father said, "That's ridiculous. He hears whatever he wants to hear. He just chooses to ignore grown-ups most of the time." Robert's mother said, "His doctor hasn't ever mentioned a problem, and I don't see any reason to think anything is wrong."

Sarah continued caring for and working with Robert, but she still had a nagging feeling that his behavior was just not up to par for a child who seemed very bright in many ways. She noticed that his relationship with his parents had deteriorated and that he was almost constantly in trouble with adults or other children. Robert's behavior became worse. Other parents complained loudly about bite marks and bruises their children received from Robert. Finally, Sarah set up an appointment to talk again with Robert's parents.

Sarah, with kindness and respect in her voice, said, "I have become very attached to Robert. He is so bright and so full of creative energy. However, much of the time, his behavior is inappropriate and I don't feel successful in working with him. I am not an expert but I worry that he may not be able to hear as well as he should. I don't feel comfortable caring for him without screening to rule out a hearing problem. I respect

that you should do whatever you think is right for Robert, but I also have to do what I think is right for me and for the other children in my care."

Robert's father blurted out, "Fine! We'll just find someone else to care for him. We are not about to set out on some wild goose chase, looking for problems that don't exist." Sarah responded, "I understand. You have every right to do only what you believe is the best thing for your child. I'm sure that I would do the same myself. As much as I care about Robert, and as much as I would love to keep him here with me, I am happy to accept your decision. I'll do anything I can to help with the transition to a different child care situation. The important thing is for each of us to feel comfortable with what we do."

Robert's mother was not eager to find new child care for Robert. She really liked the way Sarah cared for the children. Robert's mother called her child's doctor. She had several long discussions with her husband. Robert's mother finally convinced her husband that Robert should have his hearing tested in a medical clinic that could do specialized hearing testing on very young children.

A few weeks later, Robert's father stopped by to talk to Sarah. He said, "You know, I was so sure that nothing was wrong with Robert's hearing that I really resented your insisting on a hearing test. I can't believe it, but the doctor says he has a profound hearing loss in one ear and significant loss in the other. I just didn't know."

Sarah responded, "I could have been right, or I could have been wrong. I'm no expert on hearing, but I do appreciate knowing more about why he has been having such a hard time behaving. It is good to finally know what was bothering Robert. I think we can all work together to help Robert learn some new skills now."

As Robert's father turned to leave, he patted Robert's head and said softly, "Thank heaven for Sarah."

Case Discussion Questions

1. Do you think Sarah's actions were within her role as a caregiver?

2. Do you think Sarah went too far in insisting that Robert's hearing be checked?

3. How do you think this story would have ended if nothing had been wrong with Robert's hearing?

4. Specifically, what things did Sarah say or do that made her assertiveness more tolerable to Robert's parents?

5. How do you feel about very young children being "expelled" from child care centers and preschools for inappropriate behavior?

IDEA guarantees that persons ages 3–22 determined to have an ability difference fitting the IDEA definition of a "disability" will have an educational program best suited to their needs. To assure this program, they are given an **Individualized Education Program (IEP)** or an **Individualized Family Service Plan (IFSP)**. Each IEP or IFSP must be designed individually to meet the specific needs of the child. Both of these processes require effective teamwork.

6-2a What Are the IEP and IFSP Processes?

An IEP requires parents, teachers, other school staff— and the child, if he is old enough—to come together, communicate, share their commitment and expertise, and gather further information about the child's unique needs. Then they collaborate to design a support plan that will help the child be successful.

IDEA specifies rules concerning IEPs in public schools, charter schools, and some private schools or child care programs that accept public funding.

IDEA requires states to provide early intervention services for children birth to age 3 years with disabilities and developmental delays. To plan and provide services for infants and toddlers, an IFSP is required. Both the IEP and the IFSP processes are based on meeting the child's individual needs. However, the IFSP additionally gives in-depth family support services, nutrition services, and case management.

6-2b What if My Program Isn't Required to Provide an IEP?

Even if a formal IEP is not required, common sense dictates that a plan be put in place. Every child with significant ability differences deserves an individualized plan for success, whether it is legally required or not. *In any DAP program, there should be a plan in place to bring parents of a child with special needs together with teachers/caregivers and any other relevant resources to identify the child's needs, set goals, plan strategies for success, and track progress.*

Meetings with families can be informal in small, intimate programs, or they might be quite formalized and follow virtually every step of the IEP or IFSP format in a setting with many resources. The important thing is the quality and depth of the communication among parents, teachers, the child (when appropriate), and resource personnel (a community volunteer, a social worker, a therapist, and so on). This communication has the potential to generate creative approaches to troublesome problems, release pent-up emotions, provide warmth and support for all the parties involved, and keep the child's needs foremost in everyone's minds.

Additionally, parents need to know that just because their child is in a private school or child care center, they have not necessarily given up their right to free services. If the child has an ability difference that falls under IDEA's definition of a disability, free special education support services, such as speech therapy or social interaction therapy, may be provided in addition to or actually in the private child care center or school. States (and cities) vary dramatically in what services they provide and how their services are delivered. Parents should be encouraged to fully explore what services might be available and to take advantage of this valuable help.

As professionals, we must make every effort to work collaboratively with families and community resources. Perhaps we can help young families ease their way through the process of getting IDEA help for their child. Too often parents find it overwhelmingly frustrating as they struggle through the IDEA system, which is bound by government regulations and the attendant paperwork.

Parents of babies and young children newly diagnosed with serious medical conditions or ability differences may be strained to the breaking point emotionally. Cooperating with social workers and therapists, who are focused on following a set procedure, may seem unbearable to parents, who are caught up in anguish, grief, and anger. Parents can also be terribly disappointed by the limitations of services available when their needs are so great. We should evidence compassion and patience in our interactions with families of children with serious medical or ability concerns.

free appropriate public education (FAPE)
A directive requiring that school districts provide children with ability differences access to general education as well as specialized educational services to accommodate special needs. It also requires that children with ability differences receive support free of charge, the same as is provided to non–differently abled students.

least restrictive environment (LRE)
The requirement in IDEA law that children with ability differences receive their education, to the maximum extent appropriate, with non–differently abled peers and that special education pupils not be removed from regular classes unless, even with supplemental aids and services, education in regular classes cannot be achieved satisfactorily.

Child Find
A component of IDEA law that requires state agencies to locate, evaluate, and identify children between the ages of 3 and 21 who are in need of early intervention or special education services.

Individualized Education Program (IEP)
A written plan that describes exactly how teachers, parents, school administrators, related services personnel, and the student from 3–22 years of age with a disability will work together to improve the student's educational results. (Miller, 145)

Individualized Family Service Plan (IFSP)
A written plan that is intended to assist families and professionals in their combined efforts to meet the developmental requirements of young children from birth to age 3 with special needs.

6-2c What if My Program Doesn't Accept Children with Ability Differences?

Some private child care programs and private schools feel that it is outside their scope to care for children with ability differences. They may be surprised to learn that they may be held legally responsible if they turn away a child because of a disabling condition. We are each responsible to ensure that doors are open for children with ability differences.

For a differently abled child to succeed, there must be an effective plan. Part of the IEP or IFSP plan might include public funding for an aide or therapist to accompany a child with extensive needs to child care. Every child is different, every community has different resources and guidelines, and every set of possibilities is different.

6-3 How Do Various Health Conditions Affect Behavior?

Because irritability and discomfort are likely causes of misbehavior, any number of physical illnesses or conditions could result in behavior changes. Muscular differences could affect a child's ability to carry out tasks, or developmental delays could make it impossible for a child to perform as expected. Parents, teachers, and caregivers can assist screening personnel in evaluating a child who has behavioral difficulty by observing and keeping daily records of behaviors that might indicate problems.

All children behave inappropriately from time to time, no matter how well they seem to be developing and how cooperative, competent, and confident they are generally. Some children, however, behave inappropriately often enough to cause us serious concern. Although inappropriate behavior usually has simpler roots, we should consider the possibility of physical causes for severe, persistent misbehavior. Various cues or signals could be red flags that something is awry. Parents, teachers, and caregivers should never attempt to diagnose physical ailments or developmental delays. They should, however, watch carefully for indications that a child needs expert evaluation to rule out or confirm physical or psychological problems.

6-3a What Type of Ability Differences Am I Most Likely to Encounter?

About 13 percent of all 3- to 21-year-olds are receiving special education services (Aud et al., 2013). Behavior problems distress parents and teachers and are a common reason children are referred to specialists for assessment and support. Fox (2008) reports that 10 to 15 percent of typically developing children have mild to moderate behavioral concerns. He reports that children from low-income communities often have rates double or triple that number. Studies by Fox and others indicate that if these behavior issues are not addressed, they may cause serious problems for children at school and at home (Briggs-Gowan et al., 2001; Fox, 2008; Zeanah, 2000). See Positive Focus 6.8.

Positive Focus 6.8 — Troublesome Problems that Interfere with Learning

Parents and teachers agonize especially over the following five categories of disorders, which can wreak havoc with children's educational success (Dobbs, Doctoroff, Fisher, & Arnold, 2006; Kataoka, Zhang, & Wells, 2002; McGoey, Eckert, & Dupaul, 2002; Warner & Pottick, 2006):

- Behavior problems
- Attention problems
- Anxiety problems
- Mood problems
- Social problems

Many medical and physiological conditions can cause children to behave inappropriately. It is impossible to list every possibility, but in this chapter we will cover conditions that typically cause the most worrisome classroom issues.

6-3b Hearing Impairment and Deafness

Gallaudet Research Institute (2010) estimates that two to three of every 1000 children in the United States are born deaf or hard of hearing, and nine of every 10 children who are born deaf are born to parents who can hear. **Hearing impairment** (which includes deafness and difficulty hearing and is described by the terms *deaf* and *hard of hearing*) is the most common type of sensory ability difference.

Research has shown that children whose hearing loss is identified while they are still babies learn to communicate more easily and more completely than those whose hearing loss is identified later. Additionally, children who are deaf or hard of hearing from birth are able to develop and learn more effectively if they receive appropriate intervention starting early in life. Because early detection and early intervention are key to prevention of developmental delays, some states require hearing tests for infants soon after birth. See Positive Focus 6.9.

6-3c Sensory Processing Disorder

Sensory processing disorder (SPD) is a condition characterized by the inability of the brain to correctly process information brought in by the senses. SPD is associated with autism, cerebral palsy, ADHD, and other neurological conditions, or it can be present by itself (Kranowitz, 2010; Ostovar, 2010). See Positive Focus 6.10.

hearing impairment
The term "Hearing Impaired" is a medically accurate description of persons who are hard of hearing or who have no hearing. Many deaf, hard of hearing and late deafened people, however, don't like to be called impaired. Most expect to be identified as deaf or hard of hearing when the need arises to identify their hearing status, but many resent these terms being used as to identify them as people. Nearly 10 percent of human beings have some level of hearing loss.

sensory processing disorder
A neurological disorder causing difficulties in receiving, processing, and responding appropriately to sensations one's body takes in from the surrounding environment.

Guiding Children Who Are Deaf or Hard of Hearing

Positive Focus 6.9

- Get the attention of the child before speaking to her (tap her shoulder).
- Speak naturally at normal volume.
- Partner the child with or near a willing peer "buddy" during projects as a visual role model.
- Give preferential seating during circle time to make sure the child can see your face.
- Use a circle or semicircle whenever possible for any size group activities so that the hearing impaired child can see others' faces.
- Be sure lighting is adequate and free of glare (the hearing impaired child relies on vision).
- Reduce visual distractions by reducing excessive artwork, limiting mobiles, and removing clutter.
- If the child has hearing aids, she may be extremely sensitive to sounds such as aquarium pumps, computers, air conditioners, heaters, open doors, or windows. Try to eliminate or minimize such noises.
- Find out if the child has a "better" ear so you and others can speak to the child on that side.

TeachSource Digital Download

Guiding Children with SPD

Positive Focus 6.10

- Adjust chairs to the proper height for individual children so their feet are flat on the floor.
- Adjust tabletops so that they are just below children's elbows if children rest their fists under their chins.
- Present and reinforce learning through hands-on, sensory materials to increase understanding and memory.

(Continued)

- Minimize extraneous visual and auditory distractions.
- Give a child a simple picture chart (for a younger child) or a written note (for an older child) to help her stay on track when she needs to perform specific tasks.
- Provide pencil grippers for children who have trouble holding pencils and crayons.
- Tape down paper for younger children when they draw or write.
- Show older children how to use their nondominant hand to hold down paper when they draw or write.
- Provide thick paper to help prevent frustrating paper tears, and provide and thick crayons to prevent the frustration of broken crayons for a child who may press hard on pencils and crayons.

NOTE: Although it sounds contradictory, a child with SPD may be oversensitive to external stimuli, but at the same time the child may need to feel hand, mouth, or body stimulation before she can become calm and to organize her behavior.

For children who are oversensitive to stimuli, you may find it helpful to do the following:

- Approach the child from the front so you don't surprise him with your touch.
- Use firm pressure when you need to touch the child because a light, unexpected touch may distress him.
- Help the child find a workspace that is removed from the main flow of classroom traffic; doing so can help the child anticipate other children's movements.
- Provide soft pillows or a bean bag chair in the reading center as a retreat from too much stimulation.
- Help the child find a comfortable space in crowded situations (such as when he is in line or during circle time) so he can avoid unexpected jostles from other children.
- Be aware that smells (perfume, paint, cleaning products) may cause the child distress.
- Be aware that "scratchy" clothing, tags in clothing, or any uncomfortable objects or textures touching the child's body may be perceived as intolerable.

For children who need intensified sensory stimulation to organize their behavior, you may find it helpful to do the following:

- Understand that fidgeting, chewing clothing, tapping feet, rocking, and other random movements are simply the child's way of coping.
- Periodically take the child outside for 5 minutes of running and climbing.
- Have a rocking chair in the classroom and invite frequent rocking.
- Direct the child toward movement-oriented learning activities.
- Help the child find work that is physically challenging, such as carrying heavy buckets of sand in the sand box, pushing a friend on a tricycle, or washing tables.
- Select an appropriate object or squeeze ball the child can use as a way to redirect fidgeting.
- Coordinate with parents to select an appropriate object for the child to carry around and chew (go to Sensory University online to find appropriate therapeutic objects for chewing and fidgeting).
- Allow the child to sit on a partially inflated air pillow so she can rock as she works.

TeachSource Digital Download

Down syndrome
A congenital disorder involving chromosome 21 that causes intellectual disability and distinct physical differences such as a broad facial profile and short stature.

6-3d Down Syndrome **Down syndrome** causes children some degree of cognitive and developmental delay (there is a wide range). Children with Down syndrome tend to be endearing and affectionate, but they desperately need consistent, loving, and solid guidance or they, too, can be out of control and disrespectful. See Positive Focus 6.11.

Guiding Children with Down Syndrome

- Set limits that are within the child's capability and then firmly but gently see that they are kept. Although children with Down syndrome are often perceived as gentle and mild tempered, they are at risk for developing significant behavior problems.
- Support the development of self-competence, self-esteem, and self-determination that can bring about social and emotional well-being.
- Support healthful dietary and active physical patterns to avoid obesity.
- Be alert to the possibility of hearing problems.
- Provide closeness, attachment, and personal interaction.
- Assist the child in developing friendships with peers.

TeachSource Digital Download

The presence of an extra chromosome causes Down syndrome. Children with Down syndrome usually have a small head, a face that is flat and broad, slanting eyes, and a short nose. The tongue tends to protrude, and the ears are set low on the head and may be small. The hands are short and broad, with a single distinct crease through each palm (Hanson, 1996).

Infants with Down syndrome tend to be passive and have somewhat limp muscles. The intelligence quotient (IQ) among children with Down syndrome varies but averages about 50, as compared with that of typically developing children, whose average IQ is 100. Children with Down syndrome have better visual-motor skills (such as drawing) than skills that require hearing. Consequently, their language skills usually develop very slowly. Early intervention with educational and other support services significantly increases the functioning of young children with Down syndrome (Pueschel, 2000).

Any family from any racial or ethnic background may give birth to a child with Down syndrome, although it's more likely in mothers older than 35. Children with Down syndrome are especially vulnerable to colds, ear infections, and pneumonia. They usually have heart defects and a range of other underlying health problems that lead to a shorter than usual life expectancy (Stray-Gundersen, 1995).

In the past, Down syndrome was sometimes called "mongolism" because the features of people with Down syndrome were thought to resemble those of Mongolian Asians. This term is now considered offensive and should never be used.

6-3e Fetal Alcohol Spectrum Disorders

The umbrella term **fetal alcohol spectrum disorders (FASDs)** covers a cluster of individual **syndromes**, each caused by prenatal alcohol exposure. FASD includes fetal alcohol syndrome (FAS), partial fetal alcohol syndrome (PFAS), alcohol-related neurodevelopmental disorder (ARND), alcohol-related birth defects (ARBDs), and fetal alcohol effect (FAE). Children with FAS are the most severely affected among this group; those with FAE are the least affected, but they usually have significant behavioral and learning issues (National Task Force on Fetal Alcohol Syndrome and Fetal Alcohol Effect, 2004).

Alcohol use during pregnancy is a leading preventable cause of physical, cognitive, and behavioral problems—one in 10 U.S. women drinks alcohol while pregnant (Gmel & Rehm, 2003; Jones et al., 2010; Sood et al., 2001).

There is no known safe amount of alcohol for a woman who is pregnant (Sood et al., 2001). Sadly, even one drink per week

fetal alcohol spectrum disorders (FASDs)
A group of permanent birth defects caused by a mother drinking alcohol during pregnancy.

syndromes
Diseases or disorders that have more than one feature or symptom.

▶❚❚ **TeachSource** Video

© 2013 Cengage Learning®

Fetal Alcohol Syndrome

Watch this Video Case on preschool attendance, and then answer the following questions:

1. What is fetal alcohol syndrome (FAS)? What causes it?
2. List three symptoms of FAS described in this video.
3. Is FAS easily diagnosed by children's doctors?

Children with ADHD need learning activities that allow them to be physically active while they are learning. These children often have an extreme capacity for focused concentration when they discover their own special areas of interest and talent.

during the first 3 months of pregnancy increases the risk of low birth weight, prematurity, delayed or irregular development, behavior problems, and learning disabilities. Infants of heavy drinkers can suffer a wide range of devastating, lifelong physical, behavioral, and intellectual loss (Gunzerath et al., 2004; Jacobson & Jacobson, 2002; Jones et al., 2010).

Research connects maternal smoking during pregnancy to behavior risk. Children whose mothers smoked while pregnant have been identified as more likely to be socially defiant and impulsively aggressive (Huizink & Mulder, 2006; Kahn et al., 2003; Wakschlag et al., 2002, 2006; Weitzman et al., 2002). As advocates for children, we can raise health awareness of potential parents.

6-3f Attention Deficit/Hyperactivity Disorder (ADHD)

Attention deficit/hyperactivity disorder (ADHD) is one of the most common behavioral disorders. It has forms that are characterized by inattention, impulsiveness, or extremely high levels of physical activity. ADHD has had different names in past years. Children with this disorder have been called hyperactive and hyperkinetic. Those terms are no longer considered appropriate or accurate (Bramer, 2006).

ADHD is often marked by excessive physical activity at inappropriate times. Obviously, children with ADHD need special support to achieve their maximum potential. These children often need safe things to chew on and twiddle with their fingers. Their little bodies may seem to be constantly in motion. See Positive Focus 6.12.

Parents or teachers may question a diagnosis of ADHD. How can a very bright child be unable to pay attention to a lesson but be able to focus on something that strongly interests him? This is not a matter of willpower. Bramer (2006) explains that the **executive system** of the brain controls the child's attention. ADHD causes malfunctions of the brain's executive system, which can prevent the child from being able to deal with tasks that challenge him, even though he can succeed at easier tasks. Consequently, ADHD can significantly disrupt cognitive, behavioral, social, and educational parts of the child's daily life. See Positive Focus 6.13.

attention deficit/ hyperactivity disorder (ADHD)
A common developmental disorder that appears during childhood and is characterized by a persistent pattern of inattention as well as forgetfulness, poor impulse control, and distractibility.

executive system
A theorized system of the brain that controls and organizes other mental processes. It manages processes such as planning, abstract thinking, rule learning, screening out irrelevant sensory information, and inhibiting inappropriate actions; also referred to as executive function or the central executive.

Positive Focus 6.12 Children with ADHD Have Special Challenges

Although children with ADHD may be very capable, they typically experience the following:

- Extraordinary difficulty concentrating or paying attention most of the time
- Extreme, inflexible concentration on self-selected topics
- Rigid periods of concentration that cause them not to hear anyone or anything
- Intense distractibility and forgetfulness
- An extremely short interest span except when in rigid concentration
- Constant fidgeting, bouncing, and squirming
- Impulsiveness, lack of self-control, poor decision making
- Excessive, uncontrolled talking
- Difficulty waiting for a turn
- Problems getting along with peers
- Problems with erratic eating or sleeping

Guiding Children with ADHD

- Pause before the beginning of a potential problem situation to talk about what is going to happen and what is needed from the child.
- Role-play to practice handling difficult situations.
- Help the child learn to talk and think about the cause and effect of potential actions.
- Give the child more immediate and more frequent feedback about his behavior.
- Avoid rescuing the child from the consequences of her behavior (see Chapter 11 for more information on consequences).
- Regularly focus the child's attention on the consequences of his actions.

TeachSource Digital Download

Myths about ADHD abound. ADHD is a complex biologic disorder; bad parenting, inadequate teachers, too much television, food allergies, or excess sugar don't cause ADHD, but certainly can intensify the symptoms. A massive amount of international research shows that ADHD occurs in some children regardless of culture and parenting. Still, how parents and teachers respond goes a long way in bringing about a calmer, happier child. The child will need support through childhood, adolescence, and possibly adulthood to function at her best (Sherman et al., 2006).

Life is challenging for children with ADHD. They get in trouble with adults, get into quarrels with friends, and bump into one frustration after another. School-age children spend agonizing hours struggling to keep their minds on homework and then forget to bring it to school the next morning.

Siblings and classmates of a child who has ADHD are challenged too. They may feel neglected as their parents or teachers try to cope with the child with ADHD. They may resent their brother, sister, or classmate who is distressingly active, leaves messes, throws tantrums, and doesn't listen. They may especially resent that the child with ADHD doesn't behave properly but seems to have a disproportionate amount of the adult's time and attention.

Some children with ADHD unleash their pent-up annoyance and frustration by having tantrums, being aggressive, or destroying property. Others hold the frustration inside and begin to have stomach aches, headaches, or other physical symptoms (Bramer, 2006; Sherman et al., 2006).

A child with ADHD is in trouble with adults so often that he often develops poor self-esteem. The adult should find a way to make the majority of interactions with the child positive. Early childhood professionals must break the cycle of negative interactions with the child and find a way to build mutual respect and caring. Respect and caring create the foundation for self-esteem.

It's also hard for the adult. She may feel helpless and frustrated. Guidance techniques don't seem to work. The adult may be tempted to resort to negative discipline techniques, but these are even more troublesome and ineffective for the child with an ability difference than for other children. The child needs more calm and less stress—and, most importantly, caring, consistent, assertive positive guidance.

Medications prescribed for ADHD increase activity in parts of the brain that aren't working properly. They aren't tranquilizers or sedatives and they aren't addictive (Bauermeister, 2003; Manassis, 2007; MTA Cooperative Group, 2004). Parents and doctors make choices about what therapies they believe are appropriate for the children in their care. Many will approach treatment very differently. The goal of all these approaches—medication, diet, and therapy—is to help children with ADHD to be happier and more at peace with their environment and the expectations of others.

Our role as early childhood professionals is to provide and explain objective observations of the child's classroom behavior, to caringly support the family, and to give objective information about relevant resources. We overstep the bounds of professionalism if we ever make comments such as, "I don't think parents should put their children

TeachSource Video

Autism and a Bike

Watch this Video Case on preschool attendance, and then answer the following questions:

1. How does learning to ride a bike support:
   a. Motor control and balance?
   b. Independence?
   c. Self-esteem?
   d. Social skills?
   e. Feelings of inclusion?
2. Do you think these particular qualities are especially important for children with significant ability differences? Why or why not?

on drugs," or, "I don't think the therapy you have Mimi on is working. Why don't you just put her back on her ADHD pills?"

Parents of children with ADHD have plenty of stress to deal with without having to fend off teachers who give personal opinions about medical treatments. Many parents of children with special needs are overwhelmed by unsolicited advice from in-laws, friends, neighbors, and sometimes even complete strangers. Families we work with will appreciate our professionalism as we listen respectfully and stay objective.

6-3g Intellectual Disability (ID)

The traditional term *mental retardation* has an objectionable social stigma. Because of this negative connotation, doctors, health care practitioners, and educators now use the term **intellectual disability** (AAIDD, 2011). Because this transition is fairly recent, the combined term *intellectual disability* (*mental retardation*) is sometimes used as a clarification (Byrne, 2000).

Intellectual disability is not a specific medical disorder or illness like chicken pox or diabetes, and it is not a mental health condition like depression or obsessive-compulsive disorder. ID can be caused by a specific medical disorder or illness, but ID itself is simply a mismatch between the capabilities of an individual and the demands that daily life in the inclusive community make on community members.

A person is intellectually disabled if her ability to manage the basic activities of daily living is significantly limited.

Positive Focus 6.14 Guiding Children with Intellectual Disability

- Look at the individual child instead of focusing on the disability.
- Adjust to the child's unique needs and abilities.
- Use simple, short sentences.
- Repeat instructions or directions and ask the child if she understands.
- Use literal language; avoid expressions that won't make sense to the child.
- Be patient! Model and practice coping strategies.
- Keep distractions and transitions to a minimum.
- Emphasize consistency.
- Reinforce positive behavior.
- Maximize the child's inclusion with peers and help her make friends.
- Break skills into small steps; slowly demonstrate and practice one step at a time, allowing for much repetition.
- Specifically demonstrate and practice organizational skills.
- Provide an encouraging, supportive learning environment that will give the child success and support his self-esteem.
- Change the environment and the materials to assure the child's challenge and success.
- Modify teaching strategies and assessment methods to match the child's abilities.
- Avoid doing anything for the child that she can do for herself.
- Encourage independence.

© 2013 Cengage Learning®

Essential daily activities include communicating, performing self-care and hygiene, participating in community life, making decisions, solving problems, carrying out tasks, and following safety rules. Children with this disorder need a great deal of specialized support and guidance throughout their schooling to prepare them for maximum independence (Bogdan et al., 1982; Bouras, 1994, 1999; Byrne, 2000; Koskentausta, 2006). See Positive Focus 6.14.

Disability is a matter of perception. If you can do just one thing well, you're needed by someone.

—Martina Navratilova

6-3h Pervasive Developmental Disorders

Pervasive developmental disorders (PDDs) are a group of disorders affecting brain development that are characterized by delays in the development of socialization and communication skills. Autism is the most characteristic and best-studied PDD. Other types include fragile X syndrome, Rett's syndrome, and Asperger's. The diagnosis of Asperger's syndrome is currently in the process of being redefined by the medical community. The American Psychiatric Association (2010) has proposed that the diagnosis of Asperger's be eliminated and replaced by a diagnosis of autism spectrum disorder with a severity scale.

Parents sometimes notice PDD symptoms as early as infancy, but the usual age for diagnosis of these disorders is approximately 3 years of age. Children with PDDs have mild to severe difficulty using and understanding language, difficulty relating socially to others, unusual play with toys and other objects, difficulty with changes in routine or familiar surroundings, and repetitive body movements or behavior patterns (Gupta, 2004; Schaefer & Mendelsohn, 2008).

Autism 自閉症

Autism, sometimes called **mind blindness**, is a brain disorder that affects a person's sense of self. The minds of people on the autism spectrum are unusually detail oriented. Many children with this disorder are bright and analytical. Children with the disorder have difficulty sensing other people's moods. They are unable to distinguish themselves as separate and have trouble picking up language. They often avoid eye contact and sometimes even avoid physical contact. See Positive Focus 6.15.

intellectual disability (ID)
Mismatch between an individual's capabilities and the demands of daily life to communicate, handle self-care and hygiene needs, participate in community life, make appropriate decisions, solve problems, carry out tasks, and follow safety rules.

pervasive developmental disorders (PDDs)
A group of neurodevelopmental disorders characterized by severe delays in the development of socialization and communication skills.

autism
A developmental brain disorder characterized by impaired social interaction and communication skills, avoidance of eye-to-eye gaze, and a limited range of activities and interests.

mind blindness 精神盲
A brain disorder that impairs one's ability to "read minds" by noticing gestures, facial expressions, and changes in tone of voice. An inability to fathom what is in the mind of another person.

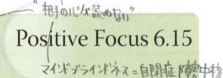

Positive Focus 6.15

Guiding Children with Autism

- Avoid insisting on eye contact.
- Be patient and supportive whether the child has stereotyped and repetitive, delayed, or no language at all.
- Help this highly sensitive child avoid upsetting sensations—glaring lights, startling sounds, scratchy textures, unpleasant smells.
- Realize that at times the child might be unresponsive to voices and sounds, even if her hearing is normal.
- Avoid pointing, because doing so probably won't help the child understand what you mean or what you want him to see.
- Avoid cuddling, touching, or hugging unless you really sense that it is invited by the child.
- Understand that the child will have difficulty expressing her needs and may use negative behavior to get your attention instead.
- Recognize that the child will lack the ability for spontaneous, make-believe play.
- Be aware that the child doesn't know what your facial expressions and body language mean.
- Remember that the child is not sure if you are happy with her or upset with her.
- Coach the child carefully to help him learn to interact with other children more appropriately.
- Help the other children learn that the child with autism will sometimes act and speak in a manner that is different from how the other children act and speak.

(Continued)

- Although the child may be preoccupied with restricted areas of interest, slightly broaden his interest by introducing related objects or topics.
- Understand that the child's obsessive need to spin or line up objects is beyond her control.
- Realize that the child's brain is forcing her to follow rigid routines or rituals, hand-flapping, rocking, or flicking fingers, and those actions may not make sense to us.
- Plan for difficulty helping the child transition from one activity or setting to another.
- Make as few changes in the environment, routines, or schedule as possible and help the child prepare for these changes.
- Plan for frequent tantrums or meltdowns as stresses become too much for the child to handle.

hypersensitivity
Overreaction to sensory input from one of the senses (for example, sight, sound, taste, smell, touch).

auditory figure-ground dysfunction
An inability to distinguish between levels of sounds in the environment, to focus on significant sounds and tune out irrelevant sounds. This is a common characteristic in PDDs and some learning disorders.

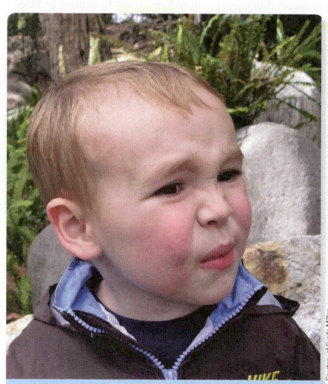

Children with autism are extremely fragile emotionally. They tend to develop repetitive behaviors to help sooth themselves, such as flapping their arms. This child needs opportunities to learn and feel valued just like any other child.

Even very young children can be diagnosed with and treated for autism; in fact, the sooner the disorder is identified in a child, the better the outcome (American Psychiatric Association, 2004). It is easy to see why these children are emotionally fragile. They begin with a special risk for developing inappropriate behaviors to help soothe themselves, such as flapping their arms, bumping their heads, or running around in circles.

Children with autism are likely to become agitated if you give them what most children long for—eye contact at eye level with warm physical touch. Nonetheless, children with autism want and need adult attention. The world is frightening, overwhelming, and overstimulating.

It may be helpful for this child make a stable connection with one consistent staff member. Spending a few minutes of quiet time with that person when problems arise may alleviate some of the stresses the child encounters day to day. Once the level of stress is reduced and the child is more relaxed, she may become more responsive to guidance suggestions and be able to cope with problem solving.

Often, this child's behavior can stay on track if her life stays predictable. A child with autism has a difficult time coping with changes in her environment, routine, or schedule. Disruptions can cause her to become uncooperative and out of control. Plan for, talk about, and move carefully into necessary changes. See Positive Focus 6.16.

Many children with autism have **hypersensitivity**. Such children may also overreact to smells, food textures, sounds, or other sensory stimuli they may not be able to explain (Bogdashina, 2003; Bonnice, 2004). A simple change, such as switching to daylight saving time, changes the environment (less light) and may cause such a child to feel extreme distress. The sensation of milk unexpectedly dripping on the child's skin at lunch may cause a "meltdown." His anguish may be expressed in tantrums or other inappropriate behavior.

Children with autism also experience a phenomenon referred to as **auditory figure-ground dysfunction**. The child may hear a distant siren on the freeway, the class singing in the next room, and the hamster scratching in the cage all at the same volume as the teacher speaking directly to him. Most of us would tune these other background noises out and notice only the voice of the speaker. The autistic child is incapable

Guiding Children with Autism

- Consistently follow a daily routine.
- Make sure the child knows the daily routine at the start of each day.
- Lay out the day's scheduled activities on a felt board.
- Make frequent reference to the schedule throughout the day.
- Give 5-minute warnings before any switch of activity or change in the day's routine.
- Teach, practice, and model appropriate social behavior and social skills (such as taking turns and maintaining social distance).
- Intentionally include the child in activities/projects with other children.
- Help the child learn how to be a friend and have a friend (practice, role model, bibliotherapy).
- Use short sentences to ensure understanding.
- Use literal, precise language; avoid tongue-in-cheek humor (the child won't understand phrases such as "I'm so hungry I could eat a horse").
- Call the child by her name (she may not realize that an instruction given to the whole class also includes her).
- Include multiple learning styles, and emphasize sensory learning.
- Make extra efforts to protect the child from teasing and bullying.

TeachSource Digital Download

of tuning out the unneeded sounds (Bogdashina, 2003). For the child with autism, the extra sounds can be unbearably distracting.

Echolalia, a speech disorder, is the compulsive repetition of words spoken by someone else or heard on television or radio. In most cases, echolalic speech is cyclical self-stimulation (like hand flapping or rocking) that is not really intended as communication to anyone. The child with echolalia is able to repeat language she has heard and memorized even though she cannot generate her own speech to express her thoughts. Occasionally echolalia is intended as communication.

For example, a first grader with autism might tell me in a monotone, "I will tie your shoes," when she is actually asking for me to tie her shoes. She can't create the words she needs to say, but she has memorized the words "I will tie your shoes." That is what she hears when her shoes get tied (Frith, 2003).

Children with autism often have dramatic differences in behavior compared with their peers. The techniques that consistently help us to bond socially with typically developing children may frustrate and frighten a child with pervasive developmental disorders like autism or Asperger's. Eye contact at eye level, speaking, smiling, touching, and offering an interesting object may actually cause these children extreme distress rather than security.

6-3i Tourette's Syndrome

Children with **Tourette's syndrome** have multiple **motor tics** and **vocal tics**. These tics occur many times throughout the day and may be aggravated by stress. Tourette's syndrome is often accompanied by ADHD or obsessive-compulsive disorder. A child with Tourette's often suffers self-esteem difficulties and may be severely embarrassed by her tics. Some children with Tourette's may be able to restrain their tics for short periods, but doing so takes their full concentration and a great deal of energy and causes them stress. See Positive Focus 6.17.

Children must be closely supervised in early childhood programs, classrooms, or any other group situations when the group includes a child with Tourette's. Allowing children to tease, bully, or stigmatize a child with tics is not only cruel, but is also damaging to the child's social and emotional development and can leave lifelong scars (Lin et al., 2007; Waltz, 2001). See Positive Focus 6.18.

echolalia
A speech disorder that causes compulsive repetition of words spoken by others. In most cases, echolalic speech is a habitual form of cyclical self-stimulation that is not intended as communication, but in some cases echolalia may be used as the child's only available tool in an improvised attempt at communication.

Tourette's syndrome
A disorder characterized by multiple motor and vocal tics.

motor tic
A sudden involuntary muscular contraction, often of the facial, shoulder, or neck muscles. Complex motor tics include distinct, obsessively repeated, intricate actions or behaviors such as twirling, hopping, or obsessively lining things up in straight rows. Tics tend to become more pronounced when one is under stress.

vocal tic
A sudden involuntary vocalization such as a yip, whistle, grunt, or cough. A complex vocal tic is a distinct, obsessively repeated phrase or the intricate obsessive use of words, such as repeating everything other people say.

Positive Focus 6.17 Children with Tourette's Syndrome

Children with Tourette's often experience the following:

- Simple vocal tics—uncontrollable repetitive sounds
  - Coughing, throat clearing
  - Whistling
  - Grunting ブタのような鳴き声、のどの奥からめくような声
  - Hissing
  - Barking
- Complex vocal tics—uncontrollable, compulsive, repeated intricate verbalizations
  - Repetitions of clichés such as "Wow," "Yup, that's it," "but, but . . ."
- Simple motor tics—uncontrollable repetitive actions
  - Neck twisting
  - Excessive blinking
  - Clapping
  - Hopping
  - Arm flailing → 激しくゆれる
  - Lip biting
  - Head banging (this and some other tics are harmful to the child)
- Complex motor tics—uncontrollable, compulsive, repeated intricate actions
  - Sorting and lining up items obsessively
  - Drawing over letters again and again until the paper tears

TeachSource Digital Download

Positive Focus 6.18 Guiding Children with Tourette's

- Give the child unconditional acceptance.
- Try to see the child and not her tics.
- React calmly to tics.
- Give the child time for short, private breaks so he can relax and release his tics.
- Remember that the child didn't choose to have tics, and he may be very embarrassed by them.
- Gather information and appropriate books for children and staff.
- Help everyone understand tics.
- Prevent or stop ridicule and teasing.
- Protect the privacy and safety of others (tics cause unwanted touching).
- Help the child find ways to work around problems.

TeachSource Digital Download

coprolalia 汚言症

Copro is the Greek term for "feces" and *lalia* is Greek for "babbling, meaningless talk." Literally, it means "manure talking." People with coprolalia make sudden, unexpected outbursts of inappropriate words or phrases.

copropraxia 7

Praxia is the Greek word for "act or action." Combined with *copro*, it means "manure behavior." People with copropraxia act out involuntarily, producing obscene, offensive, or shocking gestures and actions.

bipolar disorder 双极性障害 躁鬱

A disorder in which episodes of depression alternate with mania.

Coprolalia and **copropraxia** are rare, but characteristic, offensive outbursts from individuals with Tourette's syndrome. The words or actions are not done out of anger. The child bursts out uncontrollably, almost always to her embarrassment and dismay. It is almost as if the very mechanism in the brain that suppresses disturbing or inappropriate thoughts instead forces them to be yelled or acted out. Although these outbursts are 感情がどっとあふれること closely linked with Tourette's syndrome in the public consciousness, the vast majority of people with Tourette's never experience either type of outburst (Singer, 2009).

6-3j Bipolar Disorder

Bipolar disorder (also known as manic depression) causes episodes of mania followed by depression. Research indicates that bipolar disorder that begins in childhood may be more severe than older-adolescent and adult-onset bipolar disorder (Carlson et al., 1998; Geller & Luby, 1997). A child who appears to be depressed for a significant period and also has extreme temper outbursts, has persistent moodiness, and is extremely fidgety and distracted should be referred for medical evaluation. See Positive Focus 6.19.

Children with Bipolar Disorder

Children with bipolar disorder typically experience the following:

- Stark changes in mood—irritability, rage, extreme silliness, or intense euphoria
- Overblown, grandiose sense of self
- Difficulty falling asleep, waking after only a short sleep
- Increased talking; won't let anyone else speak
- Extremely short attention span
- Intense energy, nonstop physical activity
- Agitation; disregard for risk
- Depressive symptoms
- Irrational feelings of inadequacy
- Disproportional bouts of rage and frustration

TeachSource Digital Download

Bipolar disorder is different in children than it is in adults. Children usually have a continuing mood disturbance that is a mix of **mania** and **depression**. This quick but severe rotation between manic and depressive moods produces chronic irritability and few noticeable periods of wellness between episodes. Mania causes a worrisome combination of fearlessness, an overblown belief in one's abilities, racing thoughts, poor judgment, irritability, and anger. Children with this difficult disorder are often treated with medication and counseling, for the child as well as the parents (Frye, 2011; Mackin & Young, 2004).

Early identification, diagnosis, and treatment of bipolar disorder will help children reach their full potential. However, children who have bipolar disorder are at a greater risk of having anxiety disorders or ADHD, and having these disorders often contributes to a misdiagnosis or lack of diagnosis of bipolar disorder in young children. See Positive Focus 6.20.

mania
A mental state characterized by abnormally elevated mood, extraordinary energy, and bizarre thought patterns.

depression
A mental state characterized by pessimism, feelings of inadequacy, despondency, and lethargy.

Guiding Children with Bipolar Disorder

- Remember that bipolar disorder is a medical condition.
- Communicate often with the child's parents; they know their child and may be able to tell you how to keep him calm.
- Provide a well-structured and predictable classroom environment.
- Plan for and talk about any changes in the environment, routine, schedule, or transitions as far in advance as you can.
- Be flexible in your own expectations.
- Break tasks into smaller chunks, and allow the child plenty of time to complete his work.
- Reduce exposure to stress such as fatigue, discomfort, unexpected change, and boredom.
- Reduce unnecessary distractions in the classroom.
- Use role modeling to help the child practice social skills and rehearse situations.
- Avoid power struggles; never give threats or ultimatums.
- When dealing with an angry or defiant child, think "safety first."
- Make available a private area where the child can have some quiet time under adult supervision when he needs to calm down.
- Take seriously indication or talk of the child hurting herself, and tell the child's parents/guardians about such talk.

TeachSource Digital Download

oppositional defiant disorder (ODD) 反抗的行为障害
A condition in which an ongoing pattern of disobedient, hostile, and defiant behavior toward authority figures goes well beyond the bounds of normal childhood behavior.

self-regulation 自制心
A critical developmental process by which one learns to function without external control; being able to deal with problems appropriately and independently.

intermittent explosive disorder (IED)
A mental disorder typified by outbursts of violent and aggressive behavior that may harm others or destroy property.

conduct disorder
A mental condition typified by a repetitive and persistent pattern of socially unacceptable behavior that violates the rights of others. Typical symptoms include strongly aggressive behavior, bullying, cruelty, and destructiveness.

6-3k Oppositional Defiant Disorder and Intermittent Explosive Disorder

Oppositional defiant disorder (ODD) can seriously interfere with a child's day-to-day functioning. At a glance, it may seem difficult to tell the difference between a particularly strong-willed child and a child who has ODD. There is a big difference, however. Children afflicted with ODD are disobedient, hostile, and defiant to a degree not seen in typically developing children. See Positive Focus 6.21.

Most children have tantrums as toddlers. But by the preschool years, most children develop the social skills and **self-regulation** necessary to handle frustrating situations without resorting to tantrums—at least not very often. For reasons not yet well understood, the child with ODD is not able to develop essential self-regulation. These children regularly lose control of their emotions and feel compelled to defy authority. Children with ODD are clearly disruptive to home, community, and school environments. ODD is frequently identified in combination with other behavioral or mental health problems, such as ADHD, anxiety, and depression. These children need educational, medical, or therapeutic intervention to support them in managing this very challenging disorder (Greene et al., 2008; Keenan & Wakschlag, 2000).

Intermittent explosive disorder (IED) is a behavior disorder characterized by sudden extreme expressions of anger, often to the point of uncontrollable rage. These outbursts are totally out of proportion to the provocation and are sometimes accompanied by outbursts of physical aggression (Franz, 2004). See Positive Focus 6.22.

Because the child with ODD or IED may be argumentative, defiant, negative, and annoying to others, she isolates herself and may begin to feel rejected and unloved. Much of her time is spent in conflict with others at home, at school, and in child care (Greene et al., 2008: Lavigne et al., 2001; Loeber et al., 2000). Adults must be able to show unconditional caring so they can nurture this troubled child. This is not always easy to accomplish, especially when the child's previous negative behavior patterns have become ingrained habits. See Positive Focus 6.23.

Positive Focus 6.21   Children with ODD

Children with ODD typically experience the following:

- Frequent loss of temper
- Low tolerance for frustration
- Argumentativeness, anger, and resentfulness
- Spitefulness, vindictiveness
- Inability or unwillingness to follow direction or rules
- Placement of blame on others

Positive Focus 6.22   Children with ODD and IED

Children with ODD and IED typically need the following:

- A calm, supportive environment
- Clear boundaries
- Calm, stable guidance
- Quick interruption and firm redirection of inappropriate behavior
- Opportunities to make amends
- Help developing a sense of conscience
- Help learning how to put feelings into words

6-3l Conduct Disorder

Conduct disorder is a severe form of ODD that may, if not resolved, lead to adult antisocial personality disorder. Conduct disorder is a complex cluster of severe behavioral and emotional problems in children and adolescents. Children with this disorder have never learned to behave in a socially acceptable way. Children with conduct disorder typically exhibit aggression to people and animals, destroy property, are deceitful, lie, steal, and defy authority. Some children with conduct disorder may be drawn to violent gang involvement as young as 11 or 12 years of age (Allen et al., 2005; Frick & Dickens, 2006).

Adults, teachers, and peers might perceive children with conduct disorder to be juvenile delinquents rather than children who are differently abled, emotionally disturbed, mentally ill, and deserving of compassion. Many factors can contribute to a child developing conduct disorder. See Positive Focus 6.24.

Many children with conduct disorder have earlier experienced ODD or ADHD. In some cases, we may never know why this condition evolved in a particular child (Boxer et al., 2005; Dupéré et al., 2007). We do know that the younger the child's age when we intervene with assertive positive guidance, appropriate resources, therapies, counseling, medication, or whatever is needed to help the child, the better the chances this child can grow up to enjoy a productive adulthood (Lier et al., 2007; Welsh & Farrington, 2007). Physically punishing or socially rejecting the child with a conduct disorder pushes him further into his disorder. Finding some way to accept and include the child may open communication with the child (Green, 1998; Hutchings & Lane, 2005).

© 2013 Cengage Learning®

Children with ODD are troubled and troubling—to themselves, schools, and communities. These children need educational, medical, and therapeutic interventions to support them in addressing this challenging disorder. Now is the time to save their future.

The future for most children with conduct disorder is often very grim if they don't get early intervention and a great deal of support. A consistent, nurturing, and structured home environment is believed to be the best protection for children with conduct disorder. Child abuse and neglect are great risk factors for conduct disorder. Children with ADHD, behavior disorders, learning disabilities, or general difficulties in school need special help to avoid having these problems escalate. Addressing problems when they first appear helps prevent the frustration and low self-esteem that may lead to conduct disorder later on. See Positive Focus 6.25.

Summary

- Children with ability differences sometimes need special accommodations.
- Children with ability differences need exemplary DAP and positive guidance.
- Behavior disorders are the most common reason children are referred to specialists.
- Families learning that their young child has a serious medical condition or ability difference go through phases of shock and pain.
- Learn as much as possible about a child's ability difference(s).
- Show respect for a child and her family as they struggle to deal with a medical condition or ability difference in their own way.
- Avoid being overprotective. Never do anything for the child that he can reasonably do for himself.
- The child with an ability difference needs calm, assertive, positive child guidance as much as does any typically developing child.
- It's good to be optimistic, but have realistic expectations in guidance. Appreciate the uniqueness of each child. Never compare children.

- Focus on each child's strengths. Every child has positive characteristics and **assets**.
- Show unconditional affection to every child.
- Teach all of the children how to celebrate differences, show compassion, and express caring.
- Prevent bullying and stigmatizing.
- Have a sense of humor. Make sure that the environment is filled with joy.

- Any person from the ages of 3 to 22 years who has ability differences meeting IDEA's definition of a "disability" are guaranteed an appropriate education.
- In any developmentally appropriate program, there will be a plan in place to bring parents together with teachers to set goals, plan strategies for success, and track progress over time.
- We are each responsible to ensure that doors to education are always open for children with ability differences.

Key Terms

ability differences

accommodations

attention deficit/hyperactivity disorder (ADHD)

auditory figure-ground dysfunction

autism

bibliotherapy

bipolar disorder (manic depression)

bullying

Child Find

conduct disorder

coprolalia

copropraxia

depression

disabilities

Down syndrome

echolalia

executive system

fetal alcohol spectrum disorders (FASDs)

fight or flight response

free appropriate public education (FAPE)

hearing impairment

hypersensitivity

Individualized Family Service Plan (IFSP)

Individualized Education Program (IEP)

Individuals with Disabilities Education Act (IDEA)

intellectual disability (ID)

intermittent explosive disorder (IED)

learning disability

least restrictive environment (LRE)

mania

mind blindness

motor tics

oppositional defiant disorder (ODD)

pervasive developmental disorders (PDDs)

self-regulation

sensory processing disorder (SPD)

syndromes

teasing

Tourette's syndrome

vocal tic

Student Activities

1. Offer your services as a volunteer for an organization in your community that serves children with ability differences (Special Olympics, Down Syndrome Buddy Walk, a local hospital program, and so on).

2. Interview the parent of a child with an ability difference.
   a. How did the parent first discover that the child had an ability difference?
   b. What has been most difficult for the parent in caring for the child and meeting the child's needs?

   c. What has the parent found most rewarding?
   d. What does the parent think is the child's greatest strength?
   e. What does the parent think is the child's greatest weakness?
   f. Are there any community resources that the parent takes advantage of? If so, have they been helpful?

Related Resources

Readings

Bertin, M. (2011). *The family ADHD solution: A scientific approach to maximizing your child's attention and minimizing parental stress*. New York: Palgrave Macmillan.

This guide for parents of a child with attention deficit hyperactivity disorder can undoubtedly be useful in helping them grasp the nature of the disability and practical approaches toward treatment. Dr. Bertin approaches the topic with warmth and understanding as well as a research-based knowledge of the topic.

Twachtman-Cullen, D., & J. Twachtman-Bassett. (2011). *The IEP from A to Z: How to create meaningful and measurable goals and objectives*. San Francisco, CA: Jossey-Bass.

This guide shows teachers and parents how to develop an education plan for children with ADHD, autism/Asperger's, emotional/behavioral disturbance, and other conditions. It gives easy-to-understand explanations of the special education process, along with sample IEPs. It explains concepts educators and parents need to keep in mind during IEP development.

Websites

United States Department of Education

Questions about IDEA and ADA? For more information about IDEA regulations, contact the Department of Education or visit the department's website. You will also find answers to commonly asked questions about the Americans with Disabilities Act and practical information on child care professionals' legal responsibilities.

Kids on the Block

Kids on the Block provides programs addressing various disabilities, educational and medical differences, and social concerns. A curriculum accompanies each topic area, including scripts, answers to questions children ask, background information on the topic, character biographies, resource materials, follow-up information, and additional support.

The Future of Children

The Future of Children is a partnership developed by Princeton University and the Brookings Institution. The partnership's mission is to translate research about children and youth into information that is useful to parents and teachers. Because The Future of Children tries to reach a wide audience, its articles and webcasts avoid using overly technical language.

UNICEF

This organization strives to build a world where the rights of every child are realized. UNICEF works worldwide to support children's health, safety, and psychological well-being. UNICEF's work on disability is guided by a human rights–based approach, with a focus on equity and reaching the most marginalized individuals.

Autism Single Moms Blog Spot

This site offers conversation and insights from single moms who are raising children with autism. Moms share advice about coping, dating, and helping their children develop.

CHAPTER

7

Designing Developmentally Appropriate Environments Inside and Out

naeyc Standards

The following NAEYC Standards are addressed in this chapter

Standard 5   Using content knowledge to build meaningful curriculum

5a Understanding content knowledge and resources in academic disciplines

5b Knowing and using the central concepts, inquiry tools, and structures of content areas or academic disciplines

5c Using [your] own knowledge, appropriate early learning standards, and other resources to design, implement, and evaluate meaningful, challenging curricula for each child

The Preschool at Claremont United Methodist Church

Objectives

After reading this chapter, you should be able to do the following:

7-1 Explain how an environment can nurture appropriate behavior.

7-2 Design developmentally appropriate indoor environments.

7-3 Create a calm, peaceful classroom environment.

7-4 Design a DAP outdoor environment.

7-5 Create a nurturing social environment.

7-6 Demonstrate nurturing behaviors.

(def)
↑ care for and encourage the growth or development of.

7-1 How Does the Environment Nurture Appropriate Behavior?

育成

Infants do not fully grasp that others have feelings and needs similar to their own. They are not likely to postpone immediate gratification to work cooperatively with others toward a common goal. And, of course, children do not come into the world equipped with the **prosocial** skills to generously share a toy with a friend (Warneken & Tomasello, 2009).

Children adopt prosocial behaviors only after much experience and practice in an **environment** that demonstrates and nurtures positive social interaction (Holmes-Lonergan, 2003). All parts of the environment come together to create the child's early experience. Everything the child sees, hears, touches, smells, and tastes is a part of her environment. We are an important part of the child's environment. To plan for appropriate behavior, we must prepare ourselves, the indoors, and the outdoors to create an environment that will support prosocial behavior.

7-1a Three Key Elements of Prosocial Behavior

Prosocial behavior benefits others and demonstrates the presence of a social conscience. **Antisocial** behavior harms others and indicates a disregard for the rights and needs of others. See Positive Focus 7.1.

prosocial 向社会的な
Behavior that improves the welfare of others or has a generally positive effect on persons with whom one comes in contact.

environment
The circumstances or conditions that surround one; in the context of early childhood education, we think of the environment as everything the child experiences, including objects, activities, routines, and people.

antisocial 反社会的
Behavior that detracts from the welfare of others or has a generally negative effect on persons with whom one comes in contact. Antisocial personality behaviors are typically marked by lack of ethical restraint, lack of moral control, impulsiveness, and an inability to experience feelings of guilt.

· Lack of ethical restraint 理倫的拘束
· Lack of moral control
· Impulsiveness 衝動的
· Inability to experience feelings of guilt.

Positive Focus 7.1 Prosocial Behavior Consists of Positive Social Relations

- **Cooperation**—working with others unselfishly toward a common goal
- **Empathy**—putting oneself into others' shoes to understand what they feel, to have insight into their thoughts and actions *"build empathy" "put yourself in our shoes"*
- **Altruism**—behaving generously, acting in a way that benefits others with no motive of personal gain *kindness other without expectation*

(of) ... practice of ... selfless concern for the well-being of others

egocentrically
Babies and very young children see themselves in a self-centered, selfish manner that is considered to be egocentric. This point of view is a perfectly normal development characteristic for this age.

learning community
Group of individuals who share similar educational principles, who work toward common goals, whose activities are linked, and whose collaborative efforts create a synchronized energy in which the power of the group is more profound than that of any one individual. For children, a group that nurtures a sense of belonging among the children and adults in a program where children learn that all contribute to each other's learning.

DAP

Because patterns of natural human growth and development teach us that young children always begin life **egocentrically** focused on their own sensations, we know that prosocial behavior is not an inborn trait, but is rather a slowly learned way of acting. Prosocial behavior helps the child gain his sense of connection to his family, child care center, neighborhood, play group, and/or school.

If the child goes to school and contributes nothing, just sits and passively receives information, there is no community at her school. But if every child has a responsibility to contribute and everyone has a role to play, then the children become a **learning community**.

Children learn to cooperate and to contribute not to avoid punishment or to get rewards, but simply because it is the right thing to be generous, just as, in the home, the child learns to set the table because it is his responsibility, not to receive money or to avoid being yelled at. He learns that his friends and family need and appreciate his effort.

7-1b The Vital Role of Play in Childhood

An American Academy of Pediatrics report noted that play is so vital to child development that it has been recognized by the United Nations as a basic human right of every child (Ginsburg, 2007). Play is fun for children and it gives adults a chance to share pleasurable interactions with children. But play also accomplishes significant learning objectives. It contributes to the cognitive, physical, social, and emotional well-being of children (Ginsburg & Jablow, 2006).

Play encourages children to be creative in using their imaginations. They move freely, practicing physical dexterity. And, because play is social, children at play hone their emotional and social skills. DAP environments support playful learning. Play allows children to pretend, create, and explore a world they can control. They can practice adult roles and act out situations that scare, confuse, or worry them. This role-playing helps them master their fears in the real world. Play helps children develop new skills, confidence, and the resiliency to face future challenges (Ginsburg, 2007; McWayne, Fantuzzo, & McDermott, 2004).

Child-directed play helps children to learn sharing, negotiation, and self-advocacy skills. Free play lets children discover their own passions and talents. Joy-filled active play builds healthy bodies. Play is essential to academic environments. It ensures that school settings meet the physical, social, and emotional needs of children, as well as their intellectual needs. Research has shown that children achieve academically better in school when they set aside time for active free play and social interaction (Elias & Arnold, 2006; Ginsburg, 2007; Gurian & Stevens, 2005; Zarrett & Lerner, 2008).

Courtesy of Geneviere De Casero

Play is so vital to child development that it has been recognized by the United Nations as a basic human right of every child.

7-2 How Will I Design a DAP Indoor Environment?

We give subtle messages to children about how we expect them to behave by the surroundings we plan for them. We can prevent many behavior problems before they begin by careful planning, by understanding children's developmental needs, and by creating a perfect match between their needs and the settings around them.

Parents need to adapt home environments to make them safe, childproof, and interesting for children of various ages. Periodically, as a child grows, parents must re-examine their child's bedrooms, playrooms, and play yards to see that the space matches the child's growing skills and interests. Children can gradually deal responsibly with and reliably use and put away more complicated equipment and furnishings.

Adults planning space for groups of children also face a challenging task. The well-planned early childhood environment is orderly but not rigid, clean but not sterile, interesting but not overstimulating. In other words, it is carefully balanced. The only way to ensure that balance is to carefully observe the children who live, play, and work there, to see whether the environment seems overwhelming, boring, frustrating, or just right. (Refer to Chapter 4 for effective observation strategies.)

7-2a What Effect Does the Classroom Environment Have on Guidance?

Some early childhood classroom settings have an atmosphere that seems halfway between a festival and a flea market. Almost every square inch of the walls is plastered with pictures, posters, signs, crafts, and notices. Things dangle from the ceiling like a swarm of butterflies, and furniture and toys form a wall-to-wall obstacle course on the floor. Walls and furniture are painted in taxicab yellow, stoplight red, and iridescent lime green. The rugs are also bright with dizzying patterns of letters, numbers, and game boards to "stimulate learning."

This kind of environment invites loud, wild, unrestrained activity. Children will probably feel comfortable running, jumping, and yelling across the room. Adults will probably have great difficulty guiding children into quiet concentration on a puzzle or book or teaching children to use soft "inside voices."

If the environment has long, open pathways or open circular pathways around furniture, these **traffic patterns** may invite children to run amok rather than settle down with the learning materials. If children must cross through learning centers as they move through the room, they may disrupt other children. If there is a long, open pathway, toddlers and preschoolers will be tempted to run. An uninterrupted circular pathway around furniture or walls seems to capture the imagination of toddlers. They will run repeatedly in a circle, surprised each time that they come back to the same place. (This has learning value for toddlers, so you'll just have to decide when and where you can support it safely.)

① Children may initially have great fun in this environment but will likely become bored, tired, and overwhelmed. Because adults are likely to have difficulty coping with the children's level of intensity, they may become irritable and restrictive and fall into negative power struggles with the children.

② Other early childhood settings have an atmosphere like that of some dentists' waiting rooms. They are stark white, lacking in any color. The sparse furnishings have an eerie appearance. The room may look as if human hands have never touched it. The adults may seem anxious that the children "don't mess anything up." Painting, water play, paint, and messy clay may be either out of the question or controlled strictly by adults. Insipid elevator

traffic patterns
The most obvious routes children will take as they move around the classroom.

The Preschool at Claremont United Methodist Church

The well-planned early childhood environment is orderly but not rigid, clean but not sterile, interesting but not overstimulating.

music may be piped in softly, and any toys or books seem to be on display rather than intended for actual use (they may actually be arranged out of the children's reach). The children may be limited to large-group activities the whole class does together.

Little about this environment invites children to explore freely. Children become passive recipients of the experiences adults provide, and they are pressured to sit still, be quiet, and not touch anything without permission. The children may at first be subdued, restrained, even intimidated, but they will become bored, restless, and, eventually, either rebellious or submissive.

7-2b What Effect Does DAP Have on Child Guidance?

DAP environments are like baby bear's porridge in the Three Bears story—always just right, not too much and not too little. There is color and stimulation in the environment, but not too much, just the right amount. There is orderliness and predictability, but not to the point that it is overwhelming.

Behavior problems are minimized because children are challenged and their needs are met. They are busy and excited about their accomplishments. At the beginning of the year, adults often have to simplify an environment so children can manage independently and successfully. Gradually, as the children develop new skills, adults add new materials and increase the complexity of the environment to continually challenge the children.

Adults are constantly searching for materials that match children's skills, somewhere right in the middle between materials that are so simple that they are boring and materials that are so complex that they are overwhelming. Adults allow children to carry out play activities individually or in small groups of their own choosing rather than marching them lockstep to do the same activities at the same time.

Children in a DAP environment spend much of their time in discovery learning. They don't spend their time sitting in desks listening to a lecturing adult or reciting memorized information. Large-group activities for preschoolers are limited to short periods of sharing, singing, and story time. Group activities are avoided for infants and toddlers. Adults do, however, frequently sit on the floor and read, sing, and do finger plays for babies and toddlers who voluntarily cluster around them.

DAP teachers constantly look for ways to increase children's independence and mastery of their environment. For example, they may teach preschoolers how to spread their jackets on the floor, stand with feet near the collar or hood, stick hands in the armholes, and then flip the jackets over their heads. Like magic, children know how to put on their own coats without help. Teachers may use color-coding to help children know where things go. For instance, everything in a yellow container goes in the art center, which is marked with yellow tape; everything red goes in the science center, which is marked with red tape. See Positive Focus 7.2.

DIVERSITY

Positive Focus 7.2 Planning for Positive Behavior Checklist

- Arrange shelves and furniture to clearly identify learning centers.
- Route children's traffic patterns so children don't interrupt each other.
- Make sure teachers can observe every part of the room without obstruction.
- Select learning materials that appeal to the senses, encourage movement, and reflect diverse life experiences.
- Begin with simple materials, adding more complex materials as children begin to understand the ground rules: be safe, be respectful, be responsible.
- Consider and prepare for the special needs of any children with ability differences.
- Display materials so they are visually appealing to and are at a height easily accessible to all the children.
- Place no materials on top or in front of other materials; space them out so they are not too close to each other.

How Can I Improve Transition Times

- Put learning materials that have multiple parts into baskets, on trays, or into small plastic tubs so children can put them away easily.
- Color-code, label, or use pictures so children can put their learning materials away on the shelves without help.
- Separate noisy areas from quiet ones (for example, reading area and puzzles on one side of the room, blocks and housekeeping center on the other).
- Place learning centers near necessary resources (for example, water source, trash can, drying rack).
- Place emphasis on variety, not duplication (only one or two duplicates of a few highly sought-after materials such as markers, tricycles, dolls).
- Change the environment routinely to reflect the changing interests and abilities of children over time.

TeachSource Digital Download

In some areas the teacher may have taped pictures of toys and games on shelves to remind children where to put things away. Children may be allowed to rearrange the playhouse furniture and get out all the dishes and toys in the housekeeping center as long as they remember to be good citizens and put everything away when they are finished. The children know the environment belongs to them. They feel pride and self-confidence. They know the adult is their ally, not their enemy.

7-3 Creating a Calm, Peaceful Classroom Atmosphere

Dewey (1959) argued that the single most important purpose of schooling was to prepare children to become responsible citizens. He believed that children needed to learn social skills, empathy, perspective taking, and problem solving to become competent adults. Dewey made a good point. Character values are very important. But also, children need to become competent in these skills to create a peaceful, calm climate in the classroom so academic learning can take place (Berkowitz & Bier, 2005; Cohen, Jonathan, & Pickeral, 2009; Cohen, Shapiro, & Fisher, 2006). See Positive Focus 7.3.

Sometimes we get so busy thinking about our academic goals for children that we forget about the impact of the social and emotional climate. As children go through the school day, however, they are taking in social information about the environment around them. A kindergarten girl may interpret her teacher's body language and facial expression

We plan for positive behavior by organizing the right materials in the right way for children to use independently.

(fatigue, stress, headache, muscle tension) incorrectly as anger and respond with inappropriate behavior. A fourth-grade boy may interpret a look or gesture from a child he doesn't know as hostility and lash out aggressively (Blum, 2005; Cohen, 2006a).

Research shows that if children are not being proactively taught social–emotional skills, their tendency to assume what they see is negative increases throughout their elementary school years. The more a child sees his world as hostile, the more likely he is to respond aggressively. Children who have been given specific training in social–emotional skills are taught how to solve their own problems independently, to see other perspectives, to negotiate, and to make compromises.

Ultimately, when conflict does arise, instead of fighting or giving up, children who have learned positive, assertive skills have another option. They are able to negotiate confidently to get what they need while being responsible and respectful (Cohen, 2006b; Cohen, Pickeral, & Levine, 2010; Devine & Cohen, 2007).

These skills must be taught in a proactive, focused way, not in the heat of the moment after a problem has occurred. Children need to practice using these skills when they're calm. Then when a problem does occur, the teacher can support children in putting their skills into action (Schwartz, 2007). (See Chapter 8 for more on supporting the development of children's conflict resolution skills.)

7-3a Developmentally Appropriate Activities, Materials, and Routines

Bored children become irritable and mischievous. Children who are pushed beyond their limits into irrelevant memorization or tedious busywork may become antagonistic and rebellious. Unhappy children are more likely to behave in antisocial ways. When adults hold unrealistic expectations for children, stressful, even angry, relations erupt. This friction becomes contagious, and soon, interactions among the children themselves are tinged with irritability and annoyance. This is obviously not a situation in which children can learn and practice prosocial behavior.

The secret to a cooperative, caring, and generous atmosphere among young children lies in our meeting children's basic needs: social, emotional, physical, and intellectual. An overwhelming need of early childhood is the need for fascinating, authentic, and challenging activities. John Dewey, Maria Montessori, Jean Piaget, and other experts have shown us that children love to learn. These experts have made it clear that children learn easily through spontaneous as well as guided play experiences. Children become deeply involved in their play and are amazingly relaxed and compliant when their need for fulfilling activity is met. Children find joy and satisfaction in activities that are developmentally appropriate (Harms, Clifford, & Cryer, 2005; Hatch, 2005; Helm, 2004; Rimm-Kaufman et al., 2005; Sanders, 2002; Worth & Grollman, 2003; Zigler et al., 2004).

Montessori believed that children loved challenging learning.

7-3b Why Is Consistency Important?

Teachers, parents, and child care providers quite often are trapped by the idea that if something does not work the first time, then it will never work. Children eventually change a behavior when they finally comprehend and remember that the action will quickly and consistently be stopped or redirected. A caregiver who decides that preschoolers should learn to scrape their plates independently after lunch may feel exasperated when the children mistakenly throw away their plates and utensils.

A kindergarten teacher may throw up his hands after disastrously introducing finger painting for the first time to rowdy 5-year-olds who leave school looking like splotchy rainbows. And any adult who has ever dealt with toddlers knows that the point does not get across the first hundred times 1-year-olds are told that sticks and leaves should not go in their mouth.

Children learn positive ways of interacting with others when we can be consistent and persistent, not angry or impatient. We can avoid a great deal of irritation by recognizing that it takes time for children to absorb new skills and habits. Our task is to structure a consistent and predictable environment where children are allowed adequate periods to develop new skills introduced in tiny, bite-size bits.

7-3c What Is Special about a DAP Environment?

Developmentally appropriate early childhood settings are warm and homey. There may be special points of interest, holiday decorations or decorative touches, but they are not overwhelming. Children's artwork and other displays are not up at the adult's eye level; they are down where the children can see and touch them. Ceilings, walls, and floors are in muted, neutral tones so that what you notice first are the learning materials and the children's artwork. Instead of a chaotic mishmash, your eye should automatically go to the colors and shapes of the objects we want the children to select for their learning experiences. Children should be visually drawn to the blocks, puzzles, dress-ups, puppets, books, matching games, plants, and art materials (Harms, Clifford, & Cryer, 2005).

In the case of learning materials, more is not always better. Hundreds of paper signs on the wall are hardly noticed by the children, have minimal learning value, and detract from the environment. One real object with interesting sensory qualities (texture, color, smell) has authentic learning value when the child is allowed to explore it freely.

The DAP environment is well lighted with plenty of windows. Acoustical ceiling tiles or other materials soften the sound level. Furniture and equipment break the floor space into clearly defined learning centers to discourage running; to encourage focused attention on learning materials such as books, puzzles, and blocks; and to allow easy supervision (Harms, Clifford, & Cryer, 2005). See Positive Focus 7.4.

Messy activities such as food preparation, clay projects, water play, and painting are regularly available for children 2 years of age and older, and they are carefully structured for successful and independent use. See Positive Focus 7.5.

Analyze Classroom Traffic Patterns

Positive Focus 7.4

- At busy times, how do children move around the room?
- Where do clusters of children collect?
- Are there any specific problem areas?
- How can I change the traffic patterns to discourage running?
- How can I attract children to learning centers that are underused?

TeachSource Digital Download

Use Picture Symbols to Demonstrate Behavior

Positive Focus 7.5

A preschooler who wants to finger paint knows that a chart posted at her eye level will show, in picture symbols, each step of the process:

1. **Put on apron**
2. **Use clothespins to hold paper**
3. **Paint with hands**
4. **Use sponge to clean area**
5. **Wash hands**
6. **Dry hands**
7. **Hang up apron**
8. **Put picture on drying rack**

TeachSource Digital Download

Not only is the child enjoying a creative expression, she is also learning to deal with symbols, to follow a sequence of tasks in a specific order, and to be responsible for herself. These are important skills for children to master over time if they are to become successful in school and in life. The child may not follow all the tasks in the same order every time, but she is exposed to the idea of symbols, instructions, and independent responsibility.

If the child gets into trouble with the finger paint and has a mess she can't handle, she may ask another child or an adult for help. The adult's role is to support and guide the child through problem solving. "Let's see. What do you think you should do first?" "What about this apron on the floor? Where should it go?" "Should you get a sponge to wipe off the table?" "Hmmmm, I wonder how you can you get the sponge wet?"

In a developmentally appropriate preschool classroom, painting may be routinely set up with a day's supply of paper available to be fastened with clothespins onto a child-sized easel. Just an ounce or two of fairly thick paint in a couple of nontip containers with short, fat paintbrushes makes the activity almost goof proof for a young child wanting to paint all by herself. A clothesline or drying rack at the child's height is ready nearby for placing wet paintings to dry.

Plan for appropriate behavior by limiting quantities. It may be tempting to put paint, glue, and Play-Doh® out for children in their original containers, but that is often a mistake. Maria Montessori developed a concept that can be very helpful in preventing inappropriate behavior. She called her idea **control of error** (Montessori & Hunt, 1989). Montessori observed that children prefer to correct their own mistakes instead of having their mistakes pointed out by others. She believed that making mistakes was a valuable part of learning and that developing self-correction skills helped children develop confidence and decision-making abilities. She proposed that children's learning materials be designed so that children could see for themselves when they made an error.

If I put a large, economy-size bottle of glue on the child's shelf, the child is likely to squirt glue until the bottle is empty. Young children are more focused on the process than on the end product. The child may not even notice that glue is pouring off the edge of the table and dripping onto her shoe. She has been enthralled with the sight, smell, and process of squeezing and watching the white glue oozing out of the tip of the bottle. If I intervene, she is bound to feel a letdown from the pleasure of her activity. No matter how tolerant I am, I am bound not to be too thrilled about a bottle's worth of glue on the table, her shoes, and the floor. Yikes!

On the other hand, if I place one ounce of glue in a collection of tiny glue bottles and put two on the shelf at a time, I have created control of error. If the child uses too much glue, she runs out of glue. No adult has to intervene to tell her she has made a mistake—she hasn't made a mistake. She can simply report that the glue is empty and more glue is needed. Instead of 100 sheets of paper, put out 10 at a time and invite children to report when more paper is needed.

When practicing control of error in the classroom, an adult will have to fill up a tiny pitcher of milk, water, or juice frequently, but that is fine. If a child spills the pitcher, little is lost and it is manageable for the child to clean it up by himself. If children are making their own snacks, be sure to put out small quantities, and ask them to let you know when they are ready for more.

Classroom pets allow children to be involved in real-life activities. Adults should structure independent pet feeding so that no more food is available to children on the shelf on a given day than would be appropriate for the fish, bird, or animal. All activities are geared to meet the children's ability levels and to enhance independence. Food preparation for toddlers, for example, may consist of simply removing the peel from cut sections of bananas, peeling tangerines, or washing apples.

control of error
A teaching strategy originally developed by Maria Montessori and also known as self-correction. Materials are designed to provide instant feedback to the child if he has made a mistake, or they are designed to make it impossible to make a mistake. This puts control in the hands of the learner and protects the child's self-esteem and self-motivation.

The Preschool at Claremont United Methodist Church

Provide small, manageable containers of paint and glue so that spills are minimized.

Whether a DAP environment is designed for infants, toddlers, preschoolers, or school-age children, individual levels of development and interests are taken into consideration. Toddlers cannot function properly in environments that are arranged with hazardous and inappropriate furniture and toys, even though that same equipment may be perfectly suited to preschoolers. Infants and toddlers need unstructured toys and materials for sensory exploration and safe motor skills practice.

School-age children will be bored and offended if they are placed in a room filled with preschool blocks, picture books, and baby dolls. They too need a space suited to their individual needs and interests. In after-school care settings, children need a clubhouse environment with games, music, and quiet places to study. See Positive Focus 7.6.

2–5 Years: Play in Early Childhood

Watch this Video Case on play in early childhood, and then answer the following questions:

1. What are the four kinds of play described in the film?
2. Describe one example of each kind of play you saw in the film.
3. What kind of play is the simplest play?
4. What kind of play is the most complex?

7-3d How Do Schedules Support Positive Behavior?

Schedules are vitally important for a DAP environment. Young children adamantly resist being hurried, and they can barely tolerate standing around and waiting. They have their own pace. Adults are well advised to respect the individual pace of babies and young children. You may be wondering, "Okay, at home with my own baby I can be flexible and follow her schedule. But at school, I have too many preschoolers to do that. How can I possibly adapt to all their needs? Some zip around at a million miles an hour. Some move like a snail, studying every detail as they go."

Child-directed activity is an essential part of DAP scheduling. Different children definitely have different paces, but with large blocks of time for child-directed activities, children are able to work and play at their own pace. One child may take only 3 seconds to paint a paper plate turkey to her satisfaction; another child may want to spend 20 minutes painting it just the way he wants; and a third may not want

child-directed
Learning activity instigated by the child's natural curiosity and desire to learn rather than by the adult's direction, manipulation, or coercion.

How Can I Promote Prosocial Behavior?

Positive Focus 7.6

- **Teach prosocial skills.** Read prosocial children's books and plan age-appropriate social–emotional learning activities such as role-playing with puppets to act out appropriate behavior in specific social situations.
- **Encourage individual responsibility using DAP activities and materials.** At a young age, children can gain a sense of competency by learning to be responsible for their actions, making choices, and solving problems.
- **Assign simple chores.** Have children take on age-appropriate responsibilities; break tasks into small steps; avoid nagging.
- **Model prosocial behavior (nurturing role models).** Take advantage of children's natural tendency to imitate. Become the children's role model for cooperation, empathy, and generosity.
- **Help children see the effects of their behavior.** Help the child begin to notice the results his actions. How did his action affect others?
- **Teach compromise.** Adults can help children learn to talk calmly about possible compromises and alternatives.

(Adapted from Landy, 2002)

to paint one at all. Children appreciate having blocks of time devoted to their own pace. Regularly scheduled blocks of child-directed activity give children a secure, predictable schedule while allowing enough time to meet an individual child's needs.

If children are forced into lock-step group activity, the fast child will be bored and tempted to get into mischief as he waits for others to finish. The slow child will be forced to stop the activity before he has fully benefited from its learning value. He may be frustrated and irritated because he was unable to finish a project he cared about. Individualized, self-paced, child-directed learning is DAP—it supports authentic learning, strengthens self-esteem, and enables positive guidance.

Parents too should pay close attention to scheduling activities at home to reinforce positive child guidance. Taking a young child shopping in the late afternoon when she is likely to be tired and irritable is less likely to be successful than a mid-morning trip, for example. Allowing a school-aged child to begin watching a television show and then abruptly intervening to say that it is bedtime also shows poor planning.

For a happier family life, Bill and Irene will have to reschedule evening activities to make sure they and the children have adequate rest. They will also have to wake the children earlier, rather than as late as possible, so the children have time to wake up and plenty of time to eat and dress. Rushing a sleepy child is almost guaranteed to create an unmanageable child.

Bill and Irene both work. They hate getting their three children up in the morning. Because evenings are so hectic, the children often do not get to bed until 9:30 or 10:00 p.m. Of course they are cranky and out of sorts when their parents try to wake them at the crack of dawn. Bill and Irene are so rushed that they wait until the last possible moment to get the kids up. Then there is a mad rush to get them dressed and fed. Almost always, there is conflict with the children.

Preschool Full-Day Child Care Schedule

The following is typical of a developmentally appropriate preschool child care schedule. It includes large blocks of time to allow children the flexibility to select materials of interest to them and to work at their own pace.

6:30–9:30—Breakfast and Learning Activity Center Time
Children arrive at the center and go to the appropriate classroom. Learning centers are open for play, and breakfast is available until 9:00.

9:30–9:45—Circle Time
Children and teachers come together at circle time to sing, dance, play a game, do an activity together, read books, tell stories, discuss events, or decide who will be selected for jobs such as feeding the class pets and watering class plants.

9:45–10:45—Learning Activity Center Time
Activity is primarily child-initiated but sometimes teacher-assisted. Play in the learning centers encourages both cooperative and individual activity. Centers include areas such as housekeeping, dramatic play, music, art, blocks, science, nature, reading, writing, and math. (Bathroom assistance is provided on an individual basis throughout the day.)

10:45–11:00—Circle Time (Indoors or Outdoors)
11:00–12:00—Outdoor Play
Children need an outdoor play area in which to develop their gross and fine motor skills. They need to learn to negotiate with others, work out conflicts, and explore the world around them.

12:00–1:00—Lunch
1:00–1:30—Circle Time

Transitions

Transitions are those difficult changeovers between activities when children may balk at moving from one thing to the next. Special attention must be paid to transition periods to hold children's attention, to keep them on task if clean-up is needed, and to gently nudge them to the next activity. Excellent planning, organization, and an upbeat, optimistic attitude can go a long way to help ease children along.

Some children have far more trouble than others with transitions. Bright children become especially engrossed in their activities and may have a particularly difficult time tearing themselves away. A parent may confide, "I can't get her to stop playing with her toys to get in the bath; then once she is in the bath, I can't get her out. I finally get her in bed to read her a goodnight story and she cries for me to read more. Help!" See Positive Focus 7.7.

Young children seem to live every moment of their lives to the fullest. They are eager to learn and are wonderfully self-directed, but during transitions they need special support to avoid excessive dawdling, resistance, tears, or even a tantrum.

transitions Phases in daily activities in which a child must give up or leave one activity and begin another activity. These difficult phases between activities may cause children to balk at moving from one thing to the next. Additionally, the confusion and stress of the changeover may trigger misbehavior.

Consistent, Predictable Routines

Children are naturally inclined to resist when confronted with a sudden, unexpected demand that they change a long-standing behavior. Likewise, we adults sometimes put up quite a fuss when we are asked to change a habit. We argue, "But it feels weird . . . but I'm not accustomed to it . . . but I don't want to change" (McKenry & Price, 2005).

How Can I Improve Transition Times?

Positive Focus 7.7

For calm transitions:

- Give advance notice: "Five minutes till clean-up!"
- Assure that transitions are predictable and timely.
- Follow a routine during transitions.
- Keep transitions unrushed and peaceful.
- Eliminate boring waiting times: "While we are waiting for the other children to wash their hands, let's sing a song!"
- Add a physical component for fun and engagement ("Tip-toe like a dancer to your nap mat." "Hop like a frog to the bathroom.")
- Plan and rehearse difficult transitions: "What should you remember when your dad gets here?" "That's right—be calm and use words."
- Consider individual children's needs: "Johar, let's put your name on that puzzle so you can finish it after nap time."

(Adapted from Feldman & Jones, 1995)

TeachSource Digital Download

Giving gentle guidance and being consistent and predictable help children accept and gradually adapt to community expectations.

For example, a toddler who has never had a worry in the world about when or where to relieve himself might well feel those same feelings when we insist that he ought to keep his pants dry by urinating in a toilet. Setting reasonable expectations and then being consistent and predictable help children accept and gradually adapt to community standards.

Children do not instantly develop an ability to take turns or to resist greedily grabbing a toy. Slowly and persistently, however, we can nudge children into behaving in a more responsible and prosocial manner.

For months, toilet training may consist only of talking about the potty, looking at it, exploring it, and sitting for a second or two on it, just as a playful part of a diaper-changing routine. It may be months before the child's consistent, predictable routines expand to include actually using the potty. The important thing is that the child keeps moving in the right direction.

This is true for most significant changes in children's routines. We need to give them time to adjust gradually and learn new ways of doing things. *Someday, nobody will remember or care how fast or slow the learning took place. But it will matter to the child that it took place joyfully.*

PRACTICAL APPLICATION CASE

William and the Nature Walk

Brenda's 3-year-olds were ready to go outside. Several days of heavy autumn rains had kept them indoors in the child care center, so today's clear sky and bright sun were a welcome invitation to break away from usual morning routines and release some pent-up energy.

Brenda and her assistant teacher, Theresa, decided that the playground was out of the question because there were still big puddles in the sandbox and under the swings. "A nature walk," Theresa suggested, "would be perfect. There are lots of pretty fall leaves, and we could walk to the park to collect acorns and leaves for our science center."

The children excitedly prepared for their walk. Each child chose a buddy to hold hands with, and the pairs of young children danced and wriggled with anticipation as Brenda and Theresa helped them get into a straight line on the sidewalk.

"Remember," said Brenda, "we need to hold hands with our partners and walk very carefully on the sidewalk until we get to the park." Before they had gone even a few feet, however, William, who had just turned three, saw a bright yellow leaf and, dropping his partner's hand, bent down to pick it up. Louisa, the older 3-year-old directly behind William, immediately tumbled on top of him.

Brenda helped William and Louisa up, and then, kneeling at eye level to William and gently taking his hand, said politely but firmly, "Excuse me, William, you must wait until we get to the park before looking for leaves. Remember, be safe! Hold hands with your partner." She then gave William a little pat on the shoulder and a smile as she announced, "Okay, is this train ready to go again? Let's chug, chug, chug down the railroad track! Whooo, whoo! Ding, ding, ding!"

Within minutes, William was again distracted and stooped to pick up an irresistibly bright red leaf, and poor little Louisa was sprawled on top of him just like before. This time, however, she quickly scrambled to her feet, took William's hand and said in a confident voice, "Exsqueeze me, Weeyum! When you do dat, I faw down!" (Excuse me, William! When you do that, I fall down!)

Case Discussion Questions

1. Why do you think Louisa was able to use words to express her frustration rather than biting or hitting?
2. How should Brenda respond to the interaction between William and Louisa? Should she do anything further to correct William's behavior? Should she attempt to reinforce Louisa for remembering to use words?
3. What should Brenda and Theresa do if William continues to disrupt the nature walk? Can you think of anything preventive that could stop the problem and avoid difficulty on future walks?
4. Are these children learning prosocial behavior? If so, how?
5. Did Brenda and Theresa seem playful, consistent, assertive, and sensitive to the children's basic needs? Did it appear that developmentally appropriate activities and routines were being carried out?

7-4 How Will I Design the Outdoor Environment?

Playgrounds should support children's developing physical, intellectual, emotional, and social skills. Everything on the playground must be age appropriate. Playgrounds should be separated for infants and toddlers, 3- to 5-year-olds, and school-agers (Olsen, Hudson, & Thompson, 2005).

Playground equipment and materials are designed to support the way children of different ages develop skills. Many different kinds of important activities go on during playground time. Playground free play gives children time to play any way they choose, to run about and use a range of structures and spaces according to their own natural tendencies. They learn from one another as they interact with their outdoor environment (Elkind, 2007; Erikson, 1963; Fromberg, 2007).

During playground time children often play alone, alongside others, or in small groups. Occasionally teachers plan small- or large-group activities for the outdoor area that range from quietly reading books under a tree to actively building an obstacle course, throwing bean bags or balls, dancing, marching, singing, and playing musical instruments.

© 2013 Cengage Learning®

In a DAP outdoor environment, children initiate vigorous physical exercise, give-and-take social play, imaginative pretend play, and play with objects they find. Importantly, all of these activities are intellectually stimulating for young children.

Free play is not wasted time. Play is the work of the child (Montessori, 1986). Children playing naturally in a well-planned outdoor environment will initiate vigorous physical exercise, give-and-take social play, imaginative pretend play, and play with objects they find. Importantly, all of these activities are intellectually stimulating at this age (Leong & Bodrova, 2009).

To prepare the outdoor environment properly, we must focus on what we know about child development. We must think about the child's body, social–emotional self, and mind. We will design the playground specifically to meet the needs of these three areas of the child's being.

7-4a Supporting Physical Development

First and foremost, the playground must support the development of strong, healthy bodies by giving opportunities for physical exercise and skill development. Children's development of gross and fine motor skills is closely related to body awareness and their growing ability to regulate their own behavior (Bodrova & Leong, 2008).

Children need lots of exercise (Thigpen, 2007). Lack of adequate exercise has brought health problems to today's children that were unheard of in former generations. Fortunately, exercise is natural and pleasurable for children. As they joyfully stretch their bodies outdoors to pretending, socializing, and challenging themselves, they also become more confident, secure, and self-assured (Frost et al., 2001).

Play on equipment such as slides, swings, balance beams, climbing structures, and ladders helps children learn specific motor skills as well as refining coordination and balance. Additionally, vigorous exercise allows children to work off excess energy, enabling them to settle and concentrate more effectively on quieter classroom learning activities afterward. Sadly, many elementary school administrators have cut back on or eliminated playground time thinking this change would help children reach academic goals more effectively (Miller & Almon, 2009).

7-4b Supporting Social/Emotional Development

The playground is a wonderful place for children to develop social–emotional skills. They naturally explore social relationships, talk, have conflicts, and begin to figure out how to have a friend and how to be a friend. Teachers have an important role on the playground in supporting young children through the sometimes painful ups and downs of playground friendships. We may feel annoyed by these disruptive squabbles, but this is how young children learn how friends get along and negotiate disagreements. Children begin to learn valuable skills like compromise. We are there to guide them on their essential journey (Goleman, 1995).

We humans are social beings. From birth we have a basic human need to belong. At first we attach to our primary caregivers, our family. Babies have to feel connected to thrive. By preschool age, children need friends. Playing together gives children a chance to take into account viewpoints that differ from their own (Hallowell, 2003).

Sometimes children must regulate their behavior if they want to continue playing with a friend. They begin to learn self-control. They begin to learn how to deal with strong feelings, their own and those of others. At all levels of development, play helps children learn self-control by teaching them to express strong feelings in acceptable ways and resolve disagreements appropriately (Smagorinsky, 2007).

Additionally, play teaches many valuable social skills and helps children become sensitive to others' needs and feelings. Through social interactions, children begin to learn to deal appropriately with exclusion and dominance. They begin to learn how to share power, space, objects, and ideas. These are all important life skills and help children develop a strong sense of belonging in their various communities (Vygotsky, 1978).

The outdoor environment stimulates learning by presenting a natural environment full of interesting living and nonliving objects to observe, collect, compare, sort, and test.

7-4c Supporting Cognitive Development

The outdoor environment stimulates intellectual learning by presenting a natural environment full of interesting living and nonliving objects to observe, grow, collect, compare, sort, and test (Charles et al., 2008; Louv, 2008). Research shows that young children's play results in cognitive development. Understanding cause-and-effect relationships is fundamental to making sense of our world. This capacity enables us to develop moral judgment, come to terms with our past, and plan for our future. Piaget believed that young children learn cause-and-effect relationships primarily through actively exploring their environment—through play (1930). More recent research suggests that even younger children know much more about cause and effect than Piaget realized (Saxe, Tenenbaum, & Carey, 2005).

Bower (1982) showed that babies were able to demonstrate object permanence much earlier than Piaget expected. Infants at 3.5 months of age showed surprise (an elevated heart rate) when a screen was removed to reveal an object that had disappeared. Another researcher, Willatts (1989), found that at much earlier ages than Piaget's theory would suggest possible, babies use intention and planning to remove obstacles to find desired objects.

The idea, however, at the heart of Piaget's theory—that children "construct" their own knowledge (and particularly cause and effect knowledge) through active exploration—is basic to our work. Children naturally explore anything that captures their curiosity. Exploratory play may be unsystematic. Children may just seem to be playing with rocks, sand, and water, but they are little scientists looking for evidence (Masnick & Klahr, 2003; Sodian, Zaitchik, & Carey, 1991). Toddlers, preschoolers, and school-agers identify repeated patterns, make mental predictions, experiment using different problems and solutions, and practice logical reasoning techniques (Gopnik & Schulz, 2007; Kushnir & Gopnik, 2007; Schulz, Gopnik, & Glymour, 2007).

In addition to all-important free play, the outdoors offers opportunities for planned learning activities. When severe weather prevents outdoor play for long stretches of time, beautiful weather may be an opportunity to spend much of the day outdoors. Because outdoor play tends to be especially active and sensory, children with all learning styles can benefit. In nice weather, many learning activities can be taken outdoors. See Positive Focus 7.8.

The playground and everything on it must be age appropriate to the children using it.

Expand Outdoor Learning

Positive Focus 7.8

- Life science: exploring wind, clouds, effect of seasons, identifying insects, plants; gardening; studying weather
- Physics: exploring qualities of water, sand, rocks, and wood; studying how equipment such as swings, teeter-totters, and tricycles operates
- Math: counting and manipulating natural objects (pinecones, acorns, sticks, pebbles)
- Art: painting, shaping clay, pasting collages of found objects, building creative structures with natural materials
- Language: labeling objects, making up stories related to nature, using puppets, putting on skits
- Social studies: building cities in sandbox, drawing maps showing playground, making traffic signs for tricycle path
- Self-help/independence skills: preparing and serving snack, picking up litter, scrubbing tricycles and other objects

What Can We Do when the Weather Is Unpleasant?

- Invite a class visitor—Bookmobile, ZooMobile, firefighter, etc.
- Enjoy extra-long free play in the learning centers
- Set up a science table exploring weather
- Arrange a seasonal arts and crafts table
- Set up a special table with food preparation activities
- Introduce a new basket of donated dress-up clothes for dramatic play
- Declare spring cleaning—have small buckets, water spray bottles, and sponges and invite children to help wash shelves, toys, and windows
- Turn out the lights at circle time, listen to the sounds of the weather, talk about it, turn the lights on and read related books

TeachSource Digital Download

Positive Focus 7.9   Design a DAP Playground

The three most critical issues of playground design are as follows:

- Age-appropriate design—Infants and toddlers must have a specially designed area; preschoolers and younger school-agers need different equipment from older school-agers
- *Zones for play*—Grassy running zone, climbing equipment zone, sand and water play zone, tricycle riding zone
- *Open sight lines*—Visibility for adults to see all children in all parts of the playground at all times

Playground Checklist

- Availability of water fountain and bathroom
- Trees, grass, and other vegetation
- Variety of movement opportunities, running, climbing, crawling, sliding, balancing
- Safety surfaces under and fall zones around equipment
- Manipulative area for sand and water play, and for objects to be moved, carried around, rearranged
- Structures to provide shade, lean against, sit on and in
- Different spaces that offer a feeling of privacy (but allow proper supervision)
- Natural colors and textures
- Raised gardening boxes
- Accessibility

(Hudson, Thompson, & Olsen, 2003)

Please don't turn on a television. Many children already spend more time watching television than they spend in school. Researchers have shown that watching television can damage children's physical health and intellectual development (Bener et al., 2010; Schmidt et al., 2008; Sellers et al., 2005; Todd et al., 2008). As early childhood professionals, we must not contribute to the epidemic of electronic overload on children. We should set a positive example for parents.

7-4d Environmental Elements of a DAP Playground

The outdoor environment should help children develop an appreciation of their local environment. The structures and equipment don't all have to be commercially manufactured. Whenever possible, the structures should take advantage of the landscape and include natural materials such as stumps, logs, and boulders. The location of the playground should offer direct access to the classroom and be away from traffic, excess noise, pollution, flooding, or other hazards. See Positive Focus 7.9.

Safety

We must address current outdoor safety standards while assuring opportunities for exploration and challenge. Taking all equipment and materials off the playground might seem to make it safer, but doing so would destroy critical opportunities for learning. Our task is to provide maximum opportunities for learning while making every effort to assure safety (Pellegrini, 2009).

The playground and everything on it should be age-appropriate to the children using it. Equipment

Photo courtesy of the Preschool at Claremont United Methodist Church

Sidewalk chalk provides an opportunity for both art expression and large motor coordination practice.

should provide levels of challenges for children to explore, interact, and experience developmentally appropriate risk at their own pace. Children should not be pushed to take physical risks before they feel ready. The adult should not help them onto climbing equipment before they are able to climb onto it themselves (Thompson, Hudson, & Olsen, 2007).

The beauty of natural play is that children can challenge themselves and learn under the watchful eye of the adult. Practice and learning, however, involve making mistakes. A safely designed playground makes it okay for children to fall a short distance onto the soft surface provided beneath playground equipment. Schools usually choose surfacing based on what will match area weather conditions and what is available locally. Most child care centers rely on surfacing such as sand, wood mulch, rubber mulch, or pea gravel, but some use special materials designed especially to maximize accessibility for anyone using walkers, wheelchairs, or other support devices (Olsen, Hudson, & Thompson, 2005).

Supervision

An adult-sized bench may be placed on the playground to allow visiting parents a comfortable spot to observe their children. Effective teachers and caregivers, however, will be far too busy supervising the playground to have time to sit on a bench, chat with other adults, and use outdoor time as a teacher break. Staffing ratios specified by child care licensing regulation determine how many adults must be supervising children on the playground. We must always space ourselves around the zones of play so that we are sure someone can see every child.

We must keep special watch on gates, doors, play equipment, climbing structures, and any children who might need special assistance. We must stay close and give our full attention to the children. If we move around our area of responsibility, our eyes and ears will help keep us aware of the children's needs (Hudson, Olsen, & Thompson, 2002; Kern & Wakeford, 2007).

If the design of the playground allows open sight lines for one adult to see the whole area, a second adult can sit down and focus with a small group of children on games, crafts, painting, or other learning activities. Proper supervision and excellent teaching gives children the best of both worlds (Thompson, Hudson, & Olsen, 2007).

Our goal as playground supervisors is to be available, to support independence, and to ensure that ground rules are followed at all times—be safe, be respectful, be responsible. We don't want to solve children's problems for them; we want to guide them to resolve their own problems; we want to serve as sensitive coach and mentor. Children's learning comes from figuring out how to solve their problems appropriately. We will not allow them to harm themselves or others, disrespect others, or be irresponsible. We will gently but firmly guide them toward appropriate decision-making skills (Hughes, 2008).

It's a beautiful day. Antonio is one of three teachers supervising his school's well-designed playground, where 3-, 4-, and 5-year-olds are playing together. He is supervising the "equipment zone."

Suddenly he hears a high-pitched sound he recognizes immediately as Nida and Marcia shrieking. Instantly Antonio surveys the situation and sees 3-year-old Logan clumsily clamoring up from the bottom of the slide.

Calmly, Antonio responds to the 5-year-old girls who are still screeching at the top of the slide. He asks them what he can do to assist. They scream that Logan is in their way and is breaking a class rule. "No climbing up the slide," they yell.

Antonio says, "Would you girls like to climb down and come with me to talk to Logan? He's pretty small and maybe he doesn't understand the rule." The girls come marching down, eager to confront Logan. Antonio gathers Logan. Little Logan is very unhappy about losing his spot on the slide, but Antonio gently coaxes him into talking to the girls. They tell him in no uncertain terms that he has to go up the ladder and then down. In very animated voices they say, "It's not fair, and besides someone might crash into you and hurt you if you climb up like that."

Logan looks as if he is about to cry and says, "Yeh, but I'm too scared to climb up the ladder." Antonio says, "Hmmm. I wonder how Logan can solve this problem?" Marcia thinks a moment and then says softly, "Well, will you be scared if we help you? We could get behind you and you could go really, really slow."

Nida invites Logan to come climb the ladder with them. Logan thinks about it and decides not to join them. He goes to play in the sandbox instead. The girls return to the slide without Logan. Antonio feels pretty good. He feels successful in guiding the children toward making independent prosocial decisions.

Inclusion

DIVERSITY

Of course, playgrounds should invite the participation of children with differing abilities in social, intellectual, and physical activities. There should be something fun for everyone. Depending on needs, there can be all sorts of things to consider. An individual child's therapist is usually the best resource to recommend what accommodations are needed on the playground.

In general, accessible playgrounds may provide such things as swings with back and side supports, specially designed riding toys, and activity transfers to allow children using mobility devices access to play on equipment that might otherwise be inaccessible. Accessible playgrounds may also provide handrails, grab bars, or similar devices for children with motor difficulties.

playscape
For a playground to be considered a playscape, it must be natural, relying on native plants, trees, grassy slopes, stumps, and rock formations rather than on manufactured equipment and more.

Inclusive playgrounds always have barrier-free pathways to and around the playgrounds. An accessible platform with levels may be available. Fragrant herb gardens and other multisensory features add a special dimension of inclusiveness for children with sensory needs (Flynn & Kieff, 2002; Schappet, Malkusak, & Bruya, 2003).

▶❚❚ TeachSource Video

Obese Children

Watch this Video Case on obese children, and then answer the following questions:

1. Why should we be concerned about obesity in children?

2. List three suggestions for parents that would help reduce the chance of obesity for their children.

3. What can we as educators do to reduce childhood obesity?

7-4e What Is a Green Playscape?

A green **playscape** is a special kind of playground that is designed to give children the experience of being in nature. Playscapes emphasize creative play and learning interactions with insects, plants, trees, winding trails, grassy slopes, fallen logs, stumps, water play, gardening, and all sorts of other natural possibilities (Faber Taylor, Kuo, & Sullivan, 2001).

Children today are increasingly obese and play outside far less than did children of previous generations. Television, video games, computers, and other electronics cause our children to become passive and inactive. Robin Moore, a researcher in landscape architecture at North Carolina State University, says that natural spaces and materials entice children to play outside longer and in more creative ways (Cosco, Moore, & Islam, 2010; Louv, 2008; Moore & Cooper Marcus, 2008).

University of Illinois Researchers who are studying the relationship between children and nature have found that green playscapes not only ease the symptoms of attention deficit disorders, but also improve the quality of play and the quality of interactions between children and adults. They found dramatic differences in the way children use flat surface playgrounds with big steel and plastic equipment and the way they use versatile green playscapes. Children used the playscapes longer, more creatively, and more peacefully (Faber Taylor & Kuo, 2009; Kuo & Faber

The Preschool at Claremont United Methodist Church

This little parent-made playhouse is surrounded by a stump, interesting rocks, and potted plants for the children to tend.

Taylor, 2004; Panksepp, 2007; Schottelkorb & Ray, 2009; U.S. Department of Health and Human Services, 2009).

Additionally, growing public and professional interest in green playscapes builds on the belief that encouraging children to become engaged in gardening and in appreciating the earth at an early age enhances a lifelong appreciation of the outdoors. In 2007, the National Wildlife Federation began hosting the Green Hour, a national campaign to persuade parents to encourage their children to spend an hour a day in nature (Keeler, 2008; Louv, 2007; McLennan, 2009). See Positive Focus 7.10.

The Preschool at United Methodist Church

Children using green playscapes play longer, more creatively, and more peacefully.

Positive Focus 7.10

Design a Green Playscape

- Create natural children's gardening features (sun flowers, fragrant herbs, vegetables).
- Create natural sloping features (grassy hills).
- Create natural path features (stepping stones, woodchips, pea gravel).
- Create natural climbing features (boulders, logs, stumps, hay bales).
- Create natural water features (sand, water, rocks).

(Continued)

- Create natural sound features (bamboo and seashell wind chimes).
- Make available moveable features (sticks, stones, containers, shovels).
- Teach the children facts about birds, insects, and plants.
- Avoid chemical weed and feed to green the grass. Use organic and nontoxic alternatives.
- Use eco-friendly playground equipment; for example, equipment made with certified lumber that is sustainably harvested or recycled content. Be sure the manufacturer has a green philosophy.

TeachSource Digital Download

7-5 The Nurturing Social Environment

Adults who hope to stimulate prosocial behavior in young children must first establish a nurturing social environment, a setting in which children feel safe enough and comfortable enough to be cooperative, empathetic, and altruistic. Children who worry about being hurt, feel stressed to perform beyond their capability, or feel pushed into competition with playmates will probably have little interest in prosocial behavior. Children who are afraid that their own needs will not be met may not be able to be generous with others. Children may behave in a prosocial manner in one setting but not in another; day-to-day behavior depends to a great extent on the surroundings (Berk, 2001; Carr et al., 2002; Charney, 1997, 2002; Hartshorne & May, 1928; Katz & McClellan, 1997).

7-5a The Importance of Playful Learning

Early childhood is a special time in life. The young of other mammals (puppies, kittens, colts, and so on) frolic and play as they develop the skills they need to survive in adulthood. Adults of various species go about the serious work of providing food, shelter, and protection while the young chase around pouncing on bugs, climbing trees, rolling in the grass, and having pretend fights. Their gleeful freedom enables them to coordinate muscles and practice skills.

Young human beings also need a protected period of childhood in which to play and explore. If children are forced into somber, little-adult behavior, they may turn sour and critical. Instead of taking pleasure in their friends' playful antics, they may feel compelled to report, or tattle, to adults about even the most trivial misdeed of another child. Children should feel free to complain to adults when personal rights have been violated and to report misbehavior to authorities (adults) when rules have been broken or hazardous behavior is taking place. That kind of telling-on is sincere and should never be labeled as tattling. Frivolous or malicious telling, however, is a different matter. The child who obsessively tells, hoping to get peers in trouble, may expect adults to stamp out or punish every silly or childish behavior and to reward him for telling, for being little Mr. Goody-Goody. This behavior is inappropriate and should be addressed.

A child who persists in telling on others for no good reason will seem antisocial to playmates who have been told on. The child who tattles, however, will probably have inferred from adult criticisms of childish behavior that it is not okay to be a child, to be one of the gang. This child may feel aloof and apart from other children: he may actually view himself as a little adult. These feelings hinder the development of friendships that lead to wholesome cooperative play and to optimal social and emotional development, so we need to let the child know that it is definitely okay to be a silly kid sometimes. Children can be helped to refrain from tattling when they are taught to help a friend who made a mistake. "Yes, Shelley, I see that James forgot to take his turn. How can we help him remember?"

A relaxed, playful atmosphere for babies and young children helps them develop tolerance and a sense of humor. Exposure to tolerant adults who do not take themselves too seriously greatly aids children in developing the ability to feel empathy. Adults sometimes forget to step into children's shoes to imagine what they feel and see things from their perspective.

Adults consider sitting back, staring into space, and doing nothing an indulgent luxury. Children consider sitting and doing nothing a dreadful punishment. Adults have a slower, quieter rhythm than do children and may feel annoyed by children's squealing, wriggling, wrestling, and running. Intolerant adults force children to function within the adult's comfort zone for noise and movement. In contrast, when young children sense the generosity and tolerance of adults who gently redirect the bustling chaos of active, noisy children, the children in turn learn to demonstrate generosity and tolerance for others.

Instead of expressing exasperation, Allen, a young daddy, sits down and has a good laugh when his toddler walks in wearing underwear on his head rather than on his bottom. Mrs. Farrell, a long-time member of Weight Watchers, grins and takes it as a sincere compliment when little Jennifer says, "I think you're beautiful. You're the prettiest fat lady in the whole world." Miss Cindy laughs good-naturedly with her school-agers after the gruesome spider that has startled her turns out to be nothing more than a plastic Halloween party favor.

We might be tempted to take normal childish behaviors more seriously than necessary or even become angry and punitive. In a relaxed, playful atmosphere, however, children can learn discipline, but they can also learn that it is okay to be generous and forgiving (Webster-Stratton, 2000; Wilcox-Herzog & Ward, 2004). Children learn that it is okay to make mistakes because parents, teachers, and caregivers are allies, not enemies. It is okay to be playful and silly at times because others can let down their barriers and share in a good laugh.

Clearly, there is a boundary between silliness and genuine misbehavior, between playfulness and antisocial activity. Playfulness is neither hurtful nor mean-spirited; maliciousness is both. Silly behavior that is not totally appropriate can be dealt with patiently and with a sense of humor, even though it may need to be firmly redirected if it begins to interfere with necessary routines or to annoy others.

7-5b Creating a Cooperative Setting

When we say things such as "See if you can put your lunch box away before anyone else" or "Whoever is quietest can be first in line," children are encouraged to be competitive rather than cooperative. We are often tempted to use competitive challenges because they work more powerfully and effectively than does nagging or threatening, and they seem less negative. Remember, though, even if a strategy works well to achieve short-term goals, it may not necessarily achieve the long-term goals we seek. In the long run, getting children's coats on quickly or having trash picked up without a second reminder is not nearly as important as fostering cooperative and caring relationships among children who will someday be adult citizens.

By urging children to win at the expense of others, we may be establishing patterns of greediness and lack of regard for the feelings of others. It is far more helpful to redirect children's natural competitive urges into competition with their own best records: "I wonder if you can build these blocks even higher than you did yesterday?"

We live in an instant society. When we feel a child is old enough to behave in a certain way, we want that behavior instantly. One popular paperback book confidently tells parents that children can be toilet trained in a day. In reality, children cannot master toilet training in a day, a week, or even a month. A 2-year-old may seem to go from diapers to dry pants overnight, but this only happens after the child has mastered hundreds of prerequisite skills. Children need a lot of time, patience, and positive guidance to master the skills and self-control necessary for consistent cooperativeness.

In a learning community, children play cooperatively rather than competitively.

Positive Focus 7.11 What Is Involved in Toilet Learning?

To be independent, a child must be able to do the following:

- Recognize body sensations
- Inhibit sudden impulses
- Stop playing (this is really difficult)
- Find a bathroom
- Manage clothing (parents sometimes forget how hard this is)
- Balance on top of a big scary bowl of water
- Consciously manipulate the muscles that control elimination
- Deal with toilet tissue
- Flush

Only when these prerequisite skills have been mastered can the child take control of her bowel and bladder functions and the self-help skills necessary for true toileting independence. Parents who are very sensitive to their infant's elimination habits are able to reliably "catch" their baby's urine and bowel movements, but this is not the same thing as toilet independence. See Positive Focus 7.11.

We grown-ups can sometimes be pretty impatient about toilet learning. Many children will be 3 years or older before they have gained reliable toilet independence. And even then they may need an occasional reminder or help in the bathroom.

7-6 The Nurturing Adult

One might jump to the erroneous conclusion that a nurturing parent, teacher, or caregiver is one who is either a saint or a pushover. The word *nurture*, however, means to train, to educate, or to nourish. The truly nurturing adult is simply an honest, emotionally healthy person who has learned how to be both assertive and caring at the same time. See Positive Focus 7.12.

Positive Focus 7.12 Tips for Being a Nurturing Adult

Effective teaching and caring staff do the following (Berry, 2006):

- Maintain positive attitudes
- Keep high expectations for all children
- Have the skills to help children learn
- Make sure the classroom, activities, and materials are prepared
- Are creative and flexible
- Are warm and personal in their interactions
- Give children a sense of belonging
- Show children and parents respect
- Are tolerant and forgiving of others' mistakes
- Are willing to admit their own mistakes
- Have compassion for others
- Are fair, impartial, and unbiased
- Maintain a good sense of humor

Teaching children in a way that nourishes them does not mean pointing out every flaw, criticizing every imperfection, and punishing every lapse in judgment. In fact, the first step toward positively shaping children's behavior is simply setting a good example.

Unbeknownst to us, many of children's most upsetting misbehaviors are little more than instant replays of our own behavior in a context we do not expect. Children imitate some adult's own practice of hitting to communicate displeasure. We hit children and then we tell them not to hit others. Think about how confusing and hypocritical we are when we say, "If you don't stop hitting your brother, I'm going to spank you. Hitting is not nice!"

7-6a What about Physical Punishment?

Research tells us that physically punishing children is an inappropriate and ineffective method of disciple (Bender et al., 2007; Benjet & Kazdin, 2003 Socolar, Savage, & Evans, 2007). Spanking other people's children is almost always against regulations. Although a few Southern U.S. states still paddle children in public schools, many countries have banished physical punishment of any kind, at home and at school, Nevertheless, striking a child in a child care or school setting in anger can ruin a career, a reputation, and a financial future (lawsuits do happen). And, hurting children is never acceptable in DAP (Copple & Bredekamp, 2009).

Slapping, pinching, biting, and shaking children are dangerous and clearly unacceptable ways for us to guide children in any situation. Abusive head trauma and other kinds of abuse far too often begin with the notion that punishing a baby, toddler, or young child will make her behave better (Christian & Block, 2009; Christian & Poppe, 2007). When physical punishment does not work, frustration and anger may lead to physical abuse. About two-thirds of child abuse cases begin as physical punishment for misbehavior (Donnelly & Straus, 2005; Straus, 2008; Straus & Douglas, 2008).

Adults sometimes incorrectly think that if mild punishment doesn't work, more punishment and harsher punishment will. "If I hit just a little bit harder I will get through." By choosing never to strike a child, we avoid that whole ugly business. You and I wouldn't like for anyone to inflict physical pain on us to teach us things, and neither do children. There are much better ways to learn. But the primary reason to avoid physical punishment is that it is *not* effective in producing children who grow up behaving in a positive, prosocial ways. Children who are disciplined primarily by hitting are more likely to grow up and use hitting to resolve disagreements with their adult sexual partners (Cast, Schweingruber, & Berns, 2006; Gershoff, 2002, 2008).

Research demonstrates that children fail to develop well when their parents and caregivers come across as angry, cold, mean-spirited, or callous (Berlin et al., 2009; Bugental, Martorell, & Barraza, 2003; Carr et al., 1999; Larzelere, Cox, & Smith, 2010; O'Leary, 1995).

Researchers have found that some parents begin spanking as soon as their babies begin crawling and exploring. Some parents are routinely spanking and slapping babies' hands by 18 months of age. One study of toddlers found that babies who were spanked as 1-year-olds were more likely to have significant behavioral problems by age 3. These toddlers also scored lower on tests of mental development. The toddlers with the most severe outcomes were both spanked and treated with less warmth and sensitivity (Berlin et al., 2009; Bugental, Martorell, & Barraza, 2003; Gershoff & Bitensky, 2007; Taylor et al., 2010). Research on the effects of physical punishment on young children tells us that it not helpful for raising capable, cooperative, and responsible children (Ember & Ember, 2005; Fontes, 2005; Gershoff, 2008; Lansford et al., 2005; Socolar, Savage, & Evans, 2007; Straus, 2005). See Positive Focus 7.13.

The more children have been spanked, the more likely they will become more aggressive over time. Other studies have reported similar results (Grogan-Kaylor 2005; Lansford et al., 2009; Mulvaney & Mebert, 2007). Negative effects may be especially marked for kids who are physically punished as they get older. Jennifer

DIVERSITY

Lansford and her colleagues studied children who were spanked or paddled at home through the elementary school years and children who were not. She tracked the children for more than a decade. The children who were physically disciplined had the worst behavior problems and the least positive relationships with parents (Lansford et al., 2009).

Twenty-four countries have banned all physical punishment of children. In the U.S, thirty states, plus Washington D.C. and Puerto Rico, have banned any physical punishment of children in public schools. Twenty states still allow physical punishment in their schools, although only a few still use paddling on a frequent and routine basis to discipline children (Lynch, 2010). See Positive Focus 7.14.

Surveys looking at many studies of physical punishment have concluded that even mild physical punishment—if that is the primary method of discipline—is linked to negative outcomes. Research tells us that parental/caregiver warmth, sensitivity, and understanding support positive emotional, social, and intellectual development. Frequently expressed anger, coldness, disgust, and insensitivity are linked with poor emotional, social, and intellectual development. The expression of negative feelings that accompanies hitting may be far more damaging to the child's development than the actual hitting (Chang et al., 2003; Larzelere et al., 2010; Larzelere & Kuhn, 2005).

If Spanking Doesn't Work, Why Is It So Common?

Lots of children who are spanked manage to grow up to be respectful, bright, healthy, and responsible. That number undoubtedly includes many readers of this book. Generations of our parents and grandparents had great faith in a phrase some of us heard growing up: "I'll blister you till you can't sit down and then you'll remember not to touch other people's things" or ". . . you'll learn to be nice to your brother" or ". . . you'll remember not to run out in the street again." Sure enough, fear, pain, and intimidation turned out to be pretty good deterrents. But some of us may also remember problems and resentments as we grew up.

Although **corporal punishment** or **verbal abuse** may seem to work quite well at first, when children are small and easily intimidated, these actions model aggressive behavior and accustom children to being controlled by physical force. After a child has been harshly punished on many occasions, he becomes so accustomed to the way it feels that it no longer has the same effect. It may make him furious, but it probably will no longer scare him. This creates a difficult situation for everyone as children grow bigger and stronger. In any case, eventually the child will be too large to control physically.

corporal punishment
Corporal punishment is the use of physical force to cause pain but not injury and is intended to control a child's behavior.

verbal abuse
Verbal abuse happens when words ridicule, distain, humiliate, and taunt a child.

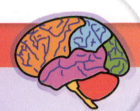

BrainFacts

What Can We Learn from Neuroscience?

Corporal punishment and brain development

- Harsh corporal punishment may be associated with permanent changes in the brain that interfere with learning (Larzelere, 2000; Larzelere & Kuhn, 2005; Mulvaney & Mebert, 2007; Straus & Paschall, 2000).

- Despite the American Academy of Pediatrics' recommendations against the use of corporal punishment, about 90% of preschool-age children are spanked (Teicher, Anderson, & Polcari, 2012).

- Research suggests that harsh corporal punishment too frequently contributes to unwanted outcomes—aggression, violence, antisocial behavior, depression, suicidal thoughts, anxiety, alcoholism, and substance abuse (Aucoin, Frick, & Bodin, 2006; Baumrind, Larzelere, & Cowan, 2002; Gershoff, 2002).

- Corporal punishment has long been considered a necessary and effective way to control and socialize children, but we now know that harsh treatment is not effective and can lead to a wide range of developmental problems (Frodl et al., 2010; Teicher, Anderson, & Polcari, 2012; Tomoda et al., 2011).

- When parents use corporal punishment (hitting, slapping, paddling with objects, pinching, and shaking) to reduce inappropriate behavior, the long-term effect is usually the opposite (Grogan-Kaylor, 2004, 2005).

- Reducing early childhood exposure to bullying and intimidating caregiver behaviors could dramatically improve children's health, development, and school success (Cohen et al., 2009; Frodl et al., 2010; Teicher et al., 2010).

BrainFacts

What Can We Learn from Neuroscience?

Verbal abuse and brain development

- Verbal abuse causes more than hurt feelings; it can cause lasting damage to a child's growing brain structure (Choi et al., 2009; Hanson et al., 2010; Taylor, 2010; Teicher, Anderson, & Polcari, 2012; Teicher et al., 2010).

- Harsh verbal reprimands are widely considered a useful way to control and socialize children, but we now know that harsh treatment is not effective and can lead to a wide range of developmental problems (Frodl et al., 2010; Polcari et al., 2014; Teicher, Anderson, & Polcari, 2012; Teicher et al., 2006; Tomoda, 2011).

- Research suggests that if parents used peaceful, supportive methods of discipline instead of enraged verbal confrontations and physical punishment, the children's life-long risk for emotional, physical, and behavioral problems would decline and school success would increase (Choi et al., 2009; Cohen et al., 2009; Larzelere, 2000; Hanson et al., 2010; Polcari et al., 2014).

Experienced teachers know they must pay special attention to the child of a parent who often uses corporal punishment and/or verbal abuse to handle behavior problems. The child may seem well controlled by the parent. Typically, as soon as the parent's back is turned, this child is out of control. Often the child will severely test teachers' patience as they begin using authoritative positive guidance strategies. The child expects to be spanked and scolded. She expects to be controlled *externally*. When she isn't punished, she feels compelled to test how far out of control she can go before the adult becomes enraged and aggressive. The child will test this process many, many times before she begins to trust the teachers. With trust, support, and caring, assertive role models, she will eventually begin the process of learning how to control her impulses and choices *internally*.

> *Mrs. Young cares for 1-year-olds in a parent's-day-out program. When a toddler bites, she does whatever she has to—as firmly as necessary but as gently as possible—to stop the biting and to get the bitten child free from the biter. In a deeply concerned (but not angry) voice, she tells the biter assertively, "Stop, please." She then takes great pains to model touching the bitten child gently. Mrs. Young delicately strokes the bitten child's arm, saying in a soothing voice, "Gentle. Be gentle." Often, the biter will imitate her and touch the other child, and then she responds, "That was so gentle. Thank you." Slowly, the toddlers begin to absorb the gentleness they see in Mrs. Young every day. See Positive Focus 7.15.*

The point is not that one spank will ruin a child's life. It is that relying on hitting children to control them interferes with their development of inner control. Spanking is simply not as effective for winning a child's cooperation as guiding the

Why Do Parents Spank?

- Parents don't really know what else to do when a child misbehaves.
- Parents have trouble controlling their own anger and frustration.
- Unusual stress can cause even a gentle parent to become angry.
- Financial stress, workplace problems, marital stress, or being an overwhelmed single parent can cause a loss of emotional control.
- Violence in the media tends to desensitize parents to aggressive behavior—hitting, slapping, and using hurtful, demeaning, humiliating language.
- Drug or alcohol use frequently leads to loss of parents' good judgment.
- A parent's family, religious, or cultural teachings may favor spanking, and the parent may not know about potential problems that result from spanking.

(Douglas & Finkelhor, 2005; Marshall, 2002; National Center for Children in Poverty, 2004)

child with positive assertive methods. Spanking and yelling increase stress for children and raise many other negative concerns if we are truly committed to providing a healthy environment where children can grow and learn to their highest potential.

7-6b How Does a Nurturing Adult Respond to Aggression?

Nurturing adults stop the aggression immediately, making sure everyone is okay, then help children resolve their own problems independently and appropriately. This is all done calmly, supportively, and with optimism. Nurturing adults try hard to find and deal with the roots of persistent aggression. Most importantly, nurturing adults establish emotional connections with children. They develop caring, sensitive, and understanding relationships with children.

When the children are older, Mrs. Young will begin emphasizing another concept: using words rather than aggression to express anger. Because she uses the word no very sparingly and only when she really intends for an action to stop, the children learn through observation that it is a powerful and important word. We will not hear Mrs. Young snapping at a child, "Don't you dare say no to me!" She allows children to express their thoughts and feelings orally.

When Mrs. Young deals with an unhappy toddler, she acknowledges the child's feelings, even if the child cannot reasonably be allowed to have his way. She says, "I know you don't want to wash your hands right now, but you must have clean hands to be allowed to eat." She actually coaches her toddlers in the skill of saying no. She prompts them, "Tell Marcus 'No'; say, 'No, Marcus. My cracker. Mine.'" In time, children learn by direct teaching as well as by imitation to use words rather than aggression to express their anger.

7-6c Can Children Learn Appropriate Behavior through Imitation?

Although babies and toddlers are able to mimic only bits and pieces of behaviors they observe, even these first attempts are critically important to their development. Preschoolers imitate entire sequences of behavior. Preschoolers are in a particularly sensitive period of their lives for imitation. As they mime adult actions, we get to see them re-enact their world as they perceive it (Bodrova & Leong, 2010; Brown & Vaughan, 2009; Gladwell, 2000; Mayes & Cohen, 2001; Piaget, 1962). These glimpses into their world range from the delightfully funny to the downright alarming. Children's

imitative play discloses their innocent misconceptions of the adult world, as well as the fears and pains they sometimes feel.

School-age children also imitate, but they are more selective in choosing role models. They are constantly (but unconsciously) absorbing subtle behavior characteristics from those around them. But they are not likely to mimic the behaviors of adults or children they do not like. They will make conscious attempts, however, to talk, dress, and act like those they admire (Bandura, 1977). We can enhance positive imitative learning by becoming respected and admired members of the child's immediate world rather than aloof and distant authority figures.

Imitation is an important and logical tool for teaching prosocial behavior. We waste a great opportunity to influence children if we do not become particularly aware of our own actions and attitudes as well as those communicated by cultural media such as television. If children spend long periods watching television, they are bound to internalize the language and behavior they see. The nurturing adult will closely monitor and limit programs to avoid overexposure to violent, irresponsible behaviors (Buijzen & Valkenburg, 2003; Linder & Gentile, 2009; Manganello & Taylor, 2009; Pagani et al., 2010; Rosenkoetter, Rosenkoetter, & Acock, 2009).

Rather than focus all our attention on correcting children's behaviors, we must take a hard look at ourselves and correct some of our own problems. Even if we are unsuccessful in weeding out all of our personal flaws, we will certainly become more sensitive to the child's dilemma of wanting to stop an undesirable behavior but not being able to. If our goal is to develop children's self-discipline and self-control, then we had best see how much of those admirable characteristics we are able to muster so we can show children (rather than just tell them) how people should behave. See Positive Focus 7.16, 7.17, and 7.18.

Positive Focus 7.16 **Ask These Questions about Annoying Behaviors**

- What specific aspects of the behavior are particularly annoying to me?
- Is there any way I might have been setting an example for that behavior?
- What positive behavior could be modeled and reinforced to replace the undesired behavior?
- How can I model appropriate behaviors so the child will be sure to notice and respond?

Positive Focus 7.17 **Positive Role Model Checklist**

- Remember that as a teacher I am automatically a role model.
- Identify the qualities in myself that I want children to develop and work on the qualities in myself that I don't want children to imitate.
- Provide learning materials and toys that represent values I want children to learn.
- Demonstrate calm and peaceful conflict management.
- Demonstrate cooperation, empathy, and generosity in my day-to-day actions.
- Read books to children that express moral values such as forgiveness, honesty, persistence, responsibility, respect, and fairness.

We occasionally set unreasonable goals. We focus our attention on children's behavior in fits and starts. We ignore messiness for months or years, then suddenly insist on neatness—this minute! We can help children by taking things one step at a time.

> *Nothing is so strong as gentleness, nothing so gentle as real strength.*
> —*St. Francis de Sales*

> *Three-year-old Fernando had always traipsed around the house after his bath in a big, soft bath towel. When he was ready to get dressed, he had a habit of dropping the damp towel in a heap on his bedroom floor. Freshly scrubbed little boys wrapped in towels are so endearing that his parents had quietly tolerated his towel-dropping ritual. One day, however, his poor mom reached the end of her patience and yelled, "Fernando, get this wet towel into the bathroom, and I mean step on it!" After she cooled off a bit, she peeked into the bathroom to check on Fernando. There he stood in the middle of the bathroom, crying pitifully but standing obediently on the towel. He had, indeed, "stepped on it," just as instructed.*

How Can I Be More Attentive to Children's Individual Needs?

Nurturing adults respond to children's individual needs. Parents generally have no difficulty in seeing their own children as individuals. Family intimacy and shared history make it likely that there is at least awareness of (if not respect for) individual differences. A key problem for parents may be accepting individual differences among their children and resisting the temptation to compare them to one another. A parent may say, "I'm sure that Ramona will love taking piano lessons just like her older brother did" while knowing full well that little Ramona would much rather do wheelies on a bicycle than learn to play the piano.

In a group setting, sadly, young children may be seen as tiny cogs in a very large machine. Babies' diapers may be changed not when they become wet or soiled, but at routinely scheduled times. Eating, playing, and sleeping may take place on a schedule for the whole group rather than in response to children's individual feelings of hunger, playfulness, or fatigue. A child may not be hungry for breakfast on a given day or may be ready for a nap before nap time. It is easy for a child to feel overlooked in a group. Although routines are essential to sanity and survival for group caregivers, nurturing adults will find ways to be sensitive and make allowances for children's individual needs.

A nurturing adult will not be callous to children sleeping face down on uncovered plastic mats in sweaty August heat or make little ones nap with their shoes on

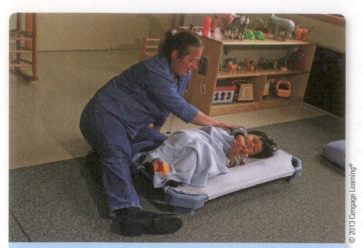

A nurturing adult really cares about the comfort and feelings of individual children.

because taking shoes off and putting them back on is too much bother. The nurturing adult would not be inclined to toss snack crackers unceremoniously onto a bare table without even the dignity of a napkin or paper plate. A nurturing adult will really care about the comfort and feelings of individual children. Even if each child's need cannot reasonably be met this instant, the nurturing adult will express awareness of and concern for individual circumstances. For example, "I know you are very hungry. As soon as we can get everyone's hands washed, you will have some lunch. I promise." Showing attentiveness to children's individual needs is an excellent way to demonstrate cooperative behavior.

Unconditional affection is communicated to a baby by his caregiver's facial expression during such routines as diaper changing. If the baby looks up and sees disgust or annoyance in the caregiver's face, he will sense that it is not okay to be a baby and to need a dirty diaper changed. If he sees a relaxed smile, he will know that he is welcome and his needs are okay. If a preschooler accidentally tramples a flower bed while trying to pull weeds like his daddy, he will sense affirmation as his dad patiently acknowledges the child's good intentions and teaches him how to weed the garden without harming it.

Nurturing adults are not afraid to show affection to children (Hoffman, 1979). Smiles, warm hugs, and sincere interest let a child know she is unconditionally accepted. Appropriate affection should never be intrusive, overwhelming, or one sided but rather respectful and reciprocal. A basic human need is for a sense of belonging. We are essentially social creatures. We cannot really be happy or functional without a secure feeling that we have a place in the social order around us. The most desirable social position is one in which we feel admiration, acceptance, and approval from the important people around us.

If that situation cannot be found, people (children as well as grown-ups) may substitute negative relationships to find recognition and acceptance. People assume leadership by becoming gang members, achieve recognition by defying rules, and hold others' attention by shocking, frightening, or angering them. The very last thing children will settle for is being ignored and left out. Only the most emotionally disabled members of society retreat into and accept a life of total social isolation.

To stimulate prosocial behavior, the nurturing adult will be generous in making sure children know that they are accepted and approved. Instead of focusing only on children's unacceptable behaviors, the nurturing adult makes a point of noticing and commenting on positive behaviors, thanking the child for remembering to wipe his feet, commenting on the bright colors in his crayon drawing, and listening with interest to his excited but rambling account of a weekend camping trip. The nurturing adult is careful to distinguish clearly between inappropriate actions and people: "I don't like hitting, but I like you very much. You are a good person. You can learn to use words rather than fists." In spite of the inevitable guidance interventions from time to time, the nurtured child always knows he is a good and worthwhile human being (Brady et al., 2003).

7-6d Can I Be Both Assertive and Caring?

The nurturing adult is willing and able to be both assertive and caring at the same time. Lackadaisical permissiveness cultivates antisocial and aggressive behavior in children (Bersamin et al., 2008; Goldthorpe, 2007; Whittle et al., 2008). A truly nurturing adult earns children's respect by being firm and fair in a way that reminds children that a sturdy, protective wall of reasonable limits surrounds them and keeps them safe. They also need to know, of course, that this "wall" can and will be broken in specific situations if it becomes an obstacle rather than a protection for the child's well-being.

Mr. Leone really enjoys children. He is tender-hearted and kind but has trouble being assertive. When Jenny runs to him complaining, "Anna pulled my hair and broke my crayons," Mr. Leone shrugs and says, "I'm sure it was just an accident." When children throw food during lunch, Mr. Leone pretends not to notice but tries to distract the ringleaders by talking loudly about the weather, "Listen, I think I hear thunder. Do you hear that?" Mr. Leone is kind, but he is definitely not assertive. His permissiveness is a hindrance, not a help to children.

Miss Juana responds immediately when she sees two boys wrestling. "Excuse me," she says. "What seems to be the trouble?" Homer yells out that Tony has had the yellow dump truck for a long time and won't share it. Tony yells back that he had it first. Tony shoves Homer and the wrestling begins again. Miss Juana kneels and gently but firmly interrupts the wrestling: "Please stop now." She says in a firm, but not harsh, tone, "Thank you. I know you are both really good friends. I think we can find a way to figure this out. Let's sit down on the step for a minute and talk about it together." As they sit together, Miss Juana helps the boys negotiate their problem and work out their own solution to their problem. When they find a solution they both accept, they go back to play.

A child should never be the target of adult anger or retaliation. The child relies on adults to be reliable and in control. Children feel especially vulnerable because they have not yet developed the self-control to manage themselves when they become angry. Children feel nurtured and safe when they know they can trust a strong adult to stop them before they behave aggressively or destructively.

| **7-6e Am I Willing to Protect Individual Rights?** | Children want to know with certainty that their safety and rights will be protected. The nurturing adult is not hesitant to enforce appropriate rules fairly and firmly. The permissive approach does not serve children's developmental needs. Children need a consistent, authoritative guide. |

Mary Beth is the mother of two young children, a 5-year-old boy, Trey, and a 3-year-old girl, Betsy. Betsy adores her big brother and attempts to follow every step he takes. Sometimes, when Trey is alone, he seems proud of Betsy's attention and plays with her for hours, but when he has friends his own age to play with, he chases Betsy away and tells her to leave him alone. One day, while Mary Beth is waxing the kitchen floor, she hears a loud altercation in the backyard. Betsy is crying because Trey and his chums will not let her play with them and are taunting her by chanting, "Betsy is a tagalong! Betsy is a tagalong!"

Because Mary Beth's mind is on the waxy yellow buildup in her kitchen, she is tempted for a moment to order Trey to entertain his little sister and stop the silly nonsense with his friends. Luckily, however, she stops to assess the individual rights of everyone involved. As a parent, she has a right to do her housework without interruption, but of course, she also has an obligation to care for her children (she thinks children are considerably more important than waxy yellow buildup). Trey has an obligation to treat his sister with kindness and to help out by entertaining her from time to time, but he also has a right to lead his own life and to play with his friends. Betsy has a right not to be called names, but she also has an obligation to respect her brother's privacy and to learn to play alone sometimes.

After Mary Beth patiently listens to complaints from all sides, she says, "Trey, Betsy feels hurt when you call her names. You have a right to play with your friends, but name-calling can't be allowed. Let's make a compromise. Please push Betsy on the swing for a few minutes so that I can finish my work in the kitchen. Then I will bring Betsy in the house, and you and your friends can have the backyard to yourselves until your friends go home. Betsy, you may play with Trey for a few minutes, then you and I will go inside and I will show you how to give your dolls a bath."

Because Mary Beth is a nurturing parent, she is able and willing to make an extra effort to see that everyone's rights are protected and that everyone behaves responsibly. She does not do only what seems expedient or convenient, but tries hard to create an environment of fairness and mutual respect for the rights of others.

Summary

- The concept of prosocial behavior focuses on three critical elements of beneficial, or helping, interactions with others: cooperation, empathy, and altruism.
- Prosocial behavior helps the child gain his sense of connection to his family, child care center, neighborhood, play group, and/or school.
- To develop prosocial behavior, children must interact with peers in a nurturing social environment.
- Play contributes to the cognitive, physical, social, and emotional well-being of children.
- Children who are afraid that their own needs will not be met will not be able to develop prosocial skills.
- All materials and equipment in indoor and outdoor environments support children's developing physical, intellectual, emotional, and social skills.

- Environments are designed to support safety, inclusion, and prosocial behavior.
- The nurturing adult is an honest, emotionally healthy person who is both assertive and caring.
- Modeling is an important and logical tool for teaching prosocial behavior.
- Encouraging children to compete with each other reduces cooperativeness.
- Recognition and encouragement are appropriate alternatives to an overabundance of praise.
- The permissive role does not serve children's developmental needs; children need a consistent authoritative guide.

Key Terms

antisocial

child-directed

control of error

corporal punishment

egocentrism

environment

learning community

prosocial

traffic patterns

transitions

verbal abuse

Student Activities

1. Observe an NAEYC accredited classroom and playground.
   a. Identify examples of prosocial behavior.
   b. Identify indications of a nurturing social environment.
   c. Identify examples of adult behaviors that are nurturing.
   d. List indoor learning materials that seemed most interesting to children.
   e. List outdoor equipment that seemed most appealing to children.

2. What surprised you most during your observation?

3. What did you see that you most expected?

Related Resources

Readings

Brown, S., & C. Vaughan. (2009). *Play, how it shapes the brain, opens the imagination, and invigorates the soul*. New York: Penguin Group.

These authors have made a career of studying the effects of play on people and animals. They conclude that play is important for human survival, not just for enhancing our quality of life.

Copple, C., & S. Bredekamp, Eds. (2009). *Developmentally appropriate practice in early childhood programs serving children from birth through age 8* (3rd ed.). Washington, DC: NAEYC.

This book is designed to assist teachers in implementing developmentally appropriate practice. The text is organized into "environments" for each developmental stage to help focus on specific appropriate responses and to nurture overall development.

Keeler, R. (2008). Natural playscapes: Creating outdoor play environments for the soul. Redmond, Washington: Exchange Press.

This book describes a new idea in children's outdoor play areas—natural playscapes. The entire playground is filled with art, hills, pathways, trees, herbs, open areas, sand, water, music, and more.

Websites naeyc

Earthplay   Earthplay is a community-built site to teach parents, grandparents, teachers, park directors, caregivers, landscape architects, students, nature enthusiasts, play advocates, builders, and educational program managers how to create green playscapes for children.

Action Alliance for Children   This policy brief explains how play is the essential foundation for developing children's potential for success in school and life.

The National Wildlife Federation   The National Wildlife Federation launched the GreenHour.org website as a resource to give parents the inspiration and tools to make the outdoors part of daily life.

Building Relationships through Positive Communication

naeyc Standards

The following NAEYC Standards are addressed in this chapter

Standard 4 Using developmentally effective approaches to connect with children and families

4a Understanding positive relationships and supportive interactions as the foundation of their [your] work with children

4b Knowing and understanding effective strategies and tools for early education

4c Using a broad repertoire of developmentally appropriate teaching/ learning approaches

4d Reflecting on their [your] own practice to promote positive outcomes for each child

Courtesy of Geneviere De Casero

Objectives

After reading this chapter, you should be able to do the following:

8-1 Demonstrate positive communication.

8-2 Identify feelings and emotions underlying communication.

8-3 Communicate using positive statements of instruction rather than negative commands.

8-4 Describe the characteristics of assertive communication.

8-5 Describe the characteristics of nonproductive communication.

8-6 Use the components of crucial conversations to resolve conflict.

8-1 Building a Foundation for Positive Communication

Positive communication is like a dance filled with expressive and responsive give and take. Children begin this interactive dance early in life, but effective communication skills are acquired gradually over many years. Children can learn to communicate effectively by interacting with nurturing role models of effective communication. We help children by participating with them in both conversational roles: speaking and listening, and leading and following.

8-1a How Can I Support Early Communication Skills?

We may lead by talking to an infant in a way that is sensitive to the baby's mood and attention span. An infant will participate in this interaction by watching and responding as we speak. In time, babies learn to mimic bits and pieces of our communication such as inflection, intonation, facial expression, and timing, as well as the give and take of dialogue. When the interaction becomes tiring, the infant will look away, grimace, or yawn to signal fatigue and the need for a brief rest (White, 1995; Yoshinaga-Itano, 2004).

A sensitive adult will follow the baby's lead, waiting until she looks back, which indicates that she is ready to interact again. We follow the infant by repeating the baby's gurgling, cooing, or babbling sounds. This form of baby talk (or "parentese"), in which the baby leads, is very useful for helping babies get a sense of conversational give and

Courtesy of Geneviere De Casero

This dad is following his baby's lead, waiting until she looks, which indicates that she is ready to interact. He follows his baby daughter by repeating her gurgling, cooing, and babbling sounds. This playful baby talk is called "parentese," and it will help this baby learn conversational give and take long before she is able to say or understand words.

DAP

TeachSource Video

© 2013 Cengage Learning®

Infants and Toddlers: Communication Development

Watch this Video Case. After viewing the clip, answer the following questions:

1. What is the difference between expressive and receptive language? Which develops more fully first?

2. Give an example of telegraphic speech.

3. Give an example of an adult recasting and expanding on a toddler's speech.

take long before they are able to say or understand words (Bruner, 1978a, 1978b; Tomasello, 2003).

When adults pace their interactions with infants, babies learn that a specific behavior elicits a predictable response. Babies get a sense that their environment is controllable and predictable, which stimulates their motivation and learning. Infants who sense they are powerless over interactions may become distressed, irritable, or passive and withdrawn (Zeanah & Zeanah, 2001).

Older babies learn to look back and forth between an object and a caregiver, and they grunt, point, or reach to indicate a desire for the object. This effort to communicate reflects the child's dawning ability to bring about a desired action by communicating with adults. Well-developing toddlers grasp the essential elements of conversation: meaningful words, intonation, inflection, facial expression, gesture, and give and take. It may be impossible, however, to make much sense of what the toddler is trying to say. An adult who is tactful will find ways to avoid repeated requests that the toddler repeat herself (Clarke-Stewart, Malloy, & Allhusen, 2004).

Supportive responses to children's early attempts at speech encourage continued efforts. Adults in DAP environments avoid excessive correcting or prodding, which discourages children from practicing their language. Even after 2-year-olds have mastered many phrases, they may need a bit of gentle encouragement to carry on a dialogue. We can help by asking simple questions: "Is this your big teddy bear? What is your teddy bear's name?" (Markus et al., 2012; Uomini, 2010; Wittmer & Honig, 1997).

8-1b How Do Young Children Communicate?

Toddlers seem oblivious to the notion that one should speak only when a listener is present. One- and two-year-olds sometimes carry on animated self-talk while engaging in solitary play. In fact, toddlers may stare blankly and silently when urged to talk, then jabber freely later when alone or with a very trusted caregiver. Toddlers who are new to a group care setting may attend for weeks or months before trying to talk with a nursery school teacher, even though parents report they talk a great deal at home with family members.

Three- and four-year-olds gain the vocabulary needed to understand and express many ideas and feelings, and they become more concerned that there is an audience present for conversations. A preschooler who thinks we are not listening may move directly into our line of vision or may even try to hold our face to keep us from looking away. It is not uncommon, however, for two preschoolers to be looking straight at each other and chatting excitedly at the same time without either of them seeming to notice that neither is listening. Preschoolers also talk to inanimate objects such as stuffed animals and television characters without seeming to be bothered that these objects are not very responsive listeners (Birchmayer, Kennedy, & Stonehouse, 2010).

School-age children become more refined in their communication. They finally recognize that communicators must take

BrainFacts

What Can We Learn from Neuroscience?

How Do Babies and Young Children Learn Language?

- How do babies make sense of the sounds in their native language and learn to express their thoughts and needs? The young child's exploding ability to express ideas through words is an astounding accomplishment of the human mind that babies and toddlers accomplish without a thought (Dunbar, 1998; Eimas, Siqueland, Jusczyk, & Vigorito 1971; Kuhl, 2010).

- By 10 months of age, researchers can identify differences in the babbling of infants raised in different countries (de Boysson-Bardies, 1993), and by 20 weeks, typically developing babies are able to imitate vocal sounds (Kuhl & Meltzoff, 1982). The speaking patterns babies develop early in life last a life-time (Flege, 1991).

- Researchers believe that language evolved because communicating helped us survive. Evolution linked language capacity and social capacity in our brain design (Adolphs, 2003; Dunbar, 1998; Kuhl, 2007; Pulvermuller, 2005).

- Babies and very young children learn language best in close social interaction. Hearing language on television or radio doesn't help babies and toddlers learn language and, in fact, tends to slow babies' language development (Conboy & Kuhl, 2011; Kuhl et al., 2003).

- As babies and toddlers learn language, they pay close attention to the faces, actions, and voices of caregivers and other children. Their little brains sort out and begin to make sense of the patterns they hear (Bialystok & Hakuta, 1994; Birdsong & Molis, 2001; Bruer, 2008; Flege et al., 1999; Johnson & Newport, 1989; Knudsen, 2004; Kuhl, 2004; Newport et al., 2001).

- Infants and young children are better language learners than adults, in spite of adults' greater knowledge. Language is one of the best examples of a "critical" or "sensitive" period in neurobiology (Birdsong, 1992; Ferguson et al., 1992; Johnson & Newport, 1989; Kuhl, 2008; Kuhl et al., 2012; Mayberry & Lock, 2003; Neville et al., 1997; Weber-Fox & Neville, 1999; White & Genesee, 1996; Yeni-Komshian et al., 2000).

- Babies' language learning involves both sensory and motor practice (Kuhl & Meltzoff, 1996). This ability to imitate vocally may also depend on the brain's mirroring system that guides babies' social and emotional development (Hari & Kujala, 2009).

- No computer in the world can listen, sort out, and create meaning from the complex inventory of sounds in a language. But babies and toddlers routinely do just this. They can learn not just one but two or three languages if they have enough social interactions with speakers of those languages (Abramson & Lisker, 1970; Rabiner & Huang, 1993).

- Babies are helped by hearing "parentese," the simplified, high pitched, and ex-aggerated speech that adults universally use when interacting with babies (de Boer & Kuhl, 2003).

(Continued)

An important discovery in the 1970s was that infants can hear all the unique phonetic differences that exist in any language, a feat we adults cannot do. But as infants begin to recognize sounds they hear daily, they lose the ability to notice sounds that are not meaningful in their own language (Abramson & Lisker, 1970; Eimas, 1975; Eimas et al., 1971; Lasky et al., 1975; Lotto et al., 2004; Werker & Lalonde, 1988; Werker et al., 2007).

turns listening and speaking if anyone is to be heard. Their growing vocabulary and maturity increase their capacity for communication. Toddlers and younger preschoolers tend to be physical in their expression of feelings. Anger may be expressed by biting or hitting and affection by bear hugs and moist kisses. In contrast, school-agers use words more expertly to express affection or to lash out when they feel angry. They tend to use insults, threats, or name-calling to express anger and promises of friendship to show affection. Although school-agers are no longer as sensitive to adult modeling as younger children (who seem to absorb everything they see), school-agers emulate role models, and thus will be influenced by adults and children they admire (Bandura, 1977).

8-1c How Does American Sign Language Support Child Guidance?

There are many reasons today's parents and early educators should be taking a hard look at adding American Sign Language (ASL) to their list of routine child guidance skills. A wider public knowledge of sign language would not only help bring deaf children and their family members into the mainstream, but would also allow babies and toddlers to use their hands to express their needs much earlier than they can use spoken words. The discovery that babies and toddlers can learn to understand signing has sparked a sign language educational crusade by parents and early educators who find ASL extremely valuable in facilitating communication in young children (Acredolo et al., 2002; Briant, 2004; Daniels, 2001; Glazer, 2001; Goodwyn et al., 2000; Jaworski, 2000).

A particularly important guidance reason for using sign language with toddlers and young preschoolers is that it is often easier for very young children to move their hands when they are angry or excited than to think up words. We often tell them, "Use your words," but in their excitement, their words don't come. Unfortunately, their hands are still free for grabbing and hitting. By instilling the habit of sign language, toddlers have something urgent to do with their hands, something easy and memorized, something that takes the place of hitting and pushing.

8-1d Why Is Communication Important for Child Guidance?

As children develop and their communication style changes from stage to stage, we must recognize and adapt to changing ability levels. The achievement of effective child guidance hinges on the child's feeling a sense of connection, and that requires meaningful communication. The goal of positive discipline is not to control or manipulate children externally but to develop the child's inner control and his own sense of responsibility and respect for the rights of others. This inner control begins through understanding the needs and expectations of others through open, honest dialogue (Dreikurs, Cassel, & Ferguson, 2004; Hallowell, 2003).

Preparing children to function as adults in a democratic political system requires that children become competent communicators. In an autocracy, citizens can blindly and ignorantly follow leaders without ever discussing or questioning

The achievement of effective child guidance hinges on the child's feeling a sense of connection, and connection requires close, attentive communication.

Communication Supports Positive Guidance

We need communication skills to do the following:

- Understand children's needs
- Clearly express expectations
- Model effective communication

To help children listen more effectively, we should do the following:

- Provide eye contact at eye level
- Limit distractions
- Slow down and stick to the point
- Pick one thing to deal with at a time
- Use simple, meaningful speech
- Use gestures to clarify meaning

TeachSource Digital Download

commands. For a democracy to work, citizens must accept responsibility for their actions and take a stand on issues. These goals are achieved by communication: listening, reading, and discussing (Caspary, 2000).

The most effective tools children use to learn communication skills are modeling and practicing. Children learn effective skills as they watch, listen to, and interact with consistent adults who set a good example. Children are able to make those skills a part of their own behavior by practicing what they have observed. See Positive Focus 8.1.

Randy pulls his chair up to the table close to his teacher and spreads out a large sheet of drawing paper and an assortment of crayons. He says, "Hi, Miss Katie. I'm gonna color me a big picture." Miss Katie glances at him and smiles briefly, saying, "Uh-huh, that's nice." Miss Katie's attention is focused on a group of children playing across the room. She does not seem to notice Randy as he repeats, "Look, Miss Katie, look here!"

Finally, Randy tugs at her sleeve and says, "Look at this. I'm drawing great big mountains. My daddy took me camping, and I found lots of rocks. Wanna see my real mountain rocks?" Randy jumps up from his chair and begins emptying his pockets onto the drawing paper. Miss Katie suddenly sees his small pile of rocks and pebbles. She says in a stern voice, "Randy! What is all this? Get these dirty rocks off here. Go throw them in the trash. You can't color with rocks all over your paper."

Randy stammers, "But, but…," as tears fill his eyes. Miss Katie insists, "Randy, would you quit making such a fuss, and just do what I said."

Randy hangs his head and drags his feet as he slowly shuffles across the room to the trash can. One by one he ceremoniously drops his pebbles, his "real mountain rocks," into the trash. Miss Katie did not listen.

8-1e How Does Attentive Listening Nurture a Sense of Belonging?

Human beings have an intense need to feel connected to other human beings. We can't thrive without that connection in our lives. If a child is routinely ignored, she will begin to feel invisible. Much of what is called misbehavior is simply an attempt by the child to become visible one way or another. A child who does not feel a sense of belonging may gradually become alienated, rebellious, or withdrawn (Hallowell, 2003).

The more sure a child is that she is an accepted member of a group, the more confident and cooperative she will be. Polite, attentive listening not only gives children the confident feeling that what they have to say is important enough for us to listen, but also

We have two ears and one mouth so that we can listen twice as much as we speak.
—Epictetus (Greek philosopher)

Listening attentively and waiting for the child to find words to express herself encourage her to continue expressing herself and practicing her language skills.

© 2013 Cengage Learning®

teaches children by modeling how they should listen to others. Also, careful listening will help us understand children's needs. Every day we can show our recognition and acceptance of children by listening attentively (Close, 2002; Egan, 2002). See Positive Focus 8.2.

8-1f Three Basic Human Needs Underlying Requests for Help

Gazda and colleagues (2006) define three causes for communication that indicate a desire for some kind of response or help. Adults and children have the same basic human urge to get their needs met. Young children (and occasionally older children and adults) may function at an unconscious level in which they react to a vague feeling of need without recognizing or understanding that need. See Positive Focus 8.3.

Time, effort, and practice are required to become skilled at recognizing the underlying needs hidden in everyday communications. A question such as "Where is my mommy?" may be a simple request for information, or it may be an emotion-packed request for understanding and attention by a child who knows very well where mommy is. A major source of miscommunication is the tendency of persons in the helping role to jump to the wrong conclusion and respond in a way that does not meet the need of the person requesting help. Listening carefully and waiting for the child to find words to express herself encourage the child to practice speaking.

The communication method presented here can be most effective only if it is applied to adult-to-adult, adult-to-child, and child-to-child interactions. We can't say, "Do as I say and not as I do." Children learn to listen well by experiencing respectful listening as a regular part of daily life. Simply telling children to listen is not enough.

"I'll Leave You Here Forever"

Marlene pauses in the shopping mall waiting for her 2-year-old to catch up with her. Her 4-month-old, who is asleep on her shoulder, is beginning to feel very heavy. "Crystal," she calls to her 2-year-old, "Please come on. We need to get home."

Crystal stalls as she climbs on and off benches and stops to look at other shoppers. Her mother loses patience, "Crystal! You come here now or you're going to be sorry." Crystal ignores her.

Marlene walks quickly back to Crystal and, taking her firmly by the wrist says, "Let's go." Crystal responds with the rubbery-legs strategy toddlers use when they rebel. Her legs go limp as she slumps to the floor; her mother clutches her wrist as her body dangles from it and she whines, "Don't want go home."

Marlene realizes that she cannot safely carry her baby and Crystal both out of the shopping mall. In exasperation, she snaps, "That's it, I'm leaving. If you won't come, then I'll just leave you here forever. Good-bye!"

She turns and begins to walk briskly out of the mall. She hears Crystal howling and running to catch up with her.

Case Discussion Questions

1. What would you have done in Marlene's place? Why?
2. What has Crystal really learned from the interaction?
3. Could anything have been done to prevent Marlene's predicament?
4. Role-play the scene using positive, assertive communication and appropriate guidance, and then compare possible outcomes.

Children learn as if by **osmosis.** They absorb information simply by living day-to-day in an environment (Atherton, 2005). Effective listening is not only a learning objective for children but is also a necessary component of children's daily lives to be used directly with children as well as among the various adults who interact with children. For example, an ancient proverb says "Tell me and I forget; show me and I remember; involve me and I understand." I hope you will begin practicing the skills you are studying in this chapter in your daily life as well as with young children. As you master these skills, young children will naturally imitate your behavior and internalize your communication strategies.

osmosis 浸透

The gradual, unconscious mental process of absorbing ideas and taking in information that resembles the tendency of fluids to gradually soak through absorbent material.

8-1g Appropriate Responses to Requests for Action or Information

Requests may also be hidden or masked. What sounds like a simple statement may really be intended as a request for action. "I can't sleep," may really mean, "Come sit by me and read me a story." A comment may really mask a request for information. "Latecia's mama is too fat" may really mean, "Latecia told me there is a baby in her mama's tummy, and I am very frightened and confused." Because children do not have fully developed communication skills, adults must accept additional responsibility for keeping the channels of communication open and clear.

Joey, an 18-month-old, sits on a small stool, rocking and crying. "Beah, beah, ma beah," he sobs. Miss Rosario squats beside him and gently coaxes him to show her what he wants. Joey quickly leads her to the bathroom. He stretches his arm toward a high shelf where diaper bags are kept. Urgently, he opens and closes his hand pleading, "Beah, beah!"

Miss Rosario takes his diaper bag from the shelf. Immediately she sees that Joey's fuzzy white teddy bear is inside. She says, "Oh, you want your bear. Is that right, Joey, bear?"

Joey nods and says, "Ma beah." He hugs his bear and toddles away dragging it by one leg.

Even though Miss Rosario could not understand Joey's words, she recognized that Joey was requesting action from her. People who work with young children spend a great deal of time responding to requests for action or information. Some requests are straightforward and simple to understand: "Is it time for snack yet?" or "Tie my shoe, please." Other requests, such as Joey's request for his bear, are difficult to interpret.

Five-year-old Malika is standing on the playground beside her teacher, Mrs. Johnson. She sees a caterpillar crawling toward her and starts to shriek. Mrs. Johnson bends down and gently allows the fuzzy caterpillar to crawl onto a leaf she is holding. Malika screams, "It's gonna kill you! Is it gonna kill you?"

Mrs. Johnson says, "No, Malika. This little caterpillar has a very tiny mouth and no teeth and no poison. He likes to eat leaves. When he gets very fat, he will wrap himself in a cocoon that is like a little blanket. While he is inside, he will change into a beautiful butterfly. Then, after a long time, that beautiful butterfly will come out of the cocoon and fly away." Mrs. Johnson helps Malika make a suitable home for the caterpillar in a large jar. Later, at circle time, she reads the book The Very Hungry Caterpillar.

Mrs. Johnson has redirected Malika's fear of bugs to curiosity about science and nature. Mrs. Johnson recognized that underneath Malika's shrieking and screaming was a need for information. Mrs. Johnson responded to a hidden request for information.

After a birthday party, 4-year-old Seth sees that his mother is wrapping leftover cake. He says, "Mommy, I want more cake, please." His mother says, "No, Seth. No more cake." Seth begs, "Please, I'm hungry. I want more cake."

Seth's mother bends down to Seth's eye level and takes his hand gently. In a sympathetic voice, she says, "Seth, I understand that you really want more cake. That cake tasted great, didn't it? But a lot of cake is not good for you. I love you and I want you to have a healthy body and healthy teeth, so I have to say no. No more cake."

Seth pulls his hand away, bouncing up and down, whining and flapping his arms like an angry old hen (the preschooler's dance of frustration and impending tantrum). Seth's mother does not flinch a muscle. She bends back down, and in a very calm tone she says, "It's okay to feel angry. Sometimes I feel angry, too. Sometimes I get so angry I feel like crying. Sometimes I feel so bad that I just need a hug."

Without looking at her face, Seth climbs into his mother's arms and gets a long hug. Suddenly, he brightens and says, "How 'bout apples. They make you get strong teeth like Superman." His mom smiles and replies, "You know, Seth, that sounds like a great idea." Seth's mother clearly understood her son's request for action, but she also knew that providing what he wanted was not in his best interest. Seth's mother loved him enough to say no to his request and enough to accept an appropriate compromise.

Adults are ultimately responsible for the health, safety, and welfare of children in their care. Complying with potentially harmful or unfair requests hurts children and, eventually, damages adult–child trust and respect. Sometimes, we are tempted to comply with questionable requests to avoid conflict or in a misguided attempt to win the child's affection. Seth's mother not only stood firm in making the decision that is in Seth's best interest, but also taught her son a valuable lesson.

Her gentle strength has shown Seth an example of self-discipline, doing the right thing even though it would be easier to give in and avoid a fuss. Through her calm, patient persistence, even when he threatens a tantrum, she serves as a positive role model for Seth. Seth can learn positive coping skills, to stay calm, and to persist in finding a solution when he feels upset. (Some adults inadvertently reinforce children's tantrums by pitching tantrums of their own.) And most importantly, Seth's mother's sensitive understanding of his feelings helps him know that he is loved and respected, even while a limit is being enforced.

Seth didn't have a tantrum, but if he had, that would have been okay. Most young children have a certain number of tantrums before they discover that tantrums don't really achieve what they want. The best thing a parent can do during a tantrum is to stay calm, make sure the child is not injured, and assure the child that he will feel calm soon.

Some requests may appear on the surface to be requests for action or information, but are not. The real need at the core of this type of communication is for someone to listen and show interest.

Mr. Wilke watches as his kindergartners work and play in various learning centers. Angelica, a shy 5-year-old, is alone in the art center. As Mr. Wilke walks past, she calls out, "Mr. Wilke, I need some help." He smiles and perches his tall frame on the little chair beside her. Angelica hands him her paper and plastic scissors and says, "Help me cut, I don't know how."

Mr. Wilke has always made careful observations and kept records of his students' levels of skill with learning center materials. He is sure that Angelica does know how to use scissors. He looks at the situation and mentally rules out possibilities such as broken scissors or thick paper. He decides that Angelica may not really be seeking action (cutting for her) or information (teaching her how to cut), but instead is seeking understanding and attention.

Mr. Wilke knows it will not help Angelica to embarrass her by confronting her in a harsh way. He also knows that he does not want to reinforce her perception that she can get the attention she needs by feigning incompetence. He says, "Sometimes cutting seems really hard, doesn't it?" He gently pats her shoulder and adds, "Would you like for me to sit beside you while you try cutting this yellow paper?" Angelica eagerly cuts her jagged paper while Mr. Wilke watches attentively. After a few minutes, as he gets up to leave, he says, "Angelica, you must really feel proud that you cut that out all by yourself."

Mr. Wilke was correct in his assumption that Angelica was really requesting understanding and attention. Seeking attention is not a perverse behavior that must always be extinguished in children. At our core, we human beings are social beings; we all need attention from others to thrive. The goal with young children is not to stop attention-getting behaviors but to teach children how to get an appropriate amount of attention in a socially acceptable manner. If Mr. Wilke observed that Angelica continued in a pattern of pretending ineptness to get attention, it might become necessary for Mr. Wilke, privately and tactfully, to address her behavior by saying, "Angelica, you seem to need some attention. It's okay to need attention. Please say, 'Mr. Wilke, I need some attention.' That will help me know exactly what you need." (See "How Should I Respond to Requests for Inappropriate Interaction?" p. 209)

In an environment in which needs are respected, children come to know that it is okay to have needs and feelings. Sometimes we inadvertently give children the impression that their needs or emotions make us angry. This problem often occurs when we are having a difficult time getting our own emotional needs met.

A particularly helpful strategy for dealing with feelings and needs honestly and respectfully is active listening (also referred to as mirroring, reflective listening, empathetic listening, or responsive listening). In active listening, the listener refrains from lecturing, advising, or informing. She simply listens and reflects the feelings she perceives from seeing and hearing the other person. This gives the listener plenty of time to really hear the other person, to let the other person know her feelings and needs are important and respected, and to think of ways to help the person resolve the problem (Cronen, 2001; Egan, 2002, 2006).

When a child's needs are respected, the child learns that it is okay to have needs and feelings. Through communication, teachers often discover the cause of inappropriate behaviors.

© 2013 Cengage Learning®

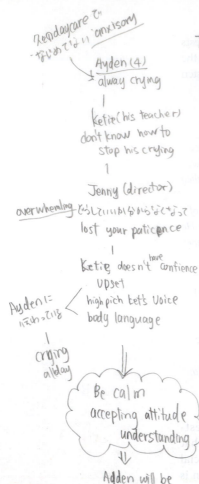

Jenny, who directs an infant and toddler child care program, treats the teaching and caring staff with the same respect and dignity she expects them to extend to the babies. She knows that even infants and toddlers are unconsciously absorbing the behaviors around them. She also knows that caring for little ones can be incredibly stressful.

Ayden, a 4-month-old whose mother has just returned to work after her maternity leave, is crying. He has attended the child care program for only a few days and has cried most of the time. Kate, his primary caregiver, has tried everything she knows to calm him. She has walked him, patted him, and rocked him, and she is now at the end of her patience.

Kate storms into the director's office and demands, "What is that child's problem? Nothing I do works. What am I supposed to do?" Luckily, Jenny realizes that Kate is not really seeking action or information. What Kate needs most is understanding, so Jenny offers her a chair and closes the door for privacy. Instead of focusing on solving baby Ayden's problem, Jenny focuses on hearing and understanding Kate's feelings. In a caring voice, Jenny says, "Kate, you seem really frustrated."

"You bet I am," replies Kate, "I don't think I can deal with his crying another minute. I don't even know if I ought to work with children. I am really at my wit's end."

Wisely, Jenny refrains from making judgments, giving information, or taking action. Gazda and colleagues (2006) note that rushing to give someone a quick solution is "cheap and dirty" advice, because the helper has not had a chance to learn all the facts. If problems were so easy to solve that an "off the top of the head" solution was adequate, one would wonder why the person suffering with the problem had not already thought of it.

Instead of rushing to tell Kate why she has a problem or how to solve it, Jenny simply mirrors to Kate (through active listening) what she hears Kate saying.

She responds with nonjudgmental active (or reflective) listening statements that begin with the following:

"What I'm hearing you say is…"

"In other words, you are saying that…"

"It sounds as if you feel…"

Jenny says, "Kate, it sounds like what you're saying is that you're feeling so frustrated that you're afraid you've lost your patience. You seem to be wondering if you're really cut out to work with children." Calmness settles over Kate as she realizes that she is not being judged or told what to do, but that her director is really listening and understanding what she is saying. She thinks for a moment and says, "I guess I'm just having a bad day. I really do love working with babies. It's just that Ayden keeps screaming no matter what I do." Jenny leans close and touches Kate's arm. "You know, it sounds as if you feel inadequate because you can't stop Ayden's crying. I think Ayden is lucky to have someone like you to care so much and try so hard to comfort him."

Streams of tears spill down Kate's face. She feels enough trust to let go of her feelings and let everything out that has been bottled inside her. Now that her own needs for understanding and attention have been met, she can return to her nursery classroom and try again to meet Ayden's needs for understanding and attention.

Even though Ayden did not see or hear the adult interaction (and would have been too young to make sense of it if he had), he undoubtedly sensed the tension and frustration in Kate's voice and body language when she was upset. He will feel and benefit from the calmer, more accepting attitude Kate will have when she returns to care for him. By sensing the patience and understanding of his caregiver, Ayden will begin to learn the coping skills he will need to develop confidence and self-esteem as he grows older.

8-1i How Should I Respond to Requests for Inappropriate Interaction?

We often have difficulty knowing where understanding ends and dependency begins. A child begs, "Hold me," "Put my coat on for me," or "Help me finish my puzzle." We sometimes struggle to know what is right for the child. Are holding, helping, and nurturing meeting the child's needs or reinforcing a pattern of dependency?

Under usual circumstances, as soon as children are able, they spontaneously break away from various levels of dependence on adults. Toddlers stubbornly resist the hovering care that was necessary to their survival as infants. Adolescents rebel against the close parental attachment that protected them in childhood. For most children, achieving independence is the motivating force behind the process of growing up. But this force does not always move steadily forward. Even highly competent, well-developing children regress from time to time and need the security of someone to depend on. A bit of babying, on infrequent occasions, does little harm to well-developing children. This regression only seems to recharge young children's energy and desire for independence. But for the chronically dependent child, coddling undermines self-esteem and destroys initiative.

In certain situations, children learn to be helpless (Altenor et al., 1977; Haith & Benson, 2008). We may have difficulty accepting change and may fail to recognize a child's emerging capabilities. At times we may inadvertently interfere with children's efforts at learning to function independently because we don't realize the importance of self-reliance.

Children's first efforts to do things by themselves are often messy and fraught with mistakes. Babies learning to feed themselves splatter, smear, and spill food. Toddlers learning to dress themselves put both feet in the same leg hole of their training pants. Preschoolers learning to tie their own shoes create nightmarish knots in their shoelaces. And school-agers learning gardening walk on the seedlings they have just planted. Little mishaps such as these are a necessary part of learning by experience. In a demanding, perfectionist, or punitive atmosphere in which a child begins to fear making mistakes, she may learn to avoid risk by becoming passive, by not attempting anything that requires initiative or involves the chance of failure.

Children sometimes express requests for dependency through such actions as persistent whining, clinging, or regularly demanding special favors such as being first in line, sitting in the teacher's lap, or being carried. Indulging these inappropriate requests is not helpful for children. A 6-month-old on the floor who whines for help after one attempt at reaching toward a toy needs to be left alone rather than having the toy handed over.

We help the child more by encouraging her than by doing her work for her. A preschooler who whines, claims exhaustion, and begs for help putting blocks away may respond to a game, such as "I'll close my eyes. You tell me when to open them, and I'll count how many blocks are on the shelf." Or a kindergartner who follows the teacher, clinging and asking for help, may need to be given some important responsibility such as helping a younger child.

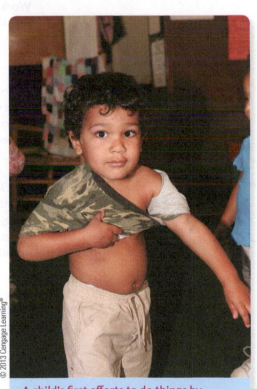

A child's first efforts to do things by himself are often fraught with mistakes, but mistakes are important for his learning. We wait patiently and avoid interfering in his efforts to learn independence. We encourage the child's persistent struggle toward self-reliance and only intervene to help when the child has reached the limit of his tolerance for frustration.

In some cases, redirection is not enough. It may be necessary to clearly communicate unwillingness to participate in interactions that indulge or solicit inappropriate dependency, spread gossip, reinforce inordinate complaining, or involve actions that turn adults or children against one another. Gazda and colleagues (2006) tell us that if we support inappropriate behavior, even by remaining silent, we may not only lose our opportunity to be helpful, but also inadvertently become a model for negative or hurtful behavior.

Gazda further adds that this rule is easier to "preach" than to practice because it is necessary to end the inappropriate interaction without offending the person initiating it. Offending a child or other adult damages trust, closes off communication, and projects an image of arrogance. The recommended response is a polite but firm refusal to be part of the inappropriateness accompanied by a straightforward, warm, and respectful indication of caring about the person as an individual. Tactfulness eases the sting of a refusal to participate in an inappropriate interaction (Gazda et al., 2006).

Mr. Hernandez arrives one afternoon and prepares to teach his after-school gymnastics class. Sarah and Cynthia, twin third graders, eagerly volunteer to help spread mats. As Sarah and Cynthia help, they confide to Mr. Hernandez how much they dislike James, one of the least popular boys in the gymnastics class.

Sarah says, "Ugh! We can't stand James. He's fatter than an elephant." Cynthia chimes in, "Have you ever listened when he laughs? He sort of snorts and makes some weird sound." They giggle uproariously.

Mr. Hernandez values the positive relationship he has with Sarah and Cynthia and does not wish to embarrass them, but he also knows that to smile and say nothing would be tacit approval of their remarks about James. That would be hurtful to James and would fail to guide Sarah and Cynthia toward more appropriate behavior.

Mr. Hernandez carefully chooses his words and then bends down, touching each girl lightly on the shoulder. He says gently, "I don't feel good talking about James." Then his tone brightens and he deftly changes the subject, "But, you know what, I surely do like all this great help. How about this balance beam, girls? Do you think you both can get at that end and help me move it? Thanks."

Mr. Hernandez has not been judgmental or critical. He has simply and politely declined to participate by focusing on his own feelings. The girls probably felt a moment of embarrassment, but they also knew their teacher accepted and cared about them. As a result of this encounter, the girls may become more thoughtful about ridiculing others, not because of an external fear of punishment or chastisement, but from a growing internal sense of right and wrong bolstered by a strong and admired role model in the person of Mr. Hernandez.

8-1j Do Listening and Helping Strategies Work with Babies and Toddlers?

The complexity of words and sentences must always be adjusted to the listener's level of maturity. However, the integrity and basic content of a message need not be lost to simplification. Physical actions, facial expressions, tone of voice, and gestures help convey our messages to babies and toddlers.

Mrs. Wang, who cares for infants in her church's mother's-day-out program, hears 11-month-old Gavin crying. He is banging on a low cabinet door that is locked with a child-guard latch. Mrs. Wang perceives the baby's cry is a request for action. Gavin wants the cabinet door opened. Mrs. Wang tries to distract him with several toys, but he continues to cry and pull at the door.

Mrs. Wang picks Gavin up as he is kicking and screaming, and she carries him to her big rocking chair. She rocks and pats Gavin as she says in a caring voice, "I really understand that you want to explore that cabinet, but the things in there could hurt you. I can't let you play there because I like you and I want to keep you safe." As Gavin begins to calm down, Mrs. Wang carries him around the nursery and shows him alternative areas to explore as she continues to talk to him.

Gavin does not understand her words but he definitely can sense her warmth and empathy, and he can sense the firmness of the limit she has set. He may test the limit many more times, but Mrs. Wang's warmth will communicate to him that he is still accepted as a person. Her consistency will communicate to him that limits are sometimes a part of life. She recognizes that babies explore boundaries because they have a limited capacity to understand or remember rules and because they learn through trial and error. She will refuse Gavin's demands that she open the locked cabinet, but his actions will not change her feelings about him.

Additionally, by talking to Gavin, Mrs. Wang is able to focus her own thoughts and feelings on the situation. She, as well as Gavin, needs to hear the words she has said. By expressing in words the reasons she is doing what she is doing, she feels reassured that she is doing the right thing. Also, by putting her feelings into words, she is able to make sure her facial expression and body language are consistent with the message she wants to convey to Gavin.

Mrs. Wang, knowing that Gavin could not really understand her words, might have said instead, "Listen, I'm tired of fooling with you. Are you just trying to bug me?" However, it is nearly impossible to say these words in a sincere, warm, and caring way.

Mrs. Wang's face and tone would probably have conveyed sarcasm, impatience, and blame to Gavin. In an unconscious way, he would have absorbed those negative feelings and reflected them in his behavior. Also, words such as *fooling* and *bug* are ambiguous words that do not help Gavin learn language. Luckily for Gavin, Mrs. Wang would not think of behaving rudely to him any more than she would be rude to anyone else she respected and valued.

8-2 Addressing Underlying Feelings

Most people who work with children would agree that child care and early childhood education are emotionally draining occupations. Young children ride an emotional roller coaster. They can go from laughter to tears in the blink of an eye. Responsive adults who are closely involved in the lives of young children are pulled along in the wave of emotions from the elation of a new discovery to the heartbreak of a best friend who says, "I hate you."

Children's emotions are real. Before 6 months, infants are capable of only three undifferentiated emotions: pleasure, wariness, and rage. By 9 months, the baby has a dramatically increased range of emotional responses. By age 3 years, children have developed the entire panorama of human emotions (Haith & Benson, 2008).

An important part of early childhood learning is the child's gradually developing awareness of feelings and the child's growing ability to express those feelings. Very young children react unconsciously. A toddler may whine and act out in an aggressive way without realizing that she is feeling hunger, discomfort, fatigue, and so on. We play an important role in identifying, labeling, and explaining children's feelings to them. We also give children important feedback about certain behaviors by expressing relevant feelings (Kottler, 2000).

8-2a When and How Should Adults Express Their Feelings to Children?

We should think carefully when expressing strong feelings to others. Young children can be overwhelmed if we unload too much on them or if feelings we express are too intense. Simple, nonjudgmental statements of our own feelings are more useful than accusatory statements. See Positive Focus 8.4.

Giving "I Messages"

Following is a fill-in-the-blank statement, called an "I" message. It is used to state feelings appropriately and in a nonthreatening way:

When _____ happens, I feel _____

because _____.

Positive Focus 8.4

This statement does not contain the word *you*. Statements such as "You make me angry" or "You are hurting my ears with your yelling" suggest blame. They may set off an unnecessary feeling of guilt. Positive guidance should bring about positive feelings of confidence and responsibility, not negative feelings of guilt. We can say simply, "When there is loud screaming I feel concerned because the noise interrupts your friends who are busy. I need for you to use a soft voice."

With a toddler we would say, "When your friend gets bitten she cries because it hurts so much. It's okay to bite crackers and apples. We're gentle with people. Touch gently. Let's get a cool, wet paper towel for your friend to help her feel better."

We must establish a warm, caring relationship with the child to be effective in guiding the child.

If we consistently use assertive yet controlled words to express strong feelings, then children will eventually imitate by using words instead of physical attacks to express their own anger and frustration. A child will also feel more compliant when our feelings are focused on the action rather than on the child.

Additionally, we can clarify and express positive feelings beginning with the same sample sentence. For example, "When I see you share a special toy, I feel proud because I know you are learning how to get along." "When the sun is shining, I feel excited because we can go outside and enjoy the grass and trees." "When I discovered that you had put every single block away all by yourself, I felt like jumping up and down because I was so happy and proud."

Positive and negative expressions of feelings can have a powerful effect on a child's behavior, but only when the person expressing those feelings is emotionally connected to the child. We must have established a relationship with the child. Neither adults nor children are particularly concerned about the feelings of someone who is not liked or respected. In fact, knowing that a disliked adult's ears hurt with loud noise might stimulate more screaming from children who mischievously intend to cause discomfort.

8-3 Positive Instructions versus Negative Commands

In positive communication we focus on identifying and stating desired behaviors rather than focusing on inappropriate behaviors. Children and adults tend to respond more cooperatively to positive requests than they do to negative admonitions. For example, a parent would probably feel more responsive to a request from a child care worker that was worded as "Please check to see that Kelly has enough diapers for the day" rather than "You never bring enough diapers for Kelly." The difference in children's and adult's responses to positive requests rather than negative commands is stark.

Additionally, toddlers are so limited in their comprehension of language that they tend to hear and respond only to key words in sentences. If an adult tells a toddler, "I do not want you to touch this cake," the toddler may actually hear, "Do…want…touch…cake." And, of course, because the toddler wants to touch the cake, she probably will. We could bring about better communication by designating a desired activity to replace touching the cake. We could provide paper and crayons at a location away from the cake and say, "Please color on this big piece of paper," which the toddler may accurately interpret as "Color…big…paper."

Toddlers and young preschoolers have difficulty hearing and interpreting every word of sentences and also have difficulty thinking about a behavior and then inhibiting that behavior. Thinking and doing are almost inseparable at this stage of development. For example, if we say firmly, "No spitting" to a young child who has not even yet thought of spitting, she may comprehend both words but, as she thinks about not spitting, it is likely the child will act out the spitting. The statement "Don't wet your pants" causes the child to have a mental image of wetting pants, which may trigger urination. The statement "It is time to use the potty" evokes a mental image of the toilet, which is much more effective in gaining a child's cooperation. See Positive Focus 8.5.

Once you replace negative thoughts with positive ones, you'll start having positive results.

—Willie Nelson

Positive Requests versus Negative Commands

Compare the examples below:

Negative Commands	Positive Requests
Don't run in the hall.	Walk slowly, please.
Don't spill your milk.	Use both hands, please.
Quit poking at Jimmy.	Hands in your lap now.
Shut up.	Please listen quietly.
Stop interrupting me.	It is my turn to talk now.
Don't talk with a full mouth.	Swallow first, then talk.
Quit shoving in line.	Walk carefully, please.
Stop yelling my name.	Please say my name softly.

TeachSource Digital Download

Negative commands are strongly entrenched as habit patterns. Time, commitment, motivation, and persistence are needed to break any habit pattern, and communication habits are no exception. Often as we begin to improve our communication style, we hear ourselves using ineffective phrases but cannot seem to stop using them. Think about a beautiful, innocent toddler, standing in a puddle of urine with a surprised look, saying, "Go potty!" He is taking the first tentative step toward changing a habit pattern, too. An adult who feels remorse for saying "shut up" to a child is taking the first step toward consciously controlling and changing an ineffective communication strategy. She, like the toddler, recognizes she made a mistake, a critical phase of learning.

8-4 Characteristics of Assertive Communication

Communication is always intended to convey a message, just as a radio transmitter is intended to transmit a radio program. For the music of a radio program to be heard, the waves sent from the transmitter have to match the receiver equipment of the radio. The communication transmitted from an adult must match the mental and emotional ability of the child or the message will not be received.

Children, and adults as well, will close off communication that is incomprehensible, threatening, vague, or rude, just as they would tune out or turn off a radio with unpleasant static. Although we may sometimes feel justified in lecturing or lashing out, there is no value in conveying a message if the message is rejected. Our goal is to have messages accepted and acted on.

Carolyn is a child care professional teaching and caring for a group of 4-year-olds. As her children leave the playground and come inside for a snack, she says, "Mmmm, I feel hungry. Do you feel hungry, Clay?" Clay agrees, and the children expand on Carolyn's expression of hunger: "I am as hungry as a tiger." "I'm so hungry I could eat this whole building." "I'm so hungry I could eat the whole world!"

The children giggle about eating the whole world as they find their seats at the table. Clay rushes to sit by his best friend Misha, but Ellen has already taken the chair. Clay stamps his foot and complains loudly as he shakes the back of the chair he wants. The child in the chair stubbornly holds on.

Carolyn quickly comes to intervene in the brewing fight. She kneels down at eye level to Clay and says, "You feel angry because someone took the chair you wanted. Can you use words to tell Ellen how you feel?"

Clay shouts, "I want that chair. Gimme it, now!" Ellen grips the chair tighter and ignores him. Carolyn turns to Ellen and says, "Ellen, can you tell Clay how you feel?" Ellen looks at the floor and shakes her head no. Carolyn asks her, "Would you like me to tell Clay how you feel?" Ellen vigorously nods yes.

Carolyn says, "Clay, Ellen is feeling very upset because you are shaking her chair and yelling at her. She got here first and she doesn't want you to take her chair away." Clay begins to shake the chair again, so Carolyn firmly removes his hands from the chair. Then, restraining his hands, but with concern and empathy in her voice, Carolyn says, "Clay, I know you feel really frustrated, but you have two choices. You may choose another chair and have a snack, or you may come out in the hall and talk with me until you feel better. What do you choose?"

From experience, Clay knows Carolyn is gentle and caring, but he also knows that she always means what she says. He does not relish the idea of throwing a tantrum that will only succeed in delaying his snack. Carolyn sees a look of indecision on his face and quickly says, "Look, Clay. There is an empty chair right at the end of the table by Joey. Would you like to sit there?" Clay decides that Joey would not be so bad to sit by after all and shuffles along to take a seat. Carolyn smiles and pats his shoulder.

If we stand across the room from a child and casually look over a shoulder, saying, "Letecia, don't touch those scissors; you'll cut yourself," Letecia will probably interpret that we are not too concerned about the danger of the scissors and we will probably not enforce the instructions. It is likely that Letecia will continue to touch the scissors while keeping an eye on us for more direct cues about the scissors.

If we stop what we are doing and bend down to the child's eye level, hold out a hand for the scissors, and say, "Please give me the scissors. These are too sharp. They could cut you. We'll find you a plastic pair," then our assertive nonverbal communication matches our verbal communication. Letecia is likely to perceive that we are serious and are willing to follow through to see that the sharp scissors are removed.

As Letecia decides whether to comply with the instructions she has been given, she will read our facial expression (is there a playful twinkle in the eye or a look of concerned resolve?), tone of voice (is there a weak tone of uncertainty or a tone of absolute confidence?), and hand gestures (are hand motions assertive or physically threatening?). If the adult's nonverbal cues are too playful or casual, Letecia will assume that she really does not have to comply. If they are too threatening and intrusive, Letecia may be likely to bristle and resist the command. If they are assertive, caring, confident, and no-nonsense, Letecia may decide that it is a good idea to comply quickly and willingly.

8-4a Key Factors in Assertive Communication	Assertive communication is a way of expressing ideas and feelings that allows a person to stand up for rights while fully respecting the rights of others. Nonassertive communication may be either passive or aggressive.

Simplicity Is the First Rule for Assertive Communication

Although babies, toddlers, and young children need plenty of opportunities to hear the rhythm and flow of complex adult language, assertive statements need to be short and to the point. Decide what needs to be said and say it in as few words as possible. Verbal clutter gets in the way of stating a desired action.

The younger the child, the more essential simplicity becomes. Toddlers need simple two- or three-word sentences, such as "Sit, please" or (if a child has already bitten) "No biting. Biting hurts." Preschoolers need only slightly longer sentences, such as "Apples are for eating, not for throwing," "Please hold your glass with two hands," or "A chair is for your seat, not your feet."

Honesty Is Essential for Assertive Communication

Children quickly identify adults who do not really mean what they say. Empty threats are counterproductive. They teach children only that adults cannot be relied on to do what they say, no matter how many times they insist that "This time I really mean it!" It is never acceptable to lie to children or to trick them into compliance. They should be told honestly when a parent is leaving, even if that causes tears. Feeling sad is a natural and healthy response; feeling tricked is not.

Directness Helps Communicators Get Right to the Point

Rambling, hinting, and insinuating are of little value to adult listeners and are totally lost on children. Instead of saying, "The art area is getting pretty sloppy, children," say, "Please pick up all of the scrap paper and put it in the trash can. Thank you. Now get a sponge and wipe the table." Instead of saying, "Let's keep it down now," say, "Please walk softly and speak quietly." Words used with children should be literal words with clearly definable meanings. A phrase such as "You need to cut it out now" should be reserved for occasions when scissors and paper are involved.

Tact Keeps Channels of Communication Open

Gushing sweetness is usually not any more palatable to young children than it is to adults, but tactfulness and sincerity are greatly appreciated. It is tactful to say, "Your glass may tip off the table. Please push it back away from the edge. Thank you." It is not tactful to say, "Stop being so careless with your glass of milk." It is overly patronizing to say, "Here, sweetheart, let's push our little glass back so we don't spill it, okay, honey?" Children can be given affection and kindness without being drowned in cloying sweetness.

Concreteness Makes Communication Clear

Abstractions such as *good* and *bad* can be very confusing to children. The statement that lying is bad, for example, may cause a child to think she is a bad person. It is more concrete to say, "If you lie, other people may not trust you. They may learn not to believe things you say." With younger children, concreteness is expressed through actions. It is not concrete to tell a toddler, "Be nice to your friends." A toddler or preschooler has no real concept of the word *nice.* It is a vague, value-laden term for which no two adults have exactly the same definition. A toddler or preschooler would not know precisely what to do to be nice. It is concrete to repeat "Touch softly" while demonstrating stroking the friend's arm gently. The toddler can see and comprehend exactly what action is expected.

Respect Is an Integral Part of Assertive Communication

It is impossible to have open, honest communication with someone for whom one has disgust and disdain. In a democracy, a garbage collector deserves as much respect as the president, even though each has distinctly different roles and responsibilities. Similarly, the person and human rights of a newborn are as deserving of respect as they are for any other member of society. Respect for children is expressed by recognizing and protecting their dignity and rights. A police officer may stop a citizen and issue a citation that makes the citizen feel very unhappy, but the officer has no right to hurt, humiliate, or threaten the citizen. Respectful adults assertively teach ground rules. A respectful adult approaches a child privately to deal with problem behavior and focuses on improving behavior rather than on punishing.

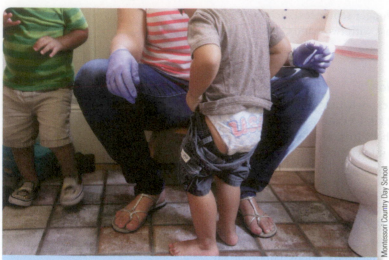

We express respect for children when we recognize and protect each child's dignity.

Optimism Boosts Cooperation by Sharing Hope

A child trying to cope with an assertive adult needs to know that the adult really has confidence the child will succeed. Interactions with adults are softened and made more acceptable by reassurance that problems can indeed be solved. After approaching Jennifer, you might say, "Jennifer, everyone makes mistakes. Our mistakes help us learn. Perhaps tomorrow you can help by reminding the younger children how important it is not to run out of the gate without permission."

Flexibility Is Necessary to Distinguish Assertiveness from Stubbornness

No matter how firm your intention to carry out a plan of action, the possibility always exists that additional information could indicate the need for a change in plans. Young children need consistency to make sense of what is expected of them, but that need is not contradictory with their need for flexibility. (The trick is finding the right balance.) Effective, assertive guidance requires that adults provide not only as much consistency as possible but also as much flexibility as needed to make discipline humane and reasonable.

Adults must constantly seek a balance between firm, predictable limits and the flexibility to listen, adapt, and compromise appropriately. For example, an adult might firmly refuse to talk about or compromise a stated rule while a child is having a tantrum or behaving very inappropriately. Later, however, when the child is calm and able to explain logically her problem with the rule, the adult might decide that justice is best served by bending or eliminating the rule. With a very young child, we may rely on direct observations rather than on verbal discussions to determine whether a rule is fair and reasonable.

Confidence Projects Assurance That What Is Said Is Really Meant

Children are especially sensitive to cues from facial expression, intonation, body positioning, and the use of hands and feet. Adults who do not really believe children will do what is asked of them project an air of uncertainty and weakness. A clear-eyed look of confidence greatly increases the probability of compliance from children as well as from listeners of any other age. Fidgeting, speaking in a weak or shrill voice, and avoiding eye contact hint to the child that compliance is not really expected.

When adults say sarcastic things such as, "Well, let's see if you can keep from being a little monster as usual, running around and tearing everything up while we wait for the doctor," children know immediately that they are expected to behave badly. In contrast, a confident adult might say firmly but caringly, "Here is a book to look at quietly while we wait. We must sit very still. People are not allowed to be rowdy and noisy in a doctor's office." This indicates assurance that the adult believes the child can and will behave appropriately.

Punishing, threatening, and intimidating get quick results on the surface but undermine discipline in the long run. Assertive communication does not always bring about an immediate solution, but persistence over time makes it an effective and lasting technique for solving problems. Adults are sometimes tempted to surrender to children's demands when first efforts at communication do not bring about an immediate resolution. A generous amount of persistence, however, will reap important benefits by letting children know that we really mean what we say. A child may stubbornly reject a rule on a whim, but if we persist in letting her know we expect the rule to be followed, she will almost surely comply eventually. As with the tortoise and the hare in their fabled contest, slow and steady wins the race.

How Can I Be Authoritative Rather Than Authoritarian?

- Listen carefully.
- Avoid giving directives to solve children's problems: "Do this and your problem will be solved."
- Avoid statements such as, "I'm the expert" or "I know what's best for you."
- Ask, "How can I be helpful?"
- Remind school-aged children that they will make important choices and decisions as they get older, regardless of what others say or do. They must learn to be in charge of their own bodies and their own minds.

TeachSource Digital Download

Empathy May Seem Out of Context with Assertiveness But Is Essential

Sympathy means feeling sorry for others; empathy means walking in their shoes, understanding what they feel. Assertiveness without empathy is hollow and insincere. Assertiveness with empathy is strength and love rolled into one. A little person with grimy hands, a runny nose, and a knack for creating havoc does not always trigger feelings of warmth and empathy in parents and caregivers. Nonetheless, effective communication requires sincere understanding and caring. Empathy is expressed to listeners, from infancy to adulthood, primarily through the eyes and face, but all other verbal and nonverbal cues can also express empathy (or the lack of it). See Positive Focus 8.6.

We can begin reprimands by making an initial positive statement of some kind to show empathy. We might take a child by the hand and say, "I know you just want to play with the kitty, but chasing him and pulling his tail really frightens him. Would you like to feed him to show him you're his friend?"

8-5 Characteristics of Nonproductive Communication

Adults use many different communication styles. Of course, some styles are more effective than others. The least effective styles usually deal only superficially with the content of the communication and fail completely to address the feelings or emotions of the persons sharing in the communication. It is most important that we avoid the communication pitfalls that inhibit dialogue and alienate children (or others of any age).

Gazda and colleagues (2006) list nine stereotypes of ineffective communication styles. Although two-dimensional stereotypes do not reflect the complex facets of real people, they are helpful in identifying characteristics that real people display from time to time. One stereotype may be the predominant way an individual responds, but others might recognize a little bit of each stereotype in their behavior occasionally. The purpose of these stereotypes is not to label children or adults, but to better recognize and understand ineffective communication styles.

8-5a How Do These Stereotypes Show Up as Problems?

Read each of the following descriptions and reflect on your own interactions with others who are seeking help, information, involvement, or inappropriate interaction from you. Most of us will see a bit of ourselves in one or more of the descriptions.

- *Florists* do not see any problems. If a child communicates that she has been hurt by another child, the florist ever so sweetly croons, "Why, Carlos, I'm sure he didn't mean to hurt you!" If a tearful child sobs, "I hate my mommy," the florist teacher just smiles knowingly and says, "Of course you don't hate your mommy. Children don't hate their mommies." The florist loses many opportunities to communicate by tossing garlands of optimism rather than by assertively dealing with the problems.
- *Detectives* want answers: "Why did you do that?" "Who did it first?" "Did I tell you not to do that?" "What do you think you're going to do now?" The listener is not only dazed by the battery of questions, but also tempted to lie or to give whatever answers the detective seems to want.
- *Magicians* dismiss issues conveniently. If a child says, "Someone pushed me off the swing," the magician says with flourish, "Yes, but playtime is over now so it really doesn't matter, does it?" If a father expresses concern that his baby's pacifier is lost, the magician responds, "That's okay. Emma really doesn't need a pacifier. She'll scream for an hour or two then forget all about it."
- *Drill sergeants* do not have time to communicate; they are too busy barking orders. The drill sergeant nursery school teacher hears a heated argument in the block center. Instead of encouraging communication, she says, "Get these blocks picked up off the floor. Kaleb, tuck in your shirt. Samantha, you wouldn't have these problems if you'd pay attention and mind your own business."
- *Bosses* keep everyone so busy that they cannot think about problems. A mother confides to her child's kindergarten teacher that her husband has left her and she has lost her job. She is worried that her son, Joshua, is being affected by her stress and depression. The boss teacher responds, "You need to get out of the house and stop feeling sorry for yourself. Take an art class. Volunteer at the hospital. Throw a party." The mother leaves feeling even more guilty and overwhelmed.
- *Naysayers* dish out blame. The naysayer's favorite phrase is "Well, I'm not surprised. You know, it's your own fault." When Jamey asks his naysayer preschool teacher, Miss Judy, for help printing his name, she says, "If you had paid attention last week, you would already know how to do this." When the director asks Miss Judy for help with a new child who is crying for his mother, Miss Judy says, "Of course he's crying. What do you expect? Did you see the way his mother let him manipulate her? She's to blame for this."
- *Gurus* have a mental storehouse of meaningless clichés to scatter like rose petals over problems. A mother asks her toddler's nursery teacher whether she thinks speech therapy is needed for the child. The guru teacher answers brightly, "Well, a stitch in time saves nine!" A 9-year-old boy asks his guru dad why countries have scary things such as nuclear bombs and is told "An ounce of prevention is worth a pound of cure." A 4-year-old cries, "Nobody likes me. I don't have any friends." Her guru teacher responds, "Well, you have to be a friend to have a friend." The guru's pat answers end dialogue rather than stimulate insight and understanding of problems.
- *Psychics* are not exactly a comfort in time of need. A psychic is always prepared to predict all the terrible and hopeless things that will probably happen as a result of the listener's actions. When a 3-year-old runs into the house crying because she has a splinter in her finger, her psychic mother says, "I told you not to play on that seesaw. Now you're going to get an infection and I'm going to be stuck with a big doctor bill. Look at this, your fingernail will probably turn black and fall off." And of course, there is the classic psychic response, "Johnny, when you fall out of that tree and break both your legs, don't come running to me."

Managing crucial conversations in a positive way is a skill that we all can learn. This teacher is guiding a preschooler through simplified conflict negotiation steps so he can begin resolving his own conflicts independently, assertively, and positively. The teacher says, "Would you like me to walk with you to tell Alvaro how you feel when he calls you a poopoo baby?"

- *Sign painters* make quick work of problems by assigning labels. A nursery school teacher complains to her coworker that she is having difficulty with one of her toddlers having temper tantrums. The sign painter coworker shrugs his shoulders and says, "I don't know of anything you can do about terrible twos. They're just that way." In a parent conference with child care staff, a single mother asks, "What is happening to my son? He seems to be trying to hurt everyone and everything around him." A sign painter teacher pats her on the shoulder and says, "Hey, all hyperactive kids do that." Meaningful communication is hindered by sign painters. There seems to be hardly any reason to discuss a problem after a label has been stamped on it with such finality.

In each of the preceding stereotypes, the communicator avoids, dismisses, evades, or thwarts feelings. An effective, assertive communicator addresses feelings with kindness, respect, and honesty. Often, it seems easiest to do whatever is expedient to stop a child's crying, end a dispute, or make a parent or coworker feel better. Unfortunately, when strong feelings are pushed under the rug, they can fester into even more unmanageable feelings.

> Peace cannot be kept by force. It can only be achieved by understanding.
> —*Albert Einstein*

8-6 Resolving Confrontations Peacefully with Conflict Resolution

When we feel attacked verbally or physically, we may react in a way that doesn't resolve the problem. Some adults and children back away from disagreements. Some lash out aggressively. Either way, we fear confrontations for a reason. Most of us handle emotionally upsetting confrontations poorly; we get angry or silent—we yell, we withdraw, or we say things we later regret. Children who lack adequate vocabulary bite, scratch, shove, and kick to express their anger.

Emotions don't prepare us to hold crucial conversations well. Nature has given us bodies that naturally want to respond to perceived threats by fighting back or running away. Our brains, however, can be trained (starting at any point in our lives) toward respectful listening and honest communication (Patterson et al., 2002).

Crucial conversations give us an effective tool for **conflict resolution**. These conversations are always about difficult issues. When we are angry or emotionally upset, things happen inside our bodies—the hairs on the back of our necks stand up; two tiny organs on top of our kidneys pump adrenaline into our bloodstream. Our brains divert blood from activities that it deems less essential, such as thinking, to high-priority tasks, such as hitting and running. Unfortunately, as the large muscles of the arms and legs get more blood, the higher level reasoning sections of our brains get less (Patterson et al., 2002).

So, we begin our crucial conversation with a brain and body that is prepared to fight or take flight. Probably, the other person also has a body prepared the same way. It's no wonder crucial conversations often go badly. Calming everyone physically, emotionally, and mentally is the first order of business. Creating a setting for the crucial conversation that feels warm, inviting, safe, and welcoming is a good starting point (Patterson et al., 2002).

Managing crucial conversation is a skill we can practice and learn. The purpose of the crucial conversation is to bring people together for respectful conversation in a planned structure with a planned outcome. At the end of the crucial conversation, the people involved in the conversation should feel valued. They should feel their views were taken seriously. Individual participants may or may not have gotten what they originally wanted out of the negotiation, but they should all feel good about the process. Every participant should go away feeling satisfied that she had a voice.

crucial conversations
Discussions that occur when there is a lot at stake, when emotions are strong, or when opinions clash. Crucial conversations offer a strategy for handling discussions with a clear sense of desired outcomes as well as a clear sense of the desired relationships when the crucial conversations are concluded.

conflict resolution
A problem-solving strategy to help two disagreeing parties dissipate their frustration and bring their opposing views to a common solution. The method requires active listening and respectful, nonjudgmental communication.

We should model peaceful negotiations of minor issues in front of the children whenever possible so they can see this process in action. We should also use this process away from children to appropriately resolve significant issues that come along with parents and fellow staff members. We will teach children simplified conflict negotiations so they can resolve their own conflicts from the time they are old enough to communicate (Patterson et al., 2002; Sharmin, 2006).

Often children and adults become locked in a struggle over who will be in control. Power struggles become win–lose situations in which the only way the adults get their needs met is for children to submit to control, and the only way for children to get their needs met is for adults to submit to control. This tug-of-war pits adults and children against each other. See Positive Focus 8.7.

Positive Focus 8.7

Crucial Conversations

Before crucial conversations, I analyze my motives:

Am I trying to:

Be right (*Negative*)
Win (*Negative*)
Punish others (*Negative*)
Get revenge (*Negative*)
Avoid feeling embarrassed (*Negative*)

Am I trying to:

Build a foundation of mutual respect, trust, and cooperation (*Positive*)
Find a solution we all find acceptable (*Positive*)
Find an ethical, legal, and moral solution (*Positive*)

Do I accept responsibility for the crucial conversation?

I am reasonable in what I expect (*Positive*)
I avoid sugarcoating or faking in my communication (*Positive*)
I make sure the other person knows I care about his goals (*Positive*)
I make sure the other person knows I respect him (*Positive*)
I make sure the other person knows we share a mutual purpose (*Positive*)
I make sure the other person trusts my motives (*Positive*)

Follow courtesy guidelines:

I will use "I" statements or "I" messages; start sentences with "I feel, I need, I want…"
I will own my own feelings and avoid blaming or scapegoating; "I personally would let you, but (licensing, my boss, other parents, etc.) don't approve."
I will recognize and respect others' feelings
I will listen attentively and avoid interrupting others
I will be respectful (avoid ridicule, sarcasm, judging)
I will stick to the topic

To carry out crucial conversations, I will follow these six steps:

1. *Listen:*

   Use respectful active listening.

2. *Agree:*

   Agree where you can. Disagreement typically is over a small portion of information.

3. *Tell your story:*

   This is what I need, this is how I see it, and this is how I'm feeling.

   Factual documents can be spread out and presented for objective consideration and discussion: "This is not me; this is a document. Let's look at it."

4. *Compare:*

   When you don't agree, just compare views; don't suggest others are wrong.

5. *Build:*

   Decide what you both want and agree on and then build on that; for example, "We both agree that we want Peter to be happy and to do well in school."

6. *Move to action:*

   Agree that we have two perspectives; let's decide how to move forward: "I have an idea for a compromise." "Would you be willing to give this a try?"

   A person in charge must take responsibility for actions and decisions: "I value your views, but this is the decision I must make for this school at this time."

Watch closely for these unhelpful stereotypes:
Victim: "It's not my fault."
Villain: "It's all your fault."
Underdog: "There's nothing else I can do."

As a role model, which of these will *you* do?
Clam up: Hold everything inside and suffer silently.
Blow up: Explode at others in a hurtful and insulting way.
Speak up: Use positive communication to appropriately express frustration, annoyance, or distress and begin healthy, problem-solving discussion (Patterson et al., 2002).

Crucial Conversation Example:

1. *Listen*

   Teacher: "Michonda, you seem really angry and in a bad mood."

   Michonda: "I hate Amy!"
   Teacher: "Michonda, are you feeling angry because Amy pulled on your swing?"
   Amy: "I hate you too!"
   Michonda: "Well, I don't want to dig in the sandbox."

2. *Agree*

   Michonda: "Yes. She keeps pulling on me, and she won't leave me alone."
   Michonda: "Amy, why are you being so mean to me and making me mad?"

3. *Tell your story*

   Amy: "Because you won't play with me. You just keep swinging all the time. I don't like swinging anymore."

4. *Compare*

   Teacher: "So, Michonda, you want swinging, and Amy wants to dig in the sand?"

   Michonda: "But, I like swinging!"

5. *Build*

   Teacher: "Do you like playing with Amy?"

   Michonda: "Yes, of course, she's my very best friend."

   (Continued)

6. *Move to action*

Teacher: "What are some things you could do to solve this problem?"

Michonda: "I could tell her I will give her a toy if she will swing with me."

Teacher: "Do you think that will work?"

Michonda: "I don't think so. She would probably just start chasing me."

Teacher: "Hmmm…what else could you try?"

Amy: "Will you play with me if we play under the tree like we're dinosaurs in the jungle?"

Michonda: "Okay…but can I be *Tyrannosaurus Rex* this time?"

Amy: "Sure! I'll be a flying dinosaur with big sharp claws…okay?"

What If No Solution Can Be Found?

- Agree to disagree.
- Walk away from the source of disagreement and find other activities.
- Try to negotiate again at another time.

Typically, power struggles result in misbehavior patterns becoming well established. Antagonism between adults and children can also begin to interfere with the pleasurable, nurturing interactions that strengthen self-esteem and help children feel connected at school and at home. We find ourselves chronically annoyed with children, and children become more and more resistant and noncompliant.

Additionally, we sometimes find ourselves becoming annoyed with squabbling children who come to us. Children often come to us begging to be rescued from various unhappy situations. Children have a right to call on someone bigger, stronger, and with more authority when their rights have been violated, just as I have a right to request legal help if my rights have been violated. See Positive Focus 8.8.

Positive Focus 8.8   Adult Expectations for Help

If I call a police officer for help because my purse has been stolen, I will feel very resentful if the officer responds by saying things like

- "Don't tattle!"
- "Don't be so stingy. The thief probably needs the money more than you do anyway."
- "You got what you deserved. You shouldn't have been carrying a purse that would tempt people anyway."
- "Well, did you tell the purse snatcher you didn't like that?"

We are a bit embarrassed by some of our frequently used expressions when we step back and compare them with what we expect from children. There are times when we must intervene as the authority figure to ensure that children's rights are protected. Nevertheless, to foster independence, children must be helped to do as much for themselves as possible.

When confronting difficult issues, use active listening first to allow the child or adult to identify, explore, and express feelings related to the situation. Advice should not be tossed out lightly. Instead, persons being helped can be guided to recognize the choices they have and the possible outcomes of those choices. Only then can a person be assisted in solving her problem. We must assume responsibility for solving our own problems before we can help others. Imposing unwanted help on another grown-up is almost always counterproductive.

Helping children is another matter. If a child does not show motivation to solve a problem, we have a responsibility to guide the child. We gently assist the child to address behavior problems. We can sit down and have crucial conversations with school-aged children. This not only helps them resolve behavior problems, but also models an important communication skill (Patterson et al., 2002; Tannen, 2002).

When confronting difficult issues, use active listening and conflict resolution strategies to communicate positively and professionally.

8-6a When Is a Critical Conversation Needed?

Albert's dad successfully avoided the stereotypes described previously. He did not avoid dealing with the problem by saying, "We'll talk about it later." He did not say yes to something he knew he would regret. He did not squelch the whole issue by saying, "I don't want to hear another word about this. Hush right now or I won't let Joshua stay with you next week either." He did not try to force Albert to comply by arguing with him, and he did not try to make Albert stop being angry. He knew Albert had a right to his feelings, so long as he behaved reasonably.

Albert is waiting excitedly for his dad to pick him up from his child care center. He and his buddy, Joshua, have been planning to ask whether they can spend the night together. As they dig in the sand, they giggle and scheme about the fun they will have watching television and eating grape popsicles.

Finally, Albert sees his dad. Both boys run to the gate and watch as Albert's dad parks his car. Before his dad is even inside the gate, Albert is talking so fast that his dad cannot understand him. Albert's dad hoists him into the air, saying, "How's my big boy?" Albert excitedly says, "Daddy, can Joshua spend the night? Can he? Huh? Can he?"

Albert's dad takes both boys by the hand, and as they walk up the sidewalk, he says quietly, "No, son, I have some paperwork I need to do tonight. This is not a good day. I will be happy to call Joshua's parents, though, and arrange for him to stay over one night next week." Albert pulls his hand away and starts to cry. His dad bends down and says, "You really had your heart set on having Joshua spend the night, didn't you?" Albert nods yes through his tears. His dad continues, "You feel sad and angry because next week seems a long time away." Albert nods again.

His dad hugs him and says, "It's okay to cry. Even grown people cry sometimes. I bet Joshua feels pretty bad, too." Albert stops rubbing his eyes and looks at Joshua. Albert throws his arms around his dad's neck for one last round of begging, "Pleeeeease, Daddy, I promise we won't bother you." His dad's expression remains calm and empathetic. He says, "Albert, it is okay to ask, and it is okay to cry and feel sad, but the answer won't change. Joshua can't spend the night tonight."

Albert's next tactic is pouting, but his dad remains calm and firm as he gathers Albert's belongings and prepares to leave. As his dad buckles him into his child safety seat, Albert plants a wet kiss on his cheek and says, "I love you, Daddy." His dad grins and says, "I love you, too, son."

Positive Focus 8.9   Ways Children Can Make Amends

- Get a damp paper towel for a friend to place on his bumped knee
- Bring the friend a bandage
- Share a toy
- Give a hug
- Pick up the blocks that were knocked over
- Ask whether the friend would like to sit at your table
- Draw a picture
- Make a homemade card that says, "Be my friend"
- Sit by the friend until he feels better
- Say, "I'm sorry," if it is sincere

TeachSource Digital Download

Instead, Albert's father used positive critical conversation strategies to resolve this conflict. He spoke to Albert simply, directly, and immediately. He showed a great deal of empathy and respect. He listened, allowed Albert to express his feelings appropriately, and recognized and reflected Albert's feelings. He made what he believed was a fair decision and stuck by his decision without anger. In the end, children need to know a parent is a strong authority figure to be relied on—not a pushover to be manipulated or a tyrant to be dreaded.

8-6b Should We Force Children to Apologize?

It seems odd that we tell children, "Be honest; always tell the truth," and then insist that the child apologize without wondering whether he actually feels remorse. It may be helpful to say, "Would you like to tell Ricky that you're sorry about what happened?" It is even more important for us to find some way to help the child make amends to Ricky. He will feel positive about himself if he has a chance to make things right. We discourage children when we imply, "You have made such a mess of things that there is no way you can undo what you've done." We may need to intervene at first to help the children brainstorm appropriate ways to make amends. See Positive Focus 8.9.

Summary

- Children can learn to communicate effectively by interacting with nurturing role models of effective communication.
- The achievement of effective child guidance hinges on the child's feeling a sense of connection, and that requires meaningful communication.
- Gazda and colleagues define three needs at the heart of communications that indicate a desire for some kind of response or help.
- Children and adults tend to respond more cooperatively to positive requests than they do to negative admonitions.
- Although we may feel justified in lecturing or lashing out, there is no value in conveying a message that will be rejected.

- Assertive communication is a way of expressing ideas and feelings that allows a person to stand up for rights while fully respecting the rights of others.
- The least effective communication styles deal superficially with the content of the communication and fail to address feelings.
- The purpose of a crucial conversation or conflict resolution is to bring people together for respectful conversation in a planned structure with a planned outcome.
- It is more valuable for children to make amends for a wrongdoing than to make an apology that is not sincere.

Key Terms

osmosis

conflict negotiation

crucial conversations

Student Activities

1. Practice active (reflective) listening in day-to-day interactions.

2. Identify interactions you have had in which another person asked you for information or action without any underlying emotional needs or messages.
   a. What did you do?
   b. Give examples.

3. Identify interactions you have had in which another person talked to you, but you sensed that what the person really was asking for was understanding and involvement.
   a. How did you respond?
   b. Did you use active listening?
   c. Give examples.

4. Identify interactions you have had in which another person talked to you, but you sensed that the person was seeking an inappropriate interaction.
   a. How did you respond?
   b. Was the interaction inappropriate because the person was overly clinging and dependent?
   c. Was it inappropriate because it was gossip or some kind of negative undermining communication?
   d. Was it inappropriate because it was racist, sexist, or demeaning to some person or group?
   e. Did you clearly communicate your refusal to participate in the interaction, but in a kind, caring manner that did not come across as arrogant?
   f. Give examples.

Related Resources

Readings

MacDonald, J., & Stoika, P. (2007). *Play to talk: A practical guide to help your late-talking child join the conversation.* Madison, WI: Kiddo Publishing.

This book gives step-by-step instructions to help children of any age develop skills needed for conversational relationships and social interactions. This approach turns play sessions and social interactions between child and adult into opportunities to foster language development, relationship skills, and positive behavior.

White, M. (2002). Teachers on teaching. A lesson on listening. *Young Children, 57*(3), 43.

The author argues that young children be allowed to mull over ideas and construct theories of their own. By listening to the children and following their lead, teachers can encourage investigation and support learning.

Websites

Talk With Your Kids This site offers information about and encouragement to talk with children about sensitive issues.

Winning Ways: To Talk with Young Children (Children's Administration Office of Child Care Policy) This free online booklet offers a beautifully illustrated overview of "I" messages, attentive listening skills, and positive requests.

Fundamental Causes of Positive and Negative Behavior

naeyc **Standards**

The following NAEYC Standards are addressed in this chapter

Standard 4 **Using Developmentally Effective Approaches to Connect with Children and Families**

4a Understanding positive relationships and supportive interactions as the foundation of their [your] work with children

4b Knowing and understanding effective strategies and tools for early education

4c Using a broad repertoire of developmentally appropriate teaching/ learning approaches

4d Reflecting on their [your] own practice to promote positive outcomes for each child

Montessori Country Day School

Objectives

After reading this chapter, you should be able to do the following:

9-1 Describe moral development in young children.

9-2 Identify methods to support children's moral development.

9-3 Define negative behavior.

9-4 Explain the role of temperament in children's behavior.

9-5 Evaluate underlying causes of problem behavior.

9.1 Moral Development Builds a Core for Positive Behavior

A critical priority for parents, schools, communities, and even entire countries is the moral development of children and future citizens. Morality is the ability to distinguish right from wrong and to act accordingly. Moral development is the process by which people learn to monitor their own actions and to decide whether a tempting behavior is the right or wrong thing to do. In other words, morally developed people are able to stop themselves from doing things they know are wrong (Nucci, 2001; Snarey & Samuelson, 2008).

Moral behavior is not just for children. If we are tempted to respond harshly to a young child's misbehavior, then we can think about how hard it is for us to stop our own negative impulses day to day. Sometimes we have difficulty resisting the temptation to gossip, smoke cigarettes, speed in the car, or tell fibs to get out of tight spots. Remember that children learn by imitation. It is important for us to set the best possible example of the behaviors we want children to follow (Gurian, 2007; Nucci, 2001).

As children observe our behaviors and experience the cause-and-effect sequences that are a part of interacting with others, they take on the character attributes and ethical standards of the important role models in their lives. Attachment, love, and respect for an adult trigger the child's internalization of that adult's values. When a child has internalized the standards of his adult role models, he begins to experience the emotional

moral affect
The ability to feel guilt or shame—feelings associated with a guilty or clear conscience—indicate whether behavior was appropriate and guide one to choose appropriate or desired behaviors.

moral reasoning
The thinking processes that guide people in deciding what is or is not moral behavior.

component of morality, or **moral affect**. Having moral affect means that when he behaves in a way that he knows to be wrong, he has feelings of guilt and shame. When he behaves properly, he feels pride. Moral affect serves as an internal regulator that guides a child or adult toward appropriate behavior and away from misbehavior.

Feelings of guilt play a role in regulating moral behavior, but it is not helpful to push guilt on a child by saying such things as "Aren't you ashamed of yourself, you naughty boy?" Forcing guilt on a young child may actually harden him emotionally and delay his development of moral affect. Conscience that comes from inside us is always more meaningful than guilt imposed on us by someone else. Two specific child-rearing practices are known to help children internalize values and prosocial moral judgment:

- Nurturing and affectionate adult guidance
- Consistency in explaining reasons for rules and expectations

We help children develop moral behavior by being loving and gentle and by putting into words the rationales for imperatives. Instead of just saying, for example, "Don't touch that!" we say, "Please choose a different crayon, that one belongs to your friend" (Blandon & Volling, 2008).

Another important component of moral development is **moral reasoning**. The way children think about right and wrong changes dramatically as their intellectual capacity matures (Piaget, 1952). Children younger than 7 years tend to focus on the concrete consequences of actions rather than on the abstract motivations behind them. As they get older and their moral capacity increases, they are better able to take intentions into consideration (Broderick & Blewitt, 2010).

9-1a Building Moral Intelligence

Carnegie (1936), considered by the business community to be the grandfather of people skills, theorized that financial success is due only 15 percent to technical knowledge and 85 percent to the ability to express ideas, to earn trust, to assume leadership, and to arouse enthusiasm among people (Carnegie, 1936, p. xiv). Instead of focusing solely on cognitive intelligence, we must also help children develop emotional and **moral intelligence** (Cherrington, 2008). In early childhood children can learn to cooperate and care about the welfare of others (Halverson, 2004).

Morality means caring about others and making good decisions about what is right and wrong based on that caring. Moral behavior is much more than memorizing rules. Moral behavior requires critical thinking, developing sensitivity to others, and making judgments about what is appropriate in various circumstances (Kostelnik, 2014). See Positive Focus 9.1.

Empathy, conscience, and self-control form children's moral core. Children must develop a moral core to have moral intelligence. A moral core gives children the strength to deal with peer pressure and other temptations but still make moral decisions.

The moral values of respect and kindness give children compassion and an awareness of the value of relationships. According to Borba, the final virtues of tolerance and

Positive Focus 9.1 Moral Intelligence

Borba (2002) described "seven essential virtues" that are basic to moral intelligence:

- Empathy
- Conscience
- Self-control
- Respect
- Kindness
- Tolerance
- Fairness

fairness are the foundation to integrity, justice, and citizenship. Together, all these moral values become the child's moral compass (Borba, 2002).

By using positive guidance, we begin teaching moral intelligence from the very beginning through value-oriented ground rules—be safe, be respectful, be responsible. When parents and teachers have supported children in DAP surroundings, children naturally begin developing the mental ability to think inductively between the ages of 7 and 11 years. **Induction** is a powerful influence on children's development of moral intelligence. Induction can be a powerful tool for the child to figure out, for example, that she needs to change her behavior because of the negative effect her behavior is having on others (Kochanska et al., 2008; Kuhn & Franklin, 2006; Kuhn, Katz, & Dean, 2004).

When children stray outside the ground rules, we have the opportunity to teach children what is right and wrong and, more importantly, *why* certain behaviors are preferable to others. This rather simple process is an important force for shaping children's moral development because it helps children internalize standards for moral behavior.

Children develop a conscience most easily when they live and go to school in an environment of mutual respect, empathy, and affection. Parents and early childhood professionals can support conscience development by making sure children know that they are willing to listen, really care about the children's feelings, and respect the children's individual needs and interests (Lefton, 2000; Santrock, 2008).

As children develop a conscience, they naturally feel guilt when they have done something wrong, not because we have shamed the child, but because the child sincerely feels his own conscience. His conscience urges him to do better the next time (Groenendyk & Volling, 2007; Kochanska et al., 2004, 2005, 2009).

Empathy has been identified by Kagan (1984) as one of the "core moral emotions." To develop empathy in young children, talk frequently with them about behavior and feelings. Talk about the consequences of their positive and negative actions on others. Help children identify and talk about how others' actions affect them (Hoffman, 2001). To support the development of values, set a good example. Regularly talk with children about values.

Ask children questions and help them think through moral perspectives. They need to understand the principles that are foundational to our guidance. (Be safe, be respectful, and be responsible.) See Positive Focus 9.2.

Authoritative guidance, especially with its focus on open, supportive communication, most effectively nurtures children's moral development. Encouraging inductive thinking, nurturing, limit-setting, being a positive model, allowing democratic discussions, and using conflict resolution all support the development of morality (Baumrind, 1967, 1971; Grusec, Goodnow, & Kuczynski, 2000).

induction

The process of reasoning from a part to a whole, from day-to-day events to major life concepts. Because children learn best from "hands-on" experiences, we invite them to think and talk about each inappropriate behavior so they will be able to figure out larger moral concepts through induction.

© 2013 Cengage Learning®

During early childhood, children can learn to respect and care about the well-being of others. And they can learn to make good decisions based on their respect and care for others.

Honesty is the first chapter in the book of wisdom.

—*Thomas Jefferson*

Sarah, a 4-year-old, was told that Jimmy broke four plates and three glasses while trying to help, and Annie broke one cookie jar lid while trying to sneak a cookie. She insisted that Jimmy was naughtier and deserved more punishment than Annie. Sarah has focused on the idea that breaking a lot of dishes is worse than breaking one dish.

A young child is not yet able to think about all features of a situation or to understand motive. Piaget (1952) studied children's sense of right and wrong through a series of interviews in which he approached children of various ages with moral questions such as the one in the description above. He found that young children's responses were very different from the responses of older children. The moral reasoning of young children tends to be simple and limited to enforcing the letter of the rule literally rather than understanding the spirit, or intent, of the rule.

Kohlberg (1969, 1976) described the stages through which human beings develop moral reasoning. He describes three levels and six stages. See Positive Focus 9.3.

Positive Focus 9.3   Kohlberg's Theory of Moral Development

Level One—Preconventional Morality (early childhood)

- *Stage One:* The child obeys rules only to avoid punishment and to gain rewards. For example, a toddler examining an electric outlet may reach for it, then look up at us while saying, "No, no. No touch." The toddler will probably resist the urge to touch the outlet only if we appear attentive and ready to enforce the rule (or if the child has unfortunately discovered the pain of an electric shock).

- *Stage Two:* The child bargains to have her needs met. Prosocial behaviors are intended to bring about favors from others. For example, "If you let me ride the tricycle, I'll be your best friend."

Level Two—Conventional Morality (9 Years to Young Adulthood)

- *Stage Three:* There is an emphasis on gaining approval by being "nice" or "good"— the focus is on getting positive attention from authority figures. For example, when we tell one child to taste just a bite of green beans, another child nearby may hurriedly stuff her mouth full of beans, saying, "See me? I'm eating my vegetables!"

- *Stage Four:* The focus is on law and order. At this stage, the child is concerned that everyone do his duty and follow the letter of the law. It is okay to break a rule only if everyone else is doing it. For example, school-age children become very indignant when rules are broken. They may resent that a child suffering from diabetes is given a candy bar by the teacher. Never mind that the child is ill; it is just not right. We sometimes rely on conventional morality when we say, "I can't let you do this, or I would have to let everyone do it." We are assuming that "a rule is a rule," and there could never be a moral reason to deviate from the rule or make an exception.

Level Three—Postconventional Morality (Adulthood)

- *Stage Five:* At this stage, correct behavior is defined in terms of individual rights according to widely held moral beliefs of society. For example, a teacher at this level would recognize that the urgent health need of a child with diabetes is more important than the usual fair and reasonable rules about candy at school. Protecting the health of a child is more valued in this situation than following a rule.

- *Stage Six:* Individuals decide whether a behavior is moral on the basis of a personal decision of conscience in accordance with personal ethical principles that are logical, consistent, and universal. For example, a child care center director might risk the solvency of her business by testifying in accordance with her conscience in a child abuse case against a powerful and popular community member.

An Alternative Perspective on Moral Development

Carol Gilligan brought an alternative approach to studying moral development. She started as a research assistant for Lawrence Kohlberg, but after studying his theories she became critical of his work because he studied only privileged white men and boys. She believed his stage theory of moral development represented a male perspective, which more highly valued individual rights and rules than would a woman's point of view. She thought females were more likely to value caring in human relationships and that Kohlberg's theories were skewed by gender bias.

Gilligan carried out her own studies and found that women were taught to care for other people and to expect others to care for them. She helped to form a new psychology for women by listening to women and girls and rethinking the meaning of self and selfishness. She outlined three stages of moral development that progress from selfish to social, or conventional, morality and finally to postconventional, or principled, morality (Gilligan, 1982).

Gilligan found that males approached morality with the assumption that individuals have certain basic rights, and thus morality imposes restrictions on persons. Females approach morality assuming that people have responsibility toward others, so morality is an imperative to care for others. Gilligan summarizes this by saying that male morality assumes a justice orientation and female morality assumes a responsibility orientation.

Gilligan believed that girls and women needed to learn to tend to their own interests and to the interests of others. She found that women and girls were often hesitant to judge others because they were more likely to see the complexities of interpersonal relationships. Gilligan noticed that boys were more likely to argue through a dispute so that they could finish a game, but girls were more likely to simply stop and choose to do something different to keep from arguing and hurting each others' feelings (Kimmel, 2000, 2004).

One distinct characteristic of more advanced levels of moral reasoning is the ability to consider motivation when evaluating the outcome of a behavior. Young children may not achieve this, but we must achieve this level of moral judgment if we wish to be effective in positive child guidance. If we blindly enforce rules just because rules are rules, regardless of circumstances or motives, we would also be functioning at a low level of moral development. If, for example, Alicia tries to knock someone off the jungle gym but no one gets hurt, and Albert is being silly and accidentally knocks someone off who is hurt badly, the morally mature adult will recognize that Alicia's behavior was more inappropriate than Albert's.

© 2013 Cengage Learning®

We collaborate with children to create rules that assure children are safe, respectful, and responsible. And we help children learn to use critical thinking to evaluate the appropriateness of our rules in various situations. For example, we might make a rule that says, "Only touch your own backpack." But what if someone couldn't see and needed to touch other people's backpacks to find her own? Would that be okay?

justice orientation
Perspective in which integrity tends to be the dominant moral compass for making autonomous, independent, and self-oriented ethical and principled decisions.

responsibility orientation
Perspective in which sensitivity to others, loyalty, responsibility, self-sacrifice, and peacemaking reflect interpersonal involvement and caring and ethical and moral decision making.

BrainFacts

What Can We Learn from Neuroscience?

Brain Development and Moral Behavior

- An expanding body of research focuses on how brain structures affect moral behavior (Koenigs et al., 2007).
- Researchers have learned that damage to specific areas of the brain can impair specific functions without affecting other functions.

(Continued)

- Damage to our prefrontal cortex results in impaired moral judgment and negative behavior (Anderson et al., 1999; King & Mayhew, 2002; Koenigs et al., 2007).
- Our brain's executive function manages our capacity to plan and control behavior (Sapolsky, 2004).
- Our ability to regulate our emotions is critical to social and moral reasoning (Damasio et al., 1994).
- The brains of babies and young children develop rapidly, but the prefrontal cortex is the last area of the brain to finish development.
- Brains change as people age (Giorgio et al., 2008). These changes in the structure of the brain relate to impulse control, emotional control, and consequently moral behavior (Silveri et al., 2006).

9-2 Methods to Support Children's Moral Development

demandingness
Requiring certain behaviors from children. Having high expectations for children that are reasonable and supported with encouragement and optimism.

Authoritative guidance supports the development of morality (Baumrind, 1978). Research confirms that authoritative guidance fosters social sensitivity, self-awareness, and respect for rules and authority (Blandon & Volling, 2008; Laible & Thompson, 2002). Authoritative child guidance provides a perfect balance of nurturing and limit-setting, and it is both gentle and firm. This style of guidance is very different from authoritarian disciplinary interactions with children, which tend to be more negative and sometimes antagonistic or combative (Baumrind, 1978).

Warm, responsive guidance communicates to children that they are valued and appreciated. As children learn that they are worthy of such treatment, their self-esteem blossoms. They also learn that people in general deserve respectful treatment and that it is wrong to hurt others. Authoritative adults routinely discuss moral issues with children in a respectful and emotionally supportive way (Black, 2005; DeVries & Zan, 2003).

▶❚❚ **TeachSource** Video

© 2013 Cengage Learning®

Early Childhood: Positive Guidance

Watch this Video Case and then answer the following questions.

1. Was this adult's intervention in the inappropriate behavior authoritative or authoritarian?

2. Did this adult require the children to say they were sorry? Why or why not?

3. What do you think might have happened if this adult had been permissive and had simply walked away from the two children who were fighting?

9-2a Set Limits An important part of authoritative child guidance is something called **demandingness**. See Positive Focus 9.4.

9-2b Model Appropriate Behavior How we live our lives in front of children, how we treat others, and how we handle our own frustrations and problems all influence children's behavior (Lickona, 1983). Children observe the adults in their lives and imitate their behavior. We can model respect and compassion toward others, or we can model behavior that is harmful and abusive by belittling, coercing, or physically dominating others. Even if children do not directly imitate the specific behaviors they observe, their beliefs and attitudes about how to treat other people may well be shaped by these experiences. The fact that these lessons are unintended makes them no less powerful. Adults who model prosocial behaviors teach their children to treat others with respect (Spinrad, Eisenberg, & Bernt, 2007).

9-2c Rely on Democratic Processes

Rely on group processes—conflict negotiation, consensus building, compromise, and discussion—to plan and to solve problems. Decisions and rules developed this way are more likely to have a sense of ownership from everyone in the group. Participating in the democratic group processes helps children learn the skills necessary to function in a democracy (Schou, 2001). Using these processes produces compliance, moral reasoning, conscience, self-esteem, and altruism in children (Lickona, 1983). Children begin to develop a strong sense of "fairness," as well as greater respect for the feelings, ideas, and needs of others (Snarey & Samuelson, 2008; Stables, 2003).

9-3 Defining Negative Behavior

Through a process called **socialization**, babies begin to learn what parents and others expect of them. Infants have no comprehension of appropriate or inappropriate behavior. Babies have no ability to inhibit their impulses even if they understood what was expected. Gradually over the first few years of life, however, if all goes well, children develop self-control and learn how to get along with others. They learn how to follow the accepted rules of their family and community. Before self-control develops, children are totally impulsive in following their feelings and desires. They act like children (of course), making mistakes, acting on impulse, and stubbornly resisting external control, actions we consider to be problem behaviors. We have defined three basic ground rules and recommend interrupting or redirecting any child behavior that

- Presents a clear risk of harm to the child or anyone else (be safe)
- Infringes on the rights of others (be respectful)
- Involves mistreatment of objects or living things (be responsible)

Those three guidelines were used for defining basic ground rules for children: Be safe! Be respectful! Be responsible! Next, we need to ask ourselves why children might behave in an unkind, unsafe, or careless manner. **Misbehavior**, **problem behavior**, and **inappropriate behavior** are used interchangeably, and all three terms tend to be misinterpreted as meaning naughtiness and mischief. Many inappropriate behaviors, however, are not at all mischievous in intent. A child may not even realize that we will consider a particular behavior naughty. Positive child guidance requires that we gauge children's reaction to misbehaviors by looking at the child's level of understanding, the severity and frequency of the behavior, and possible underlying causes.

socialization
The process by which children learn acceptable behavior.

misbehavior
Inappropriate, troublesome, and sometimes unsafe behavior.

problem behavior
Difficult and troubling behavior that causes inconvenience for others.

inappropriate behavior
Behavior that is out of place, immature, unproductive, or socially inept.

It is always easier to change the environment than to change the child. First we look at possible changes in things like the curriculum, scheduling, guidance strategies, and ourselves.

A baby who has innocently climbed on top of a coffee table must be dealt with differently than a 5-year-old who knowingly uses the couch as if it were a trampoline, although both must be redirected because the behaviors present a clear risk of harm to the children and involve the mishandling of objects in the environment. To get positive results, we must have reasonable expectations for children at various ages and recognize whether they can really be expected to control their actions in particularly difficult or tempting situations.

In many cases, it is far more effective to change the situation than to try to stop a child's behavior. By removing the baby from the coffee table and taking him to a safe piece of play equipment designed for climbing, we can change an inappropriate behavior to an appropriate behavior (even though the child may not yet recognize any difference in the two situations). We assume that the 5-year-old knows the difference between a living room sofa and a trampoline, so our emphasis is on giving the child a clear understanding of pertinent facts, choices, and consequences.

For example, we might say, "The couch is not for jumping. If you want to jump, you may jump outside on the soft grass." If the action continues, we should give the child our close, undivided attention at eye level and add in an assertive but sincere tone, "I know jumping on the couch is fun, but it could break the couch, or you could fall on something hard or sharp in here." "I will go outside with you to help you find something fun to do. Let's go find the ball. We can play catch."

Assessing the appropriateness of any individual child's behavior requires us to step into his shoes and see the world from his perspective, and doing so requires accurate insight and wise judgment. We are prone, sometimes quickly and flippantly, to label actions that are inconvenient, annoying, or embarrassing to us at the moment as misbehavior, regardless of reasons the child might have for behaving in such a manner.

Children are confused when they do not expect a negative reaction from us and when they cannot make sense of our logic in requiring different behaviors in different situations. They are bewildered when a behavior is praised in one setting but reprimanded in a situation they do not recognize as being very different. Mrs. Perez was exasperated with three of her toddlers, who persisted in climbing up on the picnic table in the toddler playground. She had not realized that the wood of the picnic table looked exactly like the wood of the climbing structure nearby. Although the adults could clearly see the differences between a climbing structure "fort" and a picnic table, a closer look would reveal that both objects are just boards nailed together. Young children's inexperience and naivete are just two of the many reasons they behave in ways that adults perceive as naughty.

dysfunctional
Inappropriate or self-destructive behavior that does not serve any positive or productive function in a child's life.

functional
Appropriate actions or behaviors that serve some productive or positive function in a child's activities and patterns of interactions.

9-3a What Do We Mean by Functional and Dysfunctional Behaviors?

When children evidence a compulsive and chronic pattern of inappropriate or self-destructive behavior, the behavior can be termed **dysfunctional**. In contrast, **functional** behaviors are appropriate actions that serve some productive or positive function in a child's life. Functional behaviors help a child get his needs met. Dysfunctional behaviors produce a negative reaction that may be opposite to the outcome desired by a child. The child's strategies for coping and for interacting with others do not work, causing the child increasing stress and unhappiness and creating a vicious cycle. A lonely child lacking in social skills may relentlessly tease other children to get their attention, but the teasing is dysfunctional because it does not attract friends; instead it causes the child to be disliked. Consequently, the child becomes more isolated and lonely and even more trapped in the existing cycle of dysfunctional behavior.

9-3b The Adult-Centered Definition of Misbehavior

Adult-centered definitions of misbehavior focus on the effect a child's behavior has on the adult. Individual actions are evaluated according to the seriousness of their effect on things the adult cares about, as well as the adult's emotional state or mood. If a child spills his juice in the grass during a picnic, the adult may hardly notice because nothing has to be cleaned up. If the same child spills juice on the kitchen floor, the adult may be annoyed and may reprimand the child. If, however, the spill is grape juice on brand-new dining room carpeting, the adult may be very angry and punish or spank the child.

The child learns that his behaviors are not always met with a consistent or predictable adult reaction. Children may learn that they can get away with inappropriate behaviors when their caregiver is in a relaxed and playful mood. They may also perceive that nothing they do makes any difference when the adult is in a bad mood. They may believe that they will get in trouble regardless of what they do or do not do. We never want children to think they have no control over their circumstances—that things just happen to them randomly.

Because adult-centered definitions of misbehavior focus on the adult's needs and desires, appropriate behaviors may be perceived to be actions that are convenient and desirable to the adult. Being quiet, staying out of the way, and performing on cue the role of a cute (but undemanding) little kid may be seen as the hallmarks of a "good" child. Crying, squealing with joy, being frightened, or being a chatterbox may be perceived as naughty if such behaviors are annoying, embarrassing, or inconvenient for the adult.

9-3c The Child-Centered Definition of Misbehavior

In contrast, a child-centered definition of misbehavior focuses on the ability level, motives, and long-term well-being of the child in evaluating the appropriateness or inappropriateness of actions. If an action is wrong or inappropriate, it is judged to be wrong because it infringes on the rights of others, is unsafe, or is unnecessarily damaging to the environment, not because the action is a bother or because the adult happens to be in an intolerant mood. Defining behaviors this way brings about consistency and a sense of fairness. Children learn to be responsible for the consequences of their own actions. They learn that there is a direct relationship between their actions and the reaction they receive from authority figures.

By taking into consideration the ages and developmental stages of children, we can recognize that exploring, or getting into things, is normal and beneficial learning behavior for a baby or toddler, not misbehavior. It is our responsibility to childproof the environment so that everything accessible to the baby is safe and appropriate. If the baby gets into something inappropriate, the baby is simply moved to an area that is safe for exploration.

Children who are allowed to become actively involved in daily processes will undoubtedly make mistakes more often than children who are encouraged to stand by passively while things are done for them. Allowing young children to help with food preparation, for example, will be messy and time-consuming. It is quicker and easier for us to do it alone, but the confidence and skill children gain from such experiences are well worth the effort. Dropping an egg and spilling flour are not mischief rather but important opportunities for children to learn responsibility and independence. Instead of being scolded for making a mess, the child can be taught how to accomplish daily tasks and how to clean up after himself.

9-4 Temperament

Why does an event motivate one person but cause another person in the same situation agonizing stress? Knowing temperament patterns helps us identify children's needs and helps identify potential talents we may assist children in developing. Temperament is an important part of a person's distinct personality. The traits that make up temperament have a profound effect on a child's style of interacting with people and things in his environment. From infancy, temperament helps shape a child's unique approach to learning about the world.

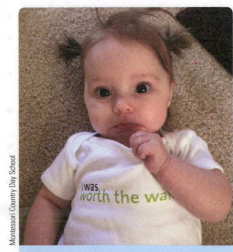

From infancy, temperament helps shape a child's unique approach to learning about the world.

Montessori Country Day School

Human beings are complex, and experts have devised many different ways to look at and understand our inner workings. One temperament assessment designates more than a dozen different personality types. Another focuses on the qualities of introvert versus extrovert. Actually, my multifaceted personality can't be reduced to a neat, easy-to-read category on a chart, and neither can yours—but a chart might help me discover some useful things about myself.

Using assessment testing to learn more about your own temperament type can help you notice things you didn't realize about yourself, including what you need in your surroundings to be truly satisfied. Knowledge about a specific child's temperament may pinpoint how to guide her more successfully.

9-4a How Do Infants Show Differences in Temperament?

Noted psychologist Mary Rothbart carried out ground-breaking studies of temperament. She developed a Measurement of Temperament in Infancy that assessed areas of infant temperament such as activity level, soothability, fear, distress when faced with limitations, smiling and laughing, and length of time paying attention to single objects (Rothbart et al., 2000). See Positive Focus 9.5.

Rothbart's inventory is useful in helping identify and understand differences in babies' temperaments so we can better address their needs. The better we know the children in our care, the better we can meet their individual needs and guide their behavior.

What Has Jerome Kagan's Research Taught Us about Temperament?

Jerome Kagan (2004), a retired professor emeritus at Harvard and considered one of the top psychologists of the twentieth century, has devised an interesting test. Present a

---

Positive Focus 9.5   Rothbart's Inventory of Babies' Temperament Differences

- *Activity Level*—Constantly moves arms and legs, squirms
- *Distress to Limitations*—Fusses, cries, or shows distress when in a confining position, being cared for, or unable to perform a desired action
- *Approach*—Approaches objects quickly, shows excitement and positive anticipation of pleasurable activities
- *Fear*—Startles and becomes upset at sudden changes, novel objects, or new people; inhibited approach to novelty
- *Duration of Orienting*—Pays attention to or interacts with a single object for long periods
- *Smiling and Laughter*—Smiles and laughs easily in caregiving and play situations
- *Vocal Reactivity*—Frequently vocalizes (cooing, babbling, and making early attempts at words) during daily activities
- *Sadness*—Experiences low moods or lowered moods because of discomfort, because an object is lost, or because of an inability to perform a desired action
- *Perceptual Sensitivity*—Detects slight, low-intensity stimuli from the external environment
- *High-Intensity Pleasure*—Enjoys high-intensity stimuli (finds pleasure in varying rate, complexity, novelty, and incongruity)
- *Low-Intensity Pleasure*—Prefers low-intensity stimuli (may be upset by too much variation in rate, complexity, novelty, and incongruity)
- *Cuddliness*—Enjoys being held by a caregiver and molds body to caregiver's
- *Soothability*—Reduces fussing, crying, or distress when the caregiver uses soothing techniques
- *Falling Reactivity or Rate of Recovery from Distress*—Recovers quickly from distress or excitement; falls asleep easily

4-month-old baby with a series of colorful new toys—ones she's never seen before—one after another, for 20 seconds each. Does she stare calmly and wait for more toys or start crying madly and shaking her arms and legs? If the baby finds this experience extremely distressing, Kagan found that she would be at higher risk for developing anxiety over social interactions as she grows older.

Kagan also found that although the baby who calmly accepts more toys was more likely to experience a future of relaxed and comfortable social interactions, she was at slightly more risk for getting into trouble later because she may be unfazed by warnings from parents and teachers.

Kagan and associates (1999) carried out their study of temperament by dangling toys in front of 500 babies. Twenty percent of the babies showed distressed "crying and vigorous pumping of the legs and arms, sometimes with arching of the back" on at least 40 percent of the trials. These were described as high reactive. Forty percent showed little motion or emotion and were described as low reactive. The remaining babies' reactions fell somewhere in the middle.

Many of the children from the original test were given follow-up tests at 2, 4, and 7 years of age. Then 237 of these children, at some point between the ages of 10 and 12, were given a full battery of brain scans, heart-rate analyses, and body-temperature readings, both at rest and during moments of stress (such as when they were asked without warning to give a speech).

Kagan's key finding was that about 20 percent of the children who had been labeled high reactives as infants still did not like things that were new and strange as they grew older. They gave off biologic signals indicating they were stressed when they were confronted with unexpected situations. The quality that had been labeled high reactive when they were infants was now manifested in these children as shyness.

Kagan found that the third of the children who had been labeled low reactives as infants remained calm and relaxed in the face of strange situations as they grew older. The study also established that as they grew up, many infants drifted away from the extreme and toward more moderate temperaments—a sign of the importance of parents and the children's environment, Kagan explained. Only a few infants, 5 percent in each category, switched to the opposite extreme in temperament as they grew up.

9-4b How Can We Support the Spirited Child?

In her book *Raising Your Spirited Child,* Mary Sheedy Kurcinka (2009) identifies five temperament traits that children she described as spirited often have in common. Compared with the typical child, these children are more intense, persistent, sensitive, and perceptive, and are slow to adapt to new situations. Also, according to Kurcinka, many but not all spirited children also may seem irregular in their day-to-day patterns, exceptionally energetic, cautious in new surroundings, and unusually serious. In DAP programs, we need to know and understand the multiple influences, such as temperament, on early development and learning. See Positive Focus boxes 9.6 to 9.10.

The Spirited Child Has Intensity

Positive Focus 9.6

- Laughs and cries loudly
- May shriek so loudly in play that it is almost overwhelming for parents and teachers
- Can become extremely upset
- Is physically passionate and dramatic
- Is very easily frustrated
- May take toys from others

(Continued)

- Can experience emotional meltdown at the drop of a hat
- May be prone to fiery name-calling or swearing
- Can create earsplitting disturbances when he doesn't get his own way

To Bring Down the Volume:

- Pay close attention to the child's cues.
- Intervene before the child's intensity builds too high.
- Change the scene.
- Learn what kinds of things send the child's intensity spiraling so they can be prevented.
- Learn what kinds of things effectively calm the child so those activities can be made available.
- Put on soothing background music.
- Initiate a relaxing physical activity (for example, walk, jump rope, climb, swing, rock a doll).
- Introduce a pleasurable project that takes concentration (for example, put together a puzzle, paint a box, feed the rabbit, cut strawberries for snack).
- Provide some relaxing one-on-one attention to get the child talking about her feelings.
- Find and tap into the child's natural sense of humor (for example, invite all the children to show their funniest face, ask who can jump like a bunny, or pretend you are confused about something the children know the answer to: "Hey, why doesn't this shoe fit my foot?" "Ha, ha, ha! That's Jimmy's shoe, not yours!").

TeachSource Digital Download

Positive Focus 9.7   The Spirited Child Has Persistence

- Has a really hard time taking no for an answer
- Because he is so sure he is right, he may argue to his last breath, "But why not? Huh? Why not?"
- Has a one-track mind; once she is committed to an activity or project, it is extremely difficult to get her to move on to anything else
- Often has his own mental plan of how everything should be (for example, he can become distraught when his mental plan doesn't match reality: "I expected my peanut butter sandwich in triangles, but you cut it in squares.")
- Wants to do everything independently and persists in spite of obvious difficulties

To Avoid Power Struggles:

- Remember that persistence is a positive virtue; honor every child's uniqueness.
- Pick your battles wisely, prioritize expectations, and stay focused.
- Try to find acceptable ways to make no into yes through appropriate compromise (for example, "It would not be safe for you to do that, but what if we did this instead? How would that be?").
- Frequently talk with the spirited child to ask about her plans and expectations so she won't be surprised.
- Help the child find stopping points by giving a 5-minute warning before clean-up time, a reminder that playtime will be over in 3 minutes, and a heads-up that as soon as the book is finished it will be time for a nap.

- Allow flexibility in scheduling so that children who need longer periods with the same learning project can be protected and encouraged in their concentration.
- Don't allow external interruptions to interfere with the child's natural patterns of persistence (for example, turn off the television, radio, and phone during mealtimes, homework, chore time).
- Stay focused on basic ground rules—be safe, be respectful, be responsible.
- Kurcinka (2009) suggests breaking the standoff of a tug-of-war by asking the child to "give you five" (that is, give you five alternative ideas so together you can choose one on which you both agree). For a very young child or a child with an ability difference, you may offer to help the child think of five alternatives.

TeachSource Digital Download

The Spirited Child Has Sensitivity

Positive Focus 9.8

- Probably becomes overstimulated by parties, crowds, shopping malls, and amusement parks
- May have food likes and dislikes, perhaps taking pickiness to the extreme
- Often overreacts to smells, sounds, lights, and textures in the environment
- May be overly sensitive to the moods of others around her
- Can become disproportionately annoyed by seams in his underwear or tags in his shirts

To Boost Coping:

- Talk with the child to help her describe and label the sensations she feels.
- Model appropriate oral expression of feelings in "I" messages when you are feeling frustrated, tired, or annoyed.
- Affirm the legitimacy of the child's feelings (that is, feelings are not right or wrong, they are just feelings).
- Try to eliminate or avoid triggers that irritate the sensitive child.
- Change the environment to reduce triggers that can't be avoided.
- Let the child practice coping with triggers that can't be changed—when he is ready and at his own pace.

TeachSource Digital Download

The Spirited Child Has Perceptiveness

Positive Focus 9.9

- Is very easily distracted
- Finds it hard to focus with other things going on
- Because of scattered concentration, often loses things
- Forgets what he was doing because something else catches his attention
- Has high levels of curiosity and attentiveness that force him to notice every detail
- Becomes exhausted when he does become absorbed in long periods of uninterrupted concentration

(Continued)

To Channel Focus:

- Modify the environment to reduce distractions.
- Get down at eye level and make eye contact when you give instructions.
- Give simple, one-step instructions and follow-up to ensure the child doesn't become distracted.
- If telling her doesn't work, show her (demonstrate for her) what you expect.

Positive Focus 9.10   **The Spirited Child Has Adaptability**   適応力のすろ

- Has a hard time coping with changes in environment, routine, schedule, food, and important people
- May dig heels in and refuse to comply with adult requests, becoming negative even when it doesn't make sense (for example, "Do you want some ice cream?" "No!!")
- Can seem obstinate, bossy, and stubborn at times
- May be quick to irritation and slow to get over being angry

To Alleviate Stress:

- Plan flexible classroom scheduling that eliminates nonessential transitions by allowing children to move from learning center to learning center at their own pace.
- Talk with the child ahead of time about plans and give him time warnings before transitions.
- Role-play and rehearse changes and new activities in advance.
- Give the child adequate time and encouragement to deal with the process of stopping and moving through a transition to a new activity.
- Acknowledge the child's feelings, and encourage him to express himself in words.
- Sometimes it helps to sit down and start the new activity with the child to help him adapt to the new activity with less stress.

Think about and evaluate your own intensity, persistence, sensitivity, perceptiveness, and ability to adapt to new situations. Temperament may have a hereditary component from one or both parents. What happens if a spirited adult is matched with a spirited child? What happens if an easy-going adult is matched with a spirited child? A spirited adult with an easy-going child?

Understanding a child's temperament can help us avoid pitfalls and develop guidance strategies that match individual children in specific situations. We can gain insight into why a child behaves the way she does in certain circumstances. We might also begin to understand why a child's behaviors intensely irritate and exasperate us.

Knowing what to expect gives us power over situations. Instead of being surprised and taken off guard, thinking the child's behavior is intended personally to annoy us, we can step back and think about why the child is behaving the way she is.

Remember, if we can forecast a child's looming breakdown, we can plan for it and, perhaps, even avoid it. Knowing more about what makes a child tick emotionally enables us to help the child learn the skills she needs to get along successfully in the world.

Is a "Really Good Spanking" Really Good?

Charlotte and Jeff stopped at a neighborhood fast-food restaurant for a quick hamburger on Saturday afternoon. The place was buzzing with activity, and children of all ages were everywhere.

Charlotte and Jeff had no children of their own, but they watched in amazement as many different types of adults talked to, played with, and reprimanded children.

Jeff was especially curious about one harried woman who seemed to be in charge of a half-dozen youngsters. One of the children, a 6-year-old, shook salt into her hand, licked it, then laughed as she brushed her salty hands over the children near her. The children shrieked with laughter as they dodged the salt, throwing napkins to defend themselves. The woman looked sternly at them and threatened to make them sit in the car if they did not settle down.

Jeff leaned over and whispered to Charlotte, "What those children need is a really good spanking!"

Case Discussion Questions

1. What could be possible reasons for the inappropriate behavior of the children Jeff and Charlotte were watching?
2. What do you think would be the most effective and appropriate thing for the harried woman to do in the preceding situation?
3. Why do you suppose Jeff believed spanking would be helpful?

9-5 Underlying Causes of Problem Behavior

Lying on a couch and watching cartoons for hours on end is not a desirable use of a child's time. To redirect the behavior, we may need to think through any potential reasons why the child is not involved in healthier, more active play. Is the child's quiet and passive behavior positively reinforced? Do we respond negatively to active play that is sometimes messy or noisy? Are interesting toys and challenging play equipment accessible to the child? Does the child need someone with whom to play? We must always take into account possible reasons for undesirable behavior if we are to have a chance at changing the situation and preventing the behavior from happening. In child guidance, as in health care, the best cure is always prevention.

9-5a Inappropriate Expectations

Sometimes, children's misbehavior is the direct result of inappropriate expectations on our part. We expect children to be able to do things that they are not yet capable of doing.

Helena and Ray are sitting in the pediatrician's waiting room with their 18-month-old son Billy. The little boy is dressed in his very best clothes and wearing shiny black shoes and a tiny bow tie. He is sitting on his dad's knee looking like a fashion model for baby clothes. Billy sits silently for a while, then looks around at the room and at his mom and dad, who are preoccupied in their discussion of the questions they want to ask Billy's doctor.

After a few more minutes of sitting, Billy points to a large aquarium with huge tropical fish swimming around and says, "Yook!" (his word for look). After a few seconds, he gestures insistently and looks at his mother, repeating, "Yook, wha' dis?" (What's this?) Helena straightens Billy's tie and says, "Yes, they're fish. Shhh, be still now. You'll get your clothes all messed up."

Billy stares at the aquarium a few seconds longer, then scrambles to get down off his dad's lap. His dad pulls him back in his lap and says firmly, "Those aren't for you to touch. You need to stay here and sit still. If you get down, you'll break something for sure." Billy begins to whine and rub his eyes with his fist, periodically struggling to get down from his dad's lap. His mother pulls a bottle out of her diaper bag and offers it to Billy, but he throws the bottle on the floor and begins kicking and crying loudly.

As the nurse comes in to announce that the doctor is ready to see Billy, Helena and Ray seem to be at their wit's end. With great frustration in her voice, Helena says, "Why does he act like this? What are you supposed to do when they get like this? He's just impossible to deal with sometimes."

Little can be done to resolve the situation at this point except to remove Billy from the setting and wait for him to wind down. A great deal could have been done to prevent the situation. If Helena and Ray had known in advance more about what to expect from a toddler, they might have anticipated that he could not sit still for 30 minutes to an hour.

They could have brought some of his favorite toys or books. Or, perhaps, they could have distracted him by playing peek-a-boo, allowed him to scribble on a notepad from his mother's purse, and followed up on his interest in the aquarium. Ray could have supervised Billy closely and talked with him about the fish as he looked at and touched the aquarium.

9-5b Misunderstanding Expectations

Sometimes, children misunderstand what is expected of them.

Miss Jean, a preschool teacher, was dismayed to discover that her preschoolers had left the bathroom in a mess. Water was all over the floor, and paper towels were everywhere except in the trash can. Miss Jean turned to 3-year-old Misha and said, "I'm going to go get a mop. Can you please put all of the paper towels into the trash can where they belong?"

When Miss Jean returned with her mop, she found poor little Misha struggling to pull clean paper towels out of the dispenser and stuffing them by the handfuls into the trash can. In a pitiful voice, Misha said, "It too much, Teacher. It too much paper towels."

Luckily, Miss Jean recognized that although the outcome of Misha's behavior was not the desired one, her intentions were good. Misha simply took her teacher's instructions literally when she said, "Put all the paper towels into the trash can." Miss Jean had not specified "wet paper towels on the floor."

Miss Jean thanked Misha warmly for trying to help and then proceeded to say matter-of-factly, "Let's put the wet, dirty paper towels in the trash can. The dry ones are good for us to use next time we wash."

If Miss Jean had scolded Misha or snapped, "Now look what you've done, you silly thing," Misha might not have been so eager to cooperate the next time someone asked her to help. Instead, she would have felt shamed for her good intentions, hard work, and inability to read the adult's mind.

9-5c Immature Self-Control

Sometimes, it seems that children really want to abide by our request, but somehow they just cannot seem to manage the self-control needed to accomplish what we expect.

Eloise provides child care for four children in her licensed family day home. She is committed to being an early childhood educator, not just a babysitter. To help her children learn about science and nature, she has bought a baby guinea pig.

The guinea pig caused a flurry of excitement on Monday morning as the children arrived for the day. Eloise sat by the cage with the two toddlers on her lap and talked with the two preschool-age children about the new pet. While the guinea pig ran around in circles making high squealing sounds, the boys decided that he should be named Squeaky.

Eloise explained that Squeaky would be frightened if people made too much noise or shook his cage. She also explained that, although Squeaky was very gentle, he might be confused if he saw a finger sticking into his cage and try to nibble on it. The children talked excitedly about Squeaky and tried to keep their hands behind their backs or in their pockets so they would not forget about shaking the cage or sticking their fingers through the bars.

Eloise stepped into the bathroom to help one of the toddlers. Suddenly she heard a commotion with shrieks and squeals. The children had gotten a bit too excited and had accidentally tipped the cage off the table. Squeaky was running around squealing, the children were running around shrieking, the toddlers had started crying, and water and guinea pig food were spilled everywhere.

Eloise quickly captured the terrified guinea pig and then, gently stroking poor Squeaky, said in a calm voice, "Listen boys and girls, can you hear the little sound Squeaky is making? He's very scared. Let's sing a quiet lullaby to Squeaky so he won't be frightened." Softly, the older children joined Eloise in singing "Rock-a-Bye Baby" to little Squeaky. The toddlers watched wide-eyed. When everyone was calm and quiet, Eloise put Squeaky back into his cage and said, "We'll put Squeaky's cage in the storage room for a while so he can rest. After naptime, we'll get him out and watch him again."

Eloise realized that the children had not maliciously intended to harm or frighten Squeaky; they were so excited that they could not manage the necessary self-control to deal with the situation successfully. Eloise felt confident that with enough time, patience, and practice, the children could eventually develop the self-control they needed to watch the guinea pig properly. She also knew that until that time, she needed to remove Squeaky, except during the times that she was able to supervise the children very closely as they watched him. Eloise recognized that reprimanding or punishing the children for their lack of self-control was not appropriate or helpful, because the children, at that point, were not yet capable of behaving in a more mature or controlled way. Instead, she helped them identify with Squeaky's feelings and needs so they could understand why they needed to watch without touching. She also knew that it was better to change the environment temporarily rather than trying to change the children's behavior.

9-5d Silly Playfulness, Group Contagion

Close your eyes for a minute and try to remember the exhilarated sensations you felt as a young child at a terrific birthday party, in a basement full of laughing cousins at a big family celebration, or maybe at a school Halloween carnival. Can you remember you and your friends or siblings going a little berserk? You knew you would get a stern lecture from your parents later, but it just felt so good you could not stop yourself. Whenever we have come to the end of our rope with gleeful, goofy children, it may help for us to pause for a second and remember those magical moments in our own childhoods. I know I would love to feel that way again—totally uninhibited and free.

Tuesday mornings are always lively at the Elm Street Public Library. The sleepy little library comes to life as neighborhood children troop in for the children's story hour.

Mrs. Asaad, the children's librarian, spends hours choosing just the right books and practicing reading them to make sure her program is interesting and fun for the children. One Tuesday morning, Mrs. Asaad helped a very young group of children get seated on the floor and ready for story time. She began singing a song about three little ducks.

One of the preschoolers folded his hands under his armpits (to make duck wings) and helped her with the "quack, quack, quack" part of the song. The other preschoolers caught on and began wagging their arms and quacking too. The first quacking preschooler began giggling and falling over on the floor. Of course, all the other preschoolers imitated by giggling and falling down and kicking their feet in the air.

Mrs. Asaad finished her song and good-naturedly helped Chris, the preschooler who appeared to be the leader of the gang, to sit up. "Are you ready to hear a story about a little duck named Ping?" she asked. Chris vigorously nodded his head and shouted yes. Of course all of the other preschooler began vigorously nodding their heads too.

Mrs. Asaad, with great suspense in her voice, began the story. "Once upon a time in a faraway land, there was a little duck named Ping." All of the children leaned forward to hear every word. When Mrs. Asaad, however, got to the very exciting part of the story where Ping gets into mischief, the preschoolers were overcome with their enthusiasm. Several began stamping their feet on the floor and Chris let out a squeal. As the other preschoolers joined in the squealing, Chris began shaking his head so vigorously that his hair stood out all around his head.

*Mrs. Asaad stood helplessly watching the preschoolers, who were seemingly possessed by this gleeful **group contagion** of head shaking and foot stamping. Suddenly, it dawned on Mrs. Asaad that the preschoolers were more interested in the social presence of the other children than they were in her planned story. She laid down the book and stood up, saying, "Who can stretch high toward the sky? Great! Now, who can stamp your feet? Terrific! Let's sing 'Head and Shoulders, Knees and Toes.'"*

group contagion
Typical toddler group behavior in which one child's gleeful action—for example, foot stamping, head shaking, or squealing—is quickly imitated by the whole group of toddlers.

Mrs. Asaad was very insightful to recognize that the preschoolers' rowdy behavior was not a personal affront to her. Chris and the others were not naughty but just immensely happy. They were thrilled to be in a group of children at an exciting event and did not have a clue about the life of a duck from a faraway land. Singing and moving as a group met their needs at this particular time, not hearing good literature.

9-5e Boredom

Boredom is one of the most predictable causes of misbehavior.

Neighborhood Nursery School was closed for the day, but staff members' children hung around, waiting for their parents' staff meeting to end. The nursery school staff took pride in their professionalism and high standards, and to reach their goals for quality, the staff met every Thursday afternoon after nursery school closed to discuss concerns.

Because most of the staff members were also parents, their own children had no alternative but to wait around while the parents met. Staff members took turns bringing a snack for the "staff kids" and attending to their needs and disagreements during meeting times, but it was clear that the staff kids dreaded the long Thursday afternoons. In early December, a meeting went on for hours as the staff planned special Christmas events. The staff kids had eaten their snack, colored pictures, and gone through stacks of puzzles and books. Shelley, age 5, and Jasmine, age 4 and a half, were terribly bored and beginning to get a little silly. They were going through familiar books, making up ridiculous things for the characters to say, and then laughing uproariously at themselves.

Next, they decided that they were Harriet the Spy, so they sneaked around under tables and behind furniture, trying to get a peek at the adults without being seen, and then retreating to the restroom to roll on the floor in laughter. The spies decided that the next time they made a foray into enemy territory (the staff meeting room) they would attack the grown-ups' coffee table. Ever so slowly, Shelley crept under the refreshment table while Jasmine crouched excitedly in the hall, watching with both hands clasped over her mouth to stifle her giggles. While the adults talked on, a little hand slowly made its way up to the box of sugar cubes by the coffee pot and a strange sound—a muffled giggly sort of chortle—burst from Jasmine in the hall. The adults droned on, not noticing a thing.

The little hand (now grasping a whole handful of sugar cubes) slowly made its way back down the table. Unfortunately, it snagged the cord to the coffee pot on its way, and abruptly, the whole great adventurous fantasy came crashing down around little Shelley.

While Jasmine watched from the hall in horror, Shelley huddled under the table, her hands full of sugar cubes, surrounded by a dented coffee pot and huge puddles and rivulets of coffee. Her face flushed with embarrassment as the room full of astonished adults rushed toward her. Her mother looked the most shocked of all. Shelley was the kind of child no one ever expected to misbehave. Fortunately, no one was injured in this mishap. The adults' assumption that their children would behave appropriately without supervision, however, might just as easily have resulted in a real disaster.

Boredom, especially when coupled with lax supervision, is an open invitation to errant behavior (as well as to some extraordinary bursts of "creativity"). Diligent supervision is essential to positive child guidance. Attentive adults can identify the first indications of boredom and take steps to correct it.

9-5f Fatigue and Discomfort

If we do not feel well, we may have difficulty behaving appropriately.

The Jacobsons had spent a wonderful day at the zoo. They had left home before sunrise and had driven several hours to a large city nearby to expose their four children to the wonders of a first-class zoo. The youngsters, three boys and a girl, ranged in age from 15 months to 8 years. They had enjoyed a near-perfect day. The weather was great, the orangutan had hung upside down and delighted the children with wonderful ape tricks, and Allison, the toddler, had learned to say "monkey" and "bird" and make lots of new animal sounds. By the end of the day, the car trip home seemed particularly long and tedious. Al drove, and his wife, Regina, and the kids fell asleep shortly before the family reached home.

As they pulled into the driveway and everyone woke up, it was clear that the children were hungry, crabby, and generally exhausted. Al said, "I think I'll make pancakes for supper. That won't take long at all." Regina got the children bathed and dressed for bed, and everyone sat down to big fluffy pancakes, applesauce, and bacon, usually one of the kids' favorite meals.

Regina collapsed into a chair as Al lifted Allison (in her cute little footy pajamas and thick overnight diaper) into her high chair. He began to cut her pancake. Suddenly, Allison began to whine, shake her head, and push the high-chair tray. Al said, "What's wrong? Didn't you want me to cut up your pancake?" Allison stiffened and struggled, getting louder and louder. Al said, "Here, I'll trade pancakes. Mine isn't cut up." Allison took a swipe at the pancake and it landed on her brother William, causing him to start crying.

Al tried to calm William as Regina lifted Allison out of the high chair and said, "Honey, I know you're tired. We're all tired, but you may not throw food." Allison stiffened, struggled, and screamed even louder. Over her screams, Al and Regina racked their brains to figure out what to do. Nothing they tried seemed to help, and every effort just seemed to make matters worse. They finally decided that the only thing to do was to put Allison in her crib for the night. She sobbed herself to sleep, finally making the little rhythmic gasping sounds children make after they have cried hard.

After the boys were fed and asleep, Al and Regina puzzled over Allison's tantrum but could not decide whether this was a new stage or just the result of her being overstimulated and exhausted from the busy day.

The next morning, Regina leaned over Allison's crib to say good morning. Allison was all smiles while her mother unsnapped her pajama bottoms and pulled off her diaper. Then Regina stopped. She discovered to her dismay that a little plastic toy dinosaur had somehow gotten stuck down in Allison's diaper, poking sharply into her skin. Allison had a bright red spot where it was stuck. Regina removed the offending toy. "Why," she asked herself, "didn't I think to check her diaper last night?"

Fatigue or anything that causes discomfort can cause children (and adults) to lose control and act aggressively, defy rules, or behave inappropriately. Being hungry, cold, hot, sick, or hurt are all reasons for children to be cranky and uncooperative. Very young children usually do not even realize that the source of their misery is a waistband that is painfully tight, a sock thread twisted around a toe, or scratchy sand in a wet diaper. Even older children sometimes become negative without recognizing that they just do not feel good. We need to remember that what appears on the surface is not always the whole story.

9-5g Desire for Recognition

Being ignored hurts at any age.

At 3 years, Kelley was the middle child. His big sister, Kathryn, brought home papers from her elementary school teacher saying how smart and wonderful she was. She also had lots of girlfriends who came and knocked on the door asking to play with her almost every day. Whenever Kelley tried to play with Kathryn and her friends, they would tell him to go away, and Kathryn would yell, "Mother, make Kelley go away and leave us alone!"

Kelley's baby brother, Nick, in comparison, always seemed to be in mommy's arms, getting fed, or burped, or bathed, or rocked. When Kelley asked his mother to read him a book or push him on the swing, she said, "Kelley, please go play with your toys. The baby's crying, and I can't play with you right now." Kelley thought his mother did not love him anymore and that she loved only that stupid baby (and Kathryn with all her important homework).

Kelley wet his pants. His mother said, "Kelley! You're such a big boy. You know how to go to the potty." Kelley said, "Nobody loves me!" and ran out the back door. Kelley pushed an old lawn chair against a tree and climbed up into the tree. Even though it was very scary, he climbed higher and higher until he could not climb any farther. Then he started to cry.

Kelley's mother ran outside when she heard Kelley crying. "Oh, my soul!" she yelled, "Kelley, how in the world did you get up there?" She called Kelley's dad, and it took an hour to get Kelley safely out of the tree. When his dad got him to the lowest branch, he handed Kelley down to his mother. She hugged him so hard he could hardly breathe, but he did not mind. He was just glad to be out of that tree.

Kelley's dad sat down on the grass. He was still panting and sweating from all the climbing and worrying. He motioned for Kelley to come sit on his lap. "Son," he said, "your mother and I love you. You're the only Kelley we have. Did you think we could put a penny in a gumball machine and out would roll another Kelley just exactly like you? That I could just go down to the grocery store and put a shiny new penny in there and, POP, out would come a new Kelley? No siree! We couldn't get a new Kelley that way. You're the only one exactly like you in the whole world."

Kelley sat in his dad's lap, encircled by his dad's strong arms, his face snuggled so close to his dad's chest that he could hear the sound of his dad's big heart thumping, the deep voice, and rumbly laughter. Kelley imagined brightly colored gumballs with his face on them rolling out of a grocery store gumball machine. He took a deep breath and grinned.

Feeling ignored is far more painful and frightening for young children than being in trouble and having everyone angry or upset. All human beings need to feel a sense of belonging, to feel that they are wanted and needed. If a child feels unwanted or left out, he may not be able to cooperate and follow rules.

9-5h Discouragement

Becoming overwhelmed by discouragement can cause anyone to feel depressed and angry.

Fiona's family moved to a new neighborhood. In her old school, she had already started second grade and had really liked the teacher there. She got good grades on her schoolwork, and the teacher often let her help other children when her own work was finished. The teacher had praised Fiona for her careful block printing and often put Fiona's papers on the bulletin board for all to see. In her new school, however, Fiona did not think that the new teacher, Miss Crane, was very happy to have her in class. On the first day she attended the new school, Miss Crane acted annoyed, and Fiona heard her complain bitterly to another teacher about having to take a student from a different school district in the middle of the year. When Fiona began carefully printing her name in the new workbook Miss Crane gave her, Miss Crane snapped, "Young lady, in this school, second graders do not print! We write in cursive."

Fiona hung her head and stared at her feet, wondering what cursive was. She knew she had heard her mother say many times that she did not like cursing at all. Miss Crane gave Fiona a little workbook filled with grown-up writing and pale blue straight and dotted lines. She said, "I don't have time to teach you everything I've already gone over with the rest of the class. Just go through this workbook and write the words on each page like the ones in the examples. I don't ever want to see you doing printing in this class again. Do you understand?"

Fiona sat at the back of the room by herself, feeling terribly dejected but struggling to copy the weirdly shaped letters in the workbook. Finally, it began to make sense to her that some of the words were made of familiar letters. The letters were just hooked together in a long string like beads on a necklace. She printed the letters she knew and then connected them to make them look like the examples.

Miss Crane did not like Fiona's work at all. "This is not how you write in cursive! Can't you see how the other children are writing?" Fiona was too embarrassed to look around. She hoped none of the other children were staring at her.

Fiona became very quiet at home. She did not bubble with stories about her day. She stopped looking forward to school and began to have stomachaches almost every morning. She begged her mother to let her stay home. She also seemed unusually irritable and often had angry fights with her sisters and brothers. At school, Fiona went to the pencil sharpener every time she thought Miss Crane was looking or walking in her direction. With so much sharpening, the pencil lead was always too pointed so it snapped every time she nervously pressed down on the paper. She erased until she finally wore holes in the sheets of paper in her workbook, which began to look like Swiss cheese and made her work look even more awful. Miss Crane became exasperated with Fiona and began to wonder whether Fiona was a slow learner or just a difficult, uncooperative little girl.

Actually, Fiona was not sick, slow, or difficult, but she was very, very discouraged. Her self-esteem had slipped, leaving her vulnerable and disorganized and not at all able to do competent schoolwork, make friends, or live up to the teacher's expectations. Being harshly criticized and subjected to put-downs makes it harder, not easier, for a child to accomplish difficult tasks.

 **9-5i Frustration**   No matter how old or how young, we all risk losing control when we hit a certain level of frustration.

Much of Benny's aggression probably stemmed from the stress and pressure he was encountering in his daily life. His mother, Virginia, had a lot of frustration building up in her as she tried to survive financially and emotionally as a single parent, as a working mother of a toddler, and as a student. She felt frustrated in her efforts to be a perfect mother while also trying to deal with her own personal and social needs. Benny "caught" some of her stress like a contagious illness. He did not know why he felt so tense and stubborn all the time, and he did not know how to make the feelings go away.

Benny was 2 years old. Hardly a day went by without his mother, Virginia, pointing out to someone that he was a "typical terrible two." He vacillated between acting like a baby and trying to act like a grown-up. He whined, "Me do it," whenever his mother tried to tie his shoes. When Virginia became exasperated with him over the shoelaces, she said, "Okay, you tie them." Of course Benny did not know how to tie them, but he stubbornly worked for 15 minutes, twisting the laces into a scrambled mass of knots.

Virginia said, "Now look what you've done. I told you that you didn't know how to tie them. Be still so I can get these knots out and tie them right." Benny kicked and fought hard to keep his mother from touching his shoes. She finally spanked him to make him let go of his shoes so she could tie them.

Even though Virginia was a single mother with a demanding job and classes two nights a week, she kept her apartment perfectly clean and went to garage sales and resale shops on weekends to see to it that Benny had all the toys and clothes a toddler could need. Every day, he was dropped at his child care center looking freshly scrubbed and starched, with every hair in place.

When Virginia got Benny home on the weekday evenings that she did not have to go to class, she always had a lot of work facing her. She usually put Benny on the floor and told him to play with his basket of toys while she cooked, cleaned, and studied. Most often, Benny abandoned the toys and followed his mother around, getting into her schoolbooks or the kitchen cabinets and making messes. When her patience with him wore thin, she would smack his hand and say, "No," or give him a firm swat on the bottom.

Tension built in their little household between the busy, frazzled mother and the clingy, insistent toddler. At his child care center, Benny began biting other children when they refused to give him a toy or let him have a turn on the tricycle. Even being made to sit on the "thinking chair" for a time-out by his teachers seemed to have absolutely no effect on stopping his biting. In fact, it seemed to make him more stubborn and agitated.

One day, Benny had been in trouble several times, so he was sitting by himself playing with a jack-in-the-box. He cranked the tiny handle and listened to the tune as it played "around and around the cobbler's bench the monkey chased the weasel…" until out popped the little clown.

Benny watched attentively, then tried to push the little clown back into the box to close the lid so that he could do it again. He pushed the little clown's head down into the box and mashed hard on the lid, but the toy clown's two little flat, plastic hands were sticking out and the lid would not close. Benny pushed on the lid as hard as he could, but his hand slipped and the little clown popped back out.

Benny glared at the uncooperative toy clown and then bent down and bit the little clown's hand. Benny bit so long and hard that his whole body shook with the effort, and he left a clear imprint of his teeth on the plastic hand.

No matter how old or how young, we all risk losing control when we hit a certain level of frustration. The DAP curriculum specifically plans for materials and activities that are not so easy that they are boring, but not so challenging that they are frustrating.

Stress is a very real crisis for many children and families today. Children can absorb stress unknowingly from their parents and caregivers or develop stress symptoms directly from their own lifestyles. Today there are children who, from earliest childhood, spend their days going from classroom to tutoring to individual lessons to social events, virtually every day from dawn to dusk. Whatever the cause of stress, its symptoms often include inappropriate behavior (along with health, appetite, and concentration problems).

反抗

9-5i Rebellion

Under repressive enough circumstances, even the most docile of us might be inclined to rebel.

Coach Sam, a tall, muscular 19-year-old, had just been hired as the gymnastics instructor in a large, inner-city community center that provided after-school care for 6- through 12-year-olds. His childhood dreams of reaching the Olympics had been dashed by a troublesome back injury, so he found himself teaching gymnastics to small children, something he had never particularly wanted to do.

He decided that to create discipline in his class he would start from the very beginning with his class by being very tough and demanding. He assembled his group of first, second, and third graders on the floor and, towering in front of them with his hands on his hips, announced in a booming voice, "If you talk without my permission, you're out of here. If you don't pay attention and follow my instructions, you're out of here. And if you even think about being lazy or careless, you're history. Is that understood?" The children chorused back in unison, "Yes, Coach."

At first the children seemed very intimidated by Coach Sam and did everything he said. They were serious and attentive and jumped when he said jump. Gradually, their obedience became more and more strained. Coach Sam never praised the children's accomplishments other than to make a curt comment such as, "Well, finally you're paying attention." He was, however, very quick to mete out caustic criticism such as "If that's the best you can do, just go sit by the wall. You're not worth me wasting my time." These comments hurt, and the children grew to dislike Coach Sam intensely.

The children wondered why Coach Sam so frequently threatened to kick them out of class but never followed through on the threat. They did not know that he lacked the authority to expel students from class. They did, however, begin to recognize that most of his threats were empty gestures. In his annoyance and frustration, Coach Sam became colder and more demanding with the children. They became more callous and uncooperative with him. Coach Sam regularly punished children by making them sit by a wall for long periods. They found ways to use this sitting time to create more mischief and disruption for Coach Sam. They expressed their dislike of him and his tactics by causing him endless frustration and interruption.

Coach Sam was filled with feelings of rage and helplessness. He knew he would be fired instantly if he struck any of the children, but he was overwhelmed with the urge to show them he had control over them. If he could not use physical force to control them, then he simply did not know how to maintain discipline and order. Coach Sam did not know that positive discipline can best be achieved by establishing an atmosphere of fairness, trust, honesty, and mutual respect, not by trying to create fear and submission.

Certain conditions trigger rebellion and tempt children to defy authority in spite of the risk of punishment (Devine, 2002; Nelson, 2006; Psunder, 2005; Stafford, Laybourn, Hill, & Walker, 2003; Wyness, 2006). See Positive Focus 9.11.

Conditions That Set the Stage for Rebellion

- Children feel anger and contempt rather than affection and respect for the authority figures in their lives who set and enforce rules.
- Children resent that they are given no voice in rules that seem arbitrary or unfair to them.
- Children find it too difficult to abide by rules and live up to adult expectations.
- Children realize that rules are just hollow threats that will not be consistently or fairly enforced.
- Children are discouraged to such an extent and feel they are in so much trouble that they believe nothing else they do can make things any worse for them.

Positive Focus 9.11

→ 子どもは、ルールを設定して強制する生活の中で権威のある人物に対して愛情や尊敬女よりもむしろ怒りや軽蔑を感じる

→ 子どもは自分達にとって恣意的で不公平と思われる規則に対して自分たちが発言を与えられないことに憤りを感じる

→ 子どもはルールを守り、大人の期待に応えることが難しいと感じている

TeachSource Digital Download

Summary

- Moral reasoning is the thinking that guides children in deciding what is right or wrong.
- High but reasonable moral standards that are consistently modeled, expected, and caringly enforced will develop core values in children.
- The child's moral intelligence becomes her compass, guiding her to choose positive behaviors over negative ones.
- Knowing temperament patterns helps us identify children's needs and helps identify potential talents we may assist them in developing.
- Spirited children need special support and understanding.
- Adult-centered definitions of misbehavior focus on the effect a child's behavior has on the adult.
- Child-centered definitions of misbehavior focus on the ability level, motives, and long-term well-being of the child in evaluating the appropriateness or inappropriateness of actions.
- Positive child guidance requires us to gauge our reaction to misbehaviors by looking at the child's level of understanding, the severity and frequency of the behavior, and possible underlying causes.
- We must always take into account possible reasons for undesirable behavior to have a chance at changing the situation and preventing recurrence.
- We focus on the child's ability level, the severity and intent of the behavior, and possible reasons for the behavior.

Key Terms

demandingness

dysfunctional

functional

group contagion

inappropriate behavior

induction

justice orientation

misbehavior

moral affect

moral reasoning

problem behavior

responsibility orientation

socialization

Student Activities

1. To be authoritative, you must set high but realistic goals for children.
   a. Think of a troubling behavior problem in a child of a specific age.
   b. Figure out potential reasons for the behavior.
   c. Decide how to go about setting a goal for improved behavior.
   d. Create a hypothetical plan to guide the child and support any behavior improvements.
   e. Decide on a plan for tracking and evaluating progress toward the goal.

2. Authoritative adults must help children achieve high and realistic goals by carefully supporting, encouraging, and monitoring progress. Interact with one or more preschoolers.
   a. Determine a guidance goal for a preschooler that is optimistic and realistic.
   b. Use positive guidance techniques to gently nudge the child toward the guidance goal.
   c. How have you encouraged the child in making small steps toward the goal?

3. Authoritative adults must provide consistent follow-up to evaluate whether children achieve goals.
   a. How have you made sure to provide consistent follow-up? Give examples.
   b. After a period of time, assess to see whether the preschooler has made progress toward the goal.
   c. Do you still believe the goal you set is appropriate (both optimistic and realistic)?

4. If you were a teacher, what would be the most effective way to collaborate with parents to work toward child behavior goals?
   a. Tell parents what they are doing is wrong and you know what is best for their child.

b. Talk to the parent in front of the child while the parent is rushing to leave for work in the morning.

c. Meet with parents at a convenient time away from the child to discuss the child's behavior and work together to decide what goals are appropriate.

d. Make it a point to really listen to what the parent has to say about the child.

e. Show respect for the parents and ask for their input in thinking through the problem and agreeing on developmentally appropriate methods with which to respond to the behavior.

Related Resources

Readings

Kurcinka, M. (2007). *Kids, parents, and power struggles*. New York: HarperCollins.

This book offers parents a better way to help their children express frustration, anger, jealousy, and other emotions. Kurcinka also helps us understand how temperament, both our own and our child's, influences family life. Guidance success depends on our respecting our differences.

Kurcinka, M. (2009). *Raising your spirited child*. New York: HarperCollins.

Kurcinka provides vivid examples and a positive approach to raising spirited children. She features up-to-date research and effective strategies for positive guidance.

Websites

Parenting: MedlinePlus   This parenting site is the National Institutes of Health's Website. It is produced by the National Library of Medicine, and it brings reliable information about effective parenting and child wellness.

National Parent Teacher Association (PTA)   National Parent Teacher Association (PTA) is the largest volunteer child advocacy association in the nation. It provides parents and families with a voice and the tools they need to help children be safe, healthy, and successful—in school and in life.

CHAPTER

10

Effective Guidance Interventions

naeyc Standards

The following NAEYC Standards are addressed in this chapter

Standard 5   Using Content Knowledge to Build Meaningful Curriculum

5a Understanding content knowledge and resources in academic disciplines

5b Knowing and using the central concepts, inquiry tools, and structures of content areas or academic disciplines

5c Using their [your] own knowledge, appropriate early learning standards, and other resources to design, implement, and evaluate meaningful, challenging curricula for each child.

Montessori Country Day School

Objectives

After reading this chapter, you should be able to do the following:

10-1 Distinguish when guidance intervention is not appropriate.

10-2 Explain when and how to intervene appropriately.

10-3 Determine appropriate methods to shape positive behavior.

10-4 Evaluate strategies to remove causes of problem behavior.

10-1 Ignore Mildly Annoying Behavior That Is Not Against the Ground Rules

Sometimes we need to step away and let children work out simple matters on their own. Children are not helped by intrusive and overwhelming attempts to change too much of their behavior at one time. We do well to focus our guidance on priorities. Typically, we should ignore mildly annoying behavior unless it is dangerous, disrespectful, or damaging. In other words, we should ignore any behavior that is within the ground rules. Before we ask children to stop a behavior, we need to ask ourselves, "Is this child really breaking a ground rule or am I just feeling annoyed with what she is doing?" We have so much important work to do in guiding children, and we can't afford to get sidetracked. Let's stay focused on priorities—safety, respect, and responsibility.

For example, a child has aggressively shoved her friend and is now sitting by herself biting her fingernails and rocking her chair back and forth. Perhaps we should intervene only regarding the aggression problem now. We can make a mental note to work with her on the other less critical issues in a tactful and supportive manner at some later time, well after the aggression has been resolved. If we overwhelm a child with too many expectations, especially when we are both upset, she may respond withdrawal or rebellion.

10-1a Focus Attention Elsewhere

When a child does something that is mildly annoying or embarrassing (but not unacceptable), simply focusing the child's attention elsewhere may resolve the problem. A baby who is banging a spoon on a metal high-chair tray in a restaurant may be redirected by a parent who plays peek-a-boo or dangles a softer, quieter toy. A thumb-sucking toddler may be redirected from the sucking by being given an interesting toy to explore. A curious preschooler may be redirected from handling items on shelves in the grocery store by being invited to help push the grocery cart and to help carry foods to the basket as they are selected.

replaces

Substitutes one action for another when both cannot be done at the same time, so that an undesired behavior must be given up or suspended for the new action to take place.

10-1b Discreetly Redirect Slightly Annoying Behavior to More Positive Substitute Behavior

Slightly annoying behaviors can also be redirected by involving the child in an activity that **replaces** the undesirable behavior. For example, a child who is picking at her nose can be directed to use a tissue to blow her nose. Without mentioning the nose picking, we can explain how using a tissue, throwing away the tissue, and then washing hands may keep others from catching a cold.

To redirect slightly inappropriate behaviors, we can identify activities that involve the part, or parts, of the child's body currently used in the undesirable action; then an alternative action involving those body parts can be substituted. For example, a child who is using her hands to feel the blossoms of a neighbor's delicate and expensive garden plants could be shown how to put her hands behind her back or in her pockets while she leans over to smell the wonderful fragrance of the gardenias. She could also be redirected to use her hands to gather interesting leaves and acorns from the ground.

This helps the child know that it is okay to explore and enjoy nature, but not okay to damage another person's property. Snapping, "Don't touch those plants!" discourages curiosity, a key factor in the child's long-term ability to develop intellectually. Of course, standing by passively while your child damages a neighbor's prized gardenias would be rude and disrespectful.

10-1c Assist the Child in Recognizing the General Effects of Positive Behaviors

Another method for gently redirecting minor misbehaviors involves focusing the child's attention on the positive outcome of more desirable behaviors. We give information to the child. We might say, "If you put your glass of milk on the top corner of your place mat, it will be safely out of your way until you want to drink it." Or, we might say, "If you erase mistakes slowly and lightly, your paper will look very nice." We can tell a preschooler, "I like to hear 'thank you.' How thoughtful! Brett remembered to say 'thank you.' "

10-1d Dealing with Genitalia-Related Issues

Genitalia-related issues often need to be dealt with early in childhood. Questions do come up about activities related to children's genital areas. Toddlers or preschoolers may rub their genital areas to fall asleep at naptime. Preschoolers or early school-agers may show curiosity about each other's genitalia. Occasionally, children may demonstrate disturbing behavior. Parents and teachers are sometimes at a loss regarding how to respond, how firmly to respond, or even whether they should respond. With society's grave concerns about sexual abuse ever present, we must be extremely alert to authentic signs of abuse. DAP programs use developmental knowledge to create healthy, respectful, and supportive environments for children, so great care is taken to assure that sensitive issues are handled professionally. See Positive Focus 10.1.

Take Time to Think Before Reacting to Genital Touching

What to Look For

- Does the behavior appear to be simple, childlike curiosity?

    Toddlers or preschoolers take a moment in the bathroom to compare, touch, explore, or talk about their genitals. A preschooler whose mother is breast-feeding pulls off her shirt to "breast-feed" the doll in the house-keeping center.

- Does the behavior appear to be cyclical self-stimulation?

    Like thumb sucking, nail-biting, and hair-twisting, masturbation may become a child's stress reduction habit. A young child rubs his or her genitals when extremely tired or upset or simply as a habit when falling asleep.

- Does the behavior appear to be stressed, sleepy behavior, or playfulness to entertain others?

    Preschoolers stuff bark mulch in their underwear and waddle around the playground giggling and chanting, "We got big butts!" Children taunt each other with bathroom insults such as "I saw your wee-wee" or "You're a pooh-pooh diaper baby."

- Does the behavior appear to be oddly unchildlike? Does it seem to be a childish imitation of adult sexual behavior?

    You find two preschoolers hiding behind a bush with one on top of the other imitating adult sexual activity. A child playing dolls invents a pretend scenario that involves graphic sexual behavior or language.

What to Do

- Take care not to overreact.

    These behaviors are perfectly normal expressions of healthy curiosity. Acknowledge the differences and take advantage of teachable moments. Say, "Yes, boys and girls have different bodies, but everybody's special. Girls grow up to be women, and boys grow up to be men." If necessary, the behavior can be gently and matter-of-factly redirected to a different activity.

- If the child is an infant or toddler, there is little to do but ignore the behavior and focus your energy on removing sources of stress. If the child is a preschooler, be more proactive. For example, "Would you like to hold this teddy bear when you fall asleep to help you remember not to rub your bottom?"

    "You must go into the bathroom when you need to touch your bottom."

- Rule out the possibility of a urinary tract or other infection.

    Be understanding, firm, and consistent. Taunting must always be stopped. Say, "Be respectful; use kind words.'"

- Have you noticed any other warning signs? Does the child seem to be delayed in social-emotional development? Does the child seem to be withdrawn? Does the child seem to be aggressive or rebellious? If the answer to any of these questions is yes, it may be necessary to contact child protective services.

TeachSource Digital Download

What Is Sexual Harassment?

Sexual harassment is unwelcome attention of a sexual nature. It includes a range of behavior from disruptive annoyances to serious abuses and even forced sexual activity. Sexual harassment is not only morally wrong but is also *illegal*.

There have been a few highly publicized cases of young children being expelled from child care and elementary school programs for "sexual harassment" because they

sexual harassment
Unwelcome attention given for sexual gratification; for personal sexual stimulation; or to antagonize, bully, and dehumanize another person through behavior of a sexual nature.

hugged a teacher inappropriately or pinched another child on the bottom. Fortunately, these bizarre situations have been rare.

Young children before puberty are by definition incapable of sexually harassing anyone. They *are* capable of bullying, misbehaving, and behaving in a socially inappropriate manner. And they *can* be molested or sexually harmed by an adolescent or adult. So we should always be alert to those concerns. But if a child is not yet physiologically, hormonally, or psychologically capable of sex, touching another child's genitals *is not of a sexual nature*. It may be from curiosity. It may be in imitation of inappropriate things the young child has seen. It may simply be silly play. But whatever it is—*it is not sexual harassment*.

A third grader who has pinched his teacher on the bottom should accept responsibility for this inappropriate behavior. We should find out why a child this age behaved this way so we can help him change his behavior. Perhaps this child was acting out as class clown because of an unmet need for attention from the teacher or from other children. Perhaps he was imitating something he had seen. Pinching a teacher on the bottom clearly is not appropriate, but children make mistakes. That's why we supervise them. They are immature. They are children!

Donnie is an energetic 5-year-old in a university lab school preschool. His practice student today is Chiquitha, a university sophomore. She is giving him a lesson in geometric shapes. "Donnie," she says, "This is a square. Can you look around the room and find anything that is shaped like this?" Donnie looks around and points to a window. "Right, Donnie. That window is shaped like a square. This is a circle. Can you find something that looks like a circle?" Donnie looks around the room for a long time. Then he brightens, grabs both of Chiquitha's breasts with his hands, and, with earnest sincerity, says, "Your breziz is round." Chiquitha is stunned. She quickly moves Donnie's hands. "Uhhh, yes, ummm, round, umm . . . let's put this away, and you can go build with the blocks now."

*Chiquitha rushes out to the director, completely distraught and a little angry, to report that Donnie has grabbed her breasts. The director explains that Donnie's behavior is perfectly normal **age-typical behavior**. She notes that Chiquitha handled the situation tactfully by redirecting Donnie to another activity when it occurred. The director explains that Donnie's behavior should simply be ignored. If the behavior persists, she is told that she should redirect it again. Focusing any attention on the behavior would reinforce it and increase the likelihood of it being repeated.*

The director also explains that Donnie's family has a new baby who is breastfeeding. Donnie has been very interested in the process and has asked his mother lots of questions about how the baby gets milk from her breasts. Donnie's behavior was not of a sexual nature. He was simply being a typical inquisitive child, innocently learning about his world.

age-typical behavior
Behavior that is characteristic to specific developmental stages; thus it is typically seen in children of a certain age.

10-2 Immediately Interrupt Behavior That Is Harmful or Unfair

Children rely on us to enforce rules and protect individual rights. Children will be willing to follow rules only if they come to believe that the rules are meaningful. Consistency and fairness in the enforcement of rules help children learn to trust authority figures. Behaviors that are harmful or unfair must be interrupted immediately by a responsible adult.

We do not help children become cooperative and respectful by passively watching them fight, saying, "They'll just have to learn to stand up for themselves. When Jimmy has had enough of Gerald hitting him, he'll learn to hit back." We also fail to help children when we say, "Don't come tell me that someone hit you. I don't want to hear about it!" Children can be helped to resolve their own disagreements, but they must know that we will reliably stop unacceptable, hurtful behavior.

10-2a What Do I Do about Biting?

Biting is a worrisome issue for parents and teachers of toddlers. In the case of biting, the inappropriate behavior dramatically affects a child other than the biter. Not only does the teacher have to worry about how to deal with responding to the biter, the teacher also has to contact the parents of the bitten child to inform them of the bite. The parents of the child who has been bitten will undoubtedly feel concerned; perhaps they will feel frustrated; maybe (if this has happened before) they will feel angry. The parent of the child who was bitten wants to know our plan to keep her child safe in the future.

Babies and toddlers lack self-control and communication skills. They don't know how to express their anger in a socially acceptable manner. Biting isn't the fault of the baby or toddler. Parents and caregivers teach toddlers more appropriate behaviors. We communicate compassionately and caringly with parents and collaboratively plan new strategies to change this unacceptable behavior.

A very disturbing trend has been for child care centers to solve the problem by expelling the biting toddler from the child care center. This is a shocking way to dismiss this problem: It leaves a family with no child care and a toddler with a behavior problem unsolved. Yale researcher Walter Gilliam (2004) studied preschool expulsions and found that pre-K students are expelled at a rate more than three times that of children in grades K–12. He found that black children were getting expelled at alarming rates and that boys were expelled 4.5 times more often than girls.

Babies and toddlers bite because they lack self-control and communication skills. We should communicate professionally and compassionately with all involved parents anytime biting occurs. Positive guidance offers many strategies that can be used to address biting. See Positive Focus 10.2.

The DAP environment protects children's psychological safety. Children should feel happy, relaxed, and comfortable rather than disengaged, frightened, worried, or stressed. Dealing with biting challenges us to maintain a peaceful, caring toddler learning community. See Positive Focus 10.3.

Positive Focus 10.2

Responding to Toddler Biting

- **Increase supervision**—Ensure that proper ratios of adult supervision are maintained.
- **Look at the environment**—Is DAP in place? Are the babies or toddlers bored?
- **Focus attention**—Use eye contact at eye level, use the child's name, and use appropriate touch while saying, "Gentle, be gentle!"
- **Role-play**—"Ouch! Be gentle, Dolly! No biting! Biting hurts!"
- **Teach sign language**—Signing may be helpful as a way to help the baby or toddler express feelings and needs.

TeachSource Digital Download

Positive Focus 10.3 Take Time to Think before You Respond to Biting

What to Look For

- Did the biting seem spontaneous?

  Babies younger than 1 year have limited self-awareness and almost no conscious control over their behavior. A baby beginning to cut teeth may bite unexpectedly while breastfeeding.

  An older baby may bite when emotionally overwhelmed with discomfort, excitement, fatigue, or fright. In fact, an older baby involved in an overly exciting game of peek-a-boo may be laughing wildly one moment and suddenly bite anyone handy the next moment.

- What were the circumstances just before the biting?

  Toddlers in the second and third year of life have begun to gain a bit of control over their behavior, but they have limited communication skills and may feel powerless when they are frustrated, angry, in pain, or frightened.

  Tiny teeth can make even a grown-up flinch and howl. Kicking and screaming may be ignored, but a bite is sure to get immediate attention from just about anyone.

  Remember that toddlers are just beginning to develop the cognitive ability to think about an action and then consciously choose *not* to do it.

  Learning takes time, consistency, and patience. In the initial stages of learning, a toddler may bite, then immediately look up, shake her head, and say, "No, no bite!"

- Has the biting become chronic?

  A preschool-age child who still bites is a source of serious concern. Biting is painful, it can be a source of infection, and others must be protected.

  Ask yourself the following questions:
  Are the child's physical and emotional needs met?
  Is she getting adequate sleep, nutrition, and health care?
  Are there other indications that the child may be experiencing emotional or health problems?
  Are there reasons the child might be feeling overwhelmed and helpless?
  Is the child developing as generally expected for her age?

What to Do

- Be calm, firm, and consistent.

  Establish eye contact at eye level, make gentle physical contact with the child, and calmly but urgently say, "Be respectful. Biting hurts." Then immediately redirect the child's attention to a different activity. Gently stroke the bitten child or adult while soothingly saying, "Gentle . . . be gentle."

  If needed, carry the biter to a different location and engage her in a totally different activity. Trying to have a baby or toddler sit in time-out is not appropriate. (Remember, biting a child back is never okay!)

- Prevention is the key.

  Focus your energy on preventing that first bite by providing close supervision and by removing sources of frustration and stress.

  Biting is contagious. A toddler who gets bitten is highly likely to try out this new tactic on others. Biting spreads in a toddler classroom faster than a runny nose in January.

  Diligent supervision and DAP will help adults prevent biting outbreaks. Be sure children are getting plenty of rest, are in a calm environment, and are receiving plenty of emotional nurturing.

  Boredom is a major source of stress for babies and toddlers, so ensure a safe, accessible DAP environment.

- Convene a "summit meeting" of teaching staff and parents.

  Successful resolution is most likely when adults resist the temptation to point fingers. Meeting cooperatively to discuss progress and strategies has an amazingly positive effect on chronic misbehavior.

  Medical experts and counselors who specialize in evaluating and treating developmental problems can be a tremendous asset to families and teachers. Don't hesitate to call on them.

10-2b Intervene as Firmly as Necessary but as Gently as Possible

When we find it necessary to stop an unacceptable behavior, we should always proceed as firmly as necessary to stop the unacceptable action, but as gently as possible to remind the child that he is accepted and respected as a person, even if his behavior must be ended.

As Miss Melanie firmly pries a toddler's clenched fingers one by one out of another screaming toddler's hair, she says with a facial expression and tone of urgent concern (not anger) in her voice, "Ouch! Pulling hurts. Touch gently, please." After the toddlers are safely separated, she softly strokes each toddler's hair saying, "Gentle, be gentle. Please touch hair gently." Miss Melanie has interrupted a harmful behavior as firmly as necessary but as gently as possible.

Roger grabs a little car from his friend Chris and runs away. Chris yells and starts to cry. Mr. Reese follows Roger (persistently but without chasing him), saying in a deeply concerned tone, "Stop, please. Roger, I need you to stop so we can talk about Chris's car." When Roger finally pauses for a second, Mr. Reese says, "Thank you for waiting. Let's sit down and talk about Chris's car. You like Chris's car, don't you? It's really a neat car."

Mr. Reese does not immediately attempt to snatch the car away from Roger. He patiently asks, "What should you do if you want to play with someone else's toy? Should you ask, 'May I play with your car?'" Roger hangs his head and says, "But if I ask him, he might say no." Mr. Reese answers, "You're right. He might say yes or he might say no. Would you like for me to come with you so you can ask? If he says no, I will help you find a different toy to play with. Remember, taking things without asking is not allowed, so when you choose a toy, no one will be allowed to take your toy away without asking you first, right?"

Roger's unfair action has been stopped, firmly but gently, and Roger has had a chance to learn a very important lesson. Although rules sometimes stop him from doing what he wants to do, they also ensure that his own rights are protected.

10-2c Maintain Objectivity

Positive child guidance is a teaching process. As in any educational process, powerful emotions such as anger, disgust, or the threat of harm interrupt rather than assist learning. People, children included, are better able to concentrate and absorb information when they are reasonably calm. A terrified child may remember vividly the look of daggers in a parent's eyes but completely forget the whole point of the reprimand and not be able to recall what behavior caused the problem in the first place.

Marilyn's 3-year-old daughter, Stephanie, waited patiently (although she was becoming very bored) while her mother shopped for new towels in a department store. Stephanie caught sight of a little boy about her age shopping with his mother on the other side of a large pillow display. Stephanie peeked around the edge of the pile of pillows to get a better look at the little boy. He grinned at her. Embarrassed, she quickly scrambled back behind the pillow display. Unfortunately, in her haste, she dislodged the display, and an avalanche of pillows piled down on top of her. Two salespersons rushed over (looking very annoyed), and several other shoppers stared at the mess. Marilyn was startled and horrified to see what Stephanie had done. She grabbed Stephanie by the arm and marched her off to the ladies' lounge to have a "few words."

Marilyn did not manage to stay objective about her daughter's behavior. She took her own feelings of embarrassment out on Stephanie. She could have been more helpful to Stephanie if she had been able to maintain a more objective and less emotional perspective.

BrainFacts

What Can We Learn from Neuroscience?

Children's Brains and the Development of Self-Control

- Executive function has a protracted developmental timetable, but most children make dramatic gains in self-control over thoughts, behaviors, and emotions in the preschool period (Carlson, 2005; Goldman-Rakic, 1987; Kopp, 1982; Zelazo & Müller, 2002).

- Our executive functions give us the capacity for self-control, self-discipline, compliance, and self-regulation. Human beings rely on these basic skills in all areas of our lives. Executive control makes it possible for us to do the following (Center on the Developing Child at Harvard University, 2011):
  - Recognize and correct our mistakes
  - Control our impulsive behavior
  - Resist things we want but know are not good for us
  - Make wise decisions
  - Solve complicated problems
  - Persist in completing challenging tasks
  - Make plans
  - Determine goals and monitor progress toward achieving them

- Children with well-developing executive function are able to become socially competent (Hughes, 1998), moral (Kochanska, Murray, & Harlan, 2000), and academically successful (Riggs, Blair, & Greenberg, 2003).

- Children diagnosed with autism, attention deficit/hyperactivity, intellectual disability, and several other disorders typically have significant disruptions in their development of executive function and need professional support to learn self-control (Tottenham, Hare, & Casey, 2011).

- A critically important aspect of a young child's executive function is theory of mind development. Theory of mind gradually begins to develop in babies and toddlers. At first it is only a vague and intuitive sense, but as language develops it becomes more reflective and specific (Astington & Dack, 2008; Astington & Hughes, 2013; Harris, 2006).

- Theory of mind helps human beings see the world from the perspective of another. It gives us the capacity to think about "what ifs." What happened last time I did this? What possible consequences may result from my doing this? What might be possible for me to do in the future? (Carlson, Mandell, & Williams, 2004; Carlson & Moses, 2001; Hughes, 1998; Perner & Lang, 1999).

- Language plays a critical role in theory of mind development and consequently in the development of self-control. Research indicates that a child's theory of mind (and, with it, executive function) develops earlier in bilingual compared to monolingual preschoolers (Goetz, 2003; Hughes, 1998). Using sign language to help babies and young toddlers communicate also has been shown to significantly assist executive function development (Emmorey, Luk, Pyers, & Bialystok, 2008).

- We often tell children, "use your words" to help them calm down and communicate. Research shows that using our words turns on our brain's braking system and sets self-control processes in motion. A study by Lieberman and his fellow researchers (2007) found that putting feelings into words increased one's capacity to maintain self-control. As children improve in their ability to use emotional words to describe their feelings, they have fewer emotional outbursts and have more friends and better academic performance.

- Researchers have found that the following also support development of self-control (Fox, Levitt, & Nelson, 2010):

  - Make sure children get plenty of rest. Fatigue interferes with self-control.

  - Allow breaks so children can exercise vigorously; exercise may have an immediate and positive effect on children's impulse control.

  - When a child is losing control, teach him to stop and focus on slow breathing for two minutes. Show him how to breathe in through his nose and exhale the day's stress through his mouth.

  - Minimize the number of choices the child has to make so that her strength is conserved for self-regulation.

  - Never make the child feel guilty for bad decisions. Research shows that guilt is *not* a good motivator for better behaviors. Instead, focus on moving forward.

We can greatly assist the development of self-control in children by staying focused on the reality of the situation rather than on adult feelings that are not relevant. Marilyn's guidance will be more effective if she can push aside her feelings of humiliation and fear that complete strangers will think she is a bad mother. Marilyn should focus on the reality of the situation—Stephanie had been trying to wait patiently, she did not intentionally do anything wrong, and she was obviously feeling very upset and embarrassed already.

It is perfectly normal and healthy for us to feel waves of sheer fury now and again. Because of our size and power, however, it is appropriate for us to release most of those feelings of frustration and rage away from young children by jogging, punching and kneading bread dough, or by pounding out melodies on a piano. It is neither fair nor helpful to blast powerful and scary expressions of anger at children. We can learn to be honest without being overpowering.

Children require guidance and sympathy far more than instruction.

—*Anne Sullivan*

10-2d Remove the Child from a Problem Situation

Removing a child from the scene of a conflict allows a cooling-off period for the adult and child, removes whatever temptation the child is having difficulty with (out of sight, out of mind), and ensures that a gawking or giggling audience of children is not watching and triggering further misbehavior. Although compromise should never be considered during the heat of a full-blown tantrum, compromise after the child has gained control may serve as an effective role model for the child to imitate as she learns to talk rather than scream to get what she wants.

Occasionally, we may have no choice but to pick up a young child who may be kicking and screaming and carry the child (as gently as possible but as firmly as necessary) away from the scene of a conflict.

A preschooler who is having a tantrum in a grocery store because she cannot have the candy bar she wants should probably be escorted or, if necessary, picked up and carried out of the store. She can be helped to understand that she has two, and only two, choices: she can sit and cry for a long, long time in the car with her patient but assertive father, or she can return to the grocery store and continue the shopping trip, accepting the fact that there will be no candy bar.

If the father, through consistent verbal and nonverbal communication, convinces his daughter that he will not become angry or argumentative, and that he will also absolutely not back down, the little girl will soon recognize the futility of a long, dramatic, exhausting fit of crying. She will learn that a tantrum simply does not work.

When the child seems ready to throw in the towel, recognizing that she cannot bully or manipulate her father, she should be given an opportunity to save face. At this point, restraint, tactfulness, empathy, and perhaps an appropriate compromise (letting her choose a nutritious snack to take home) would keep the situation from having a winner and a loser. The little girl's future cooperativeness will hinge on her feeling confident that she can be cooperative without losing her dignity and autonomy and without having her past mistakes thrown in her face.

PRACTICAL APPLICATION CASE

Will and the Cream Cheese Wonton

Renee and Tom are loving and assertive parents. They have taught their children to respect the rights of others.

One evening, the entire household is aflutter with excitement because the children's grandparents have arrived for a short visit. Because Renee and Tom both worked that day, Renee had picked up the children from child care and Tom had picked up Chinese food for dinner from a favorite restaurant. Tom made sure to include an order of cream cheese wontons; the children were not too wild about Chinese food, but they especially loved the restaurant's specialty: cream cheese wontons.

Everyone sat around the table chatting and enjoying dinner. Will, who is 5 years old, perched on his knees in the big dining chair so he could see everyone. He listened attentively to grown-up conversation as he slowly nibbled at the food on his plate.

As the adults finished eating, they pushed back their plates and continued to sit at the table, laughing and talking, catching up on family news and funny stories about the children and all their great adventures and escapades. Tom leaned back in his chair, stretched out his long legs, and draped an arm across the back of Will's chair. As he laughed and talked, he happened to glance at Will's almost empty plate. He noticed one last cream cheese wonton pushed to the back of the plate. Absentmindedly, he picked up a fork, stabbed the wonton, and popped it into his mouth.

The instant Tom swallowed the wonton, he saw a stricken look fall across Will's face, and he knew he had made a big mistake. Will leaned close to his dad's ear and whispered intently, "Dad, we have to go to a lonely place and talk." Quietly, Tom got up from the table and followed Will to the bathroom. Tom sat down on the side of the bathtub while Will ceremoniously closed the bathroom door and then, with big tears sliding down his cheeks, said, "Dad, you're not supposed to take other people's things without asking. That was the only cream cheese wonton left, and I was saving it for last. You did a wrong thing."

Tom lifted Will into his lap, and they hugged each other long and hard. Tom said, "You're right, son. I did do a wrong thing and I apologize."

Tom didn't know whether to laugh or cry, but his heart was filled with pride that his son had been able to stand up for his rights and also had made a special effort to spare his dad's dignity by asking to talk in a "lonely place."

Case Discussion Questions

1. Why do you suppose Tom ate Will's wonton? Have you ever inadvertently hurt a child's feelings? How did the child respond?

2. How do you think Will learned to resolve problems the way he did? Why do you think he asked for a lonely place to talk with his father?

3. How would it make you feel if a child responded to you the way Will responded to his father? How do you imagine Will's father felt? What do you suppose he was thinking during his conversation with Will?

10-3 Assertively Shape Positive Behavior

When a child must be subjected to an unpleasant occurrence, the situation should be discussed squarely and honestly to give the child a chance to cooperate voluntarily. The situation should not, however, be allowed to stall or become a stalemate if the child refuses to cooperate. For example, when medicine must be applied to a scrape on an unwilling child's knee, we matter-of-factly explain what has to be done and then get the unpleasant task over with. The longer whining, crying, and arguing are engaged, the more unpleasant and stressful the task of applying medicine will become.

Separation is a good example of a necessary but unpleasant occurrence in the lives of toddlers. Before a separation, parents must be given all the time they want to visit with their child and express affection. A parent should not be rushed but should clearly indicate to the caregiver when she is ready to leave (and willing to actually walk out the door). At this decisive moment of separation, a skilled caregiver will firmly but lovingly state, "Mommy needs to leave now. You may give mommy a hug and wave bye-bye through the window, or if you need, I can hold you while mommy leaves." If the child is clearly not willing to hug mommy and wave good-bye, then the parent and caregiver can move caringly and assertively to make a quick separation, even if the child resists loudly and has to be held.

The caregiver can express empathy: "Yes, you love your mommy. You miss her when she leaves. Sometimes I miss my mommy too. Did you know I have a mommy? Let's go find the dolls. Would you like to see what our rabbit is doing this morning? Would you like to give some lettuce to our rabbit?" Shape positive behavior by making sure that it happens.

We can often help children avoid situations in which they may experience failure by quickly and decisively making the right thing happen and then rapidly moving on to happier activities, all this without giving an appearance of frustration, anger, or disgust with the child's inability to actively cooperate or comply. Children's negative feelings should be acknowledged and accepted, but they should not be dwelled on (Claxton & Carr, 2004).

10-3a Teach Ground Rules

Children need to know exactly what is expected of them. We have established simple, basic ground rules—be safe, be respectful, be responsible. Consistently ensuring that ground rules are followed helps children develop a sense of order and consistency in their lives. Children must have our help if they are to learn and remember ground rules. Following are several ways we can successfully teach children ground rules.

Role-Play

Give children a chance to act out, or practice, the correct following of rules. For preschoolers, role-play so that the child can see and experience an appropriate response. Use a puppet to be the child's troublesome friend; for example, have Bert, the puppet, very, very gently, but dramatically, pull the child's hair. "Oh, no! Bert just pulled your hair! Can you look right at Bert, and say in a big voice, 'Be respectful. That hurt.'"

Repetition

Children need many opportunities to hear a rule repeated before knowledge of that rule has fully reached their long-term memory. For those of us who have experienced electrical power failures, we know that having knowledge of a thing does not necessarily mean we can immediately change a habit. We mindlessly continue attempting to turn on appliances and lights knowing full well that the electricity was off. We have to remind ourselves over and over, "Oh, yes, I can't listen to the radio. . . . Oh, the electric can opener won't work. . . . Oh, the clock is not right." Children need and deserve patient reminders of rules and expectations so they will be able to change their habit patterns. Repetition is natural to children's learning. We can provide pleasurable repetition and support child guidance learning with appropriate children's books (bibliotherapy).

Discussion

Rules have a great deal more meaning for children when children really understand reasons for the rules. We should get rid of that age-old phrase "because I said so." Some of our parents used that phrase as an all-inclusive explanation. Positive guidance requires that we explain things to children simply and honestly. We should say things like, "You must use the blunt knife instead of the sharp knife. I don't want you to get cut." "You may not open the gate without permission because the street is busy and dangerous." "You must wash your hands with soap and water before you eat because you could get sick from getting germs in your mouth."

Although the basic ground rules don't change, school-age children feel ownership when they create and routinely change their own classroom rules. Classroom rules, of course, are subcategories—the ground rules are generic and cover the basic categories of behavior. By thinking about and talking about ground rules and class rules, children learn to think about rules, to process rules, and to make good decisions.

10-3b Clarify Expectations

If we want children to follow our instructions, we must make sure they really understand what we intend for them to do. We sometimes speak in vague, general terms. We say things such as, "Be good," "Be nice," "Act like a big girl." What children need are simple but specific statements of our expectations. See Positive Focus 10.4.

Repetition is a natural part of children's learning.

At first we have to remind him every day, "Be responsible—hang up your jacket." After a while, being responsible for his own jacket becomes an automatic part of his routine.

Positive and Specific Statements of Our Expectations

- Sit down, please. Make sure your bottom is in the chair and your feet are on the floor."

- "Please hold your milk with both hands."

- "Please wait at the bottom of the slide until the person in front of you has gone down the slide. Then you may climb up and have your turn."

- "Please use a soft, slow voice to talk to me about your sister. I can't understand whining and screaming."

TeachSource Digital Download

Additionally, we sometimes assume that children automatically know how objects are intended to be used. Instead, children older than age 3 need to be told specifically what various objects are for. Babies and toddlers put bowls on their heads, try to eat decorative plastic fruit, and attempt to pull T-shirts on like underpants. (That's why they're so much fun to be around.) Gentle guidance helps them toward the proper use of objects, but they also need a great deal of freedom to explore safe objects thoroughly, using all their senses and muscles to discover their world. If a baby or toddler stands up in a chair that could fall, she should tactfully be redirected to a safer place to climb or else the chair should be removed. A child older than age 3, however, can be told, "Be safe; a chair is for your seat, not your feet."

Toys, Tools, and Weapons

Preschoolers can be taught the difference among toys, tools, and weapons; for example, "A *toy* is something you can play with, a *tool* is something useful to help you do things, but a *weapon* is meant to hurt people. At school we use toys and tools but not weapons." A ball can be used as a toy to play kickball, or it can be used as a tool to knock a kite out of a tree, but it must not be used as a weapon to hit someone in the face. A fork should be used as a tool to pick up food, not as a toy to wave around or as a weapon to poke another child. School-age children are especially capable of comprehending and identifying categories of objects and will spontaneously point out to one another, "That pencil is a tool. It's for writing. You mustn't use it like a weapon!"

10-3c Maintain Consistency

If we want children to behave appropriately, we need to provide consistency in our expectations. Discipline should not be enforced based on our mood or coincidental circumstances. For example, it would be inconsistent to indicate to a young child through our actions, "You can walk around the house eating and dropping crumbs, except when I am too tired and crabby to clean up after you or when we have company." There should be a consistent day-to-day rule either that eating takes place at the table or that eating at various places in the house is allowed as long as family members clean up after themselves.

Older children, who have a clear understanding and acceptance of specific rules, can deal with occasional exceptions to those rules. They can understand that family members are expected to eat in the kitchen, even though breakfast in bed is a perfect Mother's Day surprise, and a pizza around the coffee table might be a perfect treat for a slumber party. Toddlers and young preschoolers, in contrast, do not have a full grasp of rules. They view the world in very literal black-and-white terms. An action either is or is not allowed. They become very frustrated and confused and tend to ignore a rule altogether if it seems to them to be inconsistently enforced. For example, little ones should never be allowed, even once, to ride in a car without being properly buckled into an appropriate car seat. If they believe there is absolutely no chance the car will move unless they are belted into a car seat, they will accept the car seat as a fact of life rather than something to be negotiated every time they get into the car.

To be consistent, we should make very sure that a child's behavior is not laughed at on one occasion and reprimanded on another. Bathroom terms that brought giggles at home may not be nearly so funny when announced loudly at a family gathering. The toddler with spaghetti in his hair may be adorable the first time, but if he receives a great deal of attention (laughter, photographs, calling the neighbors to come see), he may be inclined to repeat the behavior, which will not be nearly so entertaining to harried parents the second, third, or fourth time. In the early childhood setting, consistency, with reasonable flexibility, is essential.

10-4 Adapt Objects, Events, and Attitudes to Remove Possible Causes of Problem Behavior

It is almost always easier to change the environment around the child than it is to change the child. Additionally, it is more nurturing and less stressful for everyone involved if we focus on setting the stage for positive behavior rather than on correcting children after they have behaved improperly. Rather than raising our voices to get the attention of rowdy children, we can use a dramatic whisper. Children will pay more attention to a whisper than to a rude, bellowing voice.

For example, if children are running in the classroom, it will be better and easier to change the room arrangement to make running difficult than to endlessly remind children to walk. If toddlers always spill their milk, we can give them smaller cups with only an ounce of milk at a time. That way, if they do have a spill, very little milk is wasted and very little effort is needed to clean it up.

We began to realize that if we wanted to change the situation, we first had to change ourselves.

—*Stephen R. Covey (author of Seven Habits of Highly Effective People)*

Children have to make mistakes to learn. Making small day-to-day mistakes stimulates thinking and problem solving in children's brains (Deak, 2010). Our job is to assure that children know they can be responsible. They can clean up messes and make amends to others they have offended. And they can figure out how to avoid future mistakes. Mistakes are critically important teachable moments for independent self-learning as well as for supportive teacher guidance.

If children in a preschool program consistently become tired and irritable on field trips, then perhaps field trips can be rescheduled to a different time of day or for a shorter time period. Or perhaps trips can be made less often but to more carefully chosen places. When confronted with troublesome behavior problems, we should ask ourselves, "Instead of trying to change the child, how can I can change the environment, my actions, or my attitudes to solve the problem?"

10-4a Offer Assistance and Encouragement

Children thrive on positive attention. They usually become more cooperative when we say, "What things can we do to make it really easy for you to remember your homework?" "Let's talk about some appropriate things you can do when you feel angry with your friends." We involve the child in creating his own solutions; we let the child feel ownership. Positive guidance means that we work alongside children preventively to help and encourage them to behave appropriately. Our role is not just to deal with children after they have done the wrong thing but instead to be their partners in success. We can celebrate each tiny step toward more mature, safe, respectful, responsible behavior.

10-4b Give Undivided Attention

Children immediately recognize whether we are serious enough about what we are saying to stop and see that a request is followed. Even toddlers and preschoolers know that instructions do not mean much when we casually glance back across our shoulder and make an offhanded comment across a room, such as, "Come on now, put those toys away."

In contrast, children sense that instructions mean a great deal when we stop what we are doing, walk over to the child, bend down to eye level, gently touch the child's shoulder, look directly into the child's eyes, and say in a gentle but firm tone, "Sherrie, please stop now and put the blocks away." *A half hour of nagging and threatening from across the room will not have the impact of one gentle touch and one quiet statement made eye-to-eye at eye level using the child's name.* Undivided attention is a special kind of magic in child guidance.

Of course, we must stay close and provide follow-through with Sherrie. As soon as Sherrie picks up the first block, I will smile and say, "Thank you." I will stay near her and give attention until her task is finished if I am worried that she will not be able to do without my help and/or nudging. I will offer whatever it takes for success. My hope is to help Sherrie build her own inner routine for putting materials away. Eventually, when her putting materials away routine is well established, she won't need my close attention anymore. She will put her materials away because that is her routine. Additionally, Sherrie's ground rules help her learn that when she gets something out, she has to "be responsible" and put it back away.

Undivided attention has a powerful effect on children. In positive child guidance, attention focused directly on children will be assertive, be positive, and build self-esteem rather than be negative, angry, and destructive of pride and confidence. The following four actions can be carried out in a positive way to show children that they have our undivided attention and that we really care about their behavior:

Eye Contact

Move close and try to establish eye contact. A shy child or a child who has experienced eye contact as part of threatening, angry interactions will feel compelled to look away. Do not force the child to look you in the eye, but rather attempt to win the child's trust by associating eye contact with positive, caring interactions. If the child does look you in the eye, sincerely commend him: "Thank you for listening so well."

Body Positioned at Child's Level

Bend down to the child's eye level. Staring down your nose at a child tempts the child to look away and may also seem cold. Bringing our body to the child's level gives an indication of our full attention.

Appropriate Touch

Touch clearly must be adapted based on the child's age level. Touch that is appropriate for standoffish older school-agers is not at all the same as that needed for babies and toddlers, who need loads of hugging and snuggling. Nevertheless, touch can be meaningful during guidance. While talking to a preschooler, gently placing a hand on the child's shoulder or arm, or lightly holding one or both of the child's hands, might focus her attention. If the child is sitting on the floor, gently touching a foot or knee might obtain the child's attention and communicate caring concern. Appropriate touching is *never* grabby or forced. Pay attention to the child's signals. Children usually make it pretty clear whether they find our touch unpleasant or comforting.

▶❙ **TeachSource** Video

© 2013 Cengage Learning®

Guidance for Young Children: Teacher Techniques for Encouraging Positive Social Behaviors

Watch the Video Case on teacher techniques for guiding young children. After watching the clip, answer the following questions:

1. Describe three things the teacher in this video does to prevent behavior problems in her class.

2. Based on what you read in this chapter, list three methods the teacher uses to gain the children's cooperation? (*Hint:* By letting children know they are valued, they are more likely to cooperate.)

Use of Child's Name

Using a child's given name or accepted nickname is more personal and appropriate than are general terms of endearment such as "sweety" or "honey." We must learn every child's name very quickly if we are to be effective. Sadly, some young children hear their names yelled so often as a reprimand that they fail to respond as we would expect when their name is used in a positive context. They do not recognize their name as a symbol for who they are, but only as a negative word that means they are in trouble. We can make sure children hear their names in positive contexts many times each day.

10-4c Redirect Inappropriate Behavior Firmly and Respectfully

When a child's inappropriate behavior must be stopped, cooperation can be gained and resentment avoided by offering the child an acceptable alternative activity. A child who is pouring milk back and forth from cup to bowl during a meal may be told, "You may not play with your food, but after lunch (or after nap) I will show you a good place for pouring." The child could then be directed at an appropriate time to pour, squirt, dribble, and splash to her heart's content with dishes and toys at a sink, commercial water table, outdoor wading pool, or plastic basin placed within her reach and containing an inch or two of water.

When children feel angry, they hit, kick, pinch, and scratch. These typical aggressive behaviors must be stopped. The child's anger should, however, be given an appropriate outlet. When we tell the child, "Be respectful. Hitting hurts Jessica," we should also add, "Use words. Tell Jessica you don't like it when she steps on your fingers. Can you show Jessica your fingers that hurt?" *[handwritten: ×your hitting と個人ター話した らダン‼]*

Common sense and knowledge of the basic principles of child development will guide our effective use of **redirection**. The idea is to replace misbehavior with a desired behavior so that the focus is on what the child *should* do rather than on what the child *should not* do. It is important, however, to ensure that the replacement activity does not become a reward for inappropriate behavior. Remember that operant conditioning is the process of reinforcing or strengthening a behavior by reinforcing it with a pleasurable response.

redirection
The process of offering a substitute focus to distract the child from a current undesirable one. For example, a child may be offered a developmentally appropriate water play activity to refocus his or her inappropriate interest in pouring milk from a cup onto the floor.

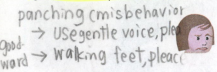

[Handwritten notes:]
panching (misbehavior → use gentle voice, plea
good ward → walking feet, pleac

prevention techniques
A specific procedure or special type of action taken to make it difficult or impossible for someone to do a certain thing or for a certain type of thing to happen.

quick response
A specific procedure or special type of action done swiftly in reaction to a situation.

Miss Seraphina, a toddler caregiver in a child care center, was concerned about the biting that was happening almost daily in her room. She thought that perhaps the toddlers were biting because their gums were uncomfortable with teething and they needed strong oral stimulation. She decided to offer hard crackers for the toddlers to bite as a substitute for biting each other. Within a few days, she discovered, to her dismay, that the toddlers were attacking and biting each other whenever they felt hungry for crackers. They had become conditioned to expect crackers in response to biting.

Fortunately, Miss Seraphina decided to resolve the biting problem instead with **prevention techniques** and **quick response** techniques. She added interesting new activities and materials, moved snack time to a bit earlier in the day, and heightened her supervision efforts. She decided to respond quickly, caringly, and firmly to the first indication of a toddler using teeth. Her efforts worked. See Positive Focus 10.5.

Positive Focus 10.5   Prevention Techniques

It is easier to prevent inappropriate behavior than to stop it. The following techniques are helpful in preventing inappropriate behavior:

● Maintain DAP activities and environments.
● Create calm, stress-free surroundings.

- Observe children to anticipate problems before they happen.
- Listen to children.
- Teach children to express their feelings appropriately.
- Maintain a warm, friendly, optimistic attitude—smile.
- Express requests in positive rather than negative statements.
- Sincerely recognize children's progress.
- Keep expectations realistic.
- Keep the big picture in mind—don't fret over trivia.

Quick Response Techniques

Sometimes, despite your best efforts at prevention, inappropriate behavior occurs. The following responses are designed to be used either during or as soon as possible after the inappropriate behavior.

- Make eye contact.
  - Position yourself so that you can establish eye contact with a child who seems to be having trouble.
  - Facial expressions should be caring rather than annoyed.
- Make physical contact.
  - Avert trouble by sticking close to a child who seems to be having problems.
  - Sit down next to the child and place an arm on his shoulder or make other appropriate contact.
  - Be calm and firm rather than menacing.
- Offer assistance.
  - Ask, "May I help you?"
  - Intervene, taking the child's hand gently and saying, "You seem to be having a problem. What is happening?"
  - "I'm sorry, Raul, you seem to have forgotten our ground rule. How can we make this right?"
- Give choices.
  - "Hussein, first you may help me tape these pages back in the picture book, then we'll find another activity for you. When you are ready to read books again, let me know and I'll show you how to turn the pages really carefully, okay?"
  - "Emma, you may swing safely or you may pick out a different activity. Which would you like to choose?"
- Remove the child from the problem and help him express feelings.
  - Physically remove a child from the situation that has triggered an outburst so that he can begin to calm down.
  - If the child has been aggressive, find ways to help him verbalize his feelings. "I understand that you feel really angry, but hitting is not acceptable."
  - Acknowledge the child's feelings while clarifying boundaries. "What are some other things you could do when you feel angry with Zachary? What are some words you could say? You could say, 'I feel . . .'"

TeachSource Digital Download

This toddler teacher is using prevention techniques. She has prepared a DAP environment that keeps the children engaged, she is warm and optimistic, she creates opportunities for the toddlers to express their feelings appropriately, and she keeps the tone of the classroom calm and comforting.

10-4d Clearly Express Appropriate Feelings

Although it is appropriate for us to be honest in our expression of feelings to children, our expression of anger would be too overwhelming for a young child to handle. Rage has no place in positive child guidance. When confronted by a large, snarling, furious grown-up, a young child has two possibilities: recoil in fear and try to stay out of the grown-up's way, or fight back by being rebellious and insubordinate. Neither of those options helps the child become a more confident, competent, and cooperative person. Children who are frequently shamed develop a general sense of guilt and unworthiness.

Rather than focus on feelings of anger, we can identify the underlying feelings that caused the anger. We can ask, "Am I feeling angry because I was startled, disappointed, worried, frightened, or frustrated?" Instead of saying, "I am furious with you," we can say, "I felt really frightened when I didn't know where you were. I was afraid you were hurt or lost. I was so upset I felt like crying." See Positive Focus 10.6.

10-4e Explain the Natural Consequences of Unacceptable Behavior

Children older than 3 years are usually perfectly capable of mentally connecting the cause-and-effect relationship between their conscious actions and potential consequences. If simple, polite, assertive statements of rules and expectations do not bring about an appropriate response from children, then it is time to discuss potential consequences. Explaining potential consequences is not the same as bribing, intimidating, or giving idle threats. It is intended to inform the child, to give an honest, sincere warning of an impending consequence. It is not intended to manipulate, coerce, or trick the child into behaving a certain way, but rather to give the child forewarning of natural things that happen, "If you do this, this is likely to happen." For example, "Blocks are hard. Throwing them could hurt someone. You may use them safely for building something really fun."

The cliché "you can lead a horse to water, but you can't make him drink" fits children well. We can offer a well-balanced meal to a young child, but we cannot force the child to eat it. We can say, "You may select what you would like to eat from the nutritious foods we have available if you feel hungry. If you are not hungry enough to eat now,

Appropriate Verbal Expressions of Adult Feelings

- *Surprise, disbelief*: "Oh my! This beautiful plant has had its leaves torn off. Plants can die if their leaves are harmed."

- *Sadness, disappointment*: "I feel very sad when I find books with the pages torn out. Books are beautiful and fun to read, but they aren't of any use when they are ripped apart."

- *Concern, worry*: "I feel worried when I see you scratching your mosquito bite. Scratching may cause it to become infected and sore. Let's cover it with a bandage."

- *Apprehension, fear*: "I feel very frightened when I see you climbing on the top rail of the fort. You must stay off the rails or else choose a different place to play on the playground."

- *Distress, frustration*: "I feel very frustrated when I find the door has been left open. We can't keep our house warm and comfortable inside when a door is left open. Please check the door each time you go out to make sure it's properly closed."

TeachSource Digital Download

then you may wait until you feel hungrier. I will put your plate in the refrigerator in case you change your mind." This statement is assertive, confident, and reasonable, but not threatening or punishing. It is merely recognition that the child has choices about his own body, and the adult has choices and responsibilities about what foods are healthy and appropriate to offer.

It is never acceptable to say, for example, "If you don't come with me this instant, I will leave you here in the store by yourself." This is an idle threat that leaves us only two options: lose credibility or what? Abandon the child? Our motto should be, "Say what you mean, and mean what you say."

> The drops of rain make a hole in the stone not by violence but by oft falling.
> —*Lucretius, Roman poet and philosopher (ca. 99 B.C.–ca. 55 B.C.)*

10-4f Provide Persistent Follow-Up

There is no magic wand or bag of tricks in positive child guidance, only persistence, persistence, persistence. When we persevere in firm, assertive, respectful, and caring discipline, we will surely see positive results in the children we care for and teach. Children may be very persistent in their patterns of misbehavior. We, however, must be even more persistent in our supervision and follow-up.

The consistency of small but persistent nudges toward appropriate behavior is far more effective than erratic and inconsistent explosions of anger, harsh punishments, or intimidating threats. A gentle, rippling stream etches deep patterns in solid rock. Pounding on rocks with sledge hammers changes the shape of the rocks but risks a lot of damage in the process.

10-4g Emphasize Unconditional Caring and Affection

Unconditional caring, the giving of affection without any strings attached, is the foundation on which good discipline is built. Unconditional caring lets children know that they do not have to perform or achieve or submit to be loved and respected. We may disagree with things they do and work hard to change them, but we will still love and care for them. We should create an environment that lets children know in ways they can understand that they are valued (Bardige & Segal, 2005; Ciaramicoli & Ketcham, 2000; Honig, 2000).

10-4h Maintain and Express Confidence That a Problem Will Be Resolved

Guiding children can be frustrating and distressing at times. We look at our children and shake our heads, wondering whether they will ever gain self-control and self-discipline. We must, however, firmly maintain and express confidence that specific problems will be resolved and our children will learn to behave appropriately, at least most of the time. Our confidence will strengthen children and convince them that control over their own behavior is a reachable goal.

10-4i Protect Children's Dignity and Privacy

When positive but assertive disciplinary measures are necessary, children should be afforded the dignity of being talked to in private. They are humiliated by being corrected in front of their friends, or even in front of other adults. We should refrain from discussing, in front of a child, all the careless, immature, and improper things the child might have done. We should refrain from talking and laughing about the child's past mistakes. Most of all, we should treat children the way we like to be treated—with dignity and respect.

10-4j Be Willing to Start Over to Forgive and Forget

In positive child guidance, adults should do the best they know how to do and then never look back. Worrying about the past, carrying grudges, or keeping mental lists of past misdeeds all undermine positive child guidance. For young children, every day is a new day. No matter what happened yesterday, today can be a good, successful day. When children know that adults are willing to forgive and forget, they will be more compliant and more willing to admit it when they know they are wrong. Forgiveness encourages honesty in children and motivates them to try harder to meet adult expectations.

Summary

- Children are not helped by intrusive and overwhelming attempts to change too much of their behavior at one time: We do well to focus our guidance on priorities.
- Children can be helped to resolve their own disagreements, but they must know that we will reliably stop unacceptable, hurtful behavior.
- We can greatly assist the development of self-control in children by staying focused on the reality of the situation rather than on adult feelings that are not relevant.
- Removing a child from the scene of a conflict allows a cooling-off period.
- Children need to know exactly what is expected of them.

- Children need many opportunities to hear a rule repeated before knowledge of that rule has fully reached their long-term memory.
- Children older than 3 years learn the difference among toys, tools, and weapons.
- To be consistent, we should make very sure that a child's behavior is not laughed at on one occasion and reprimanded on another.
- Explaining potential consequences is not the same as bribing, intimidating, or giving idle threats.
- Unconditional caring, the giving of affection without any strings attached, is the foundation on which good discipline is built.

Key Terms

age-typical behavior
prevention techniques
quick response

redirection
replaces
sexual harassment

Student Activities

1. Use your critical thinking skills to process what you've read in this and previous chapters:
   a. Create one DAP interaction to help an 18-month-old grasp our "Be safe" rule.
   b. Create one DAP interaction to help a 5-year-old remember to "Be respectful."
   c. Create one DAP interaction to help a fourth-grader remember to "Be responsible."

2. Go to the library, search online, and visit schools and/or child care centers to review children's books on topics related to feelings, anger, biting, and children's bodies:
   a. List your favorites that would be helpful for bibliotherapy.
   b. Did you find books that you thought were inappropriate for children?

3. Positive guidance requires ongoing change, in us, as well as in the child:
   a. List one thing you view differently than you did when you began studying this textbook.
   b. Describe one view you held when you began studying this textbook that you believe even more strongly now.

Related Resources

Readings

Brooks, R., & S. Goldstein. (2002). *Raising resilient children: Fostering strength, hope and optimism in your child*. New York: McGraw-Hill.

Harris, B. (2004). *When your kids push your buttons: And what you can do about it*. New York: Grand Central Publishing.

Websites

Parenting from Boys Town   This site offered by Boys Town offers parenting guides and an Ask an Expert section.

Parenting Center: Parenting Tips and Advice from WebMD   Here you'll find parenting tips and informative information including expert parenting advice for each age and stage of children's development.

11 Mistaken Goals, Motivation, and Mindfulness

naeyc Standards

The following NAEYC Standards are addressed in this chapter

Standard 4   Using Developmentally Effective Approaches to Connect with Children and Families

4a Understanding positive relationships and supportive interactions as the foundation of their [your] work with children

4b Knowing and understanding effective strategies and tools for early education

4c Using a broad repertoire of developmentally appropriate teaching/learning approaches

4d Reflecting on their own practice to promote positive outcomes for each child

Photo courtesy of the Preschool at Claremont United Methodist Church

Objectives

After reading this chapter, you should be able to do the following:

11-1 List mistaken goals that cause children's inappropriate behavior.

11-2 Describe signs of child abuse and neglect.

11-3 Generate adult coping strategies.

11-4 Differentiate punishment and positive guidance.

11-5 Explain when and how children should accept consequences of behavior.

11-6 Summarize Maslow's theory of motivation.

11-7 Give examples of situations in which external reinforcement would be effective.

11-8 Demonstrate strategies for expanding children's social–emotional intelligence.

11-9 Plan activities to help children move toward mindfulness.

11-1 Can Misbehavior Be Caused by Mistaken Goals?

Adler (1931), a colleague of Freud, theorized that sometimes an inadequate sense of self-worth causes children to adopt inappropriate behavior as a means to exert control and feel more competent. Dreikurs and colleagues (2004) refined Adler's theory, pulling together for us an approach based on four **mistaken goals** that they considered the root of troubling behavior. He theorized that persistent, chronic misbehavior is based on children's need to

1. Get attention
2. Get a sense of control
3. Get revenge for their own perceived hurts
4. Get away from frightening or painful situations

Each of these four mistaken goals is directed toward getting an emotional need met. Unfortunately, each behavior may seem to make the child feel a little better temporarily, but it actually compounds his emotional problem in the long run. The child's inappropriate behavior increases the negativity in his environment, which in turn increases his emotional neediness and the likelihood of his behaving more and more inappropriately in the future. His mistaken behavior increases the negative cycle that continues to cause him to behave more inappropriately. This pushes him away from others and makes others feel even more unhappy with him.

mistaken goals
The motivation that Dreikurs theorized caused children to behave inappropriately. The mistaken logic that causes children to misbehave to get attention from others, gain a sense of control, get revenge for their own perceived hurts, and remove themselves from frightening or painful situations.

Unfortunately, we sometimes respond in a way that is *opposite* to the response this child needs. For example, we are tempted to ignore the child who is acting out to get attention, but that will cause her to have even more need to act out. We are tempted to get into an angry power struggle with the controlling child, "to show her who's boss," but this makes her feel even more powerless and out of control.

We are tempted to inflict pain on the aggressive child who harms another child, but hurtful aggression on our part will make the child even more resolved to get revenge. And, sadly, we are tempted to shrug our shoulders and give up on the withdrawn child who hides under a table, twisting her hair or bumping her head on the wall, but our abandonment only allows her to sink deeper and deeper into isolation.

 To bring about real change, we directly address the needs causing persistent patterns of unproductive behavior. Our job is to help the child learn appropriate methods to get her emotional needs met. See Positive Focus 11.1.

11-1a Mistaken Goal Number One: Attention-Seeking Behavior

Children who are deprived of opportunities to gain status through useful contributions often seek attention by acting helpless, silly, bratty, artificially charming, lazy, inept, or obnoxious.

Positive Focus 11.1 Addressing Emotional Causes of Misbehavior

To improve behavior, we develop strategies to help the child feel

- Accepted and valued
- Influential in his environment
- Confident of respectful and fair treatment
- Optimistic that he can achieve expectations

When the child's emotional needs are met, the child will no longer need to rely on inappropriate behavior for emotional survival. At that point we can guide the child to begin breaking nonfunctional habit patterns. We can teach the child effective ways to get along with others.

Dreikurs recommends that children 5 to 12 years old be talked to in a caring, noncritical way at a relaxed time (not during a time of conflict). The child can be engaged in conversation that explores the motives for her nonproductive behavior; she can be tactfully asked any of the following questions that seem relevant:

- I wonder if you feel you need more attention?
- I wonder if you feel you need to have more control?
- I wonder if you have felt so hurt by others that you are feeling a need to hurt back?
- I wonder if you feel so overwhelmed you just want to be left alone?

If the child is able to help us understand her needs better, we can go right to the heart of the matter. If attention is the goal of the misbehavior, we can make sure she gets abundant attention, not as a reward or reinforcement, just as pleasant shared time. We can make sure we don't inadvertently reinforce unproductive behavior by giving attention in response to poor behavior.

If revenge is the goal, we can assist the child in making friends and experiencing successful accomplishments. If solitude is the goal, we must find some way to connect with the child. We can nudge the child to join activities, offer encouragement, suggest medical assessment, and explore ways to help the child feel worthwhile.

Clinging, Feigning Ineptness

Clingy children feel comfortable and loved only when they are being fussed over and cared for. They long for the adult to cuddle them and to rescue them from their responsibilities. We must focus on helping the child feel a stronger sense of independence.

Artificial Charm, Competitiveness

Children who are insecure in their sense of belonging go out on a limb to fit in. The child may find a role to play or a competition to win. His Mr. Nice Guy role may vanish instantly, however, whenever he feels threatened by attention directed toward someone else. He may turn from charmer to cold competitor in a split second. We can focus on developing the child's sense of security and self-esteem by giving sincere affection and encouragement at appropriate times. We also need to set firm limits and help the child know that he is loved for himself, not for his fake charm.

Clowning, Acting Out, Silliness

Children use clowning, acting out, and silliness to get attention not only from adults but also from other children. Some children seem to feel sure that they are loved and appreciated only when they are at the center of attention with everyone looking at them and either laughing or chiding. Children may be especially likely to get silly when they feel embarrassed or pushed into a corner. For some children, being a clown is a way of saving face and protecting damaged self-esteem.

We need to allow clowning children to save their dignity. They should be helped privately and respectfully. We will give them opportunities for responsibility and leadership in positive settings as well as chances to entertain others in appropriate ways. For example, a child might be encouraged to plan a skit for classmates, be chosen to pass out napkins or refreshments during a celebration, or be allowed to sing, dance, or act out a story at group time.

Laziness, Compulsiveness, Obnoxiousness

Lazy, compulsive, or obnoxious behaviors may be a child's unconscious way of forcing adults to pay attention. They also signal a lack of self-esteem in the child. The child labeled as lazy may receive negative attention when adults nag, take over the child's responsibilities, or insist that other children help or do the child's work for her. Children who overeat, bite their nails, tease, or purposely disgust other children and adults are also giving strong indications that they do not feel good about themselves.

Persistent, assertive, and loving guidance will build the child's respect for herself by helping her know that the adult cares deeply enough to become actively involved in redirecting her inappropriate behaviors. For example, a child who persists in running around the playground terrifying other children with bugs and worms could be firmly redirected from poking the creatures in others' faces to constructing a terrarium for the science center.

Photo courtesy of the Preschool at Claremont United Methodist Church

We will give children opportunities for positive leadership so they can get attention from others in appropriate ways. We can help this child build a terrarium for the science center so he can proudly share his earthworm.

11-1b Mistaken Goal Number Two: Controlling Behavior

Children who do not feel they are really accepted by their family or social group may seek power by acting bossy, rebellious, stubborn, vengeful, or disobedient.

Manipulativeness, Vengefulness

Being **manipulative** usually involves trying to trick someone into doing something that she really does not want to do. Sometimes we improperly set an example for this behavior in our attempts to gain control over the children's behavior. We unfortunately tell

manipulative
Using clever or devious ways to control or influence another person into doing something that he or she may not want to do. (Be aware that *manipulative*, when used by early educators as a noun, refers to small objects that are used for fine-motor development. The fingers manipulate the objects or move them around.)

children things such as "Eat your bread crusts because they will make your hair curly." It is a typical age-appropriate behavior for preschool children to try to influence their friends, as in "Give me your toy and I'll be your best friend forever." They don't really understand that they can't keep that promise. Sometimes, however, manipulativeness becomes excessive and vengeful as children struggle to gain control of the children and adults around them.

Adults need to define clear limits and help children become aware of the feelings and reactions of those around them. Adults can recognize and verbalize feelings. For example, "Mia, I know you really want Alvie's doll, but the doll belongs to Alvie. Alvie doesn't like to play with you when you try to take her doll. You may choose a different toy, or you may play in a different area."

Pouting, Stubbornness

Children who want control but fail to get their way with others may react by pouting, stubbornly refusing to participate, or causing a scene. The toddler who wants (but does not get) ice cream for dinner, for example, may push his plate off the high-chair tray, kick his feet, scream, shake his head, and generally refuse to have anything to do with carrots and roast beef.

Parents and early educators do no favor either by giving in to the toddler (and thus encouraging his controlling behavior) or by forcing nutritious food on him against his will. They can, however, avoid a power struggle by simply removing the toddler from the high chair and allowing him to express his anger. The adults can express sincere empathy but allow the child to be stubborn without showing a great deal of attention or concern.

For example, the adult may say, "It's okay to cry. When you feel better, your dinner is right here waiting for you." When the child has finished screaming, he may or may not want dinner. Either way, he will not starve before the next meal. The child's need for a sense of control can be met by allowing him to choose when he is ready to eat, not by letting him succeed in demanding things that are not in his best interest. Between the lines, the adult is saying, "You may make your own choices—within reasonable limits—but you must also deal with the consequences of your choices."

Bullying, Rebelling

Some children, when they fail to gain control by other means, resort to bullying or rebelling. They gain control over smaller children by overwhelming them physically with their size and strength. Grown-ups are not usually so easy for a small child to bully.

Each day we find ways to build positive, caring relationships with children so each child feels a strong sense of belonging.

Photo courtesy of the Preschool at Claremont United Methodist Church

A child, consequently, might be tempted to control adults by being so rebellious, so out of control that adults feel totally helpless. It is important, however, that adults not allow themselves to lapse into feelings of inadequacy. The child needs strong, reliable adult support to succeed in giving up inappropriate behaviors and forming new habits.

It is also essential for adults to avoid power struggles with the bullying or rebelling child. Head-to-head confrontation will trigger an increase in angry rebellion and will not solve the problem. Angry behavior on our part further establishes a role model for undesirable behavior. Instead, we must find ways to build a positive relationship with the child and help the child feel a sense of belonging. Clear limits are essential, but the most important step is for the child to discover that she is loved, respected, and appreciated (Stutzman Amstutz & Mullet, 2005). See Positive Focus 11.2.

11-1c Mistaken Goal Number Three: Disruptive Behavior

Children who feel pushed down may have abandoned the struggle for power and now resort to retaliation. They seek revenge by hurting others the way they feel they have been hurt. They may injure peers, destroy property, express contempt, distrust others, and defy authority.

Destructiveness, Aggressiveness

Children whose self-esteem is lacking may develop destructive and aggressive habit patterns. These behaviors tell us that the child feels a sense of hopelessness. She may believe that she has already been rejected by others so that it really does not matter what she does; nobody will like her no matter how she behaves. These feelings discourage her from developing self-control over her impulses.

The destructive or aggressive child must know that she will be stopped and that others' rights will be protected. In an extreme situation, we may have no choice but to restrain a child to prevent her from harming herself or others. If we feel helpless and intimidated by a child, we do great harm to that child by allowing her to bite, kick, shove, pinch, or scratch other children and destroy shared toys. But more importantly, in allowing the child's destructive behavior, we deny her the confidence of knowing there is a strong adult in charge who will keep everyone safe. Every child deserves that. See Positive Focus 11.3.

In dealing with a very difficult child, behavior modification may help regain a manageable relationship with the child, if the child agrees to this. A reinforcer (token reward) must be selected that is meaningful and desirable to the child; the specific desired behavior goal must be identified in concrete terms; and a schedule of when, how,

> Even a little rabbit will bite when it feels cornered.
>
> —*Chinese Proverb*

and under what circumstances the reinforcement will be given should be planned with the child. Reinforcement must always be immediate. As the child makes little steps of progress toward the desired behavior, he is instantly reinforced with a reward (such as a sticker, a plastic disk, or checks on a chart) that can be exchanged at a set number for special privileges or treats.

Behavior modification will be most successful (especially with an older child) if he has enthusiastically agreed to participate in the plan. If the child likes and respects the adult and really wants to change, he may be surprisingly willing to participate in a voluntary behavior modification plan, at least during the periods in which he is calm and logical. During the entire process of behavior modification, the child must be helped toward eventual weaning from external reinforcement and toward increasing internal control.

The child can be told from the very beginning, "Changing habits is very, very hard for anyone! These little prizes are just to help you get started, to help you remember not to lose your temper. After a while you can't rely on prizes anymore. You have to do it because it is the right thing. You can't go around in life losing your temper. Right? Your best prize of all will be learning how to have fun with your friends without having fights."

extrinsic motivation
Performance of an activity to attain an outcome. Common outcomes are rewards (money, grades) for showing the desired behavior, and the threat of punishment following misbehavior. Competition is in an extrinsic motivator, because the performer desires to win and to beat others.

intrinsic motivation
A driving force that comes from internal interest, desire, or enjoyment rather than from external pressures or to get a reward.

BrainFacts

What Can We Learn from Neuroscience?

Intrinsic Motivation versus Extrinsic Motivation
Intrinsic and **extrinsic motivation** can both impact behavior, but in different ways.

- Although neuroscientists don't fully understand human motivation yet, we do know our intrinsic motivation has deep roots. Our survival depends on our powerful impulse to optimize our well-being by avoiding physical discomfort, seeking pleasure, conserving energy, and learning how to adapt to our surroundings, (Bechara & Damasiom, 2005).

- Inborn impulses motivate us to eat, sleep, procreate, avoid danger, and adapt. I may decide to create a garden just because I enjoy the pleasure of doing the activity. I am intrinsically motived to garden (Ryan & Edward, 2000).

- The other primary reason we act is because we expect our action will bring satisfying external rewards. For instance, I may garden to simply avoid being criticized by my neighbors or to win their admiration (Pritchard & Ashwood, 2008; Reeve, 2006; Wigfield, Guthrie, Tonks, & Perencevich, 2004).

- In intrinsic motivation, people decide that they want to engage in activities based on the presence of spontaneous self-satisfactions (fun, personal interest, sense of accomplishment, personal value, or just feeling good). In extrinsic motivation people decide that they want to engage in activities based on socially acquired values (money, gold star, candy, extra credit, grade, or prize) (Lepper, Greene, & Nisbet, 1973; Steel & König, 2006).

- Research shows that we make relatively quick "gut felt" decisions about intrinsic reasons for acting. You invite me to work on a project where we will learn about dinosaurs. I love dinosaurs so I instantly raise my hand. However, we make very calculated cost–benefit decisions about extrinsic reasons for acting. Is the reward is attractive enough to be worth my effort? If you are going to give me a gold star for finishing my assignment, I may think about how much I really want this star compared with how intrinsically rewarding it is to impress my friends by chatting (Bechara & Damasio, 2005; Bray, Shimojo, & O'Doherty, 2010; Xiang, McBride, & Guan, 2004).

- Intrinsic motivation is produced by the presence of positive feelings, which come from self-satisfactions (Deci & Ryan, 2011), whereas extrinsic motivation is produced by the culturally learned rewards the activity is expected to generate (Bray, Shimojo, & O'Doherty, 2010).

- Research shows that external rewards can undermine intrinsic motivation. Rewards can backfire and decrease interest in doing tasks. We can't entirely dismiss extrinsic motivation because it has some important uses, especially in motivating children who have significant learning differences. External rewards are also very useful when an action is routine or has become an unwanted habit. But when it comes to creative tasks, extrinsic motivation often destroys interest in the task (Murayama et al., 2010; Murayama & Kitagami, 2014).

- Clearly, the best way to motivate young children is to create conditions that support their intrinsic motivation. And in early childhood this means simply making sure *not to get in the way* of how children are naturally motivated.

- Children come into the world with extremely limited ability to manage their surroundings—they can't move around, they can't communicate except with crying, they don't know much at all about their physical and social surroundings. Babies and young children have the highest intrinsic motivation they will ever have in their lives to develop skills and learn how to adapt to their world. Our job is to create a safe, challenging environment (DAP) in which they can explore the physical world, practice emerging skills, and learn how to interact with others (Corpus, McClintic-Gilbert, & Hayenga, 2009; Haimovitz, Wormington, & Corpus, 2011; Hayenga & Corpus, 2010; Lepper, Corpus, & Iyengar, 2005).

- Compared to extrinsic motivation, intrinsic motivation is associated with strong academic performance. Research suggests that a high ratio of intrinsic to extrinsic motivation gives the most benefits, particularly for younger children. Unfortunately, children tend to lose intrinsic motivation as they progress through the elementary and middle school years (Murayama et al., 2010; Deci & Ryan, 2011).

- Daniel Pink (2009) outlined the seven deadly flaws of using rewards and punishments to motivate people. Rewards and punishments can do the following:
  - They can extinguish intrinsic motivation.
  - They can diminish performance.
  - They can crush creativity.
  - They can encourage cheating, shortcuts, and unethical behavior.
  - They can become addictive.
  - They can foster short-term thinking.

Contempt, Mistrust

Contempt and mistrust in children sadden and dismay us. The child filled with contempt has so much mistrust of others that she seems to despise everyone. We may find it necessary to backtrack and work on the basic development of trust that most children develop as babies. Just as a first grader who lacked visual discrimination would need remedial work before she could learn to read, the child who feels contempt must relearn the essential lesson of infancy—to trust others, to believe that grown-ups are reliable, predictable, and accepting—before she can learn to behave appropriately.

A child who feels that she has received a great deal of hurt and unfair treatment in her life will not easily place trust in adults. We will try to connect with this child to earn that trust. Our open-mindedness, attentiveness, and active listening open the door to a trusting interaction. We can also support the development of trust in the child by modeling trust. We can look for opportunities to place our trust in the mistrustful child.

Fits of Anger, Tantrums, Defiance

Children who regularly indulge in fits of anger, tantrums, or defiance need to know we are not cowed by this behavior, and also that we will not explode into our own anger. We must take steps to build a cooperative relationship with the defiant child during calm times.

Create a positive, calm environment. A well-planned, orderly, developmentally appropriate environment sets the stage for calm behavior. Additionally, calm, supportive adults provide excellent role models for children. Strictly limit television, movies, and other electronic stimulation to infrequent experiences that are age appropriate and feature positive behavior. Television, movies, and electronic entertainment are not appropriate for children under 3, even if they seem to be mesmerized by it. Research indicates that very young children's brains and bodies need active, hands-on exploration and human interaction rather than electronic stimulation (Christakis & Garrison, 2009; Christakis, Zimmerman, & Garrison, 2006; Rideout & Hamel, 2006; Zimmerman & Christakis, 2007; Zimmerman, Christakis, & Meltzoff, 2007).

We can help a child let go of explosive behaviors by responding matter-of-factly but steadfastly to the child's eruptions. We may be forced to remove the child, but we can be very sure the child recognizes that there is no anger or punitiveness in those actions—we are firm and caring.

The unusually challenging child needs to learn that defiant tantrums are a waste of time because they have no effect. The child's tantrums will not bring rewards from the adult, and his tantrums will not succeed in causing the adult to lose her temper. Because persistently disruptive behavior is unconsciously intended to hurt others, the child may be happy to see the adult frustrated, angry, and helpless. When we stay calm, the tantrum has no reward, absolutely no reinforcement. Young children know if we are just putting on an act. Out loud we can say, "I don't like tantrums, but I do care very much for you. When you are finished crying we can talk about what is making you feel so unhappy."

No adult wants to be spit at or see a child spit on others, but our own angry outburst will make the child's problem worse, not better. Instead, we might say, "If you need to spit, you may spit in the sink. Spitting on people makes them feel angry, and it could get germs on them. Spitting in the sink is okay. Please spit at the sink if you would like to spit some more. Thank you."

Photo courtesy of the Preschool at Claremont United Methodist Church

Young children's brains and bodies need active, hands-on exploration and human interaction rather than electronic stimulation. Because children are typically exposed to excessive hours of TV, we should avoid adding more. Television is not developmentally appropriate for children under 3 years of age.

Rude Language

Also, we must avoid overreacting to what we in a school environment would call rude language or inappropriate language for school. We want to teach socially appropriate alternatives for the school setting. Children need to express their strong feelings. Their strong feelings aren't wrong or bad. Children just need to know how to express feelings in a way appropriate to different cultural settings.

The child may have adopted rude language from his home environment, television, music, and other cultural sources. We shouldn't be judgmental about those cultural settings or even about the rude language—it is a part of culture. However, rude language is not appropriate for the school setting. We will need to enlist the child's cooperation to change what may already be a deeply engrained habit. We will also have to help him find a new method to express his feelings effectively that fits in with the culture of school (Greene, 2001).

> **11-1d Mistaken Goal Number Four: Withdrawn, Passive Behavior**
>
> Children who become accustomed to passive behavior because of nonsupportive backgrounds may be discouraged. They may have given up hope and expect only failure and defeat. They may seek only to be left alone. They may be immobilized by feelings of inadequacy.

Cyclical Self-Stimulation

When a child is overwhelmed by fear, stress, and anxiety, she may withdraw into her own little world. Although most children do things to make themselves feel better from time to time, the withdrawn child may sink into constant self-stimulation. This pattern is referred to as cyclical, because the child repeats the behavior cycle over and over. The cycle may consist of excessive thumb-sucking, nail-biting, hair-twisting, overeating, head-banging, or any number of other self-stimulating actions.

We frequently find these behaviors embarrassing and may focus on forcing the child to end the behavior without addressing the cause of the behavior. These behaviors tell us the child is feeling too stressed and overwhelmed to participate in activities. By focusing on reducing stress in the child's life and drawing the child out into pleasurable, nonthreatening activities, the child may be eased into more active involvement with things and people around her (Nelson et al., 2005).

Rejection of Social Interaction

The severely withdrawn child may avoid eye contact, refuse to talk or play, and stay apart from others most of the time. We may mistakenly focus all of our guidance efforts on children whose inappropriate behaviors are forceful and annoying. We may view the child who is a loner as a quiet child who never bothers anyone. In reality, the child who is a loner may be more at risk emotionally than the difficult, loud, aggressive child. Self-esteem, trust, and a sense of belonging are all essential to building connections with the child who seems to have no interest in others. Rejection of social interaction is a very frightening and serious state for a child to be in. The child needs screening, intervention, and help.

Internalization of Stress

Inhibited children sometimes turn all their bad feelings inward. Fear, anger, and frustration are not expressed; they are just held inside, and they may chip away at the child's sense of competence and self-worth. These children need opportunities to learn that they do not have to be perfect, it is okay to disagree, and they have a right to be who they are. As they develop stronger self-esteem, they will feel more comfortable expressing their feelings and actively standing up for themselves.

Display of Ineptness and Hopelessness

Feelings of depression are not the exclusive territory of adolescents and adults. Even young children can show signs of depression. Overwhelming disruption in the child's daily life may contribute to her listlessness and display of ineptness and hopelessness.

These children do not involve themselves in spontaneous play or creative expression. They seem to have no energy. They may sleep too much or too little. They are clearly at risk and need special guidance to rebuild self-esteem and give them the spark of hope that fuels healthy curiosity, spontaneous play, and active involvement with others. A child who seems depressed should be referred for medical screening.

11-2 Can Behavioral Problems Indicate Child Abuse or Neglect?

A serious potential cause of physical, developmental, or behavioral problems may be the presence of abuse or neglect in a child's life. Although virtually any normally developing child can experience a rare incidence of inappropriate treatment, children who lead lives filled with violence or neglect are profoundly affected by that experience. The consequences of maltreatment are far reaching and affect the whole child—intellectually, physically, socially, and emotionally (Brophy, 2007; Douglas & Finkelhor, 2005; Vesneski, 2009; Whittaker, 2009).

Calmly responding in a positive and supportive way to children's day-to-day crises can be emotionally draining. We must find ways to unwind and recharge our batteries so that we can stay relaxed, enthusiastic, and happy.

11-2a How Can Child Abuse Fatalities Be Prevented?

We can help prevent child abuse deaths by fully supporting our child protective services agencies. Child abuse is against the law. Every state has a designated agency that is mandated by federal law to receive and to investigate reports of suspected child abuse and neglect. Reporting is a means of getting help for a child and family, not just a way to stop an abuser. You do not need to know that child abuse has occurred. That is up to the investigator to determine. To report a suspected case of child abuse, you should notify the designated agency in the state where the child lives. The agency is listed in the telephone directory. If you have difficulty finding the agency in your community, call your local police department or call the ChildHelp USA/IOF Foresters National Child Abuse Hotline, 1-800-422-4453 (4-A-CHILD), which keeps national listings of child protective service agencies. See Positive Focus 11.4.

Abused and neglected children's behaviors tend toward extremes. There seems to be no happy middle ground for these children. They may be diagnosed as learning disabled, or they may be compulsive overachievers. They may be hyperactive or lethargic. They may be physically inept and weak, or they may be street-smart daredevils. They may cling to others or shun social interaction. They may appear dirty and unkempt or spotlessly scrubbed. They may defy authority or compulsively try to please everyone at all times. They may always play the role of victim or brutally victimize others. The one characteristic that is shared by all abused and neglected children is their stunted sense of self. They do not have the positive feeling of self-worth that comes with self-esteem (U.S. Department of Health and Human Services, Administration on Children, Youth, and Families, 2007).

Positive Focus 11.4 Child Abuse Fatalities

- Each day in the United States, more than four children die of child abuse.
- About 70 percent of the children who die are younger than 4 years.
- Many who die are babies younger than 1 year.
- Actual deaths of babies and children up to age 4 that are attributable to abuse or neglect are believed to be twice as high as reported in death records.

(U.S. Department of Health and Human Services, 2013).

11-3 Meeting Adult Needs

Children definitely have needs, but we have needs too. Caring for children is demanding, exhilarating, frustrating, and rewarding, but it is also exhausting. We can best care for children if our own social, emotional, physical, and intellectual needs have been met. We must set aside time for our own rest and recreation, and we must be able to admit to ourselves at times that we are not able to deal with children in a positive and productive manner. If children are dealt with in a caring and respectful manner most of the time, they will be likely to cope well and respect our own need when we say, "I'm too frustrated and angry to talk about this right now. I just want to be alone for a few minutes."

We can be patient and reasonable with ourselves, recognizing that we, too, are imperfect. It is easy to sit down and think carefully about an ideal response to a misbehaving child, but it is not so easy to respond perfectly when the response is instantaneous and in the heat of conflict with that child. It is important for us to be supportive, calm, respectful, and consistent. We need to step back and give ourselves a moment when we need to.

> Ever tried? Ever failed? No matter. Try again. Fail again. Fail better.
>
> —Samuel Beckett

When we attempt to change our ways of dealing with children, we go through the same stages of learning that children go through when they learn new behaviors. For example, a toddler who has no concept of toileting will simply show no awareness when she makes a puddle on the floor. When she has developed recognition of the desired behavior but lacks practice carrying it out, she will make a puddle, look down, smile sweetly, and say, "Go potty!" Of course, it will be too late to go to the potty then. Finally, when she has fully developed both the awareness and the skill to carry out the new behavior, she will notice the sensation of a full bladder and do what needs to be done to successfully use the toilet. See Figure 11.1.

We go through that same process. At first, we may be totally unaware of the negative, destructive, and hurtful things we say or do with youngsters in the name of disciplining them. As we discover more productive and effective ways to guide them, we begin, for the first time, to notice ourselves saying or doing negative things. We feel frustration because we seem to become aware of these actions only after we have done them. We become aware of our inappropriate actions, but only after it is too late. Gradually, however, with persistence and practice, we are able to anticipate and respond more skillfully and appropriately—before we have done wrong. Eventually, our new behaviors become so natural to us that we can behave in the new way with almost no thought or effort. See Positive Focus 11.5.

FIGURE 11.1

Keep Your Life in Balance

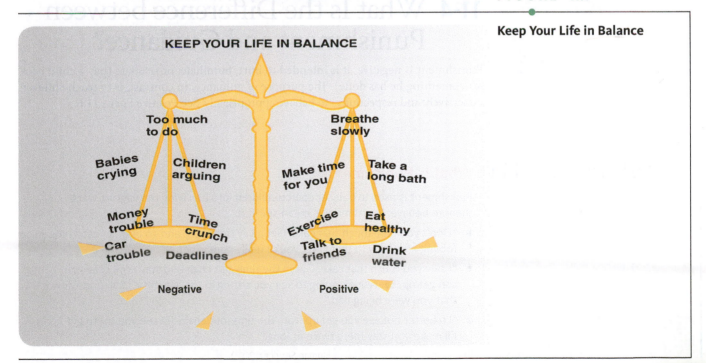

Positive child guidance is a tool that can be used to help us teach young children the skills they need to lead productive, happy lives (Thompson et al., 2001).

11-4 What Is the Difference between Punishment and Guidance?

Punishment is negative. It is intended to hurt, humiliate, or retaliate (pay a child back for something he has done). The purpose of guidance, in contrast, is to teach children (assertively and respectfully) to behave appropriately. See Positive Focus 11.6.

In this photograph the boy on the right holds a toy in an assertive stance as the boy on his left leans toward him anxiously. Two children at the outer edges are listening and watching. All four children will learn a positive lesson in appropriate behavior as this teacher assures a peaceful resolution.

At this point, you might respond by saying, "Those lists are fine, but when Devin is completely out of control and pushes over the block shelf on purpose, I'm furious. I don't care about enhancing his self-image, I just feel like taking all his privileges away and making him sit in time out until he's 20!"

Actually, Devin's infuriating behavior gives us an excellent opportunity to put positive child guidance into practice. We can show Devin, through our own behavior, that feeling angry is natural and normal but that hurting, humiliating, or belittling others is not okay.

Socially accepted guidelines for appropriate behavior do not apply only to children—they apply to all of us. Our first step is to interrupt the unacceptable behavior. Then we use active listening to see if we can understand what feelings are causing Devin's behaviors. There may be something we can do to help solve underlying problems. Having Devin participate in picking up the shelf and working with him to assure that the blocks are all put back properly is the next step. We may want to redirect Devin to a different activity away from the block area to give him a fresh start. Our attitude is optimistic and assertive rather than mean-spirited or punitive. Our focus is on helping him succeed in behaving appropriately as he moves back into class activities.

"Please Wear This Dress!"

The day Minh Hoa Thi Nguyen started child care, both her mother and father took the morning off work to take her to school to make sure that she made a good transition into the early childhood program. The parents are extremely successful businesspeople. They had studied all their options and put Minh's name on the waiting list for Apple Valley Child Development Center when she was only a few months old.

Minh had always been cared for by her grandmother while her parents worked. Grandmother has moved away now and it is time for Minh to become part of a group of children. Minh is 3½ years old, but she arrives at Apple Valley carried in her father's arms and sucking on a pacifier. She is a beautiful little girl with wide dark eyes, porcelain skin, and shiny black hair. She is dressed in an expensive pink baby-doll-style dress that makes her look even younger than she is.

Over the first few weeks at Apple Valley, Minh seems to have a good time, although the teachers have to spend a lot of time reminding her to use words instead of just screeching when she needs something. Minh's parents, however, are at their wits' end.

In a meeting with the teachers, the parents report that mornings are a nightmare. Minh's mother says, "Every morning I get a nice dress out for Minh to wear and I say, 'Let's wear this one.' But Minh grabs it and runs down the hall and stuffs it into the laundry hamper. After we go through that for 45 minutes, I try to feed her some breakfast. It is awful! I give her eggs, and she throws them on the floor and says, 'No, I want oatmeal.' Then we go through that for a half hour! We don't believe in spanking and we don't know what to do. Please help us."

After some discussion, it is decided that Minh's favorite teacher, Miss Selena, should be invited to dinner at the Nguyens' house. At 6 p.m. on Thursday evening, Miss Selena arrives. Minh greets her at the door excitedly. The air is fragrant with the spicy Vietnamese stir-fry cooking in the kitchen. Minh says, "Miss Selena, come see my room!" Miss Selena is startled to discover that Minh's room is a perfectly appointed baby nursery, complete with beautifully decorated crib, a diaper-changing table that is no longer needed, and an adult rocking chair. The curtains and all the furniture are decorated in a frilly fabric that shows pictures of baby objects such as rattles, diapers, and baby bottles.

When the family and Miss Selena sit down to eat, Minh is placed in an infant high chair, even though her legs hang down far below the footrest. Every item of food Mr. and Mrs. Nguyen put on the high-chair tray in front of Minh is refused. She refuses to drink any milk. As soon as the dishes are cleared away, Minh announces that she is hungry; Mr. Minh makes her a peanut butter sandwich. Before she even takes one bite, Minh throws the sandwich on the floor and demands an apple. She takes one bite of the apple and throws it on the floor. Her parents look embarrassed and helpless. They look at Miss Selena and say, "What are we supposed to do?" Wisely, Miss Selena says, "Let's all meet tomorrow at school to see if we can figure this out."

As the adults sit down the next day, it is obvious that the Nguyens love their daughter and want only the best for her. But it is also obvious that they are frustrated and overwhelmed by her behavior. Miss Selena begins the conversation by thanking the Nguyens for allowing her into their home and for the lovely dinner. Then she says, "Minh is 3½. I was puzzled that she still needs a crib and a high chair." The Nguyens are surprised. "Well, we waited until we were a little older to have a child. We are both so involved in our careers that we haven't spent a lot of time around friends with babies or children. I guess it just didn't dawn on us that maybe she was outgrowing those things."

"I'm wondering," said Miss Selena, "if Minh is trying to gain control because she doesn't feel that she is completely accepted as a full-fledged, responsible member of the family. I'm wondering if there are some things that you could do at home, and that we could do at school, that would assure her that we all see her as a capable, responsible 3-year-old who really belongs in the family and in the school."

Mr. Nguyen said, "Oh my god! I think my wife and I have been accustomed to being alone for so long, we just weren't prepared for a child. Yes, we'll go today and find new furniture for her room. What should she have?" Miss Selena also talked about giving Minh a voice in the family, giving her three options and letting her make her own choice. But she also talked to the Nguyens about allowing Minh to accept responsibility for her actions. Miss Selena explained how to apply **logical consequences** appropriately.

As the Nguyens began to accept Minh as a responsible child instead of a helpless toddler, Minh's irresistible urge to control interactions with her parents began to fade. As her parents became more consistent in holding her responsible for her actions, she learned to think before she made impulsive choices. Miss Selena continued to provide the parents encouragement and information.

Case Discussion Questions

1. What mistaken goal did Miss Selena refer to? Explain.
2. Describe three things the parents could do to assure that Minh feels accepted, valued, and responsible in the family.
3. List three guidance techniques (other than time out) that you would suggest the Nguyens use when Minh puts her dresses in the laundry hamper or refuses dinner and then demands food immediately afterward.

11-4a Think Twice before You Give Time-Out

Time-out should be used rarely, if at all, in a DAP program. There are many other ways to teach coping skills and encourage appropriate behavior. Many forward-thinking DAP programs use a wide range of positive guidance strategies other than time-out (Crosser, 2002). This text gives you a wealth of positive methods that can be used. It's not that time-out can't be used positively, but in reality it most often is used negatively as a punishment. DAP programs have no place for punishment. We have the power to use time-out in a positive, supportive way. See Positive Focus 11.7 and 11.8.

DAP クラスの授業で態度が悪い
isolation 生徒に外で立っていなさいと言う

11-4b Consider "Time-Away" for Tantrums and Other Troubles

Time in

Time-away is a caring time. Time-away is appropriate even for toddlers. Time-away is simply removing a child from an overwhelming situation to provide a supportive cooling-off time. Time-away gives time for a child to be *with an adult* and aside from the group after he has lost control. A child may need to cry, express anger, talk, think about what happened, regroup, and gain composure. When he has determined how to make amends and prevent further loss of control, he will be ready to return to the group without a loss of face. A toddler needs to be removed from the source of stress and given calming support for as long as needed and then redirected to an appealing activity.

time-away
Removing a child from an overwhelming situation to provide a supportive cooling-off time with an adult present.

The purpose of time-away is *not* to provide consequences or to remove the child from the pleasurable stimulation of the classroom. It is only meant to give the child a

---

Should I Ever Use Time-Out?

Positive Focus 11.7

Time-out is *not* appropriate if

- It is used with a child who is younger than 3 years old
- It feels like a punishment
- It is used routinely or often
- It is used as a threat ("If you do that, you are going to time-out")

TeachSource Digital Download

What Is the Difference between Punishment and Guidance?

Positive Focus 11.8

Punishment	Guidance
Lowers self-esteem	Builds self-esteem
Humiliates	Strengthens character
Degrades	Respects
Hurts (physically or emotionally)	Heals
Angers	Gives hope
Frustrates	Models coping skills
Thwarts efforts	Enables efforts
Embarrasses	Gives confidence
Discourages	Encourages
Belittles	Improves self-image
Socially isolates	Creates trust
Emotionally abandons	Gives emotional support
Denies affection	Is loving and caring

logical consequence
advantage
benefit

TeachSource Digital Download

This child is being guided to make amends for hurting his friend. He is helping put a cool cloth on his friend's head to make it feel better.

little privacy, time to wind down the tantrum, to save face, to be reminded that she is valued and helped to understand how to make amends for a mistake she has made.

"Away" is typically a quiet corner of the classroom. This should be a comfortable, soft place, not a designated chair. The length of a time away is as long as it takes the child to become calm. The adult stays with the child if the child wishes. Some children (including toddlers) want and need to be held, hugged, or patted. Some children despise being touched when they are angry and want to be left alone until they feel ready to talk.

Sometimes children are so upset that they will have to be kept from harming themselves and the environment until they become calm—be as gentle as possible but as firm as necessary. We should speak soothingly and reassuringly during this ordeal. Be alert to the child's movements. You may have to stay calm, firm, and caring while you are protecting yourself from being pinched or bitten. *The child needs assurance that we are calm, in control, and will not allow the child or ourselves to be harmed.*

When the out-of-control toddler or preschooler finally calms, he usually wants to reconnect emotionally with the adult who has patiently helped him through this difficult time. The child may be eager at this point to make amends for whatever he did wrong so he can return to his play. If he is not, he may need to be coaxed gently to make some gesture at making the situation right. If he is not able to do so, we can express optimism that he will soon master the skills needed to behave appropriately.

The child who has had time-away learns that his angry outburst didn't get his needs met. It didn't send us into a tailspin (which can be emotionally rewarding to an angry child). No one gave in to the shrieking. In fact, nothing much happened. The child was just removed from the group so he could cry until he was finished. The angry outburst was anticlimactic because it didn't create any real impact except patient support and a quiet reminder about how to appropriately get needs met: "Remember to use your words next time . . . Say, 'Please don't touch my blocks,' instead of kicking and screaming." This support helps children gradually develop the skills they need to better control their impulses.

Many DAP teaching staff set up a special cozy area with pillows and stuffed animals (or they use their reading area) to be a comfortable time-away place. When a child is frustrated, angry, or needing time to "settle down" emotionally, he is invited to make himself comfortable in the resting place until he feels better and to come out whenever he feels ready. For this child, time-away involves his being able to make an independent choice to go to the resting place and stay there until he cools down and feels ready to rejoin his friends. He has matured past the time-away level where the teacher had to take him away and sit with him while he cooled down. He is now independent enough to manage himself.

11-5 Accepting the Consequences of One's Behavior

Children learn from active involvement in the environment. They learn by watching, listening, experiencing, and, most importantly, by making mistakes. In life, actions are often followed by natural consequences. If I forget to water my potted plant, it will probably die (a natural consequence). If I am regularly late to work, I may lose my job (a logical consequence). In life there are consequences for behavior. I learn that I must behave in certain ways if I want to avoid undesired results and achieve desired goals (Dinkmeyer & McKay, 2007).

natural consequence
An outcome that results from a situation without any external intervention to change or control the conclusion.

logical consequence
An outcome that results from a situation in which adults determine and control the conclusion.

11-5a Natural Consequences

A natural consequence occurs when a child is allowed to learn from a situation without any intervention from adults. This guidance technique is based on the idea that learning appropriate behavior should come from direct experience whenever possible (Dinkmeyer & McKay, 2007; Dreikurs & Grey, 1968).

For example, "If you don't eat your lunch, you may become hungry before snack time." "If you don't put your artwork into your cubby, you may not be able to find it when you are ready to go home." "If you leave your cup of milk on the edge of the table, it may fall off." We must refrain from saying, "I told you so." If the child deals with being covered in milk, copes with the frustration of her lost artwork, and feels her empty, growling stomach, she will soon make the connection between her behavior and natural consequences. We can provide tactful, positive information. "Put your cup here so it will be safe." "Put your coat on the hook so you will know where it is."

Obviously, natural consequences cannot be allowed anytime they present a safety risk, infringe on the rights of others, or threaten damage to the environment. (Be safe! Be respectful! Be responsible!) Experience is a great teacher, but we must be careful not to intervene after the negative consequence has occurred. Nagging, lecturing, or punishing the child destroys the natural learning that takes place and, even worse, may trigger a power struggle.

11-5b Logical Consequences

Although natural consequences involve situations that are allowed to take place without any intervention from us, logical consequences involve our control in selecting and imposing a consequence. The success of a logical consequence is pretty shaky. First, Dinkmeyer and McKay (2007) remind us that a consequence won't work at all unless the consequence is connected to the behavior in a way that makes sense to the child. Second, but more importantly, logical consequences must not be used as thinly veiled punishment. We will use logical consequences only to give children positive opportunities to move forward, make amends, or make right what they may have damaged. See Positive Focus 11.9.

Lecturing ruins the lesson. Patience rules the day here. Don't be shocked if the young child is so taken by the experience of sponging up his spilled milk that he purposely spills more so that he can continue to wipe up spilled milk. Simply redirect

Experiencing reasonable moments of frustration and anxiety is a normal part of learning to solve problems independently. Rushing to protect children from experiencing a moment of discomfort may rob them of the joy of solving their problem independently.

Courtesy of Montessori Country Day School of Houston

Positive Focus 11.9

Examples of Logical Consequences

- The logical consequence of tearing the pages out of a picture book is an opportunity to tape the pages back so friends can share the book.
- The logical consequence of spilling water on the floor is the opportunity to mop the floor with a child-sized mop.
- The logical consequence of coloring on the wall instead of on paper is an opportunity to clean it with a sponge and spray bottle of soapy water.

TeachSource Digital Download

まちがった行動してしたり…(handwritten notes in top margin)
* try to improve their behavior
* support
* not try to judge punishment

the child to more appropriate learning materials with which she can continue to explore sponging and wiping liquid. Remember, learning is a good thing. — logical consequence につながる

rescue
Save from accepting the consequences of one's behavior; someone has intervened to "bail out" the child from the situation he has created.

11-5c Avoid Rescuing Children from the Consequences of Their Own Actions

Sometimes, when we see a child feeling disappointed or frustrated, we may be tempted to **rescue** him from the consequences of his actions. It is not helpful for us to rescue children from the results of their own actions as long as the consequences are reasonable and safe. We would never risk a child being outside in freezing temperatures as a consequence of forgetting a jacket or allow a child to go hungry as a consequence of spilling food. But allowing children to experience safe, reasonable consequences enhances their learning. Mistakes are a critical part of children's learning from interactions with others and with the environment. Our willingness to wait for a moment to allow them to deal with the discomfort of mistakes gives them the opportunity to resolve problems independently. We must step in, however, if there is an infringement of safety, respect, or responsibility ground rules.

> While we are free to choose our actions, we are not free to choose the consequences of our actions.
> —Stephen Covey

Tina, age 7, arrived home after a family outing to a downtown restaurant and exclaimed, "Oh, no! I left my purse in the restaurant!" Her dad fumed and sputtered, "Tina, why are you carrying a purse around anyway? You're only 7 years old! It'll take me a half hour to drive back downtown, and by then the purse will probably have been stolen. You'd lose your head if it wasn't tied down." After yelling at Tina for 20 minutes while she sniffled and made excuses for her behavior, he finally called the restaurant and drove back downtown alone to search for the purse.

Even though Tina's dad scolded her loudly and angrily for a long time, he rescued her from her responsibility. He was the one who made the telephone call, drove all the way back to the restaurant alone, and did the searching. Tina had nothing to do but feel miserable and stupid. Tina's dad might have used positive consequences if the following had happened:

- Tina's dad says, "Tina, I'm sure you feel awful about losing your purse. Let's think about how we can solve this problem."
- Tina and her dad brainstorm together about where her purse might be.
- Tina helps her dad look up the phone number of the restaurant.
- Tina waits while her dad calls the number and finds that the restaurant does have her purse.
- Tina and her dad drive together to get her purse.
- Tina's dad asks, "Tina, is there anything that you learned from this experience?

In the second example, Tina's father guides her to focus on her forgetfulness as the problem, not her father's anger. Her discomfort resulted from her own forgetfulness, not from someone being upset with her. Tina will learn that it is frustrating and inconvenient to lose her possessions—not just because she is trying to appease an angry father. If Tina learns to behave appropriately only as a way to please her father, she may be tempted to behave inappropriately just to annoy him when she is angry with him or feeling rebellious.

11-5d Sometimes Intervening Is Not Rescuing Children

Children come to us wanting to be rescued from all sorts of situations. But sometimes a child's grievance is legitimate. Children have a right to call on someone bigger, stronger, and with more authority when their rights have been violated, just as I have a right to request legal help if my rights have been violated.

(handwritten margin notes, left column):
What is the rule that Adult need to use to decide. Adult need to impose
↓
Observe give a choice to children
もし snack timeに 食べたくなるへ choice
① もしたべたくないなら 食べなくていいよ。でも、みんながおわるまで座っているよね
② もし食べたくなったら 手を洗って 一緒に食べよう
⇓
give a choice
⇓
logical consequence
でも選べない時もある 2択の3が Adult TV を Youtubeでみる
⇓
No choice ダメ!!

If I call a police officer for help because my purse has been stolen, I will feel very upset if the officer responds as follows:

- *"Don't tattle!"*
- *"Don't be so stingy. The thief probably needs the money more than you. You need to share!"*
- *"You got what you deserved. You shouldn't have been carrying a purse that would tempt others."*
- *"Did you tell the purse snatcher that his stealing your purse made you feel angry?"*

We are surprised when we step back and think about what we expect when we want help.

We want to spend most of our time in the caring, supportive role of nurturing adults. We definitely do not want to assume a policing role in our relationship with children. However, we are the authority figure. We are in charge. And we must intervene as the authority figure to ensure that children's basic rights are protected.

When we intervene, we do so respectfully, caringly. We have many guidance strategies to assist children in working out their own problems, if that is at all possible. If it is not possible, we serve as the offending child's self-management helper until she can muster her own self-management.

11-5e Should We Ask Children to Apologize?

It seems very odd that we tell children, "Be honest; always tell the truth," and then require them to "tell so-and-so you're sorry" (never even wondering if they actually *feel* sorry). No child should be asked to say he feels something that he really does not feel. It is more appropriate to simply point out how the other child feels. The offending child may spontaneously give some indication of remorse or regret if he really feels it.

If a child appears to be sorry for something he has done, it may be helpful to say, "Would you like to tell Luke that you're sorry about what happened?" "Would you like me to tell him for you?" It is even more important for us to find some way to help the child make amends to Luke. He will feel good about himself if he has a chance to make things right. We discourage children terribly when we imply to them, "You have made such a mess of things that there is no way you can undo what you've done."

If a child wants to make amends, she can learn to ask the offended child, "Is there something I can do to make things right?" We may need to get involved at first to help children think about different ways they can make amends. See Positive Focus 11.10.

Ways Children Can Make Amends   Positive Focus 11.10

- Ask the friend, "What can I do to help?"
- Say, "I'm sorry," if it is really sincere.
- Get a damp paper towel for a friend to place on his bumped knee.
- Bring the friend a bandage.
- Sit by the friend until the friend feels better.
- Make a homemade card.
- Give a hug (respect the fact that some friends hate hugs).
- Pick up the blocks that were knocked over.
- Ask whether the friend would like to sit at your table.
- Invite the friend to share an activity.

TeachSource Digital Download

11-6 Motivation for Behavior— Maslow's Hierarchy

Abraham Maslow (1943) created a pyramid that shows levels of psychological and physical needs; Maslow used this pyramid to explain his theory of human motivation (see Figure 11.2). He proposed that each underlying level of need in the pyramid must be met before successive levels of need can be addressed. See Positive Focus 11.11.

A child who is hungry will be distracted from playing and learning. Her primary concern will be food. A child who is frightened and insecure will show little interest in making friends or building castles with blocks. A child who feels unloved will not be able to function independently and confidently. In fact, young children will tend to do anything that seems to work to get their needs met. *See the previous section on mistaken goals.* This is important for us to remember because, as early educators, we are hoping for calm, cooperative, and curious children (Franken, 2001; Lyubomirsky, 2008; Lyubomirsky, King, & Diener, 2005; MacDonald & Leary, 2005; Myers, 2009).

FIGURE 11.2

Basic needs must be met before we can strive for higher levels of achievement.

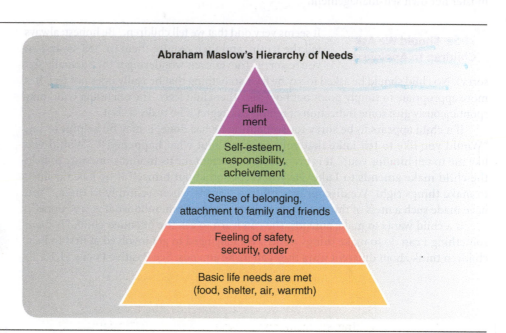

Abraham Maslow's Hierarchy of Needs

- Fulfil-ment
- Self-esteem, responsibility, acheivement
- Sense of belonging, attachment to family and friends
- Feeling of safety, security, order
- Basic life needs are met (food, shelter, air, warmth)

Positive Focus 11.11 Maslow's Hierarchy of Emotional Needs That Motivate Behavior

- Self-actualization, self-fulfillment
- Self-esteem, responsibility, achievement
- Sense of belonging, attachment to family and friends
- Feeling of safety, security, order
- Basic life needs (food, shelter, warmth)

Because unmet needs are a hidden cause of dysfunctional behavior, we want to support the development of self-esteem. Some poorly behaving children seem to be walking around with a big, black hole inside them where self-esteem ought to be. Self-esteem has been identified as a characteristic that seems closely tied to school success and social adjustment (Hill & Buss, 2006; Mruk, 2006).

We know we need to do something to foster self-esteem. Children, unfortunately, do not suddenly develop a sense of self-worth just because they sing a cute song about being special or color in between the lines on a workbook sheet that says "I am special." Authentic self-esteem activities involve valuing the child, giving the child sincere recognition, treating the child with respect every day, listening to the child, protecting the child's rights, and nurturing the child by making eye contact and using the child's name at eye level on a daily basis.

Depending on the child's age level and the child's preference, appropriate touch may be important. Hugs for babies and toddlers, an arm around the shoulder for preschoolers, or a hand on the shoulder for school-agers may be appreciated and taken as an indication of warmth and closeness. Every child has a right to achieve to the maximum of his own potential—however high or low that potential is. Our role is to support the child's achievement so he can reach for his dreams.

The perception of "value" that children place on themselves reflects the value that others who are important to them place on them. If parents and caregivers consistently see a child as lovable, capable, and worthwhile, then the child will develop positive self-esteem. Children begin to develop self-esteem from birth if attentive caregivers meet their needs while making sure they feel safe and loved and they are consistently treated with respect. Children can be given assertive guidance *and* respectful treatment at the same time. Although it is be possible to rebuild damaged self-esteem, it is easier to support the development of a positive self-concept from the very beginning (Hill & Buss, 2006; Mruk, 2006).

If a child's early experiences have been damaging to her sense of self, we must immediately begin fostering self-esteem; in doing so, we will teach the child appropriate ways to get her needs met. With a great deal of support and patience, children can unlearn old, inappropriate behaviors that may have been the only way they knew to get their needs met in a confusing or unsupportive environment. Repeated cycles of inappropriate behavior are difficult to handle, and we easily fall into behaviors that are as inappropriate as that of the children we are trying to help. Verbal abuse, yelling, sarcasm, and ridicule are all inappropriate adult behaviors.

Our key to success is to pull the child up to a more acceptable level of behavior rather than allowing the child to pull us down to the child's level of immature and inappropriate interaction. That, of course, is advice that is easy to give but never easy to put into practice.

behavior modification
A specific method for changing a child's behavior by rewarding new and desirable behaviors and making undesirable behaviors less attractive to the child, often by simply ignoring them.

When working with typically developing and gifted children, internal motivation almost always works best over time. For typically developing children, external reinforcement probably will not be effective unless it is planned in respectful collaboration with an individual child who really wants help to establish a new habit. In contrast, intellectually challenged children typically require external reinforcement to achieve fundamental learning goals.

11-7 External Reinforcement

We have looked at internal motivation. Now, however, it is time to look at the opposite side of the coin: techniques for external behavior modification. Some behaviors come from unconscious habits that are very resistant to even the most sincere desire for change. We know from our own experiences that wanting to quit smoking, lose weight, or exercise regularly is not always enough to make those things happen. I may want desperately to lose weight, but if I am unconsciously conditioned to open the refrigerator every time I pass it, I may be my own worst enemy.

Jeremy tells his mother that he does not want to practice the piano each day (as his piano teacher has asked him to do). Consequently, his mother delves into Jeremy's inner motivations. She talks with him about his hope to become a famous musician and his feelings of pride when he masters difficult pieces of music. If Jeremy really has an inner desire to play the piano and the lack of practicing is simply a matter of establishing new habits, then giving him a cute little sticker as a reward each day that he practices may work wonders. If he does not practice because he lacks inner motivation, then stickers will be a waste of time. In fact, they may be worse than a waste of time. Jeremy may base his decision not to practice on the fact that he is giving up only a little sticker that really is not very valuable anyway. Also, if Jeremy is coerced into practicing to get a reward, he may respond to future reminders of things he is supposed to do by saying, "What will you give me if I do it?"

In contrast, when Jeremy decides to train his pet chicken to "play the piano" for a county fair, he does not waste any time telling the hen how proud she will feel; he just drops a pellet of corn into her dish each time she inadvertently steps on the keyboard of the toy piano he has placed on the floor of her cage. Before long, Jeremy's chicken clucks loudly and pounds on the piano keyboard every time she sees him.

My placing money in soda vending machine every day may be as mindless as the chicken's stepping on the toy piano keyboard to get pellets of corn. I may need to change my external surroundings to break my habit cycle. Perhaps I could walk a different route so that I do not pass the vending machines, think of a reward to give myself if I resist drinking cans of soda for a whole week, or even bring water bottles with me as a substitute when I am tempted to drink soda. We can assist children in breaking undesirable habits in exactly the same way.

Stephanie runs up to her mother when her mother arrives to pick her up from her child care center. Stephanie has a handful of drawings, and she is dancing around her mother squealing, "Mommy, look what I made! Look what I made!" Stephanie's mother is busy chatting with other mothers, so she ignores Stephanie. Finally, Stephanie throws the drawings down on the ground and yells, "I hate you, Mommy!" Instantly, her mother bends down and says (in an irritated tone), "Stephanie, what do you want?"

Stephanie has learned a lesson that her mother did not intend to teach her: When you want your mother's attention, be hateful and destructive because you will get attention faster than by just asking for attention.

Children generally do whatever they need to do to get their needs met. Many unconscious habits are formed simply because they work. We need to analyze our daily procedures very carefully to identify how children get the things they want and need in the environment.

Does the child who pushes and shoves the hardest always get to be first in line? Does whining and arguing always succeed in extending bedtime or television viewing time? Does pitching a fit mean the child does not have to buckle his seat belt? Does the child who misbehaves the most during story time get almost all of our eye contact, verbal contact, physical contact, and name recognition? Remember, even negative attention is preferable to being ignored.

We also need to consider the powerful effect of **intermittent reinforcers**. People who gamble do not need to get a reward every time they put money in a slot machine.

intermittent reinforcer
A stimulus or reward given after some, but not all, occurrences of a particular behavior. The intermittency tends to increase the specific behavior that is reinforced.

They will keep feeding money to "one-armed bandits" for hours just to get a chance at one really big payoff. Children, likewise, can pester for hours on the chance that a disgusted adult will finally give in and reward their inappropriate behavior with the desired privilege or response. Without realizing it, we may reinforce and reward dysfunctional and annoying behaviors daily. By consciously looking at what a child gets out of various behaviors and changing our own behaviors, we may take big steps in preventing or resolving many frustrating misbehavior patterns.

11-7a What Is Behavior Modification and How Should It Be Used?

To use behavior modification appropriately, the adult follows a highly structured process:

- *Observe* a child's present behavior.
- *Identify* a desired future behavior.
- *Break* the distance between the two behaviors into tiny steps.

Systematically **reinforce** each small step as the child moves closer to the desired behavior.

In behavior modification, we see learning like piecing together a chain, one link at a time. The modification is external to the child, because we choose the skill to be learned and we reinforce that behavior. But, of course, the learning is internal.

Maya is a beautiful 3-year-old girl who has been diagnosed with autism. She does not speak, but she understands speech. She constantly flutters around the room flapping her arms and making small grunting sounds. Pleading with her to stop these behaviors would confuse and stress her, making her so anxious that the behaviors would increase and possibly cause a meltdown tantrum. Using behavior modification, however, might be an effective and caring way to gradually help her find a way to communicate.

Maya's teacher, Thomas, gives no attention to her flapping and helps the other children learn to do the same. Thomas has placed a special poster with laminated, Velcro-attached pictures at eye level especially for Maya. She comes close for a look and accidentally brushes a picture of Cheerios with her hand. Thomas instantly says, "Oh, you want Cheerios?" He pulls the picture off the poster and puts it into Maya's flapping hand. "Come with me, Maya, we'll get your Cheerios right now." That is Maya's favorite cereal, so she eagerly follows. Maya trades the picture for real Cheerios.

Later, Maya wanders by the poster again. She intentionally touches a picture this time. Thomas has been keeping a close eye on the poster. Instantly he says, "Oh, you would like the book about Thomas the Train. Come with me and you may trade it for your picture." Thomas had selected pictures of things that he knew Maya especially liked. By the end of the day, Maya knew how to select a picture to indicate what she wanted. Simple external reinforcement gave her the skill she needed to communicate nonverbally. Over time, Thomas will ease Maya away from rewards. Then he can create more complex picture charts to help her communicate until she masters speech.

Children with developmental delays, learning deficits, and language delays lack the skills to discuss or reflect on motivation. Behavior modification may be the best tool for guiding these children. Behavior modification can be used very successfully with well-developing, even gifted, children. It is, however, essential to enlist the bright child's voluntary and active cooperation. Adults and children who are capable of examining their own motives and those of others will feel coerced if they realize that their behavior has been manipulated without their knowledge. For example, if I suddenly realize that my boss has put an "out of order" sign on the coffee machine so I will stop drinking coffee and will be weaned from caffeine, I may not feel grateful for the help. I may feel furious at being helped without my consent. I may stubbornly drink even more coffee just to assert my autonomy.

Behavior modification works effectively with mentally capable children when we are straightforward about our plan. We might say, "Ruby, would you like to make a special book to help you remember to go to the bathroom? I can set the timer for 2 hours, and each time it rings, you could go to the bathroom and paste a sticker in your book. Do you think that would help? Would you like to try it?"

Obviously, the sticker booklet will help only if Ruby is wetting her pants because she has a habit of delaying visits to the bathroom. A young toddler will not suddenly be able to master toilet training just to get stickers if he does not yet understand the signals his body is giving him or how to control those sensations.

The strategy also will not work if Ruby has inner motivation problems (such as needing to be a baby to compete for attention with a new baby in her family). If, however, Ruby really wants to stop wetting her pants and she just needs a little boost to break a bad habit, she is likely to cooperate fully and feel very proud of herself when she succeeds. The sticker tokens will give her just the boost she needs to be successful.

11-7b Behavior Modification Does Not Work All the Time

Behavior modification is a useful tool when used appropriately. Reinforcement is a powerful tool for changing habit patterns. A valid concern for us, however, is that we do not let ignoring inappropriate behavior become an excuse to give up responsibility for children's unacceptable behavior. Tactfully overlooking inappropriate behaviors may be helpful as long as those behaviors are not outside our ground rules. We can try to make our behavior modification collaborative with capable children so that it doesn't seem manipulative and aloof. Our attempts at behavior modification could become hurtful if we forget to be respectful of individual children.

In our efforts to avoid punishments, we sometimes turn to the use of stickers and stars as awards or to privileges to induce children to master skills and obey us. Rewards can result in temporary compliance but are not effective in creating self-directed learners or caring, cooperative, responsible people (DeVries & Zan, 2003; Wien, 2004). In short, good values have to be grown from the inside out. Attempts to short-circuit this process by dangling rewards in front of children are at best ineffective and at worst counterproductive. Children are likely to become enthusiastic, lifelong learners as a result of being provided engaging DAP learning environments; a safe, caring learning community in which to discover and create; and choice about how they go about learning.

Dedicated teaching staff who support mindful self-control help children develop a lifetime love of learning. Through mindful exploration, children discover who they are and what possibilities they possess.

Photo courtesy of the Preschool at Claremont United Methodist Church

11-8 How Can We Expand Children's Social–Emotional Intelligence?

Previous generations thought knowledge was something permanent and absolute. Now we know that knowledge is a dynamic, changing interaction with the world and the universe around it. Knowledge is constantly changing. Many of the critical skills required in today's highly technical workplace are different from those of a decade ago. The pace of knowledge advancement requires constant updating of knowledge and skills.

Thinking of education as the mastery of a body of knowledge has become outmoded. Learning no longer ends at graduation. Today, quality education teaches children thinking skills so they can become effective lifelong learners. Historically, the focus has been on assessing children's capability through instruments such as the Wechsler Intelligence Test, typically called an intelligence quotient or IQ test.

IQ by itself, however, has proved not to be a very good predictor of life or job performance. Meanwhile, interest in social justice has brought interest in developing intelligence assessments that are not distorted by cultural bias. Peter Salovey and John Mayer studied the social and emotional aspects of intelligence and first coined the term "emotional intelligence" in 1990. Their work was popularized by Daniel Goleman (1995) and Reuben Bar-On (1997).

Social–emotional intelligence refers to the personal and social skills that lead to improved performance in the workplace and better social functioning. These skills are a necessary prerequisite for social competency. The Bar-On model of **social–emotional intelligence (EQ)** measures a set of emotional and social skills that determine how effectively we can express ourselves, understand others, relate with others, and cope with daily social and emotional demands (Bar-On, 2000, 2005). See Positive Focus 11.12.

Research has expanded rapidly in this field. Brain research includes exploring the brain circuitry that controls emotional awareness (Lane, 2000) as well as other emotional and social functions (Lane & McRae, 2004; Young & Saxe, 2009). Findings from these

© 2013 Cengage Learning®

▶❚❚ TeachSource Video

Preschool: Emotional Development

Watch the Video Case on teacher techniques for guiding young children. After watching the clip, answer the following questions:

1. Explain how the teacher in this video taught children to express strong feelings in a socially appropriate manner.

2. List three specific methods the teacher used to help the children calm themselves.

3. What special role did the puppet play in the teacher's activities?

social–emotional intelligence quotient (EQ)
The level of one's self-awareness, mood management, self-motivation, empathy, and understanding of one's inner feelings.

Positive Focus 11.12

Ten Habits of Emotionality Intelligent People

1. **They label their feelings, rather than labeling people or situations.**

   "I feel impatient." vs. "This is ridiculous."

   "I feel hurt." vs. "You are a jerk."

   "I feel worried." vs. "You are an idiot."

2. **They distinguish between thoughts and feelings.**

   Know when to say: "I feel . . ." instead of "I think . . ."

3. **They take responsibility for their feelings.**

   "I feel angry." vs. "You are making me angry."

(Continued)

4. **They use their feelings to help them make decisions.**

"How will I feel if I do this?" "How will I feel if I don't?"

5. **They show respect for other people's feelings.**

They ask, "How will you feel if I do this?" "How will you feel if I don't?"

6. **They feel energized, not angry.**

They use what others call "anger" to become energized to take productive action.

7. **They validate other people's feelings.**

They show empathy, understanding, and acceptance of other people's feelings.

8. **They practice getting a positive value from their negative emotions.**

They ask themselves "How do I feel?" and "What would help me feel better?"
They ask others "How do you feel?" and "What would help you feel better?"

9. **They don't advise, command, control, criticize, judge, or lecture others.**

They realize it doesn't feel good to be on the receiving end of such behavior, so they don't give it.

10. **They avoid people who invalidate them or don't respect their feelings.**

When possible, spend time around people who have high social–emotional skills.

(Hein, 1999)

studies provide physical evidence of structures in the brain that become active during social and emotional attentiveness (Matthews et al., 2002, 2003; Young & Saxe, 2009; Zeidner et al., 2001).

He who knows others is learned; he who knows himself is wise.

—Lao-tzu, Tao te Ching

DAP

11-8a How Do We Teach Children Social–Emotional Intelligence?

DAP early childhood programs make a difference in children's EQ. We can help children learn to interact in socially appropriate ways. We can help children learn to be in charge of expressing their emotions appropriately, and we can help children to learn socially intelligent behavior through positive child guidance. Strategies such as these have been shown to increase self-awareness and reduce stress (Bar-On, 2005).

It may have dawned on you as you read the list in the preceding paragraph: all of the things we have discussed in this book have built a foundation for the preceding list. Our use of ground rules lets children know from the time they are toddlers that we value respect and responsibility. As we say "Gentle, touch gently please," we are introducing early lessons in social–emotional development. As we use bibliotherapy to help preschoolers understand their feelings, we are giving lessons in social–emotional development. And, very importantly, when we teach school-agers the process of conflict negotiation, we are honing their social–emotional skills. Positive child guidance supports the social and emotional development of the child. See Positive Focus 11.13.

11-9 Moving toward Mindfulness

Harvard's Ellen Langer transformed the field of psychology with her research on mindfulness. Her remarkable studies showed that our minds have the capacity to transform our bodies. Before Langer's studies, the dominant view in psychology assumed that decision making was a logical process. Her research developed a new model for how people think. Lager contends that mindfulness expands creativity and innovation. Not paying attention to their lives makes people careless, narrow minded, and complacent (Langer, 2009).

mindfulness
Focused awareness without judgment; being completely in touch with and aware of the present moment.

Components of Social–Emotional Intelligence

Elias and Arnold (2006) state that social–emotional learning is characterized by the following traits:

Knows Oneself

- Understands feelings
- Learns to be responsible
- Recognizes strengths
- Manages emotions
- Understands social situations
- Engages in a creative, disciplined exploration
- Overcomes obstacles
- Solves problems

Cares for Others

- Shows empathy
- Respects others
- Appreciates diversity

Knows How to Act

- Communicates effectively
- Builds relationships
- Negotiates fairly to resolve conflict
- Refuses provocations
- Seeks appropriate assistance and support in pursuit of needs and goals
- Acts ethically

11-9a What Does Mindfulness Mean?

Babies and toddlers may seem to be on automatic pilot. Maria Montessori (1988) described the child's developing mind from birth to age 3 as the "unconscious absorbent mind." The behavior of babies and toddlers, however, is very close to the definition of mindfulness. Mindfulness involves full sensory involvement and attention to one's environment. A key difference between children under 3 and the rest of us is the unconsciousness Montessori described. After age 3 we lose the unconscious absorbent mind, but we can strive for mindful awareness. Mindful awareness helps children and adults gain better self-control and self-management.

Babies and toddlers are naturally nonjudgmental and open to every new experience. The child under age 3 is totally absorbed in everything she experiences. She looks at it, touches it, feels it against her cheek, tastes it, smells it, shakes it, and bangs it on the table. Babies and toddlers experience everything as if it was the first time. In mindfulness we strive to achieve that same "beginner's mind."

Mindfulness involves full sensory involvement and attention to one's environment. We strive to reach *mindful* awareness so we can accomplish better self-control.

Photo courtesy of the Preschool at Claremont United Methodist Church

Babies and toddlers live within the moment. They can express powerful emotions, and then quickly move on to the next experience. You may have observed a toddler having a tantrum who suddenly spotted a toy, stopped crying, and toddled off to play. Babies and toddlers let go of the past. They never take any baggage with them. With mindfulness training, we work toward learning from our mistakes and then moving on, ready for our next experience just like that relaxed and happy toddler (Burke, 2010; Singh et al., 2010).

11-9b How Can Mindfulness Help Me?

Mindfulness practice has been found to be helpful for children with concentration problems as well as those with ADHD and intellectual disabilities (Flook et al., 2010; Jennings, 2011; Joyce et al., 2010; Liehr & Diaz, 2010; Singh et al., 2010). It has been shown to help children with behavior problems develop self-control and self-management (Coatsworth et al., 2010; Singh et al., 2010). Additionally, mindfulness training appears to help with social and emotional problems such as anxiety, depression, and insecurity (Bazzano et al., 2010; Brown & Ryan, 2003; Coatsworth et al., 2010; Kee, & Liu, 2011). However, most remarkably, with training in mindfulness, we caregivers, teachers, and parents are likely to become more authoritative and less authoritarian (Duncan & Bardacke, 2010; Williams & Wahler, 2010).

You may want to consider yoga as a way to teach mindfulness training to staff and parents. Everyone should check with their doctor before beginning a yoga program or any other exercise program. Luckily, most regions of the country have YMCAs, health clubs, or other organizations that teach yoga. If meditation is more appropriate for you, look for meditation groups in your community or read Goleman (1997, 2003) to learn how to meditate.

Mindfulness practice for children from 3 to 12 years of age helps them keep, or regain if they have already lost, the wonderful qualities of curiosity and openness to new experiences they had early in life. See Positive Focus 11.14 through 11.19.

Positive Focus 11.14 Mindfulness of the Environment

This mindfulness exercise focuses children's mindfulness on an object:

- "Today we are going to think about an object."
- "Please walk around the classroom and pick up any small object."
- "Bring the object you choose with you and sit in a circle."
- "Hold the object with both of your hands and look at it very carefully on all sides."
- "I want you to close your eyes now and use your other senses to think about your object. Think about its weight, its smell, its sound, its texture."
- "Open your eyes. Put the object behind your back."
- "Close your eyes again. Imagine you are looking at your object."
- "Who would like to raise your hand and tell us how you felt about this exercise?"
- "Raise your hand if you could see your object in your mind the last time you closed your eyes."
- "Does paying close attention make it easier to remember things?"

Younger children may wish to use construction paper and art materials to draw and paste together a little booklet about their special object. Older children may be invited to write an imaginary story that uses their special object in the plot.

Mindfulness of the Body

This mindfulness exercise can be done with any small food item—typically, three raisins are used. It is an exercise focused on awareness and nonjudgmental experience:

- Have the children wash their hands and then come sit in a circle.
- Have "helper" children pass around napkins or paper towels for each child and invite children to place exactly three raisins on their napkin.
- "Today we are going to think about the process of eating. We are going to explore this process as if it were the first time we had ever tasted any food."
- "Please pick up one raisin and feel its texture between your fingers and notice its color."
- "Think about any feelings of liking or not liking raisins that happen to come to you while you are looking at your raisin."
- "Hold the raisin close to your nose and smell it."
- "Bring your raisin to your lips, thinking about your arm moving your hand to bring your raisin to your mouth, and your mouth watering waiting for the raisin."
- "Take the raisin into your mouth and chew it slowly, experiencing the actual taste of the raisin. Hold it in your mouth."
- "When you feel ready to swallow, feel the swallowing."
- "When you are ready, pick up the second raisin and repeat the process, with a new raisin, as if it is now the first raisin you have ever seen."

(Burke, 2010; Greenberg & Harris, 2012; Hooker & Fodor, 2008; Kabat-Zinn, 1990)

Mindfulness of the Environment: Awareness of Movement

For this activity we need an open space where the children can move freely:

- Sit in a circle.
- "Today we are going to think about how our bodies move."
- "Stand up very slowly and begin walking around the circle."
- "Imagine we are walking on a soft layer of feathers."
- "Think about how that feels." (It will be natural for the children to laugh and comment on their reactions. A sense of humor is a good thing.)
- "Now we are walking on sticky, gooey chocolate."
- "Think about how that feels."
- "Now we are just walking around our room on the regular floor."
- "Think about what you are feeling."
- "Think about what is touching your body, . . . face, . . . hands, . . . feet."
- "Everyone please sit down."
- "Raise your hand if you would like to tell me what you felt."

(Greenberg Harris, 2012; Hooker & Fodor, 2008; Kabat-Zinn, 2003)

Positive Focus 11.17   Mindfulness through Focus on Breathing

Focus on the breath is fundamental to mindfulness training:

- Have the children sit comfortably in a circle.
- "Today we're going to think about our breathing."
- "Our lungs are like two balloons inside our chest. Our lungs keep us healthy by bringing fresh air into our body and sending used air out of our body."
- "Close your mouth. Now gently hold your hands in front of but not touching your nose."
- "Notice how cool air goes in your nose, then warm air goes out."
- (We won't make any attempt to have the children hold their breath, push it out, or change their natural rhythm—we just want them to be aware of their breath.)
- For children 3 to 5 years of age, focusing on feeling their cool and warm breath going in and out is the full mindfulness exercise.
- For children from 5 to 9 years of age, continue, "You may relax your hands and put them in your laps now."
- "We are going to count our breaths silently now. Please close your eyes and count, 'Breathing in one—breathing out one. Breathing in two—breathing out two.'" (Older children, of course, can count higher than five.)
- Repeat the process.
- "Who would like to raise your hand to tell me how you feel? When you were thinking about your breathing, how did your body feel?"
- "Do you think it might be helpful to stop and think about your breathing when you are feeling upset or angry?"

(Greenberg Harris, 2012; Hooker & Fodor, 2008; Kabat-Zinn, 2003)

Positive Focus 11.18   Mindful Contemplation

Mindfulness focuses attention on awareness of the present moment. When the child's mind wanders, we just help the child observe that fact in a nonjudgmental manner and then refocus attention to the present moment. We will help children focus on a bubble to let go of worries:

- Have the children sit in a circle and relax.
- "When I go to the store, I look at things and judge them. I don't like this—it's bad. I like this—it's good. That is judging."
- "Today we are going to focus on thoughts without any judging."
- "I want you to close your eyes and imagine a beautiful bubble."
- "Think of something that makes you feel upset or unhappy. Now put that troublesome thought inside your bubble."
- "Let's look at our thought inside the pretend bubble."
- "Remember when we blow bubbles outside how the bubbles float away and disappear?"
- "We are feeling very comfortable and relaxed as we watch this bubble slowly floating away, getting smaller and smaller, until it completely disappears."
- "But we are not going to judge our thoughts."
- "We are just going to look at them and let the thought bubbles float away."

- If the children seem focused and engaged, this process can be repeated from the beginning.
- "Raise your hand if you want to talk about your thought bubbles."
- "Raise your hand if you want a turn to talk about how this activity made you feel."
- "Raise your hand if you think of some situation where focusing on thought bubbles might help you feel better."

(Hooker & Fodor, 2008)

マインドフルネス
自分の身に起きていることに意識を集中させて
自分の感情、思考、感覚を冷静に認識して
現実を受け入れること

Practicing Mindfulness

(Greenberg Harris, 2012; Hooker & Fodor, 2008; Kabat-Zinn, 2003)

Positive Focus 11.19

As children eat, we can talk with them about the tastes and smells and how they feel as they become full. As they play, we can talk to them about what they are experiencing at the moment: How does the sand feel on your hands? How does the sun feel on your face? How does the wind feel when you swing? As children become mindful, they may talk spontaneously about sounds, sights, smells, and their own movement. Mindfulness takes practice on a regular basis. The goal is to achieve greater awareness throughout the activities of daily living.

© 2013 Cengage Learning®

We can talk to children about the things they experience day to day. What textures, temperatures, and smells do they notice? Does this material have any sound? Is it smooth? . . . Rough? . . . Dry? . . . Wet? Our goal is for children to develop a habit of mindfulness.

As children become mindful of themselves, their environment, and their physical interactions with the environment, they have a better chance of achieving disciplined control over their movements, impulses, and actions. Awareness is an important step toward control. Children may not be successful in mastering control over inappropriate impulses they vaguely notice, or notice only after a misbehavior has occurred. Thus mindfulness training offers us another powerful tool we can use effectively to guide young children toward becoming the kind of citizens who will lead our democracy and contribute positively to society in the future.

Summary

- Dreikurs proposed that mistaken goals cause children to misbehave to get attention, gain control, get revenge, or remove themselves.
- Seeing children as lovable, capable, and worthwhile supports the growth of self-esteem.
- The destructive or aggressive child must know that she will be stopped and that others' rights will be protected.
- Intervene immediately to stop bullying.
- Children who regularly indulge in fits of anger, tantrums, and defiance need to know that the adults who care for them will not explode into their own fits of anger.
- Adults must recognize their own needs and imperfections if they are to be effective in child guidance.
- Reporting child abuse and neglect can save children's lives.
- We can best care for children if our own social, emotional, physical, and intellectual needs have been met.
- Insisting that children apologize, whether or not they feel regret, is neither an honest nor effective way to guide them.
- Punishment is intended to hurt, humiliate, or pay a child back for something he has done.

- The use of time-out as a punishment does not support positive child guidance.
- Children learn from the natural consequences of their actions so long as the consequences are safe and reasonable.
- Abraham Maslow (1943) created a pyramid that shows levels of psychological and physical needs as a way to explain his theory of human motivation.
- Behavior modification is a useful guidance tool when used appropriately.
- Quality educational programs make a difference in children's EQ. Early childhood professionals can help children begin to understand their emotions.
- Positive child guidance supports the social and emotional development of the child.
- Langer contended that mindfulness can expand creativity and innovation.
- Mindfulness expands concentration, self-control, and social–emotional development.

Key Terms

behavior modification

extrinsic motivation

intermittent reinforcers

intrinsic motivation

logical consequences

manipulative

mindfulness

mistaken goals

natural consequence

reinforce

rescue

social–emotional intelligence (EQ)?

time-away

Student Activities

1. Concetta is 3 years old. She has tantrums several times a week. Typically, another child has something she wants and Concetta launches into a tantrum. What might be Concetta's misguided goal? How should you respond when Concetta has a tantrum?

2. Weimin is 5 years old. He is extraordinarily competitive. Anytime he is not first in line, first in a game, or first on the slide, he becomes upset. At times he becomes so upset that he cries and refuses to participate. He always rushes to the teacher for aid. What do you think is Weimin's misguided goal? How should you respond when Weimin cries and refuses to participate?

3. Armand is 4 years old. He is quarrelsome and begins a power struggle anytime he senses that an adult is trying to get him to do something. What do you think is Armand's misguided goal? How could you respond when Armand is belligerent and refuses to cooperate?

4. Beth is 8 years old. She is extremely silly. She follows the class leaders around making jokes and behaving outrageously. Beth is so annoying that most of her peers avoid her. What do you think is Beth's misguided goal? How could you respond when Beth is loud and silly?

Related Resources

Readings

Flynn, L. (2013). *Yoga for children: 200+ yoga poses, breathing exercises, and meditations for healthier, happier, more resilient children.* Avon, MA: Adams Media.

Rigby, Ken. (2008). *Children and bullying: How parents and educators can reduce bullying at school.* Malden, MA: Blackwell.

Websites

The Center on the Social and Emotional Foundations for Early Learning (CSEFEL)   The Center on the Social and Emotional Foundations for Early Learning (CSEFEL) promotes social and emotional development and school readiness of young children birth to age 5 years. CSEFEL is a national resource center funded by the Office of Head Start and Child Care Bureau for providing research and evidence-based practices for early childhood programs.

The National Crime Prevention Council   The National Crime Prevention Council's mission is to be the nation's leader in helping people keep themselves, their families, and their communities safe from crime. Toward this aim, NCPC produces an outstanding website on preventing and responding to bullying that has a wealth of materials for teachers, parents, and young school-aged children.

The National Center for Complementary and Alternative Medicine   The National Center for Complementary and Alternative Medicine website offers a wealth of information about yoga. Yoga is a wonderful way to develop mindfulness skills.

Appendix
Children's Books Addressing Values and Feelings

Sometimes I'm Bombaloo
by Rachel Vail. New York: Scholastic Paperbacks, 2005.

This wonderful picture book is about anger. Katie is a terrific little girl, but sometimes she loses control and "I use my feet and my fists instead of my words." This book's story, which is intended for all 3- to 7-year-olds, is that it's natural, but scary and inappropriate, for young children to lose control. Katie learns how to make amends.

Llama Llama Mad at Mama
by Anna Dewdney. New York: Viking Juvenile, 2007.

Llama llama doesn't like shopping, but Mama is too busy to notice he is losing control. Baby Llama has a tantrum. Mama helps him calm down, and she realizes they need to make shopping more fun.

No, David!
by David Shannon. New York: Blue Sky Press, 1998.

This is a rowdy romp of a book that appeals a lot more to pre-schoolers than to adults. The author explores the pent-up feelings children have about getting into trouble, as the little boy in the book, David, is outlandishly awful in every way. David drives his poor parents crazy! Children from 3 to 6 will shriek with delight at David's antics but feel relief at the end when he is assured that he is loved.

Mad at Mommy
by Komako Saka. New York: Arthur A. Levine Books, 2010.

For ages 2 to 6, this story about a very angry little rabbit who is so mad he wants to fly away but quickly returns to see if his mommy misses him. Of course, she does miss him because she loves him unconditionally. Children will realize he loves his mommy too even though he felt angry with her.

My Secret Bully
by Trudy Ludwig. Berkeley, CA: Tricycle Press, 2005.

This book for children ages 8 to 12 addresses the sometimes over-looked area of hurtful bullying by girls. Monica and Katie have been friends since kindergarten, but Katie has begun to embarrass and control Monica, which causes Monica stress and difficulty at school. Monica's mother helps her work through this troubling situation assertively and appropriately.

Get Organized Without Losing It
by J. S. Fox. Minneapolis, MN: Free Spirit Publishing, 2006.

For ages 9 through 12, this 112-page book offers tips, techniques, strategies, and examples that will empower older school-age children to conquer clutter, prioritize tasks, handle homework, prepare for tests, plan projects, stop procrastinating, and start enjoying the benefits of being organized. Children can learn how to be less stressed and more successful. Lists and steps make this little book effective while humor and cartoons make it fun to read.

Hands Are Not for Hitting
by Martine Agassi, Marieka Heinlen (Illus.). Minneapolis, MN: Free Spirit Publishing, board ed., April 2002.

For ages 2 through 5, this book stimulates children to think and talk about alternatives to hitting and other forms of hurtful behavior. The repeated phrase "hands are not for hitting" is accompanied by suggestions for positive uses for hands, such as waving, helping, drawing, and making music.

Don't Despair on Thursdays! The Children's Grief-Management Book
by Adolph J. Moser, David Melton (Illus.), Nancy R. Thatch (Ed.). Kansas City, MO: Landmark Editions (Emotional Impact Series), 1998.

This book is a useful resource for children ages 5 through 9 experiencing grief.

The Fearful Fairy
by Sheri Hood, M. Faith Shaheen (Illus.). Mount Dora, FL: StonesThrow Publishing, 2007.

The Fearful Fairy is written for children ages 4 to 9. It deals with overcoming fears and insecurities. Regardless of its purpose, however, it's an enjoyable story.

An Annoying ABC
by Barbara Bottner. Michael Emberley (Illus.). Spokane, WA: Knopf Books for Young Readers, 2011.

Adelaide's annoying act sets off a chain reaction of upsetting behavior in preschool. But when Adelaide apologizes, everything turns around. This cute book for children ages 3 to 8 will help children grasp an understanding of prosocial behavior.

Lifetimes

by Bryan Mellonie. New York: Bantam, 1983.

This book answers very basic questions about death such as what it means in the life cycle. Written for children ages 5 through 8, it is general and "gentle" enough to be appropriate for home and school settings.

One of Us

by Peggy Moss, Gardiner, ME: Tilbury House Publisher, 2010.

One of Us, for children ages 5 to 9, is focused on helping children feel comfortable embracing their own uniqueness while resisting peer pressure to conform.

It's Not Your Fault, Koko Bear: A Read-Together Book for Parents and Young Children During Divorce

by Vicki Lansky, Jane Prince (Illus.). Minnetonka, MN: Book Peddlers, 1998.

This book, for children ages 3 through 6 and parents, provides a reassuring message to children that their feelings are natural, that their parents still love and will care for them, and that the divorce is not their fault. Each page includes endnotes for parents with information and advice about what children are experiencing and tips for handling each issue as it arises.

Dear Mr. Henshaw

by Beverly Cleary, Paul O. Zelinsky (Illus.). Glenview, IL: Scott Foresman (reprint ed.), 2000.

This award-winning classic story by Beverly Cleary will be appreciated by any youngster (ages 8 through 12) who feels lonely and troubled during the difficult transition into adolescence.

How Tia Lola Came to Stay

See also: Cuando Tia Lola vino (de visita) a quedarse
by Julia Alvarez, Andrea Cascardi (Ed.). New York: Knopf, 2004.

This story for children ages 9 to 12 is about Miguel's move to Vermont after his parents separate. It is a difficult time for him, and Tía Lola, his amazing aunt from the Dominican Republic, makes his life even more confusing when she arrives to help out his mami. This story has a wonderful lesson to teach as it helps us experience the world of a child living in two cultures.

Help! A Girl's Guide to Divorce and Stepfamilies

by Nancy Holyoke, Scott Nash (Illus.). Middleton, WI: Pleasant, 1999.

An appropriate resource of stories, for girls ages 7 through 12, shared by other girls. This book will help open the doors of communication about divorce and provide comfort.

Sad Isn't Bad: A Good-Grief Guidebook for Kids Dealing with Loss

by Michaelene Mundy, R. W. Alley (Illus.). St. Meinrad, IN: Abbey Press, 1998.

Written by a school counselor, this book helps comfort children ages 4 through 7 who are facing loss.

The Fall of Freddie the Leaf: A Story of Life for All Ages

by Leo Buscaglia. Thorofare, NJ: Slack Incorporated, 1982.

Dr. Buscaglia's warm and wise story is for children ages 5 to 12. It is a simple story about a leaf named Freddie and his companion leaves who change with the passing seasons, finally falling to the ground with winter's snow. This book manages to be inspirational even though it deals with a serious topic.

Play Lady: La Senora Juguetona

by Eric Hoffman, Suzanne Tornquist (Illus.), Carmen Sosa Masso (Trans.). St. Paul, MN: Redleaf Press, 1999.

When her mobile home is vandalized, neighbors come to the aid of their friend, Senora Juguetona. The children who visit to play with her are of many cultures and colors, and one, Kayla, is in a wheelchair. The children enlist their parents' help in repairing the Play Lady's house and yard. The illustrations express the feelings of the characters and enhance the book's message of accepting diversity. This book is suitable for children ages 3 through 7.

Bright Eyes, Brown Skin

by Cheryl Willis Hudson, Bernette G. Ford (Contributor), George Cephas Ford (Illus.). East Orange, NJ: Just Us Books, 2006.

Four African-American children interact with one another in a preschool environment and, in so doing, explore their facial features, skin tones, activities, personalities, and how they learn from and appreciate each other. This book is suitable for children ages 2 through 5.

Uncle Jed's Barbershop

by Margaree King Mitchell, James Ransome (Illus.). New York: Aladdin Paperbacks (reprint ed.), 1998.

Sarah Jean's favorite relative is her great-uncle Jed, who is the only black barber in the county. Great-uncle Jed travels from house to house cutting hair. His dream is to have his own barber shop. Unfortunately, segregation and the Depression present huge obstacles, and he puts aside his dream to pay Sarah Jean's hospital bill. When he finally opens his own shop on his 79th birthday, a grown-up Sarah Jean and the whole community share the joy of his dream come true. This book is suitable for children ages 7 through 10.

Something Beautiful

by Sharon Dennis Wyeth. New York: Dragonfly Books, 2002.

A very special little girl searches through her neighborhood to find something beautiful as her teacher has instructed her, but what she sees is litter, broken glass, mean graffiti, and homeless people. This inspirational story tells how she finds something beautiful in everyone she asks.

In Daddy's Arms I Am Tall: African Americans Celebrating Fathers

by Javaka Steptoe (Illus.). New York: Lee & Low Books, 2001.

This award-winning book for ages 9 through 12 creates a beautiful series of images in mixed media—torn and cut paper, found objects, and color—to illustrate short poems about fathers.

My Dream of Martin Luther King
by Faith Ringgold. New York: Dragonfly Books, 1998.

The author looks at the life of Martin Luther King, Jr. to narrate a dream story in which King is a child who must go to a segregated school and hear his daddy called "boy." In this dream sequence, King watches police on horseback beat up protesters and he is taken to prison, where his grandmother holds him and tries to explain segregation. The book, for children ages 6 through 9, teaches about King's life through an impressionistic dream sequence.

Virgie Goes to School with Us Boys
by Elizabeth Fitzgerald Howard, Earl B. Lewis (Illus.). New York: Aladdin Books, 2005.

This family story for children ages 6 through 10 is about five brothers and one little sister growing up in Tennessee just after the Civil War. Virgie, the daughter, wants to learn to read and write like her older brothers. But the boys have to walk 7 miles to Jonesborough each Monday morning, carrying their clothes and enough food for the week in a tin pail. They stay all week at the school and walk home on Friday evening. Although her parents are frightened about letting her go to school with her brothers, she begs until her father finally gives in. He says, "All free people need learning. Old folks, young folks . . . small girls, too."

My Man Blue
by Nikki Grimes, Jerome Lagarrigue (Illus.), Toby Sherry (Ed.). New York: Puffin, 2002.

Through a series of poems, an African-American boy living in a tough neighborhood tells about his friend Blue. Damon and his mother have just moved to a new apartment when an old friend of the mother's, named Blue, befriends Damon. Blue lost one boy to the streets and is determined to keep Damon on the right track. Blue shoots hoops with Damon, listens to him, and shares laughs and hot dogs. Blue always stands steadfast in Damon's corner and keeps him headed in the right direction. This book is suitable for children ages 7 through 10.

Danitra Brown Leaves Town
by Nikki Grimes, Floyd Cooper (Illus.). New York: HarperCollins Juvenile Books, 2002.

When best friends Zuri Jackson and Danitra Brown are split up for summer vacation, Danitra goes off to the country to visit relatives and Zuri is stuck in the city. They write letters to each other all summer—in richly descriptive poetry—sharing their feelings and experiences. This book is suitable for children ages 5 through 9. We met these two unforgettable best friends in the Coretta Scott King Honor Book, Meet Danitra Brown (1994).

Have You Filled a Bucket Today: A Guide to Daily Happiness for Kids
by Carol McCloud. Northville, MI: Ferne Press, 2006.

This book uses the visual metaphor of bucket filling to emphasize to children the importance of kindness, respect, fairness, other-centeredness, responsibility, and generosity. For children ages 5 to 8.

Sister Anne's Hands
by Marybeth Lorbiecki, K. Wendy Popp (Illus.), Joy Peskin (Ed.). New York: Dial Books for Young Readers, 2000.

This touching story, suitable for children ages 8 through 12, is about a black nun in the early 1960s and the lessons she imparts and is based on the author's own childhood experiences. From the first day of second grade, Sister Anne lights up Anna's classroom. But it's the early 1960s, and not everyone in Anna's small town is ready to accept Sister. How she deals with prejudice and the profound impact she has on her students are at the heart of this beautiful, timeless story about tolerance and how a devoted teacher can change a child's life.

Pelitos/Hairs
by Sandra Cisneros, Terry Ybanez (Illus.). New York: Random House, 1997.

This bilingual story for children ages 3 through 7 describes differences between family members' hair. It helps children celebrate the experience of differences even within their own family. Classroom discussion can be extended from children's own family traditions and similarities and differences. The story encourages them children to write their own stories.

My Very Own Room/Mi Propio Cuartito
by Amada Irma Pérez, Maya Christina Gonzalez (Illus.). San Francisco, CA: Children's Book Press (bilingual ed.), 2008.

The 8-year-old telling this touching family story (for children ages 5 through 9) shares a noisy, crowded little room with her five brothers. She wishes she had her own room where she could write in her diary, read, and dream undisturbed. She claims a tiny storage closet behind a flour-sack curtain and imagines that she has a bedroom with her own bed, table, and lamp. The whole family pitches in to help her empty the closet and piece together her very own little room.

Carlos and the Cornfield/Carlos y la Milpa de Maiz
by Jan Romero Stevens, Jeanne Arnold (Illus.), Patricia Davison (Trans.). New York: Luna Rising, 1999.

Before Carlos plants seed corn, his papa warns him, "Remember, 'Cosechas lo que siembras': You reap what you sow." Carlos is so excited about earning money to buy a new red pocketknife that he plants all of the seeds in the first few rows, leaving no seed to plant in the last rows. He gives up his beloved knife to buy more seed corn for the empty rows. When the corn is harvested, the error of his ways is discovered: the last rows turn out to be blue rather than yellow corn, so mama serves blue corn cakes for breakfast. Bilingual and complete with a recipe for blue corn pancakes, this beautifully written sequel to Carlos y la Planta de Calabaza/Carlos and the Squash Plant (1993) presents a valuable lesson on being responsible for one's own actions. The book is suitable for children ages 5 through 8.

Chato's Kitchen
by Gary Soto, Susan Guevara (Illus.). New York: Paper Star (reprint ed.), 1997.

This award-winning book for children ages 4 through 8 tells the story of Chato, a sly, mustachioed "cool cat" from an East Los Angeles barrio. Five mice, the color of gray river rock, move next door. Chato promptly invites the mice over for dinner—unfortunately, as the main course. Instead of the gruesome outcome you might expect, the author creates a delightfully surprising ending.

Too Many Tamales
by Gary Soto, Ed Martinez (Illus.). New York: Puffin, 1996.

In preparation for a family Christmas fiesta, Maria and her parents are busy making tamales. Maria can't resist trying on her mother's diamond ring, but she forgets all about the ring until she realizes it has disappeared. Maria is sure the ring must be inside a tamale, so she talks her cousins into eating all 24 to help her find it. The overstuffed cousins are greatly relieved to discover that the ring really isn't lost after all. Children ages 4 and older will empathize with mischievous Maria and appreciate this playful reminder about the importance of forgiveness.

Goin' Someplace Special
by Patricia C. McKissack, Jerry Pinkney (Illus.). New York: Atheneum Press, 2001.

This 2002 Coretta Scott King Illustrator Award Winner is about Tricia Ann's first solo trip out of her neighborhood. Tricia Ann is confronted by the segregation of Nashville in the 1950s, but her confidence, intelligence, pride in her heritage, and sense of self-worth make this a victorious journey for her as she searches for truth. The story, suitable for children ages 7 through 10, is based on the author's own experiences and the many indignities she encountered during that troubled period.

Markita
by Alissa Nash, Doby London (Illus.). Chicago, IL: African American Images, 1997.

Nice stories about beautiful flowers in a colorful human bouquet offer little comfort to a young girl who never feels as special as her lighter complexioned cousins. This book for children ages 6 through 9 offers a compassionate look at diversity and self-esteem.

Oliver's High Five
by Beverly Swerdlow Brown, Margot J. Ott (Illus.). Santa Fe, NM: Health Press, 1998.

Oliver Octopus has only five arms, but he doesn't mind. Young children ages 3 through 9 with any kind of disability or difference will enjoy reading about Oliver's adventures above the sea. Through determination and a positive attitude, he changes the way others think about his uniqueness.

Imagine . . . Amazing Me!
by Libbi Chilia. Valley View, OH: Halo Publishing, 2008.

This book for children from ages 2 to 9 uses lovely photography to show typically developing kids along with a little girl with an ability difference doing everyday activities. It is an uplifting classroom resource that will help begin dialogue about respectful recognition of differences.

Harry and Willy and Carrothead
by Judith Caseley. New York: Greenwillow, 1991.

This beautiful book is a classic! Harry is a lively, confident, and popular boy. He just happens not to have a left hand. His physical difference doesn't keep him from becoming a good baseball player.

His red-headed friend Oscar is not so self-assured and is hurt by taunts of "carrot head." Harry stands up to Oscar's tormentor, Willy, and soon the three are best friends. This book is suitable for children ages 3 through 9.

We Can Do It!
by Laura Dwight. Long Island City, NY: Star Bright Books, 2005.

This picture book of children with different abilities involved in activities is an excellent book to have available for children from 2 to 9. This book is a great tool for building children's understanding of and respect for ability differences.

In Jesse's Shoes
by Bevery Lewis. Ada, MI: Bethany House, 2007.

This book for 5- to 10-year-olds is a sensitive yet realistic story. Jesse's sister struggles to understand her brother—and the thoughtless kids who bully and stigmatize him because he is different. This appealing book will encourage children to appreciate and befriend others with ability differences.

If the Shoe Fits
by Gary Soto, Terry Widener (Illus.). New York: Putnam Juvenile Press, 2002.

Rigo's home is "crowed as a bus," there's no centavo to spare, and he gets stuck wearing worn-out hand-me-downs. He's thrilled to receive a pair of brand new penny loafers for his 9th birthday, but when a neighborhood bully makes fun of his fancy shoes, Rigo hides the shoes in his closet. A few months later, he tries to wear the shoes to a party, but they no longer fit. Rigo's disappointment helps him see hand-me-downs in a new light. He thoughtfully gives the almost new shoes to Uncle Celso, who needs good shoes for his new job as a waiter. This book is suitable for children ages 4 to 9.

My Little Car (Spanish and English Edition)
by Gary Soto. New York: Putman Juvenile, 2006.

My Little Car (Mi Carrito) is an adorable and very funny story about a little girl who gets a cool pedal car from her grandpa. Child readers will laugh when she shows off her little low-rider carrito and its flames shooting down the sides. They will be appalled, however, when she lazily leaves her car destined for ruin, and they will be on the edge of their chairs when grandpa discovers the dilapidated state of the little girl's bird-dropping-covered hot rod.

Dancing in the Wings
by Debbie Allen, Kadir Nelson (Illus.). New York: Puffin, 2003.

Although tall and lanky for a ballerina, African-American Sassy loves to dance and dreams of performing on stage. She is hurt by teasing from classmates about her long legs but encouraged by her uncle's belief that she is beautiful. A Russian ballet master believes in her, and she finally finds herself on stage, in the spotlight, partnered with an even taller young man. The book is suitable for children ages 5 through 8.

Simon's Hook: A Story about Teases and Put-Downs
by Karen Gedig Burnett, Laurie Barrows (Illus.). New York: GR Lockwood, 1999.

This book for children ages 5 to 9 helps children learn appropriate ways to respond to teasing. Through his use of a fishing analogy, Burnett *shows children how to "swim free" from feeling helpless, trapped, stuck, or powerless. The book teaches alternatives to hitting back.*

Say Something

by Peggy Moss. Gardiner, ME: Tilbury House Publishers.

This book makes it clear that everyone is vulnerable to teasing and bullying, and everyone has a responsibility to take action. This book will open the door to discussions with children about how to deal with bullying and help make it stop.

The First Strawberries: A Cherokee Story

by Joseph Bruchac, Anna Vojtech (Illus.). New York: Puffin (reprint ed.), 1998.

This native Cherokee folktale, written for children ages 5 through 10, reminds people to be kind to each other. In this creation story, the first man and woman have an angry quarrel that is forgotten when they share delicious strawberries she has discovered.

Coyote: A Trickster Tale from the American Southwest

by Gerald McDermott. New York: Voyager Books (reprint ed.), 1999.

Coyote, the trickster in this native legend, is rude, boastful, vain, and always in trouble. Young children (ages 2 through 5) will identify with this foolish but very human character, who has a nose for trouble and always manages to find it.

Kids Like Me in China

by Ying Ying Fry and Amy Klatzkin, Brian Boyd and Terry Fry (Photographers). St. Paul, MN: Yeong & Yeong, 2001.

This touching, enlightening, and entertaining book provides children ages 7 through 12 with an opportunity to see China through a child's eyes. Ying Ying tells her own story as readers learn about ordinary life in China (schools, homes, and families).

Come and Abide (We Are All the Same Inside)

by Timothy D. Bellavia, Randi Cannata's 4th Grade T.A.G. @ P.S. 175 Q. District 28 N.Y.C. (Collaborator). New York: T.I.M.M.E. (Tolerance in Multi Media Education), 2002.

Come and Abide, a result of the author's collaboration with 26 fourth graders, helps children better understand tolerance and diversity.

Somewhere Today: A Book of Peace

by Shelly Moore Thomas, Eric Futran (Photographer), Shelley Moore Thomas and Abby Levine (Eds.). Grove, IL: Albert Whitman, 1998.

This simple, readable picture book reminds children ages 4 through 8 how to behave positively rather than aggressively.

Rosa

by Nikki Giovanni. New York: Square Fish, 2007.

This is a beautifully illustrated recounting of Rosa Parks's historic refusal to give up her seat on the bus that was a turning point in the Civil Rights movement. It is appropriate for children ages 7 to 11.

Harvesting Hope: The Story of Cesar Chavez

by K. Krull. Orlando, FL: Harcourt, 2003.

Cesar Chavez wanted justice for farmworkers, so he organized them into a union. He became to Mexicans what Martin Luther King, Jr. is to blacks. Although the book is recommended for children ages 6 through 9, ages 9 through 12, especially those with limited English proficiency, can benefit from this story. This book can help instill pride and understanding regarding how determination, perseverance, and hard work can overcome even the greatest odds.

The Peace Book

by T. Park. New York: Little, Brown Young Readers, 2004.

For infants to age 5, this simple, bright, colorful book gives a basic understanding of peaceful behavior.

I'm Like You, You're Like Me: A Child's Book about Understanding and Celebrating Each Other

by C. Gainer. Minneapolis, MN: Free Spirit Publishing, 1998.

This book for children ages 3 through 8 presents diversity on children's level: hair that's straight or curly, families with many people or few, bodies that are big or small—each trait unique but just right for that person. Boys and girls discover that even though people are different, they can enjoy being together and learning about each other.

Glossary

A

ability differences Out of the ordinary function in one or more basic activities of life based on medical, physical, cognitive, psychological, or other characteristics. Many believe the term *disabled* focuses on inadequacy and find the term *person with an ability difference* more empowering and appropriate.

abstract symbol An abstract symbol is a person, place, or thing that comes to represent another idea or concept; in general, anything that stands for something else. Dramatic play can help preschoolers express emotional feelings. We cannot take for granted that just because something seems obvious to us it will be obvious to preschoolers. There are a lot of things they don't know yet.

abusive head trauma (AHT) (also called shaken baby syndrome) A particularly devastating type of child abuse that can be caused by direct blows to the head, dropping or throwing a child, or shaking a child. Head trauma is the leading cause of death in child abuse cases in the United States.

accommodations Special aids for persons with ability differences that give them access to inclusive activities and environments. Accommodations can include such things as a ramp for a wheelchair, a lowered sink, special door handles, signs written in Braille, a sign language translator, or other changes to help the person with ability differences function equitably with typically developing peers.

active listening A form of attentive listening in which one concentrates on what is being said, then reflects the ideas back to the speaker to show an understanding of what the speaker is feeling and saying.

adult One who seeks not to gain control over children but rather to guide them effectively, while setting for them first-hand examples of appropriate coping and assertive negotiation.

age-typical behavior Behavior that is characteristic to specific developmental stages; thus it is typically seen in children of a certain age.

anarchy Absence of any form of control; chaos and disorder.

anecdotal record A short descriptive story about a child's specific behavior event that is of particular interest or concern. This may be firsthand information as observed by child care providers or recorded from secondhand information as provided by parents. It is qualitative, not quantitative data.

antisocial Behavior that detracts from the welfare of others or has a generally negative effect on persons with whom one comes in contact. Antisocial personality behaviors are typically marked by lack of ethical restraint, lack of moral control, impulsiveness, and an inability to experience feelings of guilt.

appropriate touch Suitable for the occasion and the person affected, nonexploitative, and having no concealed intention; physical contact that is casual, affectionate, reciprocal, and welcome, but never sexual or controlling.

attention deficit/ hyperactivity disorder (ADHD) A common developmental disorder that appears during childhood and is characterized by a persistent pattern of inattention as well as forgetfulness, poor impulse control, and distractibility.

auditory figure-ground dysfunction An inability to distinguish between levels of sounds in the environment, to focus on significant sounds and tune out irrelevant sounds. This is a common characteristic in PDDs and some learning disorders.

authentic learning A family of research efforts that explain cognition in terms of the relationship between learners and the properties of specific environments. The emphasis of research on authentic learning (or "situated cognition," as it is often called) is to study complex learning, problem solving, and thinking in a realistic environment.

authoritarian style Interactive (or control) style relying on one-way communication, rigid rules, and punishment—"the sledgehammer."

authoritative style Interactive (or control) style relying on two-way communication, collaboratively developed rules, and positive guidance—"the guide."

autism A developmental brain disorder characterized by impaired social interaction and communication skills, avoidance of eye-to-eye gaze, and a limited range of activities and interests.

autocracy Control by a single person having unlimited power.

autonomy A person's self-reliance, independence, and self-sufficiency. One's capacity to make decisions and act on them.

B

behavior modification A specific method for changing a child's behavior by rewarding new and desirable behaviors and making undesirable behaviors less attractive to the child, often by simply ignoring them.

behaviorists Those holding the view that the environment is the primary determinant of human behavior and that objectively observable behavior constitutes the essential psychological makeup of a human being.

biases One's own set of beliefs, values, perceptions, and assumptions that develop from one's upbringing, past experience, and personal philosophy of life; bias can include an unfair preference for or dislike of something or someone.

bibliotherapy The use of literature by children or adults to aid in processing specific problems (for example, depression, anxiety, stress, frustration). Many libraries have listings of bibliotherapy selections categorized by concerns (divorce, death and dying, new baby, step-parenting, and so on).

bipolar disorder A disorder in which episodes of depression alternate with mania.

body language The gestures, facial expressions, and body postures that people use to communicate along with or instead of speech.

bullying To torment physically, verbally, or psychologically by threats, hitting, shoving, name-calling, sarcasm, taking possessions, etc.

C

cephalocaudal Development in a pattern from the head downward, toward the feet (head to toe).

Child Find A component of IDEA law that requires state agencies to locate, evaluate, and identify children between the ages of 3 and 21 who are in need of early intervention or special education services.

child guidance Contrived methods for external control as well as interaction with and extension of the development of naturally unfolding internal mechanisms and motivations for self-control and self-discipline.

child-directed Learning activity instigated by the child's natural curiosity and desire to learn rather than by the adult's direction, manipulation, or coercion.

classical conditioning Teaching a new response triggered by a new stimulus by pairing it repeatedly with a stimulus for which there is a physiological reflex (sometimes called Pavlovian conditioning). This term derives from an experiment originally performed by Ivan Pavlov in which a bell was rung just as food was offered to a hungry dog. Soon the dog would salivate at the sound of the bell whether or not food was offered, demonstrating that the association had become learned.

cohesive interaction Reciprocal teamwork; sticking together to carry out tight-knit group activity.

collaborative Cooperative interaction of two or more people who are trying achieve a common goal. Although school-agers may be inclined to compete against each other to be first or best, we can find ways to encourage them to work together as collaborative team members.

community of learners A group of individuals who share similar educational principles, who work toward common goals, whose activities are linked, and whose collaborative efforts create a synchronized energy in which the power of the group is more profound than that of any one individual. For children, a group that nurtures a sense of belonging among the children and adults in a program in which children learn that all contribute to each other's learning.

concept An idea, understanding, or belief formed by organizing images or mental pictures from specific occurrences and experiences.

concrete operational In Jean Piaget's theory the third stage of cognitive development, which begins with the ability to analyze thoughts concerning a concrete idea (as opposed to an abstract idea).

conduct disorder A mental condition typified by a repetitive and persistent pattern of socially unacceptable behavior that violates the rights of others. Typical symptoms include strongly aggressive behavior, bullying, cruelty, and destructiveness.

conflict resolution A problem-solving strategy to help two disagreeing parties dissipate their frustration and bring their opposing views to a common solution. The method requires active listening and respectful, nonjudgmental communication.

constructivists Those holding the view developed by Piaget and Vygotsky that our personality and intelligence comes from both inborn cognitive structures and external experiences.

control of error A teaching strategy originally developed by Maria Montessori and also known as self-correction. Materials are designed to provide instant feedback to the child if he has made a mistake, or they are designed to make it impossible to make a mistake. This puts control in the hands of the learner and protects the child's self-esteem and self-motivation.

coprolalia *Copro* is the Greek term for "feces" and *lalia* is Greek for "babbling, meaningless talk." Literally, it means "manure talking." People with coprolalia make sudden, unexpected outbursts of inappropriate words or phrases.

copropraxia *Praxia* is the Greek word for "act or action." Combined with *copro*, it means "manure behavior." People with copropraxia act out involuntarily, producing obscene, offensive, or shocking gestures and actions.

corporal punishment Corporal punishment is the use of physical force to cause pain but not injury and is intended to control a child's behavior.

crucial conversations Discussions that occur when there is a lot at stake, when emotions are strong, or when opinions clash. Crucial conversations offer a strategy for handling discussions with a clear sense of desired outcomes as well as a clear sense of the desired relationships when the crucial conversations are concluded.

cues Indications of interest or need.

cultural adaptation The process of human societies making cultural changes to better accommodate diverse environments across the globe. Slowly evolving adaptations may have neutral or even maladaptive effects in a rapidly changing cultural environment.

cultural bias Unfair preference for or dislike of something or someone based on culture.

cultural competence Being knowledgeable about different cultures, their daily living practices, cultural values, norms, and traditions; being willing to treat others with appropriate respect regardless of race, ethnicity, religion, ability, country of origin, economic status, etc.

cultural context The situation or circumstance in which a particular cultural event, action, behavior, or imagery occurs. Actions, events, and behaviors can have different meanings, depending on their cultural context.

cultural pluralism The peaceful coexistence of multiple distinct ethnic, religious, and/or cultural groups within one community or society.

culture shock A feeling of confusion, alienation, and depression that can result from the psychological stress that typically occurs during a person's initial immersion in a new culture.

culture The traditional beliefs and patterns of behavior that are passed down from parents to children by a society; beliefs, customs, practices, and social behavior of any particular cluster of people whose shared beliefs and practices identify the particular nation, religion, ability, gender, race, or group to which they belong.

D

demandingness Requiring certain behaviors from children. Having high expectations for children that are reasonable and supported with encouragement and optimism.

democracy The principles of social equality and respect for the individual within a cohesive community.

depression A mental state characterized by pessimism, feelings of inadequacy, despondency, and lethargy.

developmentally appropriate practice Early education and care that is carefully planned to match the diverse interests, abilities, and cultural needs of children at various ages and that is carried out with respect for and in cooperation with their families.

differentiated Differences between two or more things that are made apparent and categorized.

disabilities Word currently used in a diagnostic, clinical, and legal context to describe individuals defined as requiring and eligible for services because medical, physical, cognitive, psychological, or other conditions affect one or more basic activities of life.

discrimination Participation in harmful actions toward others because of their membership in a particular group; the behavioral manifestation of negative prejudice.

doubt A feeling of questioning, uncertainty, and hesitation.

Down syndrome A congenital disorder involving chromosome 21 that causes intellectual disability and distinct physical differences such as a broad facial profile and short stature.

dual-earner couples Couples in which both partners are gainfully employed.

dysfunctional Inappropriate or self-destructive behavior that does not serve any positive or productive function in a child's life.

E

echolalia A speech disorder that causes compulsive repetition of words spoken by others. In most cases, echolalic speech is a habitual form of cyclical self-stimulation that is not intended as communication, but in some cases echolalia may be used as the child's only available tool in an improvised attempt at communication.

egocentric Seeing oneself as the center of the universe, self-centered, selfish. This point of view is a perfectly normal developmental characteristic of babies and very young children.

egocentrically Babies and very young children see themselves in a self-centered, selfish manner that is considered to be egocentric. This point of view is a perfectly normal development characteristic for this age.

emotional growth Developing self-concept and self-esteem and learning to manage the feelings that affect behavior.

empathy The ability to understand or have concern for someone other than oneself, marked by identification with and understanding of another's situation, feelings, and motives.

enculturation The way a culture teaches a child its norms and values so that the child can become an accepted member of that culture. The process of passing culture down to the child not only by direct guidance, but also by her watching and experiencing culture every day from infancy onward.

environment The circumstances or conditions that surround one; in the context of early childhood education, we think of the environment as everything the child experiences, including objects, activities, routines, and people.

ethics The ideals and the shared conceptions of professional responsibility that reflect the aspirations of a group of practitioners and affirm their commitment to the core values of their field. The basic principles that are intended to guide their conduct and assist them in resolving dilemmas encountered in their field.

ethnocentrism The deeply felt belief (possibly unconsciously held) that one's own culture is superior to all others. Being unyielding in attachment to one's own way of life and condescending and intolerant toward other cultures. Alien cultural practices are often viewed as being not just different but as silly, weird, evil, or unnatural.

ethologists Scientists who study the behavior of living creatures under normal conditions. Ethology is the scientific study of animal behavior. (*Note*: Ethnology is the study of the characteristics of cultures.)

event sampling A recording to determine the precise number of times a specific behavior occurs within a set period, as well as the pattern of occurrence.

executive system A theorized system of the brain that controls and organizes other mental processes. It manages processes such as planning, abstract thinking, rule learning, screening out irrelevant sensory information, and inhibiting inappropriate actions; also referred to as executive function or the central executive.

expressive language Communication with others verbally, in sign language, or in writing.

external environment The physical surroundings or conditions around a child that influence his or her growth, development, and learning. A young child's environment can be described as everything the child sees, hears, touches, or experiences.

extrinsic motivation Performance of an activity to attain an outcome. Common outcomes are rewards (money, grades) for showing the desired behavior, and the threat of punishment following misbehavior. Competition is in an extrinsic motivator because the performer desires to win and to beat others.

F

failure to thrive syndrome Causes a wasting away of the child's body. This condition can result from prolonged absence of emotional nurturance as well as from malnutrition, and affected infants typically show delays in motor and intellectual development.

family structures Various arrangements of people living together with children and possibly other generations of relatives.

fetal alcohol spectrum disorders (FASDs) A group of permanent birth defects caused by a mother drinking alcohol during pregnancy.

fight or flight response The body's reaction to a perceived threat or danger. Our bodies react to threats by releasing hormones such as adrenalin and cortisol into our blood stream, which give us a burst of energy and strength to fight or flee. When the perceived threat is gone, our systems are designed to go back to normal levels by means of a relaxation response. But if a child is subjected to constant stress, relaxation is impaired and damage to physical health as well as sleeping, eating, and social and emotional problems may occur.

free appropriate public education (FAPE) A directive requiring that school districts provide children with ability differences access to general education as well as specialized educational services to accommodate special needs. It also requires that children with ability differences receive support free of charge, the same as is provided to non–differently abled students.

fulfillment Completely developing one's abilities and interests; a feeling of pleasure because you are getting what you want from life.

functional Appropriate actions or behaviors that serve some productive or positive function in a child's activities and patterns of interactions.

G

goal Overarching purpose or aspiration.

group contagion Typical toddler group behavior in which one child's gleeful action (for example, foot stamping, head shaking, or squealing) is quickly imitated by the whole group of toddlers.

group contagion Typical toddler group behavior in which one child's gleeful action—for example, foot stamping, head shaking, or squealing—is quickly imitated by the whole group of toddlers.

group identity A young child constructs group identity primarily by internalizing whatever that child's family considers important in defining who is "like us." Creating a strong and positive group identity is essential for young children who happen to be part of a cultural grouping that has been devalued or stigmatized by the larger society.

H

habituated The process of becoming accustomed to frequent repetition or pattern of behavior.

hearing impairment The term "Hearing Impaired" is a medically accurate description of persons who are hard of hearing or who have no hearing. Many deaf, hard of hearing and late deafened people, however, don't like to be called impaired. Most expect to be identified as deaf or hard of hearing when the need arises to identify their hearing status, but many resent these terms being used as to identify them as people. Nearly 10 percent of human beings have some level of hearing loss.

human ecology The theory that people don't develop in isolation but rather in relation to their family, home, school, community, and society. Each of these constantly changing multilevel environments, as well as the interactions among these environments, is key to a human being's development.

hypersensitivity Overreaction to sensory input from one of the senses (for example, sight, sound, taste, smell, touch).

I

imprinting A kind of early bonding in an animal's development that normally results in significant recognition ability and social attraction to members of its own species, especially to its mother.

inappropriate behavior Behavior that is out of place, immature, unproductive, or socially inept.

individual development A particular person, distinct from others in a group, changes, advances, or progresses to a more advanced state.

Individualized Education Program (IEP) A written plan that describes exactly how teachers, parents, school administrators, related services personnel, and the student from 3–22 years of age with a disability will work together to improve the student's educational results.

Individualized Family Service Plan (IFSP) A written plan that is intended to assist families and professionals in their combined efforts to meet the developmental requirements of young children from birth to age 3 with special needs.

Individuals with Ability Disabilities Act (IDEA) A law ensuring that eligible infants, toddlers, and children with ability differences receive early intervention and special education and related services. It requires that students be provided a free appropriate public education (FAPE) that prepares them for further education, employment, and independent living. Special education must provide the least restrictive environment (LRE), which is the environment most like that of typically developing children in which the child with an ability difference can succeed.

induction The process of reasoning from a part to a whole, from day-to-day events to major life concepts. Because children learn best from "hands-on" experiences, we invite them to think and talk about each inappropriate behavior so they will be able to figure out larger moral concepts through induction.

industry One's motivation to work constructively, to be diligent and productive.

inferiority The feeling of being incapable, having a pervasive sense of inadequacy and experiencing a tendency toward self-diminishment.

inferring meaning Drawing conclusions from evidence perceived by one's senses or through communication.

intellectual disability (ID) Mismatch between an individual's capabilities and the demands of daily life to communicate, handle self-care and hygiene needs, participate in community life, make appropriate decisions, solve problems, carry out tasks, and follow safety rules.

intermittent explosive disorder (IED) A mental disorder typified by outbursts of violent and aggressive behavior that may harm others or destroy property.

intermittent reinforcer A stimulus or reward given after some, but not all, occurrences of a particular behavior. The intermittency tends to increase the specific behavior that is reinforced.

internal sensations The physical feelings that are caused by one or more of the sense organs being stimulated. The feelings sensed by one's own body such as hunger or fear.

internalize The process of taking in experiences and absorbing learning, then making them part of one's own behavior or belief.

intrinsic motivation A driving force that comes from internal interest, desire, or enjoyment rather than from external pressures or to get a reward.

J

justice orientation Perspective in which integrity tends to be the dominant moral compass for making autonomous, independent, and self-oriented ethical and principled decisions.

L

learned behavior An action repeated because it produced a favorable response or was taught via the reinforcing response of another. This develops rapidly in the early stages of cognitive growth.

learned helplessness A person's inability to take action to make his or her life better, arising out of a sense of not being in control.

learning community Group of individuals who share similar educational principles, who work toward common goals, whose activities are linked, and whose collaborative efforts create a synchronized energy in which the power of the group is more profound than that of any one individual. For children, a group that nurtures a sense of belonging among the children and adults in a program where children learn that all contribute to each other's learning.

learning disability Disorder that affects the brain's ability to receive, process, analyze, or store information.

least restrictive environment (LRE) The requirement in IDEA law that children with ability differences receive their education, to the maximum extent appropriate, with non–differently abled peers and that special education pupils not be removed from regular classes unless, even with supplemental aids and services, education in regular classes cannot be achieved satisfactorily.

logical consequence An outcome that results from a situation in which adults determine and control the conclusion.

M

mania A mental state characterized by abnormally elevated mood, extraordinary energy, and bizarre thought patterns.

manipulative Using clever or devious ways to control or influence another person into doing something that he or she may not want to do. (Be aware that *manipulative*, when used by early educators as a noun, refers to small objects that are used for fine-motor development. The fingers manipulate the objects or move them around.)

maturationists Those holding the view that internal predisposition, physiological characteristics, or inherited traits account for the essential psychological makeup of a human being.

media Materials that convey information and cultural expression. Media can bring data by paper (books, magazines), film (videos), computer (cloud storage, Internet, Podcasts, CDs, DVDs, or BluRay), electronic wires or airwaves, (TV, radio), and so on.

metacognition The ability to reflect on or evaluate one's behavior or actions.

mind blindness A brain disorder that impairs one's ability to "read minds" by noticing gestures, facial expressions, and changes in tone of voice. An inability to fathom what is in the mind of another person.

mindfulness Focused awareness without judgment; being completely in touch with and aware of the present moment.

mirror Reflecting the feelings expressed by someone else—repeating what you understood someone to say (see *active listening*).

misbehavior Inappropriate, troublesome, and sometimes unsafe behavior.

mistaken goals The motivation that Dreikurs theorized caused children to behave inappropriately. The mistaken logic that causes children to misbehave to get attention from others, gain a sense of control, get revenge for their own perceived hurts, and remove themselves from frightening or painful situations.

modeling Providing an example, being a role model. In positive child guidance, the adult is the primary role model.

modify The process of bringing about a change. In behavior modification, modifying is the process of changing a specific behavior through external reinforcement of some kind.

moral affect The ability to feel guilt or shame—feelings associated with a guilty or clear conscience—indicate whether behavior was appropriate and guide one to choose appropriate or desired behaviors.

moral reasoning The thinking processes that guide people in deciding what is or is not moral behavior.

motor tic A sudden involuntary muscular contraction, often of the facial, shoulder, or neck muscles. Complex motor tics include distinct, obsessively repeated, intricate actions or behaviors such as twirling, hopping, or obsessively lining things up in straight rows. Tics tend to become more pronounced when one is under stress.

N

National Association for the Education of Young Children (NAEYC) A professional organization for early childhood educators dedicated to improving the well-being of all young children, with particular focus on the quality of educational and developmental services for all children from birth through age 8. (See Developmentally Appropriate Practice, Figure 1.1.)

natural consequence An outcome that results from a situation without any external intervention to change or control the conclusion.

negative stereotyping To categorize individuals in a group according to an oversimplified, standardized (usually racist or sexist) image or idea that ignores the unique characteristics of the individual.

nested structures An individual's interactive experience—how the parents, their workplace, the community, society, schools, and the economy interact and affect children.

O

object permanence The knowledge that something hidden from view is not gone forever but rather is in another location at that time and likely to reappear.

objective Immediate aim or purpose.

objective observations Describing what happens without making judgments. Objective observations can be seen, heard, smelled, tasted, or touched.

on task Focused on the activities at hand; fully involved in and attentive to productive skill development or learning activity.

operant conditioning A kind of learning that occurs when a spontaneous behavior is either reinforced by a reward or discouraged by punishment. For example, mice that go through a maze the wrong way get a shock. If they go the right way, they get some cheese. So they eventually learn to go the right way every time.

oppositional defiant disorder (ODD) A condition in which an ongoing pattern of disobedient, hostile, and defiant behavior toward authority figures goes well beyond the bounds of normal childhood behavior.

osmosis The gradual, unconscious mental process of absorbing ideas and taking in information that resembles the tendency of fluids to gradually soak through absorbent material.

P

parent–teacher resource team Teachers and parents working together as a cooperative, respectful, and cohesive partnership.

permissive style Interactive (or control) style relying on neglect, abdication of responsibility, or over-indulgence— "the doormat."

personal interaction Reciprocal social activity that should express genuine interest and respect for the other individual.

pervasive developmental disorders (PDDs) A group of neurodevelopmental disorders characterized by severe delays in the development of socialization and communication skills.

playscape For a playground to be considered a playscape, it must be natural, relying on native plants, trees, grassy slopes, stumps, and rock formations rather than on manufactured equipment and more.

pluralistic culture (See *cultural pluralism*.) Cultural pluralism promotes each group's right to preserve and practice its own cultural traditions without interference or prejudice.

positive child guidance Relying on the "developmental interactionist" perspective to create guidance that is primarily based on an interweaving between external forces and internal processes.

prejudice As the name implies, prejudice is the process of prejudging someone. Racial prejudice comprises negative attitudes, beliefs, and rigid stereotypes against an ethnic group that are resistant to change despite contradictory evidence.

preoperational The second stage of cognitive development in Jean Piaget's theory that begins with the achievement of object permanence. This stage is typified by imaginative play, egocentricity, the inability to take another person's point of view, and the belief that the number or amount is changed when objects are rearranged.

prevention techniques A specific procedure or special type of action taken to make it difficult or impossible for someone to do a certain thing or for a certain type of thing to happen.

problem behavior Difficult and troubling behavior that causes inconvenience for others.

prosocial Behavior that improves the welfare of others or has a generally positive effect on persons with whom one comes in contact.

proximodistal Development in a direction from closest to the body's trunk to the farthest, such as controlling the muscles of the trunk, then the muscles down the arms, and finally the hands (close to far).

pseudoconditioning The pairing of an unconditioned stimuli with a naturally occurring stimulus–response connection.

puberty The period during which the secondary sex characteristics begin to develop and the capability of sexual reproduction is attained. Puberty is followed by a period of rapid physical growth.

Q

qualitative information Unmeasurable descriptive qualities and characteristics of behaviors.

quantitative information Measurable numerical data and statistical calculations that tell how often or to what degree behaviors occur.

quick response A specific procedure or special type of action done swiftly in reaction to a situation.

R

racism A combination of racial prejudice and discrimination. Racism makes the inflexible assumption that individual differences are biologically determined and are therefore unchangeable. Racism does not exist in a vacuum but rather is enacted and reinforced through social, cultural, and institutional practices that endorse the power of one group over another.

receptive language Comprehension of written, signed, or spoken communication expressed by others.

redirection The process of offering a substitute focus to distract the child from a current undesirable one. For example, a child may be offered a developmentally appropriate water play activity to refocus his or her inappropriate interest in pouring milk from a cup onto the floor.

replaces Substitutes one action for another when both cannot be done at the same time, so that an undesired behavior must be given up or suspended for the new action to take place.

rescue Save from accepting the consequences of one's behavior; someone has intervened to "bail out" the child from the situation he has created.

respect The process of showing regard for the rights and needs of another. To display polite expressions of consideration for another.

responsibility Individual accountability and answerability.

responsibility orientation Perspective in which sensitivity to others, loyalty, responsibility, self-sacrifice, and peacemaking reflect interpersonal involvement and caring and ethical and moral decision making.

running account A detailed commentary describing an event as it unfolds each time it occurs.

S

scapegoating Putting blame on another by someone who wants to cause harm or is unwilling to take responsibility for his or her own actions.

secure attachment Healthy emotional ties to caregiver. Typical signs include brightening at the sight of caregiver, visually following caregiver's movements, smiling or vocalizing to get attention, holding out arms to be picked up, or clinging to the caregiver. Babies develop emotional bonds to the significant caregivers in their lives.

self-concept Perception of oneself in terms of personal worth, life and school successes, and perceived social status.

self-esteem Seeing oneself as a worthwhile individual.

self-identity The set of characteristics that a person recognizes as belonging uniquely to himself or herself and constituting his or her own individuality.

self-regulation A critical developmental process by which one learns to function without external control; being able to deal with problems appropriately and independently.

sensory processing disorder A neurological disorder causing difficulties in receiving, processing, and responding appropriately to sensations one's body takes in from the surrounding environment.

sexism Historically, sexism has been male-driven and accompanied by a belief in male superiority.

sexual harassment Unwelcome attention given for sexual gratification; for personal sexual stimulation; or to antagonize, bully, and dehumanize another person through behavior of a sexual nature.

shame A negative feeling or emotion of embarrassment, unworthiness, or disgrace.

single parents Mothers, fathers, grandparents, or guardians rearing children alone.

social growth Learning to understand and function appropriately in one's social environment; learning how to effectively interact with others.

social–emotional intelligence (EQ) The level of one's self-awareness, mood management, self-motivation, empathy, and understanding of one's inner feelings.

socialization The process by which children learn acceptable behavior.

stigmatized Labeled as socially undesirable on the basis of some specific characteristic; such labeling damages the stigmatized person's self-esteem and excludes him or her socially.

stimuli Something taken in through the senses that might incite activity or thought; something seen, smelled, heard, felt, or tasted; an incentive for action.

stress The process of recognizing and responding to threat or danger.

subjective interpretations Using objective observations to think about and express ideas, explanations, and perceptions of what happened.

syndromes Diseases or disorders that have more than one feature or symptom.

T

teasing To annoy, pester, irritate, aggravate, make fun of, or mock playfully.

temperament Clusters of personality traits with individual and distinctive behavioral patterns.

time sampling A recording made at predefined intervals to determine the pattern of occurrence and the general frequency of a certain behavior either in an individual or in the entire group. Setting and sticking with specific time intervals for recording the behavior reduces the influence of observer bias.

time-away Removing a child from an overwhelming situation to provide a supportive cooling-off time with an adult present.

tokens Objects (for example, stars, points, stickers) given to children for performing specified behaviors; these objects are then exchanged at prearranged times for children's choice of activities or items from a menu of rewards (for example, toys, special food treats, field trips).

Tourette's syndrome A disorder characterized by multiple motor and vocal tics.

traffic patterns The most obvious routes children will take as they move around the classroom.

transitions Phases in daily activities in which a child must give up or leave one activity and begin another activity. These difficult phases between activities may cause children to balk at moving from one thing to the next. Additionally, the confusion and stress of the changeover may trigger misbehavior.

trust Sense of security; belief that one's needs will be met.

 U

unconditional acceptance The process of accepting someone as a worthwhile human being; recognition and appreciation without any strings attached.

unconscious conditioning A response developed through the use of all the senses; an association of things seen, felt, heard, tasted, and smelled with other meaningful sensations or events.

unconscious reactions Actions that are unplanned, devoid of forethought.

 V

verbal abuse Verbal abuse happens when words ridicule, distain, humiliate, and taunt a child.

visceral Proceeding more from instinct than from logical thinking. Characterized by or showing emotion.

vocal tic A sudden involuntary vocalization such as a yip, whistle, grunt, or cough. A complex vocal tic is a distinct, obsessively repeated phrase or the intricate obsessive use of words, such as repeating everything other people say.

References

AAIDD (2011). *Definition of intellectual disability.* Washington, DC: American Association on Intellectual and Developmental Disabilities. Accessed on January 19, 2011, at www.aaidd.org/content_100.cfm? navID=21

Aboud, F. E. (2008). A social-cognitive developmental theory of prejudice. In S. M. Quintana & C. McKown (Eds.), *Handbook of race, racism, and the developing child* (55–71). Hoboken, NJ: John Wiley & Sons.

Abramson, A. S., & Lisker, L. (1970). Discriminability along the voicing continuum: Cross-language tests. *Proc. Int. Congr. Phon. Sci., 6*, 569–573.

Ackerman, D. J. (2006). The costs of being a child care teacher: Revisiting the problem of low wages. *Educational Policy, 20*(1), 85.

Acredolo, L., Goodwyn, S., & Abrams, D. (2002). *Baby signs: How to talk with your baby before your baby can talk.* New Yo: McGraw-Hill.

Addison, J. T. (1992). Urie Bronfenbrenner. *Human Ecology, 20*(2), 16–20.

Adler, A. (1931). *The pattern of life.* London, UK: Kegan Paul.

Ainsworth, M. D. S. (1973). The development of infant-mother attachment. In B. Cardwell & H. Ricciuti (Eds.), *Review of child development research* (Vol. 3, pp. 1–94) Chicago: University of Chicago Press.

Aksan, N., Prisco, T., & Adams, E.M. (2008). Mother-child and father-child mutually responsive orientation in the first 2 years and children's outcomes at preschool age: Mechanisms of influence. *Child Development, 79*(1), 30–44.

Allen, J. P., Porter, M. R., McFarland, F. C., Marsh, P., & McElhaney, K. (2005). The two faces of adolescents' success with peers: Adolescent popularity, social adaptation, and deviant behavior. *Child Development, 76*, 747–760.

Alley, T. R. (1981). Head shape and the perception of cuteness. *Dev Psychol.* 17, 650–654.

American Academy of Pediatrics Association (AAPA). (2005). Breastfeeding Your Baby: Answers to Common Questions. Accessed on March 16, 2011, at www .aap.org/healthtopics /breastfeeding.cfm

American Diabetes Association. (2006). *American Diabetes Association complete guide to diabetes* (4th ed.). New York: Bantam.

American Foundation for the Blind. (1993). *First steps.* Los Angeles, CA: Blind Children's Center.

American Psychiatric Association (2010). *Diagnostic and statistical manual of mental disorders.* Arlington, VA: American Psychiatric Publishing

American Psychiatric Association. (2004). *Diagnostic and statistical manual of mental disorders* (DSMIV-TR, 4th ed.). Washington, DC: Author.

American Psychological Association. (2003). Guidelines on multicultural education, training, research, practice, and organizational change for psychologists. *American Psychologist, 58*(5), 377–402.

American Psychotherapy Association. (2008). Working women more likely than men to stay home with a sick child.

Annals of the APA, Spring. Accessed on March 16, 2011, at www.annalsofpsychotherapy.com/articles/spring08 .php?topic=article5

Amsterdam, B. (1972). Mirror image reactions before age two. *Developmental Psychobiology, 5*, 297–305.

Anderson, S. W., Bechara, A., Damasio, H., Tranel, D., & Damasio, A.R. (1999). Impairment of social and moral behavior related to early damage in human prefrontal cortex. *Nature Neuroscience, 2*, 1032–1037.

Aries, P. (1962). *Centuries of childhood.* New York: Random House.

Asbury, K., & Plomin, R. (2005). Nature and nurture: Genetic and environmental influences on behavior. *The Annals of the American Academy of Political and Social Science, 600*(1), 86–98.

Ashcraft, R. (Ed.) (1991). John Locke: Critical assessments. New York: Routledge.

Ashworth P. (1992) Being competent and having 'competencies.' *Journal of Further and Higher Education, 16*, 8–17.

Ashworth, M. (1992). *The first step on the longer path: Becoming an ESL teacher.* Scarborough, Ontario, Canada: Pippin Publishing Limited.

Astington, J. W., Dack, L. A. (2008). Theory of mind. In M. M. Haith & J. B. Benson (Eds.), *Encyclopedia of infant and early childhood development* (Vol 3, pp. 343–356). San Diego, CA: Academic Press.

Astington, J. W., &Hughes C. (2013). Theory of mind: Self-reflection and social understanding. In P. S. Zelazo (Ed.), *Oxford handbook of developmental psychology.* New York: Oxford University Press.

Atherton, J. S. (2005). *Learning and teaching: Piaget's developmental theory.* Accessed on May 20, 2011, at http://www .learningandteaching.info/

Aucoin, K. J., Frick, P. J., & Bodin, S. D. (2006). Corporal punishment and child adjustment. *J Appl Dev Psychol, 27*, 527–41.

Aud, S., Wilkinson-Flicker, S., Kristapovich, P., Rathbun, A., Wang, X., & Zhang, J. (2013). *The condition of education 2013 (NCES 2013-037).* Washington, DC: U.S. Department of Education, National Center for Education Statistics.

Aunola, K., Stattin, H., & Nurmi, J.E. (2000). Parenting styles and adolescents' achievement strategies. *Journal of Adolescence, 23*, 205–222.

Bachman, H. J., Coley, R. L., & Carrano, J. (2011). Maternal relationship instability influences on children's emotional and behavioral functioning in low-income families. *Journal of Abnormal Child Psychology.* 39, 1149–1161.

Bandura, A. (1977). *Social learning theory.* Englewood Cliffs, NJ: Prentice Hall.

Bar-On, R. (1997). *The Emotional Quotient Inventory (EQ-I): Technical manual.* Toronto, Ontario, Canada: Multi-Health Systems.

Bar-On, R. (2000). Emotional and social intelligence: Insights from the Emotional Quotient Inventory (EQ-I). In R. Bar-On & J. D. A. Parker (Eds.), *Handbook of emotional intelligence, 363-388.* San Francisco, CA: Jossey-Bass.

Bar-On, R. (2005). The Bar-On model of emotional-social intelligence. In P. Fernández-Berrocal & N. Extremera (Guest Eds.), Special issue on emotional intelligence. *Psicothema, 17* (Accessed on 7/18/2014, at http://www.leadership-systems.com/downloads/BarOnArticle.pdf).

Bardige, B. S., & Segal, M. M. (2005). *Building literacy with love: A guide for teachers and caregivers of children birth through age 5.* Washington, DC: Zero to Three.

Barnard, M. U. (2003). *Helping your depressed child: A step-by-step guide for parents.* Oakland, CA: New Harbinger.

Barnett, W. S., & Ackerman, D. J. (2006). Costs, benefits, and the long-term effects of preschool programs. *Community Development: Journal of the Community Development Society, 37*(2). (Accessed on 7/18/2014 at http://cnpf.ca/documents/Costs,_benefits_and_long-term_effects_of_early_care_and_education_programs.pdf).

Barnett, W. S., Jung, K., Yarosz, D. J., Thomas, J., Hornbeck, A., Stechuk, R., & Burns, S. (2008). *Early Childhood Research Quarterly, 23*(3), 299–313.

Baron, R. A. (1998). *Psychology,* 4th ed. Boston, MA: Allyn & Bacon.

Bauer, P.J., San Souci, P., & Pathman, T. (2010). Infant memory. *Wiley Interdisciplinary Reviews: Cognitive Science, 1*(2), 267–277.

Bauermeister, J. J., Canino, G., Bravo, M., Ramirez, R., Jensen, P. S., Chavez, L., Martinez-Taboas, A., Ribera, J., Alegria, M., & Garcia, P. M. (2003). Stimulant and psychosocial treatment of ADHD in Latino/Hispanic children. *Journal of the American Academy of Child and Adolescent Psychiatry, 42,* 851–855.

Baumrind, D. (1967). Child care practices anteceding three patterns of preschool behavior. *Genetic Psychology Monographs, 75,* 43–88.

Baumrind, D. (1971). Current patterns of parental authority. *Developmental Psychology Monographs, 4*(1), 1–103.

Baumrind, D. (1978). Parental disciplinary patterns and social competence in children. *Youth and Society, 9*(3), 239–276.

Baumrind, D., Larzelere, R. E., & Cowan, P. A. (2002). Ordinary physical punishment: Is it harmful? *Psychological Bulletin, 128*(4), 580–589.

Bazzano, A., Wolfe, C., Zylowska, L., Wang, S., Schuster, E., & Barrett, C. (2010). Stress-Reduction and improved well-being following a pilot community-based participatory mindfulness-based stress-reduction (MBSR) program for parents/caregivers of children with developmental disabilities. *Disability and Health Journal, 3*(2), 6-7.

Beane, A. L. (2000). *Bully free classroom.* Minneapolis, MN: Free Spirit Publishing.

Beaty, J. J. (1997). Building bridges with multicultural picture books: For children 3–5. Upper Saddle River, NJ: Merrill Education/Prentice Hall.

Beaudoin, M., & Taylor, M., (2009). *Responding to the culture of bullying & disrespect: New perspectives on collaboration, compassion, and responsibility* (2nd ed.). Thousand Oaks, CA: Corwin.

Bechara, A., Damasiom, A.R. (2005). The somatic marker hypothesis: A neural theory of economic decision. *Games and Economic Behavior, 52,* 336–372.

Beck, R. (1973). White House conferences on children: An historical perspective. *Harvard Educational Review, 43,* 4.

Belfield, C. R., & Levin, H. M. (2007). *The price we pay: The costs to the nation of inadequate education.* Washington, DC: Brookings Institution Press.

Bender, H. L., Allen, J. P., McElhaney, K. B., Antonishak, J., Moore, C. M., Kelly, H. O., & Davis, S. M. (2007). Use of harsh physical discipline and developmental outcomes in adolescence. *Development and Psychopathology, 19,* 227–242.

Bener, A., Al-Mahdi, H. S., Vachhani, P. J., Al-Nufal, M., & Ali, A. I. (2010). Do excessive internet use, television viewing and poor lifestyle habits affect low vision in school children? *Journal of Child Health Care, 14*(4), 375–385.

Bentzen, W. R. (2005). *Seeing young children: A guide to observing and recording behavior* (5th ed.). Clifton Park, NY: Thomson Delmar Learning.

Bergen, D. (2002). The role of pretend play in children's cognitive development. *Early Childhood Research and Practice, 4*(1). Retrieved February 8, 2014, from http://www.ecrp.uiuc.edu/v4n1/bergen.html

Bergeron, N., & Schneider, B.H. (2009). Explaining cross-national differences in peer-directed aggression: A quantitative synthesis. *Aggressive Behavior, 31*(2), 116–137. *Encyclopedia on Early Childhood Development.*

Berk, L. (2009). *Child development* (8th ed.). Boston, MA: Pearson Education, Inc.

Berk, L. E. (2001). *Awakening children's minds: How parents and teachers can make a difference.* New York: Oxford University Press.

Berk, L. E., & Winsler, A. (1995). *Scaffolding children's learning: Vygotsky and early childhood education.* Washington, DC: National Association for the Education of Young Children.

Berk, L., Mann, T., & Ogan, A. (2006). *Make-believe play: Wellspring for development of self-regulation.* In D. G. Singer, R. M. Golinkoff, & K. Hirsh-Pasek (Eds.), Play = learning: How play motivates and enhances children's cognitive and social-emotional growth (pp. 74–100). New York: Oxford University Press.

Berkowitz, M. W. (1997). The complete moral person: Anatomy and formation. In J. M. Dubois (Ed.), *Moral issues in psychology: Personalist contributions to selected problems* (pp. 11–41). Lanham, MD: University Press of America.

Berkowitz, M. W., & Bier, M. (2005). The interpersonal roots of character education. In D. K. Lapsley & F. C. Power (Eds.), *Character psychology and character education,* 268-285.. South Bend, IN: University of Notre Dame Press.

Berlin, L. J., Ispa, J. M., Fine, M. A., Malone, P. S., Brooks-Gunn, J., Brady- Smith, C., Ayoub, C., & Bai, Y. (2009). Correlates and consequences of spanking and verbal punishment for low-income White, African American, and Mexican American toddlers. *Child Development, 80,* 1403–1420.

Bernal, R. (2008). The effect of maternal employment and child care on children's cognitive development. *International Economic Review, 49,* 1173–1209.

Berry, B. (2006). Teacher quality and the teaching profession: New messages, new messengers. In K. Jones (Ed.), *Raising schools: A democratic model for school accountability.* Lanham, MD: Scarecrow Press.

Bersamin, M., Todd, M., Fisher, D. A., Hill, D. L., Grube, J. W. & Walker, S. (2008). *Parenting practices and adolescent sexual behaviour: A longitudinal study.*

Bialystok, E., & Hakuta, K. *In other words: The science and psychology of second-language acquisition.* New York: Basic Books.

Bigler, R. S., & Liben, L.S. (2007). Developmental intergroup theory: Explaining and reducing children's social stereotyping and prejudice. *Current Directions in Psychological Science, 16,* 162–166.

Billman, J., & Sherman, J. A. (1997). *Observation and participation in early childhood settings: A practicum guide, birth through age five.* Needham Heights, MA: Allyn & Bacon.

Birchmayer, J., Kennedy, A., & Stonehouse, A. (2010). Sharing spoken language: Sounds, conversations, and told stories. *Young Children, 65*(1), 36–38.

Birdsong, D. (1992). Ultimate attainment in second language acquisition. *Linguistic Society of America, 68*, 706–755.

Birdsong, D., & Molis, M. On the evidence for maturational constraints in second-language acquisitions. *Journal of Memory and Language. 44*, 235–249.

Birkbeck, A. K.-S. (2009). Nativism versus neuroconstructivism: Rethinking the study of developmental disorders. *American Psychological Association, 45*(1), 56–63.

Blandon, A. Y., & Volling, B. L. (2008). Parental gentle guidance and children's compliance within the family: A replication study. *Journal of Family Psychology, 22*(3), 355–366.

Bloom, B. S. (1964). *Stability and change in human characteristics.* New York: Wiley.

Blum, R. (2005). *School connectedness: Improving the lives of students.* Baltimore, MD: Johns Hopkins Bloomberg School of Public Health.

Bodrova, E., & Leong, D. J. (2008) Developing self-regulation in young children: Can we keep all the crickets in the basket? *Young Children, 63*(2), 56–58.

Bodrova, E., & Leong, D. J. (2010). Curriculum and play in early child development. In: R. E. Tremblay, R. G. Barr, R. D. Peters, & M. Boivin (Eds.), *Encyclopedia on early childhood development* [online]. Montreal, Quebec, Canada: Centre of Excellence for Early Childhood Development. Accessed on March 16, 2011, at http://www.childencyclopedia.com/documents/BodrovaLeongANGxp.pdf

Bogdan, R., Biklen, D., Shapiro, A., & Spelkoman, D. (1982). The disabled: Media's monster. *Social Policy, 13*(2), 32–35.

Bogdashina, O. (2003). *Sensory perceptual issues in autism: Different sensory experiences–different perceptual worlds.* London: Jessica Kingsley.

Bongers, I. L., Koot, H. M., van der Ende, J., & Verhulst, F. C. (2008). Predicting young adult social functioning from developmental trajectories of externalizing behaviour. *Psychological Medicine, 38*, 989–999.

Bonnice, S. (2004). *The hidden child: youth with autism. Part of the series youth with special needs.* Broomall, PA: Mason Crest.

Borba, M. (2002). *Building moral intelligence: The seven essential virtues that teach kids to do the right thing.* San Francisco, CA: Jossey-Bass.

Bouchard, T. J., & McGue, M. (2003). Genetic and environmental influences on human psychological differences. *The Journal of Neurobiology, 54*, 4–45.

Bouras, N. (Ed.) (1994). *Mental health in mental retardation: Recent advances and practices.* Cambridge, UK: Cambridge University Press.

Bouras, N. (Ed) (1999). *Psychiatric and behavioral disorders in developmental disabilities and mental retardation.* Cambridge, UK: Cambridge University Press.

Bower, T. G. R. (1982). *Development in infancy.* San Francisco, CA: W.H. Freeman.

Bowlby, J. (1958). The nature of the child's tie to his mother. *International Journal of Psychoanalysis, 39*, 350–373.

Boxer, P., Guerra, N. G., Huesmann, L. R., & Morales, J. (2005). Proximal peer-level effects of a small-group selected prevention on aggression in elementary school children: An investigation of the peer contagion hypothesis. *Journal of Abnormal Child Psychology, 33*, 325–338.

Bradley, R. H., & Corwyn, R. F. (2008). Infant temperament, parenting and externalizing behavior in first grade: A test of the differential susceptibility hypothesis. *Journal of Child Psychology & Psychiatry, 49*, 124–131.

Brady, K., Forton, M. B., Porter, D., & Wood, C. (2003). *Rules in school.* Greenfield, MA: Northeast Foundation for Children.

Bramer, J. S. (2006). *Attention deficit disorder: The unfocused mind in children and adults.* New Haven, CT, & London, UK: Yale University Press.

Branje, S., Hale, W., Frijns, T., & Meeus, W. (2010). Longitudinal associations between perceived parent-child relationship quality and depressive symptoms in adolescence. *Journal of Abnormal Child Psychology, 38*(6), 751–763.

Bray, S., Shimojo, S., & O'Doherty, J. P. Human medial orbitofrontal cortex is recruited during experience of imagined and real rewards. *Journal of neurophysiology, 103*(5), 250–12.

Bray, S., Shimojo, S., & O'Doherty, J.P. (2010). Human medial orbitofrontal cortex is recruited during experience of imagined and real rewards. *Journal of Neurophysiology, 103*, 2506–2512.

Brazelton, T. B. (1985). *Working and caring.* Reading, MA: Addison-Wesley.

Brazelton, T. B., Koslowski, B., & Main, M. (1974). The origins of reciprocity. In M. Lewis & L. Rosenblum (Eds.), *The effect of the infant on its caregiver.* New York: Wiley-Interscience.

Bremner, R. H. (Ed.). (1974). *Children and youth in America: A documentary history* (vols. 1–3). Cambridge, MA: Harvard University Press.

Briant, M. Z. (2004). *Baby sign language basics: Early communication for hearing babies and toddlers.* Carlsbad, CA: Hay House.

Briggs-Gowan, M. J., Carter, A. S., Skuban, E. M., & Horwitz, S. M. (2001). Prevalence of social-emotional and behavioral problems in a community sample of 1-and 2-year-old children. *Journal of the American Academy of Child & Adolescent Psychiatry, 40*(7), 811.

Broderick, P.C. & Blewitt, P. (2010). *The life span: Human development for helping professionals.* Boston, MA: Pearson.

Bronfenbrenner, U. (1979). *The ecology of human development: Experiments by nature and design.* Cambridge, MA: Harvard University Press.

Bronfenbrenner, U. (1988). Interacting systems in human development: Research paradigms: Present and future. In N. Bolger, A. Caspi, G. Downey, & M. Moorehouse (Eds.), *Persons in context: Developmental processes* (pp. 25–49). New York: Cambridge University Press.

Bronfenbrenner, U. (1990). Discovering what families do. In *Rebuilding the nest: A new commitment to the American family.* Family Service America. Accessed on March 16, 2011, at http://www.montana.edu/www4h/process.html

Bronfenbrenner, U. (1993). The ecology of cognitive development: Research models and fugitive findings. In R. H. Wozniak & K. W. Fischer (Eds.), *Development in context: Acting and thinking in specific environments* (pp. 3–44). Hillsdale, NJ: Erlbaum.

Bronfenbrenner, U. (1994). Who cares for the children? In H. Nuba, M. Searson, & D. L. Sheiman (Eds.), *Resources for early childhood: A handbook.* New York: Garland.

Bronfenbrenner, U. (1995). The bioecological model from a life course perspective: Reflections of a participant-observer. In

P. Moen, G. H. Elder, & K. Luscher (Eds.), *Examining lives in context: Perspectives on the ecology of human development.* Cambridge, MA: Harvard University Press.

Bronfenbrenner, U., & Morris, P. A. (1998). The ecology of developmental processes (5th ed.). In W. Damon (Series Ed.) & R. M. Lerner (Vol. Ed.), *Handbook of child psychology: Theoretical models of human development* (Vol. 1, pp. 993–1027). New York: Wiley.

Bronson, M. B. (2001). *Self-regulation in early childhood: Nature and nurture.* New York: Guilford.

Brophy, J. (2007). Child maltreatment in diverse households: Challenges to child care law, theory and practice. In S. Meuwese, S. Detrick, & S. Jansen (Eds.), *100 years of child protection.* Nijmegen, the Netherlands: Wolf Legal.

Brown, K. W., & Ryan, R. M. (2003). The benefits of being present: Mindfulness and its role in psychological well-being. *Journal of Personality and Social Psychology, 84*(4), 822–848.

Brown, S. & Vaughan, C. (2009). *Play: How it shapes the brain, opens the imagination, and invigorates the soul.* New York: Avery.

Brown, S., & Vaughan, C. (2009). *Play, how it shapes the brain, opens the imagination, and invigorates the soul.* New York: Penguin Group (USA) Inc.

Brown, T. A. (1903). *A history of the New York stage.* New York: Dodd, Mead and Company, p. 176, Accessed March 19, 2014, at http://query.nytimes.com

Brown, T. E. (2007). A new approach to attention deficit disorder. *Educational Leadership, 64,* 22–24.

Bruer, J. T. (2008). Critical periods in second language learning: distinguishing phenomena from explanation. In M. Mody & E. Silliman (Eds.), *Brain, behavior and learning in language and reading disorders.* New York: The Guilford Press, 72–96.

Bruner, J. (1978a). Learning the mother tongue. *Human Nature, 1,* 43–48.

Bruner, J. (1978b). Learning how to do things with words. In J. S. Bruner & A. Garton (Eds.), *Human growth and development: Wolfson College lectures.* Oxford, UK: Clarendon Press.

Bruns, D. A., & Corso, R. M. (2001). *Working with culturally and linguistically diverse families.* Champaign, IL: ERIC Clearinghouse on Elementary and Early Childhood Education, document no. ED455972. Accessed on March 16, 2011, at http://www.eric.ed.gov

Bugental, D. B., Martorell, G. A., & Barraza, V. (2003). The hormonal costs of subtle forms of infant maltreatment. *Hormones and Behavior, 43*(1), 237–244.

Buijzen, M. & Valkenburg, P. M. (2003). The effects of television advertising on materialism, parent-child conflict, and unhappiness: A review of research. *Journal of Applied Developmental Psychology, 24*(4), 437–456.

Bullock, B. M., & Dishion, T. J. (2003). Conduct disorder. In J. J. Ponzetti Jr., R. R. Hanom, Y. Kellar- Guenther, P. K. Kerig, T. L. Scales, & J. M. While (Eds.), *The international encyclopedia of marriage and family relationships* (2nd ed., 249–354).). New York: Macmillan Reference USA.

Burke, C. A. (2010). Mindfulness-based approaches with children and adolescents: A preliminary review of current research in an emergent field. *Journal of Child and Family Studies, 19,* 133–144.

Byrne, P. (2000). *Philosophical and ethical problems in mental handicap.* New York: Palgrave Macmillan.

Caine, R. N. (1998). Building the bridge from research to classroom. *Educational Leadership, 58*(3), 62-65.

Cairns, K. (2002). *Attachment, trauma and resilience.* London: British Association for Adoption and Fostering.

Cárdenas, J. A. (1995). *Multicultural education: A generation of advocacy.* Needham Heights, MA: Allyn & Bacon.

Carlson, G. A., Jensen, P. S., & Nottelmann, E. D. (Eds.). (1998). Special issue: current issues in childhood bipolarity. *Journal of Affective Disorders, 51,* entire issue.

Carlson, S. M. (2005). Developmentally sensitive measures of executive function in preschool children. *Developmental Neuropsychology, 28,* 595–616.

Carlson, S. M., & Moses, L. J. (2001). Individual differences in inhibitory control and children's theory of mind. *Child Development, 72,* 1032–1053.

Carlson, S. M., Mandell, D. J., & Williams, L. (2004). Executive function and theory of mind: Stability and prediction from ages 2 to 3. *Developmental Psychology, 40,* 1105–1122.

Carnegie, D. (1936). *How to win friends and influence people.* New York: Simon & Schuster.

Carr, E. G., Dunlap, G., Horner, R. H., Koegel, R. L., Turnbull, A. P., Sailor, W., Anderson, J., Albin, R. W., Koegel, L. K., & Fox, L. (2002). Positive behavior support: Evolution of an applied science. *Journal of Positive Behavior Interventions 4,* 4–16.

Carr, E. G., Horner, R. H., Turnbull, A. P., Marquis, J. G., McLaughlin, D. M., McAtee, M. L., Smith, C. E., Ryan, K. A., Ruef, M. B., Doolabh, A., & Braddock, D. (1999). *Positive behavior support for people with developmental disabilities: A research synthesis.* Washington, DC: American Association on Mental Retardation.

Carrasco, J. M., Holtz, C. A., & Fox, R. A. (2008). Development of a screening measure for behavior problems in young children. Paper presented at the annual meeting of the *Association for Behavioral and Cognitive Therapies*, Orlando, FL.

Caspary, W. R. (2000). *Dewey on democracy.* Ithaca, NY: Cornell University Press.

Cast, A. D., Schweingruber, D., & Berns, N. (2006). Childhood physical punishment and problem solving in marriage. *Journal of Interpersonal Violence, 21,* 244–261.

Caulfield, J., Kidd, S., & Kocher, Brain-based instruction in action. *Educational Leadership, 58*(3), 62–65.

Cell Press. (2013, May 2). Kids with conduct problems may have brains that under-react to painful images: May increase risk of adult psychopathy. *ScienceDaily.* Retrieved September 30, 2013, from http://www.sciencedaily.com/releases/2013/05/130502131859.htm

Center on the Developing Child at Harvard University. (2011). Building the brain's 'air traffic control' system: How early experiences shape the development of executive function: *Working Paper No. 11.* Retrieved March 8, 2014, at http://www.developingchild.harvard.edu

Centers for Disease Control and Prevention, National Center for Injury Prevention and Control. (2008). *Web-based Injury Statistics Query and Reporting System.* (WISQARS) Accessed online March 16, 2011, at www.cdc.gov/ncipc/wisqars

Champagne, F., & Mashoodh, R. (2009). Genes in context: Gene–environment interplay and the origins of individual differences in behavior. *Current Directions in Psychological Science, 18,* 127–131.

Chang, L., Schwartz, D., Dodge, K., McBride-Chang, C. (2003). Harsh parenting in relation to child emotion regulation and aggression. *Journal of Family Psychology. 17,* 598–606.

Charles, C., Louv, R., Bodner, L., & Guns, B. (2008). *Children and nature 2008: A report on the movement to reconnect children* to the natural world. Sante Fe, NM; Children and Nature Network.

Charlesworth, R. (2004). *Understanding child development* (6th ed.). Clifton Park, NY: Thomson Delmar Learning.

Charlesworth, R. (2011). Understanding child development (8th ed.). Belmont, CA: Wadsworth, Cengage.

Charney, R. S. (1997). *Habits of goodness: Case studies in the social curriculum.* Greenfield, MA: Northeast Foundation for Children.

Charney, R. S. (2002). *Teaching children to care: Classroom management for ethical and academic growth, K–8.* Greenfield, MA: Northeast Foundation for Children.

Chen, D. (1999). Interactions between infants and caregivers: The context for early intervention. In D. Chen (Ed.), *Essential elements in early intervention: Visual impairment and multiple disabilities* (pp. 22–48). New York: American Foundation for the Blind.

Chen, X. (2009). Culture and early socio-emotional development. University of Western Ontario, Canada (Published online). Accessed on March 16, 2011, at www .enfant-encyclopedie. com/pages/PDF/ChenANGxp .pdf

Chen, X., Chen, H., Li, D., & Wang, L. (2009). Early childhood behavioral inhibition and social and school adjustment in Chinese children: A five-year longitudinal study. *Child Development, 80*, 1692–1704.

Chen, X., Hastings, P., Rubin, K. H., Chen, H., Cen, G., & Stewart, S. L. (1998). Childrearing attitudes and behavioral inhibition in Chinese and Canadian toddlers: A cross-cultural study. *Developmental Psychology, 34*(4), 677–686.

Chen, X., Huang, Q., Rozelle, S., Shi, Y., Zhang, L., 2009. Effect of migration on children's educational performance in rural China. *Comparative Economic Studies, 51*, 323–343.

Chen, X., Rubin, K. H., Liu, M., Chen, H., Wang, L., Li, D., Gao, X., Cen, G., Gu, H., & Li, B. (2003). Compliance in Chinese and Canadian toddlers. *International Journal of Behavioral Development, 27*(5), 428–436.

Cherrington, S. (2008). Early childhood teaching: An ethical activity. *The space,* 11, Autumn, 4–5.

Choi, J., Jeong. B., Rohan, M., Polcari, A., & Teicher, M. (2012). Preliminary evidence for white matter tract abnormalities in young adults exposed to parental verbal abuse. *Biological Psychiatry, 65*, 227–234.

Chomsky, N. (1965). *Aspects of the theory of syntax.* Cambridge, MA: MIT Press.

Christakis, D. A., & Garrison, M. M. (2009). Preschool-aged children's television viewing in child care settings. *Pediatrics, 124*(6), 1627–1632.

Christakis, D. A., Zimmerman, F. J., & Garrison, M. M. (2006). Television viewing in child care programs: A national survey. *Communication Reports, 19*(2), 111–120.

Christian, C. W., & Block, R. (2009). Abusive head trauma in infants and children. Special report: Committee on child abuse and neglect, American Academy of Pediatrics. *Pediatrics, 123*(5), 1409–141.

Christian, L. G. (2006). Understanding families: Applying Family System Theory to early childhood practice. *Young Children, 61(1),* 12–20.

Christian, S., & Poppe, J. (2007). Protecting the youngest: The role of early care and education in preventing and responding to child maltreatment. Accessed on March 16, 2011, at www.ncsl.org/print/cyf/protectingyoung.pdf

Ciaramicoli, A. P., & Ketcham, K. (2000). *The power of empathy: A practical guide to creating intimacy, self-understanding, and lasting love in your life.* New York: Dutton/Penguin.

Hughes, C., Dunn, J., & White, A. (1998). Trick or treat? Uneven understanding of mind and emotion and executive dysfunction in "hard-to-manage" preschoolers. *Journal of Child Psychology and Psychiatry, 39*, 981–994.

Clampet-Lundquist, S., Edin, K., London, A., Scott, E., & Hunter, V. (2003). Making a way out of no way: How mothers meet basic family needs while moving from welfare to work. In A. C. Crouter & A. Booth (Eds.), *Work-family challenges for low-income parents and their children.* Mahwah, NJ: Erlbaum.

Clark, E. B., Clark, C., & Neill, C. A. (2001). *The heart of a child: What families need to know about heart disorders in children* (2nd ed.). Baltimore, MD: Johns Hopkins University Press.

Clarke-Stewart, A. (1978). Popular primer for parents. *American Psychologist, 33*, 359.

Clarke-Stewart, K. A., Malloy, L. C., & Allhusen, V. D. (2004). Verbal ability, self-control, and close relationships with parents protect children against misleading suggestions. *Applied Cognitive Psychology, 18*, 1037–1058.

Claxton, G., & Carr, M. (2004). A framework for teaching learning: The dynamics of disposition. *Early Years, 24*(1), 87–97.

Close, N. (2002). *Listening to children: Talking with children about difficult issues.* Boston, MA: Allyn & Bacon.

Coatsworth, J. D., Duncan, L. G., Greenberg, M. T., & Nix, R. L. (2010). Changing parents' mindfulness, child management skills, and relationship quality with their youth: Results from a randomized pilot intervention trial. *Journal of Child and Family Studies, 19*, 203–217.

Code of ethical conduct and statement of commitment: A position statement of the National Association for the Education of Young Children. Washington, DC: Author.

Cognitive neurosciences of human social behavior. *Nat Rev Neurosci., 4*, 165–178.

Cohen, D. B. (1999). *Stranger in the nest: Do parents really shape their child's personality, intelligence and character?* New York: Wiley.

Cohen, J. (2006a). Social, emotional, ethical, and academic education: Creating a climate for learning, participation in democracy, and well-being. Harvard Educational Review, 76(2), 201–237.

Cohen, J. (2006b). School based social and emotional learning programs. In K. A. Renninger & I. E. Sigel (Eds.), *Handbook of child psychology (6th ed.). Child psychology in practice* Vol. 4, pp. 592–618). Hoboken, NJ: John Wiley and Sons.

Cohen, J. & Pickeral, T. (2009). *The school climate implementation road map: Promoting democratically informed school communities and the continuous process of school climate improvement.* New York: National Center for School Climate.

Cohen, J., Pickeral, T., & Levine, P. (2010). The Foundation for Democracy: Promoting social, emotional, ethical, cognitive skills and dispositions in K–12 schools. *Interamerican Journal of Education for Democracy, 3*(1), 73–94.

Cohen, J., Shapiro, L, & Fisher, M. (2006). Finding the heart of your school: Using school climate data to create a climate for learning. *Principal Leadership, 7*(4), 26–32.

Cohen, R. A., Grieve, S., Hoth, K., Paul, R. H., Sweet, L., Tate, G. J., Stroud, L., McCaffery, J., Hitsman, B., Niaura, R., Clark, C. R., MacFarlane, A., Bryant Gordon, E., & Williams, L. M. (2006). Early life stress and morphometry of the adult anterior cingulate cortex and caudate nuclei. *Biol Psychiatry. 59*, 975–982.

Colby, A., & Damon, W. (1992). *Some do care: Contemporary lives of moral commitment.* New York: Free Press.

Cole, L. (1950). *A history of education.* New York: Rinehart.

Collins, A., & Halverson, R. (2009). *Rethinking education in the age of technology: The digital revolution and schooling in America.* New York: Teachers College Press.

Colvin, G. (2010). *Defusing disruptive behavior in the classroom.* Thousand Oaks, CA: Corwin.

Comer, R. J. (2004). *Abnormal psychology* (5th ed.). New York: Worth Publishers.

Conboy, B., & Kuhl, P. (2011). Impact of second-language experience in infancy: Brain measures of first- and second-language speech perception. *Developmental Science,* 242–248.

Condon, W. S., & Sander, L. (1974). Neonate movement is synchronized with adult speech: Interactional participation and language acquisition. *Science, 183,* 99–101.

Cook, S. C., & Wellman, C. L. (2004). Chronic stress alters dendritic morphology in rat medial prefrontal cortex. *Neurobiology, 60*(2), 236–248.

Cooper, A., & Jenson, G. (2009). Practical processes for teaching habits of mind. In A. L. Costa and B. Kallick (Eds.), *Habits of mind across the curriculum: Practical and creative strategies for teachers* (pp. 17–35). Alexandria, VA: ASCD.

Copple, C., & Bredekamp, S. (Eds.). (2009). *Developmentally appropriate practice in early childhood programs serving children from birth through age 8* (3rd ed.). Washington, DC: NAEYC.

Corbett, B. (1988). *A garden of children.* Mississauga, Ontario, Canada: The Froebel Foundation.

Corpus, J. H., McClintic-Gilbert, M. S., & Hayenga, A. O. (2009). Within-year changes in children's intrinsic and extrinsic motivational orientations: Contextual predictors and academic outcomes. *Contemporary Educational Psychology, 34,* 154–166.

Corsaro, W. (1988). Peer culture in the preschool. *Theory into Practice, 27*(1), 19–24.

Corsaro, W. A. (1981). Friendship in the nursery school: Social organization in a peer environment. In S. R. Asher & J. M. Gottman (Eds.), *The development of children's friendships.* New York: Cambridge University Press.

Cosco, N. G., Moore, R. C., & Islam, M. Z. (2010). Behavior mapping: A method for linking preschool physical activity and outdoor design. *Medicine & Science in Sports & Exercise, 42*(3), 513–519.

Costa, A., & Kallick, B. (2014). *Dispositions: Reframing teaching and learning.* Thousand Oaks, CA: Corwin.

Costley, D., & Todd, R. (1987). *Human relations in organization* (3rd ed.). New York: West.

Cotton, N. (1983). The development of self-esteem and self-esteem regulation. In J. E. Mack & S. L. Ablon (Eds.), *The development and sustaining of self-esteem in childhood.* New York: International Universities Press.

Crone, D., Hawken, L., & Horner, R. (2010). *Responding to problem behavior in schools, Second Edition: The Behavior Education Program.* The Guilford Practical Intervention in the Schools Series. New York: Guilford Press.

Cronen, V. E. (2001). Practical theory, practical art, and the pragmatic-systemic account of inquiry. *Communication Theory, 11,* 14–35.

Crosnoe, R., Morrison, F. Burchinal, M. Pianta, R., Keating, D., Friedman, S, Clarke-Stewart, A., & NICHD Early Child Care Network. (2010). Instruction, teacher-student relations, and math achievement trajectories in elementary school. *Journal of Educational Psychology, 102*(2), 407–417.

Crosser, S. (2002). *Time out: insights from football.* Published online by Earlychildhood News. Accessed on March 16, 2011, at www.earlychildhoodnews.com/earlychildhood/article_view.aspx?ArticleID=129

Cunnington, P., & Buck, A. (1965). *Children's costume in England.* New York: Barnes & Noble.

Cutler, A., & Mehler, J. (1993). The periodicity bias. *Journal of Phonetics, 21,* 103–108.

Daly, K. (1996). *Families and time: Keeping pace in a hurried culture.* Thousand Oaks, CA: Sage.

Damasio, H., Grabowski, T., Frank, R., Galaburda, A. M., & Damasio, A. R. (1994). The return of Phineas Gage: Clues about the brain from the skull of a famous patient. *Science, 264,* 1102–1105.

Daniels, M. (2001). *Dancing with words: Signing for hearing children's literacy.* Westport, CT: Bergin & Garvey.

Davis, E. P., & Gunnar, M. (2000). Stress, coping & caregiving. In L. Gilkerson (Ed.), *Teaching and learning about the brain and early development.* Chicago, IL: Erikson Institute.

de Boer, B., & Kuhl, P. K. (2003), Investigating the role of infant-directed speech with a computer model. *ARLO, 4,* 129–134.

de Boysson-Bardies, B. (1993). Ontogeny of language-specific syllabic productions. In B. de Boysson-Bardies, S. de Schonen, P. Jusczyk, P. McNeilage, & J. Morton (Eds.). *Developmental neurocognition: Speech and face processing in the first year of life* (pp. 353–363).Dordrecht, Netherlands: Kluwer.

De'Melendez, W., & Beck, V. (2010). *Teaching young children in multicultural classrooms: issues, concepts, and strategies.* New York: Wadsworth/Cengage.

Deak, J. (2010). *Your fantastic elastic brain: Stretch it, shape it.* Belvedere, CA: Little Pickle Press.

Dean, A. L., Malik, M. M., Richards, W., & Stringer, S. A. (1986). Effects of parental maltreatment on children's conceptions of interpersonal relationships. *Developmental Psychology, 22,* 617–626.

Decety, J., & Michalska, K. J. (2010). Neurodevelopmental changes in the circuits underlying empathy and sympathy from childhood to adulthood. *Developmental Science, 13,* 886–899.

Deci, E., & Ryan, R. M. (2011). Self-determination theory. *Handbook of theories of social psychology, 1,* 416–433.

Dennis, R., & Giangreco, M. F. (1996). Creating conversation: Reflections on cultural sensitivity in family interviewing. *Exceptional Children, 63,* 103–116.

Dennis, W. (1973). *Children of the creche.* New York: Appleton-Century-Crofts.

Derman-Sparks, L. (2013). An updated guide for selecting anti-bias children's books. *Teaching for Change's Bookstore at Busboys and Poets.* Accessed on March 16, 2014, at http://bbpbooks.teachingforchange.org/2013-guide-anti-bias-childrens-books

Derman-Sparks, L., & A.B.C. Task Force. (1989). *Anti-Bias Curriculum: Tools for Empowering Young Children.* Washington, DC: National Association for the Education of Young Children.

Derman-Sparks, L., & Olsen Edwards, J. (2010). *Anti-bias education for young children and ourselves.* Washington DC: National Association for the Education of Young Children.

Derman-Sparks, L., & Ramsey, P. G. (2005). What if all the children in my class are white? Anti-bias/multicultural education with white children. *Young Children, 60*(6), 20–24, 26–27 SL.

Derman-Sparks, L., & Ramsey, P. G. (2006). *What if all the kids are white? Anti-bias multicultural education with young children and families.* New York: Teachers College Press.

Derman-Sparks, L. (1989). *Anti-bias curriculum: Tools for empowering young children.* Washington, DC: National Association for the Education of Young Children.

Derman-Sparks, 2013). An updated guide for selecting anti-bias children's books. *Teaching for Change's Bookstore at Busboys and Poets.* Accessed on March 16, 2014, at http://bbpbooks. teachingforchange.org/2013-guide-anti-bias-childrens -books

Devine, D. (2002). Children's citizenship and the structuring of adult-child relations in the primary school. *Childhood, 9,* 303–320.

Devine, J., & Cohen, J. (2007). *Making our school safe: Strategies to protect children and promote learning.* New York: Teachers College Press.

DeVries, R., & Zan, B. (1994). *Moral classrooms, moral children: Creating a constructivist atmosphere in early education.* New York: Teachers College Press.

DeVries, R., & Zan, B. (2003), When children make rules. *Educational Leadership, 61*(1), 64–68.

Dewey, J. (1959). *Dewey on education.* S. Dworkin (Ed.). New York: Bureau of Publications, Teachers College, Columbia University.

Dewey, J. (1966). *Experience and education.* New York: Collier.

Diamond, A., Barnett, W. S., Thomas, J., & Munro, S. (2007). *Science, 318,* 1387–1388.

Dilger, R. N., & Johnson, R. W. (2010). Behavioral assessment of cognitive function using a translational neonatal piglet model. *Brain Behav Immun, 24,* 1156–1165.

Dilger, R. N., & Johnson, R. W. (2010). Behavioral assessment of cognitive function using a translational neonatal piglet model. *Brain, Behavior, and Immunity, 24*(7), 1156–1165.

Dinkmeyer, D. C., & McKay, G. D. (2007). *The parent's handbook: Systematic training for effective parenting.* Bowling Green, KY: Step Publishers.

Dinnebeil, L. A., & Rule, S. (1994). Variables that influence collaboration between parents and service providers. *Journal of Early Intervention, 18*(4), 349–361.

Dishion, T. J., & Bullock, B. M. (2002). Parenting and adolescent problem behavior: An ecological analysis of the nurturance hypothesis. In J. G. Borkowski (Ed.), *Parenting and your child's world* (pp. 231–250). Hillsdale, NJ: Erlbaum.

Dix, T., & Meuniera, L. N., (2009). Depressive symptoms and parenting competence: An analysis of 13 regulatory processes. *Developmental Review, 29*(1), 45–68.

Dix, T., Gershoff, E. T., Meunier, L. N., & Miller, P. C. (2004). The affective structure of supportive parenting: Depressive symptoms, immediate emotions, and child-oriented motivation. *Developmental Psychology, 40,* 1212–1227.

Dobbs, J., Doctoroff, G. L., Fisher, P. H., & Arnold, D. H. (2006). The association between preschool children's socioemotional functioning and their mathematical skills. *Applied Developmental Psychology, 27,* 97–108.

Domjan, M. (Ed.) (2003). *The principles of learning and behavior* (5th ed.) Belmont, CA: Cengage/Wadsworth.

Don, A., Schellenberg, E., & Rourke, B. (1999). Music and language skills of children with Williams Syndrome. *Child Neuropsychology, 5,* 154–170.

Donnelly, M., & Straus, M. A. (Eds.) (2005). *Corporal punishment of children in theoretical perspective.* New Haven, CT: Yale University Press.

Donohue-Carey, P. (2002). Solitary or shared sleep: What's safe? *Mothering: Natural Family Living, 114,* September/October.

Donohue-Colletta, N. (1995). *What parents should know about school readiness.* Washington, DC: National Association for the Education of Young Children.

Douglas, E. M., & Finkelhor, D. (2005). *Child maltreatment fatalities fact sheet.* Durham, NH: Crimes Against Children Research Center. Retrieved on 6/29/2014 from http://www .unh.edu/ccrc/factsheet/pdf/CSA-FS20.pdf

Dreikurs, R., & Grey, L. (1968). *A New Approach to Discipline: Logical Consequences.* New York: Hawthorn Books.

Dreikurs, R., Cassel, P., & Ferguson, E. D. (2004). *Discipline without tears: How to reduce conflict and establish cooperation in the classroom.* Mississauga, Ontatio, Canada: Wiley.

Duckworth, A. L. & Seligman, M. E. P. (2005). Self-discipline outdoes IQ predicting academic performance in adolescents. *Psychological Science, 16,* 939–944.

Dunbar, R. I. M. (1998). The social brain hypothesis. *Evol Anthropol., 6,* 178–190.

Duncan, L. G., & Bardacke, N. (2010). Mindfulness-Based childbirth and parenting education: Promoting family mindfulness during the perinatal period. *Journal of Child and Family Studies, 19*(2), 190–202.

Dupéré, V., Lacourse, É., Willms, J. D., Vitaro, F., & Tremblay, R. E. (2007). Affiliation to youth gangs during adolescence: The interaction between childhood psychopathic tendencies and neighborhood disadvantage. *Journal of Abnormal Child Psychology.* Accessed on March 16, 2011, at http://www. springerlink.com/content/e162227q7l214121/

Dwivedi, K. (2000). *Post-traumatic stress disorder in children and adolescents.* London, UK: Whurr.

Dykeman, C., Daehlin, W., Doyle, S., & Flamer, H. S. (1996). Psychological predictors of school-based violence: Implications for school counsellors. *School Counsellor, 44,* 35–47.

Easter Seals Wisconsin. (2008). *Second Easter Seals study completed: Living with Disabilities.* Wisconsin: Massachusetts Mutual Life Insurance Company. Retrieved 7/1/14 from http://www.thefreelibrary.com/Second+Easter+Seals+study +completed%3a+Living+with+Disabilities.-a0250651737

Education and Advocacy Committee, Tourette Syndrome Foundation of Canada. (2001). *Understanding Tourette syndrome: A handbook for educators.* Toronto, Ontario, Canada: The TS Foundation of Canada.

Edwards, C. P. (2000). Children's play in cross-cultural perspective: A new look at the Six Culture Study. *Cross-Cultural Research, 34*(3), 318–338.

Egan, G. (2002). Exercises in helping skills for Egan's the skilled helper: A problem-management and opportunity-development approach to helping. New York: Brooks/Cole.

Egan, G. (2006). *Essentials of skilled helping: Managing problems, developing opportunities.* New York: Brooks/Cole.

Eimas, P. D. (1975). Auditory and phonetic coding of the cues for speech: discrimination of the /r–l/ distinction by young infants. *Percept. Psychophys., 18,* 341–347.

Eimas, P. D., Siqueland, E. R., Jusczyk, P., & Vigorito, J. (1971). Speech perception in infants. *Science, 171*, 303–306.

Elias, M. J., & Arnold, H. (2006). *The educator's guide to emotional intelligence and academic achievement: Social-emotional learning in the classroom*. Thousand Oaks, CA: Corwin Press.

Elkind, D. (1981). *The hurried child*. Reading, MA: Addison-Wesley.

Elkind, D. (1997). School and family in the post-modern world. In A. Hargreaves (Ed.), *Rethinking Educational Change With Heart and Mind*, 1997 Yearbook of ASCD(pp. 27–42). Alexandria VA: ASCD.

Elkind, D. (2003). Thanks for the memory: The lasting value of true play. *Young Children, 58*(3), 46–51.

Elkind, D. (2007). *The power of play: How spontaneous, imaginative activities lead to happier, healthier children*. Cambridge, MA: Da Capo Press.

Elkind, D. (2007). *The Power of play: Learning what comes naturally*. Cambridge, MA: Da Capo Press.

Ember, C., & Ember, M. (2005). Explaining corporal punishment of children: A cross-cultural study. *American Anthropologist, 107*(4), 609–619.

Emde, R. N., Wolf, D. P., & Oppenheim, D. (2003). *Revealing the inner worlds of young children*. New York: Oxford University Press.

Emmorey, K., Luk, G., Pyers, J. E., & Bialystok, E. (2008). The source of enhanced cognitive control in bilinguals. *Psychological Science, 19*(12), 1201–1206.

Erikson, E. (1963). *Childhood and society* (2nd ed.). New York: W. W. Norton.

Evans M., Harkness S., & Ortiz, R. (2004). Lone parents cycling between work and benefits. *Research Report No 217*. London: Department for Work and Pensions.

Evans, G. W. (2004). The environment of childhood poverty. *American Psychologist, 59*(2), 77–92.

Evans, G. W., & English, K. (2002). The environment of poverty: Multiple stressor exposure, psychophysiological stress, and socioemotional adjustment. *Child Development, 73*(4), 1238–1248.

Evans, G. W., & Schamberg, M. A. (2009). Childhood poverty, chronic stress, and adult working memory. *Proceedings of the National Academy of Sciences, 106*, 6545–6549.

Evans, G. W., & Wachs, T. D. (Eds.). (2010). *Chaos and its influence on children's development: An ecological perspective*. Washington, DC: American Psychological Association.

Evans, G. W., Gonnella, C., Marcynyszyn, L. A., Gentile, L., & Salpekar, N. (2005). The role of chaos in poverty and children's socioemotional adjustment. *Psychological Science, 16*(7), 560–565.

Faber Taylor, A., & Kuo, F. E. (2009). Children with attention deficits concentrate better after walk in the park. *Journal of Attention Disorders, 12*, 402–409.

Faber Taylor, A., Kuo, F. E., & Sullivan, W. C. (2001). Coping with ADD: The surprising connection to green play settings. *Environment and Behavior, 33*(1), 54–77.

Faegre, M., & Anderson, J. (1930). *Child care and training* (3rd ed.). Minneapolis, MN: University of Minnesota Press.

Fantuzzo, J., & McWayne, C. (2002). The relationship between peer-play interactions in the family context and dimensions of school readiness for low-income preschool children. *Journal of Educational Psychology, 94*, 79–87.

Farah, M. J., Shera, D. M., Savage, J. H., Betancourt, L., Giannetta, J. M., & Brodsky, N. L. (2006). Childhood poverty: Specific associations with neurocognitive development. *Brain Research, 1110*(1), 166–174.

Farver, J. M., Kim, Y. K., & Lee, Y. (1995). Cultural differences in Korean- and Anglo-American preschoolers' social interaction and play behaviors. *Child Development, 66*(4), 1088–1099.

Favez, N. (2006). From family play to family narratives. *Signal Newsletter* of World Association of Infant Mental Health, July–December.

Federal Interagency Forum on Child and Family Statistics. (2012). *America's children: Key national indicators of well-being*. Washington, DC: U.S. Government Printing Office.

Feeney, S., & Freeman, N. (1999). *Ethics and the early childhood educator: Using the NAEYC code*. Washington, DC: NAEYC.

Feldman, R., & Eidelman, A. I. (2009). Biological and environmental initial conditions shape the trajectories of cognitive and social-emotional development across the first years of life. *Developmental Science, 12*(1), 194–200.

Felitti, V., Anda, R., Nordenberg, D., Williamson, D., Spitz, A., Edwards, V., Koss, M. P., & Marks, J. (1998). Relationship of childhood abuse and household dysfunction to many of the leading causes of death in adults. *American Journal of Preventive Medicine, 14*(4), 245–258.

Ferguson, C. A., Menn, L., & Stoel-Gammon C. (Eds.). (1992). *Phonological development: Models, research, implications*. Timonium, MD: York Press.

Ferrier, B. M. (1980). Influence of oxytocin on human memory processes. *Life Science, 27*, 2311–2317.

Fifer, W. P., Byrd, D. L., Kaku, M., Eigsti, I.-M., Isler, J. R., Grose-Fifer, J., Tarullo, A. R., & Balsam, P. D. (2010). Newborn infants learn during sleep. *Proceedings of the National Academy of Sciences*. Washington, DC: NAS.

Filler J., & Xu, Y. (2006). Including children with disabilities in early childhood education programs: Individualizing developmentally appropriate practices. *Childhood Education, 83*(2), 92–97.

Findlay, L. C. (2010). Associations among child care, family, and behavior outcomes in a nation-wide sample of preschool-aged children. *International Journal of Behavioral Development, 34*(5), 427–440.

Fischer-Shofty, M., Levkovitz, Y. S., & Shamay-Tsoory, G. (2012). Oxytocin facilitates accurate perception of competition in men and kinship in women. *Social Cognitive and Affective Neuroscience, 8*(3).

Fishbein, H. D. (2002). *Peer prejudice and discrimination*. Mahwah, NJ: Erlbaum.

Flavell, J. H., Miller, P. H., & Miller, S. (2002). *Cognitive development* (4th ed.) Englewood Cliffs, NJ: Prentice Hall.

Fleer, M. (2009). Supporting scientific conceptual consciousness or learning in a roundabout way in play-based contexts. *International Journal of Science Education, 31*(8), 1069–1089.

Flege, J. E. (1991). Age of learning affects the authenticity of voice-onset time (VOT) in stop consonants produced in a second language. *Acoust. Soc. Am., 89*, 395–411.

Flege, J. E., Yeni-Komshian, G. H., & Liu, S. (1999). Age constraints on second-language acquisition. *J Mem Lang. 41*, 78–104.

Flook, L., Smalley, S. L., Kitil, M. J., Galla, B. M., Kaiser-Greenland, S., Locke, J., Ishijima, E., & Kasari, C. (2010). Effects of mindful awareness practices on executive functions in elementary school children. *Journal of Applied School Psychology, 26*, 70–95.

Flynn, L. L., & Kieff, J. (2002). Including everyone in outdoor play. *Young Children, 57*(3), 20–26.

Fonagy, P. (2001). *Attachment theory and psychoanalysis.* New York: Other Press.

Fontes, L. A. (2005). *Child abuse and culture: Working with diverse families.* New York: Guilford.

Forum on Child and Family Statistics (2009). America's children: Key national indicators of well-being. *Federal interagency forum on child and family statistics.* Washington, DC: U.S. Government Printing Office.

Fox, L., Dunlap, G., & Cushing, L. (2002). Early intervention, positive behavior support, and transition to school. *Journal of Emotional and Behavioral Disorders, 10,* 149–157.

Fox, R. A., & Holtz, C. A. (2009). Treatment outcomes for toddlers with behavior problems from families in poverty. Child and Adolescent Mental Health, 14, 183–189.

Fox, S. E., Levitt, P., & Nelson, C. A. (2010). How the timing and quality of early experiences influence the development of brain architecture. *Child Development, 81,* 28–40.

Franken, R. (2001). *Human motivation* (5th ed.). Pacific Grove, CA: Brooks/Cole.

Franz, J. (2004). *Gale encyclopedia of psychology: Intermittent explosive disorder.* White Plains, NY: Thomson Gale.

Frederickson, G. M., & Knobel, D. T. (1980). A history of discrimination. In T. F. Pettigrew, G. M. Frederickson, D. T. Knobel, N. Glazer, & R. Ueda (Eds.), *Prejudice.* Cambridge, MA: Harvard University Press.

Frick, P. J., & Dickens, C. (2006). Current perspectives on conduct disorder. *Current Psychiatry Reports, 8*(1), 59.

Friedman, S. L., Melhuish, E., & Hill, C. (2009). Childcare Research at the Dawn of a New Millennium: An update. In G. Bremner & T. Wachs, *Wiley-Blackwell Handbook of Infant Development.* Oxford, UK: Wiley-Blackwell.

Frith, U. (2003). *Autism: Explaining the enigma* (2nd ed.). Oxford, UK: Blackwell.

Frodl, T., Reinhold, E., Koutsouleris, Reiser, M., & Meisenzahl, E. M. Interaction of childhood stress with hippocampus and prefrontal cortex volume reduction in major depression. *J Psychiatr Res, 44,* 799–807.

Froebel, F. (1907). *The education of man: The art of education, instruction and training.* New York: Appleton. (Original work published 1826)

Fromberg, D. (2007). *Play's pathways to meaning: A dynamic theory of play.* Paper presented at the annual meeting of the American Educational Research Association. Chicago, IL.

Fromm, S. (2001). Total estimated cost of child abuse and neglect in the United States—statistical evidence. Chicago, IL: Prevent Child Abuse America (PCAA). Accessed on March 16, 2011, at www.preventchildabuse.org.

Frost, J., Wortham, S., & Reifel, S. (2001). *Play and child development.* Upper Saddle River, NJ: Merrill/Prentice-Hall.

Frye, M. A. (2011). Bipolar disorder—a focus on depression. *New England Journal of Medicine, 364*(1), 51–59.

Gadd, R. (2000). The relationship between parenting style and children's adjustment: The parent's perspective. *Journal of Child and Family Studies, 9*(2), 231–245.

Galinsky, E., Aumann, K., & Bond, J. (2008). Times are changing: Gender and generation at work and at home. Retrieved June 22, 2014, at: http://familiesandwork.org/site/research/reports/Times_Are_Changing.pdf

Galinsky, E., Aumann, K., & Bond, J. T. (2009). Times are changing: Gender and generation at work and at home. New York: Families and Work Institute.

Gallagher, K. C. (2005). Brain research and early childhood development: A primer for developmentally appropriate practice. *Young Children, 60* (4), 12–20.

Gallaudet Research Institute. (2010). *A brief summary of estimates for the size of the deaf population.* Washington, DC: Gallaudet University. Accessed on January 8, 2011, at http://research.gallaudet.edu/ Demographics/deaf-US.php

Garces, E., Thomas, D., & Currie, J. (2002). Longer-term effects of head start. *American Economic Review, 92*(4), 999–1012.

Gardner, H. (1983). *Frames of mind.* New York: Basic Books.

Gartrell, D. (2001). Replacing time-out: Part one—Using guidance to build an encouraging classroom. *Young Children, 56*(6), 8–16.

Gartrell, D. (2002). Replacing time-out: Part two—Using guidance to maintain an encouraging classroom. *Young Children, 57*(2), 36–43.

Gartstein, M. A., Gonzalez, C., Carranza, J. A., Ahadi, S. A., Ye, R., Rothbart, M. K., & Yang, S. W. (2006). Studying cross-cultural differences in the development of infant temperament: People's Republic of China, the United States of America, and Spain. *Child Psychiatry & Human Development, 37,* 145–161.

Gazda, G. M., Balzer, F. J., Childers, W. C., Nealy, A., Phelps, R. E., & Walters, R. P. (2006). *Human relations development: A manual for educators.* New York: Allyn & Bacon.

Geller, B., & Luby, J. (1997). Child and adolescent bipolar disorder: A review of the past 10 years. *J Am Acad Child Adolesc Psychiatry, 36,* 1168– 1176.

Gender and generation at work and home. In *National Study of the Changing Workforce,* New York: Families and Work Institute.

George, E. D., Bordner, K. A., Elwafi, H. M., & Simen, A. A. (2010). Maternal separation with early weaning: A novel mouse model of early life neglect. *BMC Neuroscience, 11*(1), 123.

Gerhardt, S. (2004). Why love matters: How affection shapes a *baby's brain.* London, UK: Routledge.

Gershoff, E. T. (2002). Corporal punishment by parents and associated child behaviors and experiences: A meta-analytic and theoretical review. *Psychological Bulletin, 128*(4), 539–579.

Gershoff, E. T. (2008). *Report on physical punishment in the United States: What research tells us about its effects on children.* Columbus OH: Center for Effective Discipline.

Gershoff, E. T., & Bitensky, S. H. (2007). The case against corporal punishment of children: Converging evidence from social science research and international human rights law and implications for U.S. public policy. *Psychology, Public Policy, and Law, 13,* 231–272.

Gilkerson, L. (2001). Integrating an understanding of brain development into early childhood education. *Infant Mental Health Journal, 22,* 174–187.

Gilliam, W. S. (2004). *Prekindergarteners left behind: Expulsion rates in state prekindergarten systems.* Yale University Child Study Center. Accessed on March 16, 2011, at http://www.med.yale.edu/chldstdy/faculty/pdf/Gilliam05.pdf

Gilligan, C. (1982). *In a different voice: Psychological theory and women's development.* Cambridge, MA: Harvard University Press.

Ginsburg, K. R. (2007). The importance of play in promoting healthy child development and maintaining strong parent-child bonds. *Pediatrics, 119*(1), 182–192.

Ginsburg, K. R., & Jablow, M. A (2006). *Parent's Guide to Building Resilience in Children and Teens: Giving Your Child Roots and Wings.* Elk Grove Village, IL; American Academy of Pediatrics.

Giorgio, A., Watkins, A. E., Douaud, G., James, A. C., James, S., De Stefano, et al. (2008). Changes in white matter microstructure during adolescence. *NeuroImage, 39,* 52–61.

Given, B. (2000). Theaters of the mind. *Educational Leadership,* 58(3), 72–75.

Given, B. (2002). *Teaching to the brain's natural learning systems.* ASCD: Alexandria, VA.

Gladwell, M. (2000). The tipping point: How little things can make a big difference. New York: Back Bay Books.

Glazer, S. (2001). Is it a sign? Babies with normal hearing are being taught sign language by parents hoping to produce a learning boost or tantrum relief. *The Washington Post,* March 13, p. 12, section 1.

Glubok, S., Ed. (1969). *Home and child life in colonial days.* New York: Macmillan.

Gmel, G., & Rehm, J. (2003). Harmful alcohol use. *Alcohol Research and Health, 2,* 52–62.

Goetz, P. (2003). The effects of bilingualism on theory of mind development. *Bilingualism* 6(1), 1–15.

Goldman-Rakic, P. S. (1987). Circuitry of primate prefrontal cortex and regulation of behavior by representational memory. In F. Plum (Ed.), *Handbooks of Physiology: A Spectrum of Physiological Knowledge and Concepts: Nervous System: Higher Functions of the Brain* (pp. 373–417). Bethesda, MD: American Physiological Society, Section 1(V).

Goldthorpe, J. H. (2007). *On sociology.* Stanford, CA: Stanford University Press.

Goleman, D. (1997). *Healing emotions: Conversations with the Dalai Lama on mindfulness, emotions, and health.* Boston, MA: Shambhala.

Goleman, D. (2003). *Destructive emotions: How can we overcome them?* New York: Bantam Books.

Goleman, D. (1995). *Emotional intelligence.* New York: Bantam Books.

Gonzalez-Alvarez, L. I. (1998). A short course in sensitivity training: Working with Hispanic families of children with disabilities. *Teaching Exceptional Children, 31*(2), 73–77.

Gonzalez-Mena, J. (1998a). *The child in the family and in the community* (2nd ed.). Upper Saddle River, NJ: Merrill Education/Prentice Hall.

Gonzalez-Mena, J. (1998b). *Foundations: Early childhood education in a diverse society.* Mountain View, CA: Mayfield.

Gonzalez-Mena, J. (2008). *Diversity in early care and education: Honoring differences.* Washington, DC: NAEYC.

Goodwyn, S. W., Acredolo, L. P., & Brown, C. (2000). Impact of symbolic gesturing on early language development. *Journal of Nonverbal Behavior, 24,* 81–103.

Gopnik, A. (2010). The philosophical baby. New York: Picador.

Gopnik, A., & Schulz, L. E. (2007). *Causal learning: Psychology, philosophy, and computation.* New York: Oxford University Press.

Gordon, T. (1970). *Parent effectiveness training.* New York: Peter Wyden.

Gosso, Y., Lima, M. D., Morais, S. E., & Otta, E. (2007). Pretend play of Brazilian children: A window into different cultural worlds. *Journal of Cross-Cultural Psychology, 38*(5), 539–558.

Graham, S., Bellmore, A., Nishina, A., & Juvonen, J. (2009). "It must be me": Ethnic diversity and attributions for peer victimization in middle school. *Journal of Youth and Adolescence, 38,* 487–499.

Grant, K. B., & Ray, J. A. (2010). *Home, school, and community collaboration: Culturally responsive family involvement.* Los Angeles, CA: Sage.

Graziano, A. M., Hamblen, J. L., & Plante, W. A. (1996). Subabusive violence in child rearing in middle-class American families. *Pediatrics, 98,* 845–848.

Green, R. W. (1998). *The explosive child.* New York: Harper Collins.

Green, V., & Stafford, S. H. (1997). Preschool integration: Strategies for teachers. In K. M. Paciorek & J. H. Munro (Eds.), *Annual editions: Early childhood education 97/98* (18th ed.). New York: McGraw-Hill. (Original work published in *Childhood Education,* Summer 1996)

Greenberg, M. T., & Harris, A. R. (2012). Nurturing mindfulness in children and youth: Current state of research. *Child Development Perspectives, 6*(2), 161–166.

Greene, R. W. (2001). *The explosive child: A new approach for understanding and parenting easily frustrated, chronically inflexible children.* New York: HarperCollins.

Greene, R. W., Biederman, J., Zerwas, S., Monuteaux, M. C., Goring, J. C., & Faraone, S. V. (2008). Psychiatric comorbidity, family dysfunction, and social impairment in referred youth with Oppositional Defiant Disorder. *American Journal of Psychiatry, 159*(7), 1214–1224.

Grodeck, B., & Berger, D. S. (2007). *The first year: HIV: An essential guide for the newly diagnosed.* Washington, DC: Marlowe.

Groenendyk, A. E., & Volling, B. L. (2007). Co-parenting and early conscience development in the family. *The Journal of Genetic Psychology, 168*(2), 201–224.

Grogan-Kaylor, A. (2004). The effect of corporal punishment on antisocial behavior in children. *Social Work Research, 28*(3), 153–164.

Grogan-Kaylor, A. (2005). Corporal punishment and the growth trajectory of children's antisocial behavior. *Child Maltreatment, 10,* 283–292.

Gronlund, G. (1997). Families and schools: Bringing the DAP message to kindergarten and primary teachers. In K. M. Paciorek & J. H. Munro (Eds.), *Annual editions: Early childhood education 97/98* (18th ed.). New York: McGraw-Hill. (Original work published in *Young Children,* July 1995)

Grusec, J. E., Goodnow, J., & Kuczynski, L. (2000). New directions in analyses of parenting contributions to children's acquisition of values. *Child Development, 71*(1), 205–211.

Gudykunst, W. B., Matsumoto, Y., Ting-Toomey, S., Nishida, T., Kim, K. S., & Heyman, S. (1996). The influence of cultural individualism-collectivism, self construals, and individual values on communication styles across cultures. *Human Communication Research, 22,* 510–243.

Gunnar, M. R., Morison, S. J., Chisholm, K., & Schuder, M. (2001). Salivary cortisol levels in children adopted from Romanian orphanages. *Development and Psychopathology, 13*(3), 611–628.

Gunnar, M. R., Frenn, K., Wewerka, S. S., & Van Ryzin, M. J. (2009). Moderate versus severe early life stress: Associations with stress reactivity and regulation in 10–12-year-old children. *Psychoneuroendocrinology, 34*(1), 62–75.

Gunzerath, L., Faden, V., Zakhari, S., & Warren, K. (2004). National Institute on Alcohol Abuse and Alcoholism report on moderate drinking. *Alcoholism: Clinical and Experimental Research, 28,* 829–847.

Gupta, V. B., Ed. (2004). *Autistic spectrum disorders in children.* New York: Marcel Dekker.

Gurian, M. (2007). Nurture the nature: Understanding and supporting your child's unique core personality. San Francisco: John Wiley & Sons, Jossey-Bass.

Gurian, M., & Stevens, K. (2005). *The minds of boys: Saving our sons from falling behind in school and life.* San Francisco, CA: Jossey-Bass;

Gutek, G. L. (1997). *Historical and philosophical foundations of education: A biographical introduction* (2nd ed.). Upper Saddle River, NJ: Merrill Education/Prentice Hall.

Hagele, D. (2005). The Impact of maltreatment on the developing child. *North Carolina Medical Journal, 66*(5), 356–359. Accessed on February 10, 2011, at www .ncmedicaljournal .com/wp-content/uploads/2010/11/Hagele.pdf

Haimovitz, K., Wormington, S. V., & Corpus, J. H. (2011). Dangerous mindsets: How beliefs about intelligence predict motivational change. *Learning and Individual Differences, 21,* 747–752.

Haith, M. M., & Benson, J. B. (Eds.). (2008). Encyclopedia of infant and early childhood development. New York: Elsevier.

Hallowell, E. (2003). *The Childhood roots of adult happiness: Five steps to help kids create and sustain lifelong joy.* New York: Ballantine Books.

Halverson, S. (2004). Teaching ethics: The role of the classroom teacher. *Childhood Education, 80*(3), 157.

Halvorsen, A. T., & Neary, T. (2009). *Building inclusive schools: Tools & strategies for success.* Boston, MA: Pearson-Allyn & Bacon.

Hamermesh, D. S., & Parker, A. (2005). Beauty in the classroom: Professorial pulchritude and putative pedagogical productivity. *Economics of Education Review, 24,* 369–376.

Hammack, P. L., Robinson, W. L., Crawford, I., & Li, S. T. (2004). Poverty and depressed mood among urban African-American adolescents: A family stress perspective. *Journal of Child and Family Studies, 13*(3), 309–323.

Handbook of Child Psychology: Theoretical Models of Human Development (5th ed., Vol. 1, pp. 993–1028). New York: Wiley & Sons.

Hanson, J. L., Chung, M. K., Avants, B. B., Shirtcliff, E. A., Gee, J. C., Davidson, R. J., & Pollak, S.D. Early stress is associated with alterations in the orbitofrontal cortex: A tensor-based morphometry investigation of brain structure and behavioral risk. *J Neurosci, 30,* 7466–7472

Hanson, M. J. (1996). *Teaching the infant with Down syndrome: A guide for parents and professionals* (2nd ed.). Austin, TX: Pro-Ed.

Hari, R., & Kujala, M. V. (2009). Brain basis of human social interaction: From concepts to brain imaging. *Physiol. Rev., 89,* 453–447.

Harlow, H., & Zimmerman, R. (1959). Affectional responses in the infant monkey. *Science, 130,* 421–432.

Harms, T., Clifford, R., & Cryer, D. (2005) *Early Childhood Environment Rating Scale,* Revised Ed. New York: Teachers College Press.

Harris, P.L. (2006). Social cognition. In D. Kuhn & R. S. Siegler (Eds.), *Cognition, perception, and language, Handbook of Child Psychology* (6th ed., vol. 2). Hoboken, NJ: Wiley.

Harrison, A. O., Wilson, M. N., Pine, C. J., Chan, S. Q., & Buriel, R. (1990). Family ecologies of ethnic minority children. *Child Development, 61,* 347–362.

Hartshorne, H., & May, M. A. (1928). *Studies in the nature of character* (Vol. 1). New York: Macmillan.

Hatch, J. A. (2005). *Teaching in the new kindergarten.* Clifton Park, NY: Thomson Delmar Learning.

Hauck F. R., Herman, S. M., Donovan, M., Iyasu, S., Merrick Moore, C., Donoghue, E., Kirschner, R. H., & Willinger, M. (2003). Sleep environment and the risk of Sudden Infant Death Syndrome in an urban population: The Chicago infant mortality study. *Pediatrics, 111,* 1207–1214.

Hawkins, J. D., Kosterman, R., Catalano, R. F., Hill, K. G., & Abbott, R. D. (2008). Effects of Social Development Intervention in childhood 15 years later. *Archives of Pediatrics and Adolescent Medicine, 162*(12), 1133–1141.

Hayenga, A. O., & Corpus, J. H. (2010). Profiles of intrinsic and extrinsic motivations: A person-centered approach to motivation and achievement in middle school. *Motivation and Emotion. 34,* 371–383.

Hayne, H. (2007). Infant memory development: New questions, new answers. In L. M. Oakes & P. J. Bauer (Eds.), *Short- and long-term memory in infancy and early childhood: Taking the first steps toward remembering* (pp. 209–239). New York: Oxford University Press.

Heckman, J., Pinto, R., & Savelyev, P. (2013). Understanding the mechanisms through which an influential early childhood program boosted adult outcomes. *American Economic Review, 103*(6), 2052–2086.

Hein, S. (1999). *Ten habits of emotionality intelligent people.* New York: The EQ Institute.

Heineman, R. V. (1998). *The abused child psychodynamic: Understanding and treatment.* New York: Guilford.

Heisner, J. (2005). Telling stories with blocks: Encouraging language in the block center. Early Childhood Research and Practice, 7(2). Retrieved February 8, 2014, from http://ecrp .uiuc.edu/v7n2/heisner.html

Helm, J. H. (2004). Projects that power young minds. *Educational leadership, 62*(1), 58–62.

Henderson, Z. P. (1995). Renewing our social fabric. *Human Ecology, 23*(1), 16–19.

Hess, E. (1972). Imprinting in a natural laboratory. *Scientific American, 227,* 24–31.

Heyman, S. (1996). The influence of cultural individualism-collectivism, self construals, and individual values on communication styles across cultures. *Human Communication Research, 22,* 510–543.

Heyne, D. (2009). School refusal. In J. E. Fisherand & W. T. O'Donohue (Eds.), *Practitioner's guide to evidence-based psychotherapy* (pp. 599–618). New York: Springer.

Hickman, G. P., Bartholomae, S., & McKenry, P. C. (2000). Influence of parenting style on the adjustment and academic achievement of traditional college freshmen. *Journal of College Student Development, 41*(1), 41–54.

Hildebrand, V., Phenice, L. A., Gray, M. M., & Hines, R. P. (1996). *Knowing and serving diverse families.* Upper Saddle River, NJ: Merrill Education/Prentice Hall.

Hill, S. E., & Buss, D. M. (2006). The evolution of self-esteem. In M. K. Kernis (Ed.), *Self esteem—Issues and answers: A sourcebook of current perspectives.* New York: Psychology Press.

Hochschild, A. R. (1997). *The time bind: When work becomes home and home becomes work.* New York: Holt.

Hodapp, R. M., Dykens, E. M., & Masino, L. (1997). Stress and support in families of persons with Prader-Willi syndrome. *Journal of Autism and Developmental Disorders, 27,* 11–24.

Hoffman, L., & Manis, J. D. (1979). The value of children in the United States: A new approach to the study of fertility. *Journal of Marriage and the Family, 41,* 583–596.

Hoffman, M. L. (1979). Development of moral thought, feeling, and behavior. *American Psychologist, 34,* 958–967.

Hoffman, M. L. (2001). Empathy and moral development: Implications for caring and justice. New York: Cambridge University Press.

Holmes-Lonergan, H. A. (2003). Preschool children's collaborative problem-solving interactions: The role of gender, pair type, and task—1. *Sex Roles: A Journal of Research, 48*(13), 505–517.

Holton, D., & Clark, D. (2006). Scaffolding and metacognition. *International Journal of Mathematical Education in Science and Technology, 37,* 127–143.

Honig, A. S. (2000). *Love and learn: Positive guidance for young children.* Brochure. Washington, DC: Author.

Honig, A. S. (2005). Infants & toddlers: Development—the power of touch. *Childhood Today, 19*(5), 25–26.

Honig, A. S., & Wittmer, D. S. (1997). Helping children become more prosocial: Ideas for classrooms. In K. M. Paciorek & J. H. Munro (Eds.), *Annual editions: Early childhood education 97/98* (18th ed.). New York: McGraw-Hill. (Original work published in *Young Children*, January 1996)

Hooker, K. E., & Fodor, I. E. (2008). Teaching mindfulness to children. *Gestalt Review, 12*(1), 75–91.

Hopkin, K. (1998). *Understanding cystic fibrosis.* Oxford: University Press of Mississippi.

Howard, F., & Toossi, M. (2001, November). Labor force projections to 2010: Steady growth and changing composition. *Monthly Labor Review,* 21–38.

Howard, G. R. (1993). Whites in multicultural education: Rethinking our role. *Phi Delta Kappan, 75*(1), 36–41.

Hsueh, J., & Yoshikawa, H. (2007). Working nonstandard schedules and variable shifts in low-income families: Associations with parental psychological well-being, family functioning, and child well-being. *Developmental Psychology, 43*(3), 620–632.

Hudson, S., Olsen, H., & Thompson, D. (2002). *SAFE Playground Supervision Manual.* Cedar Falls, IA: National Program for Playground Safety.

Hudson, S., Thompson, D., & Olsen, H. (2003). Let the children play ... and the supervisors have peace of mind—designing playgrounds to help those supervising children. *Parks & Recreation, 38*(9), 88–93.

Hughes, C. (1998). Executive function in preschoolers: Links with theory of mind and verbal ability. *British Journal of Developmental Psychology, 16,* 233–253.

Hughes, F. (2008). Sensitivity to the social and cultural contexts of the play of young children. In J. P. Isenberg & M. R. Jalongo (Eds.), *Major trends and issues in early childhood education: Challenges, controversies, and insights* (2nd ed.). New York: Teachers College Press.

Huizink, A. C., & Mulder, E. J. (2006). Maternal smoking, drinking or cannabis use during pregnancy and neuro-behavioral and cognitive functioning in human off-spring. *Neuroscience and Biobehavioral Reviews, 30,* 24–41.

Hunt, J. (1976). The psychological development of orphanage-reared infants: Interventions with outcomes (Tehran). *Genetic Psychology Monographs, 94,* 177–226.

Hurlemann, R., Patin, A., Onur, O. A., Cohen, M. X., Baumgartner, T., & Metzler, S. (2010). Oxytocin enhances amygdala-dependent, socially reinforced learning and emotional empathy in humans. *Journal of Neuroscience, 30*(14), 4999–5007.

Hutchings, J., & Lane, E. (2005) Parenting and the development and prevention of child mental health problems. *Current Opinion in Psychiatry, 18*(4), 386–391.

Imholz, S., & Petrosino, A. *Creative Education, 3,* 185–192.

Imholz, S., & Petrosino, A. (2012). Improving School Readiness Project. (2001). *Early to rise: Improving the school readiness of Philadelphia's young children.* Philadelphia, PA: United Way of Southeastern Pennsylvania and School District of Philadelphia.

Ingrassia, M., & McCormick, J. (1997). Why leave children with bad parents? In E. N. Junn & C. Boyatzis (Eds.), *Annual editions: Child growth and development 97/98* (4th ed.). New York: McGraw-Hill. (Original work published in *Newsweek*, April 25, 1994)

Isaacs, E. B., Gadian, D. G., Sabatini, S., Chong, W. K., Quinn, B. T., Fischl, B. R., & Lucas, A. (2008). The effect of early human diet on caudate volumes and IQ. *Pediatric Research, 63*(3), 308–314.

Boushey, H., & Williams, J. C. (2010). *The three faces of work-family conflict: The poor, the privileged, and the missing middle.* Washington, DC: Center for American Progress and the Center for Worklife Law. & San Francisco, CA: University of California, Hastings College of the Law.

Jacobson, J. L., & Jacobson, S. W. (2002). Effects of prenatal alcohol exposure on child development. *Alcohol Research & Health, 26*(4), 282–286.

Jaworski, M. (2000, October 3). Signs of intelligent life. *Family Circle,* 14.

Jennings, A. (2011). Promoting teachers' social and emotional competencies to support performance and reduce burnout. In A. Cohan & A. Honigsfeld (Eds.), *Breaking the mold of preservice and inservice teacher education: Successful practices for the twenty-first century* (pp.133–143). New York: Rowman & Littlefield.

Jenny, C., Hymel, K. P., Ritzen, A., Reinert, S. E., & Hay, T. C. (1999). Abusive head trauma: An analysis of missed cases. *Journal of the American Medical Association, 281,* 621–626.

Jensen, E. (1998). *Introduction to brain-compatible learning.* San Diego, CA: The Brain Store, Inc.

Jenson, T. K. (2005). The interpretation of signs of child sexual abuse. *Culture & Psychology, 11,* 469–498.

Joe, J. R., & Malach, R. S. (1998). Families with Native American roots. In E. W. Lynch & M. J. Hanson (Eds.), *Developing cross-cultural competence: A guide for working with young children and their families.* Baltimore, MD: Paul H. Brookes.

Johnson, A. D., Martin, A., Brooks-Gunn, J., & Petrill. S. A. (2008). Order in the house! Associations among household chaos, the home literacy environment, maternal reading ability, and children's early reading. *Merrill-Palmer Quarterly, 54*(4), 445–472.

Johnson, J., & Newport, E. (1989). Critical period effects in second language learning: The influence of maturation state on the acquisition of English as a second language. *Cogn Psychol., 21,* 60–99.

Johnson, J. G., Cohen, P., Chen, H., Kasen, S., & Brook, J. S. (2006). Parenting behaviors associated with risk for offspring personality disorder during adulthood. *Archives of General Psychiatry, 63*(5), 579–587.

Jones, K. L., Hoyme, H. E., Robinson, L. K., del Campo, M., Manning, M. A., Prewitt, L. M., & Chambers, C. D. (2010). Fetal alcohol spectrum disorders: Extending the range of structural defects. *American Journal of Medical Genetics, 152A*(11), 2731–2735. *Journal of Marriage and Family, 70,* 97–112.

Joyce, A., Etty-Leal, J., Zazryn, T., Hamilton, A., & Hassed, C. (2010). Exploring a mindfulness meditation program on the mental health of upper primary children: A pilot study. *Advances in School Mental Health Promotion, 3*(2), 17–25.

Jyoti, D. F., Frongillo, E. A., & Jones, S. J. (2005). Food insecurity affects school children's academic performance, weight gain, and social skills. *The Journal of Nutrition, 135*(12), 2831–2839.

Katz, L.G., & McClellan, D. E. (1997). *Fostering children is social competence: The teacher's role.* Washington, DC: National Association for the Education of Young Children.

Kabat-Zinn, J. (2003). Mindfulness-based interventions in context: Past, present, future. *Clinical Psychology: Science and Practice, 10*(2), 144–156.

Kagan, J. (1971). *Change and continuity in infancy.* New York: Wiley.

Kagan, J. (1984). *The nature of the child.* New York: Basic Books.

Kagan, J. (1998). Biology and the child. In W. Damon (Series Ed.) & N. Eisenberg (Vol. Ed.), *Handbook of child psychology: Vol. 3. Social, emotional, and personality development* (pp. 177–236). New York: Wiley.

Kagan, J. (2004). The uniquely human in human nature. *Daedalus, 133*(4), 77–89.

Kagan, J., Kagan, J., & Moss, H. A. (1962). *Birth to maturity.* New York: Wiley.

Kagan, J., Kearsley, R. B., & Zelazo, P. R. (1978). *Infancy: Its place in human development.* Cambridge, MA: Harvard University Press.

Kagan, J., & Snidman, N. (2004). *The long shadow of temperament.* Cambridge, MA: Harvard University Press.

Kagan, J., Snidman, N., Zentner, M., & Peterson, E. (1999). Infant temperament and anxious symptoms in school age children. *Development and Psychopathology, 11,* 209–224.

Kahn, R. S., Khoury, J., Nichols, W. C., & Lanphear, B. P. (2003). Role of dopamine transporter genotype and maternal prenatal smoking in childhood hyperactive-impulsive, inattentive, and oppositional behaviors. *Journal of Pediatrics, 143,* 104–110.

Kalyanpur, M., & Harry, B. (1999). *Culture in Special Education: Building reciprocal family-professional relationships.* Baltimore, MD: Paul H. Brookes.

Karpov, J. (2005). *The Neo-Vygotskian approach to child development.* Cambridge, MA: Cambridge University Press.

Kataoka, S., Zhang, L., & Wells, K. (2002). Unmet need for mental health care among US children: Variations by ethnicity and insurance status. *American Journal of Psychiatry, 159*(9), 1548–1555.

Katz, I. (1981). *Stigma: A social psychological analysis.* Hillsdale, NJ: Erlbaum.

Katz, P. A. (2003). Racists or tolerant multiculturalists? How do they begin? *American Psychologist, 58*(11), 897–909.

Kaufmann, D., Gesten, E., Santa Lucia, R. C., Salsedo, O., Gobioff, G. R., & Gadd, R. (2000). The relationship between parenting style and children's adjustment: The parents' perspective. *Journal of Child and Family Studies, 9*(2), 231–245.

Kaufmann, D., Gesten, E., Santa Lucia, R.C., Salcedo, O., Rendina-Gobioff, G., Kawamura, K.Y., Frost, R.O., & Harmatz, M.G. (2002). The relationship of perceived parenting styles to perfectionism. *Personality and Individual Differences, 32*(2), 317–327.

Kee, Y. H., & Liu, Y. T. (2011). Effects of dispositional mindfulness on the self-controlled learning of a novel motor task. *Learning and Individual Differences, 21*(4), 468–471.

Keeler, R. (2008). *Natural playscapes: Creating outdoor play environments for the soul.* Redmond, WA: Exchange Press.

Keenan, K., & Wakschlag, L. S. (2000). More than the terrible twos: The nature and severity of disruptive behavior problems in clinic-referred preschool children. *The Journal of Abnormal Child Psychology, 28,* 33–46.

Keirsey, D. (1998). *Please understand me II: Temperament, character, intelligence* (5th ed.). Del Mar, CA: Prometheus Nemesis.

Keller, H., Yovsi, R., Borke, J., Kartner, J., Jensen, H., & Papaligoura, Z. (2004). Developmental consequences of early parenting experiences: Self-recognition and self-regulation in three cultural communities. *Child Development, 75*(6), 1745–1760.

Kern, P., & Wakeford, L. (2007). *Supporting outdoor play for young children: The zone model of playground supervision. Young Children, 62*(2), 12–16.

Kerr, D. C., Lopez, N. L. Olson, S. L., & Sameroff, A. J. (2004). Parental discipline and externalizing behavior problems in early childhood: The roles of moral regulation and child gender. *Journal of Abnormal Child Psychology, 32*(4), 369–383.

Kim, S. (1999). The effects of storytelling and pretend play on cognitive processes, short-term and long-term narrative recall. *Child Study Journal, 2*(3), 175–191.

Kimmel, M. (2000). *Gendered lives.* New York: Oxford University Press.

Kimmel, M. A. (2004). *The gendered society* (2nd ed.). New York: Oxford University Press.

King, P. M., & Mayhew, M. J. (2002). Moral judgement development in higher education: Insights from the Defining Issues Test. *Journal of Moral Education, 31,* 247–270.

Kivel, P. (2002). *Uprooting racism: How White people can work for racial justice* (2nd ed.). Gabriola Island, BC, Canada: New Society.

Knudsen, E. I. (2004). Sensitive periods in the development of the brain and behavior. *J Cogn Neurosci., 16,* 1412–1425.

Kochanek, T. T., & Buka, S. L. (1998). Influential factors in the utilization of early intervention services. *Journal of Early Intervention, 21*(4), 323–338.

Kochanska, G., Kim, S., & Koenig Nordling, J. (2012). Challenging circumstances moderate the links between mothers' personality traits and their parenting in low-income families with young children. *J Pers Soc Psychol. 103*(6), 1040–1049.

Kochanska, G., & Aksan, N. (2006). Temperament, relationships, and young children's receptive cooperation with their parents. *Developmental Psychology, 41*(4), 648–660.

Kochanska, G., Aksan, N., Knaack, A., & Rhines, H. (2004). Maternal parenting and children's conscience: Early security as moderator. *Child Development, 74*(4), 1229–1242.

Kochanska, G., Barry, R., Jimenez, N., Hollatz, A., & Woodard, J. (2009). Guilt and effortful control: Two mechanisms that prevent disruptive developmental trajectories. *Journal of Personality & Social Psychology, 97*(2), 322–333.

Kochanska, G., Forman, D.R., Aksan, N., & Dunbar, S.B. (2005). Pathways to conscience: Early mother–child mutually responsive orientation and children's moral emotion, conduct, and cognition. *Journal of Child Psychology & Psychiatry, 46*(1), 19–34.

Kochanska, G., Murray, K. T., & Harlan, E. T. (2000). Effortful control in early childhood: Continuity and change, antecedents, and implications for social development. *Developmental Psychology, 36,* 220–232.

Koenigs, M., Young, L., Adolphs, R., Tranel, D., Cushman, F., Hauser, M., & Damasio, A. (2007). Damage to the prefrontal cortex increases utilitarian moral judgements. *Nature, 446,* 908–911.

Kohlberg, L. (1969). Stage and sequence: The cognitive-developmental approach to socialization. In D. Goslin (Ed.), *Handbook of socialization theory and research.* Skokie, IL: Rand-McNally.

Kohlberg, L. (1976). Moral stages and moralization: The cognitive-developmental approach. In T. Lickona (Ed.), *Moral development and behavior.* New York: Holt, Rinehart & Winston.

Kohlberg, L., & DeVries, R. (1987). *Constructivist early education: Overview and comparison with other programs.* Washington, DC: National Association for the Education of Young Children.

Kopp, C. B. (1982). Antecedents of self-regulation: A developmental perspective. *Developmental Psychology, 18*(2), 199–214.

Kosfeld, M., Heinrichs, M., Zak, P. J., Fischbacher, U., & Fehr, E. (2005) Oxytocin increases trust in humans. *Nature, 435,* 673–676.

Kostelnik, M. (2014). Guiding children's social development (8th ed.). Belmont, CA: Wadsworth Publishing.

Koskentausta, T. (2006). *Psychiatric disturbances in children with intellectual disability: Prevalence, risk factors and assessment.* Helsinki, Finland: University of Helsinki.

Kottler, J. A. (2000). *Nuts and bolts of helping.* Boston, MA: Pearson Education.

Kramer, Rita (1976). *Maria Montessori: A biography.* New York: Putnam.

Kranowitz, C. (2010). *Growing an in-sync child: Simple, fun activities to help every child develop, learn, and grow.* Peabody, MA: Perigee Trade

Kras, E. (1995). *Management in two cultures—Bridging the gap between U.S. and Mexico.* Yarmouth, ME: Intercultural Press.

Krebs, R. M., Boehler, C. N., Egner., T, & Wodorf, M. G. (2011). The neural underpinnings of how reward associations can both guide and misguide attention. *J Neurosci, 31*(26), 9752.

Kronenberg, M. (2010). Psychotherapy with infants and young children: Repairing the effects of stress and trauma on early attachment. *Infant Mental Health Journal, 31,* 113–114.

Krupinski, E., & Weikel, D. (1986). *Death from child abuse and no one heard.* Winter Park, FL: Currier-Davis.Kuhl PK. (2007). Is speech learning 'gated' by the social brain? *Dev Sci., 10,* 110–120.

Kuhl, P. K. (2010). Brain mechanisms in early language acquisition. *Neuron, 67*(5), 713–727.

Kuhl, P. K., & Damasio, A. (2012). Language. In E. R. Kandel. J. H. Schwartz, T. M. Jessell, S. Siegelbaum, & J. Hudspeth (Eds.), *Principles of neural science* (5th ed., pp. 1353–1372). New York: McGraw-Hill.

Kuhl, P. K. (2004). Early language acquisition: cracking the speech code. *Nat Rev Neurosci, 5,* 831–843.

Kuhl, P. K., & Meltzoff, A. N. (1982). The bimodal perception of speech in infancy. *Science, 218,* 1138–1141.

Kuhl, P. K., & Meltzoff, A. N. (1996). Infant vocalizations in response to speech: Vocal imitation and developmental change. *Acoust. Soc. Am., 100,* 2425–2438.

Kuhl, P. K., Conboy, B. T., Coffey-Corina, S., Padden, P., Rivera-Gaxiola, M., & Nelson, T. (2008). Phonetic learning as a pathway to language: new data and native language magnet theory expanded (NLM-e). *Philos Trans R Soc Lond, B, Biol Sci., 363,* 979–1000.

Kuhl, P. K., Conboy, B. T., Padden, D., Nelson. T., & Pruitt, J. (2004). Early speech perception and later language development: Implications for the 'critical period. Lang Learn Dev. case of Japanese acquisition of /r/ and /l/. In J. Slitka, S. Manuel, & M. Matthies (Eds.). *From sound to sense* (pp. C181–C186). Cambridge, MA: MIT Press.

Kuhl, P. K., Tsao, F. M., & Liu, H. M. (2003). Foreign-language experience in infancy: Effects of short-term exposure and social interaction on phonetic learning. *Proc Natl Acad Sci USA. 100,* 9096–9101.

Kuhn, D., & Franklin, S. (2006). The second decade: What develops (and how)? In Damon, W., Lerner, R., Kuhn, D., & Siegler, R., (Eds.), *Handbook of child psychology: Vol. 2. Cognition, perception, and language* (6th ed.). Hoboken, NJ: Wiley.

Kuhn, D., Katz, J., & Dean, D. (2004). Developing reason. *Thinking and Reasoning, 10.* 197–219.

Kumanyika, S., & Grier, S. (2006). Targeting interventions for ethnic minority and low-income populations. *Future Child, 16*(1), 187–207.

Kuo, F. E., & Faber Taylor, A. (2004). A potential natural treatment for attention-deficit/hyperactivity disorder: Evidence from a national study. *American Journal of Public Health, 94*(9), 1580–1586.

Kurcinka, M. S. (2009). *Raising Your Spirited Child: A guide for parents whose child is more intense, sensitive, perceptive, persistent, energetic.* New York: HarperCollins.

Kushnir, T., & Gopnik, A. (2007). Conditional probability versus spatial contiguity in causal learning: Preschoolers use new contingency evidence to overcome prior spatial assumptions. *Developmental Psychology, 44,* 186–196.

Kutscher, M. L. (2006). *Children with seizures: A guide for parents, teachers, and other professionals.* Philadelphia, PA: Jessica Kingsley.

Ladd, R. E. (Ed.). (1996). *Children's rights revisioned: Philosophical readings.* Belmont, CA: Wadsworth.

Laible, D. J., & Thompson, R. A. (2002). Mother-child conflict in the toddler years: Lessons in emotion, morality, and relationships. *Child Development, 73*(4), 1187–1203.

Lakhanpal, M., & Ram, R. (2008). Educational attainment and HIV/AIDS prevalence: A cross-country study. *Economics of Education Review, 27,* 14–21.

Lamb, M. E. (1978). Infant social cognition and "second-order" effects. *Infant Behavior and Development, 1,* 1–10.

Lamb, M. E. (1981). *The role of the father in childhood development* (2nd ed.). New York: Wiley.

Lamb, M. E., Gaensbauer, T. J., Malkin, C. M., & Schultz, L. A. (1985). The effects of child maltreatment on security of infant-adult attachment. *Infant Behavior and Development, 8,* 35–45.

Lancioni, G. E. (1980). Infant operant conditioning and its implications for early intervention. *Psychological Bulletin, 88*(2), 516–534.

Landreth, C., & Johnson, B. (1953). Young children's responses to a picture inset test designed to reveal reactions to persons of different skin color. *Child Development, 24,* 63–80.

Landy, S. (2002). *Pathways to competence: Encouraging healthy social and emotional development in young children.* Baltimore, MD: Paul H. Brookes.

Lane, K. L., Kalberg, J. R., & Menzies, H. M. (2009). *Developing schoolwide programs to prevent and manage problem behaviors: A step-by-step approach.* New York: Guilford.

Lane, R. D. (2000). Levels of emotional awareness: Neurological, psychological and social perspectives. In R. Bar-On and J. D. A. Parker (Eds.), *Handbook of emotional intelligence*. San Francisco, CA: Jossey-Bass.

Lane, R. D., & McRae, K. (2004). Neural substrates of conscious emotional experience: A cognitive-neuroscientific perspective. In B. M. Amsterdam & J. Benjamins (Eds.), *Consciousness, emotional self-regulation and the brain*. San Francisco, CA: Jossey-Bass.

Langer, E. J. (2009). Counter clockwise : Mindful health and the power of possibility. New York: Ballantine Books.

Langlois, J. H., Kalakanis, L., Rubenstein, A. J., Larson, A., Hauam, M., & Smoot, M. (2000). Maxims or myths of beauty? A meta-analytic and theoretical review. *Psychological Bulletin, 126*(3), 390–423.

Lansford, J. E., & Dodge, K. A. (2008). Cultural norms for adult corporal punishment of children and societal rates of endorsement and use of violence. *Parenting: Science and Practice, 8*(3), 257–270.

Lansford, J. E., Chang, L., Dodge, K. A., Malone, P. S., Oburu, P., Palmérus, K., Bacchini, D., Pastorelli, C., Bombi, A. S., Zelli, A., Tapanya, S., Chaudhary, N., Deater-Deckard, K., Manke, B., & Quinn, D. (2005). Physical discipline and children's adjustment: Cultural normativeness as a moderator. *Child Development, 76*, 1234–1246.

Lansford, J. E., Criss, M. M., Dodge, K. A., Shaw, D. S., Pettit, G. S., & Bates, J. E. (2009). Trajectories of physical discipline: Early childhood antecedents and developmental outcomes. *Child Development, 80*, 1385–1402.

Larzelere, R. E., Cox, R. B., & Smith, G. L. (2010). Do nonphysical punishments reduce antisocial behavior more than spanking? A comparison using the strongest previous causal evidence against spanking, *BMC Pediatrics, 10*(1),10.

Larzelere, R. E. (2000). Child outcomes of nonabusive and customary physical punishment by parents: An updated literature review. *Clinical Child & Family Psychology Review, 3*(4), 199–221.

Larzelere, R. E., &. Kuhn, B. R (2005). Comparing child outcomes of physical punishment and alternative disciplinary tactics: A meta-analysis. *Clinical Child and Family Psychology Review, 8*(1), 135–148.

Lasky, R. E., Syrdal-Lasky, A., & Klein, R. E. (1975). VOT discrimination by four to six and a half month old infants from Spanish environments. *J. Exp. Child Psychol., 20*, 215–225.

Latner, J. D., & Stunkard, A. J. (2003). Getting worse: The stigmatization of obese children. *Obesity Research, 11*, 452–456.

Lavigne, J. V., Cicchetti C., Gibbons, R. D., Binns, H. J., Larsen, L., & Devito, C. (2001). Oppositional defiant disorder with onset in preschool years: Longitudinal stability and pathways to other disorders. *Journal of the American Academy for Child and Adolescent Psychiatry, 40*(12), 1393–1400.

Lawhon, J., & Cobb, J. B. (2002). Routines that build emergent literacy skills in infants, toddlers, and preschoolers. *Early Childhood Education J, 30*(2), 113–118.

Lawrence, J. W., Rosenberg, L., Mason, S., & Fauerbach, J. A. (2011). Comparing parent and child perceptions of stigmatizing behavior experienced by children with burn scars. *Body Image, 8*(1), 70–73.

Lawrence, J. W., Rosenberg, L., Thombs, B. D., & Fauerbach, J. A. (2006). Measuring perceived stigmatization among pediatric burn survivors. *Journal of Burn Care & Research, 27*(2), S88.

Ledermann, T., Bodenmann G., Rudaz, M., & Bradbury, T. N. (2010). Stress, communication, and marital quality in couples. *Family Relations, 59*(?), 195–206.

Lee, S. J., Guterman, N. B., & Rice, J. (2010). Use of spanking for 3-year-old children and associated intimate partner aggression or violence. *Pediatrics, 126*(3), 415–424.

Lee, S. W. (2005). *Encyclopedia of school psychology*. Thousand Oaks, CA: Sage.

Lee, S. J., & Rice, J. C. (2010). Mothers' spanking of 3-year-old children and subsequent risk of children's aggressive behavior. *Pediatrics, 125*(5), e1057–e1065.

Lefton, L. A. (2000). Child development. In *Psychology*, (7th ed., pp. 350–351). New York: Allyn & Bacon.

Leong, D. J., & Bodrova, E. (2009). Tools of the mind: A Vygotskian based early childhood curriculum. *Early Childhood Services: An Interdisciplinary Journal of Effectiveness, 3*(3), 245–262.

Lepper, M. R., Corpus, J. H., & Iyengar. S. S. (2005). Intrinsic and extrinsic motivational orientations in the classroom: Age differences and academic correlates. *Journal of Educational Psychology, 97*, 184–196.

Lepper, M. R., Greene, D., & Nisbet, R. (1973). Undermining children's intrinsic interest with extrinsic reward; A test of 'overjustification' hypothesis. *Journal of Personality and Social Psychology, 28*, 129–137.

Lerner, J. W., & Kline, F. (2005). *Learning disabilities and related disorders: Characteristics and teaching strategies*. Boston, MA: Houghton Mifflin.

Lester, B. M., & Sparrow, J. D., Eds. (2010). Nurturing children and families: building on the legacy of T. Berry Brazelton. Hoboken, NJ: Wiley-Blackwell.

Leung, K., Lau, S., & Lam, W. L. (1998). Parenting styles and academic achievement: A cross-cultural study. *Merrill-Palmer Quarterly, 44*, 157–172.

Levy, A., Wolfgang, C., & Koorland, M. (1992). Sociodramatic play as a method for enhancing the language performance of kindergarten age students. *Early Childhood Research Quarterly, 7*, 245–262.

Lewis, M., & Carmody, D. (2008). Self-representation and brain development. *Developmental Psychology, 44*, 1329–1334.

Lickona, T. (1983). *Raising good children*. New York: Bantam.

Lickona, T. (1991). *Educating for character*. New York: Bantam.

Lieberman, M. D., Eisenberger, N. I., Crockett, M. J., Tom, S. M., Pfeifer, J. H., & Way, B. M. (2007). Putting feelings into words: Affect labeling disrupts amygdala activity to affective stimuli. *Psychological Science, 18*, 421–428.

Liehr, P., & Diaz, N. (2010). A pilot study examining the effect of mindfulness on depression and anxiety for minority children. *Archives of Psychiatric Nursing, 24*(1), 69–71.

Lier, P., Vitaro, F., & Eisner, M. (2007). Preventing aggressive and violent behavior: Using prevention programs to study the role of peer dynamics in maladjustment problems. *European Journal on Criminal Policy and Research*. Accessed on March 16, 2011, at http://www.springerlink.com/content/tu7t754485u15041/

Lin, H., Katsovich, L., Ghebremichael, M., Findley, D. B., Grantz, H., Lombroso, P. J., King, R. A., Zhang, H., & Leckman, J. F. (2007). Psychosocial stress predicts future symptom severities in children and adolescents with Tourette syndrome and/or obsessive-compulsive disorder. *Journal of Child Psychology and Psychiatry, 48*(2), 157–166.

Linder, J. R., & Gentile, D. A. (2009). Is the television rating system valid? Indirect, verbal, and physical aggression in programs viewed by fifth grade girls and associations with behavior. *Journal of Applied Developmental Psychology, 30*(3), 286–297.

Lindsay, R. L. (2002). Bedsharing/cosleeping: The data neither condemns nor endorses. *AAP Grand Rounds, 8,* 46–47.

Lipina, S. J., & Colombo, J. A. (2009). *Poverty and brain development during childhood: An approach from cognitive psychology and neuroscience.* Washington, DC: American Psychological Association.

Liptak, G. S. (2001). Cerebral palsy. In R. A. Hoekelman (Ed.), *Primary pediatric care* (pp. 468–473). St. Louis, MO: Mosby.

Liu, H., Mroz, T. A., & van der Klaauw, W. (2010). Maternal employment, migration, and child development. *Journal of Econometrics, 156,* 212–228.

Lockwood, P. L., Sebastian, C. L., McCrory, E. J., Hyde, Z. H., Gu, X., De Brito, S. A., & Viding, E. (2013). Association of callous traits with reduced neural response to others' pain in children with conduct problems. *Current Biology*; DOI: 10.1016/j.cub.2013.04.018.

Loeber, R., Burke, J. D., Lahey, B. B., Winters, A., & Zera, M. (2000). Oppositional defiant and conduct disorder: A review of the past 10 years, part I. *Journal of the American Academy for Child and Adolescent Psychiatry, 39*(12), 1468–1484.

Lorenz, K. (1966). *On aggression.* New York: Harcourt, Brace & World.

Lotto, A. J., Sato, M., & Diehl, R. (2004). Mapping the task for the second language learner: the case of Japanese acquisition of /r/ and /l. In J. Slitka, S. Manuel, & M. Matthies (Eds.), *From sound to sense* (pp. C181–C186). Cambridge, MA: MIT Press.

Louv, R. (2007). Leave no child inside: The growing movement to reconnect children and nature, and to battle "nature deficit disorder." *Orion Magazine,* March/April. Accessed on March 18, 2011, at www. orionmagazine.org/index.php/articles /article/240/

Louv, R. (2008). *Last child in the woods: Saving our children from nature-deficit disorder.* Chapel Hill, NC: Algonquin Books.

Lubeck, S. (1985). *Sandbox society: Early education in black and white America.* London, UK: Falmer.

Luby, J. L., Barch, D. M., Belden, A., Gaffrey, M. S., Tillman, R., Babb, C., Nishino, T., Suzuki, H., & Botteron, K. N. (2012). Maternal support in early childhood predicts larger hippocampal volumes at school age. *Proceedings of the National Academy of Sciences, 109,* 2854–2859.

Luijk, M., Saridjan, N., Tharner, A., van IJzendoorn, M., Bakermans-Kranenburg, M., Jaddoe, V., Hofman, A., Verhulst, F., & Tiemeier, H. (2010). Attachment, depression, and cortisol: Deviant patterns in insecure-resistant and disorganized infants. *Developmental Psychobiology, 52,* 441–452.

Lum, D. (1992). *Social work practice & people of color.* Pacific Grove, CA: Brooks/Cole.

Luria, A. R., & Vygotsky, L. S. (1992). *Ape, primitive man and child: Essays in the history of behavior.* London, UK: Harvester Wheatsheaf.

Lynch, B. J. (2000). *Guide to diagnosis, investigation and treatment of epilepsy.* Cambridge, MA: Novartis.

Lynch, E. W., & Hanson, M. J., Eds. (1998). *Developing cross-cultural competence: A guide for working with children and their families* (2nd ed.). Baltimore, MD: Paul H. Brookes.

Lynch, M. A. (2010). Punishment and child harm. *Child Abuse Review, 19*(4), 225–228.

Lyness, D. (2005). Depression. *Teens Health,* September. Accessed on March 16, 2011, at http://kidshealth.org/teen /your_mind/mental_health/depression.html

Lyubomirsky, S. (2008). *The how of happiness.* New York: Penguin Press.

Lyubomirsky, S., King, L., & Diener, E. (2005). The benefits of frequent positive affect: Does happiness lead to success? *Psychological Bulletin, 131,* 803–855.

Maccoby, E. E. (1992). The role of parents in the socialization of children: An historical overview. *Developmental Psychology, 28,* 1006–1017.

MacDonald, G., & Leary, M. R. (2005). Why does social exclusion hurt? The relationship between social and physical pain. *Psychological Bulletin, 131,* 202–223.

Mackin, P., & Young, A. H. (2004). Rapid cycling bipolar disorder: Historical overview and focus on emerging treatments. *Bipolar Disorders. 6*(6), 523–529.

Manassis, K. (2007). When attention-deficit/hyperactivity disorder co-occurs with anxiety disorders: Effects on treatment. *Expert Review of Neurotherapeutics, 7*(8), 981–988.

Manganello, J. A., & Taylor, C. A. (2009). Television exposure as a risk factor for aggressive behavior among 3 year-old children. *Archives of Pediatrics & Adolescent Medicine, 163*(11), 1037–1045.

Manganello, J. A., & Mantagu, A. (1986). *Touching: The significance of the skin.* New York: Harper & Row.

Marcus, G. F., Fernandes, K. J., & Johnson, S. P. (2012). The role of association in early word-learning. *Frontiers in Developmental Psychology, 3*(283), 1–6.

Marshall, J. (2011). Neurosensory development: Consideration for infant child care. *Early Childhood Education J, 39,* 175–181.

Marshall, M. J. (2002). *Why spanking doesn't work: Stopping this bad habit and getting the upper hand on effective discipline.* Springville, UT: Bonneville Books.

Martin, S. (2006). *Teaching motor skills to children with cerebral palsy and similar movement disorders: A guide for parents and professionals.* Bethesda, MD: Woodbine House.

Maslow, A. (1993). *The farther reaches of human nature* (Esalen Book reprint ed.). Manhattan Beach, CA: Arkana.

Maslow, A. H. (1943). A theory of human motivation. *Psychological Review, 50,* 370–396.

Maslow, A. H. (1970). *Motivation and personality* (2nd ed.). New York: Harper & Row.

Masnick, A. M., & Klahr, D. (2003). Error matters: An initial exploration of elementary school children's understanding of experimental error. *Journal of Cognition and Development, 4*(1), 67–98.

Matthews, G., Roberts, R. D., & Zeidner, M. (2003). Development of emotional intelligence: A skeptical—but not dismissive—perspective. *Human Development, 46,* 109–114.

Matthews, G., Zeidner, M., & Roberts, R. D. (2002). *Emotional intelligence: Science and myth.* Cambridge, MA: MIT Press.

Mayberry, R. I., & Lock, E. (2003). Age constraints on first versus second language acquisition: evidence for linguistic plasticity and epigenesist. *Brain Lang., 87,* 369–384.

Mayes, L. C., & Cohen, D. J. (2002). *The Yale Child Study Center guide to understanding your child.* New York: Little Brown.

McAfee, O., & Leong, D. J. (2007) *Assessing and guiding young children's development and learning* (4th ed.). Boston, MA: Pearson.

McCabe, E. M., Michelli, N. M., & Pickeral, T. (2009). *The school climate implementation road map: Promoting democratically informed school communities and the continuous process of school climate improvement.* New York: National Center for School Climate.

McCauley, J., Kern, D. E., Kolodner, K., Dill, L., Schroeder, A. F., DeChant, H. K., Ryden, J., Derogatis, L. R., & Bass, E. G. (1997). Clinical characteristics of women with a history of childhood abuse: Unhealed wounds. *JAMA, 277,* 1362–1368.

McClellan, D., & Katz, L. (2001). *Assessing young children's social competence.* Champaign, IL: ERIC Clearinghouse on Elementary & Early Childhood Education. (ERIC Document Reproduction Service No. ED450953)

McClellan, J., & Werry, J. (1997). Practice parameters for the assessment and treatment of adolescents with bipolar disorder. *Journal of the American Academy of Child and Adolescent Psychiatry, 36*(10), 157S–176S.

McClelland, M. M., Morrison, F. J., & Holmes, D. L. (2000). Children at risk for early academic problems: The role of learning-related social skills. *Early Childhood Research Quarterly, 15*(3), 307–329.

McClowry, S. G., Snow, D. L., Tamis-LeMonda, C. S., & Rodriguez, E. T. (2010). Testing the efficacy of *INSIGHTS* on student disruptive behavior, classroom management, and student competence in inner city primary grades. *School Mental Health, 2,* 23–35.

McElwain, N. L., Booth-LaForce, C., Lansford, J., Wu, X., & Dyer, W. J. (2008). A process model of attachment-friend linkages: Hostile attribution biases, language ability, and mother-child affective mutuality as intervening mechanisms. *Child Development, 79,* 1891–1906.

McGoey, K., Eckert, T., & Dupaul, G. (2002). Early intervention for preschool children with ADHD: A literature review. *Journal of Emotional and Behavioral Disorders, 10*(1), 14–28.

McGraw, M. (1941). *The child in painting.* New York: Greystone Press.

McKenry, P. C., & Price, S. J. (Eds.). (2005). *Families and change: Coping with stressful events and transitions.* Thousand Oaks, CA: Sage Publications.

McLean, M. E., Bailey, D. B., Jr., & Wolery, M. (1997). *Assessing infants and preschoolers with special needs* (2nd ed.). Upper Saddle River, NJ: Merrill Education/Prentice Hall.

McLennan, D. (2009). "Ready, set, grow!" nurturing young children through gardening. *Early Childhood Education Journal, 37,* 329–333.

McLoyd, V. C. (1990). The impact of economic hardship on black families and children: Psychological distress, parenting, and socioemotional development. *Child Development, 61,* 311–346.

McMaster, G., & Trafzer, C. (eds.) (2008). *Native Universe: Voices of Indian America.* Washington, DC: National Museum of the American Indian, Smithsonian Institution and National Geographic.

McMillan, M. (1930). *The nursery school.* New York: E. P. Dutton.

McWayne, C. M., Fantuzzo, J. W., & McDermott, P. A. (2004). Preschool competency in context: An investigation of the unique contribution of child competencies to early academic success. *Developmental Psychology, 40,* 633–645.

Meece, J. (1997). *Child and adolescent development for educators.* New York: McGraw-Hill.

Meltzoff, A. N., & Gopnik, A. (2013). Learning about the mind from evidence: Children's development of intuitive theories of perception and personality. In S. Baron-Cohen, H. Tager-Flausber, & M. Lombardo (Eds.), *Understanding other minds* (3rd ed., pp. 19–34). Oxford, UK: Oxford University Press.

Meltzoff, A. N., Williamson, R. A., & Marshall, P. J. (2013). Developmental perspectives on action science: Lessons from infant imitation and cognitive neuroscience. In W. Prinz, M. Beisert, & A. Herwig (Eds.), *Action science: Foundations of an emerging discipline* (pp. 281–306). Cambridge, MA: MIT Press.

Meyers, M., & Jordan, L. (2006). Choice and accommodation in parental child care decisions. *Community Development: Journal of the Community Development Society, 37*(2).

Miller, D. (1986). *Infant/toddler day care in high, middle, and low socio-economic settings: An ethnography of dialectical enculturation and linguistic code.* Unpublished doctoral dissertation, University of Houston, TX.

Miller, D. F. (1989). *First steps toward cultural difference: Socialization in infant/toddler day care.* Washington, DC: Child Welfare League of America.

Miller, E., & Almon, J. (2009). *Crisis in kindergarten: Why children need to play in school.* College Park, MD: Alliance for Childhood.

Milner, D. (1983). *Children and race.* Beverly Hills, CA: Sage Publications.

Miner, J. L., & Clarke-Stewart K. A. (2008). Trajectories of externalizing behavior from age 2 to age 9: Relations with gender, temperament, ethnicity, parenting, and rater. *Developmental Psychology, 44*(3), 771–786.

Mishel, L., Bernstein, J., & Shierholz. H. (2012). *The state of working America (12th ed.).* Ithaca, NY: Cornell University Press.

Moen, P., Elder, G. H., & Luscher, K. (Eds.). (1995). *Examining lives in context: Perspectives on the ecology of human development.* Washington, DC: American Psychological Association.

Moen, P., Elder, G., & Luscher, K. (1995). *Examining Lives in Context.* Washington, DC: American Psychological Association.

Montessori, M. (1968). *Reconstruction in education.* Adyar, Madras, India: Theosophical Publishing House.

Montessori, M. (1971). *Peace and education.* Adyar, Chennai, India: Theosophical Publishing House.

Montessori, M. (1986). *The discovery of the child.* New York: Ballantine Books.

Montessori, M. (1988). *The absorbent mind.* Oxford, UK: Clio Press.

Montessori, M., & Hunt, J. M. (1989). *The Montessori method.* New York: Schocken Books.

Moore, R. C., & Cooper-Marcus, C. (2008). Healthy planet, healthy children: Designing nature into the daily spaces of childhood. In S. R. Kellert, J. Heerwagen, & M. Mador (Eds.), *Biophilic design: Theory, science and practice* (pp. 153–203).New York: John Wiley & Sons.

Moore, T. (1994). *Care of the soul: A guide for cultivating depth and sacredness in everyday life.* New York: Harper.

Morland, J. (1972). Racial acceptance and preference in nursery school children in a southern city. In A. R. Brown (Ed.), *Prejudice in children.* Springfield, IL: Charles C. Thomas.

Morris, M. (1998). Truth and beauty in our times. In J. Bigelow (Ed.), *Our Cultural Heritage* (pp. 75–87). Canberra: Australian Academy of the Humanities.

Mruk, C. (2006). *Self-Esteem research, theory, and practice: Toward a positive psychology of self-esteem* (3rd ed.). New York: Springer.

MTA Cooperative Group. (2004). 24-month outcomes of treatment strategies for attention-deficit/hyperactivity disorder (ADHD): The NIMH MTA follow-up. *Pediatrics, 113*, 754–761.

Muennig, P. (2006). *The consequences of inadequate education for black males: The effects on health.* New York: Teachers College Equity Symposium, Columbia University.

Muennig, P., Schweinhart, L., Montie, J., & Neidell, M. (2009). Effects of a prekindergarten educational intervention on adult health: 37-year follow-up results of a randomized controlled trial. *American Public Health Association, 99*(8), 1431–1437.

Mukamel, R., Ekstrom, A. D., Kaplan, J., Iacoboni, M., & Fried, I. (2010). Single-neuron responses in humans during execution and observation of actions. *Current Biology, 20*, 750–756.

Mulvaney, M. K., & Mebert, C. J. (2007). Parental corporal punishment predicts behavior problems in early childhood. *Journal of Family Psychology, 21*(3), 389–397.

Murayama, K., & Kitagami, S. (2014). Consolidation power of extrinsic rewards: Reward cues enhance long-term memory for irrelevant past events. *Journal of Experimental Psychology: General, 143*(1), 15–20.

Murayama, K., Matsumoto, M., Izuma, K., & Matsumoto, K. (2010). *Neural basis of the undermining effect of monetary reward on intrinsic motivation.* Proceedings of the National Academy of Sciences of the United States of America, *107*(49), 20911–20916.

Murty, L., Otake, T., & Cutler, A. (2007). Perceptual tests of rhythmic similarity: I. Mora rhythm. *Language and Speech, 50*, 77–99.

Musher-Eizenman, D. R., Holub, S. C., Miller, A. B., Goldstein, S. E., & Edwards-Leaper, L. (2004). Body size stigmatization in pre-school children: The role of control attributions. *Journal of Pediatric Psychology, 29*, 613–620.

Myers, D. G. (2009). *Psychology in everyday life.* New York: Worth.

NACCRRA. (2010). The media: Is it good for your children? The Daily Parent is prepared by the National Association of Child Care Resource and Referral Agencies (NACCRRA), 37. Accessed on September 30, 2013, at http://elcofswfl.org /downloads/Daily%20Parent%20Media.pdf

NACCRRA. (2013). *We Can Do Better: Child Care Aware of America's Ranking of. State Child Care Center Regulations and Oversight, 2013 Update.* Prepared by the National Association of Child Care Resource and Referral Agencies. Accessed September 30, 2013, at http://www.naccrra.org/ node/3025

National Association for the Education of Young Children (NAEYC) Position Paper. (1997). *Time out for "time-out.* Washington, DC: Author. Accessed on March 16, 2011, at www.naeyc.org

National Association for the Education of Young Children (NAEYC). (2009). *Developmentally appropriate practice in early childhood programs serving children from birth through age 8: A position statement of the National Association for the Education of Young Children.* Washington, DC: NAEYC. Accessed on March 16, 2011, at www.naeyc.org/DAP

National Association of Child Care Resource and Referral Agencies. (2006). *Why care about child care?* Arlington, VA: NACCRRA.

National Association of Child Care Resource and Referral Agencies. (2004). *Child Care in America.* Washington, DC: Author.

National Association of Child Care Resource and Referral Agencies. (2009). *We can do better: 2009 update. NACCRRA's ranking of state child care center regulation and oversight.* Arlington, VA: NACCRRA.

National Association of Child Care Resource and Referral Agencies. (2010). *Leaving children to chance: 2010 update: NACCRRA's ranking of state standards and oversight of small family child care homes.* Arlington, VA: NACCRRA.

National Center for Children in Poverty. (2004). *Low- income children in the United States.* New York: Author. Accessed on March 16, 2011, at www.nccp.org/publications/pub_681.html

National Scientific Council on the Developing Child. (2004). *Children's Emotional Development Is Built into the Architecture of Their Brains: Working Paper No. 2.* http://www .developingchild.net

National Scientific Council on the Developing Child. (2005). *Excessive Stress Disrupts the Architecture of the Developing Brain: Working Paper #3.* Retrieved on March 15, 2014, at http://www.developingchild.net

National Task Force on Fetal Alcohol Syndrome and Fetal Alcohol Effect. (2004). Fetal alcohol spectrum disorders (FASDs). Accessed on March 16, 2011, at www .cdc.gov/ncbddd/fasd /index.html

Neidell, M. (2004). Air pollution, health, and socio- economic status: The effect of outdoor air quality on childhood asthma. *Journal of Health Economics. 23*(6), 1209–1236.

Nelson, C. A. 3rd, Zeanah, C. H., Fox, N. A., Marshall, P. J., Smyke, A. T., & Guthrie, D. (2007). Cognitive recovery in socially deprived young children: The Bucharest Early Intervention Project. *Science, 318*(5858), 1937–1940.

Nelson, C. A., Johnson, D. E., Guthrie, D., Smyke, A. T., Koga, S. F., Fox, N. A., & Zeanah, C. H. (2010). Growth and associations between auxology, caregiving environment, and cognition in socially deprived Romanian children randomized to foster vs. ongoing institutional care. *Archives of Pediatrics & Adolescent Medicine, 164*(6), 507–516.

Nelson, J. (2006). *Positive discipline.* New York: Ballantine.

Nelson, L. J., Rubin, K., & Fox, N. (2005). Social withdrawal, observed peer acceptance, and the development of self-perceptions in children ages 4 to 7 years. *Early Childhood Research Quarterly, 20*(5), 185–200.

Neville, H. J., Coffey, S. A., Lawson, D. S., Fischer, A., Emmorey, K., & Bellugi, U. Neural systems mediating American Sign Language: Effects of sensory experience and age of acquisition. *Brain Lang., 57*, 285–308.

Newport, E. L., Bavelier, D., & Neville, H. J. (2001). Critical thinking about critical periods: Perspectives on a critical period for language acquisition. In E. Dupoux (Ed.), *Language, brain, and cognitive development: Essays in honor of Jacques Mehlter* (pp. 481–502). Cambridge, MA: MIT Press.

Nickerson, A. B., Mele, D., & Princiotta, D. (2008). Attachment and empathy as predictors of roles as defenders or outsiders in bullying interactions. *Journal of School Psychology, 46*, 687–703.

Nucci, L. (2001). Education in the moral domain. Cambridge, UK: Cambridge University Press.

Noble, K. G., McCandliss, B. D., & Farah, M. J. (2007). Socioeconomic gradients predict individual differences in neurocognitive abilities. *Developmental Science, 10*(4), 464–480.

O'Brien, J., & Kollock, P. (1997). *The production of social reality: Essays and readings on social interaction.* Thousand Oaks, CA: Pine Forge Press.

O'Donnell, N. S. (2006). *Sparking connections phase II: A multi-site evaluation of community-based strategies to support family, friend and neighbor caregivers of children: Part I: Lessons learned and recommendations.* New York: Families and Work Institute.

O'Leary, S. G. (1995). Parental discipline mistakes. *Current Directions in Psychological Science, 4*(1), 11–13.

Ohtake, Y., Santos, R. M., & Fowler, S. A. (2000). It's a three-way conversation: Families, service providers, and interpreters working together. *Young Exceptional Children, 4*(1), 12–18.

Okami, P., Weisner, T., & Olmstead, R. (2002, August). Outcome correlates of parent-child bedsharing: An eighteen-year longitudinal study. *Journal of Developmental & Behavioral Pediatrics, 23*(4), 244–253.

Olsen, H., Hudson, S., & Thompson, D. (2005). *Child care assessment manual for outdoor play environments.* Cedar Falls, IA: National Program for Playground Safety.

Osborn, D. (1980). *Early childhood education in historical perspective.* Athens, GA: Education Association.

Ostovar, R. (2010). *The ultimate guide to sensory processing in children: Easy, everyday solutions to sensory challenges.* Arlington, TX: Sensory World.

Owens, D., & Bassity, K. (2007). *Ohio's parent guide to autism spectrum disorders.* Columbus: Ohio Center for Autism and Low Incidence (OCALI). Accessed on March 16, 2011, at www.nwoesc.k12.oh.us/Forms/SpEd/Ohio%20Parent%20Guide%20to%20Autism%20Spectrum%202007.pdf

Pagani, L. S., Fitzpatrick, C., Barnett, T. A., & Dubow, E. (2010). Prospective associations between early childhood television exposure and academic, psychosocial, and physical well-being by middle childhood. *Archives of Pediatric and Adolescent Medicine, 164*(5), 425–431.

Paley, V. G. (1992). *You can't say you can't play.* Cambridge, MA: Harvard University Press.

Panksepp, J. (2007). Can play diminish ADHD and facilitate the construction of the social brain? *Canadian Academy of Child and Adolescent Psychiatry, 16*(2), 57–66.

Park, S. Y., & Rubin, K. H. (2008). Toddler's gender and temperament by maternal stress as predictors of mothers' parenting behavior. *Korean Journal of Child Studies, 29*(2), 109–124.

Parrillo, V. (1985). *Strangers to these shores.* New York: Wiley.

Pascual-Leone, A., Amedi, A., Fregni, F., & Merabet, L. B. (2005). The plastic human brain cortex. *Annual Review of Neuroscience, 28*, 377–401.

Kuhl, P. K. (2010). Brain mechanisms in early language acquisition. *Neuron 67*, 713–727.

Patterson, K., Grenny, J., McMillan, R., & Switzler, A. (2002). *Crucial conversations: Tools for talking when the stakes are high.* New York: McGraw-Hill.

Paulussen-Hoogeboom, M. C., Stams, G. J. J. M., Hermanns, J. M. A., & Peetsma, T. T. D. (2007). Child negative emotionality and parenting from infancy to preschool: A meta-analytic review. *Journal of Youth and Adolescence, 37*(7), 875–887.

Pellegrini, A. D. (2009). Research and policy on children's play. *Child Development Perspectives 3*(2), 131–136.

Perner, J., & Lang, B. (1999). Development of theory of mind and executive control. *Trends in Cognitive Science, 3*, 337–344.

Peters, E., Cillessen, A. H. N., Riksen-Walraven, J. M., & Haselager, G. J.T. (2010). Best friends' preference and popularity: Associations with aggression and prosocial behavior. *International Journal of Behavioral Development, 34*, 398–405.

Piaget, J. (1930). *The child's conception of physical causality.* New York: Harcourt, Brace & Company.

Piaget, J. (1952). *The origins of intelligence in children.* New York: International University Press.

Piaget, J. (1962). *Play, dreams, and imitation in childhood.* New York: W. W. Norton.

Piaget, J. (1963). *The origins of intelligence in children.* New York: W. W. Norton.

Piaget, J. (1968). *On the development of memory and identity.* Barre, MA: Clark University Press.

Piaget, J. (1970). *Science of education and the psychology of the child.* New York: Orion Press.

Piaget, J. (1983). Piaget's theory. In P. H. Mussen (Ed.), *Handbook of child psychology* (4th ed.), and W. Kessen (Ed.), *History, theory, and methods* (Vol. 1). New York: Wiley.

Piff, P. K., Kraus, M. W., Côté, S., Cheng, B. H., & Keltner, D. (2010). Having less, giving more: The influence of social class on prosocial behavior. *J Pers Soc Psychol, 99*, 771–784.

Pink, D. (2009). *Drive: The surprising truth about what motivates us.* New York: Penguin Group.

Pitts, D. (2007). *Living on borrowed time: Life with cystic fibrosis.* Bloomington, IN: Author House.

Polcari, A., Rabi, K, Bolger, E., & Teicher, M. H. (2014). Parental verbal affection and verbal aggression in childhood differentially influence psychiatric symptoms and wellbeing in young adulthood. *Child Abuse and Neglect, , 91–102.

Ponitz, C., McClelland, M., Jewkes, A., Conner, C., Farris, C., & Morrison, F. (2008). Touch your toes! Developing a direct measure of behavioral regulation in early childhood. *Early Childhood Research Quarterly, 23*, 141–158.

Poole, D. L. (Ed.). (1996). *Multicultural issues in social work.* Washington, DC: NASW Press.

Popham, W. J. (2008). *Transformative assessment.* Alexandria, VA: ASCD.

Poplin, M., & Soto-Hinman, I. (2006). Taking off ideological blinders: Lessons from the start of a study on effective teachers in high-poverty schools. *The Journal of Education, 186*(3), 41–44.

Poussaint, A. F., & Linn, S. (1997, Spring/Summer). Fragile: Handle with care. *Newsweek* [Your Child: From Birth to Three, Special Issue], 33.

Pransky, J. (1991). *Prevention: The critical need.* Springfield, MO: Burrell Foundation and Paradigm Press.

Pritchard, R., & Ashwood, E. (2008). *Managing motivation* (p. 6). New York: Taylor & Francis Group.

Pritchard, R., & Ashwood, E. (2008). *Managing motivation: A manager's guide to diagnosing and improving motivation.* New York: Routledge Academic

Prothrow-Stith, D., & Quaday, S. (1995). *Hidden casualties: The relationship between violence and learning.* Washington, DC: National Health & Education Consortium and National Consortium for African-American Children.

Provence, S., & Lipton, R. C. (1967). *Infants in institutions: A comparison of their development during the first year of life with family-reared infants.* Madison, CT: International Universities Press.

Psunder, M. (2005). How effective is school discipline in preparing students to become responsible citizens? Slovenian teachers and students' view. *Teaching and Teacher Education, 21*, 273–286.

Pueschel, S. M. (2000). *A parent's guide to Down syndrome: Toward a brighter future* (2nd ed.). Baltimore, MD: Paul H. Brooks.

Pulvermuller, F. (2005). Brain mechanisms linking language to action. *Nat Rev Neurosci, 6*, 574–582.

Rabiner, L. R., & Huang, B. H. (1993). *Fundamentals of speech recognition*. Englewood Cliffs, NJ: Prentice Hall.

Raikes, H. (1996). A secure base for babies: Applying attachment concepts to the infant care settings. *Young Children, 51*(95), 59–67.

Ramey, C. T., & Ramey, S. L. (2004). Early educational interventions and intelligence: Implications for Head Start. In E. Zigler & S. J. Styfco (Eds.), *The Head Start debates* (pp. 3–18). Baltimore, MD: Brookes Publishing Company.

Ramsey, R. G., & Williams, L. R. (2003). *Multicultural education: A resource book*. New York: Routledge Farmer.

Rao, H., Betancourt, L., Giannetta, J. M., Brodsky, N. L., Korczykowski, M., Avants, B. B., Gee, J. C., Wang, J., Hurt, H., Detre, J. A., & Farah, M. J. (2010). Early parental care is important for hippocampal maturation: Evidence from brain morphology in humans. *Neuroimage, 49*, 1144–1150.

Raver, C. C. (2002). Emotions matter: Making the case for the role of young children's emotional development for early school readiness. *Social Policy Report, 16*(3), 3–19.

Raver, C. C., & Zigler, E. F. (1997). Social competence: An untapped dimension in evaluating Head Start's success. *Early Childhood Research Quarterly, 12*(4), 363–385.

Reeve, J. (2006). Extrinsic rewards and inner motivation. In C. Evertson, C. M. Weinstein, & C. S. Weinstein (Eds.), *Handbook of classroom management: Research, practice and contemporary issues* (pp. 645–664). Mahwah, NJ: Lawrence Erlbaum Associates.

Reid, G. (2003). *Dyslexia: A practitioners handbook* (3rd ed.). Chichester, UK: Wiley.

Reyes, J. W. (2007). Environmental policy as social policy? The impact of childhood lead exposure on crime. *Journal of Economic Analysis and Policy, 7*(1), article 51.

Rhode, D. L. (2010). The beauty bias: The injustice of appearance in life and law. New York: Oxford University Press.

Rideout, V., & Hamel, E. (2006). *The media family: Electronic media in the lives of infants, toddlers, preschoolers, and their parents*. Menlo Park, CA: Henry J. Kaiser Foundation.

Riggs, N. R., Blair, C. B., & T. (2003). Concurrent and 2-year longitudinal relations between executive function and the behavior of 1st and 2nd grade children. *Child Neuropsychology, 9*, 267–276.

Rimm-Kaufman, S. E., & Pianta, R. (2000). An ecological perspective on the transition to kindergarten: A theoretical framework to guide empirical research. *Journal of Applied Developmental Psychology, 21*(5), 491–511.

Rimm-Kaufman, S. E., La Paro, K. M., Downer, J. T., & Pianta, R. C. (2005). The contribution of classroom setting and quality of instruction to children's behavior in kindergarten classrooms. *The Elementary School Journal, 105*(4), 377–394.

Rose, S., & Meezan, W. (1996). Variations in perceptions of child neglect. *Child Welfare, 75*(2), 139–160.

Rosenblith, J. F., Sims-Knight, J. (1985). *In the beginning: Development in the first two years*. Monterey, CA: Brooks/Cole.

Rosenkoetter, L. I., Rosenkoetter, S. E., & Acock, A. C. (2009). Television violence: An intervention to reduce its impact on children. *Journal of Applied Developmental Psychology, 30*(4), 381–397.

Rosenthal, R., & Jacobson, L. (1968). *Pygmalion in the classroom: Teacher expectations and pupils' intellectual development*. New York: Holt, Rinehart & Winston.

Rothbart, M. K., Ahadi, S. A., & Evans, D. E. (2000). Temperament and personality: Origins and outcomes. *Journal of Personality and Social Psychology, 78*, 122–135.

Rousseau, J. J. (1893, 1979). *Emile, or On education*, Trans. Allan Bloom. New York: Basic Books.

Rubin, K. H., Burgess, K. B., & Hastings, P. D. (2002). Stability and social-behavioral consequences of toddlers' inhibited temperament and parenting. *Child Development, 73*, 483–495.

Rubin, K. H., Hemphill, S. A., Chen, X., Hastings, P., Sanson, A., LoCoco, A., Zappulla, C., Chung, O., Park, S. Y., Do, H. S., Chen, H., Sun, L., Yoon, C. H., & Cui, L. (2006). Cross-cultural study of behavioral inhibition in toddlers: East-west-north-south. *International Journal of Behavioral Development, 30*(3), 219–226.

Runyan, D., Wattam, C., Ikeda, R., Hassan, F., & Ramiro, L. (2002). Child abuse and neglect by parents and caregivers. In E. Krug, L. L. Dahlberg, J. A. Mercy, A. B. Zwi, & R. Lozano (Eds.). *World Report on Violence and Health*. Geneva, Switzerland: World Health Organization.

Rushton, S. P. (2011). Neuroscience, early childhood education and play: We are doing it right! *Early Childhood Education Journal, 39*, 89–94.

Rushton, S. P., & Larkin, E. (2001). Shaping the learning environment: Connecting developmentally appropriate practices to brain research. *Early Childhood Education Journal, 29*(1), 25–33.

Russell, A., Hart, C. H., Robinson, C. C., & Olsen, S. F. (2003). Children's sociable and aggressive behavior with peers: A comparison of the US and Australia, and contributions of temperament and parenting styles. *International Journal of Behavioral Development, 27*(1), 74–86.

Ryan, R. M., & Deci, E. L. (2000). Self-determination theory and the facilitation of intrinsic motivation, social development, and well-being. *Am Psychol. 55*, 68–78.

Ryan, R. M., Lynch, M. F., Vansteenkiste, M., & Deci, E. L. (2011). Motivation and autonomy in counseling, psychotherapy, and behavior change: A look at theory and practice. *The Counseling Psychologist, 39*, 193–260.

Sabbagh, M. A., Xu, F., Carlson, S. M., Moses, L. J., & Lee, K. (2006). The development of executive functioning and theory of mind: A comparison of Chinese and U.S. preschoolers. *Psychological Science, 17*(1), 74–81.

Sai, F. Z. (2005). The role of the mother's voice in developing mother's face preference: Evidence for intermodal perception at birth. *Infant and Child Development, 14*, 29–50.

Sailor, W., Dunlap, G., Sugai, G., & Horner, R. (Eds.). (2009). *Handbook of positive behavior support*. New York: Springer.

Salovey, P., & Mayer, J. D. (1990). Emotional intelligence. *Imagination, Cognition, and Personality, 9*, 185–211.

Sameroff, A. (2010). A unified theory of development: A dialectic integration of nature and nurture. *Child Development, 81*(1), 6–22.

Sanders, S. (2002). *Active for life: Developmentally appropriate movement programs for young children*. Washington, DC: NAEYC.

Santrock, J. W. (2008). *Educational psychology* (3rd ed.). Boston, MA: McGraw-Hill.

Sapolsky, R. M. (2004). The frontal cortex and the criminal justice system. *Philosophical Transactions of the Royal Society B, 359*, 1787–1796.

Saxe, R., Tenenbaum, J. B., & Carey, S. (2005). 10 and 12-month-old infants' capacity for causal attribution. *Psychological Science, 16*, 995–1001.

Schaefer, C. E., & Digeronimo, T. F. (2000). *Ages and stages: A parent's guide to normal childhood development*. New York: Wiley.

Schaefer, G. B., & Mendelsohn, N. J. (2008). Genetics evaluation for the etiologic diagnosis of autism spectrum disorders. *Genetic Medicine, 10*(1), 4–12.

Schappet, J., Malkusak, A., & Bruya, L. D., Eds. (2003). *High expectations: Playgrounds for children of all abilities.* Bloomfield, CT: The National Center for Boundless Playgrounds.

Scherer, A. (1988). The epilepsy foundation of America. In H. Reisner (Ed.), *Children with epilepsy: A parent's guide.* Bethesda, MD: Woodbine House.

Schiller, P. (2001). Brain Research and Its Implications for Early Childhood Programs —Applying Research to Our Work. *Exchange, 140,* 14–19.

Schiller, P. (2010). *Seven skills for school success: Activities to develop social & emotional intelligence in young children.* Buchanan, NY: Read How You Want.

Schmidt, M. E., Pempek, T. A., Kirkorian, H. L., Lund, A. F., & Anderson, D. R. (2008). The effects of background television on the toy play behavior of very young children. *Child Development, 79*(4), 1137–1151.

Schottelkorb, A., & Ray, D. (2009). ADHD symptom reduction in elementary students: A single-case effectiveness design. *Professional School Counselors, 13*(1), 11–22.

Schou, L. R. (2001). Democracy in education. *Studies in Philosophy and Education, 20,* 317–329.

Schulz, L. E., Gopnik, A., & Glymour, C. (2007). Preschool children learn about causal structure from conditional interventions. *Developmental Science, 10,* 322–332.

Schwartz, M. (2007). *Effective character education: A guidebook for future educators.* New York: McGraw-Hill.

Schwartz, S. H., & Sagiv, L. (1995). Identifying culture-specifics in the content and structure of values. *Journal of Cross-Cultural Psychology, 26*(1), 92–116.

Schwartz, S. H., & Ros, M. (1995). Values in the West: A theoretical and empirical challenge to the Individualism-Collectivism cultural dimension. *World Psychology, 1,* 99–122.

Schweinhart, L. J. (2004). *The High/Scope Perry Preschool study through age 40: Summary, conclusions, and frequently asked questions.* Ypsilanti, MI: High/Scope Educational Research Foundation.

Sears, W. (2008). *Nighttime parenting: How to get your baby and child to sleep.* New York: Plume and La Leche League International Books.

Sears, W., Sears, M., & Sears, J. (2001). *The baby sleep book: The complete guide to a good night's rest for the whole family.* Charlottesville, VA: Little, & Co.

Sears, W., Sears, M., Sears, R., Sears, J., & Sears, P. (2011). *The portable pediatrician: Everything you need to know about your child's health.* New York: Little, Brown and Co.

Seligman, M. E. P. (2004). Can happiness be taught? *Daedalus, 133*(2), 80–87.

Seligman, M. E. P. (2006). *Learned optimism: How to change your mind and your life.* New York: Vintage Press.

Sellers, K., Russo, T. J., Baker, I., & Dennison, B. A. (2005). The role of childcare providers in the prevention of childhood overweight. *Journal of Early Childhood Research, 3*(3), 227–242.

Semel, E., & Rosner, S. R. (2003). *Understanding Williams syndrome: A guide to behavioral patterns and interventions.* Mahwah, NJ: Erlbaum.

Sharmin (2006). Crucial conversations. Adhunika: Where Women Shape the Future. Accessed on February 16, 2011, at http://www.adhunika.org/archives/793

Sherman, J., Rasmussen, C., & Baydala, L. (2006). Thinking positively: How some characteristics of AD/HD can be adaptive and accepted in the classroom. *Childhood Education,* summer issue, *82,* 4.

Shidler, L. (2009). Setting an example in the classroom: Teaching children what we want them to learn. *Young Children, 64*(5), 88–91.

Shonkoff, J. P., & Phillips, D. A. (2000). *From neurons to neighborhoods: The science of early childhood development.* Washington, DC: National Academy Press.

Shonkoff, J. P., & Meisels, S. J. (2000). *Handbook of early intervention* (2nd ed.). New York: Cambridge University Press.

Shore, R. (1997). *Rethinking the brain: New insights into early development.* New York: Families and Work Institute.

Shulman, S. T. (1987). *Kawasaki disease.* New York: Wiley.

Sickle Cell Advisory Committee. (1999). *Sickle cell disease: Information for school personnel.* Trenton, NJ: New Jersey Department of Health and Senior Services.

Silveri, M. M., Rohan, M. L., Pimentel, P. J., Gruber, S. A., Rosso, I. M., & Yurgelun-Todd, D. A. (2006). Sex differences in the relationship between white matter microstructure and impulsivity in adolescence. *Magnetic Resonance Imaging, 24,* 833–841.

Singer, C. (2009). Coprolalia and other coprophenomena. *Neurologic Clinics, 15*(2), 299–308.

Singh, N. N., Singh, A. N., Lancioni, G. E., Singh, J., Winton, A. S. W., & Adkins, A. D. (2010). Mindfulness training for parents and their children with ADHD increases the children's compliance. *Journal of Child and Family Studies, 19*(2), 157–166.

Skinner, B. (1953). *Science and human behavior.* New York: Macmillan.

Skinner, B. (1974). *About behaviorism.* New York: Knopf.

Skolnick, A. (1991). *Embattled paradise: The American family in an age of uncertainty.* New York: Basic Books.

Slater, A., & Quinn, P. C. (2001). Face recognition in the newborn infant. *Infant and Child Development, 10,* 21–24.

Smagorinsky, P. (2007). Vygotsky and the social dynamic of classrooms. *English Journal, 97*(2), 61–66.

Snarey, J., & Samuelson, P. (2008). Moral education in the cognitive developmental tradition: Lawrence Kohlberg's revolutionary ideas. In L. P. Nucci & D. Narvaez (Eds.), *Handbook of moral and character education* (pp. 53–79). New York: Routledge.

Snow, D. L. (2009). Coping with work and family stress. Interview by J. Casey & K. Corday Sloan by *Work and Family Research Network,* Boston College, Chestnut Hill, MA. Accessed on March 16, 2011, at http:// wfnetwork.bc.edu/The _Network_News/65/experts.htm

Socolar, R. R. S., Savage, R., & Evans, H. (2007). A longitudinal study of parental

Sodian, B., Zaitchik, D., & Carey, S. (1991). Young children's differentiation of hypothetical beliefs from evidence. *Child Development, 62,* 753–766.

Sood, B., Delaney-Black, V., Covington, C., Nordstrom-Klee, B., Ager, J., & Templin, T. (2001). Prenatal alcohol exposure and childhood behaviour at age 6–7 years: Dose response effect. *Paediatrics, 108*(2), E34–E35.

Sparks, L., & Edwards, J. (2010). *Anti-bias education for young children & ourselves.* Washington, DC: National Association for the Education of Young Children.

Spielberger, C. (Ed.). (2004). *Encyclopedia of applied psychology.* San Diego, CA: Academic Press.

Spilsbury, L. (2002). *What does it mean to have dyslexia?* Oxford, UK: Heinemann Library.

Spinrad, T., Eisenberg, N., & Bernt, F. (Eds.) (2007). Introduction to the special issues on moral development: Part I. *The Journal of Genetic Psychology, 168*(2), 101–104.

Sprenger, M. B. (2002). *Becoming a wiz at brain-based teaching.* Thousand Oaks, CA: Corwin Press.

Sroufe, A. L. (2005). Attachment and development: A prospective, longitudinal study from birth to adulthood. *Attachment and Human Development, 7*(4), 349–367.

Stables, A. (2003). Learning, identity and classroom dialogue. *Journal of Educational Enquiry, 4,* 1–18.

Stafford, A., Laybourn, A., Hill, M., & Walker, M. (2003). Having a say: Children and young people talk about consultation. *Children & Society, 17,* 361–373.

Standing, E. M. (1957) *Maria Montessori: Her life and work.* New York: New American Library.

Steel, P., & König, C. (2006). Integrating theories of motivation. *Academy of Management Review, 31,* 889–913.

Steglin, D. (2005). Making a case for play policy. Research-based reasons to support play based environments. *Young Children, 60*(2), 76–85

Steinberg, L. (1995). *Childhood.* New York: McGraw-Hill.

Steinberg, L., Lamborn, S. D., Darling, N., Mounts, N. S., & Dornbush, S. M. (1994). Over-time changes in adjustment and competence among adolescents from authoritative, authoritarian, indulgent, and neglectful families. *Child Development, 65,* 754–770.

Stien, P. T., & Kendall, J. C. (2003). *Psychological trauma and the developing brain: Neurologically based interventions for troubled children.* Binghamton, NY: Haworth Press.

Straus, M. (2008). The special issue on prevention of violence ignores the primordial violence. *Journal of Interpersonal Violence, 23*(9), 1314–1320.

Straus, M. A., & Douglas, E. M. (2008). Research on spanking by parents: Implications for public policy. *The Family Psychologist: Bulletin of the Division of Family Psychology, 43*(24), 18–20.

Straus, M. A. (2005). Children should never, ever, be spanked no matter what the circumstances. In D. R. Loseke, R. J. Gelles, & M. M. Cavanaugh (Eds.), *Current controversies about family violence.* Thousand Oaks, CA: Sage.

Straus, M. A., & Paschall, M. J. (2000). Corporal punishment by mothers and development of children's cognitive ability: A longitudinal study of two nationally representative age cohorts. *J Aggress Maltreat Trauma, 18,* 459–483.

Stray-Gundersen, K. (1995). *Babies with Down syndrome: A new parent's guide* (2nd ed.). Bethesda, MD: Woodbine House.

Stutzman Amstutz, L., & Mullet, J. (2005). *The little book of restorative discipline in schools: Teaching responsibility; creating caring climates.* Intercourse, PA: Good Books.

Swann, A. C. (2009). An intriguing link between drawing and play with toys. *Childhood Education, 85*(4), 230.

Sweet, M. (2008). The thinking guide to inclusive childcare disability rights. *Disability Rights Wisconsin.* Accessed on March 17, 2014, at http://www.disabilityrightswi.org/wp-content/uploads/2008/02/thinking-guide-to-inclusive-child-care.pdf

Tannen, D. (2002). *I only say this because I love you.* New York: Ballantine Books.

Taylor, M. C. (2000). Social contextual strategies for reducing racial discrimination. In S. Oskamp (Ed.), *Reducing prejudice and discrimination.* Mahwah, NJ: Erlbaum.

Taylor, S. E. (2010). Mechanisms linking early life stress to adult health outcomes. *Proceedings of the National Academy of Sciences, 107,* 8507–8512.

Teaching Tolerance Project. (1997). *Starting small: Teaching tolerance in preschool and the early grades.* Montgomery, AL: Southern Poverty Law Center.

Teicher, M. H., Samson, J. A., Polcari, A., & McGreenery, C. E. (2006). Sticks, stones, and hurtful words: relative effects of various forms of childhood maltreatment. *Am J Psychiatry, 163*(6), 993–1000.

Teicher, M. H., Anderson, C. M., & Polcari, A. (2012). Childhood maltreatment is associated with reduced volume in the hippocampal subfields CA3, dentate gyrus, and associated with reduced volume in the hippocampal subfields CA3, dentate gyrus, and subiculum. *Proc Natl Acad Sci USA, 109*(9).

Teicher, M. H., Samson, J. A., Sheu, Y. S., Polcari, A., & McGreenery, C. E. (2010). Hurtful words: association of exposure to peer verbal abuse with elevated psychiatric symptom scores and corpus callosum abnormalities. *Am J Psychiatry, 167*(12), 1464–1471.

Thigpen, B. (2007). Outdoor play: Combating sedentary lifestyles. *Zero to Three, 28*(1), 19–23.

Thompson, D. S., Hudson, S. H., & Olsen, H. (2007). *SAFE play areas: Creation, maintenance, and renovation.* Champaign, IL: Human Kinetics.

Thompson, M., Grace, C., & Cohen, L. (2001). *Best friends, worst enemies: Understanding the social lives of children.* New York: Ballantine.

Thompson, R. A. (2001). Developing in the first years of life. *The Future of Children, 11*(1), 20–33.

Thomson, B. (1989). Building tolerance in early childhood. *Educational Leadership, 47*(2), 78–79.

Thornberg, R. (2009). The moral construction of the good pupil embedded in school rules. *Education, Citizenship and Social Justice, 4,* 245–261.

Thorpe, K., & Daly, K. (1999). Children, parents and time. The dialectics of control. In C. L. Shehan (Ed.), *Through the eyes of the child: Revisioning children as active agents of family life.* New York: JAI Press.

Tjaden, P., & Thoennes, N. (2000). *Full report of the prevalence, incidence, and consequences of violence against women: Findings from the National Violence Against Women Survey.* Washington, DC: National Institute of Justice (Report No. NCJ 183721).

Todd, M. K., Reis-Bergan, M. J., Sidman, C. L., Flohr, J. A., Jameson-Walker, K., Spicer-Bartolau, T., & Wildeman, K. (2008). Effect of a family-based intervention on electronic media use and body composition among boys aged 8–11 years: A pilot study. *Journal of Child Health Care, 12*(4), 344–358.

Tomasello, M. (2003). *Constructing a language: A usage-based theory of language acquisition.* Cambridge, MA: Harvard University Press.

Tomasello, M., Kruger, A.C. and Ratner, H.H. (1993). Cultural learning. *Behavioral and Brain Sciences, 16,* 495–552.

Tomlinson, C. A., & Kalbfleisch, M. L. (1998). Teach me, teach my brain. A call for differentiated classrooms. *Educational Leadership, 56*(3), 52–55.

Tomoda, A., Sheu, Y., Rabi, K., Suzuki, H., Navalta, C., Polcari, A., & Teicher, M. H. (2011). Exposure to parental verbal abuse is associated with increased gray matter volume in superior temporal gyrus. *Neuroimage, 54* Jan, S280–S286.

Tottenham, N., Hare, T. A., & Casey, B. J. (2011). Behavioral assessment of emotion discrimination, emotion regulation and cognitive control, in childhood, adolescence, and adulthood. *Frontiers in Developmental Psychology, 2,* 1–9.

Tower, C. (1996). *Child abuse and neglect.* Boston: Allyn & Bacon.

Trad, P. V. (1991). *Interventions with infants and parents: The theory and practice of previewing.* Hoboken, NJ: Wiley.

Trawick-Smith, J. (1997). *Early childhood development in multicultural perspective.* Upper Saddle River, NJ: Merrill Education/Prentice Hall.

Trawick-Smith, J. (2006). *Early childhood development: A multicultural perspective* (4th ed.). Upper Saddle River, NJ: Pearson.

Trilling, B., & Fadel, C. (2009). *21st century skills: Learning for life in our times.* San Francisco, CA: Jossey-Bass.

Twardosz, S. (2012). Effects of experience on the brain: The role of neuroscience in early development and education. *Early Education and Development, 23,* 96–119.

U.S. Census Bureau. (2010). Who's minding the kids? Child care arrangements: spring 2005/summer 2006. Accessed on March 16, 2011, at www.census.gov/prod/2010pubs/p70-121.pdf

U.S. Department of Education, National Center for Education Statistics. (2010). *Digest of Education Statistics* (NCES 2010-013), Chapter 2. Accessed on January 7, 2011, at http://nces.ed.gov/fastfacts/display.asp?id=64

U.S. Department of Health and Human Services. (2009). *Blueprint for action: Healthy Child Care America campaign.* Washington, DC: Author.

U.S. Department of Health and Human Services (US DHHS), Administration on Children, Youth, and Families (ACF). (2001). *In focus: Understanding the effects of maltreatment on early brain development.* Washington, DC: Government Printing Office.

U.S. Department of Health and Human Services (US DHHS), Administration on Children, Youth, and Families (ACF). (2003). *Child maltreatment.* Washington, DC: Government Printing Office. Accessed on March 16, 2011, at http://www.acf.hhs.gov

U.S. Department of Health and Human Services (US DHHS), Administration for Children and Families, Puma, M., Bell, S., Cook, R., Heid, C., & Lopez, M. (2005). *Head Start impact study: First year findings.* Washington, DC: Government Printing Office.

U.S. Department of Health and Human Services (US DHHS), Administration on Children, Youth, and Families (ACF). (2007). *Child maltreatment 2005.* Washington, DC: Government Printing Office.

U.S. Department of Health and Human Services, National Institute of Mental Health. (2008). *Attention deficit hyperactivity disorder (ADHD)* (08-3572). Bethesda, MD: Government Printing Office.

Ulich, R. (1954). *Three thousand years of educational wisdom.* Cambridge, MA: Harvard University Press.

University of California Los Angeles. (2010). First direct recording made of mirror neurons in human brain. *ScienceDaily,* April. Retrieved February 22, 2014, from http://www.sciencedaily.com/releases/2010/04/100412162112.htm

University of Haifa. (2013). 'Love hormone' oxytocin: Difference in social perception between men and women. *ScienceDaily,* July. Retrieved September 30, 2013, from http://www.sciencedaily.com/releases/2013/07/130731093257.htm

Uomini, N. T. (2010). Book review: Finding our tongues: mothers, infants, and the origins of language. *American Journal of Physical Anthropology, 141*(1), 164–165.

Van Ausdale, D., & Feagin, J. R. (2001). *The first R. How children learn race and racism.* Lanham, MD: Rowman & Littlefield.

Van Herwegen, J., Ansari, D., Xu, F., & Karmiloff-Smith, A. (2008). Small and large number processing in infants and toddlers with Williams syndrome. *Developmental Science, 11,* 637–643.

Vance, E., & Weaver, P. (2002). *Class meetings: Young children solving problems together.* Washington, DC: NAEYC.

Vandell, D. L., Belsky, J., Burchinal, M., Steinberg, & Vandergrift L. N. (2010). Do effects of early child care extend to age 15 years? Results from the NICHD study of early child care and youth development, and the NICHD Early Child Care Research Network. *National Institute for Early Education Research,* Rutgers, The State University of New Jersey. Accessed on March 16, 2011, at nieer.org/docs/?DocID=293

Vannatta, K., Gartstein, M. A., Zeller, M., & Noll, R. B. (2009). Peer acceptance and social behavior during childhood and adolescence: How important are appearance, athleticism, and academic competence? *International Journal of Behavioral Development, 33*(4), 303–311.

Vardin, P. A. (2003, Winter). Montessori and Gardner's theory of multiple intelligences. *Montessori Life, 15*(1), 40–43.

Vesneski, W. (2009). Street-level bureaucracy and family group decision-making in the USA. *Child and Family Social Work, 14,* 1–5.

von Frisch, K. (1974). Decoding the language of the bee. *Science, 185,* 663–668.

von Mutius, E. (2000). The burden of childhood asthma. *Archives of Disease in Childhood,* June, *82,* ii2–ii5.

Vygotsky, L. (1962) *Thought and language.* Cambridge, MA: MIT Press.

Vygotsky, L. (1978). *Mind in society. The development of higher psychological processes.* Cambridge, MA: Harvard University Press.

Wailoo, K. (2001). *Dying in the city of the blues: Sickle cell anemia and the politics of race and health.* Chapel Hill, NC: University of North Carolina Press.

Wakschlag, L. S., Pickett, K. E., Cook, E., Benowitz, N. L., & Leventhal, B. L. (2002). Maternal smoking during pregnancy and severe antisocial behavior in offspring: A review. *American Journal of Public Health, 92,* 966–974.

Wakschlag, L. S., Pickett, K. E., Kasza, K. E., & Loeber, R. (2006). Is prenatal smoking associated with a developmental pattern of conduct problems in young boys? *Journal of the American Academy of Child and Adolescent Psychiatry, 45*(4), 461–467.

Walker, L. J., & Taylor, J. H. (1991). Family interactions and the development of moral reasoning. *Child Development, 62,* 264–283.

Waltz, M. (2001). *Tourette's syndrome: Finding answers and getting help.* Sebastopol, CA: O'Reilly.

Warash, B., Curtis, R., Hursh, D., & Tucci, V. (2008). Skinner meets Piaget on the Reggio playground: Practical synthesis of applied behavior analysis and developmentally appropriate practice orientations. *Journal of Research in Childhood Education 22*(4), 441–453.

Warneken, F., & Tomasello, M. (2009). Varieties of altruism in children and chimpanzees. *Trends in Cognitive Science, 13,* 397–402.

Warner, J. (2010). The charitable-giving divide. *The New York Times Magazine,* Aug. 20.

Warner, L. A., & Pottick, K. J. (2006). Functional impairment among preschoolers using mental health services. *Children and Youth Services Review, 28,* 473–486.

Warren, S. L., Emde, R. N., & Sroufe, L. A. (2000). Internal representations: Predicting anxiety from children's play narratives. *Journal of American Academy of Child & Adolescent Psychiatry, 39*(1), 100–107.

Watson, J. (1930). *Behaviorism* (2nd ed.). Chicago, IL: University of Chicago Press.

Watson, M., Ecken, L., & Kohn, A. (2003). *Learning to trust: Transforming difficult elementary classrooms through developmental discipline.* San Francisco, CA: Jossey-Bass.

Weber-Fox, C. M., & Neville, H. J. (1999). Functional neural subsystems are differentially affected by delays in second language immersion: ERP and behavioral evidence in bilinguals. In D. Birdsong (Ed.). *Second language acquisition and the critical period hypothesis.* Mahwah, NJ: Lawrence Erlbaum and Associates, Inc.

Webster-Stratton, C. (2000). *How to promote social and emotional competence in young children.* London: Sage Publications.

Wechsler, D. (1958). *The measurement and appraisal of adult intelligence* (4th ed.). Baltimore, MD: Williams & Wilkins.

Weiser, M. (1982). *Group care and education of infants and toddlers.* St. Louis, MO: Mosby.

Weisz, J. R., Suwanlert, S., Chaiyasit, W., Weiss, B., Walter, B. R., & Anderson, W. W. (1988). Thai and American perspectives on over- and undercontrolled child behavior problems: Exploring the threshold model among parents, teachers, and psychologists. *Journal of Consulting and Clinical Psychology, 56*(4), 601–609.

Weitzman, M., Byrd, R. S., Aligne, C. A., & Moss, M. (2002). The effects of tobacco exposure on children's behavioral and cognitive functioning: Implications for clinical and public health policy and future research. *Neurotoxicology and Teratology, 24,* 397–406.

Welsh, B. C., & Farrington, D. P. (2007). Key challenges and prospects in peer-based delinquency prevention programs: Comment on van Lier, Vitaro, and Eisner. *European Journal on Criminal Policy and Research.* Accessed March 16, 2011, at http://www.springerlink.com/content/t164618n6243403p/

Werker, J. F., Pons, F., Dietrich, C., Kajikawa, S., Fais, L., & Amano, S. (2007). Infant-directed speech supports phonetic category learning in English and Japanese. *Cognition, 103,* 147–162.

Werner, E. E., Bierman, J. M., & French, F. E. (1971). *The children of Kauai: A longitudinal study from the prenatal period to age ten.* Honolulu: University of Hawaii Press.

White, B. L. (1995). *The new first three years of life* (rev. ed.). New York: Simon & Schuster.

White, B. L., Werker, .F., & Lalonde, C. (1988). Cross-language speech perception: initial capabilities and developmental change. *Dev. Psychol., 24,* 672–683.

White, L., & Genesee, F. (1996). How native is near-native? The issue of ultimate attainment in adult second language acquisition. *Second Language Research, 12,* 233–265.

Whittaker, J. (2009). Evidence-based intervention and services for high-risk youth: A North American perspective on the challenges of integration for policy, practice and research. *Child and Family Social Work, 14*(2), 166–177.

Whittle, S., Whittle, S., Yap, M. B., Yücel, M., Fornito, A., Simmons, J. G., Barrett, A., Sheeber, L., & Allen, N. B. (2008). Prefrontal and amygdala volumes are related to adolescents' affective behaviors during parent–adolescent interactions. *Proceedings of the National Academy of Sciences, 105,* 3652–3657.

Wien, C. A. (2004). From policy to participation: Overturning the rules and creating amiable classrooms. *Young Children, 59*(1), 34–40.

Wigfield, A., Guthrie, J. T., Tonks, S., & Perencevich, K. C. (2004). Children's motivation for reading: Domain specificity and instructional influences. *Journal of Educational Research, 97,* 299–309.

Wilcox-Herzog, A., & Ward, S. L. (2004, Fall). Measuring teachers' perceived interactions with children: A tool for assessing beliefs and intentions. *Early Childhood Research and Practice, 6*(2). Accessed on March 16, 2011, at http://ecrp.uiuc.edu

Willatts, P. (1989). Development of problem solving in infancy. In A. Slater & J. G. Bremner (Eds.), *Infant Development.* London: Lawrence Erlbaum.Williams, K. L., & Wahler, R. G. (2010). U.S. Department of Health and Human Services, Administration for Children and Families, Administration on Children, Youth and Families, Children's Bureau. Are mindful parents more authoritative and less authoritarian? An analysis of clinic-referred mothers. *Journal of Child and Family Studies, 19*(2), 230–235.

Williams, R. (2001). Culture is ordinary. In J. Higgins (Ed.), *The Raymond Williams reader* (pp. 10–24). Oxford, UK: Blackwell.

Wilson, H. (2002). Brain science, early intervention and 'at risk' families: Implications for parents, professionals and social policy. *Social Policy and Society, 1*(3), 191–202.

Winslade, J., & Monk, G. (2000). *Narrative mediation: A new approach to conflict resolution.* San Francisco, CA: Jossey-Bass.

Wisconsin Council on Children and Families. (July 2013). *Getting your brain around early childhood development.* Retrieved on March 5, 2014, at www.wccf.org

Wolfe, P. (1998). Revisiting effective teaching. *Educational Leadership, 56*(3).

Wolfe, P. (2001). *Brain matters.* Alexandria, VA: ASCD.

Wong, B. Y. L. (2004). *Learning about learning disabilities* (3rd ed.). Burlington, MA: Academic Press.

Woolfolk, A. (2004). *Educational psychology* (9th ed.). Boston, MA: Allyn & Bacon.

Worth, K., & Grollman, S. (2003). *Worms, shadows, and whirlpools: Science in the early childhood classroom.* Washington, DC: NAEYC.

Wortham, S. C. (2008). *Assessment in early childhood education* (5th ed.). Upper Saddle River, NJ: Pearson Merrill Prentice Hall.

Wyness, M. (2006). *Childhood and society: An introduction to the sociology of childhood.* New York: Palgrave MacMillan.

Xiang, P., McBride, R., & Guan, J. (2004). Children's motivation in elementary physical education: A longitudinal study. *Research Quarterly for Exercise and Sport, 75*(1), 71–80.

Yeni-Komshian, G. H., Flege, J. E., & Liu, S. (2000). Pronunciation proficiency in the first and second languages of Korean English bilinguals. *Bilingualism: Lang Cogn. 3,* 131–149.

Yoshinaga-Itano, C. (2004). Levels of evidence: Universal newborn hearing screening (UNHS) and early hearing detection and intervention systems (EHDI). *Journal of Communication Disorders, 37*(5), 451–465.

Young, L., & Saxe, R. (2009). Innocent Intentions: A correlation between forgiveness for accidental harm and neural activity. *Journal of Cognitive Neuroscience, 47*(10), 2065–2072.

Zahn-Waxler, C., Friedman, R. J., Cole, P. M., Mizuta, I., & Hiruma, N. (1966). Japanese and United States preschool children's responses to conflict and distress. *Child Development, 67*(5), 2462–2477.

Zarrett, N., & Lerner, R. M. (2008). *Ways to promote the positive development of children and youth.* Washington, DC: Child Trends.

Zeanah, C. H. (2000). Disturbances of attachment in young children adopted from institutions. Developmental and Behavioral Pediatrics, 21, 230–236.

Zeanah, C. H., Jr., & Zeanah, P. D. (2001). Towards a definition of infant mental health. *Zero to Three*, 13–20.

Zeidner, M., Matthews, G., & Roberts, R. D. (2001). Slow down, you move too fast: Emotional intelligence remains an "elusive" intelligence. *Emotion, 1*(3), 265–275.

Zelazo, P. D., & Müller, U. (2002). Executive function in typical and atypical development. In U. Goswami (Ed.), *Handbook of childhood cognitive development* (pp. 445–469). Oxford, UK: Blackwell.

Zigler, E. F., Singer, D. G., & Bishop-Josef, S. J. (2004). *Children's play: The roots of reading.* Washington, DC: Zero to Three Press.

Zimmerman, F. J., Christakis, D. A., & Meltzoff, A. N. (2007). Associations between media viewing and language development in children under age 2 years. *Journal of Pediatrics, 151*(4), 364–368.

Index

A

ability differences
accommodations, 134
books, in, 137–138
brain development, 136–137
bullying, 140
children's fear of, 137
defined, 133
inclusive education, 134–136, 138
individualized plans, 145–146
intervention services for, 145
legal rights of children with, 143, 145
nurturing children with, 133–135
parents, supporting, 142–143
physical appearances, 138–139
screening for, 133, 146
services for, 135, 143, 145–146
supporting, 135, 141
teaching strategies, 135, 143
teasing, 140
abstract symbols, 64, 76
abusive head trauma, 142–143, 187
accommodations, 134, 182
active listening, 66, 118, 203–208, 223, 287
activities
child-directed, 166, 173–174
child-initiated, 6
enrichment, 30
group, 168
teacher-initiated, 6
actualizing tendency, 25
Adler, Alfred, 25, 275
adolescence, 29
adult antisocial personality disorders, 159
adult-child interactions, 16–17, 26–27, 37, 125
active listening, 66, 118, 204–205, 207–208, 223
affection, unconditional, 74, 78, 194, 271
assertive communication, 213–218
behaviorist learning theory, 35
consistency, 234–235
constructivist learning theory, 36
coping techniques, 286
critical conversations, 223–224
crucial conversations, 219–223
dialogues, 36

empty threats, 215, 249
inappropriate, 209
language, 59–60
maturationist learning theory, 36
nurturing, 18, 29, 184, 186–187, 191, 193–196, 232
patience, 78
power struggles, 220, 222, 276, 278
recasting speech, 200
responsiveness, 193
time-away, 289–290
unconscious, 32
unconscious information, 32
unrealistic expectations, 170
adults
modeling behavior, 11–12, 15–16, 18–20, 53, 57, 191–192, 203, 206, 209–211, 227, 232
needs of, 285–286
self-reflection, 192
tolerance, 184–185
affection, unconditional, 74, 78, 194, 271
African Americans
cohesive interactions, 127
cultural traits, 119–120
after-school programs, 74–75
age-typical behavior, 256
aggressiveness, 187, 189, 191, 279
Ainsworth, Mary, 55
alcohol drinking
behavior problems and, 150
pregnancy and, 149–150
alcohol-related birth defects (ARBD), 149
Allport, Gordon W., 101
altruism, 166, 229
American Academy of Pediatrics, 62, 79, 166, 189
American Psychiatric Association, 153
American Sign Language (ASL), 202
Amsterdam, Beulah, 63
anarchy, 31
anecdotal records, 88, 91
antibias curriculum, 102–106
antisocial behavior, 29, 165, 184
anxiety, 61, 158
problems, 146
separation, 56–57
stranger, 56–57

appearances. See physical appearances
appropriate touch, 50–51, 267, 295
Arnold, Harriet A., 301
art, multicultural, 104
Ashley, Bernard, 101
Asian Americans, cultural traits, 119–121
Asperger's, 153, 155
assertive rule enforcement, 11–12, 74, 191, 194, 212
assessment, 82, 84–85, 87–88
associative learning, 47
attachment
to caregivers, secure, 54–56
imprinting, 55
attention, undivided, 267
attention deficit/hyperactivity disorder (ADHD), 143, 147, 155, 158
conduct disorders, 159–160
executive functions, 260
medication for, 151–152
self-esteem, 151
strategies for, 150–151
attention problems, 146
attention seeking behavior, 276
auditory figure-ground dysfunction, 154–155
authentic learning, 128
authoritarian-style interactions, 53, 125, 232
authoritative-style interactions, 53–55, 113–114, 125, 190–191, 194–195, 217, 229, 232–233
authority figures, 113–114
defying, 158
autism, 143, 147, 152–153
echolalia, 155
executive functions, 260
strategies for, 153–155
autism spectrum disorder, 153
autocracy, 30
autonomy, 62–63, 75

B

babies. See infants
baby-talk, 49, 199–201
Bar-On, Reuben, 299
Bar-On model of social-emotional intelligence (EQ), 299

behavior
  adult responsibility for, 35
  age-typical, 256
  annoying, 192, 253–254
  antisocial, 29
  appropriateness of, 12–14, 26, 86,
    133, 141, 146–147, 233–234, 257,
    268, 287, 298
  attention deficit/hyperactivity
    disorder (ADHD), 151
  attention seeking, 276
  behaviorist learning theory, 35
  causes of, 276
  conditioning, 47
  consequences of, 13, 64, 270–271,
    290–292
  constructivist learning theory, 37
  destructive, 279
  disruptive, 279
  dysfunctional, 234
  environments, 168–169
  evaluating, 88
  functional, 234
  imitative play, 191
  internalizing, 57
  learned, 47
  maturationist learning theory,
    35–36
  misbehavior, 32, 233–235, 241,
    244–246, 275–279
  motivation for, 294
  nonverbal, 26
  observations, 83–88, 146
  passive, 283
  positive, 168–169
  principles, 12–13
  problems, 5, 146, 188
  reinforcement, 35
  replaces, 254
  responses to, 81–82, 140–141,
    194, 276
  self-stimulating, 283
  tokens, 35
  typical, 41–42
behavior modification, 11–12, 35,
  279–280, 295–298
behaviorist learning theory, 11, 34–35, 37
biases, 75, 81–83, 86, 91, 102–103, 105,
  109, 118
bibliotherapy, 137–138, 264, 300
bio-ecological model, 28
bipolar disorder, 156–157
biting, 257–258
body language, 49–50, 59–60, 96, 120
books
  ability differences in, 137–138
  antibias curriculum, 105–106

author perspective, 106
author/illustrator qualifications, 106
copyright date of, 106
invisibility in, 106
lifestyles in, 106
loaded words, 106
multicultural, 101, 104–105
prosocial skills, 173, 264
relationships in, 106
self-image in, 106
stereotyping in, 105
tokenism in, 105
Borba, Michele, 228–229
boredom, 244–245
bottle feeding, 62
Bower, T. G. R., 178
Bowlby, John, 55
brain development, 84
  ability differences, 136–137
  corporal punishment and, 189
  emotional awareness, 299
  executive functions, 150, 260–261
  extrinsic motivation, 280–281
  infants, 37, 45–46, 50, 52, 112,
    117, 138
  intrinsic motivation, 280–281
  language, 201
  moral reasoning, 231–232
  play, 52, 69
  poverty, 117
  preschoolers, 69
  rapid eye movement (REM)
    sleep, 52
  self-control, 260
  social interactions, 112–113
  toddlers, 59
  verbal abuse, 190
Brain Facts: What Can We Learn from
  Neuroscience?
  Ask These Questions about
    Annoying Behaviors, 192
  Assessment helps us create effective
    learning environments, 84
  Brain Development and Moral
    Behavior, 231–232
  Children develop empathy and
    learn skills by watching role
    models, 27
  Children's Brains and the
    Development of Self-Control,
    260–261
  Corporal punishment and brain
    development, 189
  Healthy brain development requires
    nurturing social interaction
    and environmental experiences,
    112–113

How Do Babies and Young Children
  Learn Language? 201–202
Intrinsic Motivation versus
  Extrinsic Motivation, 280–281
Nurturing brain development in
  children with special needs,
  136–137
Play develops children's brain
  function enabling self-discipline, 69
Play supports children's brain
  development, 52
Positive Role Model Checklist,
  192–193
Poverty too often damages young
  children's developing brains, 117
Reliable, responsive care and
  affection supports a baby's
  developing brain, 50
Research is shedding new light on
  infant brain development, 46
Verbal abuse and brain
  development, 190
Warm and nurturing social
  relationships improve learning
  and behavior, 17
brain research, 17, 27, 46, 50, 52, 69,
  84, 112–113, 117, 136–137, 189–190,
  192–193, 200–201, 231–232, 260, 280
breastfeeding, 23–24, 62
Bronfenbrenner, Urie, 28–29, 98–99,
  107, 123
bullying, 101, 140, 155, 278–279
  strategies for, 140–141
burnout, 68

C

caregivers. *See also* teachers
  inexperienced, 74
  modeling behavior, 57
  observations, 85
  replacements, 62
  secure attachment, 54–56
  separation anxiety, 61
  successful, 193
Carkhuff, Robert R., 26
Carnegie, Andrew, 228
Catholicism, 119
cause-and-effect relationships, 58, 64,
  178, 270
Center on Media and Child Health, 77
cephalocaudal muscle development, 48
cerebral palsy, 147
checklists, 89–91
child abuse, 187, 254, 284
child care, 3–4, 20
  ability differences, children with,
    145–146

challenges of, 8, 20, 52
changes through time, 38
cultural diversity, 109–110
daily reminders, 13
economic differences, 109
environments, 16, 19, 181, 211
home-based, 144
individualized plans, 145
joy in, 19
organization in, 19
parents and, 45
quality, 52
schedules, 174–175
school-age children, 74
structured schedule, 30
traditions, 23, 62
Child Care Aware, 21
child development, 5–6, 11
    cultural context, 98
    growth in theories of, 25
    nature *versus* nurture, 34–36
    outdoor environments, 177–178
    preoperational development, 43
    readiness for learning, 36–37
    self-awareness, 27
    sensorimotor development, 42
    stages, 41–44
    theories of, 34
    through interactions, 26–27
Child Find, 143, 145
child guidance. *See* positive child
    guidance
child labor, 24, 30
child protective service agencies, 284
child rearing
    contemporary challenges,
      3–5, 7
    cultural values, 33
child-adult interactions. *See* adult-child
    interactions
child-directed activity, 173–174
childhood
    development of personality, 25
    need for, 184
    perception of, 24
children
    ability differences, 38, 133–154
    ability levels, 37, 172–173
    acting out, 277
    active exploration, 282
    affected by family instability, 28
    age-typical behavior, 256
    aggressive, 187, 189, 191, 279
    altruism, 229
    amends, making, 224, 290, 293
    antisocial behavior, 184
    apologizing, 224, 293

appreciation of the outdoors,
    183–184
artificial charm, 277
attention to, 207, 266–267
bias, 102–103, 105
bipolar disorder, 156–157
biting, 257–258
boredom, 244–245
bullying, 101, 140–141, 155,
    278–279
challenging activities, 170
character values, 169
clingy, 277
collaboration, 13
competitiveness, 11, 71–72, 185
compromise, 173, 178, 261–262
compulsiveness, 277
conduct disorders, 159–160
conflict resolution, 170, 218–220
conscience development, 229
consequences of actions, 13, 64,
    270–271, 290–292
constructing knowledge, 126
contempt, 282
cooperation, 11–12, 30–31, 166, 185
cosleeping, 53
cultural competence, 96
cultural differences, 97–98, 103, 107
cultural identity, 102
cultural transitions, 123–124
cultural values, 34
culture shock, 96–97
defiance, 282
depression, 156–157, 283–284
destructive behaviors, 279
dignity of, 271
disadvantaged, 112
discouragement, 246–247
egocentrism, 15, 57, 166
emotions, 211–212
empathy, 27, 61, 99, 101, 166,
    185, 229
empowerment of, 107
enculturation, 96, 102
evaluating, 88
expectations for, 24, 176, 233–234,
    241–242, 264–265
exploration, 179
external control, 11, 190
fatigue, 245–246
fight or flight response, 137, 219
freedom, 30
friendships, 184
frustration, 247–248
ground rules, 263–264
group contagion, 63, 244
guilt, 66, 68–69, 228–229

independence, 19, 28, 68, 168, 171,
    208–209, 277
individual development, 127
individual differences, 6, 11, 16–17
individual needs, 193–194
inner control, 74, 190
innocence of, 24
language learning, 96–97
laziness, 277
manipulative, 277–278
metacognition, 48, 58
misbehavior, 245
mistakes, 172, 266, 292
mistrust, 282
moral development, 227–232
motivation, 26
names, 124–125
neglected, 133, 160, 284
obesity, 182
obnoxiousness, 277
observing, 83–91
oppositional defiance disorder, 143,
    158–159
overstimulating, 167
passive behavior, 283
physical punishment, 189
pouting, 278
preoperational development,
    43, 69
problem-solving, 26, 70
prosocial skills, 165–166, 184,
    187, 194
psychosocial development, 43–44
rebelliousness, 248–249, 278
redirection, 209, 268
reinforcement, 279–280
removal from conflict, 261
repetition, 263–264
rescuing, 292
responsibility, 12, 14, 19, 30, 173
role-playing, 166, 263
routines, 7, 30, 176, 193
self-control, 5, 16, 178, 195, 233,
    242–243, 260–261
self-discipline, 5, 206
self-esteem, 26, 63, 70, 76–78, 100,
    141, 155, 160, 232, 247, 277, 279,
    283–284, 295
self-reliance, 30–31
sense of belonging, 203, 246
sensitivity, 15
sharing, 15
silliness, 184–185, 243, 277
social roles, 126–127
social-emotional skills, 170,
    178, 188
socialization of, 109, 233

children (*Continued*)
 spirited, 237–240
 spoiled, 10
 stigmatized, 101–102
 stress, 49–50, 97, 248, 283
 stubbornness, 278
 supervision, 181
 tantrums, 151, 154, 158, 206, 282
 on task, 90
 teasing, 140
 television viewing, 180, 192, 282
 telling on others/tattling, 184
 temperaments, 16, 235–240
 toilet learning, 185–186
 transitions, 175
 unconscious reactions, 46
 verbal abuse, 189–190
 welfare of, 8
 work habits, 31
The Children's Defense Fund, 21
children's rights, 7, 195–196, 222,
 292–293
 discomfort, 14
 empathy, 61
 fairness, 15
 play, 166
 possessions, 15
 safety, 14, 16, 256
citizenship, 7, 12, 19, 25, 30–31, 169,
 202–203
class rules, 13–14
classical conditioning, 47–48, 50
classroom learning materials
 books, 101, 104–106
 building blocks, 28
 digital recording equipment, 84
 media, 105
classroom management, 26
Cleversticks (Ashley), 101
cognitive development, 76, 178
cognitive stimulation, 34
cognitive tools, 27
cohesive interactions, 126–127
communication, 59, 74, 109
 assertive, 213–219
 baby-talk, 199–200
 concreteness, 215
 critical conversations, 223–224
 crucial conversations, 219–223
 development of, 200
 directness, 215
 echolalla, 155
 effective, 199, 217
 empty threats, 215, 249
 flexibility, 216
 of needs, 204–205, 207

 negative commands, 213
 nonproductive, 217–219
 nonverbal, 214
 parent-teacher, 8–9
 positive, 212–215
 practicing, 203–204
 respect, 215
 sign language, 202
 styles, 26, 202, 213
 verbal, 60
communities, cultural context, 98
community, 14
community kinship, 126–127
competence, 63
competitiveness, 11, 71–72, 185
compromise, 173, 178, 233, 261–262
concrete operational perspective, 75–76
conditioning, 46–47, 50
conduct disorders, 158–160
conflict resolution, 170, 218–220, 233, 261
conscience development, 229
consequences of actions, 13, 64,
 270–271, 290–292
 logical, 288, 291–292
 natural, 291
consistency, 216, 234–235, 265–266
constructivist learning theory, 34, 36–37,
 53, 117, 126
control, need for, 68
control of error, 172
cooperation, 11–12, 30–31, 166, 185
coprolalia, 156
copropraxia, 156
corporal punishment. *See physical
 punishment*
cosleeping, 52–53
creativity, 166
critical conversations, 223–224
critical thinking, 231
crucial conversations, 218–223
cues, sensory, 47, 53
cultural adaptation, 100–101
cultural assumptions, 108
cultural bias, 109, 299
cultural competence, 96
cultural context, 98, 123
cultural development, 99
cultural diversity, 101–102, 104, 107,
 109, 126, 129
 attitudes to, 102–103
 compromise, 109–110
 exposure to, 118
 prejudice, 100
 respecting, 116, 118–123
 stereotyping, negative, 113
 transitions, 123

cultural studies, 96
cultural transitions, 123–124
cultural values, 33–34, 98, 125–126
culture, 98
 body language, 96
 and child care, 109–113
 defined, 95–96
 destructive behaviors, 100
 exposure to, 96
 high, 96
 interactions, 125
 internalization of, 27
 language, inappropriate, 283
 pluralistic, 109
 traditional, 97
culture shock, 96–97
curriculum planning, multicultural, 104
cyclical self-stimulation, 283

D

dame schools, 24
deafness, 143, 147
 sign language, 202
demandingness, 232–233
democracy, 30–31, 169, 203
depression, 156–158, 283–284
Derman-Sparks, Louise, 102–103,
 105–106
destructive behaviors, 279
developmental disabilities, 135,
 142–146, 297
 pervasive developmental disorders
 (PDD), 153
developmentally appropriate practice
 (DAP), 8, 17, 125–126
 ability differences, 133–135
 assessment, 87–88
 child-directed activity, 173–174
 communication, 200, 213–219
 culturally diverse, 30
 culture and, 113, 129
 defined, 5–6
 developmental stages, 37
 discrimination prevention, 100
 emotional intelligence, 300
 environments, outdoor, 177
 environments for, 166–173, 181, 282
 flexible thinking strategies,
 101, 113
 goals, 86, 112
 implementing, 6
 individualized plans, 143, 145
 inductive thinking, 229
 learning, readiness for, 34
 learning, self-directed, 18
 learning activities, 119, 248

observations, 84–89
parental involvement, 29
play, 18, 28, 52, 111, 166, 170, 179
respect, 100, 114, 120, 122–123, 257
schedules, 173–174
self-directed learning, 115
self-identity, 100
sensitive issues, 254
social skills, 117, 170
temperaments, 237
time-away, 289–290
Dewey, John, 25–26, 31, 169–170
differentiated language, 127
Digital Download: Positive Focus
Addressing Emotional Causes of
Misbehavior, 276
Adult Expectations for Help,
222
Analyze Classroom Traffic
Patterns, 171
Appropriate Verbal Expressions of
Adult Feelings, 271
Authoritative Demandingness, 233
Avoiding Stress and Burnout, 68
Be Alert--Stop Bullying! 279
Children with ADHD Have Special
Challenges, 150
Children with Bipolar Disorder, 157
Children with Conduct Disorder,
159
Children with Conduct Disorder
Typically Demonstrate, 160
Children with ODD, 158
Children with ODD and IED,
158–159
Children with Tourette's
Syndrome, 156
Communication Supports Positive
Guidance, 203
Conditions That Set the Stage for
Rebellion, 249
Coping Techniques for Child
Educators/Teachers/Caregivers,
286
Critical Skills for Good
Citizenship, 31
Crucial Conversations, 220–222
DAP Concepts We Follow to
Support Children with Ability
Differences, 135
Design a Green Playscape,
183–184
Evaluating Using Home
Observations, 89
Evaluation by Event Sampling, 90
Evaluation by Time Sampling, 90

Evaluation Using Anecdotal
Records, 88
Examples of Logical Consequences,
291
Expand Outdoor Learning, 179
Giving "I Messages," 211
Guide Children Who Are Deaf or
Hard of Hearing, 147
Guide for Adult Role Models, 18
Guiding Children with ADHD, 151
Guiding Children with Autism,
153–155
Guiding Children with Bipolar
Disorder, 157
Guiding Children with Down
Syndrome, 149
Guiding Children with Intellectual
Disability, 152
Guiding Children with SPD,
147–148
Guiding Children with
Tourette's, 156
Handy Tips for Effective Home/
School Partnerships, 9
How Can I Be Authoritative Rather
Than Authoritarian? 217
How Can I Improve Transition
Times? 175
How Can We Empower Children
from Diverse Cultural
Backgrounds? 107
How Do Children and Adults
Communicate Their Needs? 204
How Do Young Children Learn
About Their Role in the World?
113–115
How Does Guidance Change to
Match Development? 42–43
How Multicultural is My School? 104
Interaction Styles, 53–54
Listening Attentively, 204
Maslow's Hierarchy of Emotional
Needs That Motivate Behavior,
294
Mindfulness of the
Environment, 302
Nurturing Children with Learning
Differences, 134
Objective Observations and
Subjective Interpretations, 83
Planning for Positive Behavior
Checklist, 168–169
Positive and Specific Statements of
Our Expectations, 265
Positive Requests versus Negative
Commands, 213

Prevention Techniques, 268–269
Prosocial Behavior Consists of
Positive Social Relations, 166
Responding to Toddler Biting, 257
Should I Ever Use Time-Out? 289
Spirited Child Has Adaptability,
The, 240
Spirited Child Has Intensity,
The, 237–238
Spirited Child Has Perceptiveness,
The, 239–240
Spirited Child Has Persistence,
The, 238–239
Spirited Child Has Sensitivity,
The, 239
Support Children with Ability
Differences, 141
To Support Emotional Growth, 279
Take Time to Think Before Reacting
to Genital Touching, 255
Take Time to Think Before You
Judge Others, 118
Take Time to Think Before You
Respond to Biting, 258
Use Picture Symbols to
Demonstrate Behavior, 171
Ways Children Can Make Amends,
224, 293
What Is Involved in Toilet
Learning? 186
What is Punishment? 286–287
What is the Difference Between
Punishment and Guidance? 289
What We Can Do to Help Children
Resist Bias, 103
Dinkmeyer, Don, 291
direct teaching, 101–102
disabilities, 133–135, 143
developmental, 135, 142–146, 297
identification of, 143–144
intervention services for, 145
preventing, 142
discipline, 5, 11, 14
conformity, 32
harsh, 125
inner, 12
obedience, 32
physical punishment, 187–188, 241
unconscious, 32
discovery learning, 168
discrimination, 100–101
discussion, 264
diversity. See cultural diversity
doubt, 62
Down syndrome, 148–149
dramatic play, 65, 97

Dreikurs, Rudolf, 275–276
dual-earner couples, 4

E

early childhood education
    benefits of, 7–8, 18, 20, 30, 37, 61
    challenges of, 20
    cohesive interactions, 127
    community involvement, 29
    cultural context, 123
    cultural pluralism, 119
    cultural transitions, 123
    cultural values, 33
    discrimination prevention, 100
    environments, 19, 28, 165, 167–170,
        177–181
    expectations for, 4
    expulsions, 257
    funding cuts, 8, 61
    inclusive education, 138–139
    individual development, 127
    job outlook, 7
    learning communities, 166
    life skills, 12
    linguistic codes, 33
    multicultural, 127
    parental involvement, 29
    play, 172–173
    quality, 92
    schedules, 174–175
    scrapbooks, 85
    settings, 17
    stressful environments, 211
    types of, 113–115
early childhood professionals. *See also*
    teachers
    assertive rule enforcement, 74
    burnout, 68
    child guidance skills, 5, 7
    communication, 74, 116
    control, need for, 68
    importance of, 20, 98
    job outlook, 7
    modeling behavior, 20
    observations, 85
    perfectionism, 68
    pressures on, 4
    relationships with, 113
    self-doubt, 68
    stress, 68
echolalia, 155
education
    citizenship, 7, 12, 19, 25, 30–31, 169,
        202–203
    goals, 27
    lifelong learners, 299
    reform, 26

egocentrism, 15, 57, 166
Elias, Maurice J., 301
emotional disorders, 143
emotional growth, 11, 62, 91, 111,
    279, 299
emotional intelligence, 228, 299–300
empathy, 27, 61, 99, 101, 166, 185,
    217, 229
employment insecurity, 8
enculturation, 27, 96, 102, 127–128
English as a Second/Other Language
    (ESOL), 124
environments
    age appropriate, 173
    changing, 266
    child-directed activity, 166,
        173–174
    child-sized, 28, 172
    comfortable, 171
    control of error, 172
    culturally diverse, 30
    discovery learning, 168
    external, 53
    hands-on learning, 27–28, 171
    home, 167
    interactions in, 36–37
    learning, 25, 84
    learning centers, 171–172
    lighting, 171
    maintaining, 19
    nurturing, 38, 68, 165, 184
    outdoor, 177–184
    overstimulating, 167
    peaceful, 169–170
    planning, 167–170
    stressful, 50
    traffic patterns, 167, 171
Erikson, Erik, 43–44, 50, 54, 62, 66, 75
ethics, 105, 107
ethnocentrism, 108
ethologists, 37, 55
event sampling, 90
executive functions, 150, 260–261
exercise, 177, 180
expectations, clarifying, 264–265
external control, 11, 190
extrinsic motivation, 280–281

F

Facebook, 77
failure to thrive syndrome, 38
fairness, 15, 75
families
    accepting all, 105
    culture and, 98, 103–104
    empowerment of, 8–9
    extended, 97

income decline, 8
individualized plans, 145
    instability, 28
    nuclear, 127
    structures, 4
fathers, child care, 4
feelings, expressing, 65, 202, 207,
    211–212, 270–271
fetal alcohol effect (FAE), 149
fetal alcohol spectrum disorders
    (FASD), 149
fetal alcohol syndrome (FAS), 149
fight or flight response, 17, 137, 219
First Steps Toward Cultural Difference
    (Miller), 127
flexible thinking strategies, 101
food, multicultural, 103–104
formative assessment, 84
fragile X syndrome, 153
free appropriate public education
    (FAPE), 143, 145
Freud, Sigmund, 25, 54, 275
friendships, 66, 184
Froebel, Friedrich, 28
fulfillment, 127

G

Gaben (gifts), 28
Gallaudet Research Institute, 147
Gazda, George Michael, 26
genitalia-related issues, 254–256
Gesell, Arnold, 35
Gilliam, Walter, 257
Gilligan, Carol, 231
Goleman, Daniel, 299
Gonzalez-Mena, Janet, 112
grandparents, 4
green playscapes, 182–184
ground rules, 263–264
group activities, 168
group contagion, 63, 244
group identity, 102
group processes, 233
guidance. *See also* positive
    child guidance
guidance interventions, 253–271
guilt, 66, 68–69, 228–229

H

Halloween, 122
hands-on learning, 27–28
hatred, 101–102
Head Start, 29, 98
health impairments, 143, 146, 150
healthy choices, 14
hearing impairments, 143, 147
helplessness, 209

holophrases, 60
human ecology, 98
human rights, 7
hypersensitivity, 154

I

identity, 75, 102
imprinting, 55
inclusive education, 134–136, 138, 182
independence, 19, 28, 68, 114, 168, 171, 208–209, 277
Individualized Education Program (IEP), 145–146
Individualized Family Service Plan (IFSP), 145–146
Individuals with Disabilities Education Act (IDEA), 143, 145
induction, 229
industry, 75
infants
  appropriate touch, 50–51
  attachment, 50, 54–56
  baby-talk, 49, 199–201
  biting, 258
  body language, 49
  born to heavy drinkers, 150
  bottle feeding, 62
  brain development, 37, 45–46, 50, 52, 138
  breastfeeding, 23–24, 62
  care, contemporary, 29
  care, historical, 23–24
  changes in routine, 49
  classical conditioning, 47, 50
  communication, 199–202
  cosleeping, 52
  crying, 45, 48
  Down syndrome, 149
  egocentrism, 57
  emotions, 211
  external environments, 53
  failure to thrive syndrome, 38
  habituation, 48–49
  impersonal pronouns, 29–30
  intentional behavior, 45–46
  interactions, 199–200
  internal sensations, 53
  internalizing behavior, 57
  language, 49, 59–60, 199–202
  learned helplessness, 51
  mindfulness, 301–302
  mortality rate, 23
  muscle development, 48
  newborns, 15
  nurturing environment, 38, 45, 49, 63
  nutrition, 46
  object permanence, 46, 178–179

operant conditioning, 50
pacifiers, 62
play, 52
psychosocial development, 43–44
punishment of, 45
rapid eye movement (REM) sleep, 52
reflex responses, 46
secure attachment, 54–56
sensorimotor development, 42
separation anxiety, 56–57
shaken baby syndrome, 142
sleep, 52
socialization, 233
"spoiled," 45, 51
stimuli, 46
stranger anxiety, 56–57
stress, 46, 49–50
tabula rasa, 35
temperaments, 236–237
trust, 50
unconscious conditioning, 46, 48
unconscious reactions, 46
wet-nurses, 23–24
inferiority, 75
inferring meaning, 86
initiative, 31, 66, 68–69
inner control, 74, 190
Institute of Child Welfare (Univ. of Minnesota), 24
intellectual disabilities, 143, 152–153, 260
intelligence, 26, 128
intelligent quotient (IQ), 299
intentional teaching, 6
interactions, 26, 29, 36, 58, 126. See also adult-child interactions
  authoritarian-style, 53
  authoritative-style, 53–55, 125
  construction of self, 26
  permissive-style, 53–54, 125
intermittent explosive disorder (IED), 158–159
intermittent reinforcer, 296–297
internal sensations, 53
interpersonal skills, 26
intrinsic motivation, 280–281

K

Kagan, Jerome, 229, 236–237
King, Martin Luther, Jr., 103
knowledge, 299
Kohlberg, Lawrence, 230–231
Kurcinka, Mary Sheedy, 237

L

Langer, Ellen, 300
language
  baby-talk, 49, 199–201

body language, 49–50, 59–60, 96, 120
development of, 27, 96–97, 201
differentiated usage, 127
enculturation, 127–128
English as a Second/Other Language (ESOL), 124
expressive, 59, 200
gender neutral, 118
inappropriate, 72–73, 283
infants, 49, 199–202
mind development, 260
picture symbols, 171–172
practicing, 203–204
preschoolers, 64
receptive, 59, 200
sign language, 202
telegraphic speech, 200
toddlers, 60, 200–202, 212
visceral usage, 127
Lansford, Jennifer, 187–188
Latino/a Americans, cultural traits, 119–120
learned helplessness, 51
learning
  associative, 47
  authentic, 128
  cultural differences, 125–126
  discovery, 168
  by doing, 25
  hands-on, 27–28, 171
  multicultural, 122, 127–128
  nature versus nurture, 34–36
  periods for, 28
  self-directed, 18, 175
  social, 27, 128
  strategies for, 27
  through play, 28, 36
learning centers, 171–172
learning communities, 71, 166
learning disabilities, 134–136, 143, 160
least restrictive environment (LRE), 143, 145
Lieberman, Matthew, 261
life skills, 11–12, 17, 19, 31
linguistic codes, 33
listening. See active listening
Locke, John, 23
logic, 26
logical consequences, 288, 291–292
Lorenz, Konrad, 55

M

mania, 157
manic depression. See bipolar disorder
manipulative children, 277–278

Maslow, Abraham, 25, 294
Maslow's hierarchy of needs, 294
maturation, 12
maturationist learning theory, 34–37
Mayer, John, 299
McKay, Gary, 291
Measurement of Temperament in
    Infancy (Rothbart), 236
media, 77, 105
meditation, 302
mental health, 158
mental retardation. See intellectual
    disabilities
metacognition, 48, 58
Middle Eastern cultures, cultural
    traits, 121
Milner, Caryn, 101
mind, unconscious absorbent, 301
mind blindness. See autism
mind development, 260
mindfulness, 300–302
    awareness of movement, 303
    body, of the, 303
    contemplation, 304–305
    environments, of, 302–303
    focus on breathing, 304
    practicing, 305
    training, 302–305
mirror neurons, 27
misbehavior, 32, 233–235, 241,
    244–246, 275
    emotional causes of, 276–279
mistaken goals, 275
mistakes, 172, 266, 292
mistrust, 282
Moen, Phyllis, 98
Montessori, Maria, 24, 26–28, 170,
    172, 301
Montessori education, 28
mood problems, 146
Moore, Robin, 182
moral affect, 228
moral behavior, 231–232
moral development, 227–229, 231
moral intelligence, 228–229
moral reasoning, 228, 230–232
morality, 230–231
Morris, Pamela A., 98
motherese, 49
mothers, traditional role, 4
motivation
    extrinsic, 280–281
    intrinsic, 280–281
motor tics, 155–156
multicultural education, 101, 103–104
multiculturalism, 101, 118, 122
multigenerational households, 4–5

Museum of Natural Science
    (Houston), 137
music, multicultural, 104

N

name-calling, 140
names, children's, 124–125
National Association for the Education of
    Young Children (NAEYC), 5, 21, 252
    assessment, 85
    ethics, 135
    ethics statement, 107–108
    standards, 2, 22, 40, 80, 94, 132, 164,
        198, 226, 252, 274
The National Child Care Information
    Center, 21
national standards, 2, 22, 40, 80, 94, 132,
    164, 198, 226, 252, 274
Native Americans
    cultural traits, 119, 121
    nature and, 119
    traditional infant care, 24
natural consequences, 291
nature, intrinsic, 34
nature versus nurture, 34–36
negative commands, 213
negative conditioning, 47
neglected children, 133, 160, 284
nested structures, 98–99
nonverbal behavior, 26
nurturing, external, 34

O

obedience, 24, 32
obesity, 182
object permanence, 46, 178–179
objective observations, 83, 91
objectivity, 259
observations, 83–91
    anecdotal records, 88, 91
    checklists, 89–91
    event sampling, 90
    home, 89
    running accounts, 89
    time sampling, 89–90
obsessive-compulsive disorder, 155
operant conditioning, 47–48, 50
oppositional defiance disorder (ODD),
    143, 158–159
orthopedic impairments, 143
osmosis, 205
oxytocin, 17

P

Pacific Islanders, 119
pacifiers, 61–62
Paley, Vivian, 101

parentese. See baby-talk
parents
    affluent, 30
    challenges of, 45, 98, 106–107
    child care, 3, 7–8
    communication with, 8–9, 84–85,
        107, 111, 116, 119, 122, 133, 145
    compromise, 262
    cultural diversity, 97, 109
    guidance skills, 7
    home environments, 9, 167
    individualized plans, 145
    influence on children, 8, 99
    observations, 89
    parenting styles, 97, 109
    physical punishment, 188–191
    reading to children, 9
    respect for, 106–107
    running accounts, 89
    schedules, 174
    separation from children, 263
    superchildren, 30
    supporting, 142–143
    working, 3–5, 7, 98
parent-teacher resource team
    ability differences, children with, 145
    common goals, 112
    compromise, 111–112
    defined, 8
    trust, 112, 120
partial fetal alcohol syndrome (PFAS), 149
peace, 24
Peace and Education (Montessori), 24
peer pressure, 77
peer tutoring, 128–129
people-pleasing, 68
perfectionism, 68, 87
permissive-style interactions, 53–54,
    125, 195
Perry Preschool Study, 92
personal interactions, 99
personality, 25
pervasive developmental disorders
    (PDD), 153
pets, 172
physical appearances, 138
    insensitivity towards, 139
    teacher expectations of, 139
physical punishment, 187–190. See also
    spanking
    bans on, 187–188
    behavior problems and, 187–188
    brain development, 189
Piaget, Jean, 26, 34, 76, 170
    cause-and-effect relationships, 178
    constructivism, 36
    moral reasoning, 230

object permanence, 178–179
stages, 26
picture symbols, 171–172
Pink, Daniel, 281
Plato, 35
play, 18, 28, 30, 36, 52, 59, 173
   active, 166
   brain development, 52, 69
   child-directed, 166, 173–174
   creativity, 166, 182
   cultural differences, 97
   dramatic, 65, 97
   exploratory, 179
   free, 166, 179
   gendered, 70–71
   imitative, 187, 191–192
   importance of, 111, 166
   learning through, 170
   outdoor, 177
   self-discipline, 69
   types of, 173
playgrounds
   accessible, 182
   accommodations, 182
   age appropriate, 177, 179–181
   design of, 180–184
   exercise, 177–178
   free play, 177
   intellectual learning, 177–178
   learning activities, 179
   safety, 180–182
   social-emotional skills, 178
   supervision, 181
playscapes, green, 182–184
pluralistic culture, 109
positive child guidance, 5, 7, 12, 53
   ability differences, 141
   active listening, 66, 118, 203–208,
     223, 287
   affection, unconditional, 74, 78, 194,
     271
   appropriate touch, 50–51,
     267, 295
   assertive rule enforcement, 11–12,
     74, 191, 194, 212
   assumptions, 108
   attention, 266–267
   authoritative-style interactions,
     53–55, 113–114, 125, 190–191,
     194–195, 217, 229, 232–233
   behaviorist learning theory, 11,
     34–35, 37
   biases, 75, 81–83
   biting, 257–258
   challenges of, 3
   changes through time, 38
   child-level position, 267

children's names, 268
citizenship, 7, 12, 19, 25, 30–31, 169,
   202–203
collaboration, 72
communication, 64–65, 70, 111,
   119, 203
compromise, 173, 178, 233, 261–262
conduct disorders, 159–160
confidence in, 271
conflict resolution, 170, 218–220,
   233, 261
consensus building, 233
consistency, 216, 234–235, 265–266
constructivist learning theory, 36–37
coping techniques, 286
cultural knowledge, 99
cultural values, 108, 120
daily reminders, 13
defined, 3, 5
demandingness, 232–233
developing, 285
different theories of, 109
disciplinary traditions, 32
discussion, 233, 264
empathy, 99, 185, 217, 229
encouragement, 266
expectations, clarifying, 264–265
external control, 11
eye contact, 267
fairness, 75
feelings, expressing, 202, 207,
   211–212, 270–271
flexibility, 216
forgiveness, 271
goals, 12, 16, 193, 233
group processes, 233
independence, 68
individual differences, 11–12
inferring meaning, 86
inner control, 12
intermittent explosive disorder
   (IED), 159
interventions. see guidance
   interventions
life skills, 11–12, 17, 19, 31
logical consequences, 288
maturationist learning theory,
   35–36
modeling behavior, 203–204
moral intelligence, 229
moral reasoning, 231–232
multiculturalism, 118
nonjudgmental, 76
nurturing, 42, 186–187
objectivity, 83, 259
observations, 83–91
oppositional defiance disorder, 159

parent-child separation, 263
patience, 25, 78
persistence, 271
personal interactions, 99
prevention techniques, 268–270
problem-solving, 86
prosocial skills, 165–166, 173–174,
   176, 184, 187, 190, 192, 194
purpose of, 10
quick response, 268–269
redirection, 268
reducing stigmatizing, 102
repetition, 263–264
respect, 19, 25, 76, 271
responses, 42, 83–84
responsibility, 12, 17, 19, 211
role-playing, 263
rules, 69, 229, 233, 263–264
secure attachment, 56
self-confidence, 12, 102
self-control, 12, 16
sign language, 202
social interactions, 102
social-emotional intelligence, 188,
   300
strategies, 31–32
supervision, 245
temperaments, 235–240
time-away, 289–290
tools, 265
traditions, 23
transitions, 175
trust, 50, 62, 76, 282
unconditional acceptance, 99
weapons, 265
positive communication, 212–215
positive reinforcement, 47
poverty, 4, 8, 117
power struggles, 276, 278
pregnancy
   alcohol and, 149–150
   smoking during, 150
prejudice, 70, 100–101, 105, 108
   early signs of, 101
   ethnocentrism, 108
   preventing, 102, 116, 129
Pre-K programs, 61
preoperational development, 43, 69
preschool. See early childhood education
preschoolers
   abstract symbols, 64
   brain development, 69
   cause-and-effect relationships, 64
   communication, 65, 200, 202,
     212, 215
   competent, 63
   competitiveness, 71

preschoolers (*Continued*)
    cooperation, 71
    emotional growth, 91, 299
    environments for, 68, 168
    expressing feelings, 65, 67, 202
    friendships, 66, 178
    gender awareness, 70
    guilt, 66, 68–69
    independence, 68
    initiative, 68–69
    intentional behavior, 64
    language, 64
    play, 65, 70–71, 173, 191
    preoperational development, 69
    problem-solving, 70
    relationships, 66
    rules, 69–70
    self-concept, 70–71
    self-esteem, 70–71
    sensitive issues, 64–65
    sign language, 202
    social development, 91
prevention techniques, 268–270
private schools, 145–146
problem-solving, 26, 70
program evaluation, 82
prosocial skills, 165–166, 173–174, 176,
    184, 187, 190, 192, 194
proximodistal muscle development, 48
pseudoconditioning, 47
psychologists, cognitive, 26
psychology, value-oriented, 25
psychosocial development, 43–44
puberty, 77–78
punishment, 187–190, 286–287, 289

Q

qualitative information, 91
quality indicators, early childhood
    education, 92
quantitative information, 91
quick response, 268

R

racism, 100, 105
Raising Your Spirited Child (Kurcinka), 237
rapid eye movement (REM) sleep, 52
rebelliousness, 29, 248–249, 278
receptive language, 59
Reconstruction in Education
    (Montessori), 24
redirection, 209, 268
reflex responses, 46
reinforcement, 35, 279–280, 295,
    297–298
relationships, 6, 98
religion, 119, 122–123

repetition, 263–264
replaces, 254
rescue, 292
respect, 14, 19, 100, 104, 114, 116, 120,
    122–123, 257
responsibility, 12, 14, 19, 30, 173
Rett's syndrome, 153
rewards, 296, 298
risk level, 16
Rogers, Carl, 25–26
role models, 18–19, 27, 36, 115, 173, 192,
    227, 232
role-playing, 166, 263
rote memorization, 18
Rothbart, Mary, 236
Rousseau, Jean-Jacques, 24
Russell, Lillian, 139

S

safety, 58–59
Salovey, Peter, 299
scaffolding, 72
scapegoating, 101–102
schedules, 173–174
Schiller, Pam, 128
school-age children, early
    autonomy, 75
    collaboration, 72
    communication, 200, 202
    competitiveness, 72
    concrete operational perspective, 75
    fairness, 75
    identity, 75
    imitative play, 192
    independence, 75
    industry, 75
    inferiority, 75
    inner control, 74
    intimidating, 74
    judging, 72
    language, 71–73
    observing, 72
    questioning, 71–72
    rules, 74
    self-esteem, 76
school-age children, older
    argument, 76
    clothing, 77
    communication, 200, 202
    concrete operational perspective, 76
    conversationalists, 76
    imitative play, 192
    media, role of, 77
    peer groups, 77
    peer pressure, 77
    puberty, 77–78
    rules, 77

self-confidence, 77–78
self-esteem, 77–78
scrapbooks, 85
secure attachment, 55–56
security blankets, 61
self, construction of, 26
self-actualization, 25
self-awareness, 27
self-concept, 26, 63, 70
self-confidence, 12, 77–78
self-control, 5, 16, 178, 195, 206, 233,
    242–243, 260–261
self-directed learning, 18, 175
self-discipline, 69
self-esteem, 26, 63, 70, 76–78, 100, 155,
    160, 232, 247, 277, 279, 283–284
    ability differences, 134–135
    fostering, 295
    low, 70, 76, 141
self-identity, 102
self-regulation, 69, 158
self-reliance, 30–31
sensitive issues, 64–65, 254–256
sensorimotor development, 42
sensory ability differences. *See* hearing
    impairments
sensory processing disorder (SPD),
    147–148
separation anxiety, 56–57, 61
sexism, 100, 105
sexual harassment, 255–256
shaken baby syndrome, 142–143
shame, 62
sharing, 15
sign language, 202
single parents, 4–5
Skinner, B. F., 35
sleep, 52–53
smoking, behavior problems and, 150
social conscience, 165
social constructivism, 25
social development, 62
    play and, 111
    preschoolers, 91
    toddlers, 59
social interactions, 11, 27, 69, 169–170
    brain development, 112
    language learning, 201
    nurturing, 17–18, 165
    reducing prejudice, 102
    rejection of, 283
social justice, 299
social learning, 27, 128
social problems, 146
social roles, 126–127
social-emotional intelligence, 128,
    299–301

social-emotional skills, 170, 178, 188
socialization, 109, 233
spanking, 74, 109, 187–191, 241
special education, 143, 145–146
special needs children. *See* ability
    differences
speech impairments, 143
"spoiled" children, 10, 45, 51
stepparents, 4
stereotyping, negative, 100–101, 105,
    113–114, 139
stigmatized children, 101–102
stranger anxiety, 56–57, 61
stress, 49–50, 97, 248, 283
    teachers, 68
subjective interpretations, 83
swaddling, 23–24

T

tabula rasa, 35
tantrums, 151, 154, 158, 206, 282
on task, defined, 90
tasks, 172
teacher evaluation, 82
teachers
    active listening, 118, 203–208
    anecdotal records, 91
    assertive rule enforcement, 74, 191,
        194, 212
    assessment, 87–88
    biases, 75, 81–83, 86, 118
    burnout, 68
    control, need for, 68
    coping techniques, 286
    ethics, 107–108
    feelings, expressing, 270–271
    needs of, 285–286
    observations, 83–91
    parent communication, 8–9, 99,
        151–152
    people-pleasing, 68
    perfectionism, 68, 87
    personal interactions, 99
    qualities of, 74
    record-keeping, 84–85, 88–91
    relationships, 74
    role models, 192, 282
    self-doubt, 68
    self-reflection, 107
    stress, 68
    trust, 190
teaching
    antibias curriculum, 102–106
    assessment, 82, 84
    cultural diversity, 103–104
    direct, 101–102
    ethics, 105

evaluating, 82
goals, 82
philosophies, 33
program evaluation, 82
successful, 74, 193
tolerance, 137
values, 13–14
TeachSource Video
    2-5 Years: Play in Early
        Childhood, 173
    5-11 Years: Developmental
        Disabilities in Middle Childhood,
        135
    5-11 Years: Lev Vygotsky, the Zone
        of Proximal Development, and
        Scaffolding, 72
    Autism and a Bike, 152
    Benefits of Preschool, 18
    Curriculum Planning:
        Implementing Developmentally
        Appropriate Practice in an Early
        Childhood Setting, 6
    Early Childhood: Positive
        Guidance, 232
    Ensuring High Quality through
        Program Evaluation, 82
    Fetal Alcohol Syndrome, 149
    Guidance for Young Children:
        Teacher Techniques for
        Encouraging Positive Social
        Behaviors, 267
    Infants and Toddlers:
        Communication Development, 200
    Making a Great Teacher, 74
    Montessori Education, 28
    Multicultural Lessons: Embracing
        Similarities and Differences in
        Preschool Education, 101
    Obese Children, 182
    A Parent's Viewpoint: Parent-
        Teacher Communication, 9
    Piaget's Stages and Educational
        Implications, 26
    Pre-K Funding Cuts, 61
    Preschool: Emotional Development,
        299
    Preschooler Social and Emotional
        Development, 91
    Shaken Baby Syndrome, 142
teamwork, 30–31
teasing, 140
technology, 29, 32
telegraphic speech, 200
television viewing, 77, 118, 180, 192, 282
telling on others/tattling, 184
temperaments, 16, 235–240
Thanksgiving, 121

Thomson, Barbara, 116
time sampling, 89–90
time-away, 289–290
toddlers
    autonomy, 62–63
    behavior, 63
    biting, 257–258
    body language, 59
    brain development, 59
    cause-and-effect relationships, 58
    comfort items, 61–62
    communication, 200–201, 214
    crying, 58–59
    curiosity, 58
    doubt, 62
    emotions, 57–58, 211
    expressive language, 59, 200
    feelings, expressing, 202
    group contagion, 63
    impulsiveness, 64
    intellectual development, 59
    interactions, 58
    language, 60, 62, 200–202, 212
    mindfulness, 301–302
    motor skill development, 59
    pacifiers, 61
    processes, 62–63
    receptive language, 59, 200
    safety, 58–59
    security blankets, 61
    self-concept, 63
    self-esteem, 63
    self-talk, 200
    sensory exploration, 58–59
    separation anxiety, 61, 263
    shame, 62
    shy, 61
    sign language, 202
    social development, 59
    speech, 200
    stranger anxiety, 61
    trust, 62
toilet learning, 185–186
tokenism, 105
tokens, 35
tolerance, 137
tools, 265
Tourette's syndrome, 155–156
toys, 265
transitions, 175
traumatic brain injury, 143
trust, 50, 62, 76, 282

U

unconditional acceptance, 99, 105
unconscious conditioning, 46, 48
United Nations, 166

United States Dept. of Education, 162
*An Updated Guide for Selecting Anti-Bias
Children's Books* (Derman-Sparks), 105

V

values, teaching, 13–14
verbal abuse, 189–190
visceral language, 127
visual impairments, 143

vocal tics, 155–156
Vygotsky, Lev, 26–27, 33–34, 36, 72, 128

W

Watson, John B., 35
weapons, 265
Wechsler Intelligence Test, 299
welfare reform, 5
Willatts, Peter, 179

Williams, Raymond, 96
words, loaded, 106

Y

yoga, 302

Z

zone of proximal educational
development (ZPD), 26, 72